FOR TRAN

FORTRAN

Samuel L. Marateck
New York University

ACADEMIC PRESS NEW YORK SAN FRANCISCO LONDON
A Subsidiary of Harcourt Brace Jovanovich, Publishers

ACADEMIC PRESS, INC.
111 Fifth Avenue, New York, New York 10003

United Kingdom Edition published by
ACADEMIC PRESS, INC. (LONDON) LTD.
24/28 Oval Road, London NW1

Library of Congress Cataloging in Publication Data

Marateck, Samuel L
FORTRAN.

Includes index.
1. Fortran (Computer program language). I. Title.
QA76.73.F25M37 001.6′424 76-45991
ISBN 0-12-470460-3

PRINTED IN THE UNITED STATES OF AMERICA

To my parents Harold and Rita

Contents

3

Calculations and the READ Statement

4

Functions and the IF Statement

5

The DO Loop, the IF-THEN-ELSE and the WHILE Loop

6

Subscripted Variables, the DATA Statement, and the Implied DO Loop

7

Doubly Subscripted Variables and Matrix Multiplication

8

Input/Output

9

Functions, Subprograms, and Subroutines

10

Structured Programming

11

The COMMON Statement and the EQUIVALENCE Statement

12

Significance, Double Precision, Complex Numbers

13

More Input/Output

Appendix

Preface

This book is an outgrowth of notes the author uses in a course in FORTRAN that he teaches to undergraduates at New York University. Its purpose is to teach the student how to program using the FORTRAN language, and it is written for students who have no prior knowledge of computers or programming.

The design of the book has special significance and deserves special comment. The right-hand pages contain pictorial material on programming which most students will readily understand; this is described in detail in "To The Reader." The left-hand pages contain the explanatory text. You will see that strict adherence to this design has resulted in a number of partially filled pages. It has been the author's experience with a book on BASIC, which he wrote and designed in the same way, that in many cases students who visit the computer center and have studied only the right-hand pages, have been able to write and run programs on their first visit. The student should, in order to understand all facets of the programming techniques described, also read the text on the left-hand pages.

There are other features that should help the beginning student. The author usually introduces only one new programming concept per program. Thus many of the programs in the book are first written as a series of smaller programs, each of which serves as a step in understanding the entire larger program.

Easy to understand programs have been used to illustrate the various programming techniques discussed in the book. These programs are the solutions to problems drawn from various disciplines, and all students, whatever their major field, should understand them without difficulty. After students have been presented these programs, they will have the ability to read optional sections in which these same techniques are applied to more advanced programs.

The author also includes examples of common programming mistakes made by beginning students when they are not explicit enough in translating their thoughts into programming instructions. The author has found this type of example to be an effective teaching technique.

Since one of the most difficult parts of learning FORTRAN is the mastering of the input/output statements, these statements are introduced early in the book. Their ramifications are explained as the programs demand it. Thus the reader is exposed to input/output concepts gradually. Then in Chapter 8 the author explains the input/output capability of FORTRAN in great detail.

Sound programming techniques, including programming style and its logical extension, structured programming, aid the programmer in all stages of program writing: the design, writing, debugging, and maintenance of programs. Sound programming techniques are emphasized from the beginning, and they are introduced as they are needed and as the statements being discussed allow their use. Chapter 10 is devoted to the application of structured programming in the design and writing of programs. Also discussed in that chapter are top-down design, top-down testing of programs, and the HIPO diagram.

At some point the FORTRAN programmer should understand round-off errors and significance as they relate to the bit configuration of the computer being used. The greater part of Chapter 12 is devoted to a discussion of these concepts, although the effect of round-off errors is introduced early in the book.

Almost the entire book is devoted to a discussion of American National Standard (ANS) FORTRAN. Since some students will be using Standard Basic FORTRAN, which has fewer instructions and which consequently can be used on machines which have less memory, any statement that is described and is not available in Standard Basic FORTRAN is footnoted as such.

The features of the WATFOR and WATFIV compilers are described as well as features of WATFIV-S (the IF-THEN-ELSE and the WHILE-DO) along with their ANS analogs. Many features of WATFOR/WATFIV/WATFIV-S have been incorporated into the proposed ANS X3.9 FORTRAN language revision (1977), and thus even the reader who will not be using WATFOR/WATFIV/WATFIV-S might want to take more than a casual interest in sections describing these compilers because of their applications to the proposed ANS compilers.

Those teachers who do not intend to use all the chapters in the book may be interested in knowing that the last four chapters—Chapter 10 (structured programming), Chapter 11 (The COMMON and the EQUIVALENCE statements), Chapter 12 (Significance, DOUBLE PRECISION, and COMPLEX numbers), and Chapter 13 (More Input/Output)—can be read in any order.

We have included in the appendices material that all readers might not have use for, e.g., control cards for the IBM 360/370 and time sharing.

It is a pleasure to thank Professor J. T. Schwartz and Professor Max Goldstein for their friendship, their many kindnesses and for their constant support while I was writing this book; and H. David Abrams and Professor Carl F. R. Weiman for acting as a sounding board for many of my ideas. It is also a pleasure to thank Jeffrey Akner and his computer facility staff for their cooperation and Professor Robert Richardson and Professor George Basbas for granting me free time on their computer.

To the Reader

This book has been written on the premise that it is at times easier to learn a subject from pictorial representations supported by text than from text supported by pictorial representations. With this in mind, beginning with Chapter 2 we have used a double page format for our presentation. On the left-hand page (we call it the text page) appears the text, and on the right-hand page (we call it the picture page) appears the pictorial representation, consisting mostly of programs and tables.

Each picture page was written to be as self-contained as possible, so that the reader, if he so desires, may read that page first and absorb the essence of the contents of the entire double page before going on to read the text. The text page consists of a very thorough discussion of the programming techniques presented on the picture page. It refers to parts of the programs and tables on the picture page; when reference is made on the text page to a given line of print on the picture page, that line—whenever it is feasible to do so—is reproduced in the text to promote readability. Students who have a previous background in programming languages and others who understand the picture page completely may find that in some chapters they can skip the text (left-hand) pages and concentrate on the picture pages.

The following techniques are used as aids in making the picture page self-contained:

1. As many as possible of the ideas discussed in the text are illustrated in the programs and tables. The captions beneath these capsulate much of what is said in the text.

2. Words underlined in the captions describe lines underlined in the figures. To illustrate this, part of Fig. 2.2a is reproduced below.

```
VAR1 = 11.4
VAR2 = 20.2
STOP
END
```

Figure 2.2a. In the program the number 11.4 is assigned to the variable VAR1 and 20.2 to VAR2 in the assignment statement.

The statements VAR1 = 11.4 and VAR2 = 20.2 are underlined to show that they are described by the words underlined in the caption. Thus they are both assignment statements.

3. To the right of most programs appears a table that describes what effect certain statements in the program have on the computer's memory. For instance, the following table describes the effect that VAR1 = 11.4 has on the memory:

DESCRIPTION	VAR1
VAR1 = 11.4	11.4

We see from the table that this statement caused the number 11.4 to be associated with VAR1 in the computer's memory. The line-by-line analysis afforded by these tables should aid the reader in understanding the program.

1

Introduction to Computers and Programming

1.1. General Remarks

If you wished to categorize the times we live in, in terms of the technological advance that most affects our lives, you would call our age the age of the computer; the computer is all encompassing. For instance, in business some of the uses of computers are for billing, check writing, and inventory control; every large organization uses computers to process its records. In another realm—science and engineering—there are two spectacular examples of the use of computers: (1) The multitude of calculations that enabled the space program to put a man on the moon were done by computers. (2) The pictures taken on Mars by the Viking lander were reconstructed on earth by computers.

In order to solve a problem, the computer follows a set of instructions called a *program*. The people who write these programs are called, appropriately, *programmers*. The form that the instructions in the program take depends on the programming language used. It is the purpose of this book to teach you to program in FORTRAN. The name FORTRAN is taken from FORmula TRANslation. FORTRAN was developed in the 1950s; as the name implies, it was devised as a language for solving mathematical and mathematics-related problems. FORTRAN is used today to solve problems in mathematics, the physical sciences and engineering, the social sciences and linguistics, and other related fields.

The type of computer used in an overwhelming number of applications solves problems and processes information by manipulating digits; hence, this type of computer is called a *digital computer*. A FORTRAN program is run on a digital computer.

So that you may understand the relation of FORTRAN to the computer, we first briefly describe computers. One way of picturing a computer is as a maze of on-off electrical switches connected by wires. Thus you might imagine that if a programmer wished to instruct a computer to do something, he would have to feed it a program composed of a series of on-off types of instructions. As a matter of fact, the first programs were written like this. The type of language that uses this form of instruction is called *machine language*. In its most primitive form, a program written in machine language consists of strings of 0's and 1's, where a zero represents an open switch, and a one represents a closed switch. As you can surmise from this brief description, learning to write programs in machine language can be very difficult. Moreover, even once you master it, writing in machine language can be very tedious. For this reason, computer languages closer in form to the spoken word—in our case, English—and to algebra, have been devised. The most widely used of these languages is FORTRAN. Computer languages closer to the machine are called *low level languages*. An example of a low level language is machine language. Computer languages similar in form to how we express ourselves, either by the spoken word or by mathematical symbols, are called *high level languages*. FORTRAN is a high level language.

A program written in FORTRAN cannot be directly understood by the computer; it must first be translated into machine language. A special program does this. It is called a *compiler*, and is already present in the machine when we feed the computer our program. Once a program has been translated, we say that it has been *compiled*. The original FORTRAN program is called the *source program*, and the translated program is called the *object* program.

FORTRAN has grammatical rules that must be followed by the programmer. These rules are similar to those in English that govern the sequence of words in a sentence, the punctuation, and the spelling—we shall learn these rules in later chapters. Before the compiler translates your program, it checks whether you have written your program instructions according to the grammatical rules. If you make grammatical errors in writing an instruction, don't worry; the compiler has been written so that it will inform you of these. Programmers refer to grammatical errors as *compilation errors* or *compile-time errors*. Your program must be free of compile-time errors before the compiler will translate your program.

We now describe the main components of the computer. Essentially, the computer consists of an *input unit*, a *memory unit*, a *logical unit* (or *arithmetic unit*), an *output unit*, and a *control unit*. Our program is communicated to the computer through the input unit. All the mathematics and decisions in the program are done in the logical unit. The program itself and the numbers it processes are stored in the memory unit. The computer communicates the results of our program to us through the output unit. The control unit directs the activities of the other four units. The control unit and the logical unit are referred to collectively as the *central processing unit* (abbreviated as CPU). The word *hardware* is used to describe the physical components of the computer, such as these units, whereas the word *software* is used to describe the programs. We shall use the word *system* to describe the programs, such as the compiler, that process the programs you write.

1.2. The Keypunch

The first, and still the most widely used, means of communicating a program to the computer is to punch the program instructions on a card. The device we use to do this is called a keypunch. In Fig. 1.1 we show a typical keypunch; and in Fig. 1.2, the keypunch keyboard.

Figure 1.1. The IBM 029 keypunch. (Courtesy of IBM.)

Figure 1.2. The IBM 029 keypunch keyboard. (Courtesy of IBM.)

In order to operate a keypunch, we must first place a batch of computer cards in the hopper—which is on the right of the keypunch. There is a clamp that will press the cards against the front of the hopper. When we press the FEED button, one card will be released from the hopper into the window directly beneath the hopper. If we press the FEED buttton again, a second card will be released from the hopper, and the first card will be properly positioned in the window so that we can start punching the card. An alternative approach for readying a card so that we can punch it is to press the FEED button and then the REG button.

After this preliminary procedure has been carried out, each time we press a key that has a symbol on it not only will that symbol be printed on the top of the card, but, more important, one or more rectangular holes corresponding to the symbol will be punched in the same column in which the symbol is printed. The printing on the card is of no consequence to the computer; only the holes are important. As we punch symbols on the card, the card will be advanced farther and farther into the middle window. In Fig. 1.3 we show some symbols that can be punched on a card and the holes that correspond to these symbols. As we see, a card is subdivided into 80 columns.

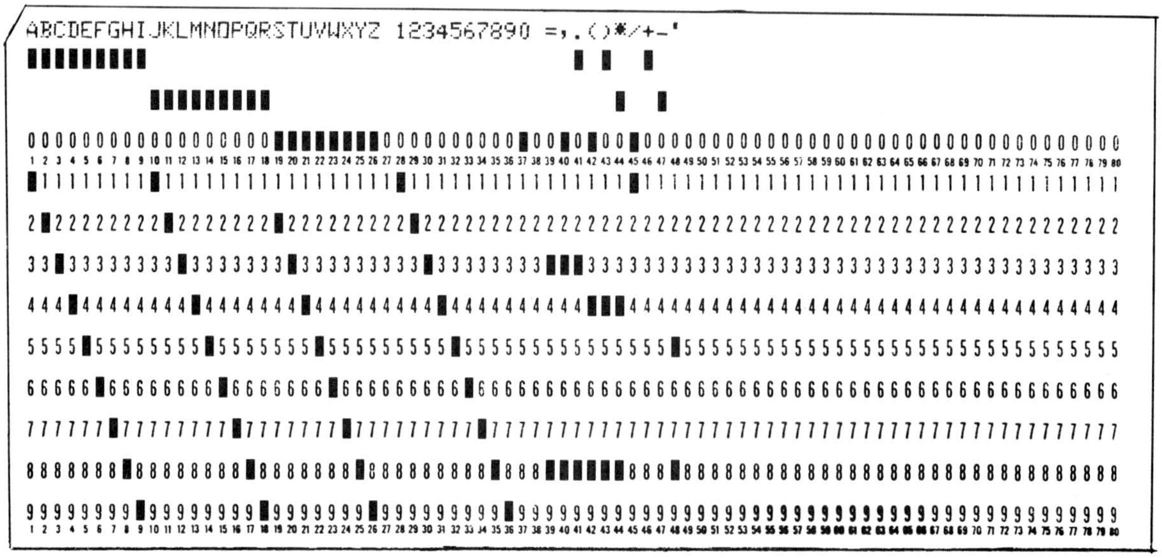

Figure 1.3. The characters punched on a card, and the holes that correspond to these characters.

The keypunch keyboard differs somewhat from a typewriter keyboard. For instance, although you can type lower-case letters—for example, a—on a typewriter, you cannot type them on a keypunch; when you depress the keypunch key marked A, a capital letter A is punched on the card.

Some keys have two symbols on them, for instance,

In order to punch the upper symbol on such a key, you must simultaneously depress the key and the NUM key.

After you have finished punching all the information you want on the card, you press the REL key. This transfers the card from the middle window to the left window. Then, if the card is not automatically ejected into the hopper above this window, press REG.

Above the middle window is a drum that rotates as the card is punched. By placing a specially punched card—called a control card—on this drum and then pressing the lever below the drum to the left, you can, for instance, instruct the keypunch to automatically make the card that you are punching skip to certain columns. If the control card is completely blank, then when you press a key that has two symbols on it, the upper symbol will be punched on the card. The keypunch is then said to be in *numeric mode*.

We now describe the function of the other keys.

ALPHA: If the keypunch is in numeric mode, then, when a given key and the ALPHA key are depressed simultaneously, the lower symbol on the key will be punched.

DUP: This allows you to duplicate the punching from the card in the middle window onto the card in the right-hand window.

BACKSPACE: This moves the card one column to the right, allowing you, for instance, to punch a symbol in a column that you accidentally skipped. The BACKSPACE key is below the middle window.

MULT PCH: This key allows you to punch more than one character in a column. If you simultaneously depress this key and a second key, the card will not advance to the left, and the symbol on the second key will be punched on the card in the same column in which you punched the last symbol.

SKIP: If you are using an appropriate control card, then when this key is depressed the keypunch advances the card to a predetermined column.

We shall explain the function of symbols that are neither numeric nor alphabetic as we encounter them in the book. In the rest of the book, we shall refer to the symbols on the keyboard as characters. There are six levers (or toggle switches) above the keyboard. Under normal conditions, the five leftmost levers should be in the "ON" position. The rightmost lever is used to clear the cards from all the windows and place them in the left hopper.

1.3. Input and Output Devices

Once all the instructions constituting a program are punched on cards, we can submit the deck of cards so that they can be processed by the computer. We take the deck of cards consisting of the program and the data and submit it to the computer center where it is read into a *card reader*. In Fig. 1.4 we show a card reader. As the card reader reads each card, it examines the holes in each column and thus determines which characters we have punched on each card. It transmits this information to the central processing unit, where the compiler determines what instruction we have punched on the card.

Once the program is compiled, unless we do not wish it, the instructions in the program will be printed. If we include the proper instructions, the results of the program will also be printed. The printing is done on the output device called a *line printer*. In Fig. 1.5 we show a line printer.

One device that can be used as both an input and output device is called a magnetic tape drive; it is shown in Fig. 1.6. It is very much like a tape recorder, but instead of recording voice patterns, it records arithmetic data in binary on magnetic tape. We can write information on a magnetic tape and then at some later time read the information as well.

The last device we discuss is called a disk. It is a metal disk on which we store arithmetic information in binary on concentric rings on the disk. We can both read information from a disk and write information on the disk. It is thus another example of a device that can be used for both input and output. Disk units are shown in Fig. 1.7.

Figure 1.4. The IBM 3505 card reader. (Courtesy of IBM.)

Figure 1.5. The IBM 3211 line printer. (Courtesy of IBM.)

Figure 1.6. The IBM 3420 magnetic tape unit. (Courtesy of IBM.)

Figure 1.7. The IBM 3350 disk storage unit. (Courtesy of IBM.)

1.4. Solving a Problem

We now describe the solution of a problem that will give us a further insight into computers and programming. The problem is to determine the regional distribution of people standing in line in a certain city. That is, we wish to determine how many people come from the north, south, east, and west sides of the city.

We begin by drawing on a piece of paper four boxes, which we label N, S, E, and W, as shown in Fig. 1.8a. These letters represent north, south, east, and west, respectively. We shall place in the appropriate box a number indicating the number of people we have encountered from the north, south, east, and west sides of the city, as we question the people in line.

The composition of the line is shown in Fig. 1.8a. The fact that the first letter on the line is a W means that the first person comes from the west; the same type of correspondence is applied to the rest of the line. The arrow indicates which person we are questioning. Before reading the next paragraph, please study all of Fig. 1.8.

We first place a zero in each of the four boxes, as shown in Fig. 1.8a. This indicates that we have not as yet encountered anyone from any section of the city. We ask the first person in line which part of the city he is from. We are told "the west." We record this by adding 1 to the 0 that is in the box marked W, obtaining 1. In order to record this result, we erase the zero that was originally in this box and replace it by the digit 1. The box for the west now contains 1, and the other three boxes still contain 0, as shown in Fig. 1.8b. We ask the second person where he is from; he answers, "the north." We thus add 1 to the 0 that is in the box marked N, obtaining 1. To record this, we erase the 0 in this box and replace it by a 1, as shown in Fig. 1.8c. We see here that the rest of the boxes still contain the numbers they contained in Fig. 1.8b. We ask the third person where he is from; he answers "the west." We now add 1 to the 1 already in the box marked W, obtaining 2. We then erase 1, the previous entry in the box, and replace it with 2, as shown in Fig. 1.8d. We continue to the end of the line, applying this same procedure to each person we question. After the last person has told us where he is from and the information has been recorded, the boxes contain the numbers shown in Fig. 1.8e.

If this problem is to be programmed, the process we just described is called *running* or *executing* the program. When the program is run on a computer, the function of the boxes—that is, to contain or "store" the numbers—is played by the computer's memory locations. Like the boxes, a memory location can store only one number at a time; moreover, when the computer places a number in a memory location, it automatically erases the location's previous contents—that is, the number that was previously stored there. The placing of zeros in all the boxes at the beginning of the problem and the addition of 1's to the correct boxes is done by the computer's logical unit. The people standing in line are called the *data* or *input* to the program. We type on the keypunch both the program that solves the problem and the data for the program. After the program is done—if we so instruct—the computer prints the results of the program on the line printer. The control unit supervises the activities of all the units (except, of course, the keypunch) as they process this problem.

Indeed, all the power of the computer is not exhibited in our example. For instance, the computer can multiply many numbers together and get the results almost immediately. It can do a multitude of complex calculations that man, without the aid of a computer, would hesitate to undertake. In the following chapters we shall give many examples of what computers can do.

SOLVING A PROBLEM

Problem: Determining the regional distribution of people standing in line in a certain city. The letter N denotes north, S denotes south, E denotes east, W denotes west. The arrow indicates which person is being questioned.

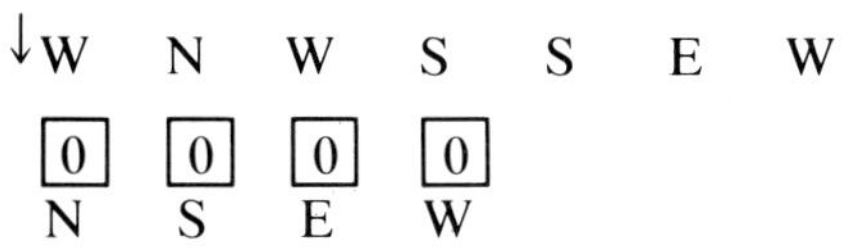

Figure 1.8a. Composition of the line and the contents of the boxes before questioning begins. The arrow is at left of line, indicating that questioning has not begun.

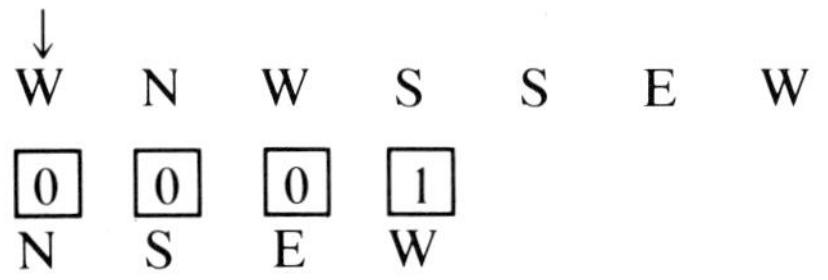

Figure 1.8b. We add 1 to the box for west after questioning the first person.

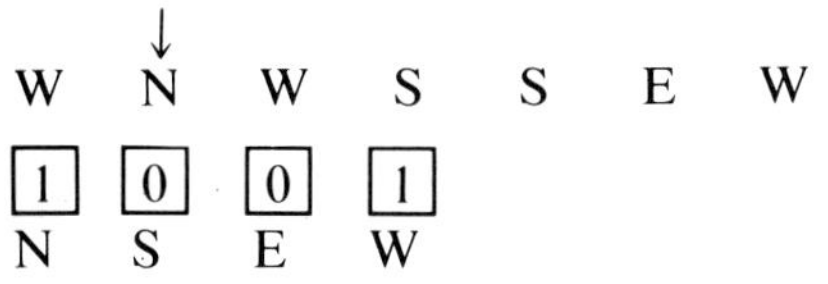

Figure 1.8c. We add 1 to the box for north after questioning the second person.

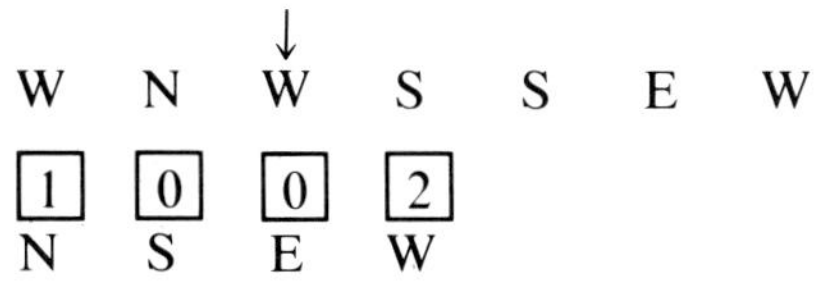

Figure 1.8d. We add 1 to the box for west after questioning the third person. It now contains 2.

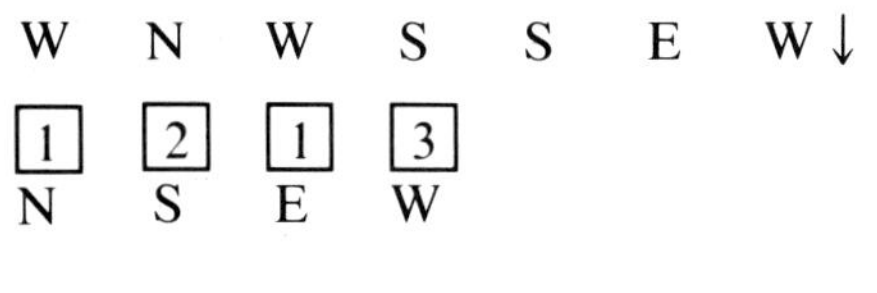

Figure 1.8e. The contents of all boxes after we have questioned each person in the line.

1.5. Algorithms

If we wanted to instruct someone how to conduct the survey discussed in Section 1.4, we would have to write a set of instructions for him to follow. In mathematics, a set of instructions written to solve a problem is called an algorithm. Assuming that the boxes have been already drawn, the algorithm for performing the survey is:

1. Place a zero in each box.
2. Ask a person which part of the city he is from.
3. Add 1 to the proper box.
4. If the person is the last one in line, stop the survey; otherwise repeat instruction 2.

Instruction 3 always follows instruction 2; and instruction 4 always follows instruction 3.

The sequence of how the instructions are performed for the first three people in line and the results of performing these instructions are as follows:

Instruction	Result
1	0 0 0 0
	N E S W
2	We are told W
3	0 0 0 1
	N E S W
4	Not the last person, so perform instruction 2
2	We are told N
3	1 0 0 1
	N E S W
4	Not the last person, so perform instruction 2
2	We are told W
3	1 0 0 2
	N E S W
4	Not the last person, so perform instruction 2

This process is continued up to and including the last person in line. Since he is from the west, a 1 is added to the box marked "W". The algorithm then terminates as directed in instruction 4.

A computer program is simply an algorithm written in a language the compiler can understand. If the algorithm on which the program is based is incorrect, the program will produce incorrect results.

1.6. FORTRAN, WATFOR, and WATFIV

The FORTRAN language has gone through several stages. The current stage, called FORTRAN IV, incorporates practically all the features of the preceding stages. Most of the computer manufacturers have their own version of the FORTRAN IV compiler in use on their computers; in fact, it is possible to have more than one version of the FORTRAN compiler used on a given computer. All these versions are similar except perhaps for some auxiliary features.

What most compilers have in common are the programming instructions incorporated in what is called ANS (American National Standards) Standard FORTRAN. If you wish to write a program that can be used on most compilers, you should write your instructions so that they conform to ANS Standard FORTRAN. When a program can be used by many compilers, we say that it is transportable. We have devoted almost this entire book to a discussion of ANS Standard FORTRAN.

Another compiler, ANS Standard Basic FORTRAN, was written with the smaller computers in mind. Many of the features of Standard FORTRAN are not included in Standard Basic FORTRAN. We note this in footnotes to the text.

A compiler developed in Canada at the University of Waterloo simplifies some of the features of FORTRAN that beginners find difficult—notably the instructions that accept data from the card reader and prepare results for the line printer. This compiler is called WATFOR. The name is taken from WATerloo FORtran. A more flexible version of WATFOR is called WATFIV (WATerloo Fortran IV). We describe both WATFOR and WATFIV.

All the instructions in ANS Standard FORTRAN were incorporated into WATFOR. And all the instructions in WATFOR were incorporated into WATFIV.

A new compiler called WATFIV-S incorporates the features of WATFIV; moreover, what is important is that it enables you to write your programs in a more elegant way using what is called structured programming. We describe structured programming features of WATFIV-S in appropriate places in this book. As of January 1977 one of these features* has been incorporated into the proposed ANS FORTRAN revision.

The reader might wish to take more than a casual interest in the parts of the book that discuss WATFOR/WATFIV and the other non-Standard features because they have been incorporated into the proposed ANS FORTRAN revision.

* This feature is the IF-THEN-ELSE statement.

2

Introduction to FORTRAN

2.1. General Remarks

A FORTRAN program is a series of statements that are instructions to the computer. Each statement is keypunched on a separate card.

In Fig. 2.1a, we see a simple FORTRAN program written on a sheet of paper called a coding form. This sheet will indicate to the person who keypunches the program, in which columns to keypunch the different characters that comprise the statements in the program. The first line of this particular program is a comment. If a C is keypunched in column 1 of a program card, the computer will not process the card any further, but will simply print what is on that card when it prints the statements in the program. Comment cards are important in that they may aid someone reading the program to understand the program; however, they are completely overlooked by the compiler. Thus a workable FORTRAN program can be written without comment cards.

The rest of the lines represent FORTRAN statements that *are* processed. These are, of course, the statements that are of primary importance in a program. (They will be discussed in this chapter and other chapters of the book.) These statements may be keypunched anywhere between columns 7 and 72 on the card; however, under normal circumstances we begin simple statements in column 7 as shown in Fig. 2.1b. Figure 2.1b indicates how the program of Fig. 2.1a would appear when keypunched on cards.

2.2. The Assignment Statement

In order to store a number in a location in the computer's memory, we give these locations names, which are called *variables*, and assign numbers to them in the program. In the program of Fig. 2.1a, the assignment of the numbers to variables is made by a statement that includes an equals sign. It is called an *Assignment* statement. In the assignment statements in this program, VAR1 and VAR2 are the variables. In the first line of the program, we assign the number 11.4 to VAR1 by keypunching

```
VAR1=11.4
```

WRITING A SIMPLE PROGRAM ON A CODING FORM

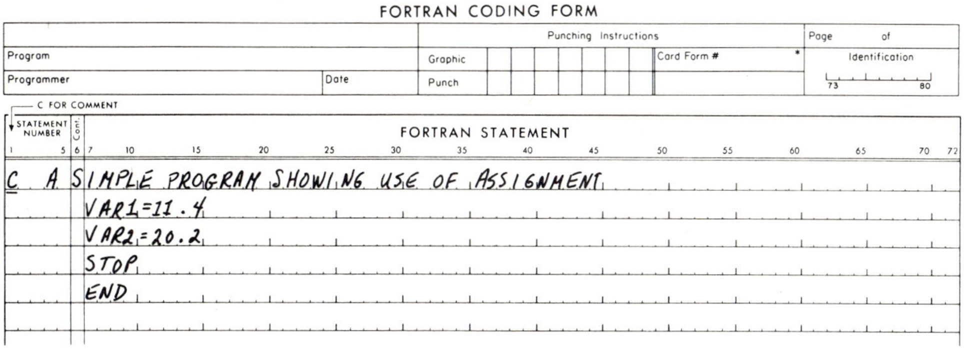

Figure 2.1a. A simple FORTRAN program written on a coding form. A program consists of statements. When a C appears in column 1, that statement is not processed by the computer. It is just used by the programmer to write comments about the program. Hence it is called a comment card.

KEYPUNCHING A SIMPLE PROGRAM

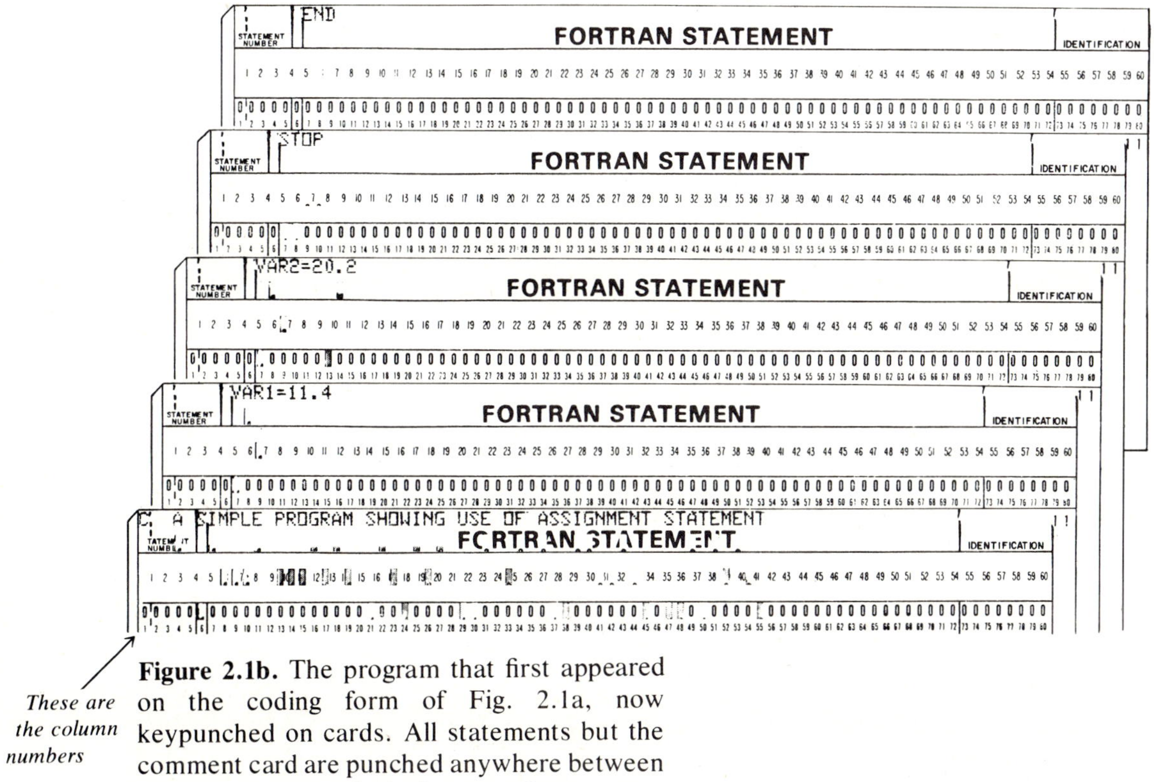

Figure 2.1b. The program that first appeared on the coding form of Fig. 2.1a, now keypunched on cards. All statements but the comment card are punched anywhere between column 7 and 72 inclusive, on the program card. The END statement instructs the compiler that the program is finished.

Thus we have instructed the computer to place the number 11.4 in the memory location named VAR1. In a similar way, we next assign the number 20.2 to VAR2 by typing

```
VAR2=20.2
```

Another way of describing what has happened in these two statements is to say that the VAR1 has the value 11.4 and VAR2 the value 20.2.

We instruct the computer to compile and then execute (run) the program by typing certain instructions on cards that are not part of the program. These cards are called *control cards,* and in general they are used to instruct the compiler how to process our program. Since different compilers require different types of control cards, we will, throughout the text, simply describe a given program and then the results of executing it. In the Appendix however, we describe how to write control cards for two systems: FORTRAN IV on the IBM system 360/370; and WATFIV on the IBM system 360/370.

2.3. The END Statement

Sometime after we have submitted our deck of cards to the computer, the computer operator will run our program. The compiler first checks each statement in our program for grammatical errors until it reaches the END statement. The END statement indicates to the compiler that we have finished writing the program, i.e., that no more cards will follow. The END statement must appear as the last statement in any FORTRAN program.

2.4. The Listing of the Program; the STOP Statement

As the compiler checks each statement for errors it prints or *lists* the statement on the line printer. In Fig. 2.2a we see a listing of the program. The program is listed exactly as we keypunched it on the program cards. Since the first card in the program is a comment card, the compiler (after it detects the C in column 1 of the card) simply prints the contents of the card and does no checking; however, the computer does check the other statements in the program of Fig. 2.2a. If a statement has an error in it, the compiler will indicate that it has found an error by printing an error message. Since none of the statements contain errors, the computer prints no error messages.

When the computer performs the task that a program statement has instructed it to perform, the computer is said to *execute* the statement. We will soon see how the computer executes the statements in the program.

After the compiler has checked the FORTRAN program for errors and has found none, it translates the program ultimately into machine language (each FORTRAN statement is translated typically into many machine language instructions). The computer will then execute the translated program, beginning with the machine language equivalent of the first noncomment card in our program and then executing the machine language equivalent of each successive card until it reaches the STOP statement. The computer follows this order unless we specifically instruct it in the program to follow a different order; we will describe how to change this order later in the book. The STOP statement instructs the computer to terminate the program.

USING THE ASSIGNMENT STATEMENT

```
C   A SIMPLE PROGRAM SHOWING USE OF ASSIGNMENT STATEMENT
      VAR1=11.4
      VAR2=20.2
      STOP
      END
```

Figure 2.2a. In the program the number 11.4 is assigned to the variable VAR1 and 20.2 to VAR2 in the assignment statements.

On most compilers, if you do not include a STOP statement in the program, the compiler will insert one directly before the END statement when it translates the program.

2.5. Executing the Program

We now follow the execution of the program in Fig. 2.2a with the help of the Table for Fig. 2.2a. This table shows the values of the variables as each card of the program is executed—the table is meant to be used as a learning aid; it is not part of the program.

Card	Description	VAR1	VAR2
1st	Comment	NOT EXECUTED	
2nd	VAR1=11.4	11.4	Undef
3rd	VAR2=20.2	11.4	20.2

We see from the table that the first card—the comment card—is not executed. When the second card is executed, the value associated with VAR1 in the computer's memory is 11.4; however, VAR2 has not yet been assigned a number. In such a case, we say that VAR2 is *undefined*. This is reflected in the table by the entry Undef. When a variable (such as VAR1 here) has been assigned a number, we say that it has been defined. When the third card is executed, we see from the third line of the table that the value associated with VAR2 is 20.2.

Once a variable is assigned a given number, it retains that assignment until the end of the program unless we assign it a new number. Thus, we see from the third line of the table for Fig. 2.2a that when the third card is executed, the computer remembers that 11.4 was assigned to VAR1.

When the computer encounters the STOP statement, it finishes execution. It usually signifies this by printing some message on the line printer, such as EXECUTION COMPLETE, or some computer memory bookkeeping about the run of the program.

The results of the execution are shown in Fig. 2.2b. We note to our disappointment that the computer has printed nothing in Fig. 2.2b except some computer memory bookkeeping information indicating that the computer has finished execution.*

```
CORE USAGE          OBJECT CODE=        192 BYTES,
```

Nothing else was printed because the computer executed the two assignment statements, encountered the STOP statement, and stopped. Since we did not include a statement in the program instructing the computer to communicate the assignments to us, it did not do so. In the next section, we remedy this situation.

* This is only the beginning of the bookkeeping information as printed by the WATFIV compiler.

EXECUTING THE PROGRAM

```
C    A SIMPLE PROGRAM SHOWING USE OF ASSIGNMENT STATEMENT
      VAR1=11.4
      VAR2=20.2
      STOP
      END
```

Figure 2.2a. This figure is reproduced for the reader's convenience.

Card	Description	VAR1	VAR2
1st	Comment	NOT EXECUTED	
2nd	VAR1 = 11.4	11.4	Undef
3rd	VAR2 = 20.2	11.4	20.2

Table for Fig. 2.2a. The status of the variable in Fig. 2.2a given by card number during execution. A comment card is never executed. In the first assignment statement, the value of VAR2 has not yet been defined. When the second assignment statement is executed, the computer remembers that 11.4 was assigned to VAR1.

```
CORE USAGE          OBJECT CODE=        192 BYTES,
```

Figure 2.2b. The results of running the program of Fig. 2.2a. Since we did not include in the program, a statement instructing the computer to print the results, it did not. It simply prints some bookkeeping information indicating that it has finished executing our program. The STOP statement instructs the computer to terminate the program.

2.6. The WRITE and FORMAT Statements

We now rewrite the program of Fig. 2.2a and add a statement instructing the computer to print the numbers that have been assigned to VAR1 and VAR2. To do this on a FORTRAN system or a WATFOR/WATFIV system, we add to the program the statement

```
WRITE(6,10) VAR1,VAR2
```

as shown in Fig. 2.3a. The first number—here 6—in the WRITE statement refers to the output unit we want information printed on; the 6 is the number most commonly designated at computer centers to represent the line printer. The 10 refers to the statement that describes the form (or format) in which we want our results to be printed. Appropriately enough, this type of statement is called a FORMAT statement. In order to make it possible for a statement (here a FORMAT statement) to be referred to by another statement (here the WRITE statement), the "referred to" statement must have a statement number—also called a label. We have chosen 10 to be the FORMAT's statement number:

```
 10    FORMAT(1X, F10.3, F9.4)
```

However, we could have chosen any integer between 1 and 99999. The statement number must be punched anywhere in the first 5 columns of the program card, as we have shown in Fig. 2.3b for the FORMAT statement. We punch these numbers, however, starting in column 2 in order to improve readability; we have not printed them starting in column 1, since we want the person reading the program to be able to immediately distinguish between statement numbers and the C in the comment statements.

The terms appearing between the parentheses in the FORMAT are called *field specifications*. Here, 1X is the first field specification; F10.3, the second; and F9.4, the third. When 1X appears at the extreme left of the FORMAT, as it does here, it instructs the line printer to vertically advance the page one line before the line printer starts printing. The 1X is said to be used for "carriage control." The F10.3 and F9.4 each describe a group of columns on a line to be printed on the line printer. These groups of columns are called *fields*. F10.3 describes the first field appearing on the left of the line printed; F9.4 describes the second field from the left. Each of the two field specifications beginning with the letter F refer to one of the variables in the associated WRITE statement:

```
       WRITE(6,10) VAR1,VAR2
 10    FORMAT(1X, F10.3, F9.4)
```

Since F10.3 immediately follows 1X, it refers to the first variable in the WRITE statement, i.e., VAR1. Since F9.4 is the second field specification to follow the 1X, it refers to VAR2, the second variable in the WRITE statement. The F in both of these field specifications indicates that the numbers that will be printed each have a decimal point in them; these

USING THE WRITE STATEMENT

```
C   PROGRAM SHOWS THE ASSIGNMENT OF NUMBERS TO VARIABLES AND
C   THEN PRINTS THEIR VALUES USING THE WRITE STATEMENT
        VAR1=11.4
        VAR2=20.2
        WRITE(6,10) VAR1,VAR2
 10     FORMAT(1X, F10.3, F9.4)
        STOP
        END
```

Figure 2.3a. Using the WRITE and FORMAT statements to print our results. In the WRITE statement, the 6 indicates that we want our results printed on the line printer. The 10 indicates that we want the variables appearing in the WRITE statement to be printed as detailed in statement 10, the FORMAT statement. The 1X, F10.3, and F9.4 in the FORMAT are called field specifications. The variables in the WRITE statement must be separated by commas.

THE FORMAT STATEMENT

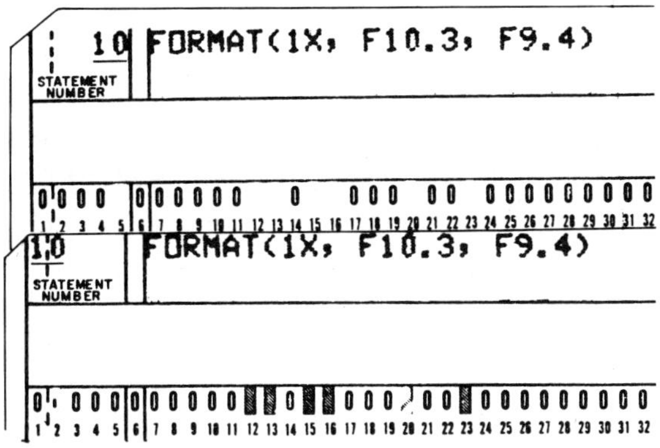

Figure 2.3b. The FORMAT statement must have a statement number. These two cards show that the statement number may appear anywhere between columns 1 and 5, inclusively. The 1X instructs the line printer to vertically advance the output page 1 space. The F10.3 refers to how we want VAR1 printed, and F9.4, to how we want VAR2 printed. Thus, here only the field specifications beginning with the letter F—called F format—refer to the variables.

field specifications are called F format. The 10 in F10.3 is called the *field width*; it instructs the computer to print the value of VAR1 in a field 10 columns wide. Since F10.3 is the first field specification, the value of VAR2 is printed in the first 10 columns on the left of the output page. The .3 instructs the computer to print 3 digits after printing the decimal point; since 11.4 (the number assigned to VAR1) has only 1 digit to the right of the decimal point, the computer inserts 2 zeros after the 4 when the value is printed. Thus it is printed as 11.400 when the program is run as is shown in Fig. 2.3c. For instructional purposes, we have labeled the columns in this figure

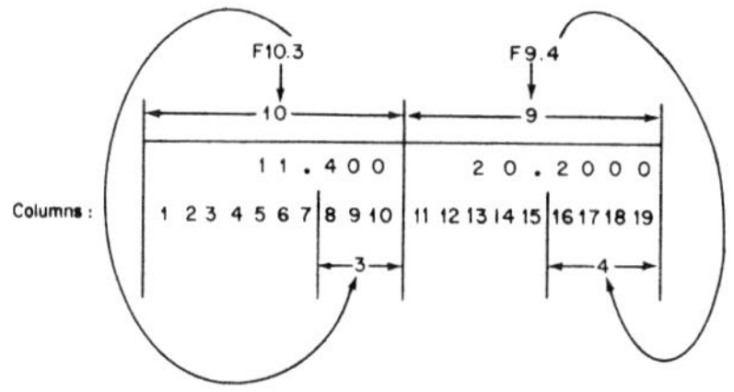

F9.4 describes the second field on the page; the 9 instructs the computer to print the value of VAR2 in a field 9 columns wide. On the output line, this field comes directly after the 10 column-wide field that 11.400 was printed in. The .4 in F9.4 instructs the computer to print 4 digits after the decimal point when it prints the value of VAR1 (i.e., 20.2). Thus it is printed as 20.2000. The computer prints all numbers so that they are shifted to the right in the field. Another way of saying this is that the numbers are *right-justified* when they are printed. Thus, 11.400 is printed in the 5th to the 10th columns, inclusively; and 20.2000 is printed in the 13th to the 19th columns, inclusively. The results as they actually appear on the line printer (without the columns being labeled) are shown in Fig. 2.3d.

```
    11.400  20.2000
```

We see from the table for Fig. 2.3a that when the WRITE statement is executed, both VAR1 and VAR2 are defined. Thus the computer will have no difficulty in printing their values. However, if either VAR1 or VAR2 had not been defined when the WRITE statement was executed, its value on any FORTRAN system would be printed as zero or some arbitrary number (depending on the system we ran the program on). Another thing to be noted in the table is that the FORMAT statement is not executed. When the WRITE statement associated with a specific FORMAT statement is executed, the computer refers to the FORMAT statement to see how the programmer wants the variables in the WRITE statement printed.

Whenever one or more variables are listed in a statement, they are collectively known, appropriately, as a *list*. Thus here the variables in the list in the WRITE statement are VAR1 and VAR2.

HOW RESULTS APPEAR ON THE PRINTER

```
C   PROGRAM SHOWS THE ASSIGNMENT OF NUMBERS TO VARIABLES AND
C   THEN PRINTS THEIR VALUES USING THE WRITE STATEMENT
       VAR1=11.4
       VAR2=20.2
       WRITE(6,10) VAR1,VAR2
 10    FORMAT(1X, F10.3, F9.4)
       STOP
       END
```

Figure 2.3a. We reproduce this figure for the reader's convenience.

Card	Description	VAR1	VAR2
1st	Comment	NOT EXECUTED	
2nd	Comment	NOT EXECUTED	
3rd	VAR1 = 11.4	11.4	Undef
4th	VAR2 = 20.2	11.4	20.2
5th	WRITE	11.4	20.2
6th	FORMAT	NOT EXECUTED	

Table for Fig. 2.3a. Status of the variable assignments for Fig. 2.3a. *Note*: Both variables must be (and have been) assigned values before they are printed by the WRITE statement. Also, FORMAT statements are not executed. They can be placed, therefore, anywhere in the program before the END statement. However, it is good programming style to place them immediately after the WRITE statement that refers to them.

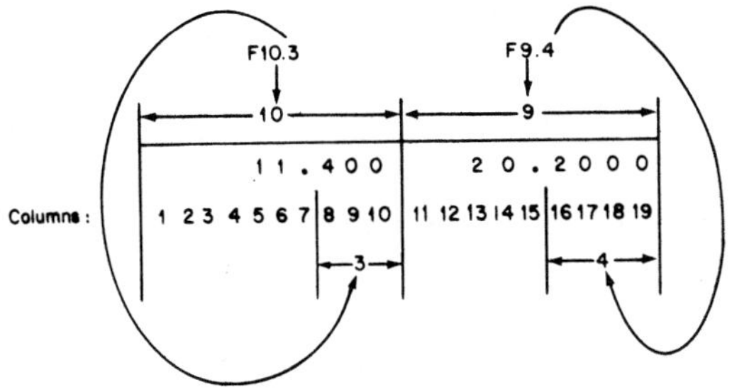

Figure 2.3c. The results of running the program of Fig. 2.3a. We have labeled the columns in order to show where the values are printed on the line printer. The 10 in F10.3 is the number of columns allotted to the printing of VAR1. These columns are called the *field* and 10 is called the *field width*. The 3 indicates how many digits will be printed after the decimal point. Thus, since the value of VAR1 is 11.4, two zeros follow the 4 when 11.4 is printed. Both numbers are printed so that they are at the right of their respective fields. This is called being right justified.

Value of VAR 1 — *Value of* VAR 2

```
11.400  20.2000
```

Figure 2.3d. The results of running the program of Fig. 2.3a as they actually appear on the line printer.

In Fig. 2.4a, we have added

```
      WRITE(6,20) VAR2,VAR1
20    FORMAT(1X, F8.3, F10.4)
```

to the previous program. Since VAR2 appears first in the WRITE statement, it is paired with F8.3. Thus the value of VAR2 is printed in the first 8 columns—again right-justified—and 3 digits follow the decimal point. Since VAR1 appears as the second variable in the WRITE statement, it is paired with F10.4. Its value will be printed so that it is right-justified in a field 10 columns wide and 4 digits will follow the decimal point in the result. All of this is shown in Fig. 2.4b. Each WRITE statement starts a new line of printing. Thus

```
11.400   20.2000
```

is printed by the first WRITE statement and

```
20.200    11.4000
```

is printed by the second WRITE. Another point that should be noted in this program is that no two statements can have the same statement number. Thus we use 10 for the first FORMAT and 20 for the second.

Although it is not necessary, we have chosen the statement numbers so that they are in ascending order. For more intricate programs, this makes the program easier for the reader to follow. However, had we wanted to, we could have labeled the first FORMAT as, for example, statement 18 and the second as statement 3. Of course, this means that the first WRITE statement would now have to be WRITE(6,18) VAR1, VAR2; and the second, WRITE(6,3) VAR2, VAR1.

We now describe the execution of the program. The computer proceeds as it did for the program of Fig. 2.3a, as is shown in the first two lines of the table for Fig. 2.4a. It is important to note that after the values of VAR1 and VAR2 are printed in the first WRITE statement, the contents of VAR1 and VAR2 are not erased—their values are simply copied from the memory onto the line printer. Thus when the next WRITE statement is executed, the computer has no difficulty in printing the results. We remark here that since the FORMAT statements are not executed, they could in fact be placed anywhere in the program before the END statement and in any order. However, it is considered good programming style to place a FORMAT statement immediately after the WRITE statement that refers to it.

MORE ON THE WRITE STATEMENT

```
C   PROGRAM USES TWO WRITE STATEMENTS TO PRINT RESULTS
C  IN THE SECOND WRITE STATEMENT, THE ORDER OF THE VARIABLES
C   IS REVERSED
        VAR1=11.4
        VAR2=20.2
        WRITE(6,10) VAR1,VAR2
 10     FORMAT(1X, F10.3, F9.4)
        WRITE(6,20) VAR2,VAR1
 20     FORMAT(1X, F8.3, F10.4)
        STOP
        END
```

Figure 2.4a. Program shows that when we reverse the order of the variables in the WRITE statement, their values are printed in reverse order. Two statements cannot have the same statement number. Thus the two FORMAT statements have different statement numbers.

Card	Description	VAR1	VAR2
3rd	VAR1 = 11.4	11.4	Undef
4th	VAR2 = 20.2	11.4	20.2
5th	WRITE(6,10)	11.4	20.2
6th	FORMAT	NOT EXECUTED	
7th	WRITE(6,20)	11.4	20.2
8th	FORMAT	NOT EXECUTED	

Table for Fig. 2.4a. We see that after the values of VAR1 and VAR2 are printed by the first WRITE statement, these values are still stored in the memory. Thus the computer will have no difficulty in executing the second WRITE statement.

```
    11.400   20.2000 ←——— Printed by WRITE (6,10) VAR 1, VAR 2
20.200     11.4000 ←——— Printed by WRITE (6,20) VAR 2, VAR 1
```

Figure 2.4b. Each WRITE statement produces a new line of results. The second WRITE statement is paired with statement 20. Thus F8.3 is matched with VAR2, and F10.4 with VAR1.

2.7. The Format-Free PRINT Statement

If the computer system we are using includes the WATFIV/WATFOR compiler, we can also write the preceding programs without FORMAT statements, using what is called a format-free PRINT. For instance, if we were writing the program of Fig. 2.4a for the WATFIV/WATFOR compiler, we could replace the two pairs of WRITE and FORMAT statements with PRINT statements as shown in Fig. 2.4c. Thus

```
PRINT, VAR1,VAR2
```

takes the place of WRITE(6,10) VAR1,VAR2 and the associated FORMAT statement. It prints the value of VAR1 and then to the right of that, it prints the value of VAR2. However, it produces the results in exponential form when the program is executed, as shown by the first line in Fig. 2.4d:

```
0.1140000E 02     0.2020000E 02
```

The E 02 in 0.1140000E 02 means that 0.114 is multiplied by 10^2, i.e., its value is 0.114×10^2 or 0.114×100, i.e., 11.4. Similarly, 0.2020000E 02 is equivalent to 0.202×10^2, or 20.2. In the second PRINT statement, we reverse the variables and get the results in reverse order. Although the PRINT statement is simpler to use than the equivalent WRITE and FORMAT statements, the programmer has no control over how the results of a PRINT statement appear.

We note that in the PRINT statement, just as in the WRITE statement, the variables (here VAR1 and VAR2) must be separated by commas. However, in the PRINT statement, a comma must precede the first variable (here VAR1) as well.

The PRINT should be of interest to non-WATFOR/WATFIV users as well, since the proposed new version of ANS Standard FORTRAN includes a format-free WRITE statement in which an asterisk replaces the format statement number. Thus, for instance, WRITE(6,*) VAR1,VAR2 would print the values of VAR1 and VAR2 without a format. This form of the WRITE statement may also be used on the WATFOR/WATFIV compiler.

USING THE WATFOR/WATFIV PRINT **STATEMENTS**

```
C   PROGRAM PRINTS THE VALUE OF TWO VARIABLES
C   USING WATFOR/WATFIV PRINT STATEMENTS
      VAR1=11.4
      VAR2=20.2
      PRINT, VAR1,VAR2
      PRINT, VAR2,VAR1
      STOP
      END
```

Figure 2.4c. The previous program written using the format-free WATFOR/WATFIV PRINT statements. No FORMAT statement is used. A comma must follow PRINT and separate the variables in the PRINT statement. The standard WRITE statement can also be used on the WATFOR/WATFIV compiler.

```
0.1140000E 02      0.2020000E 02 <—— Printed by PRINT, VAR 1, VAR 2
0.2020000E 02      0.1140000E 02 <—— Printed by PRINT, VAR 2, VAR 1
```

Figure 2.4d. The results are printed in exponential form. The E 02 indicates multiplication by 10^2. Thus 0.1140000E 02 equals 0.114×10^2, and 0.2020000E 02 equals 0.2020×10^2.

2.8. Performing an Addition

We now write a program that adds two salaries, as shown in Fig. 2.5a. The salaries will be represented by the variables SAL1 and SAL2. Their sum will be represented by SALTOT. It is considered good programming style to choose the variable names so that they indicate to you or someone else reading the program what the variables represent. In this case, SAL1 represents the first salary; SAL2, the second salary; and SALTOT, the total salary. We add the salaries and assign their result to SALTOT in

```
SALTOT=SAL1 + SAL2
```

This statement is another example of an assignment statement. The plus sign is the symbol for addition.

From the table for Fig. 2.5a, we see how the computer executes this statement.

Card	Description	SAL1	SAL2	SALTOT
7th	SALTOT = SAL1 + SAL2	346.33	287.62	633.95

It takes the value of SAL1 (which we see is 346.33) adds it to the value of SAL2 (which we see is 287.62) and assigns the result (which we see is 633.95) to SALTOT. However, after this is done, the values of SAL1 and SAL2 are still assigned to them. Thus in the next statement,

```
WRITE(6,20) SALTOT,SAL1,SAL2
```

the computer will have no difficulty in printing the values of all three variables. In statement 20, the associated FORMAT statement, we have to describe the fields for the three variables. We have thus added one field specification to those that occurred in the previous FORMAT statements we wrote. We thus write statement 20 as

```
20   FORMAT(1X, F10.2, F10.2, F10.2)
```

In Fig. 2.5b, the results are shown. We see that when the computer did the addition, it kept track of the decimal point. If we ran the program in Fig. 2.5b on the WATFOR/WATFIV system and wanted to use a format-free PRINT statement, we would write PRINT, SALTOT, SAL1, SAL2 instead of the WRITE/FORMAT statements.

PERFORMING AN ADDITION

```
C   PROGRAM ADDS TWO SALARIES AND THEN PRINTS THEM.
C   ASSIGN THE FIRST WEEK'S SALARY TO SAL1
C   ASSIGN THE SECOND WEEK'S SALARY TO SAL2
       SAL1=346.33
       SAL2=287.62
C   ASSIGN THE SUM TO SALTOT
       SALTOT=SAL1 + SAL2
       WRITE(6,20) SALTOT,SAL1,SAL2
 20    FORMAT(1X, F10.2, F10.2, F10.2)
       STOP
       END
```

Figure 2.5a. A program that illustrates a simple addition. Since there are three variables in the WRITE statement, there are three field specifications beginning with F in the FORMAT.

Card	Description	SAL1	SAL2	SALTOT
4th	SAL1 = 346.33	346.33	Undef	Undef
5th	SAL2 = 287.62	346.33	287.62	Undef
7th	SALTOT = SAL1 + SAL2	346.33	287.62	633.95
8th	WRITE	346.33	287.62	633.95

Table for Fig. 2.5a. In the 3rd line we see that the value of SAL1 is added to the value of SAL2 and the result is assigned to SALTOT. The computer automatically keeps track of the decimal point's position in the addition.

```
Value of SALTOT   Value of SAL 1   Value of SAL 2
   ↙                 ↙                ↙
633.95          346.33          287.62
```

Figure 2.5b. The results of running the program of Fig. 2.5a.

2.9. Performing a Multiplication

The symbol for multiplication in FORTRAN is the asterisk, *. We use it in the program of Fig. 2.6a, which calculates the distance, DIST, a car goes by multiplying its velocity, VELOC, by the time it has traveled, TIME. Thus in

```
DIST=VELOC*TIME
```

we multiply the value of VELOC by the value of TIME and assign the result to DIST. This statement is another example of an assignment statement. We see from the table for Fig. 2.6a that when DIST = VELOC * TIME is executed

Card	Description	VELOC	TIME	DIST
8th	DIST = VELOC * TIME	60.0	3.5	210.0

the product 210.0 is assigned to DIST. We then print all the results in WRITE(6,10) DIST, VELOC, TIME and see in Fig. 2.6b what they are.

If this program were written for the WATFOR/WATFIV system, we could substitute PRINT, DIST, VELOC, TIME for the WRITE and FORMAT statements we just used.

A calculation involving only numbers can also be done in an assignment statement. We therefore have rewritten the preceding program by eliminating the first two statements in the program and simply rewriting the final assignment statement as

```
DIST=60.0*3.5
```

This is shown in Fig. 2.6c. We print the results using WRITE(6,100) DIST. Since there is only one variable in the WRITE statement, we need only one field specification after the 1X in the associated FORMAT statement. We thus write it as 100 FORMAT(1X,F10.1). The results are shown in Fig. 2.6d. If we ran this program on the WATFOR/WATFIV compiler and wanted to use a format-free PRINT statement, we would write PRINT, DIST instead of the WRITE/FORMAT statements.

PERFORMING A MULTIPLICATION

```
C   PROGRAM CALCULATES DISTANCE A CAR GOES GIVEN ITS
C   VELOCITY AND TIME TRAVELED
C   ASSIGN A VALUE TO THE VELOCITY
        VELOC=60.0
C   ASSIGN A VALUE TO THE TIME
        TIME=3.5
C   CALCULATE THE DISTANCE
        DIST=VELOC*TIME
        WRITE(6,10) DIST, VELOC, TIME
 10     FORMAT(1X, F10.1, F10.1, F10.1 )
        STOP
        END
```

Figure 2.6a. A program that illustrates a multiplication. The symbol for multiplication is *.

Card	Description	VELOC	TIME	DIST
4th	VELOC = 60.0	60.0	Undef	Undef
6th	TIME = 3.5	60.0	3.5	Undef
8th	DIST = VELOC * TIME	60.0	3.5	210.0

Table for Fig. 2.6a. In the 3rd line we see that the value of VELOC is multiplied by the value of TIME and the result is stored in DIST. Again, the computer keeps track of the position of the decimal point.

```
Value of DIST   Value of VELOC   Value of TIME
     ↙               ↙                ↙
  210.0           60.0             3.5
```

Figure 2.6b. The results of running the program of Fig. 2.6a.

```
C   DISTANCE IS CALCULATED BY USING ONLY ONE ASSIGNMENT STATEMENT
        DIST=60.0*3.5
        WRITE(6,100) DIST
 100    FORMAT(1X,F10.1)
        STOP
        END
```

Figure 2.6c. This program shows that a calculation involving only numbers can be done in an assignment statement. Since there is only one variable in the WRITE statement, we need only one field specification beginning with an F in the FORMAT statement.

```
210.0 ←———— Value of DIST
```

Figure 2.6d. The results of running the program of Fig. 2.6c.

2.10. Restrictions and Limitations in Using F Format

When we use F format, we have to adhere to certain restrictions. The general form of F format is F*w*.*d* where *w* is the field width and *d* is the number of digits that will be printed to the right of the decimal point. For instance, in F10.4, *w* is 10 and *d* is 4. Since the field width includes, among other things, not only the digits represented by *d* but also the decimal point, then on most compilers the minimum allowable field width for a given *d* is: $w = d + 1$. Thus F5.4 is the legal format with the minimum *w* for *d* equal to 4. This field specification accommodates no digits to the left of the decimal point when the result is printed.

Adhering to the restriction that $w \geq d + 1$ (i.e., *w* must be equal to or greater than $d + 1$) will not ensure that we get the result we desire. For instance, if we calculate DIST= 0.03*0.001 as shown in Fig. 2.7a, then the result is 0.00003. When we print this, we want at least 5 digits to follow the decimal point; however, if, for instance we use F10.4 to print the result, only 4 digits will follow the decimal point. What happens when we make this mistake is shown in Fig. 2.7b when the program is run. Since the computer cannot print all the digits, it rounds the results to 0.0000 as is shown on the left of Fig. 2.7b. Thus this field gives us no idea of what the answer is. Therefore, if we expect to get a small number for an answer, we should make *d* large enough so that we get a satisfactory result. Thus, when we use F10.6, the answer is printed as 0.000030, as shown on the right of Fig. 2.7b.

We now investigate what happens if the field width is not large enough to accommodate all the digits to the left of the decimal point, as shown in Fig. 2.7c. There we calculate DIST=300.0*500.0, which yields the result 150000.0. This number has six digits to the left of the decimal point. If we use F10.4 to print the answer, since the decimal point and the 4 already specify five columns, there will only be five columns remaining to the left of the decimal point in which to print the result. Thus there is no room for the 1 in 150000. What happens is that, on most systems, the computer prints asterisks in the field, as shown in Fig. 2.7d. If we use F13.4 as the field specification, the computer prints the results without any difficulty; this, too, is shown in Fig. 2.7d.

In short, although the *d* part of the F field specification explicitly specifies how many digits appear to the right of the decimal point, the F field specification does not explicitly specify how many digits will appear to the left of the decimal point—you must allow for the digits by making *w* large enough.

One more consideration that we have not mentioned is that one column is used for the minus sign if the number printed is negative. The minus sign is printed directly to the left of the number. Thus the minimum field width needed to print −1234.5678 if we wish to see all the digits to the right of the decimal point is 10. So we could use F10.4 to print the result. The field specification with the minimum field width we could use to get any result here is F6.0. This would yield the result −1235.; no digit is printed to the right of the decimal point and the rounded result is printed. As a result of all this, our advice to the reader is: If you use F format, be sure to specify a field width that leaves ample room for the entire constant to be printed. In the beginning of Chapter 8 we present a somewhat more detailed description of printing using F format.

CHARACTERISTICS OF F FORMAT

```
C   SHOWS THAT F FORMAT ROUNDS RESULTS
      DIST=0.03*0.001
      WRITE(6,10) DIST,DIST
 10   FORMAT(1X, F10.4, F10.6)
      STOP
      END
```

Figure 2.7a. Since the value of DIST is 0.000030, the 4 in F10.4 does not provide enough columns after the decimal point to accommodate the result. The computer rounds the result to 0.0000. The 6 in F10.6 provides enough digits, so the computer prints 0.000030.

Described by F10.4 *Described by* F10.6

```
 0.0000   0.000030
```

Figure 2.7b. Running the program of Fig. 2.7a.

```
C   SHOWS THAT F FORMAT MAY NOT BE
C   ABLE TO ACCOMMODATE LARGE NUMBERS
      DIST=300.0*500.0
      WRITE(6,10) DIST,DIST
 10   FORMAT(1X, F10.4, F13.4)
      STOP
      END
```

Figure 2.7c. Since the value of DIST is 150000, F10.4 does not provide enough columns to the left of the decimal point to accommodate the 6 digits in the result. The computer thus prints asterisks. F13.4 does provide enough columns, so the computer prints an acceptable result.

Described by F10.4 *Described by* F13.4

```
 **********   150000.0000
```

Figure 2.7d. Running the program of Fig. 2.7c.

2.11. REAL and INTEGER Mode

You may have asked yourself why we wrote the value of VELOC in Fig. 2.6a as 60.0 instead of 60, i.e., without a decimal point. We now give the answer.

There are two types of numbers in FORTRAN. Those we have used in all our programs until now are called REAL numbers—REAL numbers are written with a decimal point in them; examples of REAL numbers that we can write at this time are: 16.04, 138., and 196.2316. The other type of number is called an INTEGER number—INTEGER numbers *are not* written with decimal points in them; 16, 314, and 1893 are examples.

In computer languages, numbers are called *numerical constants* or simply *constants*. The reason for this is that a constant's value does not change. The computer assigns each constant in the program to a memory location during compilation of the program. On the other hand, although the computer reserves a memory location for each variable during compilation of the program, the computer—as we have seen—does not assign values to the variables until the program is executed. Even then, the value assigned to a variable is not necessarily permanent. The value can be changed—as we shall see in Section 2.15—during the course of the program's execution; hence the term variable. We now discuss the rules for forming constants.

You are not allowed to place a comma in a constant. Thus 6,712 is not a valid constant, neither is 6,712.36. Negative constants are written with a minus sign preceding them. Thus −6712 is a negative INTEGER constant and −172.638 is a negative REAL constant.

There is a limit to the maximum number of digits you can use in a constant. This limit depends on the machine you are using. For instance, on the IBM system 360/370, the maximum number of decimal digits you can use in a REAL constant is a little more* than 7, and in an INTEGER constant it is approximately 10. In Table 2.1 we give examples of REAL constants that we can write at this time, and INTEGER constants. In Table 2.2 we give examples of illegal REAL and INTEGER constants.

* The largest REAL number you can use on the IBM 360/370 without using an exponent is 16777215., a number with 8 decimal digits.

REAL AND INTEGER CONSTANTS

REAL	INTEGER
12367.8	1234
−134.	−32162
.00085	123004

Table 2.1. Legal REAL and INTEGER constants. There are two types of numbers in FORTRAN: those written with a decimal point, called REAL numbers; those written without a decimal point, called INTEGER numbers. Because the value of the numbers does not change during the program's execution, they are called constants.

Constant	Reason for illegality
Illegal REAL	
12,364.2	Has a comma
123.6−	Has minus sign after the number
123	Has no decimal point
Illegal INTEGER	
12,364	Has a comma
123−	Has a minus sign after the number
123.	Has a decimal point

Table 2.2. Illegal REAL and INTEGER constants. Constants cannot contain a comma.

Corresponding to REAL and INTEGER constants, there are REAL and INTEGER variables. A REAL variable is the name (more accurately the address) of a memory location that contains a REAL constant. Similarly, an INTEGER variable is the name of a memory location that contains an INTEGER constant. In ANS Standard FORTRAN and in most compilers, a FORTRAN variable can consist of from one to six characters.* The first character must be a letter of the alphabet. Each of the succeeding characters may be either a digit or a letter. A REAL variable is one that begins with any letter of the alphabet but I, J, K, L, M, or N. Thus VELOC, RATE12, and A12345 are all REAL variables. An INTEGER variable is one that begins with I, J, K, L, M, or N. Thus INDEX, K, and J12345 are all INTEGER variables. On the other hand, neither VELOCITY1 nor INDEX23 are valid variables because they each have more than 6 characters. In Table 2.3 we give examples of REAL and INTEGER variables, and in Table 2.4 we give examples of *illegal* REAL and INTEGER variables. Because a REAL constant contains a decimal point and an INTEGER constant does not, the computer stores REAL variables and REAL constants, on one hand, differently than INTEGER variables and constants, on the other. It thus treats REALs differently than INTEGERs. Consequently, the computer can execute an assignment statement more easily if all the variables and constants in it are of the same type. Moreover, if both REALs and INTEGERs are used in one assignment statement, we shall see that, if you are not careful, unexpected results could be obtained. Examples of statements in which only REAL variables and constants have been used are

```
VELOC=60.0
DIST=VELOC * 3.5
DIST=60.3 * 3.5
```

We say that these statements have been written using the REAL *mode*.

Examples of statements written only with INTEGER variables and constants are

```
NUM=136
INDEX=6*41
INDEX=NUM*3964
```

We say that these statements have been written using the INTEGER *mode*.

If both REALs and INTEGERs are used in one assignment statement, we say that the statement has been written in *mixed mode*.

* On the IBM 1130 and in Standard Basic FORTRAN, the maximum number of characters that can be used in a variable name is 5. On the CDC 6600, the maximum is 7; and on the Honeywell 6000 Series, the maximum is 8.

REAL AND INTEGER VARIABLES

REAL variables	INTEGER variables
THING	INDEX
VELOC1	MASS
A2	J2
B	KOUNT
	K

Table 2.3. A REAL variable must begin with a letter other than I, J, K, L, M, or N, and an INTEGER variable must begin with the letter I, J, K, L, M, or N. Neither a REAL variable nor an INTEGER variable can contain more than 6 characters. The last 5 characters may be letters or digits.

Variables	Reason for illegality
Illegal REAL variables	
INDEX	Begins with the letter I
3MASS	Begins with a digit
A*123	Contains a *
REALVARA	Contains 8 characters
Illegal INTEGER variables	
BAR	Begins with the letter B
3IND	Begins with a digit
I*123	Contains a *
INDEXOFR	Contains 8 characters

Table 2.4. Illegal REAL and INTEGER variables.

2.12. I Format

In the programs we have written so far, we have used only REAL variables and constants; and except for the carriage control field, all the field specifications we have used began with the letter F, e.g., F10.2, F10.3. The reason for this is that when FORTRAN was first devised, the term "floating point" was used instead of REAL. Thus the *F* in the field specification indicated to the computer that we were going to print a *F*loating point number. This convention is still used today, and, as we have said, this type of format specification is called F format. When we print the value of a REAL variable in a WRITE statement, although we have indicated by our choice of variable that we are printing a REAL variable, we must also explicitly indicate in the FORMAT statement, by using F format, that we are printing a REAL value. When we print the value of an INTEGER however, we *cannot* use F format, as we shall now see.

In the next program we shall use only INTEGER variables and constants. In general, INTEGER mode arithmetic is used for counting and indexing, but in order to show the use of INTEGER format, we shall use INTEGER mode in the following program, which performs a calculation.

In the program of Fig. 2.8a we calculate the volume of a geometrical solid, called a rectangular prism, which is located on a coordinate system in which the sides can assume only integer values. The solid has the dimensions 3 × 4 × 5. In the first three cards we assign these numbers to the INTEGER variables LX, LY, and LZ, respectively. In

```
NVOL=LX*LY*LZ
```

we calculate the volume of the prism and assign it to the INTEGER variable NVOL. From the table for Fig. 2.8a we see that, for this program, all the numbers stored in memory are INTEGERs. Thus, when we print the results in WRITE(6,10) NVOL, LX, LY, LZ, although we have indicated by our choice of variables that we are printing INTEGER variables, we must also explicitly indicate in the FORMAT statement that we are printing INTEGER values. We do this in the following way. We write the WRITE and FORMAT statements

```
      WRITE(6,10) NVOL, LX, LY, LZ
10    FORMAT(1X, I5, I5, I5, I5)
```

As in all our previous FORMAT statements, the 1X is for the carriage control. The first field specification after this, I5, indicates how NVOL is to be printed. The I, as you may have guessed, indicates to the computer that it will be printing an INTEGER value. The type of field specification used here is called I format. The 5 in I5 indicates that the field will be 5 characters wide, and the value of NVOL is printed right-justified in the first 5 columns. Thus the result, 60, will be printed so that the 6 appears in column 4 and the 0 appears in column 5, as shown in Fig. 2.8b.

INTEGER ARITHMETIC

```
C   CALCULATING THE VOLUME OF A RECTANGULAR PRISM USING
C   INTEGER ARITHMETIC
      LX=3
      LY=4
      LZ=5
      NVOL=LX*LY*LZ
      WRITE(6,10) NVOL, LX, LY, LZ
 10   FORMAT(1X, I5, I5, I5, I5)
      STOP
      END
```

Figure 2.8a. A program that uses INTEGER arithmetic. In this case the variables can assume integral values only. The I in I5 indicates that we are printing INTEGER values. The 5 indicates the field width. Any field specification beginning with an I (called I format) refers to one of the variables in the WRITE statement. Since there are four INTEGER variables in the WRITE statement, we have used four I format field specifications.

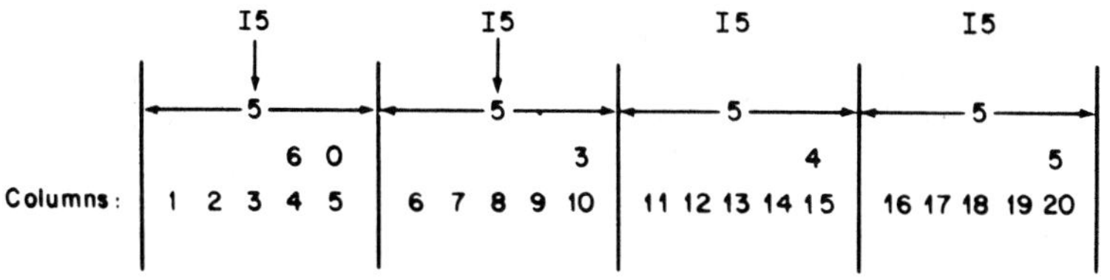

Figure 2.8b. The results of running the program of Fig. 2.8a. We have labeled the columns in order to show the field widths and where the values are printed in the fields. Note that all values are printed right justified.

The next I5 specifies how LX is to be printed. The width of the field is again 5 columns. Since the value of LX is 3, it is printed in column 10. The third I5 corresponds to LY and the fourth I5 corresponds to LZ. Thus 4 is printed in column 15 and 5 is printed in column 20. The results of running this program as they actually appear on the line printer, are shown in Fig. 2.8c.

Had we written the FORMAT statement using F format, e.g.,

```
10    FORMAT( 1X, F10.1, F10.1, F10.1, F10.1 )
```

when the program executes, the computer would either print unexpected results, an error message, or terminate the program at this point. Similarly, if we try to print a REAL variable using I format, we would encounter the same difficulty. An error that occurs during the execution of a program—as here, printing using the wrong type of format—is called an *execution-time error* or *run-time error*.

If this program is run on a WATFOR or WATFIV compiler, we could substitute the following PRINT statement for the WRITE and FORMAT pair used in Fig. 2.8a

```
PRINT, NVOL, LX, LY, LZ
```

as shown in Fig. 2.8d. Since all the variables used here are INTEGER, the results as shown in Fig. 2.8e have no decimal point in them.

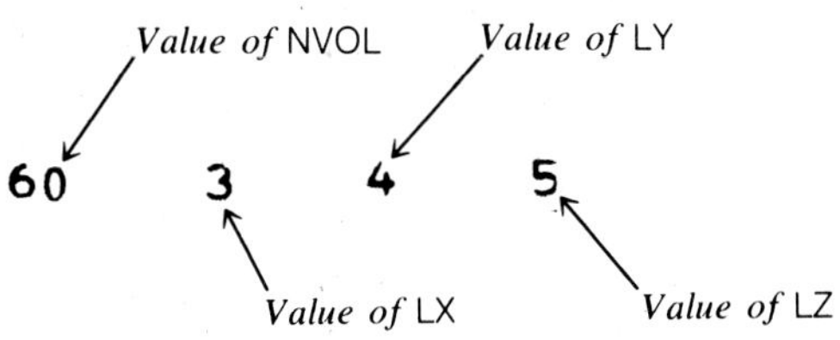

Figure 2.8c. The results of running the program of Fig. 2.8a as they actually appear on the line printer. Since we have printed the values of INTEGER variables, the results are all integers. We must use I format to print INTEGER variables; we cannot use F format. Similarly, we cannot use I format to print REAL variables.

USING INTEGER **VARIABLES IN A FORMAT-FREE** PRINT

```
C   CALCULATING THE VOLUME OF A RECTANGULAR PRISM USING
C      INTEGER ARITHMETIC AND WATFOR/WATFIV PRINT STATEMENT
       LX=3
       LY=4
       LZ=5
       NVOL=LX*LY*LZ
       PRINT, NVOL, LX, LY, LZ
       STOP
       END
```

Figure 2.8d. The program of Fig. 2.8a written using the format-free WATFOR/WATFIV PRINT statement. This statement replaces the WRITE and FORMAT statements of the previous programs.

```
    60                 3                  4                  5
```

Figure 2.8e. Running the program of Fig. 2.8d. The results of this program are printed in the same form as the results of the standard FORTRAN program shown in Fig. 2.8c.

2.13. The INTEGER and REAL Declaration Statements

In the program of Fig. 2.8a and the WATFOR/WATFIV version shown in Fig. 2.8c, in order to make the variables INTEGER, we preceded the variables, which ordinarily would have been X, Y, and Z, by the letter L; and preceded VOL by the letter N. This method of declaring variables that ordinarily would be REALs, as INTEGERs, is somewhat unnatural. A more natural method is to use the INTEGER statement

```
INTEGER VOL,X,Y,Z
```

The INTEGER statement declares any variable in its list to be an INTEGER variable independent of what letter the variable begins with. Here the list is VOL, X, Y, Z. If there is more than one variable in the list, the variables must be separated by commas. In order to make it easier for someone reading the program to find a given variable in the list, it is best to write the variables in alphabetical order. The INTEGER statement is a nonexecutable statement. However, as opposed to a FORMAT statement, it must be placed at the beginning of the program before any executable statement.

In Fig. 2.9a we have rewritten the program of Fig. 2.8a, but now use the INTEGER statement. The results of running the statement are shown in Fig. 2.9b. Corresponding to the INTEGER statement there is, as you might expect, a REAL statement. The REAL statement declares any variable that is in its list to be REAL. Thus in

```
REAL I, J, MIN, MAX
```

I, J, MIN, and MAX are all declared to be REAL. The INTEGER and REAL statements are called type declaration statements because they declare the type (mode) of the variables in their list. The INTEGER and REAL statements can be used in WATFOR/WATFIV programs.

The disadvantage of using REAL and/or INTEGER type declaration statements is that each time the person reading the program encounters a new variable, he may have to refer to the type declaration statements to determine the mode of the variable.

USING THE INTEGER STATEMENT

```
C   CALCULATING THE VOLUME OF A PRISM
      INTEGER VOL,X,Y,Z
      X=3
      Y=4
      Z=5
      VOL=X*Y*Z
      WRITE(6,10)   VOL,X,Y,Z
 10   FORMAT(1X, I5, I5, I5, I5)
      STOP
      END
```

Figure 2.9a. The program of Fig. 2.8a rewritten using the INTEGER statement. The variables listed in the INTEGER statement are all interpreted by the computer to be INTEGERs, independent of what letter they begin with. Thus we have assigned INTEGER constants to them and have used I format to print their values.

Value of NVOL   *Value of* Y

```
60    3    4    5
```

Value of X   *Value of* Z

Figure 2.9b. Running the program of Fig. 2.9a. Since VOL, X, Y, and Z have been defined to be INTEGERs, and we have used I format to print their values, their values are printed as INTEGER constants.

2.14. Restrictions Involved in Using I Format

When you use I format, you must make the field width large enough to accommodate all the digits in the constant you wish to print. If you use a field width that is not large enough, the computer will print asterisks in the field. In the program of Fig. 2.10a we first use I5 to print the constant 123456 which has 6 digits. The computer thus prints asterisks, as shown in Fig. 2.10b. When we use I10 to print the same constant, the computer prints the desired result.

If a constant is negative, besides providing enough columns for the digits in the constant, you must provide one column in the field for the minus sign. Thus in Fig. 2.10a, when we print the constant −123456, we must use a field width of at least 7 columns; otherwise, the computer will print asterisks in the field. Thus when we use I6 to print this constant, we obtain asterisks. However, when we use I10, the computer prints the desired result. All of this is also shown in Fig. 2.10b. We present a somewhat more detailed description of using I format in the beginning of Chapter 8.

CHARACTERISTICS OF I FORMAT

```
C   SHOWS WHAT HAPPENS WHEN THE FIELD WIDTH
C   IN I FORMAT IS NOT LARGE ENOUGH
        NVM=123456
        NVM1=-123456
        WRITE(6,10) NVM,NVM, NVM1,NVM1
 10     FORMAT(1X, I5, I10, I6, I10)
        STOP
        END
```

Figure 2.10a. When using I format, the field width must be large enough to accommodate all the digits in the constant being printed. If the constant is negative, one additional column must be reserved for the minus sign.

Value of NVM *Printed using* I5 — *Value of* NVM *Printed using* I6

```
*****     123456******     -123456
```

Value of NVM1 *Printed using* I10 — *Value of* NVM1 *Printed using* I10

Figure 2.10b. Running the program of Fig. 2.10a. If the field width is not large enough to accommodate all the characters being printed, the computer prints asterisks. Thus since I5 cannot accommodate the 6 digits in 123456, the computer prints asterisks. Similarly, since I6 cannot accommodate the 6 digits and the minus sign in −123456, the computer prints asterisks.

2.15. Redefining Variables

We now investigate what happens when we assign a new constant to a variable that already has been defined. This is called "redefining a variable." We do this by discussing a program that involves only REAL variables; however, the following discussion applies to the redefining of variables regardless of what type of variables and constants is used. In Fig. 2.11a, we calculate the velocity VELOC, for a constant acceleration ACCEL, but for two values of the time TIME. We use the formula: velocity = acceleration × time. TIME, which is originally assigned the value 4.0, is used in the calculation of the velocity. The results are then printed. Then the value of TIME is redefined in

```
TIME=8.0
```

We observe the consequence of this in the 5th line of the table for Fig. 2.11a

Card	Description	VELOC	ACCEL	TIME
9th	TIME = 8.0	128.0	32.0	8.0

i.e., the number now assigned to TIME is 8.0. What we are observing here is that we can place only one constant at a time in a memory location. The constant that remains is the one placed there last. We also see from this line of the table that since VELOC and ACCEL have not been redefined, they retain their old values. We thus must include a statement to recalculate VELOC for the new value of TIME. We thus repeat the calculation

```
VELOC=ACCEL*TIME
```

Thus the value of VELOC has also been redefined as is shown by 11th card in the table for Fig. 2.11a. When the computer executes the next statement in the program, it prints the redefined results. When the program is executed, we obtain two lines of results, as shown in Fig. 2.11b. In the second line of results

```
256.0    32.0    8.0
```

we see that ACCEL has been redefined so that its value is now 8.0 and thus we obtain a new value for VELOC, i.e., 256.0. As we have previously mentioned, FORMAT statements are not executed; they only detail to the computer how we want the variables in an associated WRITE statement printed. Therefore, if we want the variables in two or more WRITE statements to be printed in the same way, we may use just one FORMAT statement. We have done this in Fig. 2.11a, where

```
10    FORMAT(1X, F7.1, F7.1, F7.1 )
```

is used for the first WRITE statement as well as the second one.

Although you can use one FORMAT statement for many WRITE statements, this practice may make it difficult for someone to follow the program. Consequently, it is better to use a new FORMAT statement for each WRITE statement.

We now discuss the form of the statements we have learned so far: the END, STOP, Assignment, PRINT, WRITE, FORMAT, INTEGER, and REAL statements.

GIVING A VARIABLE A NEW VALUE (REDEFINING IT)

```
C  CALCULATES THE VELOCITY OF AN OBJECT GIVEN
C  ITS ACCELERATION AND TIME IN MOTION
C  USING VELOC=ACCEL*TIME
       ACCEL=32.0
       TIME=4.0
       VELOC=ACCEL*TIME
       WRITE(6,10) VELOC, ACCEL, TIME
C  THE VALUE OF THE TIME IS REDEFINED
       TIME=8.0
C  USING THIS, RECALCULATE THE VELOCITY
       VELOC=ACCEL*TIME
       WRITE(6,10) VELOC,ACCEL,TIME
C  WE USE ONE FORMAT STATEMENT FOR BOTH WRITE STATEMENTS
 10    FORMAT(1X, F7.1, F7.1, F7.1 )
       STOP
       END
```

Figure 2.11a. A program in which we redefine the value of a variable. In the 9th card, the value of TIME is redefined. This means that when the VELOC is calculated for the second time, it will have a new value. We use the same FORMAT statement for both WRITE statements since we want the results of both to be printed in the same form.

Card	Description	NVELOC	NACCEL	NTIME
4th	ACCEL = 32.0	Undef	32.0	Undef
5th	TIME = 4.0	Undef	32.0	4.0
6th	VELOC = ACCEL*TIME	128.0	32.0	4.0
7th	WRITE	128.0	32.0	4.0
9th	TIME = 8.0	128.0	32.0	8.0
11th	VELOC = ACCEL*TIME	256.0	32.0	8.0
12th	WRITE	256.0	32.0	8.0

Table for Fig. 2.11a. In the 9th card the value of TIME is redefined. The effect of this is shown in the 11th card, i.e., the value of VELOC is also redefined.

```
128.0    32.0     4.0
256.0    32.0     8.0
```

4.0 ← *Printed by the first* WRITE
8.0 ← *Printed by the second* WRITE

Figure 2.11b. Running the program of Fig. 2.11a. The second line of results shows the effect of redefining TIME. The results in both lines appear in the same form because we use the same FORMAT statement for both WRITE statements.

END

> The form of the END statement is the word END. The END statement cannot have a statement number (since it is not executed). Thus 100 END would be considered illegal.

STOP

> The form of the STOP statement is the word STOP. This may be preceded by a statement number. Examples:
>
> ```
>    STOP
> 30 STOP
> ```

ASSIGNMENT

> The form of the assignment statement is: a variable; followed by an equals sign; followed by what we want to assign to the variable. An assignment statement may have a statement number. Examples of assignment statements that we can write so far are:
>
> ```
>     VOL = 30.2
>     VAN = RNUM
>     NVOL = 30
> 100 DIST = 3.*SPEED
>     KOUNT = NUMBER+1
> ```
>
> We shall show in Chapter 3 that one can use both INTEGER and REAL mode in one statement.

In an assignment statement, only a variable can appear to the left of the equals sign. Thus

```
39. = SPEED
VELOC*TIME = DIST
```

are incorrect.

WATFOR/WATFIV/WATFIV-S PRINT

> The form of the PRINT statement is: the word PRINT followed by a comma; followed by the items to be printed (so far, we have seen that these items* can be variables). If there is more than one item in the PRINT statement, the items must be separated by commas. A PRINT statement may have a statement number. Each PRINT statement instructs the computer to start a new line of print on the line printer. You may have both INTEGER and REAL variables in a PRINT statement. Examples of PRINT statements that we could write so far are:
>
> ```
>     PRINT, NVOL, NAREA, LENGTH
> 100 PRINT, VOLUM, RLEN
>     PRINT, NVOL, R, LEN
> ```

* We will see that these items can also be constants, calculations and, in WATFIV, strings.

WRITE

The form of the WRITE statement is: the word WRITE followed by (; followed by the number* of the output unit; followed by a comma, followed by the statement number of the FORMAT statement you wish to use; followed by); followed by the variables to be printed. If there is more than one variable, the variables must be separated by commas. A WRITE statement can have a statement number. You may print both REAL and INTEGER variables in a WRITE statement. Examples of WRITE statements that we could write so far are:

```
      WRITE(6,100) VOL, NDAY
   30 WRITE(6,80) RLEN, DAY
      WRITE(6,100) NCOUNT, KOUNT, NINT
```

FORMAT

The form of the FORMAT statement is: statement number; followed by FORMAT(; followed by any number of field specifications. If there is more than one field specification, the specifications must be separated by commas. If the FORMAT statement is used in connection with printing results on the line printer, the first column of the first field specification used refers to the carriage control character—so far we have used 1X for this. Every FORMAT statement must end with a right parenthesis. Examples of FORMAT statements that we can write so far are:

```
1000 FORMAT(1X, F10.6, I3, F20.5)
1080 FORMAT(1X, I6, I6, I6)
```

REAL and INTEGER

The form of the INTEGER (REAL) statement is: INTEGER (REAL) followed by a list of variables. If there is more than one variable in the list, the variables are separated by commas. Examples of INTEGER (REAL) statements we can write at this time are:

```
INTEGER A, B, C, D
INTEGER A, B, I, J, K
REAL I, J, K
REAL A, B, I, J, K
```

The INTEGER (REAL) statement is nonexecutable and must appear at the beginning of the program before any executable statement. It cannot have a statement number.

In all these types of statements we can place blanks between any of the characters—they are called *embedded blanks*. Thus, although

```
P RINT(6,100)V OL,NC OUNT
```

is hard to read, it appears the same to the computer as

```
PRINT(6,100) VOL, NCOUNT
```

If we do not follow the form prescribed for these statements, or for any other type that we learn, a compile-time error will result. The next section shows what happens when we make errors in writing a program.

* We will see that this can also be an INTEGER variable representing the output unit.

2.16. Debugging Programs on the FORTRAN Compiler

In Fig. 2.12a we show a program that contains grammatical errors. During compilation, the computer checks every card of the program for grammatical errors. Since grammatical errors are discovered during compilation, they are (as we have noted) also called compilation errors or compile-time errors. On the system on which we ran this program (IBM 370 FORTRAN), the compiler prints the errors imbedded in asterisks underneath the appropriate program statements as the computer lists the program. Moreover, it prints a dollar sign ($) beneath the statement in the neighborhood that the error occurs. In Fig. 2.12a, the computer has found three errors: we used a comma in punching a constant in V = 13,4; we misspelled WRITE in WRIT(6,10); and we forgot to include the closing parenthesis in the FORMAT statement

```
10     FORMAT(1X, F10.2, F10.2, F10.2
```

If you counted the columns in the error message beneath the FORMAT statement, you would find that the $ occurs in the 72nd column, i.e., the last columns on the program card in which you could punch a character.

We note that on this system (IBM 370 FORTRAN), as well as on most other systems, the compiler numbers each noncomment statement and the number appears on the extreme left of the statement, e.g., V = 13,4 is numbered as 0001.

Although we made other errors in the program, the compiler cannot detect them: In DIST= V TIM we forgot to punch an asterisk between V and TIM; and we have spelled TIM differently than in the preceding statement. Since embedded blanks have no significance, the compiler interprets this statement as

```
DIST=VTIM
```

and finds no error.

PROGRAM WITH COMPILE-TIME ERRORS

```
                C  PROGRAM CALCULATES THE DISTANCE AN OBJECT GOES
                C  GIVEN ITS VELOCITY AND THE TIME TRAVELED
                C
                C  ASSIGN A VALUE TO THE VELOCITY
   0001                V=13,4
                       $
***********01)  IEY013I SYNTAX*****************************************************************
                C  ASSIGN A VALUE TO THE TIME
   0002                TIME=3.0
                C  CALCULATE THE DISTANCE
   0003                DIST=V TIM
   0004                WRIT(6,10) DIST,TIME,V
                       $
***********01)  IEY013I SYNTAX*****************************************************************
   0005         10     FORMAT(1X, F10.2, F10.2, F10.2
                                                                                             $
***********01)  IEY013I SYNTAX*****************************************************************
   0006                STOP
   0007                END
```

Figure 2.12a. A program that will produce compile-time errors: (1) There is a comma in 13,4. (2) WRITE is misspelled. (3) The FORMAT statement lacks a closing parenthesis. Although in DIST= V TIM we have forgotten the asterisk and have used TIM instead of TIME, the compiler does not consider these to be errors. It reads this statement as DIST= VTIM.

For pedagogic reasons, we will assume that we correct the error in the constant and punch it as 13.4, and that we discover that we omitted the asterisk in the formula for DIST; however, we do not realize that we have spelled TIME differently in two statements. We submit the partially corrected program shown in Fig. 2.12b to the computer. The listing of the program after the compilation is shown here. The compiler does not detect that there is still an error. It only checks whether TIM is a legal variable. Since TIM *is* a legal variable, the compiler finds nothing wrong with it. The compiler can detect spelling errors only in words that must be used in certain statements, e.g., WRITE and FORMAT.

Since there are no compilation errors, the program executes. The results of the program are shown in Fig. 2.12c. We see that the value of DIST calculated by the computer is zero, and not the value we expect. The reason for this is that TIM (one of the variables used in calculating DIST) is an undefined variable. The value assigned to an undefined variable is arbitrary; in this case the value assigned to TIM is 0.0. Thus the value of DIST is also 0.0.

PARTIALLY CORRECTED PROGRAM; TIM **IS STILL UNDEFINED**

```
C   PROGRAM CALCULATES THE DISTANCE AN OBJECT GOES
C   GIVEN ITS VELOCITY AND THE TIME TRAVELED
C
C   ASSIGN A VALUE TO THE VELOCITY
        V=13.4
C   ASSIGN A VALUE TO THE TIME
        TIME=3.0
C   CALCULATE THE DISTANCE
        DIST=V*TIM
        WRITE(6,10) DIST,TIME,V
 10     FORMAT(1X, F10.2, F10.2, F10.2)
        STOP
        END
```

Figure 2.12b. We correct all the errors in the program of Fig. 2.12a but still use TIM in DIST =V*TIM. The listing after the compilation is shown here. TIM is an undefined variable since it does not appear on the left in an assignment statement; the compiler, however, does not consider this an error. During the program's execution, the computer assigns an arbitrary value—in this case, 0.0—to TIM.

Value of DIST	*Value of* TIME	*Value of* V
↓	↓	↓
0.0	3.00	13.40

Figure 2.12c. Running the program of Fig. 2.12b on a FORTRAN compiler. Since the value of TIM is unpredictable, the computer produces an unpredictable value for DIST. If we were to look just at the results shown here, we would be confused since the value of TIME is given as 3.00 and the value of V as 13.4. We would have to look at DIST=V*TIM to see that we used TIM, an undefined variable. The fact that arbitrary constants are assigned to undefined variables can lead to disastrous results, since it can produce seemingly error-free output, which is in fact erroneous.

In Fig. 2.12d we see what happens when undefined variables are used in a WRITE statement. Here the REAL variable VAR and the INTEGER variable INDEX are undefined. When the computer executes

```
WRITE(6,10) VAR, INDEX
```

it prints an arbitrary value for both variables. Thus the value of VAR is printed here as 0.0 and that of INDEX is printed as 0 when the program is run (Fig. 2.12e).

2.17. Debugging Using the WATFOR/WATFIV Compiler

In Fig. 2.13a we present the same program that was shown in Fig. 2.12a, but now as compiled on the WATFOR/WATFIV compiler. We see that this compiler, also, numbers the noncomment statements and indicates the same errors as the FORTRAN compiler did. The WATFOR/WATFIV compiler, however, prints the error message for V = 13,4 directly after the comment statement that follows this assignment statement.

```
               1            V=13,4
                      C   ASSIGN A VALUE TO THE TIME
      ***ERROR***     UNDECODABLE STATEMENT
```

Also, we see that the WATFOR/WATFIV compiler considers WRIT(6,10)DIST,TIME,V to be an undecodable statement; it thus assumes that there is no WRITE statement in the program. Thus, unlike the FORTRAN compiler, the WATFOR/WATFIV compiler assumes that the FORMAT statement has no accompanying WRITE statement and, hence, that the FORMAT statement is not referred to in the program. The compiler warns us of this by printing a warning after the program

```
**WARNING**   FORMAT STATEMENT      10 IS UNREFERENCED
```

Note, a warning will not prevent a program from running, but an error will.

We have just seen an example of a situation which sometimes occurs in the compilation of a program: an error in one statement (here the WRITE) causes an error of warning to be printed referring to a second statement (here the FORMAT).

THE WATFOR/WATFIV COMPILER DETECTS UNDEFINED VARIABLES DURING EXECUTION

```
        C   PROGRAM CALCULATES THE DISTANCE AN OBJECT GOES
        C
        C   ASSIGN A VALUE TO THE VELOCITY
1               V=13.4
        C   ASSIGN A VALUE TO THE TIME
2               TIME=3.0
        C   CALCULATE THE DISTANCE
3               DIST=V*TIM
4               WRITE(6,10) DIST,TIME,V
5          10   FORMAT(1X, F10.2, F10.2, F10.2)
6               STOP
7               END
```

Figure 2.13b. We correct all the errors in the program of Fig. 2.13a but still use TIM in DIST =V*TIM. The compiler does not consider this an error. The listing after the compilation is shown here. Note: Since we have now correctly spelled WRITE, the computer no longer warns us that the accompanying FORMAT is not referenced.

```
***ERROR***   VALUE OF TIM    IS UNDEFINED

PROGRAM WAS EXECUTING LINE 3 WHEN TERMINATION OCCURRED
```

Figure 2.13c. Running the program of Fig. 2.13b. The WATFOR/WATFIV compiler detects that TIM is undefined. This is an execution error.

In Fig. 2.13d we see what happens when undefined variables are used in WRITE and format-free PRINT statements in a program compiled on the WATFOR/WATFIV compiler. When

```
WRITE(6,10) VAR
```

is executed, the compiler prints 10 U's in the field described by F 10.3 as shown in Fig. 2.13e. The U stands for "undefined." When

```
WRITE(6,20) INDEX
```

is executed, 8 U's are printed in the field described by I8. When

```
WRITE(6,30) VAR, INDEX
```

is executed, the compiler prints 10 U's in the field described by F10.3 and 8 U's in the field described by I8; but since the two fields are next to each other, the compiler prints 18 U's. When the compiler executes

```
PRINT, VAR, INDEX
```

it prints two sets of U's.

UNDEFINED VARIABLES USED IN WRITE **AND** PRINT **STATEMENTS ON THE WATFOR/WATFIV COMPILER**

```
C  DEMONSTRATES HOW THE WATFOR/WATFIV
C  COMPILER TREATS UNDEFINED VARIABLES IN
C  PRINT AND WRITE STATEMENTS
      WRITE(6,10) VAR
 10   FORMAT(1X, F10.3)
C
      WRITE(6,20) INDEX
 20   FORMAT(1X, I8)
C
      WRITE(6,30) VAR, INDEX
 30   FORMAT(1X, F10.3, I8)
C
      PRINT, VAR, INDEX
      STOP
      END
```

Figure 2.13d. A program in which undefined variables are used in WRITE and PRINT statements in a WATFOR/WATFIV program.

```
UUUUUUUUUU ←———— Printed by WRITE(6,10) VAR
UUUUUUUU ←———— Printed by WRITE(6,20) INDEX
UUUUUUUUUUUUUUUUUU ←—— Printed by WRITE(6,30) VAR, INDEX
UUUUUUUUUUUUUUUU  UUUUUUUUUUUU ←—— Printed by PRINT, VAR, INDEX
```

Figure 2.13e. Running the program of Fig. 2.13d on a WATFOR/WATFIV compiler. The compiler prints U's in the fields associated with undefined variables.

2.18. Labeling Cards

The compiler ignores columns 73 to 80 on the program card. Thus you can punch anything in these columns. It is convenient to label each card with a program identification—here DIST, as shown in Fig. 2.14—followed by a number that identifies the card, e.g., 010 on the first card. Note that the cards have been labeled sequentially. Thus, if by accident you drop the deck, you can reorder the cards quite easily simply by referring to identification numbers. We have incremented the identification numbers by 10 for each successive card, so that, if we wish to, we can insert cards in the program and identify them by a number, such as 011, without having to renumber all the other cards. Typing an identification label in columns 73 to 80 in many cases may be more trouble than it is worth. We recommend using columns 73 to 80 only for large programs which will ultimately be used by others besides the programmer.

2.19. Continuation Cards

If you need to, you may continue the punching of a statement onto another card. For instance, if you were writing a FORMAT statement that required many field specifications, you might not have enough room on one card to punch them all. You may continue punching a statement on another card if you punch any FORTRAN character but zero in column six of the second card. Once this is done, the computer interprets what has been punched on both cards, as one statement. Thus in Fig. 2.15, we have written 10 FORMAT(1X, F10.3, F20.4, F6.2) on two cards.

In ANS Standard FORTRAN you are allowed to have a maximum of 19 continuation cards. In Standard Basic FORTRAN you are allowed to have a maximum of 5 continuation cards.

IDENTIFYING CARDS

```
C  PROGRAM CALCULATES THE DISTANCE AN OBJECT GOES                      DIST010
C  GIVEN ITS VELOCITY AND THE TIME IT HAS TRAVELED                     DIST020
C                                                                      DIST030
C  ASSIGN A VALUE TO THE VELOCITY                                      DIST040
      V=13.4                                                           DIST050
C  ASSIGN A VALUE TO THE TIME                                          DIST060
      TIME=3.0                                                         DIST070
C  CALCULATE THE DISTANCE                                              DIST080
      DIST=V*TIME                                                      DIST090
      WRITE(6,10) DIST,TIME,V                                          DIST100
 10   FORMAT(1X, F10.2, F10.2)                                         DIST110
      STOP                                                             DIST120
      END                                                              DIST130
```

Figure 2.14. Columns 73 through 80 are not checked by the compiler. Thus you can punch anything in these columns. It is convenient to type a program identification label—here DIST—followed by a number that identifies the card. For example, we punch 010 on the first card. We advise, however, that students not type anything in columns 73 though 80; in most cases, doing this is more trouble than it is worth.

CONTINUING A STATEMENT ONTO ANOTHER CARD

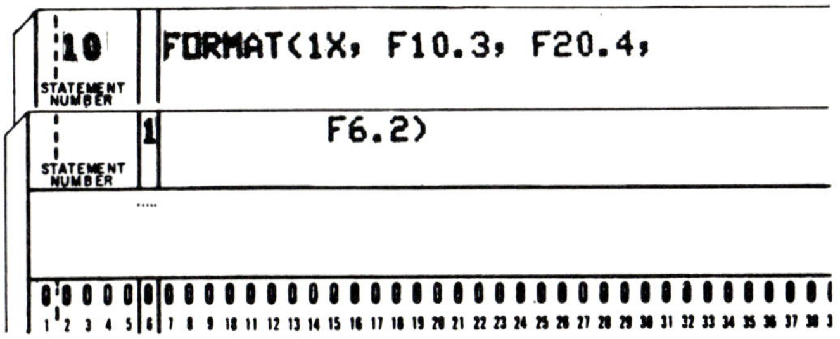

Figure 2.15. You may continue a statement onto another card by punching any nonzero character in column 6.

2.20. The Formatted PRINT

In a WRITE statement, e.g.,

```
WRITE(6,10) DIST,VELOC,TIME
```

the first number we place in the parentheses—here 6—can refer to a line printer, a magnetic tape, a disk file, or a card punch. If we want our results to be printed on the line printer using a FORMAT statement, on most systems but ANS Standard FORTRAN we can use what is called a formatted PRINT statement. Because we have no choice of what output unit we want our results to be written on, only one number appears in the PRINT statement, and this number refers to the FORMAT that will be paired with the PRINT statement. Thus the formatted PRINT that would replace WRITE(6,10) DIST, VELOC, TIME as is shown in Fig. 2.16, would be:

```
PRINT 10, DIST, VELOC, TIME
```

where 10 is the statement number of the associated FORMAT. Note that, as opposed to the WRITE statement, a comma must precede the list in the PRINT statement.

The formatted PRINT is incorporated in the revised version of ANS FORTRAN; and by substituting an asterisk for the number that refers to the FORMAT statement, you obtain a format-free PRINT statement on this system. Thus PRINT*, DIST, VELOC, TIME can be used in the revised version of ANS FORTRAN.

The Formatted PRINT

```
      V=13.4
      TIME=3.0
      DIST=V*TIME
      PRINT 10, DIST, TIME, V
10    FORMAT(1X, F10.2, F10.2, F10.2 )
      STOP
      END
```

Figure 2.16. By using a PRINT statement that includes a FORMAT statement number, and by using the appropriate FORMAT, you can produce the same output as is produced by a WRITE statement.

PROBLEMS

1. Given the partial program
   A = 12.31
   B = 60.0
   C = A * B
   WRITE (6,10) A, B, C
   write a FORMAT statement that can be used with the WRITE statement.

2. Write the WATFOR/WATFIV PRINT statement that would replace the WRITE/FORMAT statements of the previous problem.

3. Write the F format field specifications that would accommodate the printing of the following constants:
   (a) .001263
   (b) 123.78
   (c) 123456.78

4. How would the following constants be printed using the indicated formats?
   (a) .001263 by F10.2
   (b) −123.78 by F10.0
   (c) 1234567.0 by F10.4

5. Which of the following variables are legal? Indicate which mode the legal variables are written in
   (a) THINK2
   (b) VEL*T
   (c) INDICATOR3
   (d) INDI23
   (e) 6SIX
   (f) SAL$

6. Which of the following constants are legal? Indicate whether the legal constants are REAL or INTEGER.
   (a) 123.456
   (b) 12,345.2
   (c) 123,456
   (d) 1247
   (e) $1234
   (f) $12,345.00

7. Given the partial program
   I = 200
   J = 30
   K = I * J
   WRITE(6,10) I, J, K
   write a FORMAT statement that can be used with the WRITE statement.

8. Write the WATFOR/WATFIV PRINT statement that would replace the WRITE/FORMAT statements of the previous problem.

9. Write the I format field specification with the minimum field widths that would accommodate the following constants:
   (a) 12345
   (b) −123
   (c) 3621

10. How would the following constants be printed by the indicated formats?
(a) −1234 by I4
(b) 1234 by I4
(c) 1234 by I3

11. Given INTEGER VELOC, TIME, INDEX indicate whether you would use I or F format to print
(a) VELOC
(b) TIME
(c) INDEX

12. Given REAL VELOC, TIME, INDEX indicate whether you would use I or F format to print
(a) VELOC
(b) TIME
(c) INDEX

13. Write a program to calculate the sum of the integers from 1 to 10.

14. Using REAL variables and constants, write a program that calculates the product of the integers from 1 to 10.

15. What are the results of the following program?

```
       A = 1.3
       C = A * B
       WRITE(6,10) A, B, C
    10 FORMAT(1X, F10.1, F10.1, F10.1)
       B = 2.0
       C = A * B
       WRITE(6,20) A, B, C
    20 FORMAT(1X, F10.1, F10.1, F10.1)
       STOP
       END
```

16. What are the results of the following WATFOR/WATFIV program?

```
       A = 1.3
       C = A * B
       WRITE(6,10) A, B, C
    10 FORMAT(1X, F10.1, F10.1, F10.1)
       B = 2.0
       C = A * B
       PRINT, A, B, C
       STOP
       END
```

3

Calculations and the READ Statement

3.1. Performing Calculations in FORTRAN

Mathematical expressions, as they appear printed in books, in general occupy more than one line of print. As an example, it takes three lines of print to write the expression appearing in the following equation:

$$Y = \frac{(X+3)^2 \cdot (A+4)}{R+3.1}$$

(The expression is that entity which appears on the right of the equals sign—here it is a calculation.) One line is required for the exponent 2, one line for $(X+3) \cdot (A+4)$, and one line for the divisor $R+3.1$. Since in FORTRAN the program is executed statement by statement, the programmer cannot write mathematical expressions on many lines simultaneously—as he would normally do—but must use one line at a time. For this reason, some of the symbols used to express mathematical operations in FORTRAN, and some of the conventions used, differ from those in algebra. The operations available in FORTRAN are tabulated below:

Operation	Symbol used in FORTRAN
Exponentiation	**
Multiplication	*
Division	/
Addition	+
Subtraction	−

In order to enable a program to execute a mathematical expression that has more than one operation in it, a priority has been assigned to each operation, as shown in Table 3.1. The computer does not perform all the operations in an expression simultaneously.

PRIORITY OF MATHEMATICAL OPERATIONS

Operation	Symbol used in FORTRAN	Priority
Exponentiation	**	1st
Multiplication	*	2nd
Division	/	2nd
Addition	+	3rd
Subtraction	−	3rd

Table 3.1. The priority of the mathematical operations. In a mathematical expression, exponentiations are done first, followed by multiplications and divisions, followed by additions and subtractions.

The computer reads an expression as we would read an English sentence—from left to right. It starts at the equals sign and searches for an exponentiation; and if it finds it, performs that operation. If there is more than one exponentiation, the computer performs the exponentiations as it encounters them—from left to right. It then returns to the equals sign and searches from left to right for multiplications and divisions and performs them as it encounters them. Finally, it returns to the equals sign and searches from left to right for additions and subtractions and performs them, again as it encounters them.

The computer follows this same procedure whether it is evaluating a REAL expression, INTEGER expression, or mixed-mode expression. We will now consider how the computer evaluates a REAL expression: the FORTRAN equivalent of the algebraic expression for the distance a body will fall under the influence of gravity, if it is given an initial velocity V_0. The algebraic formula is

$$d = V_0t + gt^2/2$$

where g is the acceleration of gravity and t is the time that has elapsed since the body was thrown. It is not important for you to understand this formula; however, it is important to know how to translate this formula into FORTRAN. As we will explain, the FORTRAN equivalent is

```
D=VO*T + G*T**2.0/2.0
```

To help us follow the evaluation of this expression, we have assigned values to the variables: VO = 10.0, T = 2.0, G = 32.0. The computer first evaluates the exponentiation T**2.0, which equals 4.0. It then returns to the equals sign and looks for multiplications and divisions. The first one it encounters is the multiplication VO*T, which it evaluates as 20.0. The next one it encounters is the multiplication G times T**2 or 32.0*4.0, which it evaluates as 128.0. It then divides G*T**2 by 2.0 and obtains 64.0. It then returns to the equals sign and looks for additions and subtractions. It finds an addition VO*T + G*T**2/2.0 and adds 20.0 to 64.0. It obtains 84.0. All of this is shown in Table 3.2. Note: In order to make the formula in step 5

```
VO*T + G*T**2/2.0
```

easier to read, we have inserted a blank before and after the + sign, so that the other operations appear grouped together.

We note here that T**2.0 could have been written as T**2 without the expression considered to be written in mixed mode. It is easier for a person to type T**2 and easier for a person reading the program to recognize T**2 as T^2 than it is for him to recognize T**2.0. For this reason* we will always square, cube, raise to the 4th power, etc., by using an INTEGER to represent the power. If we want to evaluate an expression like $T^{1/3}$ (the cube root of T), we must use a REAL exponent. We thus write T**0.33333.

* In general, when an INTEGER is used as the exponent, e.g., T**2 or T**N, the computer evaluates the exponentiation by repeated multiplications, i.e., T*T. However, when a REAL is used as the exponent, the computer must consider the possibility that the exponent is nonintegral (i.e., T**0.5). Thus the computer evaluates an exponentiation that has a REAL exponent by using logarithms.

EVALUATING AN EXPRESSION

Example 1. Evaluating the algebraic formula $d = V_0 t + gt^2/2$

Step	Part of Expression evaluated	Value
1	T**2	4.0
2	VO*T	20.0
3	G*T**2	128.0
4	G*T**2/2.0	64.0
5	VO*T + G*T**2/2.0	84.0

Table 3.2. The evaluation of a mathematical expression in which VO=10, T=2.0, and G=32.0. If more than one operation in an expression has the same priority, it is evaluated from left to right. Note: In order to make the formula in step 5 easier to read, we have inserted a blank before and after the + sign, so that the other operations appear grouped together.

How would we write the equivalent of the interest formula $P = A(1+R)^n$ where A is the initial principal, R is the rate of interest per year, n is the number of years, and P is the principal after n years? Here we want the entire quantity $(1+R)$ raised to the nth power. Thus the addition in $1+R$ must be performed before anything else. In order to instruct the computer to do this, we place the $1+R$ between parentheses. Thus we write this expression in FORTRAN as

```
P=A*(1 + R)**N
```

In an expression, the operations enclosed in parentheses are performed before any of the operations outside the parentheses. Thus, first the computer calculates (1+R), then (1 + R)**N, and finally A*(1 + R)**N, as shown in Table 3.3. If there is more than one operation in the parentheses, the operations are performed from left to right with the priorities we previously discussed. If there is more than one pair of parentheses in an expression, the parenthesized parts are evaluated from left to right. For example, in the formula of the line which goes through the point (X_1,Y_1) and the point (X_2,Y_2), expression for the slope written in FORTRAN is

```
SLOPE=(Y2-Y1) / (X2-X1)
```

The computer, when it executes this statement, first evaluates (Y2– Y1), then (X2– X1), and finally it divides (Y2–Y1) by (X2–X1).

Parentheses can be used to make an expression easier to understand by the reader. Thus $d = V_0t + gt^2/2$, which we considered previously, can also be written

```
D=VO*T + ((G*(T**2)) / 2.0
```

However, if you do this you run the risk of forgetting to punch one or more parentheses. If the number of right parentheses does not equal the number of left parentheses, e.g., as in D= VO*T + ((G*T**2) /2.0, an error results during the compilation.

For future reference, note that the word "expression" does not have to mean a group of constants and/or variables used with mathematical operations in a calculation; it can also mean simply a constant or a variable. Thus the following are all valid expressions:

```
13.62
VAR1
NOM* (3+K)
```

We conclude this section by discussing the use of the unary minus. The unary minus makes a number negative; it is not preceded by either a constant or a variable; i.e., in −4.0, the minus sign is a unary minus, whereas in TIME −3.0 the minus sign is not a unary minus.

Two arithmetic operations cannot directly follow each other. We encounter this restriction when we use the unary minus sign. Thus V*−10.0 is illegal. Parentheses must be used in order to separate the operators. Thus the expression must be written as V* (−10.0). Similarly a^{-x} must be written as A**(−x).

Example 2. Evaluating $P = A(1 + R)^n$

Step	Part of expression evaluated
1	1+R
2	(1+R)**N
3	A*(1+R)**N

Table 3.3 When an expression has a pair of parentheses in it, the operations within the parentheses are performed first. If there are several pairs of parentheses in an expression, the operations are performed from left to right.

3.2. Peculiarities of REAL and INTEGER Arithmetic

As we have mentioned, there is a limit to the number of digits that a computer can contain in a REAL number. If the computer can contain, for instance, only 7 meaningful (significant) digits in a REAL number, it can represent repeating fractions like 1.0/3.0 to only 7 accurate digits. Therefore, it would round 1.0/3.0 to 0.3333333, and when 1.0/3.0 is used in a subsequent calculation, what is known as a *round-off error* will occur. The classic example is in the evaluation of (1.0/3.0)*3.0. One might expect the computer to evaluate this as 1. What actually happens is that after the computer calculates 1.0/3.0 and obtains 0.3333333, it then multiplies this by 3.0 and obtains 0.9999999 as the answer.

Round-off errors occur in some REAL constants that are not repeating fractions, and we now explain why.

The arithmetic for most computers is done using the binary system. This system uses 2 as its base. Thus any fraction that can be expressed as a power of 2 is internally represented exactly on the computer, as long as the fraction does not have too many digits. For example, since 0.5 is 2^{-1}, and since 0.25 is 1/4 or 2^{-2}, and since 0.125 is 1/8 or 2^{-3}, these numbers are internally represented exactly on the computer. In addition, any fraction that can be expressed as the sum of powers of 2—e.g., 0.75 equals 1/2 + 1/4—is also internally represented exactly, again as long as it does not have too many digits.* On the other hand, a number like 0.2, which is 1/5, cannot be expressed as a power of 2; thus its internal computer representation, 0.1999999, is only an approximation of its true value, and we say that a round-off error has occurred. Therefore, when we perform the calculation (1.0/5.0)*5.0 on the computer, the result is not 1. As a matter of fact, because of round-off error, the results of the calculation (1.0/R)*R, where R is any REAL number, may or may not equal 1, depending on whether 1.0/R can be expressed as a power to 2 or the sum of the powers of 2, or whether it cannot.

In Fig. 3.1a, we represent a program that performs (1.0/R)*R for R successively assuming the values 1.0, 2.0, 3.0, 4.0, and 5.0. Assuming that we are running the program on a machine on which a REAL constant can be expressed to 7 meaningful (significant) digits, we want to see at least 7 places after the decimal point when the answer is printed (the program was run using the IBM 370 FORTRAN system.) Thus the first time we print the results, we use the field specification F15.10. The results of using this format are shown on the first line of results in Fig. 3.1b. As we expect, (1.0/3.0)*3.0 and (1.0/5.0)*5.0 are not represented in the machine† as 1.000000; we see that they are represented as .9999999404. The digits to the right of the 9's are not meaningful. They arise from the fact that there is a limit to the size of a binary number that a computer can store.

The second time we print the results, we use the field specification F10.4. This time we will see only 4 digits after the decimal point. As we saw in Chapter 2, when the field specification does not permit the computer to print all the digits to the right of the decimal point, it rounds the answer. We thus now obtain 1.0000 for the results of all the calculations (as we see in the second line in Fig. 3.1b).

* We give a more detailed presentation of what is discussed in this paragraph when we discuss the binary representation of whole numbers and fractions in Chapter 12.

† Beware! On a compiler like the one used on the HP3000, even though these two numbers are internally represented as .9999999, they will always be printed as 1. followed by zeros, independent of the field width we use.

ROUND OFF ERRORS

```
C   PROGRAM DEMONSTRATES ROUND OFF ERRORS
        A=(1.0/1.0)*1.0
        B=(1.0/2.0)*2.0
        C=(1.0/3.0)*3.0
        D=(1.0/4.0)*4.0
        E=(1.0/5.0)*5.0
C   PRINT THE RESULTS OF (1.0/R)*R USING A LARGE FIELD WIDTH
        WRITE(6,100) A,B,C,D,E
  100   FORMAT(1X, F15.10, F15.10, F15.10, F15.10, F15.10)
C   PRINT THE RESULTS OF (1.0/R)*R USING A SMALL FIELD WIDTH
        WRITE(6,110) A,B,C,D,E
  110   FORMAT(1X, F10.4, F10.4, F10.4, F10.4, F10.4)
        STOP
        END
```

Figure 3.1a. Because of the limited number of digits allowed in a number, and because numbers are represented internally in the computer in binary form, round-off error occurs in REAL constants; e.g., (1.0/5.0)*5.0 is represented internally as 0.9999999.

```
(1.0/1.0)*1.0     (1.0/2.0)*2.0     (1.0/3.0)*3.0     (1.0/4.0)*4.0     (1.0/5.0)*5.0
      ↓                 ↓                 ↓                 ↓                 ↓
 1.0000000000      1.0000000000      0.9999999404      1.0000000000      0.9999999404
   1.0000      1.0000      1.0000      1.0000      1.0000
                                                  Printed using F10.4    Printed using F15.10
```

Figure 3.1b. On the first line, the results (run on the IBM 370 FORTRAN System) of (1.0/R)*R are printed so that we see all the significant digits. We see that for R = 3.0 and 5.0, the results are not equal to 1.00. On the second line we cannot see all the significant digits; in this case the computer rounds the results to 1.0000.

In Fig. 3.1c we present the results of the same program (Fig. 3.1a) when the program is run on the WATFIV compiler. We see that the values of (1.0/3.0)*3.0 and (1.0/5.0)*5.0 are now printed as 0.9999999000 on the first line of results. Thus the WATFIV compiler only prints the 7 significant digits (the seven 9s) the computer can accommodate and prints zeros to the right of the significant digits.

From all this, we see that, when we use REAL constants in a program, we should be aware that their internal representation may not be exact, even though when we print the constant, its value may appear exact. As opposed to REAL arithmetic, INTEGER arithmetic involving any operation always yields precise results—both as stored in the computer and as printed in the results. For instance, M*N is always an integer.

INTEGER division, however, may yield unexpected results, since the result of an INTEGER division is always truncated to the lowest integer. When a number is truncated, any fractional part is discarded—thus 4 3/4 when truncated equals 4. When the computer evaluates 5/3, it is actually evaluating 1 2/3 which, when truncated, is 1. As another example, when 3*(1/3) is evaluated, the result is zero, not 1, since 1/3 is truncated to zero.

In Fig. 3.2a, we present a program that performs the calculation (N/3)*N where N successively assumes the value 1, 2, 3, 4, 5, and finally, 6. Since (1/3) and (2/3) are zero; (3/3), (4/3), and (5/3) are 1; and (6/3) is 2, the results are as shown in Fig. 3.2b.

(1.0/3.0)*3.0 (1.0/5.0)*5.0

```
1.0000000000    1.0000000000    0.9999999000    1.0000000000    0.9999999000
 1.0000    1.0000    1.0000    1.0000    1.0000
```

Figure 3.1c. Running the program of Fig. 3.1a on a WATFOR/WATFIV compiler. Note that only 7 digits are outputted.

TRUNCATION IN INTEGER ARITHMETIC

```
C    PROGRAM DEMONSTRATES TRUNCATION IN INTEGER ARITHMETIC
      INTEGER A,B,C,D,E,F
      A=(1/3)*1
      B=(2/3)*2
      C=(3/3)*3
      D=(4/3)*4
      E=(5/3)*5
      F=(6/3)*6
      WRITE(6,10) A,B,C,D,E,F
 10   FORMAT(1X, I4, I4, I4, I4, I4, I4)
      STOP
      END
```

Figure 3.2a. The results of all INTEGER arithmetic (except division) is exact; i.e., no round-off errors occur. When an INTEGER division is performed, the result is truncated; i.e., any fractional part is dropped. Thus (1/3) and (2/3) are both zero; and (3/3), (4/3), (5/3) are all 1.

(1/3)*1 (3/3)*3 (5/3)*5

```
0   0   3   4   5  12
```

(2/3)*2 (4/3)*4 (6/3)*6

Figure 3.2b. Running the program of Fig. 3.2a.

3.3. Mixed Mode

One type of a mixed-mode assignment statement occurs when an INTEGER is assigned to a REAL, e.g.,

```
ACCEL=32
```

Since the computer can only store a REAL constant in the memory location named ACCEL, the computer must convert 32 to the REAL constant 32.0 before it stores the constant in ACCEL. This is called *floating* an INTEGER.

We next investigate what happens when we assign the result of an INTEGER calculation to a REAL. In V = 3/4, first the INTEGER division 3/4 is performed. Then the result, which is 0, is stored as 0.0 in the location labeled by the REAL variable V. These and another example of floating an INTEGER are shown in Table 3.4.

Another type of a mixed-mode assignment statement is the assignment of a REAL to an INTEGER

```
NUM=32.6
```

Since the computer can store only an INTEGER constant in the memory location named NUM, the computer must convert 32.6 to an INTEGER constant. In doing this, it first truncates 32.6 to 32 and then stores 32 in NUM. This is called *fixing* a REAL.

We next investigate what happens when we assign the result of REAL calculation to an INTEGER. In N = (1.0/3.0)*3.0, first the REAL calculation is performed. The result, which is 0.9999999, is truncated to zero and then stored in the location labeled by N. These and other examples of fixing a REAL are shown in Table 3.5.

The third form of mixed mode in an assignment statement is when both REALs and INTEGERs appear in a calculation. This use of mixed mode is not allowed in ANS FORTRAN. Most other compilers allow it; however, we discourage its use because it can lead to unintentional results. Internally, the computer can perform the operation +, −, /, and * only on operands of the same mode (in A*3 for instance, A and 3 are the operands). This is due to the difference in the manner of storing REALs and INTEGERs. If one operand is INTEGER and one is REAL as in

```
DIST=4*60.0
```

first the INTEGER is floated, then the calculation is performed. If there is more than one operation in a mixed-mode statement, the operations are performed according to the priorities given them: If an operation is performed on two INTEGERs, the intermediate result is an INTEGER; the result is then floated when it is used as an operand together with a REAL. This is shown in Table 3.6 for

```
R=6/4 - 12.0/5
```

The presence of the REAL constant 12.0 makes the calculation mixed mode. First the computer evaluates 6/4 as 1; it then floats the 5 and evaluates 12.0/5.0 as 2.4. It next floats 1 and then evaluates 1.0−2.4 as −1.4. It finally assigns −1.4 to R. Had we written the constant 12.0 as 12, the entire calculation would have been INTEGER, yielding the INTEGER result −1; only when the result is assigned to R would it be floated to −1.0.

MIXED MODE ASSIGNMENT STATEMENTS

FLOATING RESULTS OF INTEGER EXPRESSIONS

Statement	What is stored in V	Reason
V=10*36	360.0	The result in the INTEGER multiplication is floated
V=32	32.0	The constant 32 is floated
V=3/4	0.0	3/4 is truncated first to zero and then floated

Table 3.4. When an INTEGER constant is floated, a decimal point is included in the constant, and the result is stored in the REAL variable. The result of an INTEGER division is always truncated, i.e., the fractional part of the result is lopped off.

FIXING RESULTS OF REAL EXPRESSIONS

Statement	What is stored in N	Reason
N=32.6	32	Truncation
N= (1.0/3.0)*3.0	0	The result of the calculation is 0.9999, which is truncated to zero
N=389.0	389	Truncation
N=10.0*0.1	0	0.1 is represented in the computer as 0.09999999; the result of the calculation is 0.9999999, which is truncated to zero

Table 3.5. When a REAL is fixed, the result is truncated. Because of round-off error in the REAL arithmetic on the right-hand side of the assignment statement, some of the results shown are truncated to zero.

EVALUATION OF MIXED-MODE ARITHMETIC

Example. R = 6/4−12.0/5

Step	Operation	Result
1	6/4	1
2	12.0/5	2.4
3	1.0−2.4	−1.4

Table 3.6. For a given operation (like 6/4) in a mixed-mode expression, if both operands are INTEGER, the intermediate result is also INTEGER. Only when this intermediate INTEGER result enters into an operation with a REAL (e.g., Step 3), is it floated.

3.4. The READ Statement

We will now investigate how to write a program to evaluate the polynomial $X + A_0 + A_1T + A_2T^2 + A_nT^n$ for any set of values for A_0, A_1, A_2, A_n, T, and N. In order to do this, we introduce the READ statement. This statement enables the computer to assign values to variables by reading constants from data cards during the execution of the program. On the standard FORTRAN system (and on the WATFOR/WATFIV system if we wish), just as we use a FORMAT statement with the WRITE statement, we also use a FORMAT statement with the READ statement. However, when you read data, you do not use a control character—thus you do not begin the associated FORMAT statement with 1X. Other than that, the FORMAT statements used with READ statements are quite similar to those used with WRITE statements.

If we want to assign values to the variables A0, A1, A2, AN, T, and N by reading the information from a card, we would write

```
READ(5,10) A0,A1,A2,AN,T,N
```

The 5 refers to the numerical value assigned to the input unit (card reader) at most computer centers. The 10 refers to the FORMAT statement

```
10    FORMAT( F10.1, F10.1, F10.1, F10.1, F5.2, I5)
```

which describes the form in which the program will expect the constants to be punched on the data cards. Just as would be the case for a WRITE statement, the first four field specifications (F10.1) refer to A0, A1, A2, and AN, respectively; F5 2 refers to T and I5 to N. Thus the constant typed in the first field at the left of the card would be assigned to A0. The constant typed in the second field from the left would be assigned to A1, etc. The first four fields on the data card are each 10 columns wide, the 5th and 6th fields are each 5 columns wide. That the first five field specifications are F format and the 6th is I format is in agreement with the fact that the first five variables in the READ statement are REAL and the sixth is INTEGER. If they did not agree, the computer would print an error message. On the data card, if we punch REAL constants with decimal points, we can punch the constants anywhere in the field, as is shown in Fig. 3.3a. For example, since the first field is 10 columns wide, the constant 12.261 can be punched starting in any column up to the 5th column

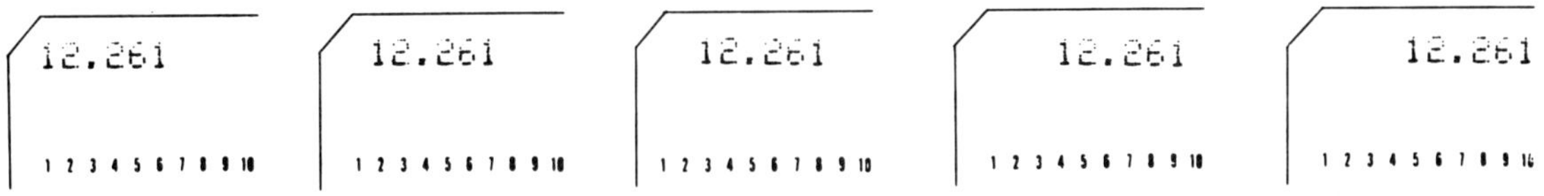

In that case, (if we punch a REAL constant with a decimal point on a data card) the 1 in F10.1 and the 3 in F5.3—and in general, the number that appears after the decimal point in F format—has no significance. Thus we could have written the FORMAT as

```
10    FORMAT( F10.0, F10.0, F10.0, F10.0, F5.0, I5)
```

VALID DATA CARDS FOR 10 FORMAT (F10.1,F10.1,F10.1,F10.1,F5.3,I5)

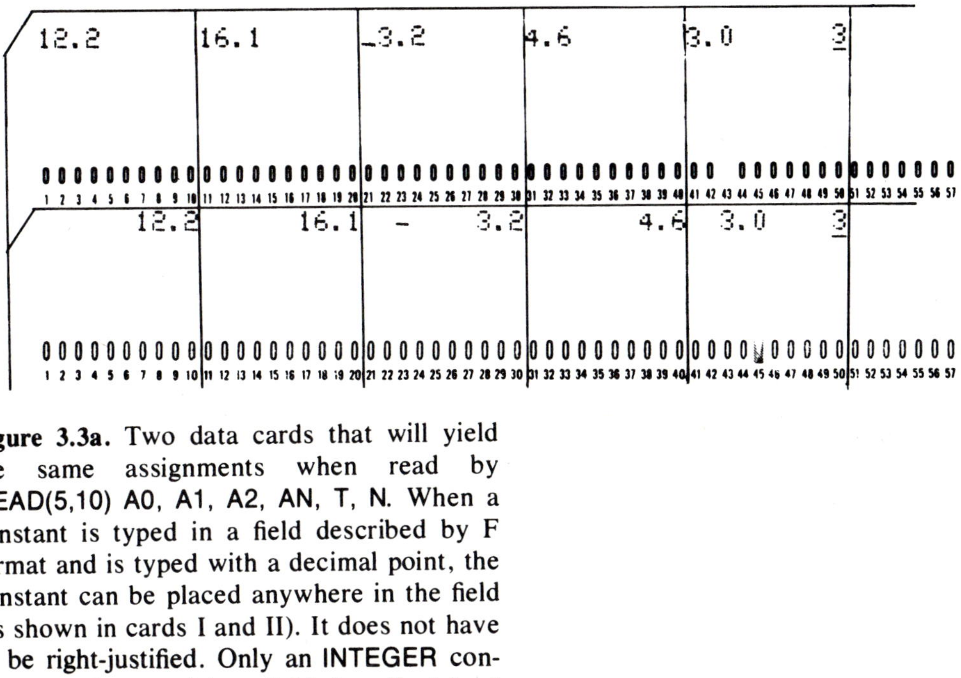

Card I

Card II

Figure 3.3a. Two data cards that will yield the same assignments when read by READ(5,10) A0, A1, A2, AN, T, N. When a constant is typed in a field described by F format and is typed with a decimal point, the constant can be placed anywhere in the field (as shown in cards I and II). It does not have to be right-justified. Only an INTEGER constant can be typed in a field described by I format. The INTEGER constant must be right-justified. If you punch a negative constant, the minus sign can appear in the field anywhere to the right of the constant, as is shown in the third field of card II.

and have obtained the same results. If you punch a constant with a minus sign, the minus sign can appear anywhere in the field to the left of the constant. Thus, for example, if the first field length is 10, then

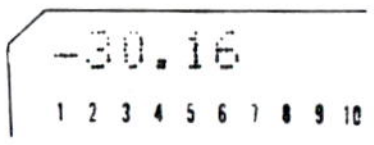

and

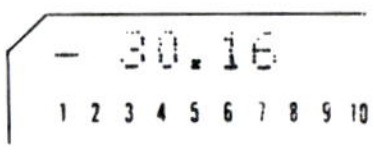

are equivalent. The reason for this is that any blanks that appear in a field are considered as zeros. Moreover, if blanks appear between the digits of the constant, they are interpreted as zeros by the computer. Thus the computer interprets

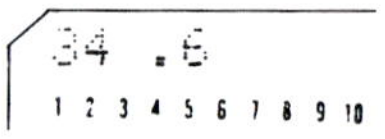

as 340.6. In fact, an entire blank field is equivalent to one that has a zero punched in it.

When we punch a constant on a data card in a field described by an I format, we have no choice as to where we place the constant in the field—the constant must be right-justified. Thus, since we are punching 3, a one-digit number, as the value of N in the polynomial we punch it in the rightmost column in the field. If we punched the 3 in column 48, as is shown in Fig. 3.3b, the computer would interpret the two blank spaces to the right of the 3 as zeros. Thus, we would be mistakenly assigning 300 to N. If we wanted to punch a negative INTEGER constant, we could punch the minus sign anywhere to the left of the constant in the field. On most systems, the data cards are usually placed after the program and separated from it by a control card.

In Fig. 3.3c, we write the program to calculate the polynomial. After we read the A's, the T, and the N into the program, we check that we have read them correctly by printing their values immediately after they have been read.

```
      READ(5,10) A0,A1,A2,AN,T,N
10    FORMAT( F10.0, F10.0, F10.0, F10.0, F5.0, I5)
      WRITE(6,20) A0,A1,A2,AN,T,N
20    FORMAT(1X, F10.3, F10.3, F10.3, F10.3, F10.3, I5)
```

This is called *echo-printing*. Thus, if we had punched the data incorrectly, we would realize it and thus understand why the program performs subsequent operations incorrectly. Beware! If you write a program without echo-printing, you are inviting disaster.

We remind the reader that, just as in the READ statement, the mode of the variables in a WRITE statement must agree with the mode of the field specification used,* as is shown in Fig. 3.3c.

When the program is executed, the assignments are made as is shown in the table for Fig. 3.3c.

Card	Description	N	A0	A1	A2	AN	T	X
4th	READ	3	12.2	16.1	−3.2	4.6	3.0	Undef

The variable X remains undefined until the value of the polynomial is calculated. The results of running the program are as shown in Fig. 3.3d.

* On one of the compilers for the CDC 6600, if you describe a REAL variable, for instance R, which appears in a READ statement, with an I format, then the computer treats R as an INTEGER variable for the rest of the program. On the other hand, if you describe an INTEGER variable, for instance K, which appears in a READ statement with an F format, then the computer treats K as a REAL variable for the rest of the program.

INTEGER **CONSTANTS MUST BE RIGHT-JUSTIFIED**

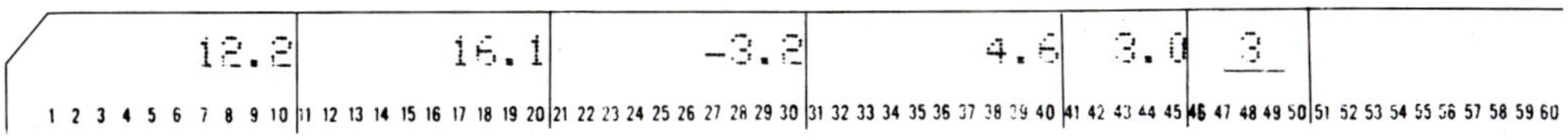

Figure 3.3b. The same data card as in Fig. 3.3a II, except that the INTEGER constant 3 is by mistake not right-justified. The 3 is punched in column 48 instead of column 50. This means that there are two blanks to the right of the 3 in the field. The computer interprets these two blanks as zeros. Thus the INTEGER is read as 300. If you punch a blank between the digits of a number, the computer interprets the blanks as zeros.

```
C    THIS PROGRAM EVALUATES THE POLYNOMIAL:
C           X=A0 + A1*T + A2*T**2 + AN*T**N
C    READS VALUES FOR THE A'S, T AND N
        READ(5,10) A0,A1,A2,AN,T,N
 10     FORMAT( F10.0, F10.0, F10.0, F10.0, F5.0, I5)
C    ECHO PRINT WHAT HAS JUST BEEN READ IN
        WRITE(6,20) A0,A1,A2,AN,T,N
 20     FORMAT(1X, F10.3, F10.3, F10.3, F10.3, F10.3, I5)
C    EVALUATE THE POLYNOMIAL
        X=A0 + A1*T + A2*T**2 + AN*T**N
        WRITE(6,30) X
 30     FORMAT(1X, F15.5)
        STOP
        END
```

Figure 3.3c. This program reads the data card we described in Fig. 3.3a and evaluates a polynomial. In order to check that we read the data correctly, we echo-print the results. The type of the field specification must agree with the variable printed, i.e., F format for REAL and I format for INTEGER. The data card is placed after the end of the program.

Card	Description	N	A0	A1	A2	AN	T	X
4th	READ	3	12.2	16.1	−3.2	4.6	3.0	Undef
7th	WRITE	3	12.2	16.1	−3.2	4.6	3.0	Undef
11th	Assignment	3	12.2	16.1	−3.2	4.6	3.0	155.9

Table for Fig. 3.3c. Shows the values of the variables used at three different statements in the program.

```
A0          A1           A2           AN           T         N
↓           ↓            ↓            ↓            ↓         ↓
12.200      16.100      -3.200       4.600        3.000      3
  155.90000 ←— X
```

Figure 3.3d. Running the program of Fig. 3.3c. The first line of results is the echo-printing of the data, and the second line is the value of the polynomial.

3.5. Some Programming Tips on FORMATs and Data Cards; Repeated Field Specifications

In general, you will find that you make fewer errors if you keypunch REAL constants left justified in their fields. This is because you keypunch from left to right. Another way to avoid errors is to specify that all fields on the input card be the same length whether they are I or F fields. In Fig. 3.4a we show a data card and a FORMAT punched using these two techniques. If you make all the fields 10 columns wide you help to eliminate the possibility that you will type a constant partially in one field and partially in another. If you do not follow this procedure and, for instance, you use the FORMAT 10 FORMAT(F8.0,I5); and then by mistake punch the constants 1234567.0 and 13 on the data card as shown in Fig. 3.4b

```
1234567. 13
1 2 3 4 5 6 7 8 9 10 11 12 13
```

the computer will see a decimal point in the field described by I5 and a run-time error will result. Thus in future versions of the program originally shown in Fig. 3.3c, it would be helpful if we typed the FORMAT that is paired with the READ as

```
10    FORMAT( F10.0, F10.0, F10.0, F10.0, F10.0, I10)
```

Because F10.0 should be repeated 5 times here, we could miscount and punch it only 4 times, for instance, and an error would result when the data card is read. We can instruct the compiler that F10.0 is repeated five times by simply placing a 5 in front of the F10.0, thus writing 5F10.0, as shown in Fig. 3.5.

```
10    FORMAT( 5F10.0, I10)
```

The "5" is called the repeat count. The repeat count can be used in front of any field specification to indicate that the field specification should be repeated. Thus 3I10 means that I10 should be repeated 3 times. A repeat count can be used both in FORMATs used for reading and FORMATs used for writing.

It is a good idea to make the field width on the data card greater than is actually required to keypunch the data. For instance, it is bad programming practice to use a field width of 5 if you are reading constants like 12.34, which occupy five columns. Thus, if you had to punch the three constants 12.34, 67.81, and 92.36 on a data card to be read using 10 FORMAT(3F5.0), the card would end up looking thus:

```
12.3467.8192.36
1 2 3 4 5 6 7 8 9 10 11 12 13 14 15
```

as shown in Fig. 3.6a. Although the computer would have no difficulty reading this card, if there were a mistake on the card, we would have a difficult time finding the error. Be generous! Use wider field widths than are required. Thus if we use the format 10 FORMAT(3F10.0), we could type the data card as

```
12.34     67.81     92.36
1 2 3 4 5 6 7 8 9 10 11 12 13 14 15 16 17 18 19 20 21 22 23 24 25 26 27 28
```

as shown in Fig. 3.6b. Certainly this is much easier for a programmer to check than is the previous card.

GOOD PROGRAMMING STYLE

```
1234567.0         13
1 2 3 4 5 6 7 8 9 10 11 12 13 14 15 16 17 18 19 20 21 22 23 24 25 26 27 28
```

```
      READ(5,10) X, K
10    FORMAT(F10.0, I10)
```

Figure 3.4a. In order to avoid errors, make each field width the same—<u>here 10</u>—and left-justify each REAL constant in its field. INTEGER constants must always be right-justified in its field. The READ and FORMAT statements for this card are also shown.

BAD PROGRAMMING STYLE

```
1234567. 13
1 2 3 4 5 6 7 8 9 10 11 12 13 14 15 16 17 18 19 20 21 22 23 24 25 26 27 28
   F8.0   I5
```

```
      READ(5,10) X, K
10    FORMAT(F8.0, I5)
```

Figure 3.4b. If you make the field widths different lengths, as here, there is the possibility that you may forget how wide each field is. You may then type a constant—here 1234567.—so that it spans two fields. The "7." part of the constant is in the field specified for the INTEGER variable K. The READ and FORMAT statements for this card are also shown.

REPEATING FORMATS

```
10    FORMAT( F10.0, F10.0, F10.0, F10.0, F10.0, I10)
               ⇕
10    FORMAT( 5F10.0, I10)

10    FORMAT( F10.0, F10.0, F10.0, I10, I10, I6)
               ⇕
10    FORMAT( 3F10.0, 2I10, I6)
```

Figure 3.5. If F10.0 is repeated 5 times it can be written as 5F10.0. The 5 is called the "repeat count." If <u>I10</u> is repeated 2 times, it can be written as <u>2I10</u>.

SPACING DATA ON DATA CARDS

```
12.3467.8192.36
1 2 3 4 5 6 7 8 9 10 11 12 13 14 15 16 17 18 19 20 21 22 23 24 25 26 27 28
```

```
      READ(5,10) X, Y, Z
10    FORMAT(3F5.0)
```

Figure 3.6a. In this data card, the constants completely fill their respective fields. This makes it difficult for the programmer to check the cards for mistakes. The READ and FORMAT statements for this card are also shown.

```
12.34     67.81     92.36
1 2 3 4 5 6 7 8 9 10 11 12 13 14 15 16 17 18 19 20 21 22 23 24 25 26 27 28
```

```
      READ(5,10) X, Y, Z
10    FORMAT(3F10.0)
```

Figure 3.6b. By making the field widths larger, we can easily visually separate one constant from the other. It also allows us to punch the REAL constants left-justified. The READ and FORMAT statements for this card are also shown.

In the program of Fig. 3.3c, we used F10.0 to read the first four constants and F10.3 to print their values

```
C   THIS PROGRAM EVALUATES THE POLYNOMIAL:
C          X=A0 + A1*T + A2*T**2 + AN*T**N
C   READS VALUES FOR THE A'S, T AND N
         READ(5,10) A0,A1,A2,AN,T,N
```

Using F10.3 here could create difficulties, since if we read a constant like 123456789., the computer would not be able to print the results—it would print asterisks instead. It is better programming practice to use F15.3 in the FORMAT associated with the WRITE, since then the computer could print any number we read. This is a simple example of writing a program (unfortunately here only part of the program) that will handle any datum, independent of its magnitude (or sign). When a program has this attribute it is said to have *integrity*.

3.6. The WATFOR/WATFIV READ Statement; Doing Calculations in the PRINT Statement

On the WATFOR and WATFIV systems and in the proposed ANS Standard FORTRAN revision, we have the option of either using a READ statement that requires a FORMAT statement or using a format-free READ statement, i.e., one that does not require a FORMAT statement. In Fig. 3.7a we rewrite the previous program (Fig. 3.3c) using a format-free READ. We have replaced the READ and its associated FORMAT statements with*

```
READ, A0,A1,A2,AN,T,N
```

The variables in the READ statement must be separated by commas, and a comma must follow the word READ. No FORMAT statement is used with this READ statement, thus we can punch the data anywhere on the data card. All the constants punched on a given data card must be separated by blank spaces or commas.† We have punched the data card using commas to separate the constants as is shown in Fig. 3.7b:

```
12.2, 16.1, 3.2, 4.6, 3.0, 3
```

The leftmost constant punched on the card is assigned to the leftmost variable in the READ statement (when that statement is executed). Thus 12.2 is assigned to A0. The next constant punched on the card is assigned to the next variable in the READ statement. Thus 16.1 is assigned to A1, etc. The constants that will be assigned to REAL variables must be punched with a decimal point in them, and the constants that will be assigned to INTEGER variables must be typed without a decimal point. How the constants are assigned to the variables in the READ are shown in the table for Fig. 3.7a

A0	A1	A2	AN	T	N
12.2	16.1	3.2	4.6	3.0	3

* In the proposed ANS Standard FORTRAN revision, we write the format-free READ as READ(5,*) A0, A1, A2, AN, T, N.

† In the proposed ANS Standard FORTRAN revision, we may use either a comma or a slash as a separator.

EVALUATING A POLYNOMIAL WATFOR/WATFIV VERSION

```
C   THIS PROGRAM EVALUATES  THE POLYNOMIAL
C    X=A0 + A1 + A2*T**2 + AN*T**N ON THE WATFOR/WATFIV SYSTEM
C   READ THE VALUES FOR THE A'S AND THE T AND N
        READ, A0,A1,A2,AN,T,N
C   ECHO PRINT WHAT HAS JUST BEEN READ
        PRINT,A0,A1,A2,AN,T,N
C   EVALUATE THE POLYNOMIAL
        X=A0 + A1*T + A2*T**2 + AN*T**N
        PRINT, T,X
        STOP
        END
```

Figure 3.7a. The program of Fig. 3.3c written as a format-free WATFOR/WATFIV program. The numbers on the data card can be typed anywhere on the card as long as the order they are in (from left to right) corresponds to the order of the variables in the READ statement. REAL constants must be typed with a decimal point on the data card; INTEGERs, without a decimal point. REAL and INTEGER constants must be assigned to REAL and INTEGER variables, respectively.

A0	A1	A2	AN	T	N
12.2	16.1	3.2	4.6	3.0	3

Table for Fig. 3.7a. How the constants on the data card in Fig. 3.7b are assigned to the variables in READ, A0, A1, A2, AN, T, N.

```
  12.2, 16.1, 3.2, 4.6, 3.0, 3
1 2 3 4 5 6 7 8 9 10 11 12 13 14 15 16 17 18 19 20 21 22 23 24 25 26 27 28 29 30 31 32 33
```

Figure 3.7b. A data card that satisfies the format-free READ in Fig. 3.7a. The constants can appear anywhere on the card. REAL constants must be punched with a decimal point in them. The order in which the constants are typed must agree with the order of the variables in the READ statement. The constants must be separated by commas or blanks.

If there are not enough constants on the first data card to assign to all the variables in the READ statement, as is shown in Fig. 3.7c,

```
12.2,   16.1
```

the computer reads the second data card, here

```
 3.2     4.6
```

and assigns the constants on that card (in the order in which they are punched) to the variables in the READ which have not yet been assigned values. Thus, since 12.2 has already been assigned to A0, and 16.1 to A1, then here 3.2 is assigned to A2 and 4.6 to AN. This process continues—the computer reading successive data cards—until all the variables in the READ statement have been assigned values. When all the variables in a list in a statement have been assigned values, or all the variables in a list in a PRINT or WRITE statement have had their values printed, we say that the *list has been satisfied.*

In Fig. 3.7c sometimes we have used a comma to separate the constants and sometimes we have used a blank, in order to show that this is allowed. However, it is best consistently to use commas or consistently to use blanks to separate the constants.

Had we wanted to, we could have punched only one constant per data card as is shown in Fig. 3.7d. Then the constant on the first card (here 12.2) would be assigned to the first variable in the WRITE statement (here A0). The constant on the second card (here 16.1) is assigned to the second variable in the WRITE statement (here A1). This process continues until the list in the WRITE statement has been satisfied.

The results of running the program with any of the sets of data we have presented (Figs. 3.7b, 3.7c, and 3.7d) are shown in Fig. 3.7e.

OTHER WAYS OF PUNCHING THE DATA FOR A FORMAT-FREE READ

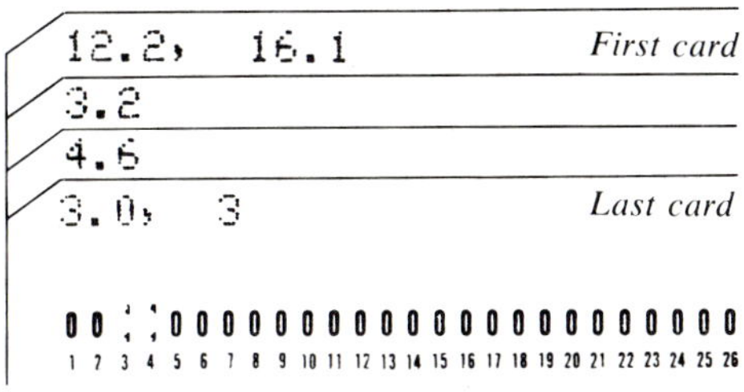

Figure 3.7c. Another way of punching the data for the program of Fig. 3.7a. The format-free READ keeps on reading data cards until all the variables in the READ are defined. How the constants on this data card are assigned to the variables in the READ is shown in the table for Fig. 3.7a.

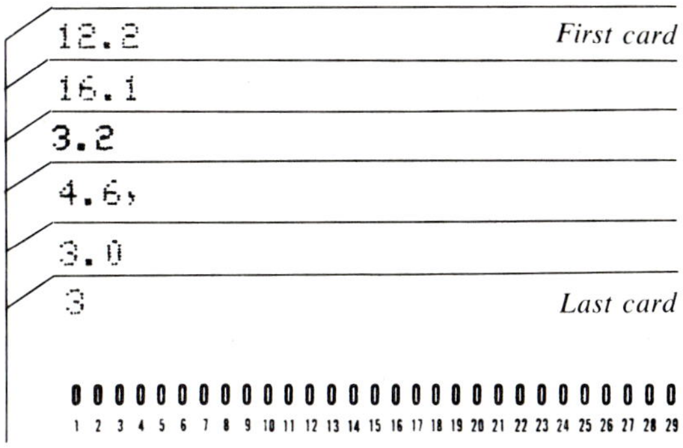

Figure 3.7d. Still another way of punching the data for the program of Fig. 3.7a.

```
      A0                A1                A2                AN                T            N
      ↓                 ↓                 ↓                 ↓                 ↓            ↓
0.1220000E 02    0.1610001E 02    0.3200000E 01    0.4600000E 01    0.3000000E 01       3
0.3000000E 01    0.2135000E 03
      ↑                 ↑
      T                 X
```

Figure 3.7e. The results of running the program of Fig. 3.7a with any of the sets of data we have presented (Fig. 3.7b, 3.7c and 3.7d).

Because a blank is used to separate constants, if by mistake you type a constant with a blank between its digits, the READ statement will consider this constant to be two constants. Thus, if you punch 136.25 as shown in Fig. 3.8a,

```
13 6.25
1 2 3 4 5 6 7 8 9 10
```

the computer will consider it to be the two numbers 13 and 6.25.

If a constant is repeated on a data card, instead of repeating the constant, you may simply write the number of times the constant is used, an asterisk, and then the constant, as shown in Fig. 3.8b. Thus 2*3.21 means 3.21 is used twice and 3*41 means that 41 is used three times. No embedded blanks are allowed here. Thus 3 *41 is incorrect.

On both the WATFOR and WATFIV systems we can rewrite the previous program so that the calculation of the polynomial is done in the PRINT statement, as shown in Fig. 3.9a

```
PRINT, T, A0 + A1*T + A2*T**2 + AN*T**N
```

When this statement is executed, both the value of T and that of the polynomial will be printed. It is tempting to place the polynomial in parentheses so that the PRINT will be easier to read

```
PRINT, T, (A0 + A1*T + A2*T**2 + AN*T**N)
```

This is illegal. You must precede any parenthesized item in a PRINT with a + sign. Thus

```
PRINT, T, +(A0 + A1*T + A2*T**2 + AN*T**N)
```

would be legal. You can also include constants in a PRINT. Thus

```
PRINT, A+3, 36.9, 31, R, +(A+B/(C-D)
```

is an acceptable statement. The results of running the program of Fig. 3.9a are shown in Fig. 3.9b.

BLANKS ON DATA CARDS IN WATFOR/WATFIV

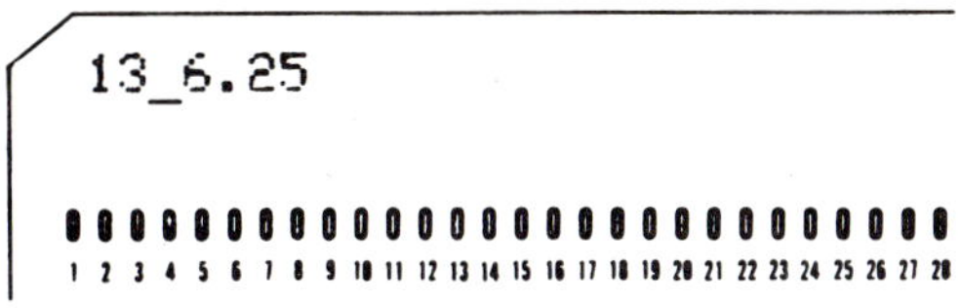

Figure 3.8a. If you leave a blank between the digits of one constant—here 136.25—the computer interprets the constant as two constants, i.e., 13 and 6.25.

REPEATING CONSTANTS ON WATFOR/WATFIV DATA CARDS

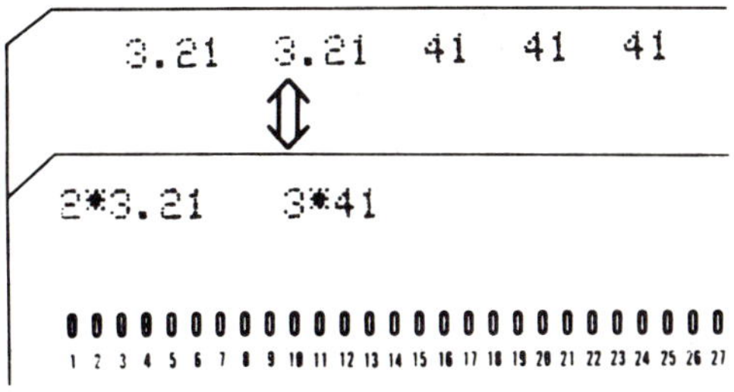

Figure 3.8b. If a constant is repeated (here 3.21 is used twice) you can represent it on a data card with a repeat count (here 2*3.21).

PERFORMING A CALCULATION IN WATFOR/WATFIV PRINT **STATEMENTS**

```
C     THIS PROGRAM EVALUATES  THE POLYNOMIAL
C        A0 + A1 + A2*T**2 + AN*T**N ON THE WATFOR/WATFIV SYSTEM
C     READ THE VALUES FOR THE A'S AND THE T AND N
         READ, A0,A1,A2,AN,T,N
C     ECHO PRINT WHAT HAS JUST BEEN READ
         PRINT,A0,A1,A2,AN,T,N
C     PRINT T AND THE VALUE OF THE POLYNOMIAL
         PRINT, T, A0 + A1*T + A2*T**2 + AN*T**N
         STOP
         END
```

Figure 3.9a. On the WATFOR/WATFIV systems you can perform calculations in a PRINT statement and have the computer print the results. If you wanted to parenthesize the polynomial, you would have to precede the parentheses with a +, i.e., PRINT, T, + (A0 + A1*T+A2*T**2 + AN*T**N). Also, you can place constants in a PRINT statement.

```
0.1220000E 02   0.1610001E 02   0.3200000E 01   0.4600000E 01   0.3000000E 01         3
0.3000000E 01   0.2135000E 03
```

Figure 3.9b. Running the program of Fig. 3.9a.

3.7. The GO TO Statement

In every program we have written until now, the order in which the statements were executed was the same as the order the program cards were in. It is possible—and often very convenient—as we will presently show, to change the order in which the statements are executed. The GO TO statement is an example of a statement that allows us to do this.

In Fig. 3.10a we use a GO TO statement

```
GO TO 10
```

to alter the previous program, so that it evaluates the polynomial for many sets of data. The computer executes this program exactly as it executed the preceding program until it reaches the GO TO statement. It then is instructed to execute statement 10 next. It then proceeds to statement 10, which is the READ statement—we say that *control has been transferred* to statement 10—and the entire process starts again. The statement number we give to the READ statement is arbitrary, but it must correspond to the number that follows the TO in the GO TO statement.

We now follow the execution of the program in more detail. When statement 10 is executed for the first time, the computer reads the first data card. All the data cards are shown in Fig. 3.10b. It then echo prints what it has just read. Next, it evaluates the polynomial. The values assigned to the variables in the program the first time the polynomial is evaluated are given in the first line of the table for Fig. 3.10a

Card	Description	Time Executed	A0	A1	A2	A3	T	N	X
10th	Assignment	1st	12.2	16.1	3.2	4.6	3.0	3	213.5

We have constructed this table slightly differently from the previous tables in that we now show the values assigned to the variables at only one statement in the program, but we show this for each of the three times this statement is executed.

After the WRITE statement, which prints the value of the polynomial, is executed, control is transferred back to statement 10. Therefore, the READ statement is executed again, and the second data card is read—thus, each time a READ statement is executed, a new card is read. New values are assigned to A0, A1, A2, AN, T, and N, and these are echo-printed. The computer evaluates the polynomial using these new values, as is shown in the second line of the table, and prints the result. Because of the GO TO

USING THE GO TO STATEMENT

```
C   THIS PROGRAM EVALUATES   THE POLYNOMIAL
C    X=A0 + A1 + A2*T**2 + AN*T**N FOR MANY SETS OF DATA
C
 10     READ(5,20) A0,A1,A2,AN,T,N
 20     FORMAT( 5F10.1, I10)
C
        WRITE(6,30) A0,A1,A2,AN,T,N
 30     FORMAT(1X, 5F10.3, I5)
C   EVALUATE THE POLYNOMIAL
        X=A0 + A1*T + A2*T**2 + AN*T**N
        WRITE(6,40) X
 40     FORMAT(1X,F15.5)
C   REPEAT THE ENTIRE PROCESS
        GO TO 10
        END
```

Figure 3.10a. Program evaluates the polynomial for many sets of data. GO TO 10 instructs the computer to execute statement 10 (the READ) next. Each time the READ statement is executed, the computer reads a new data card.

Card	Description	Time executed	A0	A1	A2	A3	T	N	X
10th	Assignment	1st	12.2	16.1	3.2	4.6	3.0	3	213.5
10th	Assignment	2nd	11.6	12.1	8.2	5.1	3.0	4	745.6477
10th	Assignment	3rd	14.2	3.6	2.1	8.2	4.0	8	537457.3

Table for Fig. 3.10a. Shows the values of the variables in the program each time the polynomial is evaluated.

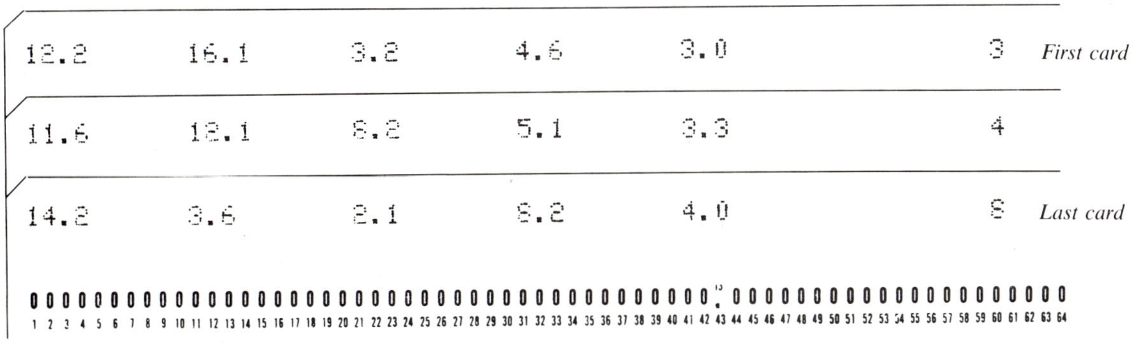

Figure 3.10b. The data cards for Fig. 3.10a.

statement, the entire process is repeated for each of the three data cards. After the result for the third card has been printed, control is transferred once again to the READ statement. This time, however, there are no more cards to be read, so the computer prints

```
***ERROR***   CONTROL CARD ENCOUNTERED ON UNIT    5 AT EXECUTION.
```

or an equivalent message, and the program is terminated. The results are shown in Fig. 3.10c. Note that we did not place a STOP statement after the GO TO statement because it would have never been executed by the computer—the GO TO always transfers control back to statement 10.

The method we have used here to end the program is not elegant, nor is it considered good programming style. We have used it simply because it allows the novice programmer early in his training to see and use one of the strengths of the computer: the ability to perform the same set of operations for many sets of data.

If you had written the previous program for the WATFOR/WATFIV system, and you did not want to use FORMAT statements, you would have to replace the WRITE and READ statements with their format-free equivalents. You could use the same data cards that we used for Fig. 3.10a. It is important to note here that, just as is the case for a formatted READ, each time a format-free READ is executed a completely new card is read. Thus if we punch all three sets of data on one data card and use it for the data for the format-free WATFOR/WATFIV equivalent of the program in Fig. 3.10a, the program would read and then process the first set of data; the other numbers on the data card would not be read. Then when the READ statement is executed for the second time, the computer would attempt to read another data card. Since there is none, the program would terminate and the computer would print

```
***ERROR***   CONTROL CARD ENCOUNTERED ON UNIT    5 AT EXECUTION.
```

3.8. Flow Charts

In the preceding program (Fig. 3.10a), the statements from the READ to the GO TO form what is called a loop. This term is used because during the execution of the program, after it has processed the first set of data, the computer returns from the GO TO statement to the READ and proceeds once again along its original path. We can pictorially depict a loop by using a flow chart. A flow chart describes the order in which instructions are executed in a program. The beginning of a flow chart is represented by an oval with the word START in it. The operations that are performed in a program in READ and WRITE statements are written inside slanted parallelograms. Assignment statements are written inside rectangles. The order in which these operations are performed is described by arrows leading from one geometric figure—at this point in our discussion of flow charts, either an oval, a parallelogram, or a rectangle—to another. In Fig. 3.10d we present a flow chart for the program of Fig. 3.10a. The arrow from the PRINT X parallelogram returns to the READ parallelogram, indicating that the reading, printing, calculating, and printing should be repeated. According to the flow chart, the entire process should be repeated over and over again. However, as we have seen, the program terminates because it runs out of data. In the next chapter we will see how to terminate programs more gracefully.

```
      12.200        16.100         3.200         4.600         3.000      3
X=→   213.50000
      11.600        12.100         8.200         5.100         3.300      4
X=→   745.64770
      14.200         3.600         2.100         8.200         4.000      8
X=→537457.30000
***ERROR***   CONTROL CARD ENCOUNTERED ON UNIT    5 AT EXECUTION.
```

Figure 3.10c. Running the program of Fig. 3.10b. The fourth time the READ statement is executed, there are no more data cards to be read. The computer therefore prints the error message.

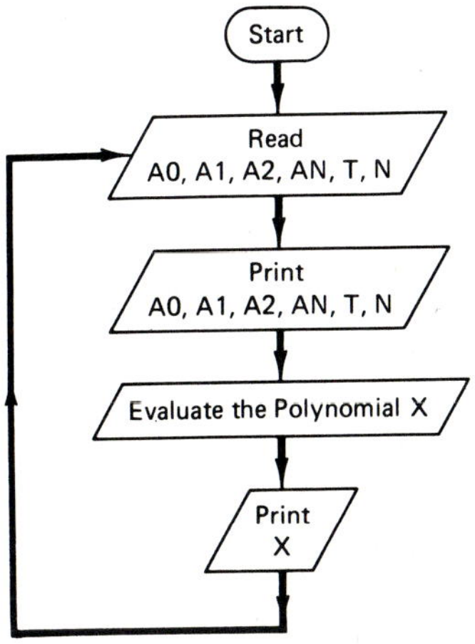

Figure 3.10d. Flow chart for the program of Fig. 3.10a.

3.9. Rounding Numbers

Sometimes when doing a calculation, it is desirable to have numbers rounded before you use them in the calculation. In Fig. 3.11a we present a program that rounds a constant to the nearest unit; i.e., 136.2 would be rounded to 136. In

```
J=X + 0.5
```

we use the property of fixing REALs to round the value of X, where X is read from a data card. The data cards are shown in Fig. 3.11b. Because of the GO TO statement, the program reads all the data cards and rounds the value of X read from each card. How the first value of X is rounded is shown in the first line of the table for Fig. 3.11a

X	X + 0.5	J
136.2	136.7	136

Since the .2 in 136.2 is less than 0.5, the addition of 0.5 does not affect the truncation of X. Thus the value of J is 136 and 136.2 has been rounded correctly. However, when the value of X is 136.8 as is shown in the second line of the table for Fig. 3.11a

X	X + 0.5	J
136.8	137.3	137

the addition of 0.5 increases the truncated value of X by 1. Thus J now equals 137 and 136.8 has been correctly rounded. The last line of the table shows how 15.16 is rounded to 15. The results of running the program are shown in Fig. 3.11c.

ROUNDING NUMBERS

```
C  ROUNDS A NUMBER TO THE NEAREST UNIT
 10    READ(5,20) X
 20    FORMAT( F10.1)
       J=X + 0.5
       WRITE(6,30) X,J
 30    FORMAT(1X, F10.1, I10)
       GO TO 10
       END
```

Figure 3.11a. Program rounds numbers to the nearest unit by fixing a REAL expression X+ 0.5.

X	X + 0.5	J
136.2	136.7	136
136.8	137.3	137
15.16	15.66	15

Table for Fig. 3.11a. How J= X + 0.5 rounds to the nearest unit. After X + 0.5 is evaluated, the result is truncated and assigned to J.

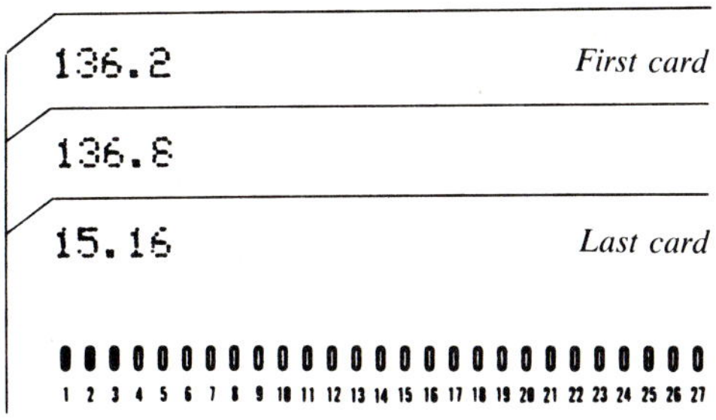

Figure 3.11b. The data cards for Fig. 3.11a.

```
         X               Rounded value of X

      136.2           136
      136.8           137
       15.2            15
***ERROR***   CONTROL CARD ENCOUNTERED ON UNIT    5 AT EXECUTION.
```

Figure 3.11c. Running the program of Fig. 3.11a.

In the next program, shown in Fig. 3.12a, we round the value of X to the nearest 100. In order to do this, we first divide X by 100.0. We then round X/100.0 to the nearest unit by writing

```
J=(X/100.0) + 0.5
```

In order to compensate for the division of 100, we now multiply by 100 in

```
NUM=100*J
```

How this works for each value of X read from the data cards shown in Fig. 3.12b, is shown in the table for Fig. 3.12a. The first line of the table shows how 1396 is rounded to the nearest 100.

X	X/100.0	(X/100) + 0.5	J	NUM
1396.	13.96	14.46	14	1400

Thus, 1396 is correctly rounded to 1400. The results of running the program are shown in Fig. 3.12c.

ROUNDING NUMBERS TO THE NEAREST 100

```
C   ROUNDS A NUMBER TO THE NEAREST 100
C
 10     READ(5,20) X
 20     FORMAT( F10.0 )
C
        J=(X/100.0) + 0.5
        NUM=100*J
        WRITE(6,30) X,NUM
 30     FORMAT(1X, F10.1, I10)
C
        GO TO 10
        END
```

Figure 3.12a. Program rounds numbers to the nearest hundred. We first divide X by 100 and round X/100 to the nearest unit. We then compensate for the division by multiplying by 100.

X	X/100.0	(X/100)+ 0.5	J	NUM
1396.	13.96	14.46	14	1400
132.	1.32	1.8	1	100
981.	9.81	10.31	10	1000

Table for Fig. 3.12a. How J=(X/100) + 0.5 works.

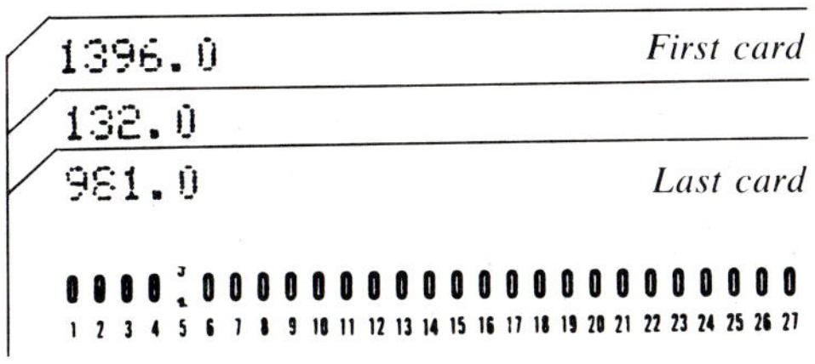

Figure 3.12b. The data cards for Fig. 3.12a.

```
    1396.0          1400
     132.0           100
     981.0          1000
***ERROR***    CONTROL CARD ENCOUNTERED ON UNIT     5 AT EXECUTION.
```

Figure 3.12c. Running the program of Fig. 3.12a.

3.10. Strings

The results of the programs we have previously discussed have been printed simply as numbers. Unless we read the program that produced the results, we have no way of knowing what these numbers represent. This situation can easily be rectified by adding to the FORMAT statement any descriptive information we want printed. This information usually appears between apostrophe marks (but on CDC systems between asterisks). Any group of characters that appears between apostrophe marks is called a *string* and is printed on the line printer exactly as it appears in the FORMAT statement. Since the apostrophe marks bracket the string, they are called the *string delimiters*. In ANS Standard FORTRAN you cannot use string delimiters. However, on most compilers and on the proposed ANS Standard revised FORTRAN, the apostrophe is used as a string delimiter.

In Fig. 3.13a we write a program that uses $Y=V_0t-gt^2/2$ to calculate the height Y of a projectile as a function of the time T it is in the air. The program first reads the value of VO (the value of the projectile's velocity when it is fired from the ground) from the first card. It then reads the values of T from the remaining cards. All the data cards are shown in Fig. 3.13b. We have used strings in the FORMAT to label the results.

```
40    FORMAT(1X, 'Y=', F10.0, ' T=', F10.0, ' VO=', F10.0)
```

The strings are Y=, T=, and VO=. Strings are separated from field specifications and from other strings by commas. When

```
WRITE(6,40) Y,T,VO
```

is executed, the first thing printed, starting in the leftmost column, is Y=; this is followed by a field 10 columns wide (corresponding to the first F10.0) in which the value of Y is printed so that it is right-justified. This is followed by T=, which is followed by a field 10 columns wide (corresponding to the second F10.0), in which the value of T is printed right-justified. This is followed by VO=, which is followed by a field 10 columns wide (corresponding to the third F10.0) in which the value of TIME is printed right-justified. All of this is shown in Fig. 3.13c.

USING STRINGS IN FORMAT STATEMENTS

```
C   CALCULATES THE  Y-COORDINATE OF A FALLING BODY
C   AS A FUNCTION OF T. VO=INITIAL VELOCITY
C   USES STRINGS
        G=-32.0
        READ(5,10) VO
 10     FORMAT( F10.0 )
C
 20     READ (5,30) T
 30     FORMAT( F10.0 )
        Y=VO*T + (G* (T**2) ) / 2.0
        WRITE(6,40) Y,T,VO
 40     FORMAT(1X, 'Y=', F10.0, ' T=', F10.0, ' VO=', F10.0)
C
        GO TO 20
        END
```

Figure 3.13a. A program in which strings are used in the FORMAT statement. Anything printed between apostrophe marks in the FORMAT statement will be exactly reproduced on the line printer when the associated WRITE statement is executed. The field specifications correspond to the variables in the WRITE statement as usual.

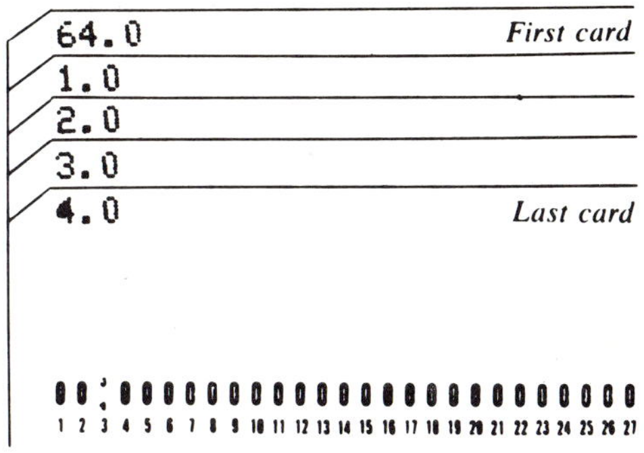

Figure 3.13b. The data for the program of Fig. 3.13a. The constant on the first card is the value of VO. The constants on the rest of the cards are the values of T. These are read and used in the loop in the program.

The reading of the values of T and the calculation and printing of Y is done in the loop

```
 20     READ (5,30) T
 30     FORMAT( F10.0 )
        Y=V0*T + (G* (T**2) ) / 2.0
        WRITE(6,40) Y,T,V0
 40     FORMAT(1X, 'Y=', F10.0, ' T=', F10.0, ' V0=', F10.0)
C
        GO TO 20
```

until all the data cards are read. The first line of results

```
Y=        48. T=         1. V0=        64.
```

shows the result for the value of T equal to 1. This, as well as the values of Y for T equal to 2.0, 3.0, and 4.0, are shown in Fig. 3.13c. When there are no more data cards to be read, the computer prints an error message indicating this. We see that the height of the projectile Y is 48 when the value of time is 1; is 64 when the value of time is 2; is 48 again when the value of time is 3; and is finally 0 when the value of time is 4, i.e., when the value of time is 4, the projectile returns to the ground.

Because the values of the variables are printed right-justified in their fields, the last digit of a constant immediately precedes the first character in the next string. That is why we have begun all but the first string with a blank, e.g., we write the second string as ' T='.

If the strings mislabel the results, the computer has no way of discovering this error. Thus the computer would not consider

```
40   FORMAT(1X, 'T=', F10.0, 'VO=', F10.0, 'Y=', F10.0)
```

an error, even though T= labels the value of Y, VO= labels the value of T, and Y= labels the value of VO.

When writing a FORMAT statement, on most compilers you do not have to separate a delimited string from the other field specifications by commas. Thus we can write the FORMAT as

```
40   FORMAT(1X, 'Y=' F10.0 'T=' F10.0 'VO=' F10.0 )
```

As we have mentioned, in ANS Standard FORTRAN you cannot use the apostrophe, or for that matter any other symbol, to bracket strings. You can only use what is called Hollerith FORMAT. In Hollerith FORMAT you must precede a string by the letter H which in turn is preceded by an integer indicating how many characters, including blanks, follow the H. Thus in Fig. 3.13d we write

```
 40    FORMAT(1X, 2HY=, F10.0, 3H T=, F10.0, 4H V0=, F10.0)
```

We have written 3H T= because of the blank that precedes the T, and 4H VO= because of the blank that precedes the V. The output of this program is the same as that shown in Fig. 3.13a.

```
Y=         48. T=          1. VO=         64.
Y=         64. T=          2. VO=         64.
Y=         48. T=          3. VO=         64.
Y=          0. T=          4. VO=         64.
***ERROR***  CONTROL CARD ENCOUNTERED ON UNIT     5 AT EXECUTION.
```

Figure 3.13c. The results of running the program of Fig. 3.13a. We see the value of Y, the height above the ground, vary as the value of T does. If the strings do not correctly label the results, no error will result. The computer has no way of checking whether the strings and values they label correspond.

USING HOLLERITH FIELDS

```
C   CALCULATES THE  Y-COORDINATE OF A FALLING BODY
C   AS A FUNCTION OF T. VO=INITIAL VELOCITY
C   USES STRINGS
C   USING HOLLERITH FIELDS
        G=-32.0
        READ(5,10) VO
 10     FORMAT( F10.0 )
C
 20     READ (5,30) T
 30     FORMAT( F10.0 )
        Y=VO*T + (G* (T**2) ) / 2.0
        WRITE(6,40) Y, T, VO
 40     FORMAT(1X, 2HY=, F10.0, 3H T=, F10.0, 4H VO=, F10.0)
C
        GO TO 20
        END
```

Figure 3.13d. In ANS standard FORTRAN you specify a string by preceding the string with an H preceded by an integer indicating how many characters—including blanks—are in the string.

3.11. Strings in WATFIV

Since there are no FORMAT statements associated with PRINT statement on WATFIV compilers, you can place strings in the PRINT statement itself if you are running your program on the WATFIV compiler. [This cannot be done on the WATFOR compiler.] Thus in Fig. 3.14a we write the PRINT statement as

```
PRINT, 'Y=', Y, 'T=', T, 'V0=', V0
```

The results are shown in Fig. 3.14b.

Formatted READ

> The form of the formatted READ statement is: READ(; followed by the number of the input unit*; followed by a comma; followed by the statement number of the FORMAT statement you want to use; followed by); followed by the variables to be read. If there is more than one variable, the variables must be separated by commas. Each time a READ statement is executed, it reads a new card. Examples:
>
> READ(5,1000) AO, N, INT, T
> READ(5,100) VARI
> READ(5,1008) I,J,K

WATFOR/WATFIV/WATFIV-S READ

> The form of the format-free READ (available only on WATFOR/WATFIV compilers) is: READ; followed by a comma; followed by the variables to be read. If there is more than one variable to be read, the variables must be separated by a comma. The format-free READ continues to read cards until all the variables in the READ are defined; however, each time a format-free READ statement is executed, it starts reading from a new card. Examples:
>
> READ, AO, N, INT, Y
> READ, VAR1
> READ, I, J, K

Just as in the WRITE and PRINT statements, the variables that appear in a READ statement are collectively called a list.

On the proposed revision of ANS Standard FORTRAN, you can use H FORMAT or constants enclosed in single quotes to express alphanumeric constants.

* As we shall see, we can use an INTEGER variable to represent the output unit.

USING STRINGS IN WATFIV PRINT **STATEMENTS**

```
C   CALCULATES THE Y-COORDINATE OF A FALLING BODY
C   AS A FUNCTION OF T. USES WATFIV
      G=-32.0
      READ, V0
 20   READ, T
      Y=V0*T + (G*(T**2))/2.0
      PRINT, 'Y=', Y, 'T=', T, 'V0=', V0
      GO TO 20
      END
```

Figure 3.14a. The program of Fig. 3.13a written as a format-free WATFIV program. Since there is no FORMAT statement, the strings must be placed in the PRINT statement. In WATFOR you cannot do this.

```
Y=     0.4800000E 02 T=     0.1000000E 01 V0=     0.6400000E 02
Y=     0.6400000E 02 T=     0.2000000E 01 V0=     0.6400000E 02
Y=     0.4800000E 02 T=     0.3000000E 01 V0=     0.6400000E 02
***ERROR***  CONTROL CARD ENCOUNTERED ON UNIT   5 AT EXECUTION.
```

Figure 3.14b. Running the program of Fig. 3.14a.

3.12. Another Form of the READ Statement

In the READ statement we have learned, e.g.,

```
READ(5,10) A, B, C, T
```

that the first number we place in the parentheses—here 5—can refer to the card reader, a magnetic tape, or a disk file. If we want to read from a card reader, on most systems, but not ANS Standard FORTRAN,* we can use the following (See Fig. 3.15):

```
READ 10, A, B, C, T
```

where 10 refers to the format to be paired with the READ. Note that a comma must precede the list in this form of the READ statement.

* This type of READ statement is incorporated into the revised edition of ANS FORTRAN; and by substituting an asterisk for the number that refers to the FORMAT statement, you obtain a format-free READ statement on this system. Thus READ*, A, B, C, T can be used in the revised version of ANS FORTRAN.

A SIMPLIFIED FORMATTED READ STATEMENT

```
      G=-32.0
      READ 10, VO
 10   FORMAT( F10.0 )
C
 20   READ 30, T
 30   FORMAT( F10.0 )
      Y=VO*T + (G* (T**2) ) / 2.0
      PRINT 40, Y, T, VO
 40   FORMAT(1X, 'Y=', F10.0, ' T=', F10.0, ' VO=', F10.0)
C
      GO TO 20
      END
```

Figure 3.15. On most systems you can use a READ statement that does not contain a number referring to the line printer. It just contains the FORMAT number followed by a comma followed by the variables in the list.

PROBLEMS

1. What value is calculated for each of the following statements?

```
A = 4.0 - 2.0 ** 2
B = (4.0 + 2.0)/4.0 - 3.0
C = 4.0 + 2.0/(4.0 - 3.0)
D = (4.0 + 2.0)/(4.0 - 3.0)
E = 4.0 * 3.0 + 2.0
```

2. What is wrong with each of the following FORTRAN statements?

   (a) `SAL + COM = 106.2 + R`
   (b) `DIST = VELOC * + TIME`
   (c) `-DIST = VELOC * (-TIME)`
   (d) `Z = T(X + Y)`
   (e) `C**2 = A**2 + B**2`

3. Write the FORTRAN equivalent of the following equations:

   (a) $A = \dfrac{3 + B}{B + 2}$

   (b) $R = \dfrac{(A + B)^2 - R}{3B}$

4. Which of the following fractions would you expect to be represented exactly on a binary machine?

   (a) 1/64
   (b) 1/25
   (c) 1/32
   (d) 1/10
   (e) 1/50

5. If a given computer prints the value of 3.0 * (1.0/3.0) as 0.999963278, what is the maximum number of significant decimal digits a REAL constant can have?

6. What values are assigned to the variables in the following statements?

   (a) `VAR = (3/2) ** 2 + 2.0`
   (b) `INTER = (3/2) ** 2 + 2`
   (c) `VAR = (3.0/2.0) ** 2 + 2`
   (d) `VEL = (3.0/2) ** 2 + 2.0`

7. For each of the following cards, write a pair of READ and FORMAT statements that will read the card

(a)

5	10	20	30
12.6	20.6	13.936	32

(b)

5	10	20	30
12.6	20.6	13.936	−30

(c)

10	20	30	40
12.6	20.612	306.312	32

8. Give examples of a data card that will satisfy the READ and FORMAT statement

```
   READ(5,10) X, Y, Z, I, J
10 FORMAT(F10.2, F10.0, F10.0, I10, I10)
```

9. A formula used in statistics to relate a variable X to a variable Z is

$$Z = (X - \mu)/\sigma$$

where all the variables are REAL. Write a program that reads values for X, μ, and σ and calculates Z.

10. What is wrong with each of the following pairs of statements?

(a)
```
   READ(5,10) X, Z, SIGMA
10 FORMAT(F10.0, I10, F10.0)
```

(b)
```
   READ(6,10) X, Z, SIGMA
10 FORMAT(F10.0, F10.0, F10.0)
```

(c)
```
   READ(6,10)
10 FORMAT(I10)
```

11. A data card in which an 8 is punched in column 10 is read by

```
   READ(5,10) INT
10 FORMAT(1X, I10)
```

What is the value of INT stored after the READ is executed?

12. Rewrite the following FORMAT statement using repeat counts:

```
20 FORMAT(1X, F10.0, F10.0, F10.2, F10.3, F10.3, I4, I4)
```

13. What is wrong with the following format-free READ statements?

(a) `READ, X, Y, Z,`
(b) `READ X, Y, Z`
(c) `READ, X ** 2, Y, Z + 2`

14. Give some example of data cards that would satisfy the following format-free READ

```
READ, A, B, I, J, C
```

15. Write a program that will round constants to the nearest 1000th, e.g., .1034 would be rounded to .103 and .1038 would be rounded to .104.

16. Write a program that will truncate constants to the nearest 1000th, e.g., both .1034 and .1038 would be rounded to .103.

17. What is wrong with each of the following statements?

(a) `20 FORMAT(1X, HZ=', F12.4)`

(b) `20 FORMAT(1X, 1HZ=, F12.4)`

(c) `PRINT 'Z=', Z`

18. Given the following table, write a program that for each sale calculates the number of square feet of plywood sold and the amount of the sale in dollars. The price per square foot of plywood is $.06.

Sale Number	Length	Width
1001	8ft	4ft
1006	12ft	4ft
1012	5ft	3ft

The information for each sale should be punched on a data card which will be read by the program.

4

Functions and the IF Statement

4.1. Library Functions

Although we can obtain the square root of a number like 180.3 by writing the FORTRAN equivalent of $Y = 180.3^{1/2}$, i.e., Y = 180.3**0.5, the computer will execute the following faster:

```
Y=SQRT(180.3)
```

More important than this, however, is that it is easier for someone reading the program to recognize this as the square root of a number. The appearance of SQRT(   ) in a program automatically activates a group of statements referred to as the SQRT library function, which is permanently stored in the computer's memory. The SQRT library function, or more simply, SQRT function, calculates the square root of whatever appears between the parentheses, be it a constant, variable, expression, or another function. What appears between the parentheses is called the argument of the function.

We will now use this function to write the FORTRAN equivalent of some algebraic formulas. The velocity V that a particle has after it has traveled a distance Y at an acceleration g, given the fact that it had an initial velocity V_0, is described by

$$V^2 = V_0^2 + 2gY$$

We could write the solution for V in FORTRAN as

```
V=SQRT(VO**2 + 2.0*G*Y)
```

One of the solutions to the quadratic equation $ax^2+bx+c = 0$ is given by

$$X = \frac{-b+\sqrt{b^2-4ac}}{2a}$$

This is written in FORTRAN as

```
X=(-B + SQRT(B*B - 4.0*A*C)) / (2.0*A)
```

Note that we have placed the term 2.0*A in parentheses, since we want this whole term to divide the numerator.*

Some of the library functions offered in FORTRAN are given in Table 4.1. For the

* Had we eliminated these parentheses, we would have divided (– B+ SQRT(B*B– 4.0*A*C)) by 2.0 and then multiplied the result by A.

ARITHMETIC FUNCTIONS THAT HAVE REAL **ARGUMENTS**

Function	Description	Restriction on X
SQRT(X)	Square root	*X* must be positive
EXP(X)	e^X	None
ALOG(X)	$\log_e{}^x$	*X* must be larger than zero
ALOG10(S)	$\log_{10}{}^x$	*X* must be larger than zero
SIN(X)	Sin*X*	*X* in radians
COS(X)	Cos*X*	*X* in radians
TAN(X)	Tan*X*	*X* in radians
ATAN(X)	$\mathrm{Tan}^{-1}X$; result in radians	None
ABS(X)	Absolute value of *X*; i.e., always gives the positive value of *X*	None

Table 4.1. The most commonly used arithmetic functions available on the FORTRAN compiler. The quantity that appears between the parentheses is called the argument of the function. The argument for these functions must be REAL and may be either a constant, a variable, a calculation, or another function. Also, none of these functions begins with the letters I, J, K, L, M, or N; thus their results are all REALs.

functions tabulated here, the arguments must be REAL; otherwise, either an error message or unexpected answer will result, depending on which compiler you are using. Also, since none of these function names begins with the letters I, J, K, L, M, or N, the functions' values are also REAL. Any function name that begins with one of these letters will have an INTEGER value.

Another library function is the exponentiation function, EXP. EXP(X) calculates e^x where e is the base of the natural logarithms, 2.71828. We now use the EXP function to evaluate the normal curve. The normal curve is shaped like a bell, hence it is also called the bell-shaped curve. Many statistical distributions, such as the distribution of male adult heights or the distribution of I.Q.s, can be described by the normal curve. The equation for the ordinate Y of the normal curve in terms of the abscissa Z is given by

$$Y = \frac{e^{-Z^2/2}}{\sqrt{2\pi}}$$

In FORTRAN we would write this as

```
Y=EXP(-Z**2/2.0) / SQRT(2.0*3.14159)
```

When a function appears in an expression in FORTRAN, the argument of the function is evaluated first. Then the function itself is evaluated. If there is more than one function in an expression, the functions are evaluated from left to right. Finally, the remaining operations in the expression are evaluated according to their priorities. Thus the compiler evaluates the above expression in the following order:

1. −Z**2/2.0
2. EXP(−Z**2/2.0)
3. 2.0*3.14159
4. SQRT(2.0*3.14159)
5. EXP(−Z**2/2.0) / SQRT(2.0*3.14159)

In −Z**2/2.0, since Z**2 is evaluated first, then Z**2/2.0 is evaluated, and finally −Z**2/2.0 is evaluated, we need not include any extra parentheses. Thus we do not have to write −(Z**2/2.0).

As we have seen, a function can be used in an expression in the same manner as a variable. Thus, if we wanted to write the FORTRAN equivalent of $Y = \sin^2(X + Z)$ we could write Y=SIN(X + Y)**2. This is equivalent to the overparenthesized version Y= (SIN(X + Y))**2. In Table 4.2 we list some algebraic expressions and their FORTRAN equivalents. All variables that are normally INTEGERs, like K, M, and N, have been declared REAL.

USING FUNCTIONS

Algebraic expression	FORTRAN expression
$T = 0.5KA^2\sin^2(wt+\delta)$	REAL K
	T=0.5*K * (A**2) * (SIN(W*T + DELTA))**2
$T = 2\pi\sqrt{(R\cos\theta)/g}$	TAU=2.0*3.14159 * SQRT(R*COS(THETA)/G)
$N = e^{-mv^2/2Kt}$	REAL K,M,N
	N=EXP(-M*(V**2) / (2.0*K*T))

Table 4.2. Algebraic expressions using functions as translated into FORTRAN. All variables in the FORTRAN expressions that are not ordinarily REAL have been declared REAL in a REAL statement.

Sometimes we want to use INTEGER values in REAL expressions; for example, if we wanted to round an integer M to the nearest unit, in order to avoid a mixed-mode expression we would have to first float M to a REAL variable X, and then use X in the statement that performed the rounding. Thus we would write

```
X=M
J=X + 0.5
```

If we did not want to save the value of X, we could write these two statements as one statement by using the FLOAT function

```
J=FLOAT(M) + 0.5
```

The FLOAT function floats the value of its argument, and thus allows you to use its argument in a REAL expression.

The IFIX function allows you to use a REAL constant or variable in an expression involving INTEGERs. However, IFIX first truncates the value of its argument. Thus if we wanted to add the truncated value of R to J and store the result in L, we would write

```
L=IFIX(R) + J
```

If the value of R is 9.3, then IFIX(R) is 9. Table 4.3 summarizes these results.

THE FLOAT AND IFIX FUNCTIONS

Function	Description	Restriction on argument	Example
FLOAT(K)	Converts the value of K to a REAL	Must be an INTEGER	J= FLOAT(M)+ 0.5
IFIX(X)	Truncates the value of X and converts it to an INTEGER	Must be a REAL	L=IFIX(R)+J

Table 4.3. These functions are used in an expression in order to avoid mixed-mode expressions.

4.2. The Logical IF Statement

In the program we wrote in Fig. 3.10a—i.e., calculating a polynomial for many sets of data—the execution of the statements in the loop continued until the last data card was processed. After the program had processed this card, the computer, because it could not read another card, terminated the program, thereby producing an error message. In other words, the program did not end because of an instruction we gave in the program; the program was ended by the compiler because of a run-time error. The ending of a program in this manner is not only aesthetically unpleasing, but also impractical because it does not allow us to perform any further calculations in the program. We now discuss a statement called the logical IF that enables us to terminate a loop from within the program. An example of this statement is given in the program of Fig. 4.1a

```
IF( N .EQ. 1) STOP
```

where EQ stands for equals. It is called a *relational operator*. Other examples of relational operators will be given in Section 4.3. A relational operator must be both preceded and followed by a period, and it is sandwiched between two expressions—in our case N and 1—which in ANS FORTRAN must both be written in the same mode, although on other compilers these two expressions may be of different modes. Everything that appears between the parentheses is called a *logical expression*, sometimes called a *condition*.

When an IF statement is executed, if the condition in the parentheses (in this case whether N equals 1) is true, then the instruction to the right of the right parenthesis (in this case STOP) is executed. If the condition is false, then the next statement—in this case GO TO 10—is executed.

The program calculates and then prints the ordinate, Y, of the normal distribution

$$Y = \frac{e^{-Z^2/2}}{\sqrt{2\pi}}$$

after each time a value of Z is read in from cards by 10 READ(5,20) Z,N. Since the field specifications for this READ are (F10.0, I10), each data card must have the value of Z punched somewhere in the first 10 columns—we have punched it left-justified. However, all cards except the last data card have nothing else punched on them, as we see in Fig. 4.1b. Thus the second field for these cards is blank, and the computer assigns zero to N when these cards are read. The last data card, however, has a 1 punched in the rightmost column of the second field.

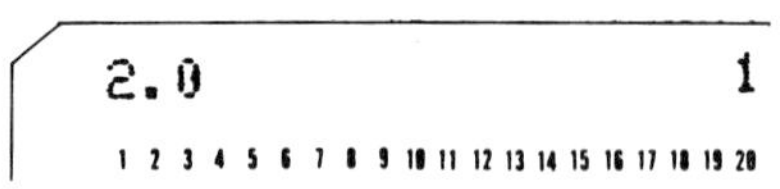

Thus when this card is read, the computer obviously assigns 1 to N.

USING THE IF STATEMENT

```
C  PROGRAM PRODUCES A TABLE FOR THE NORMAL DISTRIBUTION
C  THE INDEPENDENT VARIABLE, Z, IS READ FROM DATA CARDS
C  FOR THE LAST DATA CARD, N=1; FOR ALL OTHERS, N=0
C          ...Y IS THE HEIGHT OF THE DISTRIBUTION
C
 10    READ(5,20) Z,N
 20    FORMAT( F10.0, I10)
C
       WRITE(6,30) Z,N
 30    FORMAT(1X, 'Z=', F10.2,    ' N=', I2)
C
       Y=EXP(-(Z**2)/2.0) / SQRT(2.0*3.14159)
       WRITE(6,40) Y
 40    FORMAT(1X, 'Y=', F10.5)
C                     TEST FOR LAST CARD
       IF( N .EQ. 1) STOP
           GO TO 10
C
       END
```

Figure 4.1a. Program produces a table for the normal distribution. The IF statement is used to instruct the computer to leave the loop. The condition, N .EQ. 1, means $N = 1$. When the condition is true, the statement to the right of the right parentheses—here STOP—is executed. If the condition is false, the next statement—here GO TO 10—is executed, and the loop is executed again.

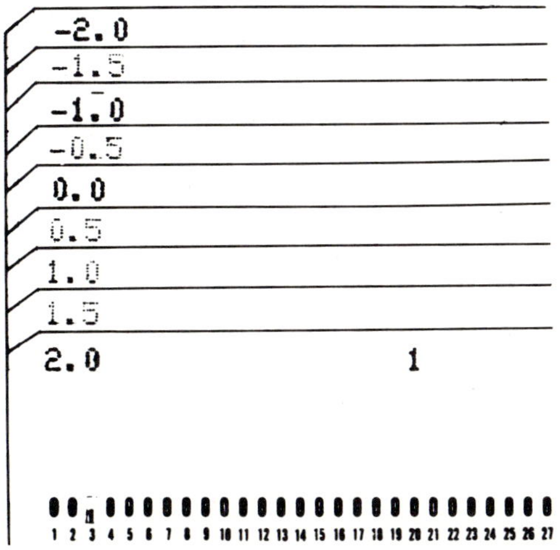

Figure 4.1b. Data cards for the program of Fig. 4.1a. On all but the last card, only one number is punched. Thus when 10 READ(5,20) Z,N is executed, since the second field is blank, a zero is assigned to N. In order to make it easier for us, we have punched the values of Z left-justified. The value of N, however, has to be punched right-justified since it is an INTEGER.

Each of the data cards but the last is processed in the following way: First, the card is read. Then after the results for each of these cards are printed, the IF statement is executed. Since the condition N. EQ. 1 is false, the statement that follows it—GO TO 10—is executed and the next card is read. This same process continues until the last card has been read. Then the computer assigns 1 to N. When the computer now executes the IF statement, the condition N .EQ. 1 is now true. Thus the program executes STOP, and the program terminates. All of this is summarized in the table for Fig. 4.1a, which shows what happens in the program each time the IF statement is executed. The results of the program are shown in Fig. 4.1c.

When you write a program, your primary aim should be to make the program as easy as possible to understand and use. This will make debugging easier for you, make future revisions easier for you or someone else, and finally, make it easier to use the program.

With this in mind, we have: (1) overparenthesized; i.e., we parenthesized Z**2 in EXP(−(Z**2)/2.0) to make it absolutely clear that Z, not −Z, is being squared; (2) both preceded and followed the division sign outside the parentheses by one blank space (i.e., . . . 2.0) / SQRT. . .) to clarify what is dividing what; (3) both preceded and followed the .EQ. in the IF statement with blanks so that it is clear what the two expressions are—thus we can plainly see that we are using 1 and not .1 after the relational operator; (4) used the same field widths for the two variables in the READ statement—F10.0 and I10; (5) used comment cards only where necessary. Too many comment cards may obscure the actual programming statements. Comment cards that state the obvious, e.g., C THE FOLLOWING READS Z AND N, do more harm than good. We have also (6) indented three spaces any statement that is executed if the condition in the IF is false. Thus we have indented the GO TO in

```
IF( N .EQ. 1 ) STOP
   GO TO 10
```

This enables anyone reading the program to determine easily which statements are executed if the condition in the IF is false.

The IF statement represents a point in the program where the computer decides which statement it will execute next. A point like this in the program is called *branch point*, and it is represented in a flow chart by a diamond. Inside the diamond, we write the condition that determines the next statement executed. For the logical IF, two arrows leave the diamond—one labeled YES and the other NO. The YES arrow is followed if the condition in the diamond is true. The NO arrow is followed if the condition is false. In Fig. 4.1d, we present a flow chart for this program.

Data card executed	Z	Y	N	N .EQ. 1	Next statement executed
1st	−2.0	0.05400	0	False	GO TO 10
2nd	−1.5	0.12952	0	False	GO TO 10
3rd	−1.0	0.24197	0	False	GO TO 10
.	.	.	.	.	.
.	.	.	.	.	. .
.	.	.	.	.	.
8th	1.5	0.12952	0	False	GO TO 10
9th	2.0	0.05400	1	True	STOP

Table for Fig. 4.1a. Status of the variables in the program when the IF statement is executed. For each data card but the last, N equals 0. Thus the condition N .EQ. 1 is false, so the statement after the IF is executed. For the last data card N equals 1. Therefore N .EQ. 1 is true, and the STOP is executed.

```
Z=       -2.00  N=  0
Y=    0.05399
Z=       -1.50  N=  0
Y=    0.12952
Z=       -1.00  N=  0
Y=    0.24197
Z=       -0.50  N=  0
Y=    0.35207
Z=        0.00  N=  0
Y=    0.39894
Z=        0.50  N=  0
Y=    0.35207
Z=        1.00  N=  0
Y=    0.24197
Z=        1.50  N=  0
Y=    0.12952
Z=        2.00  N=  1
Y=    0.05399
```

Figure 4.1c. The results of running the program in Fig. 4.1a.

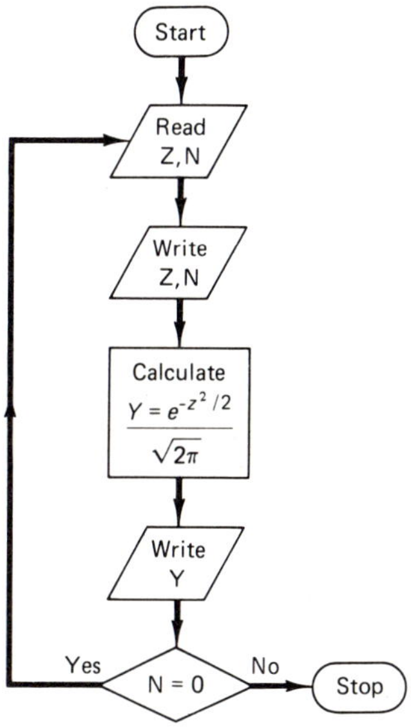

Figure 4.1d. Flow chart for Fig. 4.1a.

If we make the error of writing the program so that the IF statement immediately follows the first WRITE statement and preceding the calculation of Y, as depicted in the flow chart shown in Fig. 4.1e, and the program shown in Fig. 4.1f,

```
          WRITE(6,30) Z, N
   30     FORMAT(1X, 'Z=', F10.2, ' N=', I2)
  C          ...TEST FOR LAST CARD
          IF( N .EQ. 1 ) STOP
             Y=EXP(-(Z**2)/2.0) / SQRT(2.0*3.14159)
             WRITE(6,40) Y
```

then the program does not calculate Y for the value of Z on the last card. Thus we do not obtain all the information we want, as is shown in Fig. 4.1g when the program is run. Note: Because of the incorrect placement of the IF statement, the value of Y for Z equals 2.0 is neither calculated nor printed. For this reason, it is always a good policy to draw a flow chart—no matter how primitive—(or write some other short description of the program) and briefly analyze it before you proceed to write the corresponding program.

IMPROPER PLACEMENT OF IF

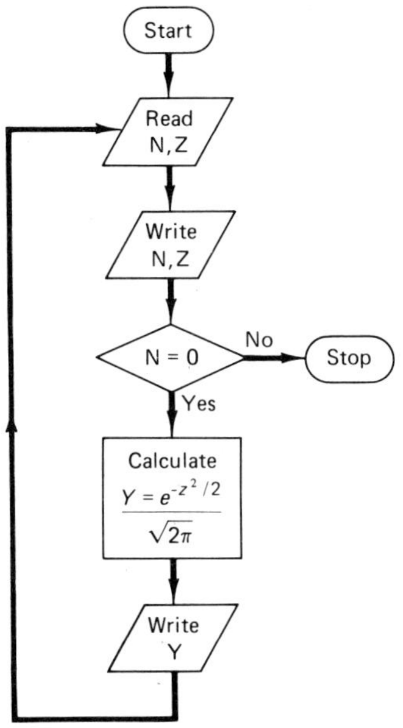

$$Y = \frac{e^{-Z^2/2}}{\sqrt{2\pi}}$$

Figure 4.1e. If we had mistakenly placed the IF statement after the first WRITE statement, as shown here, we would not have calculated or printed the value of Y for the value of Z on the last card.

```
C   PROGRAM DEMONSTRATES IMPROPER PLACEMENT OF IF
C
 10     READ(5,20) Z,N
 20     FORMAT( F10.0, I10)
        WRITE(6,30) Z, N
 30     FORMAT(1X, 'Z=', F10.2, ' N=', I2)
C           ...TEST FOR LAST CARD
        IF( N .EQ. 1 ) STOP
           Y=EXP(-(Z**2)/2.0) / SQRT(2.0*3.14159)
           WRITE(6,40) Y
 40        FORMAT(1X, 'Y=', F10.5)
           GO TO 10
        END
```

Figure 4.1f. Program corresponding to the flow chart in Fig. 4.1e. Because of the position of the IF statement, the value of Y for the value of Z on the last card is not calculated.

```
Z=      -2.00 N= 0
Y=    0.05399
Z=      -1.50 N= 0
Y=    0.12952
Z=      -1.00 N= 0
Y=    0.24197
Z=      -0.50 N= 0
Y=    0.35207
Z=       0.00 N= 0
Y=    0.39894
Z=       0.50 N= 0
Y=    0.35207
Z=       1.00 N= 0
Y=    0.24197
Z=       1.50 N= 0
Y=    0.12952
Z=       2.00 N= 1
```

Figure 4.1g. Running the program of Fig. 4.1f.

In the next program, shown in Fig. 4.2a, we have altered the preceding program so that it now counts the number of cards processed; the data cards are shown in Fig. 4.2b. The data cards are the same as those shown in Fig. 4.1a. Thus the last card has a 1 punched in the second field. This value will be assigned to N when the last data card is read.

```
2.0                              1
```

In order to count the number of data cards, we have written the IF statement as

```
IF( N .EQ. 0 ) GO TO 10
```

Thus for all but the last data card processed, the condition in the IF is true. Therefore, the GO TO 10 part of the IF is executed, and another card is read. For the last card processed, the condition is false. Thus the next statement executed is the one that immediately follows the IF in the program, i.e., the WRITE statement, and the computer prints how many cards have been processed.

The statement that enables the program to count the number of cards is

```
COUNT=COUNT + 1
```

where COUNT has been declared INTEGER. This statement would not make sense algebraically. In FORTRAN it is interpreted as follows: The value of COUNT on the right-hand side of the equals sign represents the last value of COUNT. We see from the program that the first time this statement is executed, COUNT has previously been assigned the value of zero. Thus the value assigned to COUNT (since it also appears on the left-hand side) is 0 + 1, or simply 1. Since this is done after the first card has been read, the value of COUNT indicates that one card has been read. When the second card is read, COUNT=COUNT+1 is executed again. The value of COUNT on the right-hand side of the equals sign now is 1; thus the value assigned to COUNT (since it also appears on the left-hand side) is 1 + 1 or 2. Each time a card is read, the value of COUNT is increased by

USING A COUNTER

```
C   PROGRAM PRODUCES A LABELED TABLE FOR
C   THE NORMAL DISTRIBUTION AND COUNTS THE NUMBER OF DATA CARDS
        INTEGER COUNT
        COUNT=0
C
 10     READ(5,20) Z,N
 20     FORMAT( F10.0, I10)
        WRITE(6,30) Z,N
 30     FORMAT(1X, 'Z=', F10.2, ' N=', I2)
C
        COUNT=COUNT + 1
        Y=EXP(-(Z**2)/2.0) / SQRT(2.0*3.14159)
        WRITE(6,40) Y
 40     FORMAT(1X, 'Y=', F10.5)
C           ...TEST FOR LAST CARD
        IF( N .EQ. 0 ) GO TO 10
           WRITE(6,50) COUNT
 50        FORMAT(1X, 'THE NUMBER OF CARDS IS', I4)
           STOP
        END
```

Figure 4.2a. Same as the preceding program, but this one counts the number of data cards processed. In COUNT=COUNT + 1, the number that was assigned to COUNT is increased by 1, and the result is again assigned to COUNT. Thus each time this statement is executed, COUNT indicates how many cards have been read.

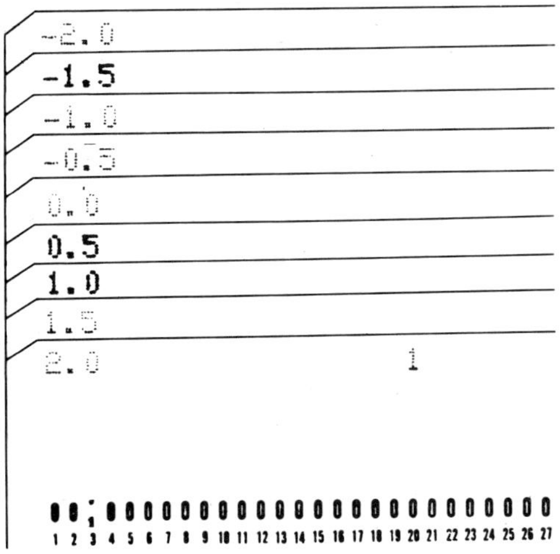

Figure 4.2b. The data cards for Fig. 4.2a. The last data card has a 1 punched in the second field.

1 as is shown in the table for Fig. 4.2a. This process is continued until the program terminates; thus the program counts how many data cards it has processed. When a variable like COUNT has its value increased in this way, it is called a *counter*. The results of the program are shown in Fig. 4.2c.

If we had used the condition N .EQ. 1 in the IF statement, the program would have been harder to follow. Because then the statements at the end of the program would have included two GO TOs

```
      IF( N .EQ. 1 ) GO TO 50
      GO TO 10
50    WRITE(6,60) COUNT
```

instead of one. The lesson we should learn from this is that, if we are not careful in choosing the proper condition, we will need extra GO TO statements that needlessly complicate the program.

The counting could have been done with a REAL variable, e.g.,

```
SUM = SUM + 1.0
```

but since INTEGER arithmetic is always more exact and faster than REAL arithmetic, we will always count using INTEGER arithmetic.

The flow chart for this program is shown in Fig. 4.2d. If we mistakenly start the loop

Data card executed	Z	COUNT	N	N .EQ. 0	Next statement executed
1st	−2.0	1	0	True	GO TO 10
2nd	−1.5	2	0	True	GO TO 10
3rd	−1.0	3	0	True	GO TO 10
.	.	.	.	.	.
.	.	.	.	.	.
.	.	.	.	.	.
8th	1.5	8	0	True	GO TO 10
9th	2.0	9	1	False	WRITE(6,50) COUNT

Table for Fig. 4.2a. The values of some of the variables in the program each time the IF statement is executed. We see that COUNT indicates how many cards have been read. For all but the last data card, N .EQ. 0 is true; so the statement after the right parenthesis—GO TO 10—is executed. For the last data card N .EQ. 0 is false, so WRITE(6,50)COUNT is executed.

COUNTER CORRECTLY INITIALIZED

```
Z=      -2.00  N= 0
Y=    0.05399
Z=      -1.50  N= 0
Y=    0.12952
Z=      -1.00  N= 0
Y=    0.24197
Z=      -0.50  N= 0
Y=    0.35207
Z=       0.00  N= 0
Y=    0.39894
Z=       0.50  N= 0
Y=    0.35207
Z=       1.00  N= 0
Y=    0.24197
Z=       1.50  N= 0
Y=    0.12952
Z=       2.00  N= 1
Y=    0.05399
THE NUMBER OF CARDS IS    9
```

Figure 4.2c. Running the program of Fig. 4.2a.

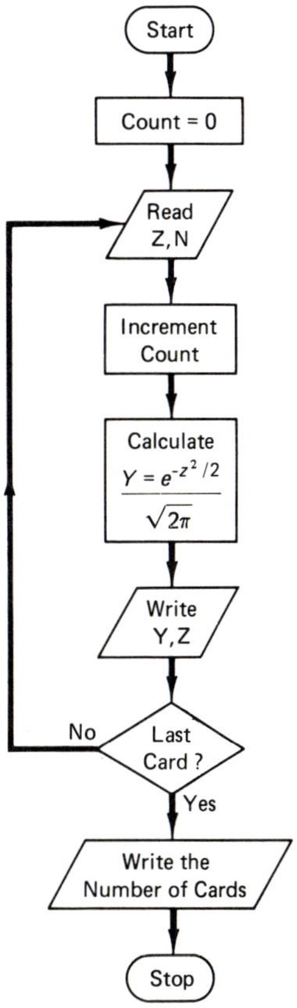

Figure 4.2d. The flow chart for the program of Fig. 4.2a.

with COUNT = 0 as indicated in the flow chart of Fig. 4.2e and the program of Fig. 4.2f,

```
 10     COUNT = 0
C
        READ(5,20) Z,N
 20     FORMAT(1X, 'Z=', F10.2, ' N=', I2)
C
        COUNT=COUNT + 1
```

an unfortunate thing occurs. The counter COUNT is assigned the value of zero each time a new card is read. Therefore the card count is 1 at the end of each loop, and at the end of the program the computer prints the incorrect result

```
THE NUMBER OF CARDS IS    1
```

COUNTER INCORRECTLY INITIALIZED

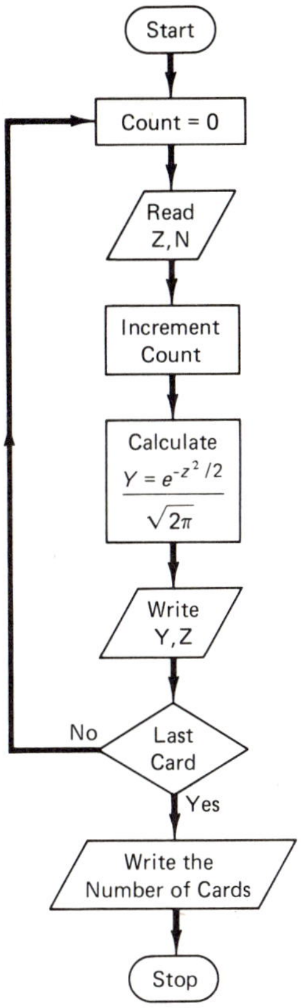

Figure 4.2e. If we mistakenly write the program so that the counter is set to zero in the loop, as shown in this flow chart and the program of Fig. 4.2f, then COUNT is set to zero each time the loop is executed. Thus the value of COUNT at the end of the program is only 1 (see Fig. 4.2g).

```
C     PROGRAM PRODUCES A LABELED TABLE FOR
C     THE NORMAL DISTRIBUTION AND COUNTS THE NUMBER OF DATA CARDS
C
C     COUNT IS INITIALIZED IN THE WRONG PLACE
      INTEGER COUNT
C
   10 COUNT = 0
C
      READ(5,20) Z,N
   20 FORMAT( F10.0, I10)
      WRITE(6,30) Z,N
   30 FORMAT(1X, 'Z=', F10.2, ' N=', I2)
C
      COUNT=COUNT + 1
      Y=EXP(-(Z**2)/2.0) / SQRT(2.0*3.14159)
      WRITE(6,40) Y
   40 FORMAT(1X, 'Y=', F10.5)
C         ...TEST FOR LAST CARD
      IF( N .EQ. 0 ) GO TO 10
         WRITE(6,50) COUNT
   50    FORMAT(1X, 'THE NUMBER OF CARDS IS', I4)
         STOP
      END
```

Figure 4.2f. The counter COUNT is set to zero in the beginning of the loop. Thus the value of COUNT is 1 each time the loop is executed.

as shown in Fig. 4.2g.

When you assign to a variable the first of many values it will assume during the execution of a program, you have initialized the variable; thus in COUNT=0 we have initialized COUNT. What has been illustrated in the preceding paragraph is that when you initialize a counter, you should do it outside the loop in which the counter is incremented.

What would happen if we had forgotten to initialize the counter, i.e., omitted COUNT=0 from Fig. 4.2a? Then COUNT would be undefined. If the computer on which we ran the program automatically assigns zero to all undefined variables, the card count printed at the end of the program would still be correct. On the other hand, on most computers, arbitrary values are assigned to undefined variables; thus the card count at the end of the program would not be correct. On the WATFOR/WATFIV system, the compiler would indicate that COUNT was undefined, in an error message during execution, and then the program would terminate.

If you wanted to run the last two programs as format-free WATFOR/WATFIV programs, not only would you have to replace the READ and WRITE statements with the format-free equivalent statements, but you would also have to punch a zero on each but the last data card.* Remember that WATFOR/WATFIV system would not consider the blanks on these cards as zero, but just as a separation between constants. If you used the unaltered data cards used for the last two programs, the READ, Z, N would read two data cards, assign the constant on the first card to Z and try to assign the constant on the second card to the INTEGER variable N. Since this constant has a decimal point in it, an error condition would result.

* You must leave at least one blank to the right of the value of Z.

```
Z=      -2.00 N= 0
Y=    0.05399
Z=      -1.50 N= 0
Y=    0.12952
Z=      -1.00 N= 0
Y=    0.24197
Z=      -0.50 N= 0
Y=    0.35207
Z=       0.00 N= 0
Y=    0.39894
Z=       0.50 N= 0
Y=    0.35207
Z=       1.00 N= 0
Y=    0.24197
Z=       1.50 N= 0
Y=    0.12952
Z=       2.00 N= 1
Y=    0.05399
THE NUMBER OF CARDS IS    1
```

Figure 4.2g. Running the program of Fig. 4.2f. Because COUNT was set to zero in the loop, the card count at the end of the program is incorrect.

4.3. Relational Operators: EQ, NE, GT, LT, GE, and LE

We now discuss the relational operators and their use in logical expressions by giving several examples. This is shown in Table 4.4. In order to make these examples easier to follow, we have assigned the following numerical values to the variables used in the logical expressions: A=1.0, B=2.2, C=3.0, I=1, J=2, and K=4. If the logical expression is true, then the statement to the right of the logical expression is executed. This statement can be any executable statement except another logical IF or a DO.* If the statement to the right is not a GO TO or a STOP, then, after that statement has been executed, the statement following the logical IF, is executed next

Example 1:

```
IF(A .EQ. B) WRITE(6,100) COUNT
   GO TO 10
```

Since 1.0 does not equal 2.2, the logical expression is false; therefore the GO TO is executed next, and the WRITE is not executed.

Example 2:

```
IF (I+J .NE. K) WRITE(6,100) COUNT
   GO TO 10
```

Since 3 does not equal 4, the logical expression is true; therefore the WRITE statement is executed, then the GO TO is executed.

Example 3:

```
IF (B*C .GT. A) GO TO 40
   WRITE(6,100) A,B,C
```

Since 6.6 is greater than 1.0, the logical expression is true; therefore GO TO 40 is executed. Since control has been transferred to statement 40, the WRITE is not executed.

Example 4:

```
IF (K .LT. I) GO TO 40
   WRITE(6,100) A,B,C
```

Since 4 is greater than 1, the logical expression is false; therefore the WRITE statement is executed.

* See Chapter 5.

THE DIFFERENT RELATIONAL OPERATORS

Evaluating conditions for $A=1.0$, $B=2.2$, $C=3.0$, $I=1$, $J=2$, and $K=4$

Example	Relational operators	Meaning	Example of use in a condition	Appearance of the condition when the IF statement which contains it is executed	Value of the condition
1	.EQ.	Equals	A .EQ. B	1.0 .EQ. 2.2	False
2	.NE.	Not equal	I+J .NE. K	3 .NE. 4	True
3	.GT.	Greater than	B*C .GT. A	6.6 .GT. 1.0	True
4	.LT.	Less than	K .LT. I	4 .LT. 1	False
5	.GE.	Greater than or equal to	C .GE. 3.0	3.0 .GE. 3.0	True
6	.LE.	Less than or equal to	K .LE. I+J	4 .LE. 3	False

Table 4.4. The use of the relational operators in different conditions. Also given are the values of the condition. If the condition is true, then the statement to the right of the right parenthesis in the IF is executed. If the statement to the right is not a STOP or a GO TO, then after it is executed, the statement after the IF is executed next. If the condition is false, then the computer immediately executes the statement after the IF. Some compilers require the expressions on either side of the relational operator to be of the same mode.

Example 5:

```
IF (C .GE. 3.0) STOP
    Y=A+B*X+C*(X**2)
```

Since 3.0 is equal to 3.0, the "greater than" part of the "greater than or equal to" is satisfied; therefore the logical expression is true and the STOP is executed. Since the program terminates here, the next statement (the polynomial) is not executed.

Example 6:

```
IF (K .LE. I*J) STOP
    Y=A+B*X+C*(X**2)
```

Since 4 is greater than 2, the logical expression is false; therefore, the polynomial is calculated next.

Suppose in example 2

```
IF (I+J .NE. K) WRITE(6,100) COUNT
    GO TO 10
```

that after WRITE(6,100) COUNT was executed, you wanted the program to stop. In a situation like this, i.e., where you want to execute two statements (here a WRITE and a STOP) if the condition in an IF statement is true, you would have to use two IF statements:

```
IF (I+J .NE. K) WRITE(6,100) COUNT
IF (I+J .NE. K) STOP
    GO TO 10
```

If the condition I+J .NE. K is true, the WRITE is executed. Then the next IF is executed and since the value of the conditions has not changed, the STOP is executed.

4.4. Other Applications of IF Statement

The program shown in Fig. 4.3a sums the constants punched on data cards which are shown in Fig. 4.3b. The statement 10 READ(5,20) NUMB, TRAIL reads the constants punched on the data cards. NUMB has been declared to be REAL. All but the last data card has nothing punched in the second field; so the value of TRAIL for these cards is zero. The last card has 1.0 punched in the second field, besides having 9.6 punched in the first field as shown in Fig. 4.3b

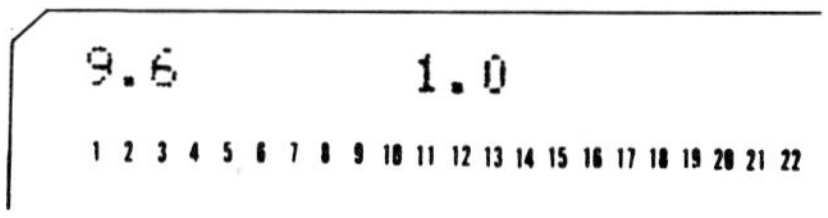

SUMMING NUMBER FROM DATA CARDS

```
C   PROGRAM SUMS THE NUMBERS FROM DATA CARDS
       REAL NUMB
       SUM=0.0
C          ...READ AND ADD THE NUMBERS
 10    READ(5,20) NUMB, TRAIL
 20    FORMAT(2F10.0)
       WRITE(6,30) NUMB
 30    FORMAT(1X, F10.2)
C
       SUM=SUM + NUMB
C          ...TEST FOR TRAILER
       IF( TRAIL .NE. 1.0 ) GO TO 10
C
          WRITE(6,40) SUM
 40       FORMAT(1X, 'THE SUM IS', F20.2)
          STOP
       END
```

Figure 4.3a. Program sums the constants read from the cards. In SUM=SUM + NUMB, the value of NUMB just read is added to the previous value of SUM, and the result is assigned to SUM.

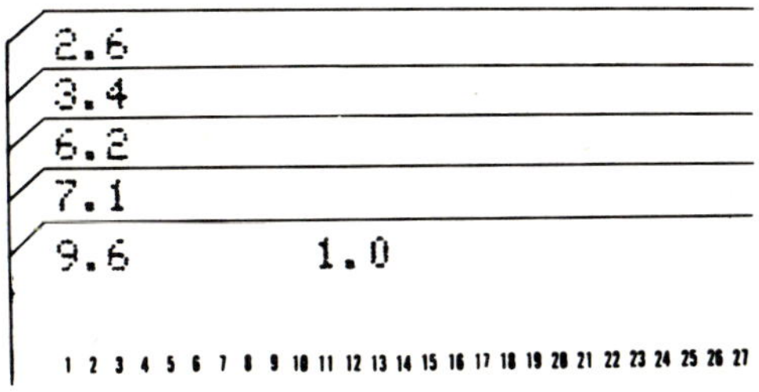

Figure 4.3b. Data cards for Fig. 4.3a. The last data card has a 1.0 punched in the second field. This signals the computer to print the results.

The first time SUM= SUM + NUMB is executed, the value of SUM on the right of the equals sign is 0.0. Thus, since the value of NUMB is 2.6, the computer assigns 2.6 to SUM because SUM is also on the left of the equals sign. This is shown in the first four columns of the first line of the table for Fig. 4.3a.

Time executed	SUM on the left of =	SUM on right of =	NUMB
1st	2.6	0.0	2.6

Since the value of TRAIL read from the first card is zero, the condition TRAIL .NE. 1.0 in

```
IF( TRAIL .NE. 1.0 ) GO TO 10
```

is true; consequently, the GO TO 10 part of the IF is executed, as is shown to the right in the first line of the table for Fig. 4.3a. Thus 10 READ(5,20) NUMB, TRAIL is executed again, and another value of NUMB and TRAIL are read. Now when SUM=SUM+ NUMB is executed, the value of SUM on the right of the equals sign is 2.6. Since the value of NUMB just read is 3.4, the value of SUM on the left is now 6.0 as is shown in the second column in the second line of the table for Fig. 4.3a. This process continues up to and including the last card. The value of NUMB for this card is added to the previous value of SUM. Since the value of TRAIL for this card is 1.0, the condition TRAIL.NE. 1.0 is now false, so the statement following the IF is executed: WRITE(6,40) SUM (as is shown in the last line of the table) and the value of SUM is printed as shown in Fig. 4.3c.

If the program were written so that the statement that does the summing and the IF statement are interchanged, i.e., their new order being

```
IF( TRAIL .NE. 1.0 ) GO TO 10
SUM=SUM + NUMB
```

then, the contribution from the last card to SUM would not be included, and thus the results would be incorrect.

IF

The form of the IF statement is: IF followed by (, followed by a condition, followed by), followed by an executable statement which is not another logical IF or a DO. Examples:

```
IF(A+B .GT. 4.0)STOP
IF(A+B .GT. C+D) GO TO 10
IF(A*B .LT. C+D) WRITE(6,10) A, B, C, D
```

Time executed	SUM on left of =	SUM on right of =	NUMB	Trail	Next statement after IF
1st	2.6	0.0	2.6	0.0	10
2nd	6.0	2.6	3.4	0.0	10
3rd	12.2	6.0	6.2	0.0	10
4th	19.3	12.2	7.1	0.0	10
5th	28.9	19.3	9.6	1.0	WRITE(6, 40) SUM

Table for Fig. 4.3a. The table shows how SUM is increased by NUMB each time SUM=SUM + NUMB is executed. The value of "SUM on right of =" for one line equals the value of "SUM on left of =" for the preceding line. The table also shows how the value of TRAIL affects which statement is executed after the IF.

```
        2.60
        3.40
        6.20
        7.10
        9.60
THE SUM IS                  28.90
```

Figure 4.3c. Running the program of Fig. 4.3a.

In Fig. 4.4a we present a program that generates and adds the integers from 1 to NMAX, where the value of NMAX is read from the data card shown in Fig. 4.4b. Thus the value of NMAX is 5. The integers are generated by

```
20     NUM=NUM + 1
```

and their sum is calculated by

```
SUM=SUM + NUM
```

where SUM has been declared to be INTEGER. The results of NUM=NUM + 1, and how this affects SUM=SUM + NUM the first time both of these statements are executed, are given in the first line of the table for Fig. 4.4a

Time executed	SUM on the left of =	SUM on the right of =	NUM
1st	1	0	1

Since the value of NMAX is 5, the computer interprets the condition NUM .NE. NMAX in the IF statement as 1 .NE. 5. This is true, therefore the GO TO 20 part of

```
IF( NUM .NE. NMAX ) GO TO 20
```

is executed, and the computer executes 20 NUM=NUM + 1 again and assigns 2 to NUM. This value of NUM is added to SUM when

```
SUM=SUM + NUM
```

is executed. Thus the value of SUM becomes 2 + 1, or 3, as shown in the second line of the table for Fig. 4.4a. This process continues up to and including the time when the value of N is 5. However, now when the computer executes the IF statement, since the value of NMAX is 5, the condition NUM .NE. NMAX is false. The computer thus executes the statement that immediately follows the IF statement: WRITE(6,30) NMAX, SUM. The program thus prints the results as is shown in Fig. 4.4c. If we wanted the value of SUM printed each time SUM=SUM + NUM is executed, we would place the WRITE statement before the IF statement.

SUMMING THE NUMBERS FROM 1 TO N

```
C   PROGRAM SUMS THE NUMBERS FROM 1 TO NMAX
       INTEGER SUM
       SUM=0
       NUM=0
C
       READ(5,10) NMAX
 10    FORMAT(I10)
C          ...COUNTS AND SUMS
 20    NUM=NUM + 1
       SUM=SUM + NUM
C          ...TEST FOR LAST NUMBER
       IF( NUM .NE. NMAX ) GO TO 20
          WRITE(6,30) NMAX, SUM
 30       FORMAT(1X, 'THE SUM OF THE NUMBERS FROM 1 TO', I4, ' IS',
      1     I10)
          STOP
       END
```

Figure 4.4a. Sums the integers from 1 to NMAX. SUM sums the numbers that the counter NUM produces.

Time executed	SUM on left of=	SUM on right of=	NUM
1st	1	0	1
2nd	3	1	2
3rd	6	3	3
4th	10	6	4
5th	15	10	5

Table for Fig. 4.4a. The values of the variables in SUM=SUM + NUM each time this statement is executed. Each new value of NUM is added to the previous value of SUM (SUM on right of =) producing the current value of SUM (SUM on left of =).

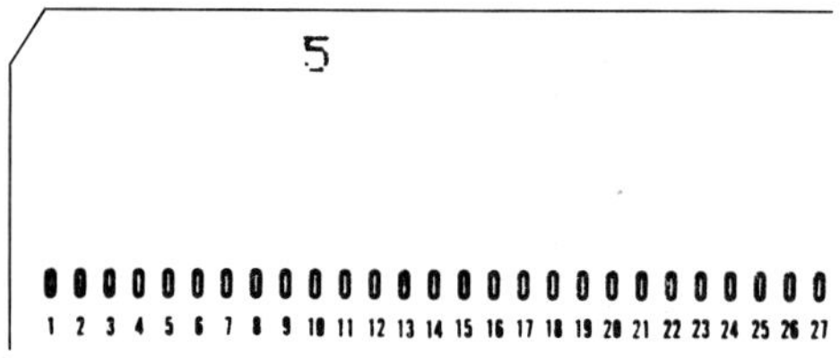

Figure 4.4b. The data read by the program. The value of NMAX will equal 5. Thus the computer interprets the IF as IF(NUM .NE. 5) GO TO 20.

```
THE SUM OF THE NUMBERS FROM 1 TO    5 IS         15
```

Figure 4.4c. The results of running Fig. 4.4a.

In Fig. 4.5a we present a program that sums the numbers 0.2, 0.4, 0.6, 0.8, and 1.0. The numbers are generated in

```
Z=Z + 0.2
```

The summation is performed in

```
10    SUM=SUM + Z
```

How these statements work is shown in the table for Fig. 4.5a. The first time 10 SUM=SUM + Z is executed, the value of SUM remains zero. The first time Z=Z + 0.2 is executed, the value of Z becomes 0.2. Since the condition in

```
IF( Z .GT. 1.0) GO TO 30
```

is false, the statement 10 SUM=SUM+Z is executed again. The value of SUM becomes 0.2. The value of the increment 0.2 cannot be expressed accurately in binary. It is stored in the computer as 0.1999999. Thus a round-off error occurs every time Z=Z + 0.2 is executed. We see this when the values of Z are printed as is shown in Fig. 4.5b. Thus, the value of Z is never actually 1.0; the closest the actual value of Z comes to 1.0 is 0.9999999.

We have written the IF statement as

```
IF( Z .GT. 1.0) GO TO 30
```

Thus, when the value of Z is 0.9999999, the condition Z .GT. 1.0 is still false, so this value of Z is added to SUM. Had we written the IF statement as

```
IF( Z .EQ. 1.0) GO TO 30
```

the program would never stop, because the value of Z is never actually 1.0. For that reason one never tests for the equality or inequality of two REALs in an IF statement. However, one can test for the equality or inequality of two INTEGERs, as we have shown in the preceding program.

You may have wondered why we did not increment Z before we incremented SUM, i.e., write the two major statements in the program in the following order:

```
10    Z=Z + 0.2
      SUM=SUM + Z
```

The reason can be seen when we analyze what happens when the value of Z is 0.9999999 (i.e., 1.0) in these altered statements. This value of Z is added to SUM as it should be; however, when IF(Z .GT. 1.0) GO TO 30 is executed the condition Z .GT. 1.0 is false, so 10 Z=Z+0.2 is eventually executed again. We would therefore add 1.2 to SUM and obtain the incorrect value of SUM.

What we learn from the preceding paragraph is that, in general, one should place the statement—here, Z=Z+0.2—that alters the condition in the IF statement, immediately before the IF statement.

SUMMING THE NUMBERS FROM 0 TO 1 IN INCREMENTS OF 0.2

```
C   PROGRAM SUMS THE REAL NUMBERS FROM 0.0 TO 1.0
C   IN INCREMENTS OF 0.2
C
        SUM=0.0
        Z=0.0
 10     SUM=SUM + Z
        Z=Z + 0.2
        IF( Z .GT. 1.0) GO TO 30
           WRITE(6, 20) Z
 20        FORMAT(1X, 'Z=', F20.8)
           GO TO 10
 30     WRITE(6,40) SUM
 40     FORMAT(1X, 'SUM IS', F20.10)
        STOP
        END
```

Figure 4.5a. The program sums 0.0, 0.2, 0.4, 0.6, 0.8, and 1.0. After each time Z=Z + 0.2 is executed, the new value of Z is added to SUM when 10 SUM+SUM + Z is executed. Because of round-off error, the value of Z produced by Z=Z + 0.2 is never actually 1.0. Thus we do not use the EQ or NE in the IF.

Time executed	SUM on left of =	SUM on right of =	Z
1st	0.0	0.0	0.0
2nd	0.2	0.0	0.2
3rd	0.6	0.2	0.4
4th	1.2	0.6	0.6
5th	2.0	1.2	0.8
6th	3.0	2.0	1.0

Table for Fig. 4.5a. The values of the variables in SUM+SUM + Z each time the statement is executed. The last time this statement is executed, the value of Z added to SUM is 1.0. Then the value of Z is increased to 1.2. Thus the condition in the IF is true and the results of the program are printed.

```
 Z=               0.19999990
 Z=               0.39999990
 Z=               0.59999990
 Z=               0.79999990
 Z=               0.99999990
 SUM IS               2.9999980000
```

Figure 4.5b. The results of running the program. We see that because of round-off error, the value of Z never equals 0.2, 0.4, 0.6, 0.8, or 1.0, but is very close to these values.

We now rewrite the program of Fig. 4.2a, which calculated the points on the normal curve. The present program, shown in Fig. 4.6a, is the same as the program of Fig. 4.2a—it calculates *Y* (the ordinate) for values of *Z*—except that the values of *Z* instead of being read from cards, as they were in Fig. 4.2a, are now generated in the program itself. The program does, however, read the following from cards: The minimum value of Z (we call it ZMIN), the maximum value of Z (we call it ZMAX), and the amount by which Z is increased (we call it DZ). We have chosen ZMIN to be −2.0, ZMAX to be 2.0, and DZ to be 0.2, and have typed these values in the appropriate fields on the data card shown in Fig. 4.6b. After the data card has been read, the statements Z=ZMIN, Z=Z+DZ, and IF(Z .LT. ZMAX) GO TO 30, when they are executed, are interpreted by the computer as being:

```
Z=-2.0
Z=Z + 0.2
IF(Z .LT. 2.0) GO TO 30
```

respectively. The loop in the program begins with the calculation of Y and ends with the IF statement. In the loop the computer first calculates Y and prints Y and Z, then increments Z, and finally decides whether to continue the loop or stop. After Y is calculated for the value of Z equal to 2.0 (actually 1.999999), the value of Z is increased to 2.2. Then the condition Z .LT. ZMAX is false, and the program stops. The results of running the program are shown in Fig. 4.6c.

EVALUATING THE NORMAL CURVE

```
C   PROGRAM PRODUCES A TABLE FOR THF NORMAL DISTRIBUTION.
C   THE LIMITS OF Z( THE INDEPENDENT VARIABLE ) ARE
C   READ FROM CARDS
C
        READ(5,10) ZMIN, ZMAX, DZ
 10     FORMAT(3F10.0)
        WRITE(6,20) ZMIN, ZMAX, DZ
 20     FORMAT(1X, 'ZMIN=', F10.3, ' ZMAX=', F10.3, ' DZ=', F10.3)
C
        Z=ZMIN
 30     Y=EXP(-(Z**2)/2.0) / SQRT(2.0*3.14159)
        WRITE(6,40) Z , Y
 40     FORMAT(1X,'Z=', F10.3, ' Y=', F10.5)
        Z=Z + DZ
        IF( Z .LT. ZMAX) GO TO 30
           STOP
        END
```

Figure 4.6a. Program produces a table for the normal distribution but generates the different values of Z in the program itself. Each time Z=Z + DZ is executed, the value of DZ (the change in Z) is added to the previous value of Z, and the sum becomes the current value of Z. When Z is greater than ZMAX, the program stops.

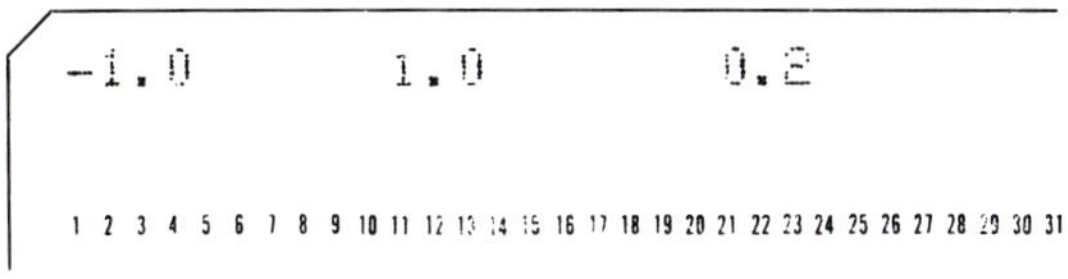

Figure 4.6b. The data card for the program of Figure 4.6a. The first field is the value of ZMIN; the second field, ZMAX; and the third field, DZ.

```
ZMIN=    -1.000 ZMAX=     1.000 DZ=      0.200
Z=     -1.000 Y=    0.24197
Z=     -0.800 Y=    0.28969
Z=     -0.600 Y=    0.33322
Z=     -0.400 Y=    0.36827
Z=     -0.200 Y=    0.39104
Z=     -0.000 Y=    0.39894
Z=      0.200 Y=    0.39104
Z=      0.400 Y=    0.36827
Z=      0.600 Y=    0.33322
Z=      0.800 Y=    0.28969
Z=      1.000 Y=    0.24197
```

Figure 4.6c. The results of the program of Fig. 4.6a. Since DZ = 0.2, it cannot be represented exactly in binary, so it is represented internally as .1999999. Thus we have not tested for equality in the IF but for "less than." Had we tested for equality, the program would continue indefinitely.

We now discuss a program which determines the area under the normal curve. If this topic does not interest you, you may skip to the next section without loss of continuity.

In order to determine the area under the curve shown in Fig. 4.7a, we partition the curve into rectangles. The height of a given rectangle is determined by the Y value of the curve. The curve and a given rectangle meet at the rectangle's upper left corner. Thus the height of a rectangle is given by Y as is shown in Fig. 4.7b. Its width is given by dZ. The area of each rectangle is ZdZ. If we add the area of all the rectangles, we get an approximation to the area under the curve. We get only an approximation because some of the area under the curve is not included in the rectangles to the left of the peak, and the upper right-hand corners of the rectangles to the right of the peak lie outside the curve. If we make dZ smaller, and thus increase the number of rectangles, the approximation becomes better. If we call the height of the first rectangle, Y_1, the height of the second rectangle, Y_2, and the height of the last rectangle, Y_L, then the approximation to the area under the curve is

$$\text{Area} = Y_1dZ + Y_2dZ + . . . + Y_LdZ$$

where each rectangle has a width dZ. If we factor out the dZ we get

$$\text{Area} = dZ(Y_1 + Y_2 + . . . + Y_L)$$

The summation which appears in the parentheses can be expressed in FORTRAN as

```
SUM=SUM + Y
```

CALCULATING THE AREA UNDER THE NORMAL CURVE

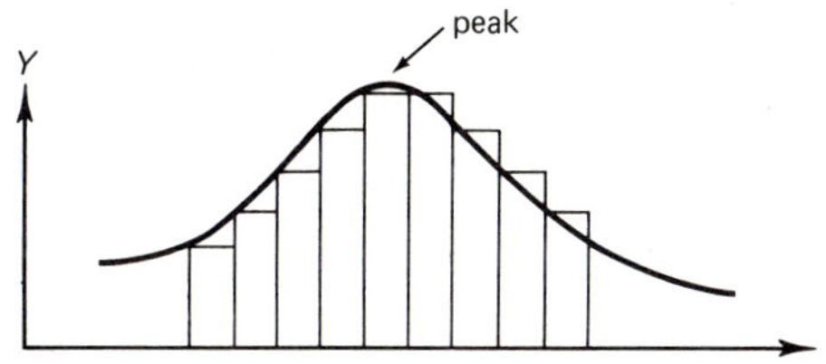

Figure 4.7a. We can approximate the area beneath a curve by forming rectangles beneath the curve.

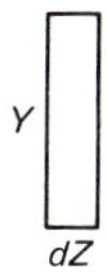

Figure 4.7b. Since the upper left corner of each rectangle touches the curve, the height of each rectangle is Y. The width is dZ. The sum of the area of all the rectangles is $Y_1dZ + Y_2 dZ + Y_tdZ$. Thus the total area is dZ times the sum of all the Ys.

Thus all we have to do is to place this statement into the loop of the program for Fig. 4.6a as is now shown in Fig. 4.7c. The values of ZMIN, ZMAX, and DZ we read into the program are −4.0, 4.0, and .001, respectively, as is shown on the data card (see Fig. 4.7d). Thus the first value of Y is calculated for Z equals −4.0. In the above discussion we called this Y_1. Then the value of Z is increased to −3.999, and we calculate a new value of Y. This we called Y_2. As we continue to increase Z, we calculate a new Y. Each new value of Y is added to the preceding one when SUM=SUM + Y is executed. The last value of Y that we want to use in the summation is the Y for the rightmost rectangle. This is, however, not the Y we would calculate for Z equaling −4.0, but for the value of Z that precedes this, i.e., ZMAX− DZ. Thus we have altered the IF statement that originally appeared in Fig. 4.6a, i.e., IF(Z .LT. ZMAX) GO TO 30 and now write it

```
IF( Z .LT. ZMAX-DZ) GO TO 30
```

The condition in this IF statement is false when Z equals 4.0, thus the statement that follows the IF is executed

```
AREA=DZ*SUM
```

and the area is calculated and then printed as is shown in Fig. 4.7e. The area, 0.9993631, is very close to 1.0. If we found the area by using integral calculus and varied Z from $-\infty$ to ∞, then the area would be exactly 1.0.

```
C PROGRAM CALCULATES THE AREA UNDER THE NORMAL CURVE.
C  THE LIMITS OF 7 (THE INDEPENDENT VARIABLE) ARE READ FROM CARDS
C
      READ(5,10) ZMIN, ZMAX, DZ
10    FORMAT(3F10.0)
      WRITE(6,20) ZMIN, ZMAX, DZ
 20   FORMAT(1X, 'ZMIN=', F10.3, ' ZMAX=', F10.3, ' DZ=', F10.3)
C
      SUM=0.0
      Z=ZMIN
 30   Y=EXP(-(Z**2)/2.0) / SQRT(2.0*3.14159)
      SUM=SUM + Y
      Z=Z + DZ
      IF( Z .LT. ZMAX-DZ) GO TO 30
C        ...CALCULATE THE AREA
         AREA=DZ*SUM
         WRITE(6,40) AREA
 40      FORMAT(1X, 'AREA IS', F20.10)
         STOP
      END
```

Figure 4.7c. Program calculates the area under the normal curve; Y is calculated for each Z. The Z is increased by Z=Z+ DZ. The sum of all the Ys is produced by SUM=SUM + Y. This enables the computer at the end of the program to calculate the area AREA= DZ*SUM.

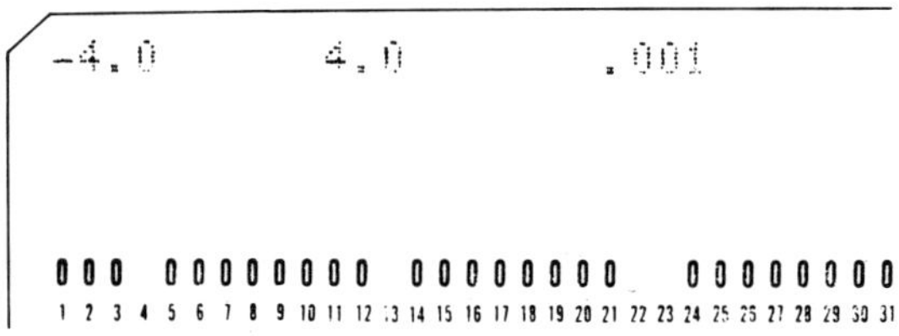

Figure 4.7d. Data card for the program. The value of ZMIN is −4.0, of ZMAX is 4.0, and DZ is .001. By making DZ this small, our approximation of the rectangles should be fairly good.

```
ZMIN=     -4.000 ZMAX=       4.000 DZ=       0.001
AREA IS          0.9993631000
```

Figure 4.7e. Running the program of Fig. 4.7c. The area under the curve should be exactly 1.0; our result is a good approximation.

4.5. Writing REAL Constants in Exponential Form

At times you may want to write a REAL constant having more digits than the computer can accommodate. For instance, on a computer that can accommodate a maximum of 7 digits in a REAL constant, you could not write the number 16 325 000 000.0. At other times, it is inconvenient to write a REAL constant in conventional form. We will now show that by writing REAL constants in what is called exponential form, you can include a number of almost any size in a program.

The number 16,325,000. is equivalent to 16.325 multiplied by one million, or 16.325 $\times$ 1,000,000. Writing the 1,000,000 part of the number is cumbersome. We can express it as 10^6, where the exponent 6 corresponds to the number of zeros in 1,000,000. Thus 16,325,000. equals 16.325×10^6—the number 16.325×10^6 is written in exponential form. Another way of looking at this is that the exponent 6 corresponds to the number of decimal places we have to shift the decimal point in 16,325,000. to the left, in order to obtain 16.325. The 16.325 part of 16.325×10^6, is called the *mantissa*, and the 6 in 10^6 is called the *exponent* or *characteristic*. When you write a number in exponential form in FORTRAN, you first write the mantissa, then the letter E, and finally the exponent. Thus 16.325×10^6 is written in FORTRAN as 16.325E6. If the exponent is positive, you may place a plus sign between the E and the exponent, thus you may also write 16.325×10^6 as 16.325E+6. You may also precede the 6 with a zero, thus writing 16.325×10^6 as 16.325E+06 or 16.325E06.

A number like 0.00000236 can be expressed in a more readable form by moving the decimal point to the right and compensating for this by using the number corresponding to the moves to the right, as the exponent. We precede the exponent with a minus sign. Thus 0.00000236 equals 2.36×10^{-6} or 0.236×10^{-5}. In FORTRAN, when you write a constant that has a negative exponent, you must include the minus between the E and the exponent. Thus 0.236×10^{-5} in FORTRAN is 0.236E−5.

In any constant written in exponential form, the maximum number of digits you can use in the mantissa is the same as the maximum number of digits you can use in a conventional REAL constant. (Remember on the IBM System 360/370 it is 7.)

In Table 4.5 we show how exponential constants can be used in calculations. We note here that the exponent must be an INTEGER. Thus 1.32E−0.52 would cause a compile-time error since 0.52 is not an INTEGER.

USING REAL CONSTANTS IN EXPONENTIAL FORM

```
X = 1.32E-05
X = 13.26E+05 + 0.46E+05
RESULT = 13.26E+05 * 7.36
```

Table 4.5. Using REAL constants in exponential form. The constant 1.32E−05 is the same as 1.32×10^{-5}. The constant 13.26E+05 is the same as 13.26×10^{5}; 13.26 is the mantissa, and the 5 in E+05 is the exponent.

4.6. How REAL and INTEGER Constants Are Stored

All REAL constants are stored in the computer's memory in exponential form regardless of whether or not we write them in exponential form in the program. The digits in the mantissa, the digits noting the power of ten, and the sign of the entire number are all stored in the same memory location, as shown in Fig. 4.8a. These memory locations are known as REAL words. The digits in the mantissa are stored without a decimal point. The decimal point is assumed to be at the left of the mantissa, and the mantissa is stored so that there are no leading zeros.* Thus the mantissa of .0001234567 would be stored as the binary equivalent of .1234567; the exponent is adjusted to compensate for the loss of leading zeros in the mantissa. Thus the exponent, if it were stored in decimal, would be stored as −3, all of which is shown in Fig. 4.8a. However, not only the mantissa but the exponent also is stored in binary. When the entire process is done, the number is said to be in normalized form.

In an INTEGER constant, just the digits in the constant and the sign are stored in the same memory location, as shown in Fig. 4.8b. Here we show how 2647263 is stored. These memory locations are known as INTEGER words. We see from all of this that INTEGER and REAL constants are represented in the memory in different ways. Thus it is no surprise that ANS FORTRAN does not allow mixed-mode calculations. Also, because of the manipulations involved in adjusting the mantissa and exponent, REAL arithmetic requires more time to perform than does INTEGER arithmetic.

* This is not quite the case on the IBM 360/370 which uses a hexadecimal representation.

HOW CONSTANTS ARE STORED

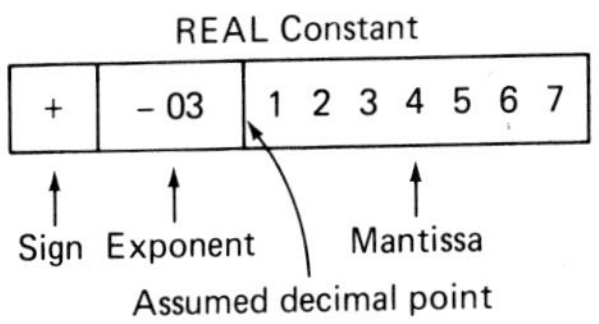

Figure 4.8a. Every REAL constant (whether it is printed in exponential form or not) is stored in the memory in exponential form. It is stored so that there are no leading zeros. Thus .0001234567 is stored as $.1234567X10^{-3}$ (actually, its binary equivalent); the decimal point is assumed to be at the left of the mantissa, as is shown here.

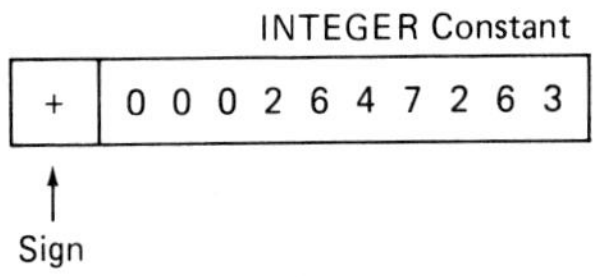

Figure 4.8b. How the INTEGER constant 2647263 is stored in the computer's memory.

4.7. Printing Using E Format

Because of the possibility that our REAL results will not fit into the fields we have specified, there is always a certain amount of uncertainty involved in running for the first time a program written using F format. Assuming that everything else in the program but the FORMATs are correct, we might obtain asterisks instead of the result we expect. For this reason, we see why it is much easier to use the format-free PRINT statement provided by the WATFOR/WATFIV compiler. However, there is a type of format available to all FORTRAN users that will enable the computer to print any REAL constant that the computer hardware can accommodate. It is called E format. When E format is used, a REAL constant which has been stored in the memory, is printed in exponential form.

Since the constant is stored in normalized form, when you use E format the result is printed in normalized form also.

When a constant is printed in E format, on most computers it is printed as follows: The computer first prints a minus sign if the constant is negative. It then prints a zero, followed by a decimal point, followed by the digits in the mantissa, followed by four characters indicating the exponent. These four characters are an E, a plus or minus, and a two-digit exponent.* Since the constant is printed in normalized form, 0.00236 would be printed as 0.236E−02 and not as 0.0236E−01 or as 2.36E−03.

In Fig. 4.9a we write a simple program which prints 1234567.0 in exponential form using three field specifications. The first field specification we use is E16.5; it produces the result 0.12346E+07 as shown in Fig. 4.9b. Here 16 is the field width and the 5 after the decimal point indicates how many digits will appear to the right of the decimal point. The mantissa was rounded to 5 digits.

The second field specification we use is E16.0. As opposed to F16.0, which specifies that no digits will be printed after the decimal point, E16.0 specifies that no digits be printed at all, so we obtain 0.E+07, as shown in Fig. 4.9b. Using an E format that has a zero following the decimal point, as we have just done by using E16.0, is a common mistake made by beginning programmers.

When printing using E format the field width must be large enough to accommodate the four characters in the exponent, the digits to the right of the decimal point, the decimal point itself, the leading zero, and the sign of the constant if it is negative. If the field width is not large enough to accommodate all this, the computer will print asterisks in the field. Thus, if we specify E8.3 to print a positive constant, the exponent (as always) requires four columns, the 0. (as always) requires two columns and there will be three digits after the decimal point. Thus a total of 9 columns will be required. Since the field width is only 8 characters wide, the computer prints asterisks in the field. This is what happens when we use E8.3 in Fig. 4.9a. If you are using a machine that can accommodate a maximum of 7 meaningful digits and you want to see all these digits in the results, then the E format with the minimum field width you can use for both positive and negative constants is E14.7.

* Many compilers print a blank instead of a plus sign.

USING E FORMAT

```
C   PROGRAM DEMONSTRATES E FORMAT
        VAR1=1234567.0
        WRITE(6,10) VAR1, VAR1
 10     FORMAT(1X, E16.5, E16.0)
        WRITE(6,20) VAR1
 20     FORMAT(1X, E8.3)
        STOP
        END
```

Figure 4.9a. If we want a REAL constant to be printed in exponential form, we use E format. The general form is E*w* .*d*. *d* indicating how many digits will be printed to the right of the decimal point.

```
                E 16.5                        E 16.0
      0.12346E+07                  0.E+07
********
          E 9.3
```

Figure 4.9b. Running the program of Fig. 4.9a. The field width must accommodate the four characters in the exponent, a decimal point, the leading zero, a possible minus sign, and the digits in the mantissa. Thus $w \geqslant d+7$.

4.8. Using X Format

By using X format, we can specify how many spaces are to be left between fields that contain printing. In the program of Fig. 4.10a we use the X formats 5X, 7X, in

```
10    FORMAT(1X, E15.7, 5X, ' K=', I4, 7X, F10.3)
```

to separate the other fields. The number that precedes the X specifies how many blank spaces we want to separate the other fields; e.g., 10X creates a field consisting of 10 blanks. If the 5X were not in the FORMAT, the string K= would immediately follow E+03 in the printed results, and we would obtain E+03K=. It is thus advisable to precede strings with X format. The results of running the program are shown in Fig. 4.10b.

If you use an X format in the beginning of the FORMAT immediately following the 1X, e.g., 10 FORMAT(1X, 5X, F10.3), you may write the FORMAT as

```
10    FORMAT(6X, F10.3)
```

i.e., the first column specified by 6X is used for the control character. When the control character is blank, as it is here, the line printer starts printing on the next line.

USING X FORMAT

```
C PROGRAM DEMONSTRATES USE OF X FORMAT
      A=3632.0E+03
      K=1234
      B=136.21
      WRITE(6,10) A, K, B
 10   FORMAT(1X, E15.7, 5X, ' K=', I4, 7X, F10.3)
      STOP
      END
```

Figure 4.10a. Shows use of X format. 5X leaves 5 blanks between the field described by E15.7 and 'K='; 7X leaves 7 blanks between the field described by I4 and the field described by F10.3.

```
0.3632000E+07      K=1234            136.210
```

Figure 4.10b. Results of running the program of Fig. 4.10a.

4.9. The Arithmetic IF Statement

The arithmetic IF is not used in any program in any other section, so you may skip to the next section without any loss of continuity.

The arithmetic IF statement enables the computer to branch to one of three statements depending on whether an arithmetic expression sandwiched between parentheses is negative, zero, or positive. For instance, in

```
IF( DETRM ) 30, 60, 80
```

if the value of the expression—here DETRM—is negative, the computer branches to the first statement number following the parenthesis—here statement 30; if the value of the expression is zero, the computer branches to the second statement number following the parenthesis—here statement 60; and if the value of the expression is positive, the computer branches to the third statement number following the parenthesis—here statement 80.

In Fig. 4.11a we write a program that solves the quadratic equation $AX + BX^2 + C = 0$. We use the variable DETRM to represent the determinant, i.e., $B^2 - 4AC$. If the value of DETRM is negative, then the two solutions are complex, so the computer branches to statement 30. There the computer calculates the real part, REAL; and the imaginary part, IMAG, where IMAG has been declared REAL. Since the value of DETRM is negative, we evaluate SQRT (−DETRM) when we calculate IMAG. The two FORMAT statements used

```
40    FORMAT(1X, 'X=', F10.3, '+', F10.3, 'I')
50    FORMAT(1X, 'X=', F10.3, '-', F10.3, 'I')
```

provide both the sign and the 'I' of the imaginary part.

If the value of DETRM is zero, the computer branches to statement 60, where it evaluates the one solution of the equation.

```
60    X=-B/(2.0*A)
```

If the value of DETRM is positive, the computer branches to statement 80, where it calculates two solutions of the equation.

```
80    X1=(-B + SQRT(DETRM)) / (2.0*A)
      X2=(-B - SQRT(DETRM)) / (2.0*A)
```

USING THE ARITHMETIC IF

```
C  PROGRAM USES THE ARITHMETIC IF
C TO SOLVE A QUADRATIC EQUATION
C          A*X**2 + B*X + C=0.0
      REAL IMAG
      READ(5,10) A, B, C
 10   FORMAT( 3F10.0 )
      WRITE(6,20) A, B, C
 20   FORMAT(1X, 'A=', F10.3, ' B=', F10.3, ' C=', F10.3)
C
      DETRM=B*B - 4.0*A*C
      IF( DETRM ) 30, 60, 80
C         ...NEGATIVE DETERMINANT
 30   REAL=-B/(2.0*A)
      IMAG=SQRT(-DETRM)/(2.0*A)
      WRITE(6,40) REAL, IMAG
 40   FORMAT(1X, 'X=', F10.3, '+', F10.3, 'I')
      WRITE(6,50) REAL, IMAG
 50   FORMAT(1X, 'X=', F10.3, '-', F10.3, 'I')
      STOP
C         ...ZERO DETERMINANT
 60   X=-B/(2.0*A)
      WRITE(6,70) X
 70   FORMAT(1X, 'X=', F10.3)
      STOP
C         ...POSITIVE DETERMINANT
 80   X1=(-B + SQRT(DETRM)) / (2.0*A)
      X2=(-B - SQRT(DETRM)) / (2.0*A)
      WRITE(6,90) X1, X2
 90   FORMAT(1X, 'X1=', F10.3, ' X2=',F10.3)
      STOP
      END
```

Figure 4.11a. Solves the quadratic equation by using the arithmetic IF statement. When IF (DETRM) 30, 60, 80 is executed, if the value DETRM is negative, then statement 30 is executed next. If the value of DETRM is zero, then statement 60 is executed next. If the value of DETRM is positive, then statement 80 is executed next.

In Fig. 4.11b we show the data card used for running the program and in Fig. 4.11c, the results.

The arithmetic IF differs from the logical IF in that the statement which follows the arithmetic IF must have a statement number so that it can be referred to. Thus in

```
IF( DETRM ) 50, 60, 70
STOP
```

the STOP could never be executed since it has no statement number.

ARITHMETIC IF

> The form of the arithmetic IF is: IF followed by (; followed by an arithmetic expression; followed by); followed by three statement numbers. These statement numbers do not all have to be different. Examples:
>
> IF (A*3+3.0) 10, 20, 10
> IF (A) 10, 20, 30
> IF (I+J) 30, 10, 30

Using an arithmetic IF makes it somewhat difficult for someone reading the program to follow it, since the arithmetic IF requires the reader to follow a maximum of three possible paths. Thus the logical IF is preferable. On the other hand, the arithmetic IF is acceptable to both the ANSI Standard FORTRAN and ANSI Standard Basic FORTRAN, whereas the logical IF is acceptable only to the ANSI Standard FORTRAN. Thus, if you wanted to write a program that would compile on both these compilers, you could not use a logical IF.

As we remember, integrity is the quality a program possesses that allows it to correctly process data of all values. The previous program did not exhibit integrity since, for instance, if the value of A is zero, the root of the equation cannot be evaluated because of division by zero and the resultant overflow. When the value of A is zero, the solution to the quadratic equation is simply $X = -C/B$. Since the inclusion of various integrity features might make the program hard to understand, we have omitted them for the sake of clarity.

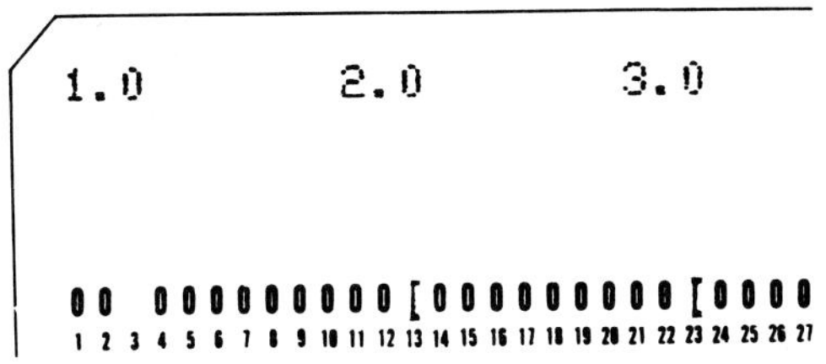

Figure 4.11b. The data card for the program. The value of A is 1.0, B is 2.0, and C is 3.0.

```
A=        1.000 B=        2.000 C=        3.000
X=       -1.000+        1.414I
X=       -1.000-        1.414I
```

Figure 4.11c. Results of running the program of Fig. 4.11a.

PROBLEMS

1. The formula for the sine of the sum of two angles is

$$\sin(x + y) = \sin x \cos y + \cos x \sin y$$

Write a program to show that the right-hand side of this equation equals the left-hand side for various values of x and y read by the program.

2. The roots of the quadratic equation $ax^2 + bx + c = 0$ are

$$x = \frac{-b \pm \sqrt{b^2-4ac}}{2a}$$

Write a program that solves the quadratic equation for values of a, b, and c read by the program.

3. Given $A = 1.0, B = 3.0, C = 3.0, D = 1.0$, what statement is executed after the IF statement in each of the following?

(a)
```
IF (A + B .GT. C) GO TO 80
WRITE (6,10) A
```
(b)
```
IF (A*B .NE. C*D) WRITE (6,10) A,B
WRITE (6,20) C, D
```
(c)
```
IF (A*B*C .GE. 9) STOP
WRITE (6,10) A, B, C
```

4. Write a program that sums the odd integers from 1 to a number the program reads.

5. Write a program that calculates

$$Y = \sum_{n=0}^{M} A_N X^N$$

where $A_N = 2N + 1$. Thus $Y = 1 + 3X + 5X^2 + 7X^3 + (2M + 1) X^M$ where the values of M and X are read by the program.

6. The series

0, 1, 1, 2, 3, 5, 8, 13, 21, . . .

is formed by adding the two previous numbers to get the present number, e.g., 3 plus 5 equals 8. Write a program to produce the first 20 terms of this series.

7. A set of data cards consists of a group of numbers, followed by a trailer (−999.0), which is followed by the same group of numbers, which is again followed by a trailer, e.g.,

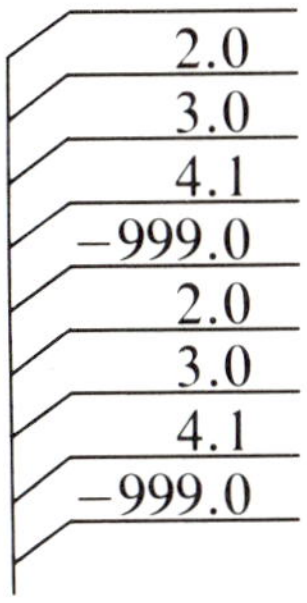

Write a program that calculates $\bar{x}$, the average of the first group of numbers, e.g., here

$$\bar{x} = \frac{x_1 + x_2 + x_3}{3}$$

but in general $\bar{x} = (x_1 + x_2 + x_3 + \ldots + x_n)/N$. Then by reading in the second group of numbers, calculate the variance V where here

$$V = [(x_1-\bar{x})^2 + (x_2-\bar{x})^2 + (x_3-\bar{x})^2]/(3-1)$$

but in general

$$V = [(x_1-\bar{x})^2 + (x_2-\bar{x})^2 + (x_3-\bar{x})^2 + \ldots + (x_n-\bar{x})^2]/(N-1)$$

Write the program so it works for any set of data cards that satisfy the description in this program.

8. Find the area between the curve $y = x^2$ and the x axis and between $x = -2$ and $x = 2$, i.e., the shaded area in

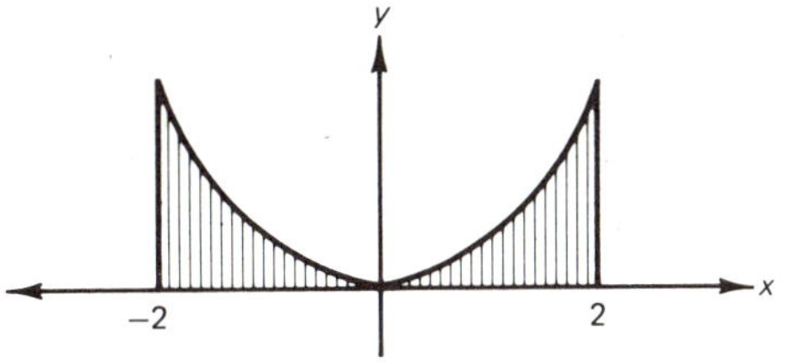

9. Given the following table, write a program that not only calculates the dollar amount of each sale, but also determines for each purchase how many sales including the present sale have been made, and the total dollar amount of sales. The price of plywood per square foot is $.06.

Sale Number	Length	Width
1001	8ft	4ft
1006	12ft	4ft
1012	5ft	3ft

5

The DO Loop, the IF-THEN-ELSE and the WHILE Loop

5.1. The DO Loop

When we previously wrote programs that had loops in them, we used an IF statement and a GO TO statement. We now introduce a new method that will make it easier for you to program loops. It is called a DO loop.

To motivate the use of the DO loop, we will first present a program that, using an IF and GO TO, prints the same line of Xs 4 times on the page. The program is shown in Fig. 5.1a; the results are shown in Fig. 5.1b.

We next write this program using a DO loop, as shown in Fig. 5.2a. We do this by sandwiching the statements in the loop of the preceding program that were not used as a counter or to terminate the loop, i.e.,

```
          WRITE(6,10)
10        FORMAT(1X,'XXXXXXXXXX')
```

between a statement which begins with the word DO and a CONTINUE statement.*

* The FORMAT because it is a nonexecutable statement can be placed anywhere in the program before the END.

MOTIVATING THE DO LOOP

```
C  PROGRAM PRINTS A LINE OF XS 4 TIMES
C  INITIALIZE THE COUNTER
      N=1
 10   WRITE(6,20)
 20   FORMAT(1X,'XXXXXXXXXX')
      N=N + 1
      IF( N .LE. 4) GO TO 10
      STOP
      END
```

Figure 5.1a. Program to motivate learning the DO loop. This program prints a string of Xs 4 times.

```
XXXXXXXXXX
XXXXXXXXXX
XXXXXXXXXX
XXXXXXXXXX
```

Figure 5.1b. Running the program of Fig. 5.1a.

The DO statement

```
DO 20 I=1,4
```

instructs the computer to execute the statements following it, up to and including statement 20

```
20    CONTINUE
```

for I=1, I=2, I=3, and finally I=4, i.e., 4 times. The number following the DO—here 20—indicates the statement number of the last statement in the loop.

The variable I which follows the 20, is called the index of the loop. It must be an INTEGER variable. What follows I—in this case the INTEGER constants 1 and 4, however, they can also be INTEGER variables—indicate the initial and limiting value of I. Thus 1 is the initial value of the index and 4 is the limit. In ANS Standard FORTRAN and on most compilers, these two quantities cannot have a negative or zero value. Thus DO 20 I= −2,4 and DO 20 I=0,3 would both be incorrect.

In using the DO loop in this program, the programmer does not have to write statements that set I=1 or increase I by 1 or test the value of I as we did in Fig. 5.1a. This is now all done "behind the scenes" in the computer, when the DO loop is translated. One can think of the statement that ends the DO loop as first incrementing I by 1 and then testing whether the new value of I is greater than the limiting value of the loop index, here 4. If the value of the loop index is not greater than 4, then the statements in the loop are executed again. If it is greater than 4, the statement that immediately follows the loop, is executed.

In order to make it clear to the reader which statements are in the loop, it is a good idea to indent the statements that are sandwiched between the DO and the CONTINUE, as is shown in Fig. 5.2a. After the statements in the DO loop are executed the required number of times, the statement following the end of the loop—the STOP in Fig. 5.2a—is executed next.

The results of running the program are shown in Fig. 5.2b.

INTRODUCTION TO THE DO LOOP

```
C   PROGRAM PRINTS A LINE OF XS 4 TIMES
C   USING A DO LOOP
        DO 20 I=1,4
           WRITE(6,10)
 10        FORMAT(1X,'XXXXXXXXXX')
 20     CONTINUE
        STOP
        END
```

Figure 5.2a. Because of DO 20 I=1,4 the statements sandwiched between the DO and 20 CONTINUE are executed for I=1, I=2, I=3, and I=4. The 20 refers to the last statement in the loop. The variable I (called the loop index) as well as 1 (the initial value of the loop index) and 4 (the limiting value) must all be INTEGERS. The executable statements sandwiched between the DO and the CONTINUE are called the range of the DO.

```
XXXXXXXXXX
XXXXXXXXXX
XXXXXXXXXX
XXXXXXXXXX
```

Figure 5.2b. Each time 20 CONTINUE is executed, the computer increases I by 1 and then checks to see whether I is greater than 4. If it is not, the statements in the loop are executed. If I is greater than 4, the statement after the CONTINUE (here STOP) is executed.

It is not necessary to end a DO loop with a CONTINUE statement.* Thus the DO loop in Fig. 5.2a could have been written as

```
      DO 10 I=1,4
   10 WRITE(6,20)
```

However, we always will end a DO loop with a CONTINUE statement, since it makes the structure of the loop easier for a reader to follow.

You will find that, years after taking the course in FORTRAN, if you have to write a program with a loop in it, most probably you will use a DO loop. The reason is that it is in general easier to use than the GO TO and IF; moreover, it is also easier for someone reading the program to understand. Because of our training in reading prose, by force of habit we tend to scan any reading matter line by line from the top down. This is also the case when we read a program. However, in order to follow a GO TO statement, we either have to go back to a previous part of the program or jump ahead to an unread part. Although this does not make a program impossible to understand, it does add to the difficulty. For this reason, whenever possible and as we develop the ability, we will avoid using GO TO statements in the programs in this book.

As we previously indicated, the initial and limiting value of the loop index can also be variables. In Fig. 5.3a we rewrite the program of Fig. 5.2a so that the limit of the index is now the variable M

```
      DO 40 I=1,M
```

where the value of M is read from a data card (Fig. 5.3b) when READ(5,10)M is executed. Since the value on the data card is 3, three lines are printed as is shown in Fig. 5.3c. This program is considered to be written in better programming style than the first (Fig. 5.2a) since it does the job that the first does and is more general but at the same time is not more difficult to understand.

* One can end a DO loop with any executable statement except another DO, a GO TO, arithmetic IF, RETURN (discussed in Chapter 9), STOP, or a logical IF containing any of these.

VARIABLE LIMIT FOR DO LOOP INDEX

```
C   PROGRAM PRINTS A LINE OF XS MANY TIMES ON THE PAGE
C   USING A DO LOOP. THE NUMBER OF TIMES THE LOOP IS EXECUTED
C   IS DETERMINED BY AN INTEGER VARIABLE READ FROM CARDS.
C
C   M WILL INDICATE HOW MANY TIMES TO EXECUTE THE LOOP.
        READ(5,10) M
 10     FORMAT( I5 )
        WRITE(6,20) M
 20     FORMAT(1X, I6, ' LINES OF XS WILL BE PRINTED')
        DO 40 I=1,M
           WRITE(6,30)
 30        FORMAT(1X, 'XXXXXXXXXX')
 40     CONTINUE
        STOP
        END
```

Figure 5.3a. The previous program written so that the upper limit on the loop index is now a variable (the INTEGER M).

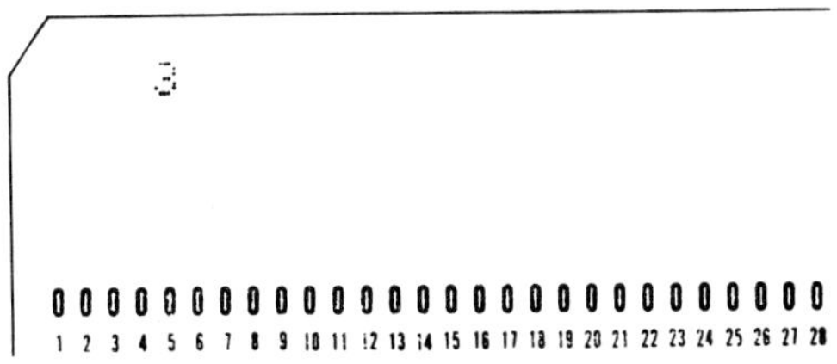

Figure 5.3b. The data card for Fig. 5.3a. Since the value on the data card is 3, we see that three lines will be printed (see Fig. 5.3c).

```
      3 LINES OF XS WILL BE PRINTED
XXXXXXXXXX
XXXXXXXXXX
XXXXXXXXXX
```

Figure 5.3c. The results of this program are the same as the previous program, as expected.

We now write a program, shown in Fig. 5.4a, which uses the loop index, J, in a calculation within the loop

```
Y=X**J
```

where X (its value here is 5.0) is read from the data card shown in Fig. 5.4b. This program calculates X^J for J varying from 1 to 10. The first time Y=X**J is executed, the computer interprets it as Y = X**1 and prints the appropriate result, as shown in the first line of Fig. 5.4c. The remaining results are also shown in Fig. 5.4c.

The executable statements that are sandwiched between the DO and the CONTINUE are called the *range* of the DO. Thus in Fig. 5.4a

```
Y=X**J
WRITE(6,20) X, J, Y
```

are the range of the DO. If we had decided to write the DO without the CONTINUE

```
   DO 30 J=1,10
   Y=X**J
30 WRITE(6,20) X, J, Y
```

then Y = X**J and 30 WRITE(6,20) X, J, Y are the range.

As we have mentioned, the DO loop index must be an INTEGER variable. This restriction did not cause any difficulty in this program because we used the loop index J as the exponent in Y = X**J. Sometimes, however, we would like to use the loop index in a REAL expression. In the next program we show how to do this.

The program of Fig. 5.5a converts a Fahrenheit temperature to centigrade using the formula C=5/9(F−32) for Fahrenheit temperatures varying from 50° to 60° in increments of 1°. Hence we write the DO statement as

```
DO 20 J=50,60
```

We see that the initial value of J is 50 and its limit is 60. The values of J represent the Fahrenheit temperatures. Since the temperatures will be used in a REAL calculation, they must be first floated; hence we write

```
F=J
```

otherwise we would have a mixed-mode calculation. The statement that calculates the centigrade temperature C is

```
C=CONV*(F-32.0)
```

The value of CONV, which is 5.0/9.0, is calculated before the DO loop.

What we have done here, in effect remove from a loop a calculation involving constants (5.0/9.0) and then using the value of the calculation (the value of CONV) in the loop, is called *folding a constant*. All compilers except the most primitive, automatically fold constants in the programs they compile, before they translate the program into machine language. Thus calculating CONV before the loop, for most compilers, is unnecessary.

Had we wanted to, we could have eliminated F = J and simply used the FLOAT function, thus writing C = (5.0/9.0)*(FLOAT (J) −32.0). Then, however, we would have to

USING THE LOOP INDEX IN A CALCULATION

```
C   PROGRAM USES THE LOOP INDEX
C   PROGRAM USES THE LOOP INDEX AS  AN
C   INTEGER VARIABLE IN A CALCULATION
        READ(5,10) X
 10     FORMAT( F10.0 )
C
        DO 30 J=1,10
           Y=X**J
           WRITE(6,20) X, J, Y
 20     FORMAT(1X, 'X=', F5.1, 4X, 'X**', I2, '=', E15.7)
 30     CONTINUE
        STOP
        END
```

Figure 5.4a. The loop index J is used as an INTEGER variable in the calculation Y=X**J.

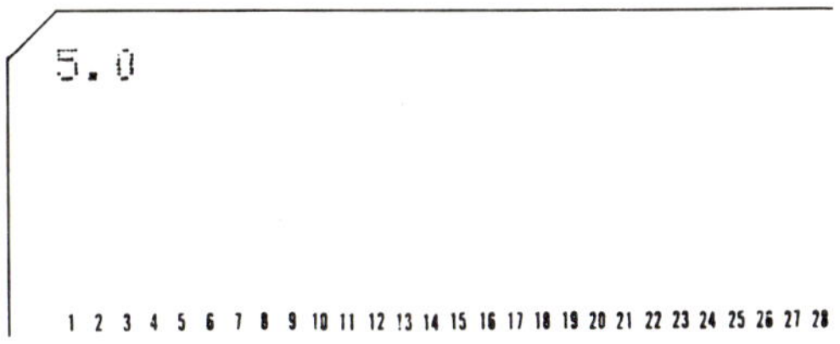

Figure 5.4b. The data card for Fig. 5.4a.

```
X=  5.0    X** 1=  0.5000000E 01
X=  5.0    X** 2=  0.2500000E 02
X=  5.0    X** 3=  0.1250000E 03
X=  5.0    X** 4=  0.6250000E 03
X=  5.0    X** 5=  0.3125000E 04
X=  5.0    X** 6=  0.1562500E 05
X=  5.0    X** 7=  0.7812500E 05
X=  5.0    X** 8=  0.3906250E 06
X=  5.0    X** 9=  0.1953125E 07
X=  5.0    X**10=  0.9765625E 07
```

Figure 5.4c. Running the program of Fig. 5.4a.

USING THE FLOATED VALUE OF THE LOOP INDEX

```
C   PROGRAM USES THE LOOP INDEX
C   AS A REAL VARIABLE IN A CALCULATION
        CONV=(5.0/9.0)
        DO 20 J=50,60
           F=J
           C=CONV*(F-32.0)
           WRITE(6,10) C, F
 10        FORMAT(1X, 'CENTIGRADE=', F10.2, 4X, 'FAHRENHEIT=', F10.2)
 20     CONTINUE
        STOP
        END
```

Figure 5.5a. The loop index J is first floated (assigned to F) and then used as a REAL in C=(5.0/9.0)*(F−32.0). In DO 20 J=50,60 the initial value of the index is given as 50 and its limit is given as 60.

change the WRITE and FORMAT statements to reflect the elimination of F from the program.

The results of the program are shown in Fig. 5.5b.

If we want to, we can instruct the computer to increase the loop index by more than 1 each time the statements in the range of the DO are executed. In Fig. 5.6a, we rewrite the program of Fig. 5.5a so that the value of J is increased by 3 each time the range of the DO is executed. We instruct the computer to do this in

```
DO 20 J=50, 60, 3
```

The first two numbers after the J are as usual the initial value of the index and its limit. The 3 is the number by which the computer will increment J each time the range of the DO is executed. The values that J successively assumes are 50, 53, 56, and 59 as is shown in the table for Fig. 5.6a.

Since the next value that J assumes, 62, is greater than the limit of the loop index, the range of the DO is no longer executed. Therefore, the statement after the loop is executed next. Since this is a STOP, the program terminates. The results of the program are given in Fig. 5.6b.

```
CENTIGRADE=       10.00      FARENHEIT=        50.00
CENTIGRADE=       10.56      FARENHEIT=        51.00
CENTIGRADE=       11.11      FARENHEIT=        52.00
CENTIGRADE=       11.67      FARENHEIT=        53.00
CENTIGRADE=       12.22      FARENHEIT=        54.00
CENTIGRADE=       12.78      FARENHEIT=        55.00
CENTIGRADE=       13.33      FARENHEIT=        56.00
CENTIGRADE=       13.89      FARENHEIT=        57.00
CENTIGRADE=       14.44      FARENHEIT=        58.00
CENTIGRADE=       15.00      FARENHEIT=        59.00
CENTIGRADE=       15.56      FARENHEIT=        60.00
```

Figure 5.5b. Running the program of Fig. 5.5a.

NON-UNIT INCREMENT IN DO LOOP INDEX

```
C   LOOP INDEX IS INCREASED BY 2 FOR
C   EACH EXECUTION OF THE LOOP
        CONV=(5.0/9.0)
C
        DO 20 J=50, 60, 3
           F=J
           C=CONV*(F-32.0)
           WRITE(6,10) C, F
 10     FORMAT(1X, 'CENTIGRADE=', F10.2, 4X, 'FARENHEIT=', F10.2)
 20     CONTINUE
        STOP
        END
```

Figure 5.6a. Same as Fig. 5.5a except that now the increment in the loop index is no longer 1. In DO 20 J=50, 60, 3 the initial value of the loop index is given as 50; its limit is given as 60. The next number, 3, is the increment in J each time the range of the DO is executed.

Time executed	J
1	50
2	53
3	56
4	59

Table for Fig. 5.6a. The values of J each time the loop is executed.

```
CENTIGRADE=       10.00      FARENHEIT=        50.00
CENTIGRADE=       11.67      FARENHEIT=        53.00
CENTIGRADE=       13.33      FARENHEIT=        56.00
CENTIGRADE=       15.00      FARENHEIT=        59.00
```

Figure 5.6b. Running the program of Fig. 5.6a. The range of the DO is executed for values of the index J successively set to 50, 53, 56, 59. The range is not executed for J equal to 62, since this value of J is greater than the limit, 60, set in the DO.

5.2. T Format

A feature of FORTRAN* that facilitates printing results in tabular form is the T format. The program shown in Fig. 5.7a uses T format to produce three columns of numbers labeled by J, K, and L, respectively. The T stands for *tab*, and instructs the computer to start the next field in the column whose column number is one less than indicated by the number† following the T. Thus in Fig. 5.7a

```
20    FORMAT(1X, T5, 'J', T15, 'K', T25, 'L')
```

T5 instructs the computer to print the string 'J' starting in column 4, T15 instructs the computer to print the string 'K' starting in column 14, and T25 instructs the computer to print the string 'L' starting in column 24. All of this is shown in Fig. 5.7b. Since we want the values assigned to J, K, and L to be printed under the proper string, we write

```
      WRITE(6,30) J, K, L
30    FORMAT(1X, T5, I2, T15, I2, T25, I2)
```

using the same T format to precede the field specifications as we used to precede the strings. Thus the field in which J will be printed will start in column 4 and extend 2 columns. Similarly the field in which K will be printed will start in column 14; and the field that L will be printed in, will start in column 24. Since the numbers are printed right-justified in the fields, the numbers are all printed one column to the right of the column in which the strings are printed.

* The T format is not available on ANS Standard FORTRAN.
† The reason for this is that T1 indicates the column used for the control character.

USING T FORMAT

```
C   USE OF T FORMAT FOR PRODUCING TABLES
        J=1
        K=2
        L=3
        WRITE(6,10)
 10     FORMAT(1X, '123456789-123456789-123456789-')
        WRITE(6,20)
 20     FORMAT(1X, T5, 'J', T15, 'K', T25, 'L')
        WRITE(6,30) J, K, L
 30     FORMAT(1X, T5, I2, T15, I2, T25, I2)
        J=4
        K=5
        L=6
        WRITE(6,30) J, K, L
        STOP
        END
```

Figure 5.7a. The fields following a T format start in the column preceded by the one specified by the T format. Thus T5, 'J' means that 'J' will be printed starting in column 4; and T5, I2 means that the field specified by I2 will start in column 4.

```
123456789-123456789-123456789-
   J         K         L
    1         2         3
    4         5         6
```

Figure 5.7b. Running the program of Fig. 5.7a. The first line of numbers indicates the column numbers. The constants printed under J, K, and L are shifted one column to the right since they are right-justified in their respective fields.

5.3. More on DO Loops

We now use the DO loop to write a program, shown in Fig. 5.8a, which produces a trigonometric table that prints the values of the SIN, COS and TAN for an angle that varies from 0° to 90° in steps of 15°. We might be tempted to do this by writing the DO statement as

```
DO 30 I=0, 90, 15
```

where I would represent the angle. However, as we have mentioned, the initial value of the loop index cannot be zero.* The way we circumvent this restriction is to add 1 to both the initial and limits of the loop index in the DO, making them 1 and 91, respectively. We thus write the DO as

```
DO 30  I=1, 91, 15
```

In order to compensate for adding the 1, we must subtract 1 from I in the first statement within the loop. We thus write

```
ANGLE=I-1
```

In order to check that we have done all this correctly, it is a good idea to check the operation of the loop for a few trial values of the loop index—typically we check the initial value and the limit of the index. When I=1, ANGLE equals zero; when I=91, ANGLE equals 90. Thus the limiting values of ANGLE are correct. We now discuss another important aspect of the program.

We remember that the argument of the trigonometric functions must be in radians. However, since it is more convenient to work with angles measured in degrees, we have written the DO statement with the index representing an angle measured in degrees. We must therefore convert the angle, ANGLE, to radians. This is done as follows: We know that there are 360 degrees in a circle. It is also true that there are 2π radians in a circle. Thus to convert from degrees to radians, we must multiply the angle measured in degrees by $2\pi/360$ or $\pi/180$, which to 7 significant figures is 3.141593/180. We assign this ratio to CONV in a statement that precedes the DO loop. In the loop we convert from degrees to radians in

```
RADIAN=CONV*ANGLE
```

The T formats used in the FORMAT which prints the table heading

```
10    FORMAT(1X, 'ANGLE', T18, 'RADIAN', T35, 'SIN', T50, 'COS',
   1          T65, 'TAN')
```

specify columns in which the labels will be printed. We note that all labels are shifted 5 columns to the right of the fields in which the numbers they label are printed

```
20        FORMAT(1X, F5.1,        T15, F10.7, T30, F10.7, T45, F10.7,
   1              T60, E16.7)
```

The reason for this is that the numbers are printed right-justified in their respective fields, and we want the labels to be approximately in line with the column of numbers they label as shown in Fig. 5.8b. Another thing to note about this last FORMAT statement is that we used F15.1 for ANGLE but F10.7 for the trigonometric functions. The reason for this is that the value of ANGLE will always be a whole number whereas the value of the trigonometric functions will always be less than 1; the 7 in F10.7 will allow us to see all the significant digits.

* On some compilers, e.g., WATFIV-S, we *can* do this by eliminating the DO and the CONTINUE and instead, beginning the loop with FOR(I=0, 90, 15) DO and ending it with END FOR.

PRODUCING A TRIGONOMETRIC TABLE

```
C   PROGRAM PRODUCES A TRIGONOMETRIC TABLE
C
C   CONVERT FROM DEGREES TO RADIANS
       CONV=3.141593/180.0
C          ...LABEL TABLE
       WRITE(6,10)
 10    FORMAT(1X, 'ANGLE', T18, 'RADIAN', T35, 'SIN', T50, 'COS',
    1        T65, 'TAN')
C          ...CALCULATE ENTRIES FOR TABLE
       DO 30  I=1, 91, 15
C          ...SUBTRACT 1 SO THAT ANGLE STARTS AT ZERO
          ANGLE=I-1
          RADIAN=CONV*ANGLE
          SINE=SIN(RADIAN)
          COSINF=COS(RADIAN)
          TANG=TAN(RADIAN)
          WRITE(6,20) ANGLE, RADIAN, SINE, COSINE, TANG
 20       FORMAT(1X, F5.1,      T15, F10.7, T30, F10.7, T45, F10.7,
    1           T60, E16.7)
 30    CONTINUE
       STOP
       END
```

Figure 5.8a. Program produces a trigonometric table. We want the angle to vary between 0° and 90°. Since the initial value of the index cannot be zero, we have to add 1 to the initial value and also to the limit, but not to the increment. Then we write DO 30 I=1, 91, 15. In the range we compensate for this by subtracting 1 from the index.

ANGLE	RADIAN	SIN	COS	TAN
0.0	0.0000000	0.0000000	1.0000000	0.0000000E 00
15.0	0.2617994	0.2588190	0.9659258	0.2679492E 00
30.0	0.5235988	0.5000000	0.8660254	0.5773503E 00
45.0	0.7853982	0.7071068	0.7071067	0.1000000E 01
60.0	1.0471970	0.8660253	0.5000002	0.1732050E 01
75.0	1.3089960	0.9659256	0.2588197	0.3732039E 01
90.0	1.5707960	0.9999999	0.0000003	0.3185560E 07

Figure 5.8b. Running the program of Fig. 5.18a. Since the argument of the trigonometric functions must be in radians, we write RADIAN=CONV*ANGLE. The conversion factor CONV is calculated before the DO loop in order to eliminate unnecessarily repeating the calculation.

In Fig. 5.9a we write a more general version of this program, which reads the increment, INCR, in the angle from the data card shown in Fig. 5.9b. The DO statement can now be written as

```
DO 40 I=1, 91, INCR
```

To ensure that the value of INCR is not negative or zero, we insert IF(INCR .LE. 0) GO TO 50 in the beginning of the program, where statement 50 and the statements which follow it are

```
50   WRITE(6,60) INCR
60   FORMAT(1X, 'BAD INPUT! INCR=', I10)
```

Thus invalid values of INCR, for instance −4, will trigger the program to print

```
BAD INPUT  INCR= -4
```

and then the program will stop.

VARIABLE INCREMENT IN DO LOOP INDEX

```
C  PROGRAM PRODUCES A TRIGONOMETRIC TABLE
C
C  CONVERT FROM DEGREES TO RADIANS
      CONV=3.141593/180.0
C          ...READ INCREMENT IN ANGLE
      READ(5,10) INCR
 10   FORMAT(I10)
      WRITE(6,15) INCR
 15   FORMAT(1X, I10)
      IF( INCR .LE. 0 ) GO TO 50
C          ...LABEL TABLE
         WRITE(6,20)
 20      FORMAT(1X, 'ANGLE', T18, 'RADIAN', T35, 'SIN', T50, 'COS',
     1         T65, 'TAN')
C             ...CALCULATE ENTRIES FOR TABLE
         DO 40 I=1, 91, INCR
C             ...SUBTRACT 1 SO THAT ANGLE STARTS AT ZERO
            ANGLE=I-1
            RADIAN=CONV*ANGLE
            SINE=SIN(RADIAN)
            COSINE=COS(RADIAN)
            TANG=TAN(RADIAN)
            WRITE(6,30) ANGLE, RADIAN, SINE, COSINE, TANG
 30         FORMAT(1X, F5.1,      T15, F10.7, T30, F10.7, T45, F10.7,
     1             T60, E16.7)
 40      CONTINUE
         STOP
 50   WRITE(6,60) INCR
 60   FORMAT(1X, 'BAD INPUT! INCR=', I10)
      STOP
      END
```

Figure 5.9a. The program of Fig. 5.8a rewritten so that the loop index increment is now a variable INCR.

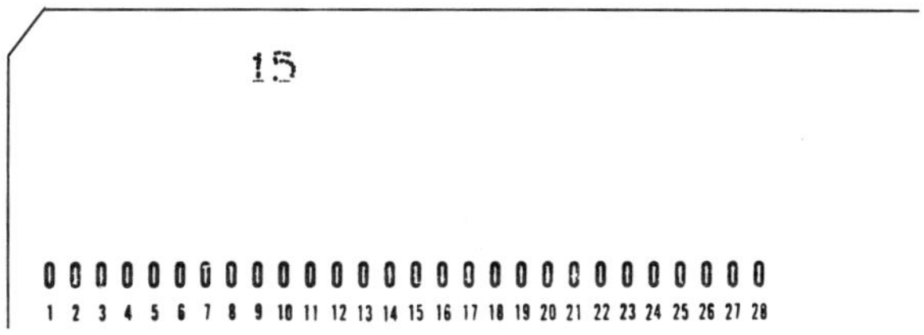

Figure 5.9b. The data card for the program of Fig. 5.9a.

The results of running the program are shown in Fig. 5.9c. Since the data card had the value 15 punched on it, the table is printed in increments of 15^0. The program just presented is not the most general, since it does not accommodate fractional increases in the angle. We leave it as an exercise to the reader to generalize this program accordingly.

The flow chart for Fig. 5.9a is shown in Fig. 5.9d. We indicate the beginning of a DO loop with a hexagon that contains the parameters of the DO. This is followed by the range of the DO, which is followed by a circle containing the statement number of the CONTINUE statement that marks the end of the loop. To indicate that these statements form a loop, an additional line goes from the circle back to the hexagon.

DO

The form of the DO statement is: DO; followed by the statement number that terminates the loop; followed by the loop index—this must be an INTEGER variable; followed by =; followed by the initial value of the index; followed by a comma; followed by the maximum value or limit of the index. This is followed by a comma, which is followed by the increment in the loop index. The initial value and the limit of the index and the increment can be either an INTEGER constant or variable* with a positive value. If the index is increased by 1 each time the loop is executed, the last comma and the increment can be omitted. The index, its minimum and maximum values, and the increment are called the *parameters* of the loop. In standard FORTRAN, the parameters† can only have positive values. Examples:

```
    DO 20 I=1, N, M
    DO 30 JK=M, 80, NMAX
100 DO 40 NUM=L1, L2, L3
    DO 50 J=3, 20, 2
    DO 60 J=3, M
    DO 70 J=N, M
    DO 10 J=5, 4
    DO 10 J=6, 2, 2
```

As long as the values of the parameters are legal, the range of the DO is executed at least once. Thus, in the last two DO statements, the loops described would be executed only once because the maximum limit is less than the minimum limit of the index.

* The limit and the increment cannot be subscripted INTEGER variables.

† On many systems, however, the initial value and limit of the index as well as increment can also be zero or negative. In fact on some systems, they can also be expressions.

15

ANGLE	RADIAN	SIN	COS	TAN
0.0	0.0000000	0.0000000	1.0000000	0.0000000E 00
15.0	0.2617994	0.2588190	0.9659258	0.2679492E 00
30.0	0.5235988	0.5000000	0.8660254	0.5773503E 00
45.0	0.7853982	0.7071068	0.7071067	0.1000000E 01
60.0	1.0471970	0.8660253	0.5000002	0.1732050E 01
75.0	1.3089960	0.9659256	0.2588197	0.3732039E 01
90.0	1.5707960	0.9999999	0.0000003	0.3185560E 07

Figure 5.9c. Running the program of Fig. 5.9a.

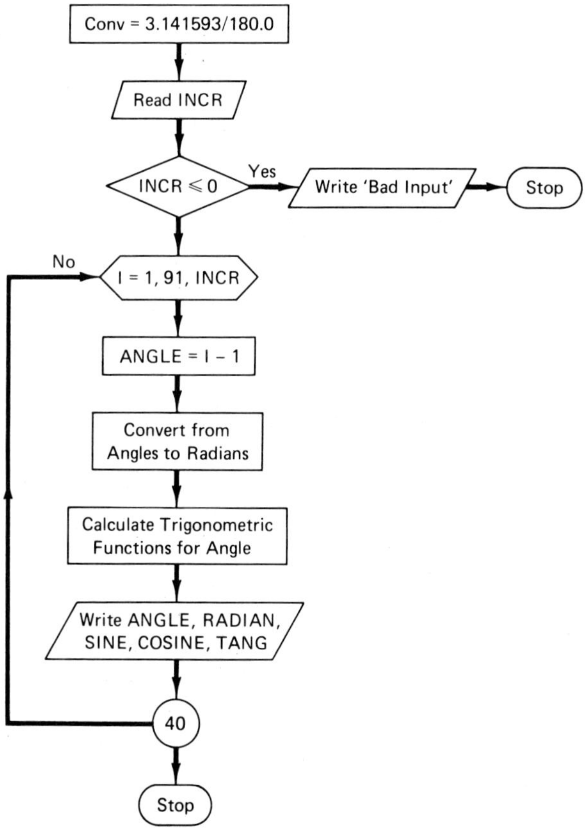

Figure 5.9d. The flow chart for Fig. 5.9a. We represent a DO loop by starting with a hexagon which has the index parameters for the loop. These are followed by the statements in the range, which are followed by a circle containing the statement number of the CONTINUE. Finally, a line leads from the circle to the hexagon to aid in depicting a loop.

CONTINUE

> The form of the CONTINUE statement is: statement number followed by CONTINUE. Besides ending DO loops, the CONTINUE statement can be placed anywhere in a program and can be referred to by a GO TO statement. Example:
>
> ```
> GO TO 10
>    •
>    •
>    •
> 10 CONTINUE
> ```

In some problems we want to continually increase the value of a variable by nonintegral increments. Although the DO statement does not allow us to do this, we can overcome this restriction and still use a DO loop, as we show in the following example.

We now investigate how to write a program in which we want the value of a variable X in the range of the DO to vary from 0.5 to 10.0 in steps of 0.5, i.e., we want X to assume the values in the sequence 0.5, 1.0, 1.5, 2.0, . . . 10.0 . If we multiply each of the numbers in the sequence by 10, we obtain 5, 10, 15, 20, . . . 100. The difference between consecutive numbers in this altered sequence is now an integer, 5. Thus if, for instance, we use 20 CONTINUE to end the loop, the following DO will produce the numbers in this altered sequence

```
DO 20 I=5, 100, 5
```

To compensate for the fact that we multiplied the numbers in the DO by 10, we must divide the values of I by 10 in the range of the DO. We thus write

```
X=FLOAT(I)/10.0
```

The effect of this statement is shown in the table for Fig. 5.10a. The purpose of this program is to sum the values of X. The results are shown in Fig. 5.10b.

NONINTEGRAL VALUES FOR DO LOOP PARAMETERS

```
C   PROGRAM USES DO LOOP TO DEMONSTRATE HOW A NON-INTEGRAL
C   INCREMENT IN A DO LOOP IS PROGRAMMED
C   PROGRAM SUMS THE 20 NUMBERS: 0.5, 1.0, 1.5, 2.0, ...10.0
        SUM=0.0
C              ...SUM THE NUMBERS
        DO 20 I=5, 100, 5
           X=FLOAT(I)/10.0
           WRITE(6,10) X
 10        FORMAT(1X, 'X=', F10.1)
           SUM=SUM + X
 20     CONTINUE
        WRITE(6,30) SUM
 30     FORMAT(1X, 'SUM=', F10.1)
        STOP
        END
```

Figure 5.10a. Programming nonintegral increments in the loop index. Since we cannot write DO 20 I= 0.5, 10, 0.5, we multiply all the parameters to the right of the equal sign by the lowest power of 10 that will make all the parameters integers. In this problem we multiply the parameters by 10 and we get DO 20 I=5, 100, 5. We must then divide I by 10 in the range of the DO.

I	X
5	0.5
10	1.0
15	1.5
20	2.0
25	2.5
.	
.	
.	
95	9.5
100	10.0

Table for Fig. 5.10a. Shows that we obtain the proper value of X for each value of I.

```
X=          0.5
X=          1.0
X=          1.5
X=          2.0
X=          2.5
X=          3.0
X=          3.5
X=          4.0
X=          4.5
X=          5.0
X=          5.5
X=          6.0
X=          6.5
X=          7.0
X=          7.5
X=          8.0
X=          8.5
X=          9.0
X=          9.5
X=         10.0
SUM=        105.0
```

Figure 5.10b. Running the program of Fig. 5.10a.

5.4. Summations and Products

The DO loop is ideal for calculating sums. In the program of Fig. 5.11a we perform $X + X^2 + X^3 + X^4$, where the value of X is read into the program from the data card shown in Fig. 5.11b. When the program was run, the value of X read was 3.6. We perform the summation by placing an accumulator in the loop

```
SUM=SUM + X**N
```

The first time the range of the DO is executed the value of N is 1 and the value of SUM on the right of the equals sign is zero, so the computer interprets this statement as SUM = 0.0 + 3.6**1. The second time, the value of SUM on the right of the equals sign is 3.6**1, and the value of N is 2. Thus the computer interprets the statement as SUM = 3.6**1 + 3.6**2. The third time, the computer interprets it as SUM = 3.6**1 + 3.6**2 + 3.6**3.

The table for Fig. 5.11a shows how the accumulator works for a general value of X. The results of running the program are shown in Fig. 5.11c.

EVALUATING A SERIES

```
C   EVALUATES SUM OF X**N FOR N EQUALS 1 TO 6
C
      READ(5,10) X
 10   FORMAT(F10.0)
      SUM=0.0
C        ...EVALUATES SUMMATION
      DO 20 N=1, 4
         SUM=SUM + X**N
      WRITE(6,15) X, N, SUM
 15   FORMAT(1X, 'SUM OF SERIES X**N, FOR X=', F10.3,
     1       ' AND N= ', I3, ' IS', E15.7)
 20   CONTINUE
C
      STOP
      END
```

Figure 5.11a. Program calculates $X + X^2 + X^3 + X^4$ using SUM=SUM + X**N. Each time the range of DO is executed, another power of X is added to SUM, as shown in the table for Fig. 5.11a.

N	SUM=SUM +X**N
1	SUM=0.0 + X**1
2	SUM=X**1 + X**2
3	SUM=X**1 + X**2 + X**3
4	Sum=X**1 + X**2 + X**3 + X**4

Table for Fig. 5.11a. We see that as the value of N increases, a new power of X is added to the previous sum: this is exactly the meaning of SUM=SUM+X**N.

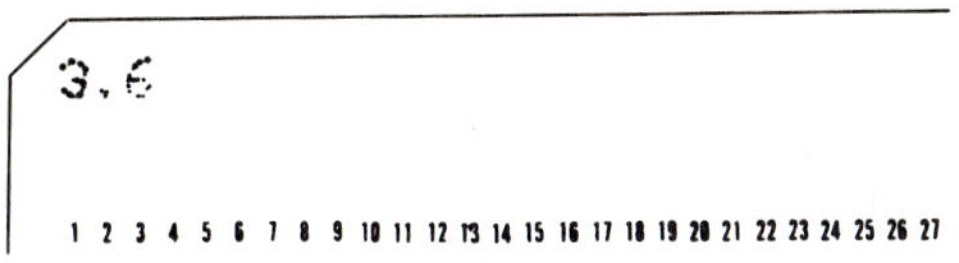

Figure 5.11b. The data card for Fig. 5.11a.

```
SUM OF SERIES X**N, FOR X=     3.600  AND N=   1 IS  0.3600000E 01
SUM OF SERIES X**N, FOR X=     3.600  AND N=   2 IS  0.1656000E 02
SUM OF SERIES X**N, FOR X=     3.600  AND N=   3 IS  0.6321600E 02
SUM OF SERIES X**N, FOR X=     3.600  AND N=   4 IS  0.2311777E 03
```

Figure 5.11c. Running the program of Fig. 5.11a.

We now write a program to calculate the product of the integers from 1 to N. In mathematics, this product is called N factorial and is written as $N!$. In order to calculate $N!$ we use a device called *multiplicative accumulator*, which we will represent by the variable PRODCT.

The program shown in Fig. 5.12a calculates 5!; it begins by setting PRODCT equal to 1. Then after floating I (the loop index) and assigning it to F, the program in PRODCT=PRODCT*F takes the previous value of PRODCT, multiplies it by 1, and again assigns the result to PRODCT. The second time this statement is executed, F equals 2.0, so 1.0×2.0 is assigned to PRODCT. The third time, F equals 3.0 and the previous value of PRODCT is 1.0×2.0, so $1.0 \times 2.0 \times 3.0$ is assigned to PRODCT. Thus the program is calculating factorials. The process is repeated each time the loop is executed, as can be seen from the table for Fig. 5.12a. If we study any two consecutive lines in the table, for instance

Time executed	F	PRODCT
2nd	2.0	2.0
3rd	3.0	6.0

we see that the value for PRODCT for the third line is obtained by multiplying the value of F for that line by the value of PRODCT for the preceding line. This is precisely the meaning of PRODCT = PRODCT*F. After the loop is executed 5 times, the results are printed as is shown in Fig. 5.12b.

In terms of the computer's hardware, one would explain PRODCT=PRODCT*F as follows: Take the contents of the location called F, multiply it by the contents of the location called PRODCT, and place the product back into PRODCT.

CALCULATING A FACTORIAL

```
C   PROGRAM CALCULATES 5!
C
        PRODCT=1.0
C           ...CALCULATES 5!
        DO 20 I=1, 5
           F=I
           PRODCT=PRODCT*F
 20     CONTINUE
C
        WRITE(6,30) PRODCT
 30     FORMAT(1X, '5!=', E15.7)
        STOP
        END
```

Figure 5.12a. Program calculates 5!. Each time PRODCT = PRODCT*F is executed, the value of the REAL counter F is multiplied by the previous value of PRODCT and the result is assigned to PRODCT. Thus the number assigned to PRODCT on the third execution of the loop is 2.0 × 3.0 or 6.0.

Time executed	F	PRODCT
1st	1.0	1.0
2nd	2.0	2.0
3rd	3.0	6.0
4th	4.0	24.0
5th	5.0	120.0

Table for Fig. 5.12a. Note that, for a given line, the value of PRODCT is obtained from the product of F for that line and PRODCT for the preceding line. This corresponds to PRODCT=PRODCT*F.

```
5!=   0.1200000E 03
```

Figure 5.12b. Running the program of Fig. 5.12a. The calculation is done in REAL arithmetic since factorials become very large.

We alter the previous program so that it now calculates *N!* for any integer *N* greater than zero, instead of simply 5!. The value of *N* is read at the beginning of the program as is shown in Fig. 5.13a, from the data card shown in Fig. 5.13b. This program also prints the factorials of all the integers up to and including *N*. We do this by now placing the WRITE statement within the loop

```
      DO 30 I=1, N
         F=I
         PRODCT=PRODCT*F
         WRITE(6,20) I, PRODCT
20       FORMAT(1X, I3, '!=', E15.7)
30    CONTINUE
```

The value of N the computer reads from the data card is 5, so the computer interprets the DO as DO 30 I=1, 5 and calculates 1!, 2!, 3!, 4!, and 5!, as shown in Fig. 5.13c.

If the value of N read is less than or equal to 0, the program stops because of

```
IF( N .LE. 0 ) STOP
```

The presence of this statement gives the program more integrity than if the statement were omitted. However, the program does not calculate 0! as 1; it would have more integrity if we substituted for IF (N .LE. 0) STOP, the following:

```
IF(N .LT. 0) STOP
IF(N .EQ. 0) WRITE(6,20) N, PRODCT
IF(N .EQ. 0) STOP
```

A factorial of a number is a much larger number than you might expect. For instance 10! equals 3,628,000. Very large numbers present difficulties for the computer. The machine cannot store REAL constants that have extremely large exponents. The largest exponent of a REAL constant that the IBM 370/360 can store is approximately 10^{75}. However, for INTEGER constants the situation is worse: the largest INTEGER* constant the IBM/370 can store is 2,147,483,647 or approximately 2×10^9. Since 10^{75} (the REAL maximum) is much greater than 2×10^9 (the INTEGER maximum) it is advisable to perform calculations involving integers that may become very large—such as calculations of factorials—using REAL quantities. Consequently we floated I in the DO loops of the preceding two programs and performed the factorial calculations using REALs.

* When a REAL constant becomes too large for the computer to accommodate, the computer on most systems will print an error message, such as OVERFLOW, but will continue to execute the program. On the other hand, if an INTEGER constant becomes too large for the computer to accommodate, the computer does not produce an error message. It drops the leftmost digits (most significant digits) and retains only the remaining, least-significant digits.

PRODUCING A TABLE OF FACTORIALS

```
C   PROGRAM PRODUCES A TABLE OF FACTORIALS
      PRODCT=1.0
C        ...READ THE VALUE OF THE HIGHEST NUMBER YOU WANT
C        ...THE FACTORIAL OF
      READ(5,10) N
 10   FORMAT(I5)
      IF( N .LE. 0 ) STOP
C        ...CALCULATE N!
      DO 30 I=1, N
         F=I
         PRODCT=PRODCT*F
         WRITE(6,20) I, PRODCT
 20      FORMAT(1X, I3, '!=', E15.7)
 30   CONTINUE
      STOP
      END
```

Figure 5.13a. Program calculates *N!*, where *N* is read by the program. Because WRITE(6,20) I, PRODCT is in the range of the DO, 1!, 2!, 3! up to *N*! is printed.

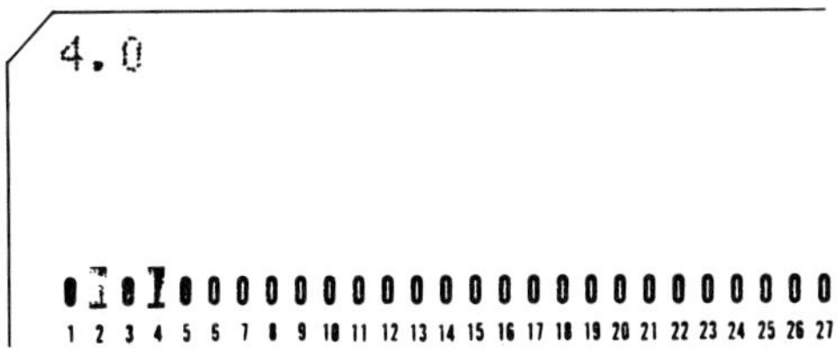

Figure 5.13b. The data card for Fig. 5.13a.

```
  1!=  0.1000000E 01
  2!=  0.2000000E 01
  3!=  0.6000000E 01
  4!=  0.2400000E 02
```

Figure 5.13c. Running the program of Fig. 5.13a.

We now use the techniques we learned in the programs of Figs. 5.11a and 5.12a, that is, using additive and multiplicative accumulators in DO loops, to write a program that will calculate the value of e, the base of the natural logarithm. The program is shown in Fig. 5.14a.

The value of e can be obtained from the expression*

$$e = 1 + 1/1! + 1/2! + 1/3! + 1/4! + \cdots + 1/N!$$

We will calculate the denominators 1!, 2!, 3!, etc., by using a multiplicative accumulator PROD, which appears in

```
PROD=PROD*FLOAT(J)
```

The addition of the terms will be done using an additive accumulator SUM, which appears in

```
SUM=SUM + 1.0/PROD
```

We have placed the WRITE statement within the loop so that we can see what contribution each term we calculate makes to SUM.

By looking at the expression for e, we see that the first three terms are 1 + 1/1! + 1/2!; however, the first two numbers that PROD = PROD*FLOAT (J) will produce are 1! and 2!, respectively. Thus we want the initial value of SUM to be 1. Thus, SUM = 1.0 precedes the loop. In the table for Fig. 5.14a we see how the expression for e is generated. For instance, the second time the range of the DO is executed

J	SUM on right of=	PROD	1.0/PROD	SUM on left of=
2	1 + 1/1!	2!	1/2!	1 + 1/1! + 1/2!

1/2! is added to the value of SUM (1 + 1/1!) giving 1 + 1/1! + 1/2!. So the Nth time the range is executed, $1/N!$ is added to the previous value of SUM. This is precisely the definition of e. The results of running the program are given in Fig. 5.14b. We see that the sum, rounded to 6 digits, rapidly converges to 2.71828, the value of e.

* In mathematics, this is called a series. The first term, 1, can actually be expressed as 1.0!, where 0! is 1. Thus the entire expression can be expressed as $e = \sum_n (1/N!)$.

CALCULATING *e*

```
      SUM=1.0
      PROD=1.0
C        ...ADD THE FIRST  9 TERMS IN THE SERIES 1/(N!)
      DO 20 J=1, 9
         PROD=PROD*FLOAT(J)
         SUM=SUM + 1.0/PROD
         WRITE(6,10) J, SUM
 10      FORMAT(1X, 'SUM OF FIRST', I2, 'TERMS IS', F15.10)
 20   CONTINUE
      STOP
      END
```

Figure 5.14a. This program calculates the base of the natural logarithm, *e*.

J	SUM on right of =	PROD	1.0/PROD	SUM on left of =
1	1	1!	1/!	1 + 1/!
2	1 + 1/!	2!	1/2!	1 + 1/1! + 1/2!
3	1 + 1/1! + 1/2!	3!	1/3!	1 + 1/! + 1/2! + 1/3!

Table for Fig. 5.14a shows how SUM=SUM+1.0/PROD works, where PROD=PROD*FLOAT(J)

```
SUM OF FIRST 1TERMS IS   2.0000000000
SUM OF FIRST 2TERMS IS   2.5000000000
SUM OF FIRST 3TERMS IS   2.6666660000
SUM OF FIRST 4TERMS IS   2.7083320000
SUM OF FIRST 5TERMS IS   2.7166650000
SUM OF FIRST 6TERMS IS   2.7180530000
SUM OF FIRST 7TERMS IS   2.7182520000
SUM OF FIRST 8TERMS IS   2.7182760000
SUM OF FIRST 9TERMS IS   2.7182780000
```

Figure 5.14b. Running the program of Fig. 5.14a.

5.5. Negative Increments; Reading a Variable Number of Data Cards

It is sometimes desirable to have a variable start at its maximum value and decrease to its minimum value.* We now show how to do this using a DO loop.

Since the increment in the loop index cannot be negative, we must program the continuing decrease of a variable within the range of the DO. As an example of this, we write a program, shown in Fig. 5.15a, that, given a constant velocity read from a data card, calculates the distance for values of the time varying from 20 to 1 in steps of −1. The data card read by the program, is shown in Fig. 5.15b.

* For instance, because of difficulties due to significance, it is generally desirable to sum series starting with the smaller terms at the end of the series and ending with the first term.

USING A NEGATIVE INCREMENT

```
C   PROGRAM DEMONSTRATES NEGATIVE INCREMENT IN
C   LOOP INDEX
        INTEGER T
C
        READ(5,10) VELOC
 10     FORMAT(F10.0)
        WRITE(6,20) VELOC
 20     FORMAT(1X, 'VELOCITY=', E15.7)
C           ...CALCULATE DISTANCES FOR VARIOUS VELOCITIES
        DO 40 T=1, 20
           TIME=21-T
           DIST=VELOC*TIME
           WRITE(6,30) DIST, TIME
 30        FORMAT(1X, 'DISTANCE=',E15.7, 4X, 'TIME =', F10.1)
 40     CONTINUE
        STOP
        END
```

Figure 5.15a. Programming a negative increment in the loop index. We would like to write DO 40 T= 20, 1, – 1 but we cannot because of the negative increment. Instead we write the initial value as 1 and the limit as 20 and write the first statement in the range of the DO as TIME = 21– T. This causes TIME to decrease by 1 each time the range is executed.

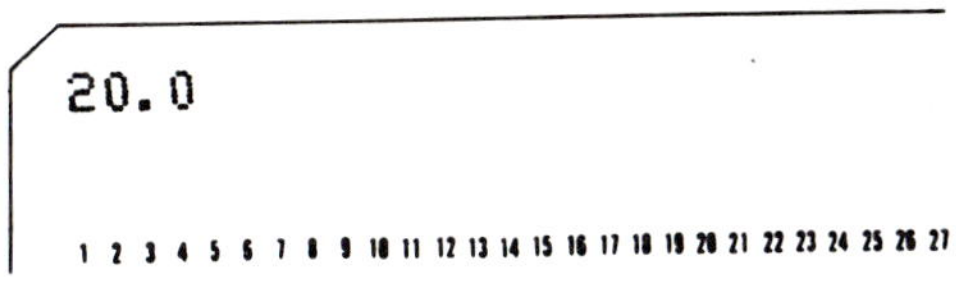

Figure 5.15b. The data card for Fig. 5.15a.

We write the DO using 1 as the initial value and 20 as the limit of the index T

```
DO 40 T=1, 20
```

where T has been declared INTEGER. In order to reverse the order, we add 1 to the limit, 20, and then subtract T obtaining

```
TIME=21-T
```

When the statement is executed for the first time, the value of TIME is 20; whereas the last time it is executed, the value of TIME is 1 as is shown in the table for Fig. 5.15a. The results are shown in Fig. 5.15c.

T	TIME
1	20
2	19
3	18
4	17
.	.
.	.
.	.
20	1

Table for Fig. 5.15a. Shows that as the loop index T increases, TIME decreases. This is a result of TIME=21−T.

```
VELOCITY=  0.2000000E 02
DISTANCE=  0.4000000E 03      TIME  =        20.0
DISTANCE=  0.3800000E 03      TIME  =        19.0
DISTANCE=  0.3600000E 03      TIME  =        18.0
DISTANCE=  0.3400000E 03      TIME  =        17.0
DISTANCE=  0.3200000E 03      TIME  =        16.0
DISTANCE=  0.3000000E 03      TIME  =        15.0
DISTANCE=  0.2800000E 03      TIME  =        14.0
DISTANCE=  0.2600000E 03      TIME  =        13.0
DISTANCE=  0.2400000E 03      TIME  =        12.0
DISTANCE=  0.2200000E 03      TIME  =        11.0
DISTANCE=  0.2000000E 03      TIME  =        10.0
DISTANCE=  0.1800000E 03      TIME  =         9.0
DISTANCE=  0.1600000E 03      TIME  =         8.0
DISTANCE=  0.1400000E 03      TIME  =         7.0
DISTANCE=  0.1200000E 03      TIME  =         6.0
DISTANCE=  0.1000000E 03      TIME  =         5.0
DISTANCE=  0.8000000E 02      TIME  =         4.0
DISTANCE=  0.6000000E 02      TIME  =         3.0
DISTANCE=  0.4000000E 02      TIME  =         2.0
DISTANCE=  0.2000000E 02      TIME  =         1.0
```

Figure 5.15c. Running the program of Fig. 5.15a.

We now write a program that averages the numbers read from data cards, where each data card contains only one number. The number of data cards is unknown, but the last card contains −12345678. This card is called a *trailer*. It is not included in the average; it simply signals the computer that no more data cards will follow.

When choosing a trailer, one should use a value that is very far from the range of values the program will encounter as data. Thus, if we were reading heights or weights, for instance, any negative number—e.g., −1—would serve as a trailer. If, on the other hand, we were reading data that can assume any value, then we would choose as a trailer a number unlikely to appear as one of the data. Thus, here we have chosen −12345678. Note that the absolute value of this number is less than 16777210, the largest REAL constant the IBM 360/370 can accommodate. Thus we will not encounter any difficulty in the program testing for −12345678.0 in the data.

The program shown in Fig. 5.16a can average a maximum of 10,000 numbers. The DO loop which reads and sums the constants is

```
      DO 20 N=1, 10001
         READ(5,10) NUMB
   10    FORMAT(F10.0)
C        ...TEST FOR TRAILER
         IF( NUMB .EQ. -12345678.0 ) GO TO 40
            WRITE(6,15) NUMB
   15       FORMAT(1X, F10.2)
            SUM=SUM + NUMB
   20 CONTINUE
```

After a card is read, the program adds the constant punched on it to the previous value of SUM. When the trailer is encountered, control is transferred from a statement in the range of the DO to

```
   40  N=N - 1
       AVER=SUM/FLOAT(N)
```

where the average is calculated. After 40 N=N − 1 is executed, the value of N is the

CALCULATING THE AVERAGE OF *N* NUMBERS

```
C   PROGRAM CALCULATES THE AVERAGE OF N NUMBERS
C   AS LONG AS N<10,000
        REAL NUMB
        SUM=0.0
C           ...READ THE CARDS AND SUM THE NUMBERS
        DO 20 N=1, 10001
            READ(5,10) NUMB
 10         FORMAT(F10.0)
C           ...TEST FOR TRAILER
            IF( NUMB .EQ. -12345678.0 ) GO TO 40
                WRITE(6,15) NUMB
 15             FORMAT(1X, F10.2)
                SUM=SUM + NUMB
 20     CONTINUE
C           ...EXECUTE ONLY IF TOO MANY CARDS WERE READ IN
        WRITE(6,30)
 30     FORMAT(1X, '10,001 CARDS READ IN, MAXIMUM IS 10,000')
        STOP
C           ...CALCULATE THE AVERAGE
C           ...WE USE N-1 IN THIS CALCULATION SO THAT WE DON'T
C           ... INCLUDE THE TRAILER
 40     N=N - 1
        AVER=SUM/FLOAT(N)
        WRITE(6,50) N, AVER
 50     FORMAT(1X, 'THE AVERAGE OF', I5, ' NUMBERS IS', E15.7)
        STOP
        END
```

Figure 5.16a. A program in which a transfer is made out of the range of a DO before the loop is finished. In a case like this, the index is still defined after the transfer is made out of the range. The program reads in an unknown number of data cards and stops reading after the last card (−12345678.0) called a *trailer*, is encountered. If more than 10,000 data cards (excluding the trailer) are read, the program stops. The trailer is not included in the average. It only indicates that no data follow.

number of cards, excluding the trailer, which the program read. The data cards for the program are shown in Fig. 5.16b. The results of the program are shown in Fig. 5.16c.

We could have punched −99999999. on the trailer instead of −12345678.0; however, we might then punch the incorrect number of 9s in the IF statement that tests for the trailer. Thus the trailer would not be detected; the program would try to read another data card, and, since there are no more data cards, an error would result.

When a transfer out of a DO loop occurs, as it has here, the value of the loop index (here N) is defined. However, if the loop is executed as instructed in the DO and then terminates normally—in this case the range would be executed 10,001 times—the loop index becomes undefined. For example, if 10,001 cards—excluding the trailer—were read, then

```
      WRITE(6,30)
30    FORMAT(1X, '10,001 CARDS READ IN, MAXIMUM IS 10,000')
```

would be executed. If we wanted to use N here, e.g., write these statements as

```
      WRITE(6,30) N
30    FORMAT(1X, I4, 'NUMBERS READ' )
```

since N is undefined at this point we would obtain the wrong result.

Figure 5.16b. The data cards for Fig. 5.16a. The trailer (−12345678.0) is not included in the average; it simply signals the computer that no data cards will follow.

```
     16.20
      3.80
     -4.20
      7.89
THE AVERAGE OF     4 NUMBERS IS  0.5922493E 01
```

Figure 5.16c. Running the program of Fig. 5.16a. The program also counts the number of cards. If the program is written correctly, the card count will always be correct. This is in contrast to the program shown in Fig. 5.17a.

We could have written the previous program as is now shown in Fig. 5.17a. The composition of the deck of cards that contains the data is now somewhat different. Instead of having a trailer at the end of the data cards, we now precede the cards containing the numbers to be averaged with one on which we have punched a constant that indicates the number of data cards to follow. We will call this first data card a *leader*. The data cards are shown in Fig. 5.17b. We read the leader in

```
READ(5,10) NMAX
```

and can now write the DO statement as

```
DO 30 N=1, NMAX
```

This allows us to eliminate the IF statement that tested for the trailer in Fig. 5.16a and thus eliminate the GO TO statement accompanied the IF. Although this change not only improves the appearance of the program but also makes it easier for someone reading the program to follow, it makes the operation of the program prone to errors. The reason is that the greater the number of data cards, the more careful we would have to be counting them. As an example, let us say we counted 5 data cards following the leader. We would thus punch 5 on the leader. What would happen if we had miscounted and there were actually only 4 data cards (excluding the leader)? Then the 5th time

```
READ(5,20) NUMB
```

was executed, there would be no data card to read and the computer would produce an error message as is shown in Fig. 5.17c. Since this program was run on the WATFIV compiler, the compiler indicates where this run-time error occurred: it occurred in READ(5,20)NUMB.

The lesson this teaches us is that we should not do manually what the computer can do better. Thus, in the preceding program (Fig. 5.16a) we are in effect programming the computer to also count the number of cards. Once that program is completely debugged, assuming that the data cards are punched correctly, the program must produce the correct results. On the other hand, even after the present program is completely debugged, if we miscount the number of data cards the program will produce incorrect results.

In the present program (Fig. 5.17a) since the loop index N is undefined after the loop is executed, we did not use N to calculate the average. We thus did not write it as

```
AVER=SUM/FLOAT(N)
```

but instead wrote it using NMAX (which is defined)

```
AVER=SUM/FLOAT(NMAX)
```

USING A HEADER

```
      C  DANGEROUS WAY OF READING THE
      C  NUMBER OF CARDS TO BE PROCESSED
1           REAL NUMB
2           SUM=0.0
3           READ(5,10) NMAX
4      10   FORMAT(I10)
5           WRITE(6,15)  NMAX
6      15   FORMAT(1X, I10)
      C           ...SUMS THE NUMBERS
7           DO 30 N=1, NMAX
8              READ(5,20) NUMB
9      20      FORMAT(F10.0)
10             WRITE(6,25) NUMB
11     25      FORMAT(1X, F12.2)
12             SUM=SUM + NUMB
13     30   CONTINUE
      C           ...CALCULATE THE AVERAGE
14          AVER=SUM/FLOAT(NMAX)
15          WRITE(6,40) N, AVER
16     40   FORMAT(1X, 'THE AVERAGE OF', I5, ' NUMBERS IS', E15.7)
17          STOP
18          END
```

Figure 5.17a. The program of Fig. 5.16a rewritten so that we have to count the number of data cards. This number is punched on the first data card and is then used as limit of the index in the DO. If we make a mistake in counting the number of data cards, the program produces the wrong results. Thus the technique employed in this program is not a good one to use.

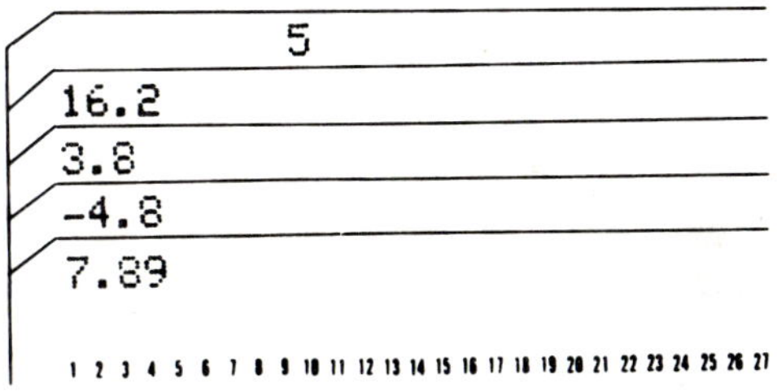

Figure 5.17b. The data cards for Fig. 5.17a. The constant on the first card should indicate how many data cards follow. Here it does not, since 4 and not 5 cards follow the first card.

```
         5
     16.20
      3.80
     -4.20
      7.89
***ERROR***  CONTROL CARD ENCOUNTERED ON UNIT   5 AT EXECUTION. PROBABLE CAUSE:MISSING DATA

        PROGRAM WAS EXECUTING LINE     8 IN ROUTINE M/PROG WHEN TERMINATION OCCURRED
```

Figure 5.17c. Running the program of Fig. 5.17a. Since the first data card is incorrect, the program attempts to read more data cards than there are. This produces an error. The WATFIV compiler indicates that the error occurred in READ(5,20)NUMB.

5.6. The AND, OR, and NOT Logical Operators

The AND operator allows us to test more than one condition in an IF statement, as the program of Fig. 5.18a shows. This program prints a row of asterisks below the echo-printed value of CARD read from a data card if the value is between 0.0 and 1.0, inclusively. Thus, we want both of two conditions in the IF statements to be true—namely, CARD .GE. 0.0 and CARD .LE. 1.0, before we print the value of CARD. When we sandwich the AND operator between two conditions, *both* conditions must be true in order for the entire condition in the IF statement to be true; if one of these conditions is false, the entire condition is false. We thus write the entire condition as

```
CARD .GE. 0.0 .AND. CARD .LE. 0.0
```

The AND operator, just as do the relational operators, must be preceded and followed by a decimal point.

The data cards for the program are shown in Fig. 5.18b. The constant on the first data card is 0.0. We see from the table for Fig. 5.18a that CARD .GE. 0.0 is true and CARD .LE. 1.0 is true. Since both conditions are true, the entire condition is true. Thus WRITE(6,40), the statement to the right of the IF, is executed and asterisks are printed beneath the echo-printing as shown in Fig. 5.18c. Then the GO TO 10 is executed and the next data card is read. The constant on this card is 1.3. Thus CARD .GE. 0.0 is true, but CARD .LE. 1.0 is false. Since one of the conditions is false, the entire condition is false—as is shown in the table for Fig. 5.18a—and thus asterisks are not printed under the echo-printing of the value of CARD. How the rest of the data cards are processed is also shown in the table. The results of running the program for the remaining data are also shown in Fig. 5.18c.

The relational operations (here GE and LE) are performed before the AND is; i.e., first CARD .GE. 0.0 and CARD .LE. 1.0 are evaluated (conditions with the same priority are evaluated from left to right) and only then is CARD .GE. 0.0 .AND. CARD .LE. 1.0 evaluated. In order to make the IF statement clear, we wrote the two conditions on separate cards. Had we wanted to write the entire condition on one line, it would have aided the person reading the program if we had over-parenthesized and written

```
IF(CARD .GE. 0.0) .AND. (CARD .LE. 1.0 )
```

When a condition in an expression in an IF statement is parenthesized as CARD .GE. 0.0 and CARD .LE. 1.0 are here, the parenthesized condition is evaluated before anything else. If there is more than one parenthesized condition, the conditions are evaluated from left to right. However, since the GE and LE are evaluated before the AND is, the parentheses in (CARD .GE. 0.0) .AND. (CARD .LE. 1.0) do not effect the evaluation of the expression.

The last data card in Fig. 5.18b is a trailer; it will not enter into the selection process in the program.

USING THE AND

```
C   PROGRAM DEMONSTRATES USE OF 'AND'
C   UNDERLINES CARDS BETWEEN 0.0 AND 1.1
C
 10      READ(5,20) CARD
 20      FORMAT(F10.0)
C
         WRITE(6,30) CARD
 30      FORMAT(1X, F10.2)
C           ...TEST FOR TRAILER
         IF( CARD .EQ. -99.0) STOP
            IF(CARD .GE. 0.0   .AND.
       1       CARD .LE. 1.0 ) WRITE(6,40)
 40                            FORMAT(1X,'**********')
            GO TO 10
         END
```

Figure 5.18a. How the AND operator works. In the (CARD .GE. 0.0 .AND. CARD .LE. 1.0), the AND is sandwiched between two conditions. Both conditions must be true if the entire condition is to be true. If one is false, the entire condition is false.

CARD	CARD .GE. 0.0	CARD .LE. 1.0	CARD .GE. 0.0 .AND. CARD .LT. 1.0	Next statement
0.0	T	T	T	WRITE(6,40)
1.3	T	F	F	GO TO 10
0.8	T	T	T	WRITE(6,40)
−1.6	F	T	F	GO TO 10

Table for Fig. 5.18a. Shows that if both conditions are true, the entire condition in the IF will be true. If either condition is false, the entire condition is false.

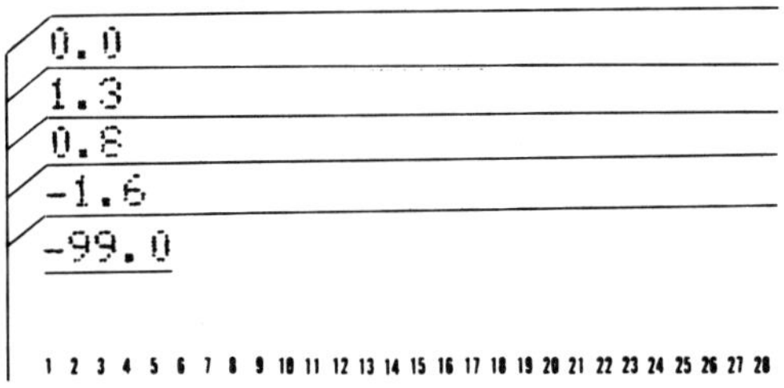

Figure 5.18b. The data cards for Fig. 5.19a. The last card is a trailer. It does not enter into the selection process. It only signals the computer that no more data cards follow.

```
      0.00
**********
      1.30
      0.80
**********
     -1.60
    -99.00
```

Figure 5.18c. Running the program of Fig. 5.18a. The program prints a row of asterisks only beneath the echo printing of those values that are between 0.0 and 1.0, inclusively.

In Fig. 5.19a we show the use of the OR operator. When we sandwich the OR operator between two conditions, if *either* condition is true then the entire condition is true. If both the conditions are true then the entire condition is true. If both conditions are false, then the entire condition is false. The program of Fig. 5.19a prints a row of asterisks beneath the echo printing of the value of CARD read from a data card if the value is either less than zero or greater than 1.0. We thus want either CARD .LT. 0.0 or CARD .GT. 1.0 to be true in order for the entire condition in the IF statement to be true. We thus write the entire condition as

```
CARD .LT. 0.0  .OR.  CARD .GT. 1.0
```

The OR operator must be preceded and followed by a decimal point. The relational operators are performed before the OR is. Thus we did not use parentheses in writing the condition.

The data cards for the program are shown in Fig. 5.19b. The constant on the first data card is 0.2. We see from the table for Fig. 5.19b that both CARD .LT. 0.0 and CARD .GT. 1.0 are false. Thus the entire condition is false. The next statement executed is GO TO 10 (as is shown in the table), and the next data card is read. The constant on this card is 1.3. Thus CARD .LT. 0.0 is false but CARD .GT. 1.0 is true. Therefore the entire condition is true. Thus WRITE(6,40) is executed, as shown in the table for Fig. 5.19a and asterisks are printed beneath 1.3 as is shown in Fig. 5.19c. How the rest of the data cards are processed is also shown in the table. The results of running the program for the remaining data are also shown in Fig. 5.19c.

USING THE OR

```
C   PROGRAM DEMONSTRATES USE OF 'OR'
C   UNDERLINES CARDS WHICH ARE NOT BETWEEN 0.0 AND 1.0
C
 10     READ (5,20) CARD
 20     FORMAT(F10.0)
C
        WRITE(6,30) CARD
 30     FORMAT(1X, F10.2)
C           ...TEST FOR TRAILER
        IF( CARD .EQ. -99.0) STOP
           IF( CARD .LT. 0.0   .OR.
     1        CARD .GT. 1.0 ) WRITE(6,40)
 40                           FORMAT(1X,'**********')
           GO TO 10
        END
```

Figure 5.19a. How the OR operator works. In (CARD .LT. 0.0 .OR. CARD .GT. 1.0) the OR is sandwiched between two conditions. If either of these conditions is true, the entire condition is true. If both are false, the entire condition is false.

CARD	CARD .LT. 0.0	CARD .GT. 1.0	CARD .LT. 0.0 .OR. CARD .GT. 1.0	Next statement
0.2	F	F	F	GO TO 10
1.3	F	T	T	WRITE(6,40)
0.8	F	F	F	GO TO 10
−1.6	T	F	T	WRITE(6,40)

Table for Fig. 5.19a. Shows that if either or both of the conditions are true, the entire condition is true. If both are false, the entire condition is false.

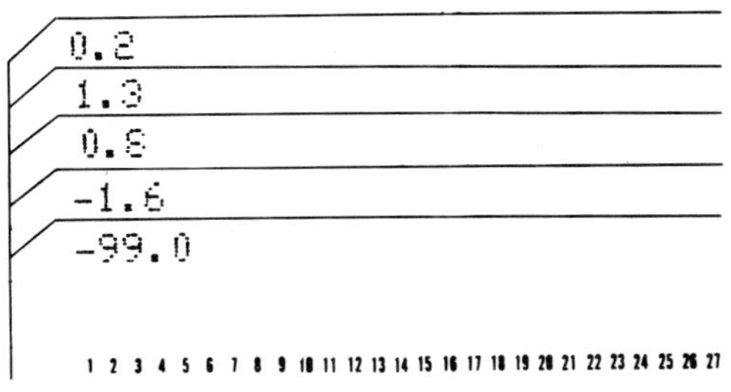

Figure 5.19b. The data cards for Fig. 5.19a.

```
      0.20
      1.30
**********
      0.80
     -1.60
**********
    -99.00
```

Figure 5.19c. Running the program of Fig. 5.19a. The program prints asterisks only beneath the echo-printing of those constants that are less than 0.0 or greater than 1.0.

We now discuss the last of the logical operators, the NOT. The NOT operator changes the logical value (true or false value) of the condition it precedes. Thus if CARD .GT. 0.0 is true, then .NOT. CARD .GT. 0.0 is false. In the absence of parentheses, the NOT operation is performed before the AND and the OR but after the relational operators. The priorities of all the operations are shown in Table 5.1.

In Fig. 5.20a we present another version of the program shown in Fig. 5.19a—it prints values of CARD less than 0.0 or more than 1.0. The present program uses the NOT statement. The data cards are shown in Fig. 5.20b, and results of running the program are shown in Fig. 5.20c. When the constant 1.3 is read, the value of CARD .GE. 0.0 .AND. CARD .LE. 1.0 is false. Since the entire condition is parenthesized the NOT operates on the entire condition and changes its value to true. Thus 1.3 is printed.

If CARD .GE. 0.0 .AND. CARD .LE. 1.0 were not parenthesized, then the precedence of the AND and NOT operators in this condition is as given in Table 5.1: The NOT is performed first, and only then is the AND performed. Thus in

```
.NOT. CARD .GE. 0.0    .AND.    CARD .LE. 1.0
```

first CARD .GE. 0.0 is evaluated; its value is true for 1.3. Thus .NOT. CARD .GE. 0.0 is false. CARD .LE. 1.0 is false, thus the entire condition is false. Therefore 1.3 would not be printed.

LOGICAL OPERATORS USED IN CONDITIONS IN AN IF

Examples:

```
IF (A+B .GT. 4.0) STOP
IF (A+B .GT. C+D .OR. A .EQ. C) GO TO 10
IF (.NOT. A+B .GT. C) WRITE(6,10)A,B
IF ((A .EQ. B) .AND. (C .EQ. D) .OR. (A .EQ. D)) STOP
IF ((A .EQ. B) .OR. (C .EQ. D) .OR. (A .EQ. D)) STOP
```

PRIORITY OF OPERATIONS

Priority	Operator
1st	**
2nd	*,/
3rd	+,−
4th	.EQ., .NE., .GT., .LT., .GE., .LE.
5th	.NOT.
6th	.AND.
7th	.OR.

Table 5.1. The priorities of the operators.

USING THE NOT

```
C  PROGRAM DEMONSTRATES THE USE OF THE 'NOT'
C  UNDERLINES CARDS WHICH ARE NOT BETWEEN 0.0 AND 1.0
C
 10     READ(5,20) CARD
 20     FORMAT( F10.0)
C
        WRITE(6,30) CARD
 30     FORMAT(1X, F10.2)
C           ...TEST FOR TRAILER
        IF ( CARD .EQ. -99.0) STOP
           IF ( .NOT. (CARD .GE. 0.0   .AND.   CARD .LE. 1.0))
     1                   WRITE(6,40)
 40                          FORMAT(1X,'**********')
           GO TO 10
        END
```

Figure 5.20a. How the NOT operator works. The NOT changes the logical value of the condition that immediately follows it, i.e., it changes false to true; and true to false.

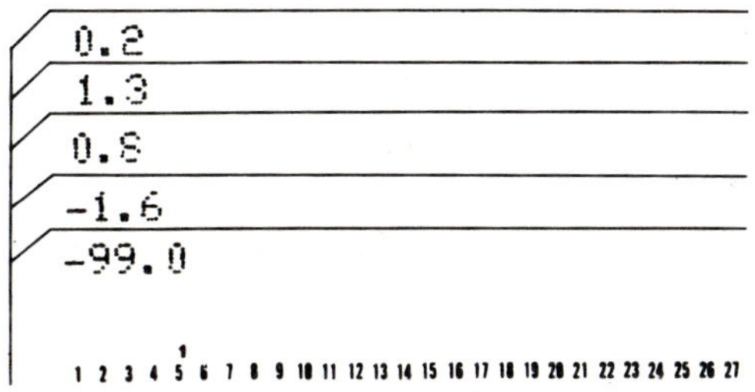

Figure 5.20b. The data cards for Fig. 5.20a.

```
      0.20
      1.30
**********
      0.80
     -1.60
**********
    -99.00
```

Figure 5.20c. Running the program of Fig. 5.20a. The program prints a row of asterisks only beneath the echo-printing of those constants which are less than 0.0 or greater than 1.0.

5.7. LOGICAL Constants and Format

In Fig. 5.21a we show a program that reads the LOGICAL constants T and F from cards and then evaluates a LOGICAL expression; T is the constant that, when punched on a data card, represents the logical value TRUE, and F is the constant that, when punched on a data card, represents the logical value FALSE. The field specification L10 describes a field 10 columns wide in which a LOGICAL constant will appear. The constant T or F can be punched anywhere within this field on the data as shown in Fig. 5.21b. If we want to use a LOGICAL constant in a statement in the program, we must type .TRUE. or .FALSE. as is shown in

```
TEST = .TRUE.   .AND. A   .OR.   B
```

When we print the value of a LOGICAL variable, we again use L format. In Fig. 5.21a we use L format to print the values of A, B, and TEST. The value of the LOGICAL variables are printed right-justified in their field. The results are shown in Fig. 5.21c; we will discuss the results for the first two data cards.

After the first data card is read, the value of A is true and the value of B is also true. Thus .TRUE. .AND. A is true and so .TRUE. .AND. A .OR. B is also true (remember that the AND is executed before the OR is). Therefore the value of TEST is printed as T. After the second data card is read, the value of A is true; but the value of B is false. Thus .TRUE. .AND. A is true and so .TRUE. .AND. A .OR. B is also true. Therefore, the value of TEST is printed as T.

When the computer reads the constant in a field described by L format, it looks for a T or F as the first nonblank character when reading the field from left to right. This is the value it assigns to the appropriate variable. Thus we could have typed the constants as TRUE or FALSE, as shown in Fig. 5.21d.

USING L FORMAT

```
C   SHOWS USE OF 'L FORMAT'
        LOGICAL A, B, TEST
C       ...READ AND WRITE LOGICAL VARIABLES
        DO 30 I=1,4
            READ(5,10) A, B
 10         FORMAT( 2L10 )
            WRITE(6,15) A, B
 15         FORMAT(1X, 'A=', L2, ' B=', L2 )
            TEST = .TRUE.  .AND. A  .OR.  B
            WRITE(6,20) TEST
 20         FORMAT(1X, 'TEST=', L2 )
 30     CONTINUE
        STOP
        END
```

Figure 5.21a. Reading and writing using L format. The constant .TRUE. represents the value "true."

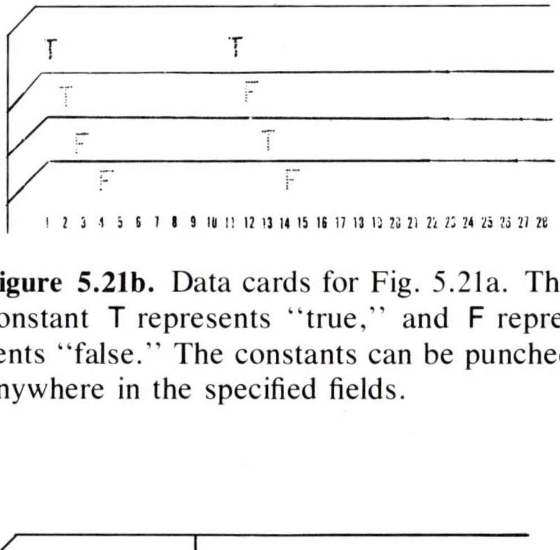

Figure 5.21b. Data cards for Fig. 5.21a. The constant T represents "true," and F represents "false." The constants can be punched anywhere in the specified fields.

```
A= T B= T
TEST= T
A= T B= F
TEST= T
A= F B= T
TEST= T
A= F B= F
TEST= F
```

Figure 5.21c. Running the program of Fig. 5.21a. The values for F and T are printed right-justified in the specified fields.

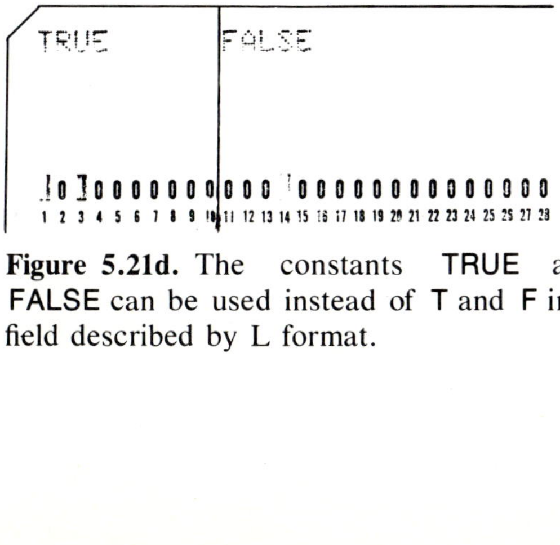

Figure 5.21d. The constants TRUE and FALSE can be used instead of T and F in a field described by L format.

5.8. The LOGICAL Declaration Statement

There is a way of rewriting the program of Fig. 5.16a without using a GO TO statement. It will allow us to read the program from the top to the bottom. We can take

```
IF( NUMB .EQ. -12345678.0 ) GO TO 40
```

and the statements that are executed if the condition in this IF statement is true

```
40    N=N - 1
      AVER=SUM/FLOAT(N)
      WRITE(6,50) N, AVER
      STOP
```

and by eliminating the GO TO, replace these four statements with statements that are now in the loop

```
M=N-1
IF( NUMB .EQ. -12345678.0 ) AVER=SUM/FLOAT(M)
   IF( NUMB .EQ. -12345678.0 ) WRITE(6,20) M, AVER
      IF( NUMB. EQ. -12345678.0) STOP
```

as shown in Fig. 5.22a. Fig. 5.22a also shows the results. We see that the trailer was printed as −12345670.00 instead of as −12345678.00 as we might expect. The reason for this is that this program was run on the WATFIV compiler on the IBM 370. This compiler only outputs at most 7 leading digits and follows the 7 digits with zeros. Note, the data for this program is the same as shown in Fig. 5.16b.

ELIMINATING GO TO **STATEMENTS**

```
C   ELIMINATING GO TO STATEMENTS
      REAL NUMB
      SUM=0.0
C         ...READS , SUMS AND AVERAGES
      DO 30 N=1, 10001
         READ(5,10) NUMB
 10      FORMAT( F10.0 )
         WRITE(6,15) NUMB
 15      FORMAT(1X, F12.2)
C        ...SUBTRACT 1 FROM N SO TRAILER IS NOT COUNTED
         M=N-1
         IF( NUMB .EQ. -12345678.0 ) AVER=SUM/FLOAT(M)
            IF( NUMB .EQ. -12345678.0 ) WRITE(6,20) M, AVER
 20         FORMAT(1X, 'THE AVERAGE OF', I4, ' NUMBERS IS', E15.7)
               IF( NUMB. EQ. -12345678.0) STOP
                  SUM=SUM + NUMB
 30   CONTINUE
C        ...EXECUTED ONLY IF TOO MANY CARDS ARE READ
      WRITE(6,40)
 40   FORMAT(1X, '10001 CARDS READ; MAXIMUM IS 10001')
      STOP
      END
```

```
          16.20
           3.80
          -4.20
           7.89
   -12345670.00
   THE AVERAGE OF    4 NUMBERS IS  0.5922493E 01
```

Figure 5.22a. By repeating an IF statement—here three times—we can avoid using the GO TO we used in Fig. 5.16a. The results of running the program are also shown here. The value—12345678.0 is printed as—12345670.0, because the WATFIV compiler on the IBM 370 prints at most 7 leading digits. Note, the data for this program is the same as in Fig. 5.16b.

We can simplify the writing of this program by using a LOGICAL variable. A LOGICAL variable is one that can assume only two values—true or false. In brief, we take a condition—the expression that we are accustomed to seeing appear in a logical IF—and assign the condition to a LOGICAL variable. We must, however, first declare the variable to be LOGICAL in a LOGICAL declaration statement. For example, in the program of Fig. 5.22a, the condition we wish to assign to a LOGICAL variable is NUMB .EQ. −12345678.0. If we first declare a variable TRAIL to be LOGICAL in

```
LOGICAL TRAIL
```

(TRAIL is an abbreviation for trailer) we can then write

```
TRAIL= NUMB .EQ. -12345678.0
```

This will allow us to now rewrite the three IF statements as

```
IF( TRAIL ) AVER=SUM/FLOAT(M)
IF( TRAIL ) WRITE(6,20) M, AVER
IF( TRAIL ) STOP
```

as now shown in Fig. 5.22b. Fig. 5.22b also shows the results of running the program. The advantage of using a LOGICAL variable in this case is that we only have to write the logical expression once—when we assign it to TRAIL. Then we can use TRAIL in place of the logical expression in all subsequent IF statements where it is required. This also makes it easier for someone reading the program to see that the same logical expression has been used in all three IF statements. As a logical expression becomes more and more complicated, this method becomes more and more useful.

Other examples of LOGICAL variables, are

```
TRAIL= (A .GT. B) .OR. (A .LT. C)
GREAT=(R+3. .GE. 4.0) .AND. ((A .GT. B) .OR. (A .LT. C))
```

If TRAIL appears prior to GREAT in a program, since the definition of GREAT includes (A .GT. B) .OR. (A .LT. C), we can simplify GREAT by writing it as

```
GREAT=(R+3. .GE. 4.0) .AND. TRAIL
```

If a LOGICAL variable LESS which comes after the appearance of GREAT in a program is defined as

```
LESS= .NOT. ((R+3.0 .GE. 4.0) .AND. TRAIL)
```

we may rewrite LESS as

```
LESS= .NOT. GREAT
```

LOGICAL **VARIABLES**

```
C  USING LOGICAL VARIABLES
      LOGICAL TRAIL
      REAL NUMB
      SUM=0.0
C          ...READS , SUMS AND AVERAGES
      DO 30 N=1, 10001
         READ(5,10) NUMB
 10      FORMAT( F10.0 )
         WRITE(6,15) NUMB
 15      FORMAT(1X, F20.2)
         TRAIL= NUMB .EQ. -12345678.0
C        ...SUBTRACT 1 FROM N SO TRAILER IS NOT COUNTED
         M=N-1
         IF( TRAIL ) AVER=SUM/FLOAT(M)
            IF( TRAIL ) WRITE(6,20) M, AVER
 20         FORMAT(1X, 'THE AVERAGE OF', I4, ' NUMBERS IS', E15.7)
                  IF( TRAIL ) STOP
                  SUM=SUM + NUMB
 30   CONTINUE
C        ...EXECUTED ONLY IF TOO MANY CARDS ARE READ
      WRITE(6,40)
 40   FORMAT(1X, '10001 CARDS READ; MAXIMUM IS 10001')
      STOP
      END
```

```
           16.20
            3.80
           -4.20
            7.89
   -12345670.00
   THE AVERAGE OF    4 NUMBERS IS  0.5922493E 01
```

Figure 5.22b. By defining a LOGICAL variable TRAIL we can substitute TRAIL for the condition in the IF statement in the program of Fig. 5.22a. The results of running the program are also shown here for the data of Fig. 5.16b.

We use Fig. 5.23a to demonstrate a common mistake made by beginning programmers. They think that a LOGICAL variable—here TEST—is automatically redefined if the variables used to define it—here L and M—are redefined. Thus, since originally the value of L is 13 and the value of M is 12, the value of TEST in TEST=L .GT. M, is "true"; consequently the program because of

```
IF( TEST ) WRITE(6,10) L, M
```

prints 13 IS GREATER THAN 12 as is shown in Fig. 5.23b. The values of L and M are then redefined (4 and 6 respectively) so that L is no longer greater than M; however, the value of TEST is not redefined, and thus its value is still "true." Therefore, when

```
IF( TEST ) WRITE(6,20) L,M
```

is executed, the computer prints 4 IS GREATER THAN 3 even though the opposite is true.

LOGICAL

The form of the LOGICAL declaration statement is: The word LOGICAL followed by a list of LOGICAL variables. A LOGICAL variable may be dimensioned in a LOGICAL statement. Examples:

```
LOGICAL TEST, TRAIL(3), COND
LOGICAL A1, A2, A3
```

Here TRAIL(3) means that TRAIL is a LOGICAL array which has 3 elements. As opposed to REAL and INTEGER variables, the first letter of a LOGICAL variable does not indicate that the variable is LOGICAL. Thus all LOGICAL variables must appear in a LOGICAL declaration statement.

ERRORS MADE WHEN USING LOGICAL VARIABLES

```
C  DEMONSTRATES A COMMON ERROR MADE WHEN USING LOGICAL VARIABLES
      LOGICAL TEST
      L=13
      M=12
      TEST= L .GT. M
      IF( TEST ) WRITE(6,10) L, M
 10   FORMAT(1X, I3, ' IS GREATER THAN', I3)
C        ...REDEFINE L AND M BUT NOT TEST
      L=4
      M=6
      IF( TEST ) WRITE(6,20) L,M
 20   FORMAT(1X, I3, ' IS GREATER THAN', I3)
      STOP
      END
```

Figure 5.23a. What happens if the variables assigned to a LOGICAL variable are redefined; but the LOGICAL variable itself is not.

```
 13 IS GREATER THAN 12
  4 IS GREATER THAN  6
```

Figure 5.23b. Running the program of Fig. 5.23a. Since TEST is not redefined when L and M are, the value of TEST is still "true" in the second IF. Thus, the wrong result is printed.

5.9. Nested DO Loops

We now investigate a program shown in Fig. 5.24a which calculates X^I for I varying from 1 to 4. This program is similar to the one we studied in Fig. 5.4a, except that the value of X is no longer read from a card—now the value of X itself varies. The program consists of a DO loop within a DO loop, a process called *nesting loops*. The inner loop is the same as the loop in the program of Fig. 5.4a except that the limit of the index is now 4

```
      DO 20 I=1, 4
         Y=X**I
         WRITE(6,10) X, I, Y
10       FORMAT(1X, 'X=', F5.1, 4X, 'X**' , I2, '=', E15.7)
20    CONTINUE
```

The value of X is defined in the outer loop as being the floated value of the outer loop index J

```
DO 40 J=2,5
   X=J
```

The first thing done in any of the loops is to set the value of the outer loop index J equal to 2. Hence the value of X is set equal to 2.0. Next, DO 20 I=1,4 is executed, so the value of I is 1. Thus the computer interprets Y=X**I as Y=2.0**1. The computer executes the WRITE statement next and prints the results

```
X=  2.0     X** 1=  0.2000000E 01
```

as shown in Fig. 5.24b.

The range of the inner DO is executed again, this time the value of I is 2; however, the value of X is still 2.0. Thus the computer interprets Y=X**I as Y=2.0**2 and prints the appropriate results. The next two times the range of the inner DO is executed, the computer interprets Y=X**I as Y=2.0**3 when I=3; and Y=2.0**4, when I=4. Since the range of the inner DO has now been executed the required 4 times, control passes to the next statement, which is WRITE(6,30). Since statement 30, which is FORMAT(1X), contains only a control character, the computer prints a blank line, i.e., skips a line. This will separate the printed results of the next execution of the inner loop from the present results so that the output is easier to read.

Control then passes to 40 CONTINUE. This means that the outer loop index J is now set equal to 3 and the range of the outer loop is executed again. Thus the value of X is now 3.0. The DO statement of the inner loop DO 20 I=1, 4 is now treated as if it had never been executed. Thus the range of the inner loop is executed for I assuming the values 1, 2, 3, and 4, successively. Thus the computer interprets Y=X**I successively as Y=3.0**1, Y=3.0**2, Y=3.0**3, and Y=3.0**4 and prints the appropriate results; then the computer skips a line. The value of J is then increased to 4 and the inner DO loop is again executed for I equaling 1 to 4. Finally, the value of J is increased to 5 and the inner DO loop is executed for I equaling 1 to 4 for the last time.

NESTED DO **LOOPS**

```
C   PROGRAM DEMONSTRATES USE OF NESTED LOOPS
        DO 40 J=2,5
           X=J
           DO 20 I=1, 4
              Y=X**I
              WRITE(6,10) X, I, Y
 10           FORMAT(1X, 'X=', F5.1, 4X, 'X**' , I2, '=', E15.7)
 20        CONTINUE
           WRITE(6,30)
 30        FORMAT(1X)
 40     CONTINUE
        STOP
        END
```

Figure 5.24a. Program uses nested DO loops placing one loop within the range of another loop to calculate X^I. The inner loop (the I loop) varies I from 1 to 4 for each value of X assigned by the outer loop.

```
X=  2.0     X** 1=  0.2000000E 01
X=  2.0     X** 2=  0.4000000E 01
X=  2.0     X** 3=  0.8000000E 01
X=  2.0     X** 4=  0.1600000E 02

X=  3.0     X** 1=  0.3000000E 01
X=  3.0     X** 2=  0.9000000E 01
X=  3.0     X** 3=  0.2700000E 02
X=  3.0     X** 4=  0.8100000E 02

X=  4.0     X** 1=  0.4000000E 01
X=  4.0     X** 2=  0.1600000E 02
X=  4.0     X** 3=  0.6400000E 02
X=  4.0     X** 4=  0.2560000E 03

X=  5.0     X** 1=  0.5000000E 01
X=  5.0     X** 2=  0.2500000E 02
X=  5.0     X** 3=  0.1250000E 03
X=  5.0     X** 4=  0.6250000E 03
```

Figure 5.24b. Running the program of Fig. 5.24a.

The table for Fig. 5.24a shows that for each value of the outer loop index J, the inner loop is executed for I equals 1, 2, 3, and 4. The flow chart for the program is shown in Fig. 5.24c.

We note here that the statement X= J could have been placed in the range of the inner DO loop; i.e., we could have written the inner DO loop as

```
      DO 20 I=1,4
         X=J
         Y=X**I
         WRITE(6,10) X, I, Y
10       FORMAT(1X, 'X=',...
20    CONTINUE
```

However, then X= J would be needlessly executed 3 times each time the I loop is executed. Thus, statements that depend only on the outer loop index and do not increase the clarity of the program if they are inserted in the inner loop—like X= J here—should be placed before the inner loop. We obviously could not have placed Y = X**I before the inner loop since then the value of I would initially be undefined and then later would be incorrectly defined.

If we had placed the WRITE statement, which skips a line, before the inner loop, we could have used one CONTINUE for both loops

```
      DO 30 J=2,5
         X=J
         WRITE(6,10)
10       FORMAT(1X)
         DO 30 I=1,4
            Y=X**J
            WRITE(6,20) X, I, Y
20          FORMAT(1X, 'X=', ...)
30    CONTINUE
```

In fact, we do not have to use any CONTINUE statement at all and could have labeled the second WRITE statement as 30 WRITE(6,20) X, I, Y. Neither of these "short cuts" demonstrate the structure of the nesting, and thus they are not considered good programming style.

In order to enable you to better understand nesting, we compare what we have done with the loops—placing the inner loop entirely within the outer loop—with the practice used by shippers of such items as wastepaper baskets. To conserve space they stack—or "nest"—the baskets one within the other. Just as we can nest many baskets one within the other, we may nest many loops within each other. In order to demonstrate the structure of the loops, we indent nested loops as we showed in Fig. 5.24a.

Iteration of outer loop	J	X	Values of inner loop index
1st	2	2.0	I=1 I=2 I=3 I=4
2nd	3	3.0	I=1 I=2 I=3 I=4
3rd	4	4.0	I=1 I=2 I=3 I=4
4th	5	5.0	I=1 I=2 I=3 I=4

Table for Fig. 5.24a. Shows that for each value of the outer loop index, J, the inner loop is executed for I equals 1, 2, 3, and 4.

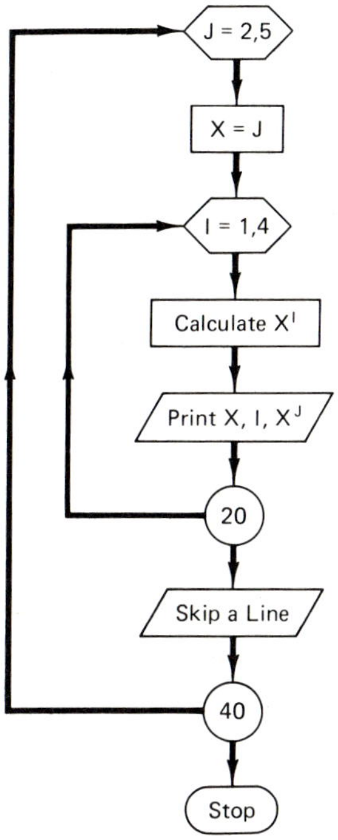

Figure 5.24c. Flow chart for Fig. 5.24a.

When nesting loops, we must take care to use a different index for each loop. If by mistake we use the same index for nested loops, we will get an error message.

A nested loop must be completely contained in the outer loop. Thus since DO 20 J=2,5 precedes DO 40 I=1,4, the reverse order must be followed in the placement of the CONTINUE statements. Thus 40 CONTINUE must precede 20 CONTINUE. However, in Fig. 5.25a we have reversed this order. As a result when the program is run, the computer prints an error message, as shown in the figure.

IMPROPER NESTING

```
      C   PROGRAM DEMONSTRATES IMPROPER NESTING OF DO LOOPS
      C
                DO 20 J=2,5
                   X=J
                   DO 40 I=1, 4
                      Y=X**I
                      WRITE(6,10) X, I, Y
         10           FORMAT(1X, 'X=', F5.1, 4X, 'X**' , I2, '=', E15.7)
         20        CONTINUE
***ERROR***   IMPROPERLY NESTED DO-LOOPS
                   WRITE(6,30)
         30        FORMAT(1X)
         40     CONTINUE
                STOP
                END
```

Figure 5.25. The CONTINUE for the inner loop must precede the CONTINUE for the outer loop. Thus 40 CONTINUE should precede 20 CONTINUE. Since we have incorrectly nested the loops, the compiler prints an error message.

In Figs. 5.26a and 5.26b we show how loops can be nested. One can transfer out of a nested loop into the range of a loop in which it is nested, as shown in Fig. 5.26a. Thus GO TO 40 is allowed. What one cannot do, however, is to transfer into the range of an inner loop, as shown in Fig. 5.26b. One must first execute the DO statement of the inner DO. Otherwise, the loop index for the inner loop would be undefined. Thus GO TO 50 and GO TO 80 in this figure are both illegal.

Once in a DO loop you cannot change the values of the loop's parameters: the value of the loop index, its initial and limiting value, or its increment. Thus given DO 20 I= L,M,N one could not write for instance any of the following in the range of the DO: I=I + 1, L=3, M=L+4, or N=A.

LEGAL TRANSFERS INTO AND OUT OF LOOPS

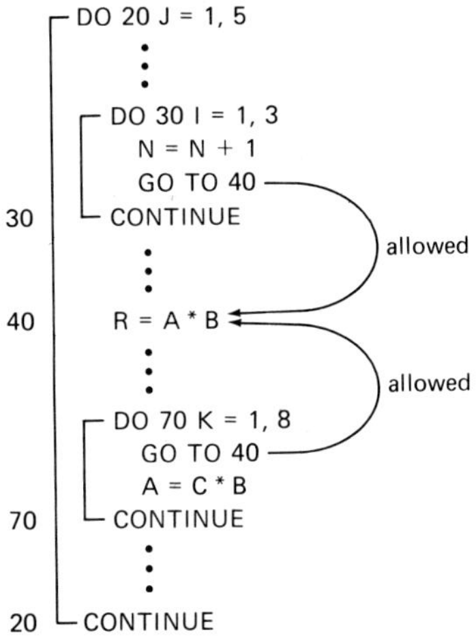

Figure 5.26a. You can transfer out of the range of an inner loop into the range of the outer loop in which the inner loop is nested.

ILLEGAL TRANSFERS INTO AND OUT OF LOOPS

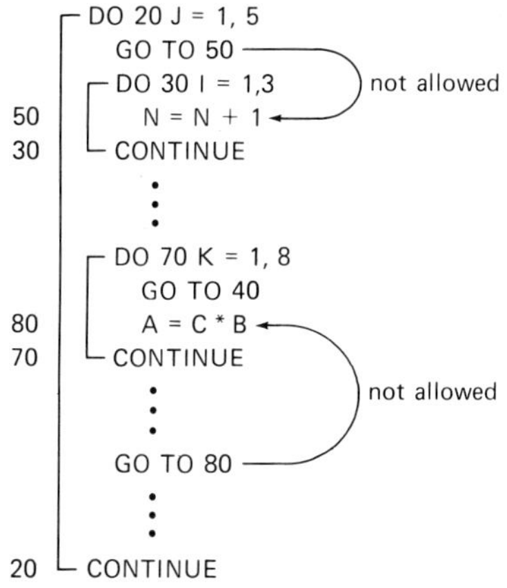

Figure 5.26b. You cannot transfer into the range of a DO loop for which the loop index is undefined, e.g., GO TO 50. Here I is undefined because its DO has not been executed. On the other hand, for GO TO 80, K is undefined because its loop has already been completely executed. On many compilers, if you transfer out of the range of a DO you can transfer back into it, the reason being that the loop index is still defined.

5.10. Applications of the DO Loop

This section is optional; the reader can skip it without interrupting the continuity of the book.

Our first application of the DO loop will be to a program that calculates the statistic called chi squared. It is written mathematically as χ^2. Chi squared enables us to test a theoretical model by comparing it with experimental data. Chi squared is defined as

$$\chi^2 = \sum_i (observed_i - expected_i)^2/expected_i$$

where observed$_i$ and expected$_i$ are the experimental and theoretical quantities in the ith interval. The symbol $\sum_i^N$ signifies that a summation will be done on the quantity that appears to the right of the summation with the index i varying from 1 to N. For instance, if $N=2$ then $\chi^2 = (observed_1 - expected_1)^2/expected_1 + (observed_2 - expected_2)^2/expected_2$.

As an example we will use χ^2 to test whether a die* is fair. In this case, since a die has 6 faces, we would be placing the observations into 6 different intervals. If we rolled the die 60 times, we would theoretically expect the die to land 10 times in each of the 6 intervals if the die is fair. Thus the expected value for each interval is 10. The observed quantities for each interval would be what we actually observe after the die is rolled 60 times: If we observed 12 ones, 8 twos, 13 threes, 7 fours, 9 fives, and 11 sixes, then χ^2 would be calculated as

$$\chi^2 = \frac{(12-10)^2}{10} + \frac{(8-10)^2}{10} + \frac{(13-10)^2}{10} + \frac{(7-10)^2}{10} + \frac{(9-10)^2}{10} + \frac{(11-10)^2}{10}$$

The program of Fig. 5.27a calculates χ^2 for up to 100 intervals. The observed and the expected quantities for a given interval are punched on one data card. The data card for the last interval is followed by a trailer that has a zero punched in the first field. Hence the number of data cards (excluding the trailer) equals the number of intervals.

* Die is the singular of dice. If a die is fair, there is equal probability that it will land on any of its six faces; otherwise, it is considered loaded.

CALCULATING χ^2

```
C    CALCULATES CHI-SQUARED FOR A MAXIMUM OF 100 DATA CARDS.
C    INITIALIZE CHI-SQUARED SUM.
       CHI2=0.0
C          ...READ AND CALCLATE CHI-SQUARED.
       DO 20 I=1,101
          READ(5,10) OBSERV, EXPECT
 10       FORMAT( 2F10.0 )
          WRITE(6,15) OBSERV, EXPECT
 15       FORMAT(1X, 2F12.2)
C          ...TEST FOR TRAILER
          IF( OBSERV .EQ. -12345678.0 ) GO TO 40
             CHI2=CHI2 + (OBSERV-EXPECT)**2 / EXPECT
 20    CONTINUE
C          ...WHEN THE DO TERMINATES BY ITSELF, YOU HAVE INPUTTED
C          ...MORE THEN THE MAXIMUM ALLOWABLE # OF CARDS
       WRITE(6,30)
 30    FORMAT(1X, 'TOO MANY DATA CARDS.' )
       STOP
C
C          ...PRINT RESULTS FOR VALID TERMINATION
C
C          ...SUBTRACT 1 FROM I SO NOT TO COUNT TRAILER
 40    INTER = I - 1
       WRITE(6,50) CHI2, INTER
 50    FORMAT(1X, 'CHI-SQUARED=', E16.7, ' FOR', I3, ' INTERVALS.' )
       STOP
       END
```

Figure 5.27a. Program calculates χ^2 for up to 100 intervals. $\chi^2 = \Sigma_i$ (observed$_i$ − expected$_i$)^2/expected$_i$.

The program calculates χ^2 using

```
CHI2=CHI2 + (OBSERV-EXPECT)**2 / EXPECT
```

Each time a nontrailer data card is read by READ(5,10) OBSERV, EXPECT, a term of the form

```
(OBSERV-EXPECT)**2 / EXPECT
```

calculated from the constants on that data card, is added to CHI2. When the trailer is read, control is transferred from a statement in the range of the DO

```
IF( OBSERV .EQ. -12345678.0 ) GO TO 40
```

to one outside the loop

```
40    INTER = I - 1
```

as shown in the flow chart (Fig. 5.27b). Then the resultant χ^2 is printed as shown in Fig. 5.27c. This result is for 6 intervals. The interpretation of χ^2 is beyond the scope of this book. This program was given simply as an example of converting a statistical test into a program.

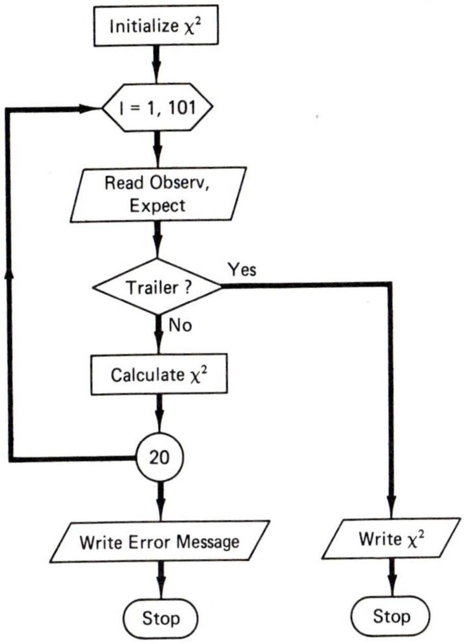

Figure 5.27b. Flow chart for Fig. 5.27a.

```
      12.00          10.00
       8.00          10.00
      13.00          10.00
      11.00          10.00
       9.00          10.00
       7.00          10.00
-12345670.00          0.00
CHI-SQUARED=     0.2799998E 01 FOR  6 INTERVALS.
```

Figure 5.27c. Results of running the program of Fig. 5.27a.

Our next application of the DO loop is to a program that calculates the X and Y coordinates of a projectile as a function of the time T elapsed since it was fired. The time will vary from T equals 1 to the time TMAX required for the projectile to land.

If a projectile is fired with an initial velocity V at an angle θ with the horizontal, it has an initial velocity VX in the X direction given by VX = V*COS(R), where R is the value of θ in radians. It has an initial velocity VY in the Y direction given as VY = V*SIN(R) as is shown in Fig. 5.28a. The X and Y motions of the projectile can be treated separately. Since there is no gravity in the X direction, the distance traveled in this direction after a time T is simply the product of the velocity VX multiplied by the time, T, i.e., X=VX*T1 where T1 is the floated value of the loop index T. The motion in the Y direction can be treated as a falling body. Its height Y, above the ground after a time T1 is given by

```
Y=VY * T1 - 16.0 * (T1**2)
```

How do we find the time TMAX the projectile is in the air? We assume the projectile is fired on a flat plane, so that it lands on the same level that it was fired from. Thus when it lands, Y would equal 0. We set Y equal to 0 and solve the previous equation for T, and we obtain T=VY/16.0. This is the value of TMAX*.

* Another solution to Y = 0 is T = 0. All this solution means is that another time that the projectile is at Y = 0, is when it is initially fired.

CALCULATING TRAJECTORIES

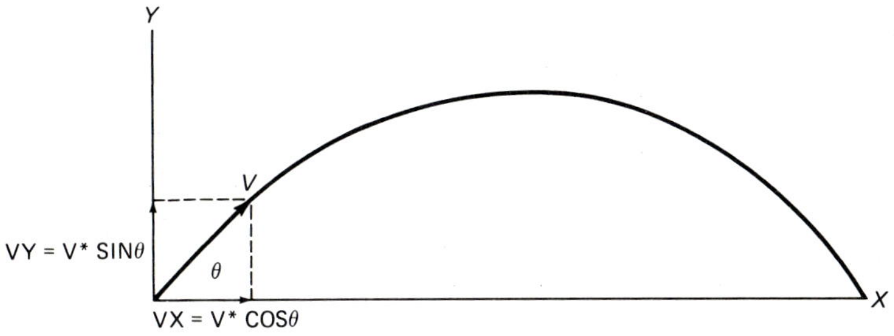

Figure 5.28a. Diagram of a projectile being fired at an angle Θ. Its velocity can be resolved into an X component and Y component.

In the program of Fig. 5.28b after we calculate VY/16.0, we add 0.5 to it. Thus when we assign the result to the INTEGER variable TMAX (the limit of the loop index in DO 50 T = 1, TMAX), the result is rounded to the nearest integer. We calculate X and Y in the DO loop. The results of running the program are shown in Fig. 5.28c.

Note we have used T and TMAX in this program because these are the variables that are usually used in physics. These variables are normally REALs. Because we are using them as the loop index and its limit, respectively, we declare them to be INTEGER in the INTEGER statement.

```
C       PROGRAM CALCULATES X AND Y COORDINATES FOR A PROJECTILE
C       TMAX= TIME TO ATTAIN MAXIMUM  X-DISTANCE (RANGE)
C
        INTEGER T, TMAX
C          ...READ INITIAL VALOCITY AND INITIAL ANGLE
        READ(5,10) V, THETA
 10     FORMAT( 2F10.0 )
        WRITE(6,20) V,THETA
 20     FORMAT(1X, 'INITIAL VELOCITY=', F15.7, 4X,'INITIAL ANGLE',F10.2)
C          ...LABEL TABLE
        WRITE(6,30)
 30     FORMAT(T9, 'X', T28, 'Y', T42, 'T' )
C          ...CONVERT TO RADIANS
           R=(3.141593/180.0) * THETA
C          ...CALCULATE X AND Y INITIAL VELOCITIES.
        VX= V * COS(R)
        VY= V * SIN(R)
C          ...CALCULATE   TMAX    AND ROUND TO THE NEAREST INTEGER.
        TMAX= (VY/16.0) + 0.5
C          ...CALCULATE X AND Y COORDINATES
        DO 50 T=1,TMAX
           T1=T
           X=VX * T1
           Y=VY * T1 - 16.0 * (T1**2)
           WRITE(6,40) X, Y, T1
 40        FORMAT(1X, 2E16.7, F10.2)
 50     CONTINUE
C          ... CALCULATE AND PRINT RANGE
        RANGE=VX * (VY/16.0)
        WRITE(6,60) RANGE
 60     FORMAT(1X, 'RANGE=', E16.7)
        STOP
        END
```

Figure 5.28b. Calculates the X and Y coordinates of a projectile fired at an angle THETA with a velocity V.

```
INITIAL VELOCITY=  0.3000000E 03     INITIAL ANGLE      40.00
        X                  Y               T
   0.2298133E 03   0.1768363E 03        1.00
   0.4596265E 03   0.3216724E 03        2.00
   0.6894397E 03   0.4345088E 03        3.00
   0.9192532E 03   0.5153450E 03        4.00
   0.1149066E 04   0.5641814E 03        5.00
   0.1378880E 04   0.5810176E 03        6.00
   0.1608693E 04   0.5658540E 03        7.00
   0.1838506E 04   0.5186902E 03        8.00
   0.2068320E 04   0.4395264E 03        9.00
   0.2298133E 04   0.3283628E 03       10.00
   0.2527946E 04   0.1851990E 03       11.00
   0.2757760E 04   0.1003540E 02       12.00
RANGE=    0.2769771E 04
```

Figure 5.28c. Running the program of Fig. 5.28a.

In Fig. 5.29a we calculate the X and Y coordinates of a projectile given its initial velocity V, but, as opposed to the program of Fig. 5.28b, we now vary the initial angle THETA so that it varies from 15 to 75 degrees in steps of 15 degrees. Thus THETA is now the index of an outer loop which begins with

```
DO 50 THETA = 15,75,15
```

TRAJECTORIES WITH VARIABLE INITIAL ANGLES

```
C       PROGRAM CALCULATES X AND Y COORDINATES FOR A PROJECTILE
C   VARYING THE INITIAL ANGLE THETA FROM 15 TO 75 DEGREES
C       TMAX= TIME TO ATTAIN MAXIMUM  X-DISTANCE (RANGE)
        INTEGER T, TMAX, THETA
C           ...READ INITIAL VALOCITY, V
        READ(5,10) V
 10     FORMAT(  F10.0 )
        DO 50 THETA = 15,75,15
            WRITE(6,20) V,THETA
 20         FORMAT(1X, 'INITIAL VELOCITY=', E15.7, ' INITIAL ANGLE', I3)
C               ...LABEL TABLE
            WRITE(6,30)
 30         FORMAT(T9, 'X', T28, 'Y', T42, 'T' )
C               ...CONVERT TO RADIANS
                R=(3.141593/180.0) * THETA
C               ...CALCULATE X AND Y INITIAL VELOCITIES.
            VX= V * COS(R)
            VY= V * SIN(R)
C               ...CALCULATE  TMAX      AND ROUND TO THE NEAREST INTEGER.
            TMAX= (VY/16.0) + 0.5
C               ...CALCULATE X AND Y COORDINATES
            DO 40 T=1,TMAX
                T1=T
                X=VX * T1
                Y=VY * T1 - 16.0 * (T1**2)
                WRITE(6,35) X, Y, T1
 35             FORMAT(1X, 2E16.7, F10.2)
 40         CONTINUE
C               ... CALCULATE AND PRINT RANGE
            RANGE=VX * (VY/16.0)
            WRITE(6,45) RANGE
 45         FORMAT(1X, 'RANGE=', E16.7)
 50     CONTINUE
        STOP
        END
```

Figure 5.29a. Program calculates the X and Y coordinates for a projectile fired at an angle THETA and velocity V. The angle THETA is the outer loop index and varies from 15° to 75° in steps of 15°. The inner loop index is the time. Both of these variables were previously declared to be INTEGER.

For each value of THETA, the inner loop which begins with

```
DO 40 T=1,TMAX
```

is executed from 1 to TMAX. In Fig. 5.29b we print only the last line of the table for each THETA greater than 45°; for smaller values of THETA we print the entire table. We see that the maximum value of X is obtained when* THETA is 45°. The reason we obtain a negative value of Y (−0.1177148E 02) for T equals 5.00 and θ equals 15° is that the maximum value of T for this set of data is actually less than 5.00. Consequently, the projectile reaches the ground for a value of T less than 5.00; and at T equals 5.00 the projectile (if it is no restrained by the ground) is below ground level. The reason that this difficulty arises is that we obtained TMAX by rounding.

* Under actual conditions, this is not true because of many factors, the easiest to understand being the air resistance. In practice, in order to obtain the maximum range, projectiles are fired at large initial angles so that they can quickly get into the region of the atmosphere where the air resistance is very small.

```
INITIAL VELOCITY=  0.3000000E 03 INITIAL ANGLE 15
          X                  Y                 T
   0.2897776E 03    0.6164571E 02          1.00
   0.5795552E 03    0.9129141E 02          2.00
   0.8693328E 03    0.8893712E 02          3.00
   0.1159110E 04    0.5458276E 02          4.00
   0.1448888E 04   -0.1177148E 02          5.00
RANGE=    0.1406249E 04
INITIAL VELOCITY=  0.3000000E 03 INITIAL ANGLE 30
          X                  Y                 T
   0.2598074E 03    0.1340000E 03          1.00
   0.5196147E 03    0.2360000E 03          2.00
   0.7794221E 03    0.3060000E 03          3.00
   0.1039229E 04    0.3440000E 03          4.00
   0.1299037E 04    0.3500000E 03          5.00
   0.1558844E 04    0.3240000E 03          6.00
   0.1818652E 04    0.2660000E 03          7.00
   0.2078459E 04    0.1760000E 03          8.00
   0.2338266E 04    0.5400000E 02          9.00
RANGE=    0.2435694E 04
INITIAL VELOCITY=  0.3000000E 03 INITIAL ANGLE 45
          X                  Y                 T
   0.2121320E 03    0.1961320E 03          1.00
   0.4242639E 03    0.3602639E 03          2.00
   0.6363960E 03    0.4923960E 03          3.00
   0.8485278E 03    0.5925281E 03          4.00
   0.1060660E 04    0.6606599E 03          5.00
   0.1272792E 04    0.6967920E 03          6.00
   0.1484924E 04    0.7009241E 03          7.00
   0.1697056E 04    0.6730562E 03          8.00
   0.1909188E 04    0.6131880E 03          9.00
   0.2121320E 04    0.5213201E 03         10.00
   0.2333452E 04    0.3974521E 03         11.00
   0.2545584E 04    0.2415842E 03         12.00
   0.2757716E 04    0.5371606E 02         13.00
RANGE=    0.2812499E 04
INITIAL VELOCITY=  0.3000000E 03 INITIAL ANGLE 60
RANGE=    0.2435695E 04
INITIAL VELOCITY=  0.3000000E 03 INITIAL ANGLE 75
RANGE=    0.1406252E 04
```

Figure 5.29b. Running the program of Fig. 5.29a. For values of THETA greater than 45°, we have listed the coordinates X, Y, and T for the maximum value of X only. The reason that the last value of Y is negative for the first set of data is that we obtain TMAX by rounding.

5.11. A WATFIV-S Feature: The IF-THEN-ELSE (The Block IF)

As of January 1977,* the proposed revision of ANS Standard FORTRAN will contain what is known as the IF-THEN-ELSE. The IF-THEN-ELSE differs from the IF statement in that if the condition in the IF-THEN-ELSE is true, more than one statement (in other words, a block of statements) are executed. Hence, the IF-THEN-ELSE is also known as the *block* IF. The present version of ANS Standard FORTRAN does not include the block IF; however, an extension of WATFIV called WATFIV-S does include the block IF.

The block IF allows you to write programs in a top to bottom manner without having to use several consecutive IF statements, as we have previously done. Writing a program in a top to bottom manner is one of the principles of *structured programming*, a subject which we will discuss in detail in Chapter 10. The S in WATFIV-S stands for *S*tructured. The simplest form of the block IF is shown in Fig. 5.30. It begins with an IF-THEN statement, here

```
IF( NUMB .EQ. -12345678.0 ) THEN
```

and ends with an END IF statement. The condition used in the block IF—here, NUMB .EQ. −12345678.0—appears in parentheses and is sandwiched between the word IF and the word THEN.

The program shown in Fig. 5.30 is the latest version of the program we have written that averages the numbers read from the data cards. The data for the program would be the same as shown in Fig. 5.16b. The statements in the block IF are

```
IF( NUMB .EQ. -12345678.0 ) THEN
   AVER=SUM / FLOAT( N-1 )
   WRITE(6,20) N, AVER
20 FORMAT(1X, 'THE AVERAGE OF ', I6, 'NUMBERS IS', E15.7)
   STOP
END IF
```

If the condition in the IF-THEN is true, then the block of statements sandwiched between the IF-THEN and the END IF are executed. Thus in Fig. 5.30, if the trailer is encountered, the IF-THEN condition is true, so the program calculates and then prints the average of all the numbers read. It then stops. If this block of statements did not contain a STOP, the computer would then proceed to the statement following the END IF.

On the other hand, if the condition in the IF-THEN is false, then control is immediately transferred to the statement following the END IF (in Fig. 5.30, SUM=SUM+NUMB); therefore, the block of statements sandwiched between the IF-THEN and the END IF are not executed. Thus, in Fig. 5.30, if a trailer is not encountered, the program does not execute the block that averages, prints the result, and then stops. Instead, it executes SUM=SUM+NUMB, where, as we remember it, it adds the number just read to SUM.

* Loren P. Meissner, *SIGPLAN Notices*, Jan. 1977, p. 93.

USING THE IF-THEN

```
C USING THE IF-THEN
      REAL NUMB
      SUM=0.0
C     ...READ AND AVERAGE
      DO 30 N=1,10001
         READ(5,10) NUMB
 10      FORMAT( F10.0 )
         IF( NUMB .EQ. -12345678.0 ) THEN
            AVER=SUM / FLOAT( N-1 )
            WRITE(6,20) N, AVER
 20         FORMAT(1X, 'THE AVERAGE OF ', I6, 'NUMBERS IS', E15.7)
            STOP
         END IF
C
         SUM=SUM + NUMB
 30   CONTINUE
C     ...EXECUTED ONLY IF TOO MANY CARDS ARE READ
      WRITE(6,40)
 40   FORMAT(1X, '1000 CARDS READ, MAXIMUM IS 10,000' )
      STOP
      END
```

Figure 5.30. The averaging program rewritten using the IF-THEN. If the condition in the IF-THEN is true, then the block of statements ending with END IF is executed. If the condition is false, then the block of statements is skipped and the statement following END IF is executed. The data for this program is the same as shown in Fig. 5.16b.

The full-fledged form of the block IF is the IF-THEN-ELSE. This allows you to execute one block of statements if the condition in the IF-THEN is true, and another block of statements if the condition is false. After one of these blocks is executed, and if the block does not contain a STOP, the program executes the statements which follow the IF END.

In Fig. 5.31 we see an example of an IF-THEN-ELSE. If the condition A .NE. B is true, then the block

```
A=A + B
C=A**2
```

is executed. Control is then transferred to the statement following the END IF, that is, WRITE (6,10) A, B, C. If the condition is false, then the block of statements following the ELSE, i.e.,

```
C=A * B
A=B + C
```

is executed. Control is then transferred to the statement following the END IF.

IF-THEN-ELSE

The form of the IF-THEN-ELSE is: IF (; followed by a condition; followed by) THEN; this is followed by a block of statements that are executed if the condition is true. This is followed by ELSE, which appears on a separate card; this is followed by a block of statements that are executed if the condition is false; this is followed by IF END which appears on a separate card. Example:

```
IF (A .NE. B) THEN
   A=A+B
   C=A**2
ELSE
   C = A*B
   A = B + C
END IF
```

If there is no second block of statements to be executed, the ELSE is omitted and the block IF becomes an IF-THEN.

USING THE IF-THEN-ELSE

```
      IF( A .NE. B ) THEN
         A=A + B
         C=A**2
      ELSE
         C=A * B
         A=B + C
      END IF
      WRITE(6,10) A, B, C
10    FORMAT(1X, 3F10.0 )
```

Figure 5.31. If the condition in the IF-THEN is true, then the block of statements preceding the ELSE is executed. Then the statements after the END IF are executed. If the condition is false, then the block of statements between the ELSE and the END IF are executed. Then the statements after the END IF are executed.

5.12. Another WATFIV-S Feature: The WHILE Loop

A feature of WATFIV-S which in many ways aids in structured programming is the WHILE-DO. The WHILE-DO is neither in the present version nor in the proposed revised version of ANS Standard FORTRAN.

In Fig. 5.32 we use the WHILE-DO in still another version of the program that averages numbers read from data cards. The data is the same as shown in Fig. 5.16b

```
WHILE( NUMB .NE. -12345678.0 ) DO
   N=N + 1
   SUM = SUM + NUMB
   READ(5,20) NUMB
END WHILE
```

The WHILE-DO and the END WHILE statements determine a loop which is called a WHILE loop. Each time, before the computer executes the block of statements sandwiched between the WHILE-DO and the END WHILE, it checks whether the condition in the WHILE-DO—here, NUMB .EQ. -12345678.0—is false. If it is false, the computer does not execute the WHILE loop. If it is true, the computer executes the loop. For this reason, one should place the statement that can alter the condition in the WHILE-DO at the end of the block, immediately before the END WHILE. Since the value of NUMB affects this condition, we place the statement which changes the value of NUMB—READ(5,20)NUMB—at the end of the block. Thus, when the trailer is encountered, its value is not added to SUM and it does not affect the card count N. As opposed to the DO loop, the WHILE loop does not have a built-in index. If we want to count the number of cards read, we must place a counter in the WHILE loop. Thus N = N + 1 is in the loop.

The variables that appear in the condition in the WHILE-DO statement must have a value before the WHILE-DO statement is executed the first time. Thus we have preceded the WHILE loop with READ (5,10) NUMB. Also since N = N + 1 and SUM = SUM + NUMB appear in the loop, we initialize N and SUM before the loop. The first value of NUMB read here is added to SUM and the value of N is increased to 1, the first time the loop is executed. The second time the loop is executed, the value of N is increased to 2. This process continues until the trailer is encountered. The computer then calculates the average, prints the results, and then stops.

We remark here, that this program does not exhibit integrity for the following reason. If the first card is the trailer, the computer will not execute the WHILE loop at all. Thus the value of N will remain zero, and the computer in evaluating AVER = SUM/FLOAT(N) will be dividing by zero. This will produce an error.

Note, if the condition in the WHILE-DO is not altered by one or more statements in the WHILE loop, the loop will continue to execute forever; so beware! The WHILE-DO can be used to advantage to rewrite the programs presented in Chapter 4. We leave this as an exercise for the reader.

WHILE-DO

The form of the WHILE-DO is: WHILE(; followed by a condition; followed by)DO. Examples:

```
WHILE(NUMB .EQ.-12345678.0 .AND. N .LT. 100) DO
WHILE(TEST) DO
```

USING THE WHILE **LOOP**

```
C  USING THE WHILE LOOP
      REAL NUMB
      SUM=0.0
      N=0
C     ...READ FIRST CONSTANT
      READ(5,10) NUMB
 10   FORMAT( F10.0 )
C     ...READ AND SUM LOOP
      WHILE( NUMB .NE. -12345678.0 ) DO
         N=N + 1
         SUM = SUM + NUMB
         READ(5,20) NUMB
      END WHILE
C     ...AVERAGING NUMBERS
      AVER=SUM / FLOAT( N )
      WRITE(6,30) N, AVER
 30   FORMAT(1X, 'THE AVERAGE OF', I6, 'NUMBERS IS', E15.5 )
      STOP
      END
```

Figure 5.32. The averaging program rewritten using a WHILE loop. If the condition in the WHILE-DO is true, then the block of statements between the WHILE-DO and the END WHILE is executed. This continues until the condition is false, then the statement following the END WHILE is executed.

PROBLEMS

1. What is wrong with each of the following DO statements?

(a) DO 10 F = 1, 3, 2
(b) DO 10 JAK = 8, 2, −1
(c) DO 10 JAK = −2, 10, 3
(d) DO 10 JAK = 1, 10, .01
(e) DO 10 JAK = 0, 10, 3
(f) DO 10 JAK = 1, J + L, 3
(g) DO 10 I = 1, 3
(h) DO 10 J = NUM, F, G

2. Using a DO loop write a program that calculates

$$Y = \sum_{N=0}^{M} A_N X^N$$

where $A_N = 2N + 1$. The values of M and X are read from data cards.

3. Using a DO loop, write a program that calculates the sum of the odd numbers from 1 to a number read by the program.

4. What is wrong with the following program that should calculate $M!$?

```
        REAL M
        READ(5,10) M
10      FORMAT(I10)
        DO 30 I=1, M
        P = P*M
        WRITE(5,20) M, P
20      FORMAT(I10, '!=', F10.3)
30      CONTINUE
        STOP
        END
```

5. Using a DO loop write a program that calculates the products of the odd numbers from 1 to M, where M is read by the program.

6. As in chapter 4, problem 7, a set of data cards consists of a group of data cards, a trailer, the same group of data cards, and a trailer. Using DO loops, write a program that calculates the average $\bar{x}$ and the variance V.

$$\bar{x} = \frac{\sum_i x_i}{N} \qquad V = \frac{\sum_i (x_i - \bar{x})^2}{N-1}$$

7. Using the data cards described in problem 6, write a program that counts how many numbers read are less than the average.

8. Using a DO loop, write a program that calculates the area between $y=x^2$ and the x-axis for x varying between -2 and 2.

9. Write a program that produces a multiplication table for the integers from 1 to 8.

10. What is wrong with the following doubly nested loop?

```
      DO  40  I = 1, 5
          DO  20 J = 1, 5
              DO 30 K = 1, 5
                  V = I * J * K
                  WRITE(6,10) V
10                FORMAT(1X, F10.0)
20            CONTINUE
30        CONTINUE
40    CONTINUE
```

11. Social Security numbers have 3 parts, e.g.,

627 - 08 - 1244

where the first part has 3 digits, the second part has 2 digits, and the third part has 4 digits. Write a program that combines these 3 parts read in 3 different fields into one number, e.g., 627-08-1244 would become 627081244.

12. Write a program that takes the output of problem 11, i.e., a 9 digit number, and breaks it down into the Social Security format.

13. A die is tossed 60 times. Since a die has 6 faces, the expected number of times each face appears is 10. Assuming the result of each toss is punched on a card, write a program that reads these cards and calculates chi square.

14. Using a WHILE loop, write a program like the one in Fig. 4.4a that sums the integers from 1 to NMAX.

15. Using a WHILE loop, write a program like the one in Fig. 4.5a that sums 0.0, 0.2, 0.4, 0.6, 0.8, and 1.0.

16. Using a WHILE loop, write a program like the one in Fig. 4.6a that produces a table for the normal distribution. The values of Z should be generated by the program itself.

17. Using a WHILE loop, write a program like the one in Fig. 4.7a that calculates the area under the normal curve.

6

Subscripted Variables, the DATA Statement, and the Implied DO Loop

6.1 Subscripted Variables

In Fig. 6.1a we present a simple program that averages the four numbers, it reads from data cards. Figure 6.1b shows the data card read by the program. The table for Fig. 6.1a shows how the variables are assigned values in the program, and the results are shown in Fig. 6.1c. There is nothing new in the program. In fact, we could have written it after Chapter 3. At present, the variable names are themselves constant; i.e., the names cannot change during the execution of the program.

MOTIVATING USE OF ARRAYS

```
C   PROGRAM CALCULATES THE AVERAGE OF 4 NUMBERS
C
        READ(5,10) A, B, C, D
 10     FORMAT(4F10.0)
        WRITE(6,15) A, B, C, D
 15     FORMAT(1X, 4F12.2)
        AVER=( A + B + C + D) / 4.0
        WRITE(6,20) AVER
 20     FORMAT(1X, 'AVERAGE=', E15.7)
        STOP
        END
```

Figure 6.1a. A simple program that reads four numbers and then calculates their average.

Statement executed	A	B	C	D
READ	10.1	7.2	3.6	9.4
Assignment	10.1	7.2	3.6	9.4
WRITE	10.1	7.2	3.6	9.4

Table for Fig. 6.1a. The values assigned to the variables in the program of Fig. 6.1a.

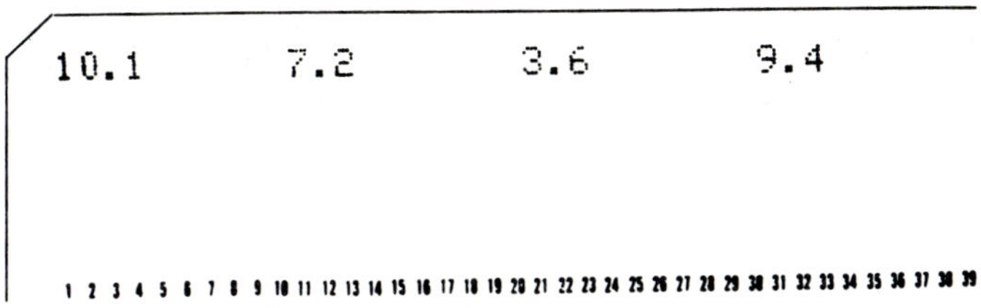

Figure 6.1b. The data cards for Fig. 6.1a.

```
        10.10        7.20        3.60        9.40
 AVERAGE=  0.7574993E 01
```

Figure 6.1c. Running the program of Fig. 6.1a.

We now present a different way of representing variables. It will enable us to make part of the variable name itself a variable and thus allow us to change the name of a variable in a given statement during the execution of the program. In Fig. 6.2a we rewrite the program using this new technique.

The variable X in

```
READ(5,10)  X(1), X(2), X(3), X(4)
```

is called an array. It consists of four parts called the *elements* of the array. They are: X(1), X(2), X(3), and X(4); in FORTRAN each element is called a *subscripted variable*. We see that part of the name of a subscripted variable—the part that appears between the parentheses—can be changed. We call that part the *subscript*. The subscript must be an INTEGER. We see in the READ statement that the subscript assumes the values 1, 2, 3, and 4. When the READ statement is executed, all four elements are defined, as shown in the table for Fig. 6.2a.

Statement executed	X(1)	X(2)	X(3)	X(4)
READ	10.1	7.2	3.6	9.4

In order for the computer to process a program that has one or more arrays in it, it must reserve a location in its memory for each element of the array. By using a DIMENSION statement, the programmer instructs the computer to do this. In a DIMENSION statement, we inform the computer what will be the largest value of the subscript of each array used in the program. Since 4 is the largest value a subscript can have in the program of Fig. 6.2a, we begin the program with

```
DIMENSION X(4)
```

We could always dimension a subscripted variable with a number larger than is required. Thus in the program of Fig. 6.2a, we could, for instance, have written DIMENSION X(6). The DIMENSION statement is a nonexecutable statement, and it must precede any executable statement in the program.

The data card for the program is shown in Fig. 6.2b. The results of running the program of Fig. 6.2a are shown in Fig. 6.2c.

INTRODUCTION TO ARRAYS

```
C       PROGRAM USES SUBSCRIPTED VARIABLES
        DIMENSION X(4)
        READ(5,10)  X(1), X(2), X(3), X(4)
 10     FORMAT(4F10.0)
        WRITE(6,15) X(1), X(2), X(3), X(4)
 15     FORMAT(1X, 4F12.2)
        AVER=( X(1)  + X(2)  + X(3)  + X(4)  )/ 4.0
        WRITE(6,20) AVER
 20     FORMAT(1X, 'AVERAGE=', E15.7)
        STOP
        END
```

Figure 6.2a. Same as the program in Fig. 6.1a except that the array X is used. It consists of four parts: X(1), X(2), X(3), and X(4); they are called the elements of X. What appears in the parentheses is called a subscript; it distinguishes the elements from each other. Thus in FORTRAN the elements are called subscripted variables. Any array must appear in the beginning of the program in a DIMENSION statement; here a constant that is the maximum value of the subscript appears in the parentheses.

Statement executed	X(1)	X(2)	X(3)	X(4)
READ	10.1	7.2	3.6	9.4
Assignment	10.1	7.2	3.6	9.4
WRITE	10.1	7.2	3.6	9.4

Table for Fig. 6.2a. The values assigned to the four elements of X. The elements of X are in effect separate variables. What distinguishes one from the other is the subscript (the constants which appear between the parentheses).

```
 10.1      7.2       3.6       9.4

1 2 3 4 5|6|7 8 9 10 11 12 13 14 15 16 17 18 19 20 21 22 23 24 25 26 27 28 29 30 31 32 33 34 35 36
```

Figure 6.2b. The data card for Fig. 6.2a.

```
       10.10       7.20        3.60        9.40
AVERAGE=  0.7574993E 01
```

Figure 6.2c. Running the program of Fig. 6.2a.

The appearance in a program of a subscripted variable with a subscript larger than the one indicated in the DIMENSION statement will usually produce an undesirable result. On some systems, e.g., WATFOR/WATFIV, the compiler will indicate, by printing an appropriate error message, that you have exceeded the dimensions of a variable; the reason for this, as we remember, is that the compiler remains in operation even while the program is being executed. In Standard Fortran IV, the system—unless something drastic occurs in the execution of the program—does not produce an error message here.

One way in which exceeding the dimensions of a variable can produce an error is by causing an incorrect value to be assigned to a variable. When memory locations are allocated to the different variables in the program, these memory locations are next to each other. For example, in the program of Fig. 6.3a, when the compiler encounters

```
DIMENSION A(2), B(2)
```

during compilation time, it reserves two locations for the array A and two for the array B. These locations are right next to each other, as shown in Fig. 6.3b.

When B(1)=0.0 and B(2)=0.0 are executed, zeros are assigned to B(1) and B(2) as shown in the first line of the table for Fig. 6.3a. When

```
READ(5,10) A(1), A(2), A(3)
```

is executed, the first two constants on the data card shown in Fig. 6.3c

```
10.3          20.6          3.6
```

are assigned to A(1) and A(2), respectively, as is shown in the second line of the table. The constant 3.6 then should be assigned to A(3), but no memory location has been reserved for A(3). The computer interprets A(3) as the location that follows A(2), but as we see from Fig. 6.3b, this is B(1). Thus the computer assigns 3.6 to B(1), as shown in the second line of the table for Fig. 6.3a.

Statement	A(1)	A(2)	B(1)	B(2)
READ	10.3	20.6	3.6	0.0

When we run the program, as shown in Fig. 6.3d, we obtain the undesired result B(1)= 3.6. For this reason, it is wise to check programs that use arrays, to see that the value of a subscript does not exceed the dimensions specified in the DIMENSION statement. One way of doing this is to run programs originally on a WATFOR/WATFIV compiler, if available, since that compiler detects arrays which have been under-dimensioned.

EFFECTS OF INCORRECTLY DIMENSIONING

```
C   PROGRAM SHOWS THE DANGER OF UNDERDIMENSIONING AN ARRAY
C
      DIMENSION A(2), B(2)
      B(1)=0.0
      B(2)=0.0
      READ(5,10) A(1), A(2), A(3)
 10   FORMAT(3F10.0)
      WRITE(6,20) A(1), A(2)
 20   FORMAT(1X,'A(1)=', F10.0,3X, 'A(2)=', F10.0)
      WRITE(6,30) B(1), B(2)
 30   FORMAT(1X, 'B(1)=', F10.1, 3X, 'B(2)=', F10.1)
      STOP
      END
```

Figure 6.3a. A program in which the dimension of A is not large enough: only two memory locations are reserved for A, but we use A(3) in the READ.

Statement	A(1)	A(2)	B(1)	B(2)
B(2)= 0	Undef	Undef	0.0	0.0
READ	10.3	20.6	3.6	0.0

Table for Fig. 6.3a. After B(1)= 0.0 and B(2)= 0.0 are executed, the values assigned to the variable are shown in the first line of the table. The computer interprets A(3) as the name of the memory location which follows location A(2). Since no memory location has been reserved for A(3), the computer assigns the constant that should have been assigned to A(3), instead to B(1). This is done since the location for B(1) follows the location for A(2) in the memory.

A(1)	A(2)	B(1)	B(2)

Figure 6.3b. How the memory locations for the subscripted variables A and B are positioned in the memory; i.e., B(1) follows A(2).

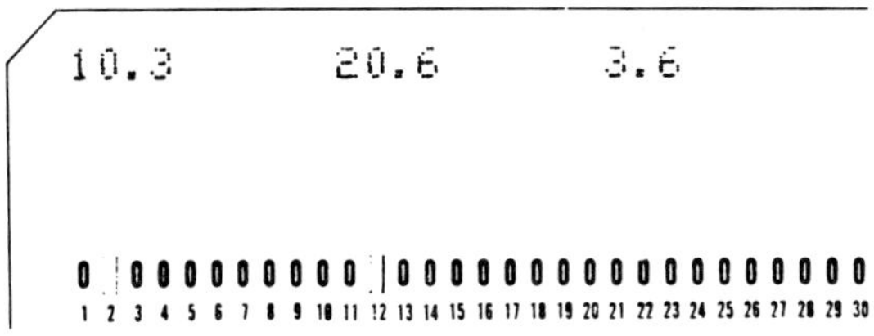

Figure 6.3c. The data card that will be read by READ(5,10) A(1), A(2), A(3).

```
A(1)=        10.    A(2)=        21.
B(1)=        3.6    B(2)=        0.0
```

Figure 6.3d. The results of running the program of Fig. 6.3a. The computer prints the wrong result for B(1) instead of B(1)=0.0. Had we correctly dimensioned A, e.g., written DIMENSION A(3), then the computer would have printed B(1)= 0.0.

In Fig. 6.4a we write a program which, once it has read the values of the constants punched on the data card shown in Fig. 6.4b, prints them out in reverse order. In doing so, the subscript of Y will itself be a variable. In the READ statement, the subscript is I.

```
READ(5,10) Y(I)
```

The first time this statement is executed, the compiler interprets it as READ(5,10) Y(1), and it assigns the number on the first data card, 13.2, to Y(1). Each time the READ is executed, a new data card is read, and the value of the constant punched on it is assigned to the appropriate Y(I). The table for Fig. 6.4a demonstrates how this is done. For instance, from the left half of the fourth line of the table

I	Form of Y(I)	Value of Y(I)
4	Y(4)	8.3

We see that when the fourth card (I=4) is read, 8.3 is assigned to Y(4).

PROGRAM PRINTS NUMBERS IN OPPOSITE ORDER THAN THEY WERE READ

```
C   PROGRAM PRINTS NUMBERS IN OPPOSITE ORDER
C   THAN THEY WERE READ INTO PROGRAM
        DIMENSION Y(4)
C           ...READ THE CARDS
        DO 20 I=1,4
           READ(5,10) Y(I)
 10        FORMAT(F10.0)
           WRITE(6,15) Y(I)
 15        FORMAT(1X, F12.2)
 20     CONTINUE
C           ...PRINT THE  CARDS IN OPPOSITE ORDER
        WRITE(6,25)
 25     FORMAT(1X, 'THE CARDS IN REVERSE ORDER FOLLOW')
        DO 40 I=1,4
           J=5-I
           WRITE(6,30) Y(J)
 30        FORMAT(1X, F10.2)
 40     CONTINUE
        STOP
        END
```

Figure 6.4a. Program demonstrates use of variables as subscripts. Each of the four times READ(5,10) Y(I) is executed a different value of Y(I) is defined, as is shown in the accompanying table. Had we written the READ as READ(5,10) Y, each time a new value of Y was read, it would destroy the previous value. In WRITE(6,30) Y(J) the value of J successively equals 4, 3, 2, 1, so the results are printed in reverse order.

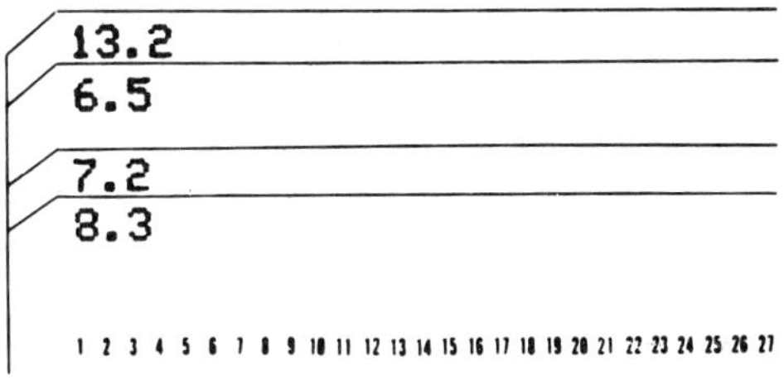

Figure 6.4b. The data cards for the program of Fig. 6.4a.

I	Form of Y(I)	Value of Y(I)	J	Form of Y(J)	Value of Y(J)
1	Y(1)	13.2	4	Y(4)	8.3
2	Y(2)	6.5	3	Y(3)	7.2
3	Y(3)	7.2	2	Y(2)	6.5
4	Y(4)	8.3	1	Y(1)	13.2

Table for Fig. 6.4a. The subscript of Y is different in the beginning of the program—Y(I)—than it is at the end—Y(J). However, it is the value of the subscript, not its name, that is important. Since the values of J are in reverse order in comparison to I, the results are printed in the opposite order than what was read.

The second DO loop in the program prints the numbers in reverse order. The subscript now is J. (We will soon see that does not affect the running of the program.) Because of

```
J=5-I
```

the subscript successively assumes the values 4, 3, 2, and finally 1. When J equals 4, WRITE(6,30) Y(J) is interpreted by the computer as WRITE(6,30) Y(4). But Y(4) has already been defined in the first DO loop as 8.3, so the computer prints the correct results. We see from this that it is the value of the subscript that is important. The name we use for the subscript—as long as it is an INTEGER and previously defined—is immaterial. The results of the program are shown in Fig. 6.4c.

In Standard Fortran, you are allowed to use an INTEGER expression as a subscript, but the expression must assume one of the following forms:

Variable
Variable + constant
Variable − constant
Constant * variable
Constant * variable + constant
Constant * variable − constant

(as shown in Table 6.1), where the variable and each constant must be INTEGER. Thus in Standard Fortran, Y(I+3), Y(3*I), and Y(4*I−2) are all acceptable ways of subscripting an array; whereas Y(3+I), Y(I*3), and Y(I*4−2) are not because the subscripts do not follow the prescribed form. On WATFOR/WATFIV and some other compilers, any form of subscript expression is acceptable, even those containing REALs and subscripted variables. Thus Y(I*4−2), Y(I**2+J**2), and Y(X(3)) would be acceptable on these compilers. When a REAL expression is used as a subscript on these systems, the expression is converted to an INTEGER, i.e., the value of the expression is truncated.

```
        13.20
         6.50
         7.20
         8.30
THE CARDS IN REVERSE ORDER FCLLOW
         8.30
         7.20
         6.50
        13.20
```

Figure 6.4c. Running the program of Fig. 6.4a. A subscript must always be an INTEGER. The name of the subscript is not important; what is important is its value. Thus when I and J have the same values, Y(I) and Y(J) have the same values.

FORM OF SUBSCRIPTS

All subscripts must be INTEGER expressions of the following form.

Form of subscript	Correct example	Incorrect example
Constant	4	4.6
Variable	J	R
Variable + constant	J+4	4+J
Variable − constant	J−4	4−J
Constant * variable	6*INDEX	INDEX*6
Constant * variable + constant	3*K+2	2+3*K
Constant * variable − constant	6*M1−3	M1*6−3

Table 6.1. On ANS Standard Fortran the above form must be followed in subscripting a variable. On WATFOR/WATFIV and some other compilers, you can use any expression for a subscript, even one that includes REAL and subscripted variables; thus R(X(I)*2.6) would be acceptable on those compilers.

In the next program (Fig. 6.5a) we use an accumulator to average the numbers read from cards (Fig. 6.5b). We then print the difference between each number and the average. We have written the program so that it processes any number of data cards up to 100. The data cards must be followed by a trailer that instructs the program to stop summing the numbers on the cards and to calculate the average. The trailer contains the number −12345678.; this is the largest negative number with a decimal point that can be punched into a field 10 columns wide. The array CARD is dimensioned to 101 because, if there are 100 data cards containing numbers to be averaged, then the trailer would be the 101st card. If there are more than 100 data cards containing numbers to be averaged, the program prints TOO MANY DATA CARDS PROCESSED and then stops.

If there are 100 or fewer data cards, the program proceeds as follows: Each time the program reads a new card, it assigns the value of the constant on the card to CARD(I), and this value in turn (if it is not the trailer) is added to SUM. Thus the first time the computer reads a data card, it interprets the READ as

```
READ (5,10) CARD(1)
```

and the last statement in the first DO loop as

```
SUM=SUM + CARD(1)
```

It would be very difficult to write this program without subscripted variables. Thus, had we written the statement that adds the numbers as

```
SUM=SUM + CARD
```

we would have obtained the correct sum, but we could not have found the difference between each value of CARD and the average because each time a new data card is read, the previous value assigned to CARD is destroyed.

PROGRAM PRINTS THE DEVIATION OF EACH NUMBER READ FROM THE AVERAGE

```
C  PROGRAM AVERAGES N NUMBERS, THEN PRINTS THE DIFFERENCE
C  BETWEEN EACH NUMBER AND THE AVERAGE
      DIMENSION CARD(101)
      N=0
      SUM=0.0
C         ...READ CARDS AND SUM NUMBERS
      DO 20 I=1,101
         READ(5,10) CARD(I)
 10      FORMAT(F10.0)
         WRITE(6,15) CARD(I)
 15      FORMAT(1X, F12.2)
         IF( CARD(I) .EQ. -12345678.0 ) GO TO 40
            N=N + 1
            SUM=SUM + CARD(I)
 20   CONTINUE
C
      WRITE(6,30)
 30   FORMAT(1X, 'TOO MANY DATA CARDS PROCESSED')
      STOP
C         ...CALCULATE AVERAGE
 40   AVER=SUM / FLOAT(N)
      WRITE(6,50) AVER
 50   FORMAT(1X, ' THE AVERAGE IS', E15.7)
      WRITE(6,60)
 60   FORMAT(1X, T9, 'X',T17, 'DIFFERENCE')
C         ...PRINT DIFFERENCE BETWEEN EACH NUMBER AND AVERAGE
      DO 80 I=1,N
         DIFF= AVER - CARD(I)
         WRITE(6,70) CARD(I), DIFF
 70      FORMAT(1X, F10.2, 2X, F10.2)
 80   CONTINUE
      STOP
      END
```

Figure 6.5a. The addition of the numbers is done in SUM=SUM + CARD(I). Each value of CARD(I) is remembered by the computer, so at the end of the program it can evaluate <u>DIFF= AVER − CARD(I)</u> where AVER is the average of all the constants the program read.

Figure 6.5b. The data cards for the program of Fig. 6.5a.

For the data shown here, the first data card contains 10.2. The value of SUM is originally zero, so the first time this statement is executed, the value of SUM to the right of the equals sign is zero. The value of SUM on the left is 0 + 10.2 or 10.2. This is shown in the first line of the table for Fig. 6.5a.

The second time the computer reads a data card, it assigns the number on the second data card—in this case 16.7—to CARD(2). The result of the execution of SUM=SUM + CARD(2) is shown in the second line of the table for Fig. 6.5a.

Time executed	SUM to the right of =	I	CARD(I)	SUM to the left of =
2nd	10.2	2	16.7	26.9

Since the value of SUM on the right of the equals sign is now 10.2, the value of SUM on the left is 10.2 + CARD(2) or 10.2 + 16.7 which is 26.9. This procedure continues until the trailer is processed; then control is transferred to statement 40. There the average is calculated.

Because N=N + 1 appears after the IF statement that checks for the trailer, the trailer is not counted. Thus the average defined by AVER=SUM / FLOAT(N) is calculated correctly. Similarly, the value of N is correct in

```
DO 80 I=1,N
```

This statement begins the loop that calculates the difference

```
DIFF= AVER - CARD(I)
```

We remember that the name of the variable we use for the index in this loop does not have to be the same as the one we used in the first DO loop. Thus we could have written the DO statement as DO 80 J= 1,N as long as we also changed the definition of DIFF to be: DIFF=AVER – CARD(J). The results of running this program are shown in Fig. 6.5c.

Time executed	SUM to the right of =	I	CARD(I)	SUM to the left of =
1st	0	1	10.2	10.2
2nd	10.2	2	16.7	26.9
3rd	26.9	3	14.2	41.1
4th	41.1	4	6.1	47.2

Table for Fig. 6.5a. Each time SUM= SUM + CARD(I) is executed, the value of a new element of CARD(I) is added to SUM.

```
      10.20
      16.70
      14.20
       6.10
-12345670.00
 THE AVERAGE IS   0.1180000E 02
        X           DIFFERENCE
      10.20            1.60
      16.70           -4.90
      14.20           -2.40
       6.10            5.70
```

Figure 6.5c. Running the program of Fig. 6.5a. If we use a nonsubscripted variable in the program—e.g., writing the READ as READ(5,10) CARD—each new value of CARD would destroy the previous value, so if it calculated DIFF= AVER − CARD, we would get the same value of DIFF for each constant read.

In the programs in this section, we have used REAL subscripted variables. The rules for naming subscripted REAL variables are the same as those for naming nonsubscripted REAL variables: Ordinarily the name of a REAL subscripted variable must begin with any letter but I, J, K, L, M, or N. If it does not, as in this case of NAME, the variable must be declared REAL in a REAL specification statement. Thus if NAME were a REAL variable which contained 4 elements, we would write

```
REAL NAME
DIMENSION NAME(4)
```

However, we could do this in one statement simply by dimensioning NAME in the REAL declaration statement

```
REAL NAME(4)
```

If we use this approach we cannot also dimension NAME in a DIMENSION statement. This and other examples are given in Table 6.2. Note, we are allowed to dimension a REAL variable in a REAL declaration statement. Thus REAL X(4) is allowed.

The computer treats a REAL subscripted variable in the same way as it treats a nonsubscripted REAL variable. For instance, when an INTEGER constant is assigned to a REAL subscripted variable, the computer first floats the constant and then assigns it to the variable. Thus when the computer executes A(3)=10, for example, it converts 10 to 10.0 and stores the result in the location named A(3).

USING THE REAL DECLARATIVE STATEMENT

Specification statements	Equivalent statement	Incorrect	Comment
REAL NAME DIMENSION NAME(4)	REAL NAME(4)	REAL NAME(4) DIMENSION NAME(4)	We may dimension array in a REAL statement. If we do, we cannot also dimension the array in a DIMENSION statement
REAL L,NAME,NUM DIMENSION L(6), NAME(4),NUM(10)	REAL L(6),NAME(4), NUM(10)	REAL L(6),NAME(4), NUM(10) DIMENSION L(6), NAME(4),NUM(10)	Many variables are dimensioned in the REAL statement. We place them in alphabetical order to aid anyone reading the program
REAL NAME,NUM DIMENSION CARD(8), NAME(3),NUM(10)	REAL NAME(3), NUM(10) DIMENSION CARD(8)	REAL NAME(3), NUM(10) DIMENSION CARD(8), NAME(3)	Those arrays not dimensioned in a REAL, or INTEGER, statement must be dimensioned in a DIMENSION statement

Table 6.2. Examples using the REAL and DIMENSION declaration statements.

6.2. The DATA Statement

Instead of reading data in from cards, we can assign constants to variables by using a DATA statement. In the program of Fig. 6.6a we use a DATA statement to calculate the average of 5 numbers. A DATA statement is not an executable statement—although it is performing the function of executable statements, i.e., assigning constants to variables. It assigns values to variables before the execution of the program. It must be placed at the beginning of a program before any executable statements. In the simplest form of the DATA statement, an example of which is shown in Fig. 6.6a,

```
DATA A, B, C, D, E / 12.6, 15.4, 6.8, 6.8, 10.0/
```

the variable to which values are to be assigned are followed by a slash. This is followed by the constants that are to be assigned to the variables. The statement ends with a slash. The variables are separated from each other by commas. The constants are similarly separated. The assignments are made as follows: The leftmost constant is assigned to the leftmost variable. Then the next constant is assigned to the next variable, etc. The mode of the constant must be the same as the mode of the variable to which it is paired in the DATA statement. Thus in this particular example of the DATA statement, since the variables are REALs, so are the constants. All that we have discussed is shown in the table for Fig. 6.6a. The result of running the program are shown in Fig. 6.6b.

If a constant is repeated in a DATA statement, e.g., 6.8 in Fig. 6.6a, you may eliminate all but one of the constants and precede the constant with an INTEGER specifying how many times the constant is repeated. Sandwiched between the constant and the INTEGER is an *. Thus the two 6.8s can be replaced by 2*6.8, and the DATA statement can be rewritten as DATA A, B, C, D, E/ 12.6, 15.4, 2*6.8, 10.0/.

USING THE DATA STATEMENT

```
C  USING A DATA STATEMENT
      DATA A, B, C, D, E / 12.6, 15.4, 6.8, 6.8, 10.0/
      AVER=( A + B + C + D + E ) / 5.0
      WRITE(6,10) AVER
 10   FORMAT(1X, 'THE AVERAGE IS', F10.2)
      STOP
      END
```

Figure 6.6a. Using the DATA statement. The constants in the DATA statement are assigned, in the order they are written, to the variables in the order that they are written. The DATA statement is a nonexecutable statement. It must precede any executable statement.

A	B	C	D	E
12.6	15.4	6.8	6.8	10.0

Table for Fig. 6.6a. How the constants in the DATA statement are assigned to the corresponding variables.

```
THE AVERAGE IS        10.32
```

Figure 6.6b. Running the program of Fig. 6.6a.

Subscripted variables can also be used with a DATA statement. Thus

```
DIMENSION X(5)
DATA X(1),X(2),X(3),X(4),X(5)/ 12.6, 15.4, 2*6.8, 10.0/
```

could replace the previously used DATA statement, as shown in Fig. 6.7a. The assignments are as shown in the table for Fig. 6.7a. The results of running the program are shown in Fig. 6.7b. The previous DATA statement can be written more simply by placing the array X instead of the subscripted variables in the DATA statement

```
DIMENSION X(5)
DATA X / 12.6, 15.4, 2*6.8, 10.0/
```

as shown in Fig. 6.7c. The fact that X is dimensioned to 5, indicates to the computer that X in the DATA statement is identical to X(1), X(2), X(3), X(4), X(5). The assignments are as shown in the table for Fig. 6.7c. The results are shown in Fig. 6.7d.

The DATA statement is useful in checking programs because the data are displayed within the program itself; it is useful in initializing variables, especially in initializing large arrays in which all or many of the elements have the same value.

USING AN ARRAY IN A DATA STATEMENT

```
C  USING A SUBSCRIPTED VARIABLE IN A DATA STATEMENT
      DIMENSION X(5)
      DATA X(1),X(2),X(3),X(4),X(5)/ 12.6, 15.4, 2*6.8, 10.0/
      AVER = ( X(1) + X(2) + X(3) + X(4) + X(5)) / 5.0
      WRITE(6,10) AVER
 10   FORMAT(1X, 'THE AVERAGE IS', F10.2)
      STOP
      END
```

Figure 6.7a. Using a subscripted variable in a DATA statement. The subscripted variable must still be dimensioned in a DIMENSION statement. The meaning of 2*6.8 is that 6.8 appears twice in the DATA statement. If there were three 6.8s, we could replace them with 3*6.8.

X(1)	X(2)	X(3)	X(4)	X(5)
12.6	15.4	6.8	6.8	10.0

Table for Fig. 6.7a. How the constants and variables in the DATA statement of Fig. 6.7a are matched.

```
 THE AVERAGE IS      10.32
```

Figure 6.7b. Running the program of Fig. 6.7a.

```
C       USING AN ARRAY IN A DATA STATEMENT
        DIMENSION X(5)
        DATA X / 12.6, 15.4, 2*6.8, 10.0/
        SUM=0.0
C          ...READ THE DATA AND SUM THE NUMBERS
        DO 10 I=1,5
           SUM = SUM + X(I)
 10     CONTINUE
C
        AVER = SUM / 5.0
        WRITE(6,20) AVER
 20     FORMAT(1X, 'THE AVERAGE IS', F10.2)
        STOP
        END
```

Figure 6.7c. If we want all the elements of a subscript variable to be assigned values, we can simply place the variable name, unsubscripted, in the DATA statement.

X(1)	X(2)	X(3)	X(4)	X(5)
12.6	15.4	6.8	6.8	10.0

Table for Fig. 6.7c. How the constants and the variables in the DATA statement of Fig. 6.7c are matched.

```
 THE AVERAGE IS      10.32
```

Figure 6.7d. Running the program of Fig. 6.7c.

6.3. The Computed GO TO Statement

The computed GO TO statement allows you to branch to one of many statements, depending on the value of an INTEGER variable called the controlling variable. In

```
GO TO (80, 85, 90, 95), J
```

the numbers in the parentheses are statement numbers and the controlling variable is J. Here control is transferred to statement 80, if the value of J is 1; to statement 85, if the value of J is 2; to statement 90, if the value of J is 3; and to statement 95, if the value of J is 4. If we had written the statement with the numbers in reverse order, i.e.,

```
GO TO (95, 90, 85, 80), J
```

then when the value of J is 1, control is transferred to statement 95; when J is 2, to statement 90; when J is 3, to statement 85; and when J is 4, to statement 80. In brief, the leftmost statement number indicated in the GO TO is executed if the value of the controlling variable (here J) is 1, the second leftmost statement is executed if the controlling variable's value is 2, etc. If the value of the controlling variable is less than 1 or greater than the number of statement numbers appearing in the GO TO, then an execution error occurs in ANS FORTRAN; however, if this happens in WATFOR/WATFIV, control is transferred to the statement directly below the computed GO TO statement.

In the program of Fig. 6.8a we use a computed GO TO statement to determine how many 1s, 2s, 3s, and 4s there are in a set of up to 1000 data cards. Each data card contains one of these constants. The last data card is a trailer and contains the number −9 as is

USING THE COMPUTED GO TO STATEMENT

```
C  USING THE 'COMPUTED GO TO ' TO COUNT HOW MANY
C  1S, 2S, 3S AND 4S THERE ARE ON THE DATA CARDS
      INTEGER COUNT1, COUNT2, COUNT3, COUNT4
      DATA COUNT1, COUNT2, COUNT3, COUNT4 / 4*0 /
C         ... HISTOGRAM VALUES
      DO 80 I=1,1001
         READ(5,30) NUM
 30      FORMAT(I2)
         WRITE(6,35) NUM
 35      FORMAT(1X, I3)
         IF( NUM .EQ. -9) GO TO 100
            IF( (NUM .LT. 1) .OR. (NUM .GT. 4) ) GO TO 80
               GO TO (40, 50, 60, 70), NUM
C
 40            COUNT1=COUNT1 + 1
               GO TO 80
C
 50            COUNT2=COUNT2 + 1
               GO TO 80
C
 60            COUNT3=COUNT3 + 1
               GO TO 80
C
 70            COUNT4=COUNT4 + 1
 80   CONTINUE
      WRITE(6,90)
 90   FORMAT(1X, 'TOO MANY CARDS, LIMIT IS 1000')
      STOP
C         ...PRINT THE RESULTS
 100  WRITE(6,110) COUNT1
 110  FORMAT(1X, 'AMOUNT OF 1S IS', I4)
      WRITE(6,120) COUNT2
 120  FORMAT(1X, 'AMOUNT OF 2S IS', I4)
      WRITE(6,130) COUNT3
 130  FORMAT(1X, 'AMOUNT OF 3S IS', I4)
      WRITE(6,140) COUNT4
 140  FORMAT(1X, 'AMOUNT OF 4S IS', I4)
      STOP
      END
```

Figure 6.8a. Program counts how many 1s, 2s, 3s, and 4s there are on the data cards. Since the variables (the counters) in the DATA statement are INTEGERS, the constants there are also integers. GO TO (40, 50, 60, 70), NUM works as follows: if NUM is 1, statement 40 is executed next; if NUM is 2, statement 50 is executed next; if NUM is 3, statement 60 is executed next; and if NUM is 4, statement 70 is executed next. As a consequence of this, the value of the appropriate counter is increased by 1. The CONTINUE statement is executed next, and thus a new data card is read.

shown in Fig. 6.8b. We use the INTEGER variables COUNT1, COUNT2, COUNT3, and COUNT4 (which are declared INTEGER in an INTEGER specification statement) to count the number of 1s, 2s, 3s, and 4s, respectively. These counters are zeroed in the DATA statement

```
DATA COUNT1, COUNT2, COUNT3, COUNT4 / 4*0 /
```

Since all the counters are INTEGER, we have written the constants assigned to the counters as 4*0, not as 4*0.0.

In the DO loop, the value of the constant read is assigned to NUM. If the value of NUM is −9, the results of the program are printed; otherwise the remaining statements in the loop are executed. The purpose of

```
IF( (NUM .LT. 1) .OR. (NUM .GT. 4) ) GO TO 80
```

is to eliminate values of NUM that would create an error when the computed GO TO statement

```
GO TO (40, 50, 60, 70), NUM
```

is executed. Since there are only four statement numbers indicated in this computed GO TO statement, it can accommodate values of NUM only from 1 through 4.

We now investigate how the program works for some of the values of NUM. The first constant read is 2. Since the conditions in both the IF statements are false, the computed GO TO is executed next. Since the value of NUM is 2, execution is transferred to the second statement number listed in the computed GO TO statement. This is statement 50. There the value of COUNT2 is increased by 1, all of which is shown in the first line of the table for Fig. 6.8a.

NUM	Next statement executed	COUNT1	COUNT2	COUNT3	COUNT4
2	50	0	1	0	0

This table shows which statement is executed after the computed GO TO and the subsequent status of the counters for each value of NUM read. After line 50, the next statement executed GO TO 80 transfers control to the last statement in the loop, 80 CONTINUE. This means that loop index I is incremented by 1 and the statements in the loop are executed again. Thus the next value of NUM is read. Since its value is 4, the fourth statement number (70) listed in the computed GO TO statement is executed. At statement 70, the value of COUNT4 is increased by 1, as is shown in the second line of the table.

When the next value of NUM is read, since its value is 6 the second IF statement instructs the computer not to count this value but to go directly to the last statement in the loop. When the trailer is read, the first IF transfers control to the WRITE statements at the end of the program. The values of all the counters at this point are shown in the last line of the table. These values are used when the results are printed, as shown in Fig. 6.8c.

It is important to note that if we had interchanged the two IF statements and had written them as

```
IF( (NUM .LT. 1) .OR. (NUM .GT. 4) ) GO TO 80
IF( NUM .EQ. -9) GO TO 100
```

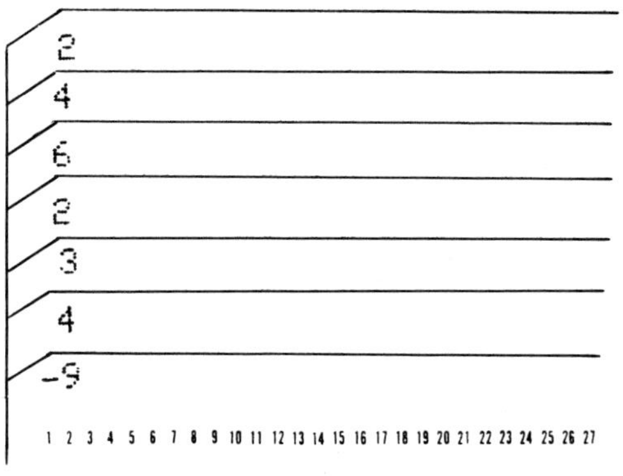

Figure 6.8b. The data cards for Fig. 6.8a. The last data card is the trailer and contains a −9. This triggers the program to print the results.

NUM	Next statement executed	COUNT1	COUNT2	COUNT3	COUNT4
2	50	0	1	0	0
4	70	0	1	0	1
6	80	0	1	0	0
2	50	0	2	0	0
3	60	0	2	1	0
4	70	0	2	1	2
−9	90	0	2	1	2

Table for Fig. 6.8a. This table shows how GO TO (40, 50, 60, 70), NUM works. If the value of NUM at this statement is not 1, 2, 3, or 4, an error occurs. Thus we have preceded this statement with IF((NUM .LT. 1) .OR. (NUM .GT. 4)) GO TO 80. Each time 80 CONTINUE is executed (except the 1001st time), the READ is executed next. This means for instance when NUM is 6, no counter is increased.

```
 2
 4
 6
 2
 3
 4
-9
AMOUNT OF 1S IS  0
AMOUNT OF 2S IS  2
AMOUNT OF 3S IS  1
AMOUNT OF 4S IS  2
```

Figure 6.8c. Running the program of Fig. 6.8a.

we would have caused an error. The reason is that, when the trailer is read, the condition (NUM .LT. 1) would be true and the next statement executed would be the CONTINUE statement. Therefore, the program would try to read another card, and an execution error would occur.

COMPUTED GO TO

The form of the computed GO TO statement is: GO TO (, followed by a list of statement numbers. These statement numbers must be separated by commas. The last statement number in the list is followed by), which is followed by a comma; followed by an INTEGER variable. If the value of the INTEGER is 1, the first statement number in the list is executed next; if the value is 2, the second statement in the list is executed, etc. Examples:

```
GO TO (20, 60, 60, 80), KOUNT
GO TO (20, 40, 50), I
```

In the first example, we see that you can transfer to the same statement number for different values of the controlling variable.

The present program, because it has a multiple branch statement in it—the computed GO TO statement—makes it somewhat difficult for the reader to follow; the multiple branch is accompanied by a proliferation of statement numbers and GO TO statements. The more statement numbers there are in a program, the harder it is to find any given one. In the next program we present a cleaner way of writing this program.

6.4. INTEGER **Subscripted Variables**

In the previous programs we have used subscripted REAL variables. We have seen that the rules for naming subscripted REAL variables are the same as for naming nonsubscripted REAL variables. Similarly, the rules for naming INTEGER subscripted variables are the same as for naming nonsubscripted INTEGER variables. Ordinarily, the name of an INTEGER subscripted variable must begin with the letter I, J, K, L, M, or N. If it does not, as in the case of, for instance, COUNT, the variable must be declared INTEGER in an INTEGER specification statement. Thus if COUNT were an INTEGER variable that contained 4 elements, we would write

```
INTEGER COUNT
DIMENSION COUNT(4)
```

or we could simply dimension COUNT in the INTEGER statement

```
INTEGER COUNT(4)
```

and not use a DIMENSION statement. This and other examples are given in Table 6.3. We are also allowed to dimension an INTEGER variable in an INTEGER declaration statement. Thus INTEGER NUM(4) is allowed.

USING THE INTEGER DECLARATION STATEMENT

Specification statement	Equivalent statement	Comment
INTEGER COUNT DIMENSION COUNT(4)	INTEGER COUNT(4)	We may dimension an array in an INTEGER statement. If we do, we cannot also dimension the array in a DIMENSION statement
INTEGER COUNT,QUANT,TIME DIMENSION COUNT(4),QUANT(10), TIME(6)	INTEGER COUNT(4),QUANT(10), TIME(6)	Many variables are dimensioned in the INTEGER statement
INTEGER COUNT,QUANT DIMENSION COUNT(4),QUANT(10), STACK(3)	INTEGER COUNT(4),QUANT(10) DIMENSION STACK(3)	Those arrays not dimensioned in an INTEGER (or REAL) statement must be dimensioned in a DIMENSION statement
INTEGER COUNT,TIME REAL NAME,NUM DIMENSION COUNT(4),NAME(6), NUM(3),TIME(10)	INTEGER COUNT(4),TIME(10) REAL NAME(6),NUM(3)	Both REAL and INTEGER variables in the DIMENSION statement

Table 6.3. Examples using the REAL, INTEGER, and DIMENSION statements.

We now use a subscripted INTEGER variable in the program of Fig. 6.9a. This program does the same thing as did the previous one (Fig. 6.8a); i.e., it counts the number of 1s, 2s, 3s, and 4s in a set of data cards; the data cards are shown in Fig. 6.9b. There is one constant per card. We will use the subscripted variables COUNT(1), COUNT(2), COUNT(3), and COUNT(4), respectively, to count the total of each of these numbers.

After we dimension COUNT, we assign zeroes to each of its 4 elements in DATA COUNT/ 4*0/. The first loop does the same thing as in the preceding program—counts how many numbers there are in each category—but in a much briefer and cleaner way. It processes the data as follows: After READ(5,20)NUM is executed and if the value of NUM is 1, 2, 3, or 4, then

```
COUNT(NUM)=COUNT(NUM) + 1
```

is executed. This one statement does the addition for all the counters. For example, the first time the loop is executed, NUM assumes the value 2. Thus the computer interprets the (counting) statement as

```
COUNT(2)= COUNT(2) + 1
```

Since COUNT(2) has originally been assigned the value zero in the DATA statement, the value of COUNT(2) is now 1, as shown in the first line of the table for Fig. 6.9a.

NUM	COUNT(1)	COUNT(2)	COUNT(3)	COUNT(4)
2	0	1	0	0

We see here that the values of the other counters are still zero. The second time the statements in the loop are executed, the value of NUM read is 4. Thus COUNT(NUM)=COUNT(NUM) + 1 is now interpreted as

```
COUNT(4)=COUNT(4) + 1
```

and is added to COUNT(4), as shown in the second line of the table

NUM	COUNT(1)	COUNT(2)	COUNT(3)	COUNT(4)
4	0	1	0	1

We see, of course, that the computer remembers that the value of COUNT(2) is 1.

The program terminates normally when the trailer is read—assuming the number of preceding data cards to be 1000 or less. If the number of preceding data cards is more than 1000, the program executes the loop 1001 times. It then executes the WRITE statement following 10 CONTINUE and prints TOO MANY CARDS, LIMIT IS 1000. It then stops.

When the program terminates because it has read the trailer, it executes the DO loop which starts at statement 40. The first time the computer executes WRITE(6,50) I,COUNT(I), it interprets the statement as

```
WRITE(6,50) 1, COUNT(1)
```

From the last line of the table for Fig. 6.9a,

NUM	COUNT(1)	COUNT(2)	COUNT(3)	COUNT(4)
−9	0	2	1	2

USING AN ARRAY TO HISTOGRAM

```
C   USING AN ARRAY TO HISTOGRAM
        INTEGER COUNT(4)
        DATA COUNT/ 4*0/
C           ...HISTOGRAM THE CARDS
        DO 30 I=1,1001
 10         READ(5,20) NUM
 20         FORMAT(I2)
            WRITE(6,25) NUM
 25         FORMAT(1X, I2)
            IF( NUM .EQ. -9) GO TO 40
                    IF( (NUM .LT. 1) .OR. (NUM .GT. 4) ) GO TO 30
                        COUNT(NUM)=COUNT(NUM) + 1
 30     CONTINUE
        WRITE(6,35)
 35     FORMAT(1X, 'TOO MANY CARDS, LIMIT IS 1000')
        STOP
C           ...PRINT THE RESULTS
 40     DO 60 I=1,4
            WRITE(6,50) I, COUNT(I)
 50         FORMAT(1X, 'THE NUMBER OF', I2, 'S IS', I4)
 60     CONTINUE
        STOP
        END
```

Figure 6.9a. This program does the same thing as the preceding one; i.e., it counts the number of 1s, 2s, 3s, and 4s on the data cards. The subscripted variables COUNT(NUM) represent all four counters. Thus when the value of NUM is 1, COUNT(NUM) is the same as COUNT(1). Consequently, all the counters can be incremented by writing one statement: COUNT(NUM)=COUNT(NUM) + 1. Thus for example, COUNT(1)=COUNT(1) + 1 adds 1 to COUNT(1).

Figure 6.9b. The data cards for Fig. 6.9a. When the value of NUM is −9, the program prints the results.

NUM	COUNT(1)	COUNT(2)	COUNT(3)	COUNT(4)
2	0	1	0	0
4	0	1	0	1
6	0	1	0	1
2	0	2	0	1
3	0	2	1	1
4	0	2	1	2
−9	0	2	1	2

Table for Fig. 6.9a. How COUNT(NUM)= COUNT(NUM)+ 1 works. Because of DIMENSION COUNT(4), the value of the subscript should not be greater than 4. On the other hand, COUNT(0) would cause an error. Therefore we precede the counting statement with IF((NUM .LT. 1) .OR. (NUM .GT. 4) GO TO 30. This means, for instance, that when NUM is 6, no counter is increased.

we see that the last value of COUNT(1) is zero. Thus the computer uses this value of COUNT(1) and prints THE NUMBER OF 1S IS 0. The second time the computer executes the WRITE statement, it interprets the statement as

```
WRITE(6,50) 2, CCUNT(2)
```

and since the last value of COUNT(2) is 2, it prints THE NUMBER OF 2S IS 2. All of this and the rest of the results are shown in Fig. 6.9c. We note here that we could have written this program using a REAL array, if we had wished to.

The process of determining how many 1s, 2s, 3s, and 4s there are in a set is called *histogramming*. The subdivisions into which we place the numbers are called *bins*. Thus we placed all the 1s in the first bin, all the 2s in the second bin, etc. In the two preceding programs, a given bin contained many integers, but they were all the same digit. In a case like this, we say that the bin width is 1 integer. How then would we change the program so that it histograms a set of numbers into bins 5 integers wide where the smallest number in the first bin is 10.0?

The general formula for determining which bin we should place a number into is

```
J=(Y-YMIN) / DY + 1.0
```

where J is the bin numbers, Y is the number to be histogrammed, YMIN, is the smallest number* in the first bin, and DY is the bin width. Table 6.4 shows how this formula works for YMIN equals 10.0, DY equals 5.0, and Y assumes the values 12.0, 14.0, 16.0, 18.0, and 20.0. To the right of the table we show the 3 bins constituting the histogram, into which the various values of Y will be placed. As J is calculated for each value of Y, we place an X in the proper bin. We thus see how the histogram develops. The first line of the table shows what happens when Y is 12.0

Y	(Y−10.0)/5.0	(Y−10.0)/5.0+1.0	J
12.0	0.4	1.4	1

The value of (Y−10.0)/5.0 is 0.4. If we did not add 1.0 to this, 0.4 would be truncated to 0, when it is assigned to J. Since this formula would eventually be followed by a statement that counted the number of integers in each bin, e.g.,

```
COUNT(J)=COUNT(J) + 1
```

and since J is used here as a subscript, it cannot assume the value zero.

In concluding this section, we remark that the computer treats an INTEGER subscripted variable in the same way that it treats a nonsubscripted INTEGER variable. For instance, when a REAL constant is assigned to an INTEGER subscripted variable, the computer first truncates the constant and then assigns it to the variable. Thus when the computer executes NUM(3)=10.6, for example, it truncates 10.6 to 10 and then stores 10 in the location named NUM(3).

We also note here that you cannot use the same name for a nonsubscripted variable and an array. Thus if X is an array, you cannot use X as a variable name, e.g., you cannot write Y = X**3.

* YMIN is the lower limiting value of the first bin.

```
2
4
6
2
3
4
-9
THE NUMBER OF 1S IS   0
THE NUMBER OF 2S IS   2
THE NUMBER OF 3S IS   1
THE NUMBER OF 4S IS   2
```

Figure 6.9c. Running the program of Fig. 6.9a.

HOW TO HISTOGRAM

How J=(Y−YMIN)/DY+1.0 works for YMIN=10.0,DY=5.0. Then J=(Y−10.0)/5.0+1.0 where the value of J is the bin number

Y	(Y−10.0)/5.0	(Y−10.0)/5.0 + 1.0	J (bin number)	Interval 10–15 (BIN1)	Interval 15–20 (BIN2)	Interval 20–25 (BIN3)
12.0	0.4	1.4	1	X		
14.0	0.8	1.8	1	XX		
16.0	1.2	2.2	2	XX	X	
18.0	1.6	2.6	2	XX	XX	
20.0	2.0	2.0	3	XX	XX	X

Table 6.4. Shows how the general formula works for determining the bin a number falls into. We have chosen YMIN= 10.0 and DY= 5.0. The graph on the right of each line of the table shows how an X is added to the proper interval or bin.

6.5. Sorting

We now learn to write a program that sorts numbers in ascending order. The first step is to write the program shown in Fig. 6.10a, which, given a list of numbers (e.g., 5,4,3,2,1) that appear in the DATA statement, will start by taking the first two numbers in the list and if necessary switch them so that the larger one is to the right. Thus 5 would be switched with 4. The modified list would now be 4,5,3,2,1. The program then takes the second and third numbers (in this case they would now be 5 and 3) and if necessary switch them so that, here again, the larger one would be to the right. This process continues until the largest number is at the extreme right of the list. Thus this program is, in effect, selecting the largest number in the list and placing it in the extreme right position.

The interchanging is done in a DO loop. Since there are only 5 numbers in the list, the program has to perform a maximum of 4 interchanges. We write the DO loop as follows

```
      DO 20 I=1,4
         IF( X(I) .LT. X(I + 1) ) GO TO 20
              TEMP=X(I)
              X(I)=X(I + 1)
              X(I + 1)=TEMP
20    CONTINUE
```

The first time the statements in this loop are executed, the value of I is 1. Therefore, the computer interprets the IF statement in this loop as

```
IF( X(1) .LT. X(2) ) GO TO 20
```

The numbers assigned to X(1) and X(2) at this point are as specified in the DATA statement. They are given in Table I for Fig. 6.10a.

I	X(I)	X(I+1)
1	5	4

The condition X(I) .LT. X(I+1) in the IF statement is false. Thus the computer executes the next statement, where it performs the first step in interchanging the subscripts of the numbers 5 and 4; it interprets this statement as TEMP=X(1) and it assigns 5 to TEMP.

It interprets the next statement as X(1)=X(2) and thus assigns 4 [which was originally assigned to X(2)] to X(1). It then interprets the next statement as X(2)=TEMP and thus now assigns 5 to X(2). The numbers assigned to X(1) and X(2) at this point in the loop are given in the first line of Table II for Fig. 6.10a. The order of the list is now 4,5,3,2,1. Thus 4 and 5 have been interchanged. The second time the statements in the loop are executed, the value of I is 2. Thus in the IF statement X(2) and X(3) (i.e., 5 and 3) are now compared. Since 5 is larger than 3, the two numbers are interchanged. Thus the order of the numbers at the end of this execution of the loop is 4,3,5,2,1. This procedure is continued until the largest number is at the right of the list; i.e., the list is now 4,3,2,1,5. The appearance of

SORTING, STEP I

```
C  FIRST STEP IN SORTING. PROGRAM FINDS THE LARGEST NUMBER IN A SET
      DIMENSION X(5)
      DATA X/ 5.0, 4.0, 3.0, 2.0, 1.0/
C         ...PLACE LARGEST NUMBER IN X(5)
      DO 20 I=1,4
         IF( X(I) .LT. X(I + 1) ) GO TO 20
            TEMP=X(I)
            X(I)=X(I + 1)
            X(I + 1)=TEMP
 20   CONTINUE
C
      WRITE(6,30) X(5)
 30   FORMAT(1X, 'THE LARGEST NUMBER IS', F10.0)
C
      WRITE(6,40)
 40   FORMAT(1X, 'RESULT OF FIRST STEP IN SORT')
      DO 60 I=1,5
         WRITE(6,50) X(I)
 50      FORMAT(1X, F10.U)
 60   CONTINUE
      STOP
      END
```

Figure 6.10a. Program interchanges adjacent numbers in a list (which is first presented in the DATA statement) so that the largest number will be at the right of the list. The interchanging is done toward the right, as shown in Table I for this figure. This is the first program in a two-step sequence that will rearrange the list so that it is in ascending order from left to right.

I	X(I)	X(I + 1)
1	5	4
2	5	3
3	5	2
4	5	1

Table I for Fig. 6.10a. The values of X(I) and X(I + 1) each time IF((X(I) .LT. X(I + 1)) GO TO 20 is executed.

I	X(I)	X(I + 1)
1	4	5
2	3	5
3	2	5
4	1	5

Table II for Fig. 6.10a. The values of X(I) and X(I + 1) each time 20 CONTINUE is executed, i.e., after the interchange is made.

the list after each interchange is shown in Table III for Fig. 6.10a. Again we remark that although there are 5 numbers in the list, we have to execute the statement in the loop only four times. The reason for this is that it takes only four interchanges to make the first number the last. The results are printed at the end of the program. They are shown in Fig. 6.10b.

In writing a program like this, it is tempting to perform the interchange by using two statements, i.e.,

```
X(I)=X(I + 1)
X(I + 1)= X(I)
```

instead of the three we used. This is wrong, as we now show. Let us assume that the value of X(I + 1) is 4 and X(I) is 5 before these statements are executed. When the first of these two statements is executed, 4 is assigned to X(I). When the second is executed, X(I) (which is now 4) is assigned to X(I + 1). Now not only is the value of X(I) 4, but also the value of X(I + 1) is 4.

If the IF-THEN is available on your compiler you can use it to eliminate the GO TO in the program of Fig. 6.10a. Thus you can rewrite the DO loop as

```
   DO 20 I = 1,4
     IF( X(I) .GT. X(I + 1)) THEN
        TEMP = X(I)
        X(I) = X(I + 1)
        X(I + 1) = TEMP
     END IF
20 CONTINUE
```

At the end of the execution of the program shown in Fig. 6.10a, we have not placed all the numbers in ascending order. All we have succeeded in doing is placing the largest number at the right end of the list. The way we sort the entire list is to repeat the entire comparison and interchanging procedure to our final list. We do this by simply placing the interchanging loop of the last program in an outer loop, as is shown in Fig. 6.11a so that the entire sorting loop is executed again and again until the numbers are in ascending

Original list:	5,4,3,2,1
I	List
1	4,5,3,2,1
2	4,3,5,2,1
3	4,3,2,5,1
4	4,3,2,1,5
Final list:	4,3,2,1,5

Table III for Fig. 6.10a. How this list appears for each value of I, each time 20 CONTINUE is executed.

```
THE LARGEST NUMBER IS            5.
RESULT OF FIRST STEP IN SORT
        4.
        3.
        2.
        1.
        5.
```

Figure 6.10b. Running the program of Fig. 6.10a.

SORTING, STEP II

```
C   SORTS NUMBERS , STEP 2
      DIMENSION X(5)
      DATA X/ 5.0, 4.0, 3.0, 2.0, 1.0 /
C         ...SORTS NUMBERS
      DO 30 J=1,4
         M=5-J
         DO 20 I=1,M
         IF( X(I) .LT. X(I + 1) ) GO TO 20
            TEMP=X(I)
            X(I)=X(I + 1)
            X(I + 1)= TEMP
 20      CONTINUE
 30   CONTINUE
C         ...PRINT RESULTS IN ASCENDING ORDER
      DO 50 I=1,5
         WRITE(6,40) X(I)
 40      FORMAT(1X, F10.0)
 50   CONTINUE
      STOP
      END
```

Figure 6.11a. Program sorts, in ascending order, the numbers that appear in the DATA statement. The DO loop of the preceding program (here the I loop) is now executed 4 times. At the end of each time, the inner loop is completely executed; the rearranged list appears as is shown in the table for Fig. 6.11a.

order. To determine how many times we have to do this, let us first examine the list as it appears originally and as it appears after each time the interchanging loop is completely executed. The list as it appears at various stages is shown in the table for Fig. 6.11a. The index of the outer loop is J.

Since the numbers were originally in *descending* order, the number of times we have to interchange adjacent numbers in order to get them in *ascending* order is a maximum and will certainly suffice for any other original order. The first two lines of the table show the list as it originally appears and as it appears in the beginning of the interchanging loop the second time it is executed.

J (ordering)	List	5−J (interchanges required to get to next ordering)
1	5,4,3,2,1	4
2	4,3,2,1,5	3

We see from the table that four interchanges of adjacent numbers are required to get from 5,4,3,2,1 to 4,3,2,1,5. However, this is just 5−J, the amount of numbers in the list minus the value of the outer loop index, which in this case is 1. From the second and third lines, we see

J (ordering)	List	5−J (interchanges required to get to next ordering)
2	4,3,2,1,5	3
3	3,2,1,4,5	2

that three interchanges are required to get from 4,3,2,1,5 to 3,2,1,4,5. However, this again is 5−J. As we look at the rest of the table, we see that the number of interchanges required to get from a given line to the next lower line is always 5−J. We also see that there are four steps required to go from the original to the sorted list. Thus in Fig. 6.11a, we write the DO statement for the outer loop as

```
DO 30 J=1,4
```

This determines how many times the complete interchanging process must be applied to the original list to obtain the sorted list. The inner loop—which starts with DO 20 I=1,M—determines how many interchanges must be done to a given list. We have seen that this is 5−J. Thus we define the limit of the index of this loop as M=5−J. This is done in the statement immediately preceding this inner DO. The results of the program are shown in Fig. 6.11b.

J (ordering)	List	5−J (interchanges required to get to next ordering)
1	5,4,3,2,1	4
2	4,3,2,1,5	3
3	3,2,1,4,5	2
4	2,1,3,4,5	1
	1,2,3,4,5	0

Table for Fig. 6.11a. The first four lines show the list as it appears at the beginning of the execution of the inner loop for each value of J (the outer loop index). The last line shows the list as it appears at the end of the last execution of the inner loop. We see that, as we descend the table, we have to perform one less interchange to get from a given line to the next lower line in the table. The number of these interchanges is given in the last column. We use this number as the upper limit of the index in the inner DO loop.

```
1.
2.
3.
4.
5.
```

Figure 6.11b. Running the program of Fig. 6.11a. The numbers are now sorted in ascending order.

6.6. Satisfying Input and Output Lists

The first WRITE statement in the program of Fig. 6.12a

```
WRITE(6,10) VAR1
```

has fewer variables in its list than there are field specifications in the associated FORMAT statement

```
10   FORMAT(1X, 'VAR1=', F7.3,'   VAR2=', F8.3, '   VAR3=', F9.3, 'END')
```

When the program is executed, the computer matches VAR1 with F7.3 and prints 10.31. The fact that no variable in the first WRITE list corresponds to F8.3 does not bother the compiler. It simply does not print anything in this field or in any of the fields that follow this field, including those described by strings. However, since VAR2= precedes F8.3, the first field specification not used, VAR2=, is printed. All of this is shown in the first line of Fig. 6.12b,

```
VAR1= 10.310   VAR2=
```

The second WRITE statement in the program

```
WRITE(6,10) VAR1, VAR2
```

also has fewer variables in its list than there are field specifications in the associated FORMAT. The computer again prints information in all the fields to the left of the field described by the first field specification that is not used—this time F9.3. The computer thus prints

```
VAR1= 10.310   VAR2= 16.810   VAR3=
```

The third WRITE statement WRITE(6,10) VAR1, VAR2, VAR3 has the same number of variables in its list as there are field specifications in the associated FORMAT. Thus the computer prints

```
VAR1= 10.310   VAR2= 16.810   VAR3= 20.210END
```

We can summarize what happened when these three WRITE statements were executed by saying that the computer uses the FORMAT statement only until all the variables in the WRITE list have been matched with field specifications; then, if there is a string which immediately follows the last field specification used, this string is also printed. Another way of saying this is that the FORMAT is used until the WRITE list is satisfied.

ASPECTS OF THE WRITE **LIST**

```
C  MORE FIELD SPECIFICATIONS THAN VARIABLES IN THE WRITE LIST
C
      VAR1=10.31
      VAR2=16.81
      VAR3=20.21
C
      WRITE(6,10) VAR1
      WRITE(6,10) VAR1, VAR2
      WRITE(6,10) VAR1, VAR2, VAR3
 10   FORMAT(1X, 'VAR1=', F7.3,'   VAR2=', F8.3, '   VAR3=', F9.3, 'END')
      STOP
      END
```

Figure 6.12a. A program in which there are more field specifications in the FORMAT than there are variables in the WRITE list. The same FORMAT is used with three different WRITE statements.

```
VAR1= 10.310   VAR2=
VAR1= 10.310   VAR2= 16.810   VAR3=
VAR1= 10.310   VAR2= 16.810   VAR3= 20.210END
```

Figure 6.12b. Running the program of Fig. 6.12a the computer uses the FORMAT up to the first field specification that is not matched with a variable in the WRITE list. If there is a string which immediately follows the last field specification used, this string is also printed.

In Fig. 6.12c we see a program in which the FORMAT

```
10    FORMAT(1X, 'RESULT=', F7.3)
```

has fewer field specifications than there are variables in the associated WRITE statement

```
WRITE(6,10) VAR1, VAR2, VAR3
```

What happens is that the computer reuses the FORMAT statement until the WRITE list is satisfied. Each time the computer uses the FORMAT statement in Fig. 6.12c, it interprets the first character in the first field as a control character. Since 1X describes the first field, the computer prints the results on a new line each time the FORMAT is used. When the computer executes the WRITE statement, it encounters VAR1 and matches it with F7.3 thus printing

```
RESULT= 10.310
```

as is shown in Fig. 6.12d. It then encounters VAR2. Since there are no more field specifications in the FORMAT, the computer reuses the FORMAT from its beginning and matches VAR2 with F7.3. It thus prints

```
RESULT= 16.810
```

on a new line. The computer then encounters VAR3 and again reuses the FORMAT statement from its beginning, thus printing

```
RESULT= 20.210
```

Now, since the WRITE list is satisfied, the computer no longer uses the FORMAT statement.

```
C   LESS FIELD SPECIFICATIONS THAN VARIABLES IN THE WRITE LIST
C
       VAR1=10.31
       VAR2=16.81
       VAR3=20.21
C
       WRITE(6,10) VAR1, VAR2, VAR3
 10    FORMAT(1X, 'RESULT=', F7.3)
       STOP
       END
```

Figure 6.12c. A program in which there are fewer field specifications in the FORMAT than there are variables in the WRITE list. The computer reuses the FORMAT specification until all the variables in the WRITE list have been matched with a field specification.

```
RESULT= 10.310
RESULT= 16.810
RESULT= 20.210
```

Figure 6.12d. Running the program of Fig. 6.12c. Each time the FORMAT is used, the 1X is used to describe the control character and then the results are printed on a new line.

When a FORMAT is used with a READ statement, the FORMAT is used only until the READ list is satisfied. Thus in Fig. 6.13a since there is only one variable in the list in

```
READ(5,10) VAR1
```

only the first field specification in

```
10    FORMAT(F10.0,F10.0)
```

is used. The fact that the data card in Fig. 6.13b has three constants punched on it does not affect the operation of the program. Only the constant punched (10.31) in the field that is used is read by the program. Thus the program ignores 16.81 and −9.6. The results of running the program are shown in Fig. 6.13c.

In Fig. 6.13d, there are more variables in the READ

```
READ(5,10) VAR1, VAR2, VAR3
```

list than there are field specifications in the FORMAT. Thus the FORMAT

```
10    FORMAT(F10.0, F10.0)
```

is reused until the READ list is satisfied. Each time the FORMAT is reused, a new card is read. The data cards are shown in Fig. 6.13e. When the computer executes the READ statement, it matches VAR1 and VAR2 with the two field specifications in the FORMAT and assigns the values of the constants on the first data card to these variables—10.31 is assigned to VAR1; and 16.81 to VAR2. Since there is no field specification to match with VAR3, the computer uses the FORMAT again. It thus reads the next card and uses the first F10.0 in assigning 20.62 to VAR3. If there were other constants punched in subsequent fields on this card, the computer would ignore these constants, since only one field specification in the FORMAT is used. The results of running the program are shown in Fig. 6.13f.

ASPECTS OF THE READ LIST

```
C  MORE FIELD SPECIFICATIONS THAN VARIABLES IN  THE READ LIST
C
       READ(5,10) VAR1
 10    FORMAT(F10.0,F10.0)
       WRITE(6,20) VAR1
 20    FORMAT(1X, 'VAR1=', F10.3)
       STOP
       END
```

Figure 6.13a. A program in which there are more field specifications in the FORMAT than there are variables in the READ list. Since only one variable appears in the READ list, only the first field specification in the FORMAT is used.

```
 10.31       16.81       -9.6
```

Figure 6.13b. The data card for Fig. 6.13a. Since only one variable appears in the READ list, only the value (10.31) in the first field on the data card is used. The other values on the data card are ignored.

```
VAR1=     10.310
```

Figure 6.13c. Running the program of Fig. 6.13a.

```
C  LESS FIELD SPECIFICATIONS THAN VARIABLES IN THE READ LIST
       READ(5,10) VAR1, VAR2, VAR3
 10    FORMAT(F10.0, F10.0)
       WRITE(6, 20) VAR1, VAR2, VAR3
 20    FORMAT(1X, 'VAR1=', F7.3, '   VAR2=', F7.3, '   VAR3=', F7.3)
       STOP
       END
```

Figure 6.13d. Now there are more variables in the READ list than there are field specifications in the FORMAT. The computer reuses the FORMAT until all the variables in the READ list have been matched with a field specification. Each time the FORMAT is reused, a new data card is read.

```
 10.31       16.81
20.62
```

Figure 6.13e. The data cards for Fig. 6.13d.

```
VAR1= 10.310   VAR2= 16.810   VAR3= 20.620
```

Figure 6.13f. Running the program of Fig. 6.13d.

6.7. Implied DO Loops

In Fig. 6.14a, we present a brief program that, using a DO loop, prints the values of an array X. The values of X are defined in the DATA statement. The results are shown in Fig. 6.14b. This program can be written so that the DO loop is incorporated into the WRITE statement itself as is shown in Fig. 6.15a:

```
WRITE(6,10) ( X(I), I=1,5)
```

This construct is called an implied DO loop. It instructs the computer to print the elements of X for values of the subscript prescribed in the implied DO. In this case the subscript varies from 1 to 5 in steps of 1. The variable I is called the index of the implied DO loop; the index must be an INTEGER variable. The implied DO in Fig. 6.15a is equivalent to

```
WRITE(6,10) X(1), X(2), X(3), X(4), X(5)
```

Since it is matched with 10 FORMAT(1X, F10.1), the value of each of the elements is printed on a different line. We recall that the reason for this is that, after the value of X(1) is printed, there is no field specification to match with X(2). The computer thus returns to the first left parenthesis it encounters. Since this is the beginning of the FORMAT and since it is followed by 1X, the computer skips to the next line and prints the value of X(2). This procedure is continued, resulting in the value of each element of X being printed on the next line. This is shown in Fig. 6.15b. If we wanted the 5 numbers printed on one line,

MOTIVATING THE IMPLIED DO

```
C   MOTIVATING THE IMPLIED DO
       DIMENSION X(5)
       DATA X/ 1.0, 2.0, 3.0, 4.0, 5.0/
C          ...USE DO LOOP TO PRINT RESULTS
       DO 20 I=1,5
          WRITE(6,10) X(I)
 10       FORMAT(1X, F10.2)
 20    CONTINUE
       STOP
       END
```

Figure 6.14a. This program uses a DO loop to print the constant shown in the DATA statement.

```
1.00
2.00
3.00
4.00
5.00
```

Figure 6.14b. Running the program of Fig. 6.14a.

USING THE IMPLIED DO FOR VERTICAL OUTPUT

```
C   INTRODUCTION TO IMPLIED DO
C   VERTICAL OUTPUT
       DIMENSION X(5)
       DATA X/ 1.0, 2.0, 3.0, 4.0, 5.0/
       WRITE(6,10) ( X(I), I=1,5)
 10    FORMAT(1X, F10.1)
       STOP
       END
```

Figure 6.15a. The implied DO loop replaces the DO loop of the previous program. The computer interprets the implied DO as WRITE(6,10) X(1), X(2), X(3), X(4), X(5)

```
1.0
2.0
3.0
4.0
5.0
```

Figure 6.15b. The results are printed one per line, since for each new element of X the FORMAT is used again. We remember that each time a FORMAT statement is used, the results are printed on a new line.

we would have to provide 5 field specifications in the FORMAT, e.g.,

```
10     FORMAT(1X, 5F10.1)
```

as is shown in Fig. 6.15c. This way, each of the 5 elements of X would be matched with one of the field specifications in 5F10.1 (see Fig. 6.15d). It is important to note that if this format had replaced the one used with the program of Fig. 5.14a, the results of that program would not have been printed on one line; the reason is that each time the WRITE is executed, the computer prints the results on a new line (only the first of the five field specifications would be used, each time the WRITE is executed).

If you are using the WATFIV compiler, you can use an implied DO in a PRINT statement, e.g., write

```
PRINT, ( X(I), I=1,5 )
```

USING THE IMPLIED DO FOR HORIZONTAL OUTPUT

```
C  THE IMPLIED DO
C  HORIZONTAL OUTPUT
      DIMENSION X(5)
      DATA X/ 1.0, 2.0, 3.0, 4.0, 5.0/
      WRITE(6,10) ( X(I), I=1,5)
 10   FORMAT(1X, 5F10.1)
      STOP
      END
```

Figure 6.15c. Same as the preceding program, but because of 10 FORMAT(1X, 5F10.1), all 5 values are printed on one line.

```
1.0       2.0       3.0       4.0       5.0
```

Figure 6.15d. Running the program of Fig. 6.15c.

In Fig. 6.16a we present a program that sorts a maximum of 100 numbers, which are punched one per data card. The last data card is a trailer on which is punched −123456789. If more than 100 cards are read, the program prints a message and then stops. Note that the test for the trailer precedes N=I, the statement that will tell us how many data cards were read. If this statement preceded the IF, the final value of N would include the contribution of the trailer. This would cause an error later in the program. After the trailer is read, control is transferred to the part of the program that does the sorting. Since the outer DO loop of the nested DO loops that perform the sorting has to be executed only N−1 times (where N is the number of items in the list to be sorted), we write N1=N−1 immediately preceding the outer DO loop. Consequently, we use N1 as the limit of the loop index for this loop, thus writing the DO as

```
DO 70 J=1,N1
```

We remember that the inner loop does the interchanging and that, each time the inner loop is completely executed, it does one less interchange than the time before. We thus precede the inner DO with M=N−J (where J is the outer loop index) and use M as the limit of the inner DO. We thus write the DO as

```
DO 60 I=1,M
```

The results of the program are shown in Fig. 6.16b.

Had we wanted to, we could have eliminated N=I from the first loop, since we know that the number of data cards, excluding the trailer, read is I−1. We would then write statement 50 as 50 N1=I−2 instead of N1=N−1.

SORTING CONSTANTS READ INTO THE PROGRAM

```
C  FULL SORT. SORTS A MAXIMUM OF 100 CARDS
      DIMENSION  X(101)
C          ...READ CARDS
      DO 30 I=1,101
         READ(5,10) X(I)
 10      FORMAT(F10.0)
         WRITE(6,20) X(I)
 20      FORMAT(1X, F12.2)
         IF( X(I) .EQ. -12345678.0 ) GO TO 50
C          ...N IS THE NUMBER OF DATA CARDS EXCLUDING THE TRAILER
            N=I
 30   CONTINUE
      WRITE(6,40)
 40   FORMAT(1X, '100  CARDS READ. SORRY, BUT THE MAXIMUM IS 100')
      STOP
C          ...SORT THE NUMBERS
 50   N1=N-1
      DO 70 J=1,N1
         M=N-J
         DO 60 I=1,M
         IF(  X(I) .LT. X(I + 1) ) GO TO 60
            TEMP=X(I)
            X(I)=X(I + 1)
            X(I + 1)= TEMP
 60      CONTINUE
 70   CONTINUE
C          ...PRINT THE RESULTS
      WRITE(6,80)
 80   FORMAT(1X,  'THE SORTED NUMBERS')
      WRITE(6,90) ( X(I), I=1,N)
 90   FORMAT(1X, F10.2)
      STOP
      END
```

Figure 6.16a. A sorting program that sorts any amount of numbers up to 100. The upper limit of the inner DO is M (which equals N−J). Thus, each time the inner loop is executed, it is executed one less time. This is further explained in the table for Fig. 6.16a.

```
      12.20
      16.30
       8.10
       3.60
      14.00
-12345670.00
THE SORTED NUMBERS
      3.60
      8.10
     12.20
     14.00
     16.30
```

Figure 6.16b. Running the program of Fig. 6.16a.

DIMENSION

The form of the DIMENSION statement is: DIMENSION, followed by the subscripted variables used in the program. If there is more than one variable, the variables are separated by commas. In the parentheses following the name of a given subscripted variable is placed the maximum value that the subscript will assume in the program. Examples:

```
DIMENSION CARD(20), STATE(4), MINE(10)
DIMENSION CARD(4)
```

If there are so many subscripted variables that they cannot be all listed on one line in the DIMENSION statement, you may continue the DIMENSION statement by continuing* the statement on the next line

```
 DIMENSION A(10), B(10), C(10), D(10), E(10)
1     F(10), G(18), H(9), I(15), J(14)
```

Or you may start another DIMENSION statement

```
DIMENSION A(10), B(10), C(10), D(10), E(10)
DIMENSION F(10), G(18), H(9), I(15), J(14)
```

Since the DIMENSION statement is nonexecutable, it cannot be preceded by a statement number. To facilitate readability, it is best to place the variables in the DIMENSION statement in alphabetical order.

INTEGER (or REAL)

The form of the INTEGER (or REAL) statement is: INTEGER (or REAL) followed by the variables that you wish to be INTEGER (or REAL). If there is more than one variable, the variables are separated by commas. If you wish to, you may dimension a variable in an INTEGER (or REAL) statement. Examples::

```
INTEGER A(10), B,C,D(18), E(6), K(8)
REAL I(15), J(14), K(8), L(6), S(10)
INTEGER CARD (4)
```

You may continue an INTEGER (or REAL) statement, e.g.,

```
 INTEGER A(10) B,C,D(18), E(6)
1     F(10), G(18), H(9)
```

or you may start another INTEGER (or REAL) statement

```
INTEGER A(10), B,C,D(18), E(6)
INTEGER F(10), G(18), H(9)
```

The INTEGER (or REAL) statement cannot be preceded by a statement number. To facilitate readability, it is best to place the variables in the INTEGER or REAL statement in alphabetical order.

* ANS Standard FORTRAN allows a maximum of 19 continuation cards, whereas ANS Standard Basic FORTRAN allows a maximum of 5 continuation cards.

I (ordering)	List	N (numbers in list)	M=N−I (interchanges required to get to next ordering)
1	5,4,3,2,1	5	4
2	4,3,2,1,5	5	3
3	3,2,1,4,5	5	2
4	2,1,3,4,5	5	1
	1,2,3,4,5	5	0

Table for Fig. 6.16a. The list is given as it appears at the beginning of the execution of the inner loop for each value of I (the outer loop index). The last line shows the list as it appears at the end of the last execution of the inner loop. We see that as we descend the table we have to perform one less interchange at each line of the table. The number of these interchanges is given in the last column. This number is the upper limit of the index in the inner DO loop.

PROBLEMS

1. Which of the following subscript forms are correct?

   (a) 3 * K + 2
   (b) 2 + K * 3
   (c) I + 2
   (d) 2 + I
   (e) K * 4 + 2
   (f) 2 * K
   (g) K * 2

2. N data cards contain N constants. Write a program that calculates the sum of these N numbers and the fraction each of these numbers is of the sum.

3. Write a program that calculates the average of numbers read from a group of cards. One number is punched per card. The program should then print those values which are less than the average.

4. Write a program that calculates the average $\bar{x}$ and the variance, V for the data cards in problem 3.
   Remember

$$\bar{x} = \frac{\sum_i x_i}{N} \qquad V = \frac{\sum_i (x_i - \bar{x})^2}{N-1}$$

5. What is wrong with the following DATA statements?

   (a) DATA/A,B,C/ 3.0, 2.4, 6.11
   (b) DATA A,B,I,C/ 4 * 3.2 /
   (c) DATA A,B,I,C/ 4.0, 3.1, 6.2, 7.8/

6. What is printed by the following program?

```
      DIMENSION X(3), Y(3)
      DATA X, Y / 1.0, 2.0, 3.0, 4.0, 5.0, 6.0 /
      DO 20 I = 1, 3
         WRITE(6,10) X(I), Y(I)
10       FORMAT(1X, 2F10.0)
20    CONTINUE
        STOP
        END
```

7. Each card in a set of data cards has punched on it an integer. The integers vary from 1 to 20. Write a program that histograms the results of reading these cards. The histogram should be divided into 4 equal intervals.

8. The statistic χ^2 is defined as

$$\chi^2 = \frac{\sum_i (\text{OBSERVED}_i - \text{EXPECTED}_i)^2}{\text{EXPECTED}_i}$$

A die is tossed 60 times. Since a die has 6 faces, the expected number of times each face appears is 10. Assuming the result of each toss is punched on a card, write a program that reads these cards and calculates χ^2. Use a 6-element array E to store the results. Thus OBSERVED_i equals E(I) and $\text{EXPECTED}_i = 10$.

9. Write the program of problem 8 so that it calculates χ^2 for N tosses of the die, where N is determined by the number of cards read in.

10. Write the program of problem 8 so that it accommodates an M-sided die tossed N times.

11. Do problem 7 so that it calculates χ^2. Since there are four intervals the EXPECTED number for each interval is just the total number of cards read, divided by 4.

12. On an exam, marks between 90 and 99 rate an A; marks between 80 and 89 rate a B; between 70 and 79 rate a C; between 60 and 69 rate a D. Marks below 60 rate an F and 100 rates an A+. The numerical grades are punched one per data card. Write a program that determines how many marks are in each category.

13. Write a program that determines the average, lowest, and highest numbers from a group of numbers read from cards.

14. The median of a set of sorted numbers is the middle number. Thus in 1,3,4,11,12 the number 4 is the median. Write a program that first sorts a set of numbers and then determines its median.

15. The mode of a set of numbers is that number which occurs most frequently. Thus in 1,4,3,2,4,1,4,3,4, the number 4 is the mode. Write a program that determines the mode of a set of numbers.

7

Doubly Subscripted Variables and Matrix Multiplication

7.1 Doubly Subscripted Variables

We now explain the use of variables that have two subscripts by using a doubly subscripted variable—also called two-dimensional arrays—in the program shown in Fig. 7.1a. This program enables the programmer to determine whether there is any connection between the result of throwing one die and the result of throwing a second die in a game in which two dice are thrown. The results of throwing the dice for any given time are both punched on a data card. The program accommodates up to 1000 data cards (i.e., 1000 throws of the dice.)

The array COUNT(F,S) is used as a counter to record the results each time the two dice are thrown. Since we are using the array as a counter, we declare it to be an INTEGER. The first subscript F, refers to the result when the first die is thrown. The second subscript S refers to the result when the second die is thrown. Since both F and S are subscripts, they are also declared INTEGER.

USE OF DOUBLY SUBSCRIPTED VARIABLES

```
C   USE OF DOUBLY SUBSCRIPTED VARIABLES
        INTEGER F, S, COUNT(6,6)
C           ...ZERO ARRAY
        DO 20 J=1,6
              DO 10 K=1,6
                 COUNT(J,K)=0
 10           CONTINUE
 20     CONTINUE
C           ...READ AND HISTOGRAM
        WRITE(6,25)
 25     FORMAT(1X, T11, 'J', T21, 'K')
        DO 40 N=1, 101
              READ(5,30) F, S
 30           FORMAT(2I10)
           WRITE(6,35) F, S
 35        FORMAT(1X, 2I10)
C          ...TEST FOR TRAILER
           IF( F .EQ. -9) GO TO 70
              COUNT(F,S)=COUNT(F,S) + 1
 40     CONTINUE
C
        WRITE(6,50)
 50     FORMAT(1X,'TOO MANY CARDS; MAXIMUM IS 100')
        STOP
C           ...PRINT RESULTS
 70     WRITE(6,80)
 80     FORMAT(1X,'RESULTS')
        DO 110 J=1,6
           DO 100 K=1,6
              WRITE(6,90) J,K, COUNT(J,K)
 90           FORMAT(1X, 'J=', I2, '  K=', I2, I6)
 100       CONTINUE
 110    CONTINUE
        STOP
        END
```

Figure 7.1a. Program determines whether there is any correlation between the throwing of a pair of dice. The elements of COUNT(F,S) are used as counters. The subscript F determines the row (horizontal line) and the subscript S determines the column (vertical line) in the result shown in Fig. 7.1d. All the counters are zeroed at the beginning of the program with a nested DO loop. A doubly subscripted (or two-dimensional) array can be dimensioned in an INTEGER statement.

The values of F and S are read by READ(5,30) F, S. If the result of throwing the first die is 3 and of throwing the second die is 4, then because of

```
COUNT(F,S)=COUNT(F,S) + 1
```

the value of COUNT(3,4) is increased by 1. In Fig. 7.1b we show diagrammatically where COUNT(3,4) would be in the array by placing an X in the appropriate position. On the other hand, if the result of throwing the first die is 4 and the result of throwing the second die is 3, then the value of COUNT(4,3) is increased by 1. In Fig. 7.1c, we show where COUNT(4,3) would be in the array. Note it is the mathematical convention to have the values of the first subscript F describe horizontal lines—called *rows*—and the values of the second subscript S, describe vertical lines—called *columns*. If you have difficulty remembering which are the columns, recall that the columns of the Greek temples were vertical. In mathematics, arrays—e.g., COUNT—are called *matrices*. The locations in the array—e.g., COUNT(3,4)—and their values, are called the *elements* of the array or matrix.

Since the number on a face of a die can be one of the integers from 1 to 6, the maximum value of both F and S is 6. Thus we dimension COUNT as COUNT(6,6). We do this in the INTEGER statement. Since COUNT has 6 rows and 6 columns, we say that it is a 6 by 6 array.

Before we can use a counter, we must assign zero to it. Since F and S can both vary from 1 to 6, the array COUNT(F,S) represents 36 counters; each of these must be zeroed. One way of doing this is to use the nested DO loops

```
      DO 20 J=1,6
         DO 10 K=1,6
            COUNT(J,K)=0
10       CONTINUE
20    CONTINUE
```

In COUNT(J,K), K assumes the values 1 to 6 for each successive value of J up to and including J equals 6. Thus when J equals 1, the computer in successive executions of this statement interprets COUNT(J,K) as COUNT(1,1), COUNT(1,2), COUNT(1,3), COUNT(1,4), COUNT(1,5), and COUNT(1,6), assigning zeros to all these elements. When J equals 2, the computer interprets COUNT(J,K) as COUNT(2,1), COUNT(2,2), COUNT(2,3), COUNT(2,4), COUNT(2,5), and COUNT(2,6). This process continues until all 36 counters are assigned zeros. As the values of J and K are read from the cards shown in Fig. 7.1d they are echo-printed as shown in Fig. 7.1e. This will enable us to check that the program has assigned the values of J and K read, to the proper element of COUNT.

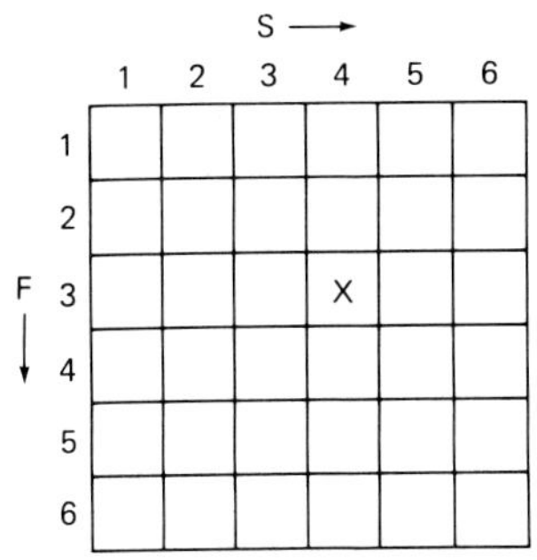

Figure 7.1b. A diagrammatic way of visualizing the array COUNT. Each time COUNT(F,S)=COUNT(F,S) + 1 is executed, a 1 is added to the contents of the appropriate element of COUNT. When F equals 3 and S equals 4, COUNT(3,4)=COUNT(3,4) + 1 instructs the computer to add 1 to the element of COUNT indicated here by an *X*.

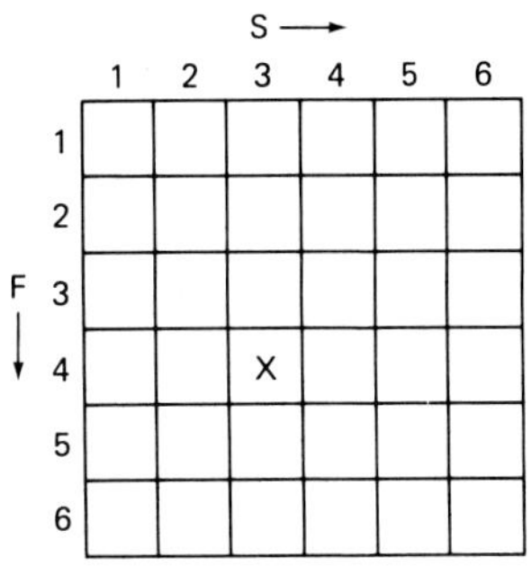

Figure 7.1c. When F equals 4 and S equals 3, the computer interprets COUNT(F,S)= COUNT(F,S) + 1 as COUNT(4,3)= COUNT(4,3) + 1 and therefore adds 1 to the element of COUNT indicated here by an *X*.

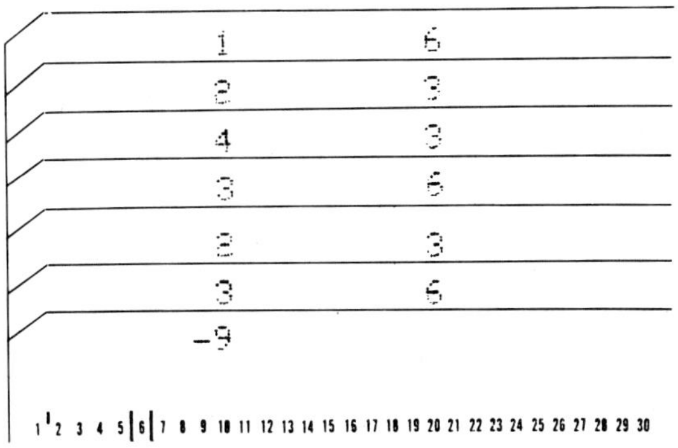

Figure 7.1d. The data cards for the program of Fig. 7.1a.

After the trailer is read, the word RESULTS is printed and the following is executed

```
          DO 110 J=1,6
             DO 100 K=1,6
                WRITE(6,90) J,K, COUNT(J,K)
90              FORMAT(1X, 'J=', I2, '   K=', I2, I6)
100          CONTINUE
110       CONTINUE
```

This group of statements prints the numbers stored in each counter at the end of the program (Fig. 7.1e). The first time the range of the outer loop is executed, the value of J is 1; therefore the computer interprets the WRITE as

```
WRITE(6,90) COUNT(1,K)
```

and as the computer executes the range of the inner loop, it prints the values of COUNT(1,1), COUNT(1,2), COUNT(1,3), COUNT(1,4), COUNT(1,5), and COUNT(1,6) down the page. Each of the values is preceded by the appropriate values of J and K. We see that the value of COUNT(1,6) is 1, whereas the values of the other counters are all zero for the first time the range of the outer DO is executed.

The second time the range of the outer loop is executed, the value of J is 2; therefore the computer interprets the WRITE as

```
WRITE(6,90) COUNT(2,K)
```

and as the computer executes the range of the inner loop, it prints the values of COUNT(2,1), COUNT(2,2), COUNT(2,3), COUNT(2,4), COUNT(2,5), and COUNT(2,6) down the page. Again, each of the values is preceded by the appropriate values of J and K. When the program is complete, it has printed all the elements of the matrix.

If the IF-THEN is available on your compiler, you can eliminate the GO TO and place the nested loop, which does the printing between an IF-THEN and an END IF. Then you can place all of this in the DO loop.

If we wanted to, we could label the results more effectively by rewriting the WRITE and its associated FORMAT as

```
      WRITE(6,90) J, K, COUNT(J,K)
90    FORMAT(1X, 'COUNT(', I1, ',', I1, ')=', I10 )
```

This would produce results that look like

```
COUNT(1,1)= 4
COUNT(1,2)=5
```

etc., assuming the other statements in the program remained unchanged.

Both of the preceding methods of labeling the results printed each element on a new line. We recall that the reason for this is that each time a WRITE statement is executed, it produces its results on a new line. Since the WRITE statement is executed 36 times—once for each element (or counter)—it produces 36 lines of results. Even if we wanted to print the value of 6 elements per line and wrote the WRITE and the associated FORMAT as

```
      WRITE(6,90) COUNT(J,K)
90    FORMAT(1X, 6I10)
```

the results would be the same. Since there is only one variable in the WRITE, only the first of the six fields indicated would be used. If we use an implied DO loop, we will not only be able to print 6 elements of the array per line, but we will also be able to eliminate the nested DO loop.

```
$ENTRY
J        K
1        6
2        3
4        3
3        6
4        2
2        3
3        6
-9       0
RESULTS
J= 1   K= 1     0
J= 1   K= 2     0
J= 1   K= 3     0
J= 1   K= 4     0
J= 1   K= 5     0
J= 1   K= 6     1
J= 2   K= 1     0
J= 2   K= 2     0
J= 2   K= 3     2
J= 2   K= 4     0
J= 2   K= 5     0
J= 2   K= 6     0
J= 3   K= 1     0
J= 3   K= 2     0
J= 3   K= 3     0
J= 3   K= 4     0
J= 3   K= 5     0
J= 3   K= 6     2
J= 4   K= 1     0
J= 4   K= 2     1
J= 4   K= 3     1
J= 4   K= 4     0
J= 4   K= 5     0
J= 4   K= 6     0
J= 5   K= 1     0
J= 5   K= 2     0
J= 5   K= 3     0
J= 5   K= 4     0
J= 5   K= 5     0
J= 5   K= 6     0
J= 6   K= 1     0
J= 6   K= 2     0
J= 6   K= 3     0
J= 6   K= 4     0
J= 6   K= 5     0
J= 6   K= 6     0
```

Figure 7.1e. We first echo-print the values of J and K read. Then, after RESULTS, we print the contents of the array after all values of J and K have been read. The first six values printed, i.e., 0,0,0,0,0,1 correspond to the values of COUNT(1,1), COUNT(1,2), COUNT(1,3), COUNT(1,4), and COUNT(1,6), respectively.

We now use an implied DO loop to rewrite the part of the program which prints the results. We write it

```
      DO 100 J=1,6
         WRITE(6,90) J, (COUNT(J,K), K=1,6)
90       FORMAT(1X, 'J=', I2, 6I6)
100   CONTINUE
```

as is shown in Fig. 7.2a. The data cards for the program are shown in Fig. 7.2b (they are the same as shown in Fig. 7.1d). Here we have placed the implied DO loop (COUNT(J,K), K= 1,6) along with the variable J in the WRITE statement. The variable K is the index of the implied DO. An implied DO is considered to be like any other variable. We have thus separated it with a comma from the variable J. It can also be placed anywhere in a WRITE statement that a variable can be placed. The first time the WRITE statement is executed, the value of J is 1, so the computer intreprets (COUNT(J,K), K= 1,6) as (COUNT(1,K), K= 1,6). This instructs the computer to print the values of COUNT(1,1), COUNT(1,2),

PLACING THE IMPLIED DO WITHIN THE RANGE OF A DO LOOP

```
C   USE OF DOUBLY SUBSCRIPTED VARIABLES
C   AND IMPLIED DO LOOP
        INTEGER F, S, COUNT(6,6)
C           ...ZERO ARRAY
        DO 20 J=1,6
                DO 10 K=1,6
                    COUNT(J,K)=0
 10             CONTINUE
 20     CONTINUE
C           ...READ AND HISTOGRAM
        WRITE(6,25)
 25     FORMAT(1X, T11, 'J', T21, 'K')
        DO 40 N=1, 101
                READ(5,30) F, S
 30             FORMAT(2I10)
                WRITE(6,35) F, S
 35             FORMAT(1X, 2I10)
C               ...TEST FOR TRAILER
                IF( F .EQ. -9) GO TO 70
                COUNT(F,S)=COUNT(F,S) + 1
 40     CONTINUE
C
        WRITE(6,50)
 50     FORMAT(1X,'TOO MANY CARDS! MAXIMUM IS 100')
        STOP
C           ...PRINT RESULTS
 70     WRITE(6,80)
 80     FORMAT(1X,'RESULTS')
        DO 100 J=1,6
            WRITE(6,90) J, (COUNT(J,K), K=1,6)
 90         FORMAT(1X, 'J=', I2, 6I6)
 100    CONTINUE
        STOP
        END
```

Figure 7.2a. The program of Fig. 7.1a rewritten using an implied DO loop. The computer interprets it as WRITE(6,90) J,COUNT (J,1), COUNT(J,2), COUNT(J,3), COUNT(J,4), COUNT(J,5), COUNT(J,6). The implied DO is treated just like a variable, so it must be separated from the preceding variable, J, with a comma. In WATFOR/WATFIV we could write this statement as PRINT,J,(COUNT(J,K), K= 1,6).

COUNT(1,3), COUNT(1,4), COUNT(1,5), and COUNT(1,6). Since these elements correspond to 6I6 in the FORMAT, the 6 values are printed on one line along with J=1 as is shown in Fig. 7.2c. The second time the WRITE statement is executed, the value of J is 2, so the computer interprets (COUNT(J,K), K=1,6) as (COUNT(2,K), K=1,6). This instructs the computer to print the values of COUNT(2,1), COUNT(2,2), COUNT(2,3), COUNT(2,4), COUNT(2,5), and COUNT(2,6) across the page.

In WATFOR/WATFIV we could, if we wanted to, write this WRITE statement without a FORMAT. Thus the DO loop would appear as

```
      DO 100 J=1,6
         PRINT, J, ( COUNT(J,K), K=1,6 )
100   CONTINUE
```

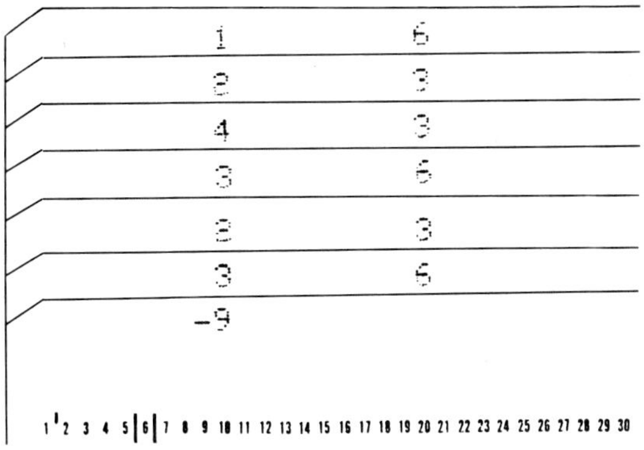

Figure 7.2b. The data cards for the program of Fig. 7.2a. (They are the same as those shown in Fig. 7.1d.)

```
          J            K
          1            6
          2            3
          4            3
          3            6
          4            2
          2            3
          3            6
         -9            0
RESULTS
J= 1      0      0      0      0      0      1
J= 2      0      0      2      0      0      0
J= 3      0      0      0      0      0      2
J= 4      0      1      1      0      0      0
J= 5      0      0      0      0      0      0
J= 6      0      0      0      0      0      0
```

Figure 7.2c. Running the program of Fig. 7.2a. Since we are using 6I6 in the FORMAT, the values of COUNT(J,K) for K equals 1 to 6 are printed on one line.

In Chapter 8 on Input/Output we will cover the implied DO loop in more detail, and we will see how we can have value of K printed across the page.

In the meantime, we will cover an aspect of the implied DO loop that will enable us to eliminate the DO loop that prints the results. We now take the implied DO loop (COUNT(J,K), K=1,6) and place *it* in an implied DO loop in which J is now the index of the loop. We thus now write the WRITE statement as

```
      WRITE(6,90) ( (COUNT(J,K), K=1,6), J=1,6)
90    FORMAT(1X, 6I10)
```

and eliminate the DO loop, all of which is shown in Fig. 7.3a. The data for the program are shown in Fig. 7.3b. Note that, since (COUNT(J,K), J=1,6) is considered grammatically to be just like a variable, it is separated from K with a comma just as any variable appearing in an implied DO would have to be separated from the index of the implied DO loop. We now have something similar to a nested DO loop—(COUNT(J,K), J=1,6) is considered to be the "inner" implied DO loop and K is considered to be the index of the "inner" loop, much the same as the situation in the preceding program. The index of the inner implied DO loop varies from its initial value to its maximum value for each value of the index of the outer implied DO loop. Thus, first the value of J is set equal to 1 and the computer interprets the inner implied DO as (COUNT(1,K), K=1,6). Because of the 6 fields specified

NESTING AN IMPLIED DO **LOOP**

```
C  NESTING AN IMPLIED DO LOOP
      INTEGER F, S, COUNT(6,6)
C        ...ZERO ARRAY
      DO 20 J=1,6
           DO 10 K=1,6
                COUNT(J,K)=0
 10        CONTINUE
 20   CONTINUE
C        ...READ AND HISTOGRAM
      WRITE(6,25)
 25   FORMAT(1X, T11, 'J', T21, 'K')
      DO 40 N=1, 101
           READ(5,30) F, S
 30        FORMAT(2I10)
           WRITE(6,35) F, S
 35        FORMAT(1X, 2I10)
C        ...TEST FOR TRAILER
           IF( F .EQ. -9) GO TO 70
           COUNT(F,S)=COUNT(F,S) + 1
 40   CONTINUE
C
      WRITE(6,50)
 50   FORMAT(1X,'TOO MANY CARDS; MAXIMUM IS 100')
      STOP
C        ...PRINT RESULTS
 70   WRITE(6,80)
 80   FORMAT(1X,'RESULTS')
      WRITE(6,90) ( (COUNT(J,K), K=1,6), J=1,6)
 90   FORMAT(1X, 6I10)
      STOP
      END
```

Figure 7.3a. Same as Fig. 7.2a, but now only implied DO loops are used to print the results. (COUNT(J,K), K=1,6) is treated as an inner DO loop, so first (COUNT(1,K), K=1,6) is executed, printing the first line of results. Then (COUNT(2,K), K=1,6) prints the second line of results, etc. (COUNT(J,K), K=1,6) is treated just like a variable, so it must be separated from K=1,6 by a comma. In WATFOR/WATFIV we could write this statement as PRINT,((COUNT(J,K), K=1,6), J=1,6).

in 6I10 in the FORMAT, the computer prints the values of the elements COUNT(1,1), COUNT(1,2) . . . COUNT(1,6) across the page, as shown in Fig. 7.3c, just as was done in the last program. The index J of the outer implied DO is then increased to 2, and the computer interprets the inner implied DO now as (COUNT(2,K), K=1,6). Since there are no more field specifications to correspond to these 6 elements of COUNT, the computer uses the FORMAT again. It thus prints the values of the appropriate 6 elements on a new line. This process is continued until 6 lines are printed—all the elements of the array—as shown in Fig. 7.3c. We did not label the output here, because doing so might have made the program harder to follow.

In WATFOR/WATFIV if we wished we could write this implied DO without a FORMAT

```
PRINT, (( COUNT(J,K), K=1,6), J=1,6)
```

If we had changed the FORMAT to

```
90     FORMAT(1X, I10)
```

then the values of the elements would have been printed one per line, the reason being that there are in effect 36 variables in the WRITE and only one field specification in the FORMAT. Moreover, the program would have to use the FORMAT 36 times, and we remember that the program prints the results on a new line each time the FORMAT is used again. On the other hand, although it would not have been desirable, we could have written the FORMAT as

```
90     FORMAT(1X, 36I3)
```

and the values of the 36 elements would have been printed on one line.

If we had written the implied DO loop in the program of Fig. 7.3a as

```
WRITE(6,90) (( COUNT(J,K), J=1,6), K=1,6)
```

instead of

```
WRITE(6,90) (( COUNT(J,K), K=1,6), J=1,6)
```

i.e., interchanging the position of J=1,6 and K=1,6, then J would become the index of the inner implied DO loop; and K the index of the outer implied DO loop. We will assume that the FORMAT is still 90 FORMAT(1X, 6I10). The computer first sets the value of K to 1 and interprets the inner loop as (COUNT(J,1), J=1,6) and thus prints the values of COUNT(1,1), COUNT(2,1), COUNT(3,1), . . . , COUNT(6,1) across the page. Thus the order the results would be printed in would be changed.

One might ask here, what would happen if we interchanged J and K in the DO statements of the nested DO loops which zeroed the elements of COUNT in the beginning of any of the programs shown in Figs. 7.1a, 7.2a, and 7.3a. If we had written it as

```
      DO 20 K=1,6
         DO 10 J=1,6
            COUNT(J,K)=0
10       CONTINUE
20    CONTINUE
```

instead of

```
      DO 20 J=1,6
         DO 10 K=1,6
            COUNT(J,K)=0
10       CONTINUE
20    CONTINUE
```

The answer is that both sets of DO loops accomplish the same thing. The reason is that the initial and limiting values of both the indices J and K are the same.

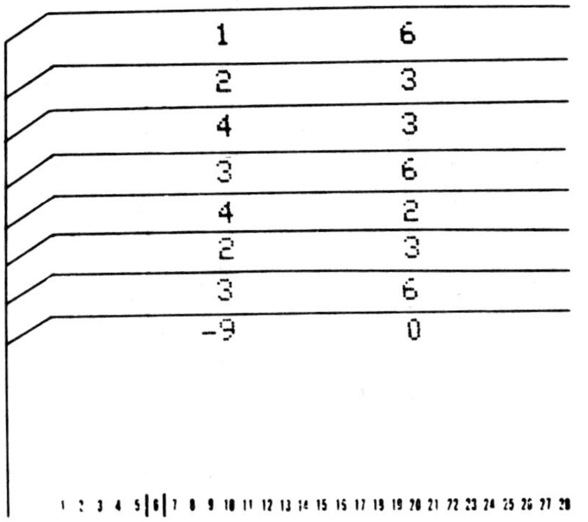

Figure 7.3b. The data cards for the program shown in Fig. 7.3a.

```
          J         K
          1         6
          2         3
          4         3
          3         6
          4         2
          2         3
          3         6
         -9         0
RESULTS
          0         0         0         0         0         1
          0         0         2         0         0         0
          0         0         0         0         0         2
          0         1         1         0         0         0
          0         0         0         0         0         0
          0         0         0         0         0         0
```

Figure 7.3c. The results of running the program of Fig. 7.3a. The elements are printed six to a line because of the 6I10 in the FORMAT. If we used 90 FORMAT(1X, I10), all the elements would be printed one per line.

In the preceding three programs we have made the tacit assumption that the values of the F and S read would be always between 1 and 6. This is an unwise and dangerous assumption to make because F and S are used as subscripts in COUNT(F,S). Because of DIMENSION COUNT(6,6), values of F and S not in this range might produce errors in the output. We omitted testing the validity of the data in the preceding three programs because inclusion of a test would have made the program slightly more complicated and might have obscured the points we were trying to emphasize. The next program we present histograms heights versus weights. We present the program in several versions. The last version will include the test for the integrity of the data. After reading that version, you should easily be able to alter the program of Fig. 7.3a so that it tests the validity of F and S.

In the program of Fig. 7.4a, we produce a two-dimensional histogram of height vs. weight. We assume that the possible values of a height read varies between 60 and 78 inches and that the bin width is 2 inches. Thus there will be 9 intervals for the height. We also assume that the possible weight of a person varies between 100 and 250 pounds and that the bin width is 25 pounds; thus there will be 6 intervals for the weight.

The elements of the subscripted variable BIN(H,W) serve as the counters, where H is the subscript for the height and W is the subscript for the weight. BIN is declared to be INTEGER. Since there are 9 intervals for the height, H will vary from 1 to 9; and since there are 6 intervals for the weight, W will vary from 1 to 6. We thus dimension it accordingly in

```
INTEGER BIN(9,6), H, W
```

Since BIN has 9 rows and 6 columns, it is called a 9 by 6 array.

Since the variables H and W will be used as subscripts, they are also declared INTEGER here. In the nested DO loops we zero all the elements of BIN. Since I in BIN(I,J) has a different limit than J, we must be careful not to interchange the limits of the indices in the DO statements. If we do, an error may result. Thus if we were to incorrectly write the nested DOs as

```
      DO 20 I=1,6
         DO 10 J=1,9
            BIN(K,J)=0
10       CONTINUE
20    CONTINUE
```

instead of

```
      DO 20 I=1,9
         DO 10 J=1,6
            BIN(I,J)=0
10       CONTINUE
20    CONTINUE
```

we would be zeroing, for instance, the element BIN(1,9). Since INTEGER BIN(9,6), H, W does not reserve space in the memory for BIN(1,9), this element might be stored in a location reserved for another variable. If this nested DO loop appeared later on in the program we might be zeroing a variable that we did not want zeroed. On the other hand, BIN(9,1) would not be zeroed because the maximum value of I in BIN(I,J) is only 6.

HISTOGRAMMING HEIGHT VS. WEIGHT

```
C  HISTOGRAMS HEIGHT VS WEIGHT
      INTEGER BIN(9,6), H, W
C        ...ZERO ARRAY  'BIN(HEIGHT,WEIGHT)'
      DO 20 I=1,9
         DO 10 J=1,6
            BIN(I,J)=0
 10      CONTINUE
 20   CONTINUE
C        ...READ AND HISTOGRAM RESULTS
      WRITE(6,25)
 25   FORMAT(1X, T7, 'HEIGHT', T17, 'WEIGHT', T31, 'H', T41, 'W')
      DO 40 N=1,1001
         READ(5,30) HEIGHT, WEIGHT
 30      FORMAT(2F10.0)
C        ...TEST FOR TRAILER
         IF( HEIGHT .EQ. -12345678.0 ) GO TO 60
            H=(HEIGHT-60.0) / 2.0 + 1.0
            W=(WEIGHT-100.0) / 25.0 + 1.0
            WRITE(6,35) HEIGHT, WEIGHT, H, W
 35         FORMAT(1X, 2F10.0, 2I10)
            BIN(H,W)=BIN(H,W) + 1
 40   CONTINUE
      WRITE(6,50)
 50   FORMAT(1X, 'TOO MANY CARDS! MAXIMUM IS 1000')
      STOP
 60   WRITE(6,70)
 70   FORMAT(1X, 'RESULTS')
      WRITE(6,80) ( (BIN(I,J), J=1,6), I=1,9)
 80   FORMAT(1X, 6I10)
      STOP
      END
```

Figure 7.4a. Histogramming height versus weight. H=(HEIGHT−60.0) / 2.0 + 1.0 determines which interval the height is in. W=(WEIGHT−100.0) / 25.0 + 1.0 determines which interval the weight is in. If W equals 3 and H equals 5, then BIN(H,W)=BIN(H,W)+1 is interpreted as BIN(5,3)=BIN(5,3)+1. Thus 1 is added to BIN(5,3). The elements of BIN are zeroed in the beginning of the program in a nested DO loop.

The data cards for the program are shown in Fig. 7.4b. Each data card but the last has one value of the height and one value of the weight punched on it. The last data card is a trailer and has the constant −12345678. punched in the first field.

The statements

```
H=(HEIGHT-60.0) / 2.0 + 1.0
W=(WEIGHT-100.0) / 25.0 + 1.0
```

will be used to determine into what bin a particular value of HEIGHT and WEIGHT will be placed. If a person's height is 69 inches, then H= (69.0 − 60.0) / 2.0 + 1.0 or 4.5 + 1.0 which is truncated to 5; thus the value of H is 5. If the person's weight is 170 pounds, then W=(170.0 − 100.0) / 25.0 + 1.0 or 2.8 + 1.0, which is truncated to 3; thus the value of W is 3, as shown in the table for Fig. 7.4a.

The next statement

```
BIN(H,W)=BIN(H,W) + 1
```

is interpreted by the computer as

```
BIN(5,3)=BIN(5,3) + 1
```

Since the original value of BIN(5,3) is zero, this statement assigns 1 to BIN(5,3). The results of the program are shown in Fig. 7.4c. We have not labeled the output because at this point in the book the statement that labels the output might confuse the reader. We will learn how to label this type of output in Chapter 8 on Input/Output.

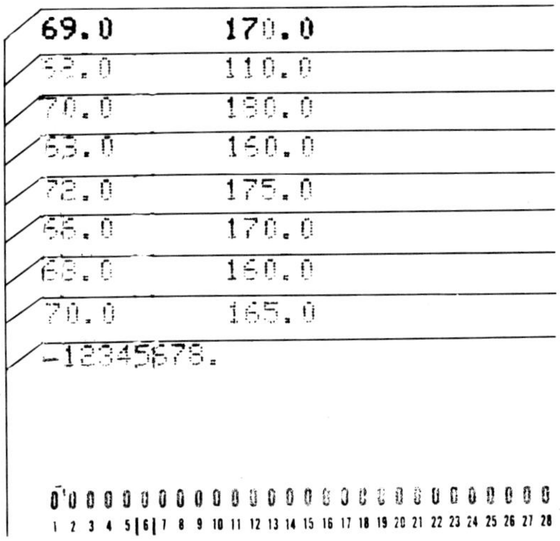

Figure 7.4b. The data cards for the program of Fig. 7.4a.

Height	(HEIGHT−60.0) / 2.0	H	Weight	(WEIGHT−100.0) / 25.0	W	Form of BIN(H,W)
69.0	4.5	5	170.0	2.8	3	BIN(5,3)
71.0	5.5	6	160.0	2.4	3	BIN(6,3)

Table for Fig.7.4a. Shows how the values of the INTEGERs H and W are determined. For a height of 69.0 the value of (HEIGHT−60.0)/2.0 + 1 is 5.5. This is truncated to 5 when assigned to the INTEGER variable H.

```
        HEIGHT       WEIGHT         H         W
           69.         170.         5         3
           62.         110.         2         1
           70.         180.         6         4
           68.         160.         5         3
           72.         175.         7         4
           66.         170.         4         3
           68.         160.         5         3
           70.         165.         6         3
RESULTS        Weight ------->
  Height   0          0         0         0         0         0
  |        1          0         0         0         0         0
  |        0          0         0         0         0         0
  |        0          0         1         0         0         0
  |        0          0         3         0         0         0
  |        0          0         1         1         0         0
  |        0          0         0         1         0         0
  |        0          0         0         0         0         0
  v        0          0         0         0         0         0
```

Figure 7.4c. Running the program of Fig. 7.4a.

The fact that one statement prints the elements of the array in Fig. 7.4a, but not DO loops as in Figs. 7.1a and 7.2a, allows us now to rewrite the program of Fig. 7.4a, in accordance with the top to bottom requirement of structured programming as is now shown in the program of Fig. 7.5a. Thus if we declare the variable LAST to be LOGICAL, we may write

```
LAST=HEIGHT .EQ. -12345678.0
```

This allows us to eliminate the GO TO that appeared in the previous program in

```
IF( HEIGHT .EQ. -12345678.0 ) GO TO 60
```

and bring the WRITE statement up to the "read and histogram" loop (the N loop). We can now write

```
IF( LAST ) WRITE(6,20) ( (BIN(I,J), J=1,6), I=1,9)
```

and since we want the program to stop after the results are printed, we follow this with

```
IF( LAST ) STOP
```

USING TOP TO BOTTOM DESIGN IN THE HISTOGRAMMING PROGRAM

```
C   HISTOGRAM HEIGHT VS WEIGHT USING A DATA STATEMENT TO
C   ZERO AN ARRAY AND USING TOP TO BOTTOM DESIGN
        INTEGER BIN(9,6), H, W
        LOGICAL LAST
C           ...ZERO ARRAY  'BIN(HEIGHT,WEIGHT)'
        DATA BIN / 54*0 /
C           ...READ AND HISTOGRAM RESULTS
        WRITE(6,5)
 5      FORMAT(1X, T7, 'HEIGHT', T17, 'WEIGHT', T31, 'H', T41, 'W')
        DO 30 N=1,1001
            READ(5,10) HEIGHT, WEIGHT
 10         FORMAT(2F10.0)
C           ...WHEN TRAILER ENCOUNTERED, PRINT RESULTS
            LAST=HEIGHT .EQ. -12345678.0
            IF( LAST ) WRITE(6,15)
 15         FORMAT(1X, 'RESULTS')
            IF( LAST ) WRITE(6,20) ( (BIN(I,J), J=1,6), I=1,9)
            IF( LAST ) STOP
 20         FORMAT(1X, 6I10)
                H=(HEIGHT-60.0) / 2.0 + 1
                W=(WEIGHT-100.0) / 25.0 + 1.0
                WRITE(6,25) HEIGHT, WEIGHT, H, W
 25             FORMAT(1X, 2F10.0, 2I10)
                BIN(H,W)=BIN(H,W) + 1
 30     CONTINUE
        WRITE(6,40)
 40     FORMAT(1X, 'TOO MANY CARDS; MAXIMUM IS 1000')
        STOP
        END
```

Figure 7.5a. Same as the preceding program but now by using a LOGICAL variable, we eliminate the GO TO statement. Also, now the elements of the array A are zeroed in a DATA statement. The elements of a two-dimensional array are stored sequentially in the computer's memory. Since there are 54 elements as determined by the INTEGER BIN(9,6), then 54*0 in the DATA statement assigns zeroes to all the elements. By using the LOGICAL variable LAST, we can move the WRITE statements up to the histogramming loop. Thus we can read the program from the top to the bottom.

The data cards for the program are shown in Fig. 7.5b and the results of running the program are shown in Fig. 7.5c.

Another thing we have done differently in this program is to zero the elements of the array BIN in a DATA statement. Since BIN is dimensioned as BIN(9,6), there are 54 elements in BIN. These 54 elements are stored in sequence in the computer's memory. Since we want zeros assigned to all 54 elements of BIN, we write

```
DATA BIN / 54*0 /
```

If the IF-THEN is available on your computer you can place the printing part of the program into the range of the DO without using logical variables.

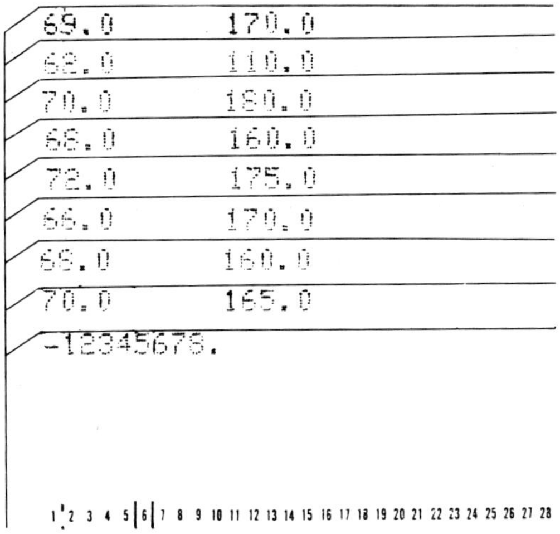

Figure 7.5b. The data cards for the program of Fig. 7.5a.

```
      HEIGHT        WEIGHT           H          W
        69.          170.            5          3
        62.          110.            2          1
        70.          180.            6          4
        68.          160.            5          3
        72.          175.            7          4
        66.          170.            4          3
        68.          160.            5          3
        70.          165.            6          3
RESULTS
         0             0             0          0          0          0
         1             0             0          0          0          0
         0             0             0          0          0          0
         0             0             1          0          0          0
         0             0             3          0          0          0
         0             0             1          1          0          0
         0             0             0          1          0          0
         0             0             0          0          0          0
         0             0             0          0          0          0
```

Figure 7.5c. Running the program of Fig. 7.5a.

In the next program, shown in Fig. 7.6a, we alter the preceding program so that by using logical expressions it now checks the data (Fig. 7.6b) for integrity; if the value of HEIGHT is too large

```
(HEIGHT .GT. 78.0)
```

or if its value is too small

```
(HEIGHT .LT. 60.0)
```

or if the value of WEIGHT is too large

```
(WEIGHT .GT. 250.0)
```

or if it is too small

```
(WEIGHT .LT. 100.0)
```

then the value of the LOGICAL variable COND is true. If this is the case, the program

TESTING FOR INTEGRITY IN THE HISTOGRAMMING PROGRAM

```
C  HISTOGRAM HEIGHT VS WEIGHT USING A DATA STATEMENT TO
C  ZERO AN ARRAY AND USING TOP TO BOTTOM DESIGN
C  TESTS FOR INTEGRITY OF DATA
      INTEGER BIN(9,6), H, W
      LOGICAL COND, LAST
C        ...ZERO ARRAY  'BIN(HEIGHT,WEIGHT)'
      DATA BIN / 54*0 /
C        ...READ AND HISTOGRAM RESULTS
      WRITE(6,5)
 5    FORMAT(1X, T7, 'HEIGHT', T17, 'WEIGHT', T31, 'H', T41, 'W')
      DO 50 N=1,1001
         READ(5,10) HEIGHT, WEIGHT
 10      FORMAT(2F10.0)
C        ...WHEN TRAILER ENCOUNTERED, PRINT RESULTS
         LAST=HEIGHT .EQ. -12345678.0
         IF( LAST ) WRITE(6,15)
 15      FORMAT(1X, 'RESULTS')
         IF( LAST ) WRITE(6,20) ( (BIN(I,J), J=1,6), I=1,9)
         IF( LAST ) STOP
 20      FORMAT(1X, 6I10)
C        ...TEST FOR BAD INPUT
            COND=(HEIGHT .GT. 78.0) .OR.
     1            (HEIGHT .LT. 60.0) .OR.
     2            (WEIGHT .GT. 250.0) .OR.
     3            (WEIGHT .LT. 100.0)
            IF(COND) WRITE(6,40) HEIGHT, WEIGHT
            IF(COND) GO TO 50
 40         FORMAT(1X, 'BAD INPUT.  HEIGHT=', F10.2, 2X, 'WEIGHT=',
     1                                                      F10.2)
C        ...HISTOGRAM RESULTS
               H=(HEIGHT-60.0) / 2.0 + 1.0
               W=(WEIGHT-100.0) / 25.0 + 1.0
               WRITE(6,45) HEIGHT, WEIGHT, H, W
 45            FORMAT(1X, 2F10.0, 2I10)
               BIN(H,W)=BIN(H,W) + 1
 50   CONTINUE
      WRITE(6,60)
 60   FORMAT(1X, 'TOO MANY CARDS! MAXIMUM IS 1000')
      STOP
      END
```

Figure 7.6a. Same as the preceding program, but now the program checks for the integrity of the data: If the value either of HEIGHT or WEIGHT is such that it would cause H or W to be outside of the range indicated by INTEGER BIN(9,6) the LOGICAL variable COND is true. When the value of COND is true, the values of H and W are not histogrammed; instead the program prints an error message and goes on to read the next data card.

does not histogram the data but prints an error message with both the values of HEIGHT and WEIGHT as is shown in Fig. 7.6c. It then reads another data card. For instance, since the value of WEIGHT on the first data card is 71.0, the computer prints

```
BAD INPUT.  HEIGHT=      69.00  WEIGHT=      71.00
```

and does not histogram this value. The program would certainly work if we omitted the statement that produces the error message

```
IF(COND) WRITE(6,40) HEIGHT, WEIGHT
```

We include this statement since it indicates which cards will not be included in the histogram. This test for the integrity of the data is placed after the test for the trailer. If this test had been placed before the test for the trailer, the constant −12345678.0 (the number on the trailer card) would be considered a small height and the condition HEIGHT .LT. 60.0 would be true; the program would then try to read another data card. A run-time error message would result, and the results would not be printed.

If the IF-THEN-ELSE is available on your compiler, you can write the test for the validity of the data in a more elegant way. First, eliminate the two IF statements involving COND and the statements which follow, up to, but not including, the CONTINUE. Substitute in their place

```
      IF ( .NOT. COND) THEN
        BIN(H,W) = BIN(H,W) + 1
      ELSE
        WRITE(6,10) HEIGHT, WEIGHT
40      FORMAT(1X, 'BAD INPUT. HEIGHT=', F10.2, 2X, 'WEIGHT=', F10.2)
      END IF
```

This is immediately followed by the CONTINUE. This IF-THEN-ELSE operates as follows: If the values of HEIGHT and WEIGHT read are in the allowable range, then the value of COND is false. Therefore, the value .NOT. COND is true and BIN(H,W) = BIN(H,W) + 1 is executed, i.e., the data just read is histogrammed. Then the program skips to the END IF and therefore executes the CONTINUE next. On the other hand, if one or both of the values read are out of the allowable range, then the value of COND is true and .NOT. COND is false. Therefore, the program does not histogram the result but goes to the block of statements sandwiched between the ELSE and the END IF, i.e., it prints the values of the offending data.

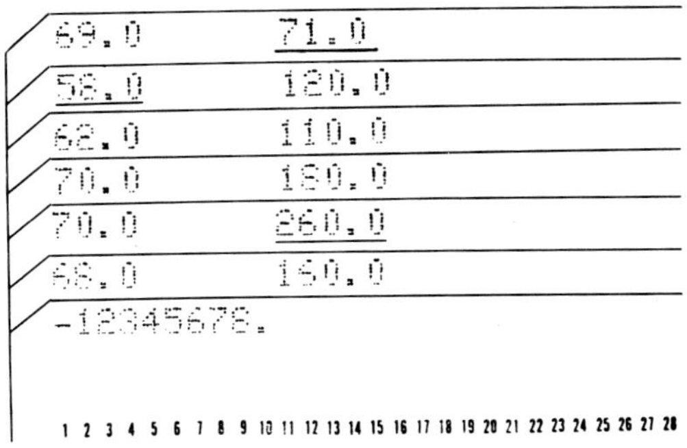
```
69.0      71.0
58.0      120.0
62.0      110.0
70.0      180.0
70.0      260.0
68.0      160.0
-12345678.
```


Figure 7.6b. The data cards for Fig. 7.6a. Some of the data cards have values on them which will cause the dimensions of BIN to be exceeded.

```
       HEIGHT       WEIGHT            H            W
BAD INPUT.   HEIGHT=        69.00   WEIGHT=        71.00
BAD INPUT.   HEIGHT=        58.00   WEIGHT=       120.00
          62.          110.        2            1
          70.          180.        6            4
BAD INPUT.   HEIGHT=        70.00   WEIGHT=       260.00
          68.          160.        5            3
RESULTS
           0            0          0            0            0            0
           1            0          0            0            0            0
           0            0          0            0            0            0
           0            0          0            0            0            0
           0            0          1            0            0            0
           0            0          0            1            0            0
           0            0          0            0            0            0
           0            0          0            0            0            0
           0            0          0            0            0            0
```

Figure 7.6c. Running the program of Fig. 7.6a.

7.2 How an Array's Elements Are Stored in the Computer's Memory

The elements of a doubly subscripted array are stored in sequence in the computer's memory such that *one column follows the other*. As an example, let us consider an array A which is dimensioned as

```
DIMENSION A(2,3)
```

We recall that in dimensioning arrays, the first subscript indicates the number of rows the array has, the second subscript indicates the number of columns the array has. We will assume that the values of the array are given as

$$\begin{pmatrix} 1.0 & 2.0 & 3.0 \\ 4.0 & 5.0 & 6.0 \end{pmatrix}$$

where we enclose the numbers in parentheses to show that they constitute an array. Since its first column is 1.0 4.0, its second column is 2.0 5.0, and its third column is 3.0 6.0, then its elements are stored in the memory as follows

1.0	4.0	2.0	5.0	3.0	6.0

as shown in Fig. 7.7a. The elements of any two by three array A are stored as shown in Fig. 7.7b.

A(1,1)	A(2,1)	A(1,2)	A(2,2)	A(1,3)	A(2,3)

Thus the elements of a doubly subscripted array are stored in sequence in the computer's memory such that the first subscript assumes all of its possible values in sequence for each successive value of the second subscript. Programmers describe this by saying that "the first subscript varies more rapidly than the second."

In a DATA statement, when we assign constants to a doubly subscripted array, we must follow the sequence in which the elements of the array are stored in the memory. Thus in order to assign the elements of the array shown in Fig. 7.7a to the array A in a DATA statement we write

```
DIMENSION A(2,3)
DATA A / 1.0, 4.0, 2.0, 5.0, 3.0, 6.0 /
```

as is shown in Fig. 7.7c. The results of running the program are shown in Fig. 7.7d. Because of

```
      WRITE(6,10) ( (A(I,J), J=1,3), I=1,2)
10    FORMAT(1X, 3F10.1)
```

the results are printed in the required array form

```
1.0          2.0          3.0
4.0          5.0          6.0
```

USING DOUBLY SUBSCRIPTED ARRAYS IN A DATA STATEMENT

$$\begin{pmatrix} 1.0 & 2.0 & 3.0 \\ 4.0 & 5.0 & 6.0 \end{pmatrix} \quad \text{Array A}$$

1.0	4.0	2.0	5.0	3.0	6.0
First column		Second column		Third column	

Memory

Figure 7.7a. The elements of a two-dimensional array are stored in the computer's memory by column. Since 1.0 4.0 is the first column, it is stored first. This is followed by 2.0 5.0, the second column. This is in turn followed by 3.0 6.0, the third column.

A(1,1)	A(2,1)	A(1,2)	A(2,2)	A(1,3)	A(2,3)

Figure 7.7b. The elements of a doubly subscripted array are stored in sequence in the computer's memory such that the first subscript varies more rapidly than the second.

```
C  USING A DOUBLY SUBSCRIPTED ARRAY IN A DATA STATEMENT
      DIMENSION A(2,3)
      DATA A / 1.0, 4.0, 2.0, 5.0, 3.0, 6.0 /
      WRITE(6,10) ( (A(I,J), J=1,3), I=1,2)
 10   FORMAT(1X, 3F10.1)
      STOP
      END
```

Figure 7.7c. In the DIMENSION statement, the first subscript of the array indicates how many rows the array will have. The second subscript indicates how many columns the array will have. Thus DIMENSION A(2,3) indicates that A has 2 rows and 3 columns. We have to write the constants to be assigned to a two-dimensional array in the DATA statement in the same order in which they will be stored in the memory.

```
    1.0          2.0          3.0
    4.0          5.0          6.0
```

Figure 7.7d. The results of running the program of Fig. 7.7b. Since the constants were written in the correct order in the DATA statement, the results are in the same form as the matrix in Fig. 7.7a.

If we were to write the constants in the array in the order given in

```
DATA A / 1.0, 2.0, 3.0, 4.0, 5.0, 6.0  /
```

as shown in Fig. 7.8a, then the results would be printed as

```
1.0        3.0        5.0
2.0        4.0        6.0
```

as shown in Fig. 7.8b.

Although ANS Standard Basic FORTRAN allows an array to have a maximum of only two subscripts, ANS Standard FORTRAN allows an array to have a maximum of three subscripts, and most compilers allow a maximum of seven subscripts. A multidimensional array is stored so that the leftmost subscript varies most rapidly and the rightmost subscript varies least rapidly. Thus, if the array A were dimensioned as A(2,2,2), then its elements would be stored in the following order:

A(1,1,1), A(2,1,1), A(1,2,1), A(2,2,1), A(1,1,2), A(2,1,2), A(1,2,2), A(2,2,2)

LISTING CONSTANTS FOR A DOUBLY SUBSCRIPTED ARRAY IN THE WRONG ORDER IN A DATA STATEMENT

```
C   CONSTANTS WRITTEN IN INCORRECT ORDER, I.E. BY ROW
        DIMENSION A(2,3)
        DATA A / 1.0, 2.0, 3.0, 4.0, 5.0, 6.0  /
        WRITE(6,10) ( (A(I,J), J=1,3), I=1,2)
 10     FORMAT(1X, 3F10.1)
        STOP
        END
```

Figure 7.8a. We write the constants in the incorrect order in the DATA statement. We have by mistake written them according to row. As a result we will get the incorrect assignment shown in Fig. 7.8b.

```
      1.0          3.0          5.0
      2.0          4.0          6.0
```

Figure 7.8b. Running the program of Fig. 7.8a. Because of the improper assignment, we do not get the array shown in Fig. 7.7a.

7.3 Matrix Multiplication

Certain problems that involve many equations can be solved quite simply by using matrix multiplication. Before we describe such a problem, we describe matrix multiplication. The reader to whom this topic is not of interest may skip to the next section.

Matrix multiplication is much different from regular (or scalar) multiplication, as shown in Fig. 7.9. In it we show how the multiplication in the matrix equation

C = A*B

is evaluated. Since the constants that form the elements of a matrix can be INTEGER or REAL, we make them all REAL. Thus we will assign the elements of a matrix to REAL subscripted variables. We will consider only matrix multiplications in which the matrix that appears on the extreme right in the multiplication—here B—has only one column.

The matrices A and B are specified as

$$\text{A} \qquad \begin{pmatrix} 1.0 & 2.0 & 3.0 \\ 4.0 & 5.0 & 6.0 \end{pmatrix} \qquad\qquad \text{B} \qquad \begin{pmatrix} 7.0 \\ 8.0 \\ 9.0 \end{pmatrix}$$

The elements are always enclosed in parentheses to show that they constitute a matrix. The elements of the matrix C will be evaluated from the matrix product, so at this point we represent them as the unknowns X and Y as shown in Fig. 7.9. Note that it is *impossible* to have an array in which some of the elements are REAL and some of the elements are INTEGER, i.e.,

$$\begin{pmatrix} 1.2 & 3 \\ 4.1 & 4 \end{pmatrix}$$

The elements must either be all REAL or all INTEGER.

MATRIX MULTIPLICATION

$$\underset{C}{\begin{pmatrix} X \\ Y \end{pmatrix}} = \underset{A}{\begin{pmatrix} 1 & 2 & 3 \\ 4 & 5 & 6 \end{pmatrix}} * \underset{B}{\begin{pmatrix} 7 \\ 8 \\ 9 \end{pmatrix}}$$

Figure 7.9. Multiplying the matrix A times the matrix B.

Terms used to describe a matrix:
The rows are the horizontal lines of numbers.
The columns are the vertical lines of numbers.
The numbers are called the elements of the matrix. Thus for matrix A

	First column	Second column	Third column
First row	1	2	3
Second row	4	5	6

In order to facilitate explaining matrix multiplication we have depicted it pictorially in Fig. 7.9, in five steps

Step 1. The matrix B, in this case

$$\begin{pmatrix} 7.0 \\ 8.0 \\ 9.0 \end{pmatrix}$$

in which the elements are in a vertical line, is physically turned so that the elements are in a horizontal line, (7.0 8.0 9.0), and is placed on the top of the matrix A so that each of the numbers in B lines up with the columns in A

Step 2. The matrix B descends on matrix A.

Step 3. When B reaches the first row of A, each element of B multiplies its corresponding element in the first row of A, i.e., 7.0 multiplies 1.0, 8.0 multiplies 2.0, and 9.0 multiplies 3.0. Then each element of B multiplies its corresponding element in the second row of A.

Step 4. The products in the first row of our new matrix are added together. They equal 50.0. The products in the second row of our new matrix are added together. They equal 122.0.

Step 5. If two matrices are equal to each other, their elements are equal. Thus, since C equals our new matrix, then X = 50.0 and Y = 122.0. Therefore C is the matrix

$$\begin{pmatrix} 50.0 \\ 122.0 \end{pmatrix}$$

We note that in order to perform the matrix multiplication A*B, the number of rows in B (here 3) must equal the number of columns in A.

Step 1. Rotate the matrix B a quarter turn to the left and place on top of A as shown.

$$(7\ \ 8\ \ 9)$$

$$\begin{pmatrix} X \\ Y \end{pmatrix} \quad \begin{pmatrix} 1 & 2 & 3 \\ 4 & 5 & 6 \end{pmatrix} \quad \begin{pmatrix} 7 \\ 8 \\ 9 \end{pmatrix}$$

$$C \quad = \quad A \quad * \quad B$$

Step 2. The matrix B descends on A.

$$\begin{matrix} & & (7 & 8 & 9)\ B \\ & & \downarrow & \downarrow & \downarrow \end{matrix}$$

$$\begin{pmatrix} X \\ Y \end{pmatrix} = \begin{pmatrix} 1 & 2 & 3 \\ 4 & 5 & 6 \end{pmatrix}$$

$$C \qquad\qquad A$$

Step 3. Each element of B multiplies the corresponding element in the first row of A, then the corresponding element in the second row of A.

$$\begin{pmatrix} X \\ Y \end{pmatrix} = \begin{pmatrix} 1*7 & 2*8 & 3*9 \\ 4*7 & 5*8 & 6*9 \end{pmatrix}$$

$$C \quad = \quad A*B$$

Step 4. Add the products in the first row, then add the products in the second row

$$\begin{pmatrix} X \\ Y \end{pmatrix} = \begin{pmatrix} 7 + 16 + 27 \\ 28 + 40 + 54 \end{pmatrix} = \begin{pmatrix} 50 \\ 122 \end{pmatrix}$$

$$C \qquad\qquad A * B$$

Step 5. If two matrices are equal their elements are equal.

$$X = 50$$
$$Y = 122$$

We now discuss the application of matrix multiplication to the calculation of total weekly sales for each of four car dealers. The number of cars of a given make that each of four dealers sells per week is shown in Fig. 7.10a. Thus dealer 1 sold 7 Chryslers, 8 Dodges, and 11 Plymouths in one week, etc. In Fig. 7.10b we show the matrix S, which represents the weekly sales of the four dealers.

In Fig. 7.11a we show the selling price of each car, and in Fig. 7.11b we show the matrix P representing these prices. To repeat, the problem is to calculate the total sales for each dealer. We can do this easily by performing the matrix multiplication S*P. We set the result equal to the total sales matrix, T, whose elements are unknown until the matrix multiplication is performed. We will refer to these elements as T_1, T_2, T_3, and T_4. When we perform the matrix multiplication shown in Fig. 7.12a, we obtain as an intermediate result what is shown in Fig. 7.12b. When we sum the numbers in each row, we get the results shown in Fig. 7.12c. The total sales for dealer 1, T_1, equals 122,000 dollars; T_2 equals 117,000, etc. We see that matrices are convenient when the same operation—here multiplication—must be performed on all the elements of a group.

APPLICATION OF MATRIX MULTIPLICATION

Dealer	Chrysler	Dodge	Plymouth
1	7	8	11
2	4	10	13
3	2	7	3
4	8	8	4

Figure 7.10a. The number of cars each of four dealers sells per week.

$$S = \begin{pmatrix} 7 & 8 & 11 \\ 4 & 10 & 13 \\ 2 & 7 & 3 \\ 8 & 8 & 4 \end{pmatrix} \text{ SALES MATRIX}$$

Figure 7.10b. Matrix for sales shown in Fig. 7.10a.

Make	Price
Chrysler	7000
Dodge	5000
Plymouth	3000

Figure 7.11a. The price of each car.

$$P = \begin{pmatrix} 7000 \\ 5000 \\ 3000 \end{pmatrix} \text{ PRICE MATRIX}$$

Figure 7.11b. Price matrix for Fig. 7.11a.

TOTAL = SALES * PRICE

$$\overset{T}{\begin{pmatrix} T_1 \\ T_2 \\ T_3 \\ T_4 \end{pmatrix}} \quad \overset{S}{\begin{pmatrix} 7 & 8 & 11 \\ 4 & 10 & 13 \\ 2 & 7 & 3 \\ 8 & 8 & 4 \end{pmatrix}} \quad \overset{P}{\begin{pmatrix} 7000 \\ 5000 \\ 3000 \end{pmatrix}}$$

Figure 7.12a. The matrix multiplication needed to obtain the total sales for each dealer; e.g., T_1 is the total sales for dealer No. 1.

$$\begin{pmatrix} T_1 \\ T_2 \\ T_3 \\ T_4 \end{pmatrix} = \begin{pmatrix} 49000+40000+33000 \\ 28000+50000+39000 \\ 14000+35000+9000 \\ 56000+40000+12000 \end{pmatrix}$$

Figure 7.12b. An intermediate result in the matrix multiplication shown in Fig. 7.12a.

T_1 = 122000
T_2 = 117000
T_3 = 58000
T_4 = 108000

Figure 7.12c. The final results of the matrix multiplication shown in Fig. 7.12a. These are the elements of the total sales matrix T.

We now discuss the matrix multiplication indicated in C=A*B as described in Fig. 7.9, but now we perform the multiplication using the general elements.

$$\begin{pmatrix} C(1) \\ C(2) \end{pmatrix} = \begin{pmatrix} A(1,1) & A(1,2) & A(1,3) \\ A(2,1) & A(2,2) & A(2,3) \end{pmatrix} * \begin{pmatrix} B(1) \\ B(2) \\ B(3) \end{pmatrix}$$

as shown in Fig. 7.13. This will help us to write a program that performs this type of matrix multiplication.

We remember that for the elements in the matrix A, the first subscript indicates the row the element is in and the second subscript indicates the column the element is in. Thus A(1,3) is in the first row and third column. Since the matrix B has only one column, it only has one subscript. The subscript indicates which row the element is in. Thus B(2) is in the second row. The same applies for C. When we perform the matrix multiplication we obtain two equations

$$\begin{aligned} C(1) &= A(1,1) * B(1) + A(1,2) * B(2) + A(1,3) * B(3) \\ C(2) &= A(2,1) * B(2) + A(2,2) * B(2) + A(2,3) * B(3) \end{aligned}$$

We see that for each element of A which multiplies B—e.g., A(1,2)*B(2)—the value of the second subscript of A equals the value of the subscript of B. The value of the first subscript of A equals the value of the subscript of C.

PERFORMING A MATRIX MULTIPLICATION

$$\begin{pmatrix} C(1) \\ C(2) \end{pmatrix} = \begin{pmatrix} A(1,1) & A(1,2) & A(1,3) \\ A(2,1) & A(2,2) & A(2,3) \end{pmatrix} * \begin{pmatrix} B(1) \\ B(2) \\ B(3) \end{pmatrix}$$

$$C(1) = A(1,1) * B(1) + A(1,2) * B(2) + A(1,3) * B(3)$$
$$C(2) = A(2,1) * B(2) + A(2,2) * B(2) + A(2,3) * B(3)$$

Figure 7.13. The matrix multiplication indicated in C=A*B in terms of general elements where A is a 3 by 3 matrix and B is a 3 by 1 matrix; and the results of the multiplication, also in terms of the general elements.

We now write a program, shown in Fig. 7.14a, that will perform the matrix multiplication indicated in Fig. 7.13. If we let I represent the subscript of C, we could write either of the equations that appear in Fig. 7.13

$$\begin{pmatrix} C(1) \\ C(2) \end{pmatrix} = \begin{pmatrix} A(1,1) & A(1,2) & A(1,3) \\ A(2,1) & A(2,2) & A(2,3) \end{pmatrix} * \begin{pmatrix} B(1) \\ B(2) \\ B(3) \end{pmatrix}$$

as

```
C(I)=A(I,1)*B(1) + A(I,2)*B(2) + A(I,3)*B(3)
```

Since the expression to the right of the equals sign is a sum, we could use an accumulator to calculate it. We will call the accumulator C(I) and write

```
        DO 50 J=1,3
           C(I)=C(I) + A(I,J) * B(J)
50      CONTINUE
```

where C(I) is originally set to zero, i.e., C(1)=0.0 and C(2)=0.0 in a DATA statement. Thus the first time the range of this DO is executed, the value of J is 1, and the computer interprets the assignment statement as

```
C(I)=C(I) + A(I,1)*B(1)
```

The second time, since C(I) is now equal to A(I,1)*B(1), the computer interprets the assignment statement as

```
C(I)=A(I,1)*B(1) + A(I,2)*B(2)
```

and the third time as

```
C(I)=A(I,1)*B(1) + A(I,2)*B(2) + A(I,3)*B(3)
```

which is what we want.

Since we want this entire operation done for I=1 and I=2, we nest this loop in an I loop

```
     DO 60 I=1,2
        DO 50 J=1,3
           C(I)=C(I) + A(I,J) * B(J)
50      CONTINUE
60   CONTINUE
```

We now explain the statements appearing in the beginning of the program. We dimension A, B, and C as follows

```
DIMENSION A(2,3), B(3), C(2)
```

The size of the matrices A and B determine how we should dimension them, but how do we know how to dimension C? The dimensions of C must equal the first dimension of A—which is here 2. Thus if we write the matrix equation so that it includes the matrices' dimensions

```
C(2)= A(2,3)*B(3)
```

and remembering that C and B both have only one column and that their subscripts indicate how many rows the matrix has, we see that the number of rows in C (i.e., 2) equals the number of rows in A. We also see that the number of columns in A (i.e., 3) must equal the number of rows in B.

PERFORMING A MATRIX MULTIPLICATION

```
      DIMENSION A(2,3), B(3), C(2)
C        ...ASSIGN VALUES TO THE MATRICES A, B, AND C
      DATA A / 1.0, 4.0, 2.0, 5.0, 3.0, 6.0 /
      DATA B / 7.0, 8.0, 9.0 /
      DATA C / 2*0.0 /
      WRITE(6,10)
 10   FORMAT(1X, 'MATRIX A')
      WRITE(6,20) ( (A(I,J), J=1,3), I=1,2)
 20   FORMAT(1X, 3F10.0)
      WRITE(6,30)
 30   FORMAT(1X, 'MATRIX B')
      WRITE(6,40) (B(I), I=1,3)
 40   FORMAT(1X, F10.1)
C        ...PERFORM THE MATRIX MULTIPLICATION
      DO 60 I=1,2
         DO 50 J=1,3
            C(I)=C(I) + A(I,J) * B(J)
 50      CONTINUE
 60   CONTINUE
C        ...PRINT RESULTS
      WRITE(6,70)
 70   FORMAT(1X, 'MATRIX C')
      WRITE(6,80) (C(I), I=1,2)
 80   FORMAT(1X, F10.1)
      STOP
      END
```

$$\begin{pmatrix} 1.0 & 2.0 & 3.0 \\ 4.0 & 5.0 & 6.0 \end{pmatrix} \quad \begin{pmatrix} 7.0 \\ 8.0 \\ 9.0 \end{pmatrix}$$

Figure 7.14a. A program that performs the matrix multiplication shown to the right of the program. When the value of I is 1, the range of the nested DO loop is interpreted as C(1)=C(1) + A(1,J) * B(J). After the inner loop is executed, this statement becomes C(1)=A(1,1) * B(1) + A(1,2) * B(2) + A(1,3) * B(3) since the value of C(1) was originally zero. Similarly when the value of I is 2, this statement becomes C(2)=A(2,1) * B(1) + A(2,2) * B(2) + A(2,3) * B(3). These are the results of the matrix equation C=A*B.

We assign the constants to A in

```
DATA A / 1.0, 4.0, 2.0, 5.0, 3.0, 6.0 /
```

To remind you how the constants are assigned to A, we show the assignments in Fig. 7.14b. We assign the constants to B in

```
DATA B / 7.0, 8.0, 9.0 /
```

We are thus doing the specific matrix multiplication that we discussed in Fig. 7.9. Since C is used as an accumulator, we must initially assign zero to its elements. This is done in

```
DATA C / 2*0.0 /
```

The results of running the program are shown in Fig. 7.14c.

1.0	4.0	2.0	5.0	3.0	6.0
A(1,1)	A(2,1)	A(1,2)	A(2,2)	A(1,3)	A(2,3)
First column		Second column		Third column	

Figure 7.14b. How the elements of A appearing in DATA A / 1.0, 4.0, 2.0, 5.0, 3.0, 6.0 / are stored.

```
MATRIX A
          1.          2.          3.
          4.          5.          6.
MATRIX B
         7.0
         8.0
         9.0
MATRIX C
        50.0
       122.0
```

Figure 7.14c. Running the program of Fig. 7.14a.

7.4 Reading Values into Arrays

In Fig. 7.15a we show a method that would enable you to read constants into an array. The arrays are dimensioned in DIMENSION A(2,3), B(3). Each element of an array is punched on a separate data card, as shown in Fig. 7.15b. Thus we require 3 data cards for B and 6 data cards for A. We read the elements of B in

```
      DO 20 I=1,3
         READ(5,10) B(I)
10       FORMAT(F10.0)
20    CONTINUE
```

When the value of I is 1, the computer interprets the READ as

```
READ(5,10) B(1)
```

and assigns the constant on the first card to B(1), as shown in the table for Fig. 7.15a. When the value of I is 2, the computer interprets the READ as READ(5,10) B(2). It reads the next card, and the constant on the second card is assigned to B(2), etc.

We read the elements of A in the nested loop

```
      DO 50 I=1,2
         DO 40 J=1,3
            READ(5,30) A(I,J)
30          FORMAT(F10.0)
40       CONTINUE
50    CONTINUE
```

The first three times the range of the inner loop is executed the value of I is 1 and the values of J are 1, 2, and 3, respectively. So the computer interprets the READ the first three times as READ(5,30) A(1,1), READ(5,30) A(1,2), and READ(5,30) A(1,3), respec-

USING DO LOOPS TO READ ARRAYS

```
C   PROGRAM READS VALUES INTO ARRAYS
        DIMENSION A(2,3), B(3)
C           ...READ ARRAY B
        DO 20 I=1,3
           READ(5,10) B(I)
 10        FORMAT(F10.0)
 20     CONTINUE
C           ...READ ARRAY A
        DO 50 I=1,2
           DO 40 J=1,3
              READ(5,30) A(I,J)
 30           FORMAT(F10.0)
 40        CONTINUE
 50     CONTINUE
C           ...PRINT THE RESULTS
        WRITE(6,60)
 60     FORMAT(1X, 'ARRAY A')
        WRITE(6,70) (B(I), I=1,3)
 70     FORMAT(1X, 3F10.0)
        WRITE(6,80)
 80     FORMAT(1X, 'ARRAY B')
        WRITE(6,90) ( (A(I,J), J=1,3), I=1,2)
 90     FORMAT(1X, 3F10.0)
        STOP
        END
```

Figure 7.15a. The program reads the elements of the arrays A and B from cards. Each time either of the READ statements is executed, a new card is read.

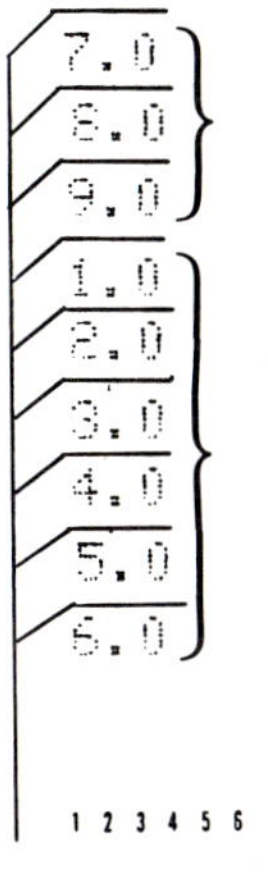

Read by

```
        DO 20 I=1,3
           READ(5,10) B(I)
 10        FORMAT(F10.0)
 20     CONTINUE
```

Read by

```
        DO 50 I=1,2
           DO 40 J=1,3
              READ(5,30) A(I,J)
 30           FORMAT(F10.0)
 40        CONTINUE
 50     CONTINUE
```

Figure 7.15b. The data cards read by the program. To the right are the statements which instruct the computer to read the group of cards to the left.

tively. As each of these READs is executed, the computer reads a new data card and assigns the constant on it to the appropriate element of A, as shown in the table for Fig. 7.15a.

The second three times the range of the inner DO is executed, the value of I is 2 and the values of J are again 1, 2, and 3, respectively. So the computer successively interprets the READ as READ(5,30) A(2,1), READ(5,30) A(2,2), and READ(5,30) A(2,3), respectively. As each of these reads is executed, the computer reads a new data card and assigns the constant on it to the appropriate element of A, as shown in the table for Fig. 7.15a. The results of running the program are shown in Fig. 7.15c.

If the constants were punched three to a data card, e.g.,

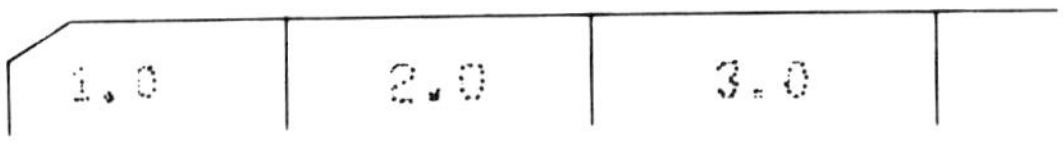

and the FORMATs were 10 FORMAT(3F10.0) and 30 FORMAT(3F10.0), both READ(5,10) B(I) and READ(5,30) A(I,J) would still only read the first constant on the card. The reason for this is that there is only one variable in each of these READs. If we wanted to read the 3 constants on the card we would have to rewrite the statements which read the data as

```
      READ(5,10) B(1), B(2), B(3)
10    FORMAT(3F10.0)
```

and

```
   DO 40 I=1,2
      READ(5,30) A(I,1), A(I,2), A(I,3)
30    FORMAT(3F10.0)
40 CONTINUE
```

7.0	8.0	9.0
B(1)	B(2)	B(3)

1.0	2.0	3.0
A(1,1)	A(1,2)	A(1,3)

4.0	5.0	6.0
A(2,1)	A(2,2)	A(2,3)

Table for Fig. 7.15a. Shows the constants assigned to the elements of the array after the READ statements are executed.

```
ARRAY A
          7.          8.          9.
ARRAY B
          1.          2.          3.
          4.          5.          6.
```

Figure 7.15c. Running the program of Fig. 7.15a.

A simpler way of doing this is to use implied DO loops, as shown in Fig. 7.16a. The first set of statements involving the use of an implied DO is

```
      READ(5,10) (B(I), I=1,3)
10    FORMAT(3F10.0)
```

The implied DO—(B(I), I=1,3)—is interpreted exactly as it is in a WRITE statement. If this READ is used to read the card shown in Fig. 7.16b, 1.0 will be assigned to B(1); 2.0 to B(2); and 3.0 to B(3). This READ is more flexible than the one shown in Fig. 7.15a

```
      DO 20 I=1,3
         READ(5,10) B(I)
10       FORMAT(F10.0)
20    CONTINUE
```

since the READ of Fig. 7.15a can read only one constant per card even if we had changed the FORMAT to 10 FORMAT (3F10.0); whereas the implied DO not only can read three constants which are punched on one card—as we have just shown—but can also be made to read three cards, each of which has only one constant on it. To do this we would have to change the FORMAT to 10 FORMAT (F10.0), thus writing

```
      READ(5,10) (B(I), I=1,3)
10    FORMAT(F10.0)
```

Here B(1) is matched with F10.0, and thus the constant on the first card is assigned to B(1). Since there is no specification to match with B(2), the computer goes back to the beginning of the FORMAT. This causes another card to be read, and the constant on the second card is assigned to B(2), etc.

The second set of statements involving the use of an implied DO is

```
      DO 30 I=1,2
         READ(5,20) (A(I,J), J=1,3)
20       FORMAT(3F10.0)
30    CONTINUE
```

When the value of I is 1, the computer interprets the READ as

```
      READ(5,20) (A(1,J), J=1,3)
```

Thus, because of 3F10.0, the three constants on the card read are assigned to A(1,1), A(1,2), and A(1,3), respectively. When I is 2, the computer interprets the READ as READ(5,20) (A(2,J), J=1,3) and the three constants on the next card are assigned to A(2,1), A(2,2), and A(2,3), respectively, etc.

If we use nested implied DO loops, we can replace the last set of statements—an implied DO used in a DO loop—with the nested implied DO as shown in Fig. 7.16c

```
      READ(5,20) ( (A(I,J), J=1,3), I=1,2)
20    FORMAT(3F10.0)
```

The inner implied DO is (A(I,J), J= 1,3), and it is executed for the value of I equaling 1 and then 2 as it was in Fig. 7.16a.

USING IMPLIED DO LOOPS TO READ ARRAYS

```
C   READING ARRAYS USING IMPLIED DO LOOPS
       DIMENSION A(2,3), B(3)
C           ...READ ARRAY B
       READ(5,10)  (B(I), I=1,3)
 10    FORMAT(3F10.0)
C           ...READ ARRAY A
       DO 30 I=1,2
          READ(5,20)  (A(I,J), J=1,3)
 20       FORMAT(3F10.0)
 30    CONTINUE
```

Figure 7.16a. The first READ is equivalent to READ(5,10) B(1),B(2),B(3); the second READ is equivalent to READ(5,20)A(I,1),A(I,2), A(I,3).

```
   1.0          2.0          3.0
```

Figure 7.16b. One of the DATA cards that would be read by Fig. 7.16a.

USING A NESTED IMPLIED DO LOOP TO READ ARRAYS

```
C   USING A NESTED IMPLIED DO TO READ
       DIMENSION A(2,3)
C           ...READ ARRAY A
       READ(5,20)  ( (A(I,J), J=1,3), I=1,2)
 20    FORMAT(3F10.0)
```

Figure 7.16c. (A(I,J), J=1,3) is the inner implied DO loop; so first (A(1,J), J=1,3) is executed and one card containing three constants is read. Then (A(2,J), J=1,3) is executed, and another card is read.

A nested implied DO is not always preferable to an implied DO used in a DO loop—for instance, if the limiting values of the loop indices were variables, as shown in the program of Fig. 7.17a. In this program an array A of arbitrary dimensions up to 10 rows and 10 columns is read and then printed. In order to accommodate up to 10 constants on one card, we have written the FORMAT used with the implied DO as 20 FORMAT(10F8.0). We read the number of rows IMAX and the number of columns JMAX the array has in

```
READ(5,10) IMAX, JMAX
```

The data cards for the program are shown in Fig. 7.17b. Since we are reading an array that has 2 rows and 3 columns, the first data card has a 2 and a 3 punched on it to indicate these dimensions. Thus the computer interprets the next READ as

```
READ(5,20) ((A(I,J), J=1,3), I=1,2)
```

Since the FORMAT is 10 FORMAT(10F8.0), the computer reads all the 6 elements of the array from the second card, even though there are only 3 constants punched on it. Thus A(1,1), A(1,2), and A(1,3) assume the values 1.0, 2.0, and 3.0, respectively, and A(2,1), A(3,3), and A(2,3) all assume the value zero. Since the implied DO is now satisfied, the third data card is not read.

The computer interprets the WRITE statement as

```
WRITE(6, 30) ( (A(I,J), J=1,3), I=1,2)
```

Since the FORMAT for the WRITE statement is

```
30    FORMAT(1X, 10F8.0)
```

All 6 values which were read into the array are printed on one line, as shown in Fig. 7.17c.

```
1.      2.      3.      0.      0.      0.
```

LIMITATIONS OF THE IMPLIED DO **LOOPS (AN INCORRECT WAY OF READING ARRAYS)**

```
C   SHOWS LIMITATION OF IMPLIED DO LOOPS
        DIMENSION A(10,10)
C           READ DIMENSIONS OF ARRAY
C           ...IMAX= # OF ROWS; JMAX= # OF COLUMNS
        READ(5,10) IMAX, JMAX
 10     FORMAT(2I10)
C           ...READ ARRAY A
        READ(5,20) ( (A(I,J), J=1,JMAX), I=1,IMAX)
 20     FORMAT(10F8.0)
C           ...WRITE ARRAY A
        WRITE(6,30) ( (A(I,J), J=1,JMAX), I=1,IMAX)
 30     FORMAT(1X, 10F8.0)
        STOP
        END
```

Figure 7.17a. Using an implied DO to read an array. Since IMAX is 2 and JMAX is 3, the implied DO in the READ has in its list, 6 elements of the array. Since the FORMAT has 10 field specifications in it, the computer tries to read all 6 elements from one card.

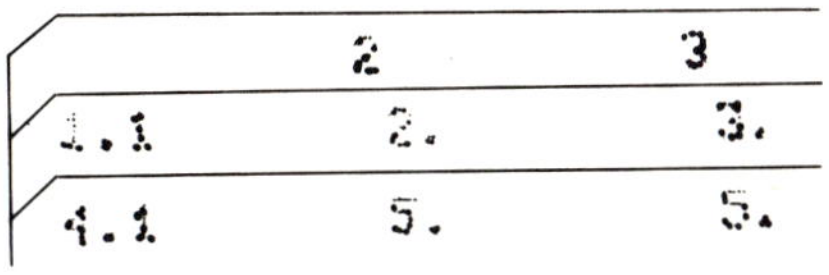

Figure 7.17b. The data cards read by Fig. 7.17a. The first data card has the values of IMAX and JMAX on it. The computer reads all 6 constants from the second card and thus assigns zeros to A(2,1), A(2,2), and A(2,3).

```
1.       2.       3.       0.       0.       0.
```

Figure 7.17c. Running the program of Fig. 7.17a. The implied DO in the WRITE describes 6 elements of the array. Since the associated FORMAT has 10 field specifications in it, all 6 elements are printed on one line.

In order to avoid reading an array incorrectly, we have rewritten the program placing READ(5,20) (A(I,J), J=1,JMAX) within a DO loop, as shown in Fig. 7.18a. After the computer reads the first card shown in Fig. 7.18b, it interprets the second READ as

```
READ(5,20) (A(1,J), J=1,3)
```

The FORMAT for this READ is 20 FORMAT(10F8.0). Since there are fewer variables in the list—A(I,1), A(I,2), A(I,3)—than there are field specifications, only the first three field specifications are used by the computer. Since the value of I is originally 1, the constants on the second card, i.e., 1.0, 2.0, 3.0, are assigned to A(1,1), A(1,2), and A(1,3), respectively. When the value of I is 2, the constants on the third card, i.e., 4.0, 5.0, and 6.0 are assigned to A(2,1), A(2,2), and A(2,3), respectively.

In order to have the array elements printed so as to show the shape of the array, we have again placed an implied DO—this time WRITE(6,40) (A(I,J) J=1,JMAX)—in a DO loop. When the value of I is 1, since the value of JMAX is 3, and since the FORMAT used is 40 FORMAT(1X,10F8.0), the computer prints A(1,1), A(1,2), and A(1,3) on one line. When the value of I is 2, the computer prints the values of A(2,1), A(2,2), and A(2,3) on the second line. All of this is shown in Fig. 7.18c.

CORRECT WAY OF READING ARRAYS

```
C   THE PROPER WAY OF READING AND WRITING AN ARRAY
C   WITH VARIABLE DIMENSIONS
        DIMENSION A(10,10)
C           ...READ ARRAY'S DIMENSION
        READ(5,10) IMAX, JMAX
 10     FORMAT(2I10)
C           ...READ ARRAY
        DO 30 I=1, IMAX
           READ(5,20) (A(I,J), J=1, JMAX)
 20        FORMAT(10F8.0)
 30     CONTINUE
C           ...WRITE ARRAY
        DO 50 I=1,IMAX
           WRITE(6,40) (A(I,J), J=1,JMAX)
 40        FORMAT(1X, 10F8.0)
 50     CONTINUE
        STOP
        END
```

Figure 7.18a. By placing an implied DO loop within a regular DO loop you can control how many elements will be either read or printed. Thus since JMAX is 3, the READ reads only 3 elements of the array and the WRITE prints only 3 elements, which is precisely what we want.

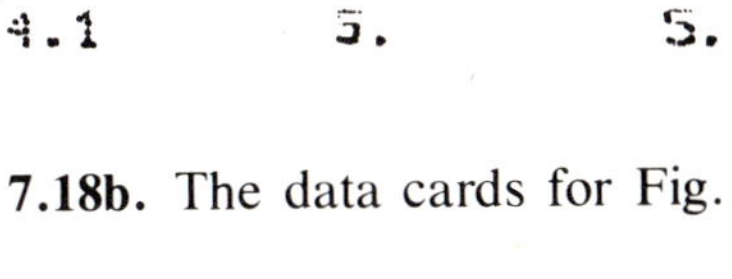

Figure 7.18b. The data cards for Fig. 7.18a.

```
   1.      2.      3.
   4.      5.      6.
```

Figure 7.18c. Running the program of Fig. 7.18a.

The program of Fig. 7.18a can be written so that the READ and WRITE statements are placed in one DO loop

```
      DO 40 I=1,IMAX
         READ(5,20) ( A(I,J), J=1,JMAX)
20       FORMAT(10F8.0)
         WRITE(6,30) ( A(I,J), J=1,JMAX)
30       FORMAT(1X, 10F8.0)
40    CONTINUE
```

as shown in Fig. 7.18d. The results of running the program with the same data shown in Fig. 7.18b, are shown in Fig. 7.18e.

```
C  READING AND WRITING AN ARRAY IN ONE LOOP
      DIMENSION A(10,10)
      READ(5,10) IMAX, JMAX
 10   FORMAT(2I10)
C         ...READ AND WRITE ARRAY
      DO 40 I=1,IMAX
         READ(5,20) ( A(I,J), J=1,JMAX)
 20      FORMAT(10F8.0)
         WRITE(6,30) ( A(I,J), J=1,JMAX)
 30      FORMAT(1X, 10F8.0)
 40   CONTINUE
      STOP
      END
```

Figure 7.18d. The program of Fig. 7.18a can be written so that the READ and WRITE statements are placed in one DO loop.

```
      1.      2.      3.
      4.      5.      6.
```

Figure 7.18e. Running the program of Fig. 7.18d with the data shown in Fig. 7.18b.

PROBLEMS

1. Rewrite the program that histograms the results of tossing a pair of dice (Figs. 7.1a–7.3a) using an IF-THEN to illuminate the GO TO. Also, test for the validity of the data.

2. Using an IF-THEN, rewrite the program (Fig. 7.4a) that histograms height versus weight so that the printing is done in the range of the DO.

3. Using an IF-THEN-ELSE, rewrite the program (Fig. 7.5a) that histograms height versus weight and tests for the validity of the data. The IF-THEN-ELSE which tests for the validity of the data should appear between the ELSE and the END-IF of the IF-THEN-ELSE which tests for the trailer. This is called *nesting IFs*.

4. Extend the program of Fig. 7.3a so that it calculates χ^2 for 360 throws of a pair of dice. The expected number of events for each element of the array is 10. See Chapter 5 for the definition of χ^2.

5. Given the matrix A whose elements are given by

$$\begin{pmatrix} 6 & 9 & 4 & 3 \\ 3 & 1 & 6 & 4 \\ 2 & 1 & 7 & 2 \end{pmatrix}$$

write the DATA statement that will assign these elements to the array A.

6. Write a program that uses a data statement and prints the following matrix:

$$\begin{pmatrix} 1 & 2 \\ 3 & 4 \\ 5 & 6 \end{pmatrix}$$

7. What changes would you have to make in the program of problem 6 so that it produces the following matrix?

$$\begin{pmatrix} 1 & 2 & 3 \\ 4 & 5 & 6 \end{pmatrix}$$

8. Which of the following matrix multiplications are allowed?

(a) $$\begin{pmatrix} 1 & 2 & 3 \\ 4 & 5 & 6 \\ 7 & 8 & 9 \end{pmatrix} \begin{pmatrix} 1 \\ 2 \\ 3 \\ 4 \end{pmatrix}$$

(b) $$\begin{pmatrix} 1 & 1 & 2 & 3 \\ 3 & 1 & 2 & 1 \\ 4 & 1 & 3 & 6 \end{pmatrix} \begin{pmatrix} 3 \\ 2 \\ 1 \end{pmatrix}$$

(c) $\begin{pmatrix} 1 & 2 \\ 3 & 4 \end{pmatrix} \begin{pmatrix} 4 \\ 6 \end{pmatrix}$ (d) $\begin{pmatrix} 1 & 6 & 3 \end{pmatrix} \begin{pmatrix} 3 \\ 2 \\ 2 \end{pmatrix}$

(e) $\begin{pmatrix} 1 & 6 & 3 \\ 3 & 6 & 1 \end{pmatrix} \begin{pmatrix} 2 \\ 3 \\ 4 \end{pmatrix}$

9. Write a program to multiply the following two matrices:

$$\begin{pmatrix} 1 & 2 \\ 3 & 4 \\ 5 & 6 \end{pmatrix} \begin{pmatrix} 1 \\ 2 \end{pmatrix}$$

10. Write a program that does the kind of matrix multiplication we have shown in this chapter but for matrices of an arbitrary size.

11. A more general matrix multiplication than we have studied is given, for example, by

$$\begin{pmatrix} 1 & 2 & 3 \\ 4 & 5 & 6 \end{pmatrix} \begin{pmatrix} 1 & 4 \\ 2 & 5 \\ 3 & 6 \end{pmatrix} = \begin{pmatrix} 1*1 + 2*2 + 3*3 & 4*1 + 5*2 + 6*3 \\ 1*4 + 2*5 + 3*6 & 4*4 + 5*5 + 6*6 \end{pmatrix}$$

$$A \quad * \quad B \quad = \quad C$$

Note each column of B separately multiplies the rows of A. The resulting matrix C is

$$\begin{pmatrix} 14 & 32 \\ 32 & 77 \end{pmatrix}$$

The elements of C are given by

$$C(I,J) = \sum_{K=1}^{3} A(I,K) * B(K,J)$$

Write a program that multiplies the matrix A times the matrix B and store the result in C.

12. Write a program that does the same matrix multiplication as shown in problem 11 but for matrices of an arbitrary size.

13. When you add or subtract two matrices they must have the same dimensions. For $C = A \pm B$, the elements of C are given by $C(I,J) = A(I,J) \pm B(I,J)$. Using this, write a program that adds two matrices. The matrices can be any arbitrary size.

8

Input/Output

8.1. Printing Using F Format

We now review how real constants are printed using F format.

The general form of F format is F*w*.*d* where *w* is the field width and *d* is the number of digits that will appear to the right of the decimal point. Thus in F9.2, the field width is 9, and 2 digits will appear to the right of the decimal point when a REAL value is printed in the field.

In order for the programmer to determine the minimum field width required to print a REAL constant, what in practice he might actually do is to write the constant with the most digits the program would produce for a given result, including *d*, the number of digits he wants printed to the right of the decimal point. Thus a typical result might be 12345.67. He then counts the number of columns the constant occupies; e.g., 12345.67, including the decimal point, occupies 8 columns. He then adds 1 to this to accommodate the constant's signs (if the sign is negative, a minus sign is printed; if the sign is positive, a blank space is printed). Thus the minimum width needed to print a constant which has the same form as 12345.67 is 9. Because the value of *d* is 2, F9.2 would accommodate the constant. This is shown in Fig. 8.1a. On most systems, if you are sure that the sign will be positive, you do not have to add 1 to the column count. Thus on these systems, F8.2 would accommodate 12345.67.

If the number to be printed has an absolute value less than one,* e.g., .12345, many systems print it with a zero preceding the number, i.e., as 0.12345, as shown in Fig. 8.1b. Thus we must add to the items mentioned in the last paragraph, one space for the zero (it is called a leading zero) which the computer prints to the left of the decimal point. Therefore, the field width needed to accommodate 0.12345 (including one column for the sign) is F8.5. On many systems, the computer does not print leading zeros, so on these systems, we do not have to provide an extra space here, i.e., we can use F7.5.

* The number is less than 1.0 but larger than −1.0.

PRINTING USING F FORMAT

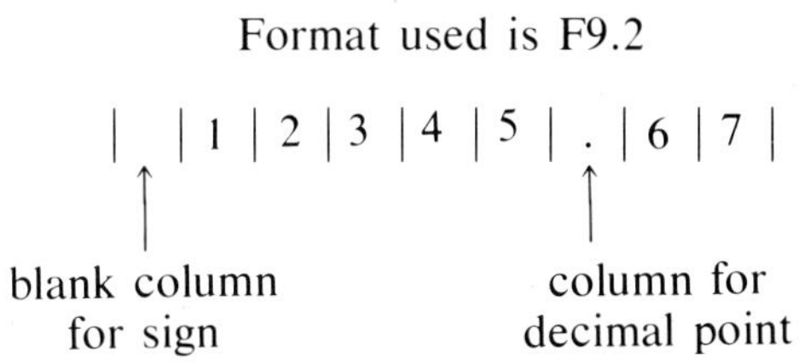

Figure 8.1a. The general form for F format is F*w*.*d*. When you print the REAL constant 12345.67 and you want the 67 to be printed, then *d* in F*w*.*d*, should be 2. The field width, *w*, must accommodate all the characters in the constant including the decimal point and the possibility that the constant's sign will be negative. Thus, here *w* would be 9, so we use F9.2.

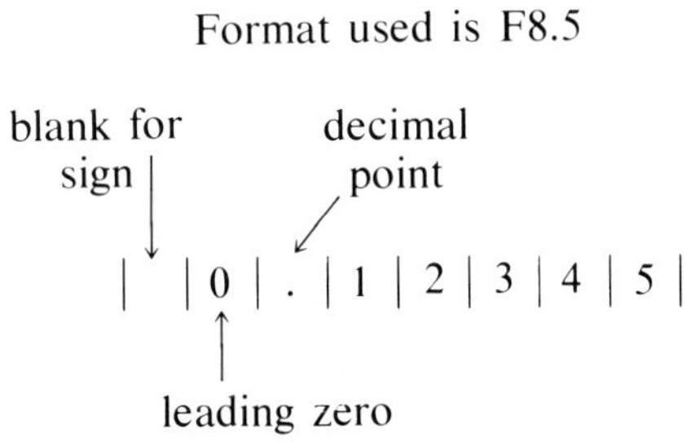

Figure 8.1b. If the absolute value of a number is less than 1, an additional space must be left for a leading zero. So for .12345 the minimum field width needed is 8 if we want the 12345 to be printed. Thus we can use F8.5 to print the constant.

If d is smaller than the number of digits to the right of the decimal point in the constant to be printed, then the rounded value of the constant will be printed. Thus if the constant 12345.67 is printed using F9.1, it is rounded to 12345.7 when it is printed. This and other examples are given in Table 8.1.

If you do not use a field width that accommodates all the digits to the left of the decimal point (plus, on many systems, the sign) the computer will print asterisks in the field. Thus if we use F7.2 to print 12345.67, asterisks will be printed, as shown in the last line of Table 8.1. However, on some systems, the computer will print only the right-most (least significant) digits that fit into the field. Thus if 12345.67 is the constant stored, and if the computer uses F7.2 to print the constant, it prints 2345.67. So, beware. To be safe, it is always wise to make the field width larger than is actually required.

8.2. Reading Using F Format

We recall the situation when a constant is read from a card and the constant is punched in a field described by F format. If the constant is punched with a decimal point, the constant can be punched anywhere in the field and the value of the constant, as punched, is assigned to the appropriate variable. In other words, the decimal point in the constant overrides the decimal point in the F field specification; e.g., F10.2 and F10.0 have the same meaning. We now describe what happens if the constant is punched without a decimal point, as in Fig. 8.2. Now the decimal point in the field specification has meaning. For instance, if we use F10.2 for the field specification, the computer assumes a decimal point was punched two columns from the left of the right end of the field; i.e., it was punched between columns 8 and 9. So the constant 1234567 punched as shown in Fig. 8.2 and read by F10.2 format, is stored as 12345.67. Table 8.2 shows how the same constant would be stored if different formats were used. For instance, if F10.4 is used, the decimal point is assumed to be between columns 6 and 7 and the constant is stored as 123.4567. When you read constants using F format, once you have chosen the field width w, you are not as restricted in choosing d (the number which indicates how many digits

THE EFFECT OF *d* IN F*w*.*d* IN PRINTING RESULTS

Number stored in memory	Field specification	How number is printed
12345.67	F9.2	12345.67
12345.67	F9.1	12345.7←rounded
12345.67	F9.0	12346. ←rounded
12345.67	F7.2	******* ←field width not large enough

Table 8.1. In F*w*.*d*, if *d* is smaller than the number of digits to the right of the decimal point in the constant to be printed, then the rounded value of the constant will be printed (see the second and third lines of this table). If the field width is not large enough to accommodate all the digits to the left of the decimal point in a constant, the computer prints asterisks in the field.

READING USING F FORMAT

Figure 8.2. If a REAL constant is punched without a decimal point on a card, the *d* in F*w*.*d* describing the field, has significance. It instructs the computer to assume that the decimal point is *d* places from the right of the field. Thus if F10.2 were used to read the constant shown here, it would be read as 12345.67. If the constant is punched with a decimal point, then the *d* has no significance.

Field specification	How number is stored
F10.0	1234567.0
F10.1	123456.7
F10.2	12345.67
F10.3	1234.567
F10.4	123.4567
F10.10	.0001234567

Table 8.2. How different field specifications affect how the constant shown in Fig. 8.2 is read.

are expected to appear to the right of the decimal point) as you are when you write constants. Thus F10.10 is allowed and if it is used, the computer stores the constant shown in Fig. 8.2 as .0001234567. On many systems, you can use formats in which $d > w$ and the computer assumes that the decimal point is punched to the left of the field. Thus if

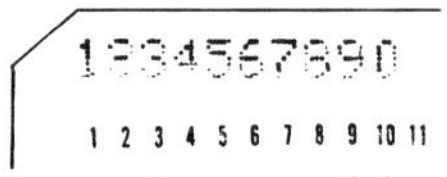

were read by F10.12 format, the computer would store the constant as .001234567890.

If the constant is not punched right-justified in the field, the blanks to the right of the constant, and still in the field, are interpreted as zeros. Thus, if we read the constant

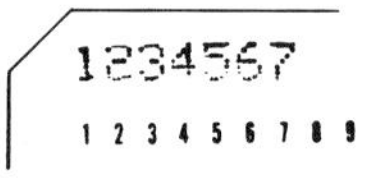

using F10.2, the constant will be stored as 12345670. This and other examples are given in Table 8.3.

8.3. I Format

We have already described how constants are read using I format. The computer assumes that they are punched right-justified in the field. When an INTEGER constant is printed using I format, the field width must be large enough to accommodate the number of digits in the constant, plus one space for the sign. If the sign is negative, a minus sign is printed; if the sign is positive, the space is left blank. Thus, if we represent the general form of I format as Iw and if there are n digits in the number we want printed, then the condition $w \geqslant n + 1$ must be satisfied in order for the field to accommodate the number. If this condition is not met, on many systems the computer will print asterisks in the field. Thus the minimum field required to print 123 is I4, as shown in Fig. 8.3. On many systems, if the sign of the constant is positive, you only have to provide space for the digits in the constants. Thus on these systems 123 could be printed using I3.

EFFECT OF NOT RIGHT-JUSTIFYING A CONSTANT

Data card	How number is stored using F10.2
Assumed decimal point:	
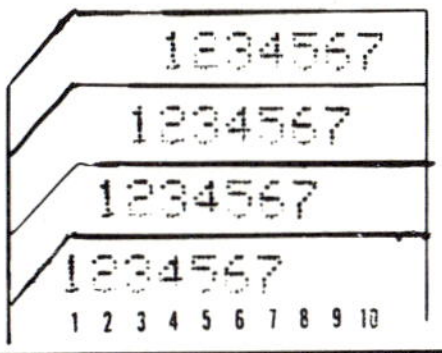	12345.67 123456.7 1234567. 12345670.

Table 8.3. If the constant is not punched right-justified in the field, the blanks to the right of the number, and still in the field, are interpreted as zeros. Each of the cards is read using F10.2. Shown to the right of each card is how the number is stored.

PRINTING USING I FORMAT

Format used is I4

blank for sign

↓

| | 1 | 2 | 3 |

Figure 8.3. When an INTEGER is printed, one column must be provided for the constant's sign. The general form of I format is Iw. If n is the number of digits in the constant, then $w \geqslant n + 1$. Thus the minimum field width needed to print 123 is 4, and we can use I4 here.

8.4. E Format

When E format is used in printing, the field width must be large enough not only to accommodate the d digits that will appear to the right of the decimal point, but also to accommodate the decimal point, a leading zero, a sign, and the four characters used to indicate the exponent (e.g., E + 02) giving a grand total of 7. Thus if Ew.d is the general form of the format, then $w \geqslant d + 7$. If this condition is not met, on many systems the computer prints asterisks.

For example, if we wanted the computer to print a number stored as $.1234 \times 10^{-2}$ and we wanted 4 digits to be printed to the right of the decimal point, the minimum field width allowed would be 11, so we could use E11.4, as shown in Fig. 8.4.

On input, if a decimal point is punched in the constant, then the mantissa can be placed anywhere in the field, as shown in Fig. 8.5a. The exponent part, however, must be right-justified; it can be punched as shown in Fig. 8.5a (E + 02) or as shown in Fig. 8.5b, i.e., if the sign is positive, it can be omitted. Thus we can punch the exponent as E02. Moreover, the leading zero can be omitted, so we can punch the exponent as E2. Furthermore, the E can be omitted, but the sign must be included. Thus we can punch the exponent as +2. All of this is shown in Fig. 8.5b.

If the constant being read were 1.234×10^{-2}, some possible ways of punching the exponent are shown in Fig. 8.5c: 1.234E − 02, 1.234E − 2, and 1.234 − 2. Note that the minus sign cannot be omitted.

Whether or not the constant is punched with a decimal point, the w in Ew.d, as always, describes the field width; thus, if for instance w is 10, then the exponent part must be punched right-justified in a field 10 columns wide.

PRINTING USING E FORMAT

Format used is E11.4

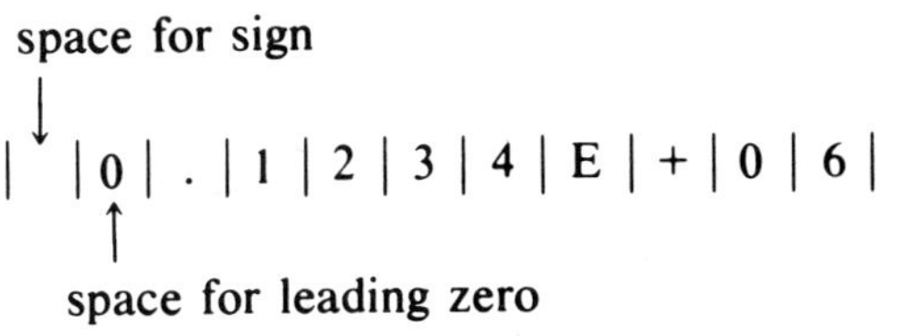

Figure 8.4. When printing a REAL constant using E format, you must leave one space each for the sign, leading zero, and decimal point; and four spaces for the exponent, giving a grand total of 7. Since E*w*.*d* is the general form of E format, then $w \geq d + 7$. For the number shown here the minimum field width is 11 so we can use E11.4.

READING USING E FORMAT

Format used is E15.5

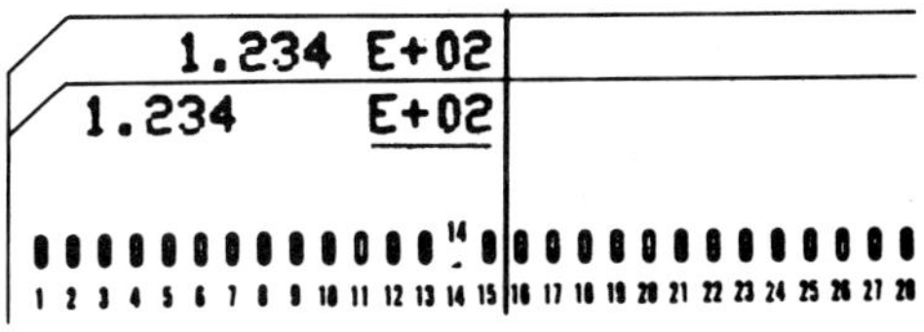

Figure 8.5a. When reading a constant in E format, if the mantissa is punched with a decimal point, the mantissa can be punched anywhere in the field (the *d* in E*w*.*d*, has no significance). The exponent part, however, must be punched right-justified in a field *w* columns wide.

OTHER WAYS OF PUNCHING A POSITIVE EXPONENT

Format used is E10.0

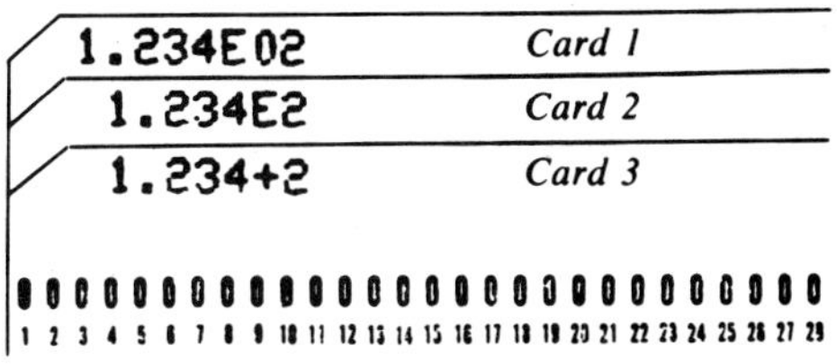

Figure 8.5b. Other acceptable forms of punching the exponential part: card 1—without the sign; card 2—without the leading zero; card 3—using only the sign and the exponent. If the sign is negative, it cannot be omitted.

SOME WAYS OF PUNCHING A NEGATIVE EXPONENT

Format used is E10.0

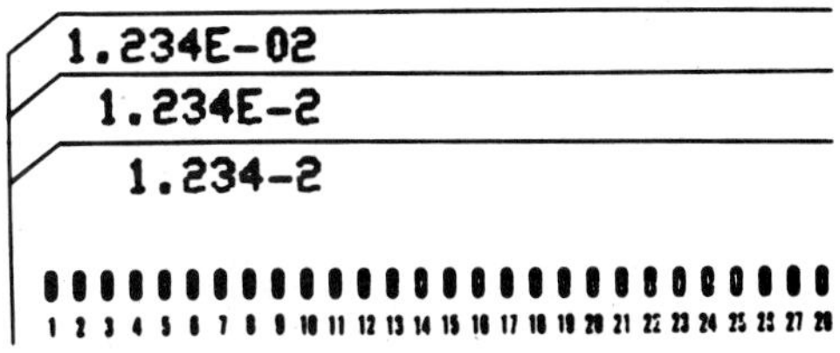

Figure 8.5c. If the number being read were 1.234×10^{-2}, the possible ways of punching the exponent are shown here. Note that the minus sign cannot be omitted.

If the constant is not punched with a decimal point, then no blanks should appear between the mantissa and the exponential part; the entire constant must be right-justified in the field. The *d* in E*w*.*d* instructs the computer to assume that the decimal point appears *d* places to the left of the E. Thus E10.0 instructs the computer to assume the decimal point is to the immediate left of the E and it thus stores the constant 1234E + 06 as 1234.0×10^6, as shown in Table 8.4. When E10.1 is used, the constant is stored as 123.4E + 06. If blanks appear between the mantissa and the exponent, they affect where the computer assumes the decimal point to be. Thus if E10.1 is used to read 1234bbE + 06 (the b indicates a blank), the constant is stored as 12340.0×10^6.

If the constant is not punched right-justified, as shown in Table 8.5, the computer interprets the blanks that follow the exponent but precede the end of the field, as zeros. Thus if we use E10.1, then 1234E + 06b is stored as 123.4E + 060 and 1234E + 06bb is stored as 123.4×10^{600}. In conclusion, we can punch a conventional REAL constant, e.g., 1.234, any place in a field described by E format, as shown in the last card of Table 8.5, and the constant will be stored as it is punched; i.e., 1.234 is stored simply as 1.234.

USING E FORMAT TO READ CONSTANTS PUNCHED WITHOUT A DECIMAL POINT

Data card	Field specification	How number is stored
1234E+06	E10.0	1234.0×10^6
	E10.1	123.4×10^6
1 2 3 4 5 6 7 8 9 10	E10.2	12.34×10^6

Table 8.4. If the constant is punched without a decimal point, the **d** in E**w**.**d**, used to read the constant, instructs the computer to assume that the decimal point is **d** places to the left of the E. Thus if E10.1 is used, then the constant is stored as 123.4×10^6 assuming the constant is punched right-justified in a field 10 columns wide.

THE EFFECT OF NOT PUNCHING EXPONENT RIGHT-JUSTIFIED

Data card	How number is stored using E10.1
1234E+06	123.4E+060
1234E+06	123.4E+0600
1.234	1.234
1 2 3 4 5 6 7 8 9 10 11 12 13	

Table 8.5. If the exponent part is not right-justified in the field, the blanks that follow the exponent, but are still in the field, are interpreted as zeros. If a constant is punched without any exponential part, it can be punched anywhere in the field.

8.5. Using Slashes in FORMAT Statements

In Fig. 8.6a we present a simple program that uses three different READ statements to read the three data cards shown in Fig. 8.6b. The results are shown in Fig. 8.6c.

In Fig. 8.7a, we rewrite the program so that we can use one READ statement to read all three cards. (The data cards to this program are the same ones shown in Fig. 8.6b.) In essence, we do this by including slashes in the FORMAT that is paired with the READ

```
      READ(5,10) A, J, C
10    FORMAT(F10.0 / I10 / F10.0)
```

When the computer executes the READ, it reads the value of A from the first card. The first slash instructs the computer to read the next card, so the computer then reads the value of J from a field described by I10. The second slash instructs the computer to read the third card, so the computer reads the value of C from the third data card. Note that when we use the slash and it is sandwiched between two fields, we do not use a comma to separate these fields. Thus writing the FORMAT as

```
10    FORMAT( F10.0,/ I10, / F10.0 )
```

would be unnecessary; however, it would not cause an error.

The results of running the program are shown in Fig. 8.7b.

INTRODUCTION TO SLASHES

```
C  INTRODUCTION TO SLASHES
      READ(5,10) A
 10   FORMAT( F10.0 )
C
      READ(5,20) I
 20   FORMAT( I10 )
C
      READ(5,30) C
 30   FORMAT( F10.0 )
C
      WRITE(6,40) A, I, C
 40   FORMAT(1X, F10.0, I10, F10.0 )
      STOP
      END
```

Figure 8.6a. A simple program that reads three cards and then prints them.

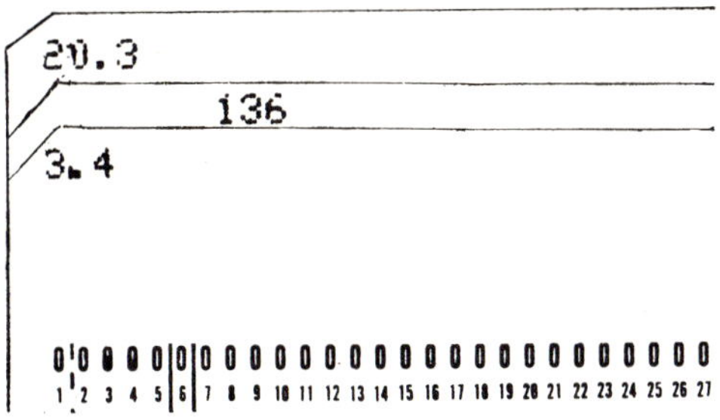

Figure 8.6b. The three cards read by the program of Fig. 8.6a.

```
 20.       136        3.
```

Figure 8.6c. The results of running the program of Fig. 8.6a.

USING SLASHES IN READ STATEMENTS

```
C  USING SLASHES IN READ STATEMENTS
      READ(5,10) A, J, C
 10   FORMAT(F10.0 / I10 / F10.0)
C
      WRITE(6,20) A, J, C
 20   FORMAT(1X, F10.0, I10, F10.0)
      STOP
      END
```

Figure 8.7a. Program of Fig. 8.6a rewritten so that the three cards of Fig. 8.6b are read by one READ statement. A slash (/) instructs the computer to read the next card. The A is matched with F10.0; the J with I10; and the C with F10.0.

```
 20.       136        3.
```

Figure 8.7b. The results of running the program of Fig. 8.7a. The constant on the first card is assigned to A; the constant on the second card, to J; and the constant on the third card, to C.

If we delete the variable J from the READ and thus delete I10 from the FORMAT as shown in Fig. 8.8a

```
         READ(5,10) A, C
   10    FORMAT( F10.0 / / F10.0)
```

the program would read the value of A (3.0) from the first data card (Fig. 8.8b). It would then read the next card, but since there is no field specification following the slash, the computer would not read any value from this card. The second slash would instruct the computer to read the third data card. The computer would do this and then assign the constant on that card (20.0) to C. What we learn from this is that when there are two slashes in the middle of a format, the computer skips one card. If there were n slashes here, the computer would skip $n - 1$ cards. However, if the n slashes came at the end of the FORMAT, e.g., FORMAT (F10.0, F10.0 / /), the computer skips n cards. The reason is that no field specification follows each of the slashes. If the n slashes came at the beginning of the FORMAT, e.g., FORMAT(/ / F10.0, F10.0), the computer also skips n cards.

The results of running the program of Fig. 8.8a are shown in Fig. 8.8c.

USING SLASHES TO SKIP A CARD

```
C  USING SLASHES TO SKIP A CARD
      READ(5,10) A, C
 10   FORMAT( F10.0 / / F10.0)
C
      WRITE(6,20) A, C
 20   FORMAT(1X, 2F10.0)
      STOP
      END
```

Figure 8.8a. If two slashes are used in the middle of the FORMAT, then the computer, although it read three cards, skips the second of these cards and assigns the constant(s) on the third card to the appropriate variable(s). If two slashes appear at the beginning or the end of a FORMAT, then the computer skips two cards.

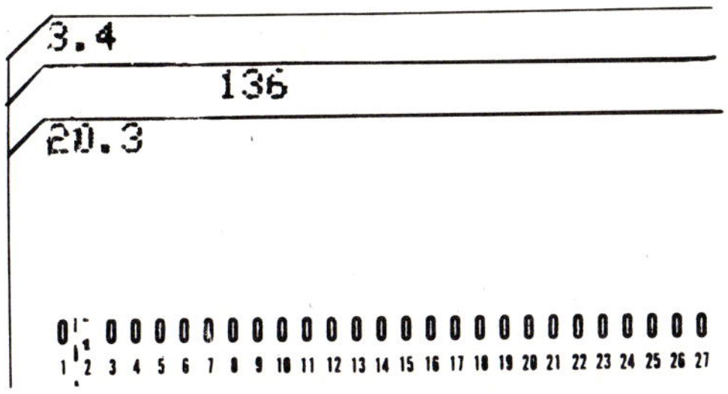

Figure 8.8b. The data cards for the program of Fig. 8.8a.

```
          3.        20.
```

Figure 8.8c. Running the program of Fig. 8.8a.

The above discussion of slashes also applies to FORMAT statements that are used with WRITE statements, as we see in Fig. 8.9a. When the computer executes

```
      WRITE(6,10) A, B, C
10    FORMAT(1X, 'RESULTS' / 1X, 'A=', F5.2, '  B=', F5.2 / /
     1         1X, 'C=', F5.2 /)
```

it prints RESULTS on the first line. When the computer encounters a slash, it determines what to do after it has examined the field immediately following the slash. If that field is blank—as in the case when the field is 1X—then the line printer continues printing on the next line. Two slashes in the middle of a FORMAT cause the computer to first skip a line and then look for the control character that follows the second slash.

Thus when the computer encounters the first slash, since it is followed by 1X, the computer prints 'A=', the value of A, 'B=', and the value of B, all on the next line, as shown in Fig. 8.9b. When the computer encounters the two slashes, since the second slash is followed by 1X, the computer skips a line and then prints 'C=' and the value of C on the next line. The next slash, since it is not followed by anything, instructs the computer to skip a line, as shown in Fig. 8.9b. The next WRITE statement prints THE END.

We can summarize this by saying that if the computer encounters n contiguous slashes in the middle of a FORMAT being used with a WRITE statement, the computer skips $n - 1$ lines. However, if it encounters n slashes at the end or the beginning of a FORMAT, the computer skips n lines.

USING SLASHES IN WRITE STATEMENTS

```
C   USING SLASHES IN WRITE STATEMENTS
      A=10.2
      B=3.6
      C=19.1
      WRITE(6,10) A, B, C
 10   FORMAT(1X, 'RESULTS' / 1X, 'A=', F5.2, '   B=', F5.2 / /
     1         1X, 'C=', F5.2 /)
      WRITE(6,20)
 20   FORMAT(1X, 'THE END')
      STOP
      END
```

Figure 8.9a. Using slashes in WRITE statements. One slash in the middle of a FORMAT instructs the computer to look for a carriage control character. If it is a blank (i.e., when 1X is used) then the computer continues printing on the next line. Two slashes in the middle of a FORMAT cause the computer to skip one line and then look for the control character. Two slashes at the beginning or the end of the FORMAT instructs the computer to skip two lines. One slash at the end of the FORMAT—as occurs here—instructs the computer to skip one line.

```
RESULTS
A=10.20   B= 3.60

C=19.10

THE END
```

Figure 8.9b. Running the program of Fig. 8.9a.

8.6. Introduction to Alphanumeric Constants

An alphanumeric constant has the same form as a string; and, like REAL and INTEGER constants, it can be assigned to a variable, but as we shall see, in fewer types of statements. An alphanumeric constant can contain any character that appears on the keys of the keypunch. When an alphanumeric constant appears in a statement in a program in ANS Standard FORTRAN, the constant must be described by a Hollerith field (H format). Three examples of alphanumeric constants are: 123, A + C$, and < −7. In a program, they would be described as: 3H123, 4HA+C$, and 3H < −7.

Although the general form of both a string appearing in a FORMAT and an alphanumeric constant is the same—any group of characters preceded by an integer and an H—there is a difference. The difference is that the number of characters you can place in an alphanumeric constant is limited by the size of the memory location the computer uses. On the IBM 360/370, under normal circumstances the maximum number of characters you can use in an alphanumeric constant is 4. On the other hand, on the CDC6600, the maximum is 10. On most other machines, the maximum varies between 4 and 10, depending on the machine.

In ANS Standard FORTRAN and WATFOR, an alphanumeric constant can appear only in a DATA statement, as we show in Fig. 8.10a

```
DATA ALPHA, BETA, MN / 1HA, 2HAB, 3HABC /
```

where A is assigned to ALPHA, AB to BETA, and ABC to MN, as shown in the table to Fig. 8.10a. However, just like REAL and INTEGER variables, the variable to which alphanumeric constants are assigned can appear almost anywhere else in the program.

An alphanumeric constant can be assigned to either a REAL or an INTEGER variable; e.g., we have used both the INTEGER MN, and the REALs ALPHA and BETA. Thus, by simply looking at the variable name, you cannot tell whether it has been assigned an alphanumeric constant. Alphanumeric constants can also be used as data to a program, as we will show in a subsequent chapter.

In order to print the value of a variable that has been assigned an alphanumeric constant, we must use the field specification called A format. Its general form is A*w* where *w* is the field width. The simplest way of using A format is to have *w* equal the number of characters in the constant. Thus, since the one-character constant A was assigned to ALPHA, we use A1 to print its value. Since the two-character constant AB was assigned to BETA, we use A2 to print its value. And finally, since the three-character constant ABC was assigned to MN, we use A3 to print its value, all of which is shown in Fig. 8.10a.

```
      WRITE(6,10) ALPHA, BETA, MN
10    FORMAT(1X, A1, 2X, A2, 2X, A3)
```

The results of running the program are shown in Fig. 8.10b.

On most systems, instead of using H format to describe an alphanumeric constant, you may simply enclose the constant in single quotes. Thus on most systems, we could write the DATA statement as

```
DATA ALPHA, BETA, MN / 'A', 'AB', 'ABC' /
```

as is shown in Fig. 8.10c.

On the proposed revision of ANS Standard FORTRAN, you can use either H format or constants enclosed in single quotes to express alphanumeric constants.

INTRODUCTION TO ALPHANUMERIC CONSTANTS

```
C   INTRODUCTION TO ALPHANUMERIC CONSTANTS
      DATA ALPHA, BETA, MN / 1HA, 2HAB, 3HABC /
      WRITE(6,10) ALPHA, BETA, MN
 10   FORMAT(1X, A1, 2X, A2, 2X, A3)
      STOP
      END
```

Figure 8.10a. An alphanumeric constant has the same form as a string, but the number of characters that can effectively be used in an alphanumeric constant depends on the machine used. Most machines allow you to use up to at least 4 characters in an alphanumeric constant. The alphanumeric constants used here are: A, AB, and ABC. An alphanumeric constant can be assigned to a REAL variable (here ALPHA and BETA) and to an INTEGER variable (here MN).

ALPHA	BETA	MN
'A'	'AB'	'ABC'

Table for Fig. 8.10a. Now the alphanumeric constants are assigned to the variables in the DATA statement. An alphanumeric constant can be assigned to either a REAL or INTEGER variable. Thus, you cannot tell whether a variable contains an alphanumeric constant simply by looking at the variable name.

```
 A  AB  ABC
```

Figure 8.10b. Running the program of Fig. 8.10a. In order to print alphanumeric constants you use A format. The general form is A*w*, where *w* is the field width. In this program, the simplest way of writing A format is to have *w* equal to the number of characters in the constant.

```
C   INTRODUCTION TO ALPHANUMERIC CONSTANTS
      DATA ALPHA, BETA, MN / 'A', 'AB', 'ABC' /
      WRITE(6,10) ALPHA, BETA, MN
 10   FORMAT(1X, A1, 2X, A2, 2X, A3)
      STOP
      END
```

Figure 8.10c. On most systems we can write an alphanumeric constant simply by enclosing the constant in single quotes.

```
 A  AB  ABC
```

Figure 8.10d. Running the program of Fig. 8.10c. The results are the same as in Fig. 8.10b.

8.7. More on the Implied DO Loop

The implied DO loop, e.g., (A(I), I=1,4) is an instruction that appears in an input (READ) or output (WRITE or PRINT) statement and instructs the computer to either read or write the quantity—here A(I)—that appears between the first left parenthesis in the implied DO, here

```
WRITE(6,10) (
```

and the comma that appears to the left of the last occurrence of an INTEGER variable—called the index—in the implied DO, here the I in

```
,I=1,4 )
```

The values of I are indicated by the numbers following the equals sign. This part of the implied DO is interpreted the same way it is in a DO statement. The implied DO is thus similar to a DO loop, the quantity we just referred to—here A(I)—being similar to the range of the DO. This quantity can consist of one or more nonsubscripted variables and/or subscripted variables.

In Fig. 8.11a we write a program that demonstrates some examples of the implied DO that do not use arrays. In

```
WRITE(6,10)  ( I, I=1,4)
```

the range of the implied DO is simply the variable I. Since the FORMAT is 10 FORMAT(1X, 4I5 /), the program prints the values of I, i.e., 1, 2, 3, and 4 on one line and then skips a line, as shown in Fig. 8.11b.

In

```
WRITE(6,20)  ( I, I=2,9,2)
```

the range of the implied DO is again I, but the initial value of the index is now 2, the limit is 9, and the increment is 2, so the computer prints the values 2, 4, 6, and 8.

In

```
WRITE(6,30)  ( I, I, R, I=1, 4)
```

the range of the implied DO is I, I, R where R has been assigned the constant value 3.2. The range will be executed four times. Since the FORMAT for this is

```
30    FORMAT(1X, 2I5, F5.1 )
```

first 1 1 3.2 is printed. Then on the next line 2 2 3.2 is printed. Then on the third line, 3 3 3.2 is printed, etc. (see Fig. 11b).

USING THE IMPLIED DO

```
C   USING THE IMPLIED DO
        R=3.2
        WRITE(6,10) ( I, I=1,4)
 10     FORMAT(1X, 4I5 / )
C
C
        WRITE(6,20) ( I, I=2,9,2)
 20     FORMAT(1X, 4I5 //)
C
        WRITE(6,30) ( I, I, R, I=1, 4)
 30     FORMAT(1X, 2I5, F5.1 )
        STOP
        END
```

Figure 8.11a. In the first WRITE, the (I, I=1,4) is the implied DO. The I=1,4 part serves the same purpose it does in a DO statement, i.e., specifies the parameters of the DO. The items that precede I=1,4—here simply I—are considered the range of the DO. If a variable that has a constant value appears in an implied DO, as R in (I, I, R, I=1,4), then the constant value of R is printed the number of times specified by the parameters of the implied DO.

```
1    2    3    4   <———— Printed by WRITE(6,10) (I, I=1,4)

2    4    6    8   <———— Printed by WRITE(6,20) (I, I=2,9,2)

1    1  3.2  ⎫
2    2  3.2  ⎬   <———— Printed by WRITE(6,30) (I, I, R, I=1, 4)
3    3  3.2  ⎪
4    4  3.2  ⎭
```

Figure 8.11b. Running the program of Fig. 8.11a. Note that the same value of R is printed four times.

In the program shown in Fig. 8.12a we place the index L of the implied DO and an array R(L), in the range of the implied DO

```
WRITE(6,20) ( L, R(L), L=1,4)
```

The values of the elements of R are assigned in the DATA statement. The first time the range of the implied DO is executed, the computer interprets it as 1, R(1). Since the FORMAT is 20 FORMAT(1X,I4,F6.1), the computer pairs L with I4; and R(L) with F6.1 and prints

```
1   1.1
```

as shown in Fig. 8.12b, where 1.1 is the value of R(1).

The second time the range of the implied DO is executed, the computer interprets it as 2, R(2). The computer thus prints

```
2   6.2
```

as shown in Fig. 8.12b. The next two lines of results are produced for the same reason.

In Fig. 8.13a we rewrite the preceding program so that the results appear as shown in Fig. 8.13b, e.g., the first line is

```
R( 1)= 1.1
```

In

```
DATA C, D / 2HR(, 2H)= /
```

we assign the characters R(to the variable C and)= to D. This will allow us to label the results rather neatly. Since

```
WRITE(6,10) ( C, L, D, R(L), L=1,4)
```

is matched with

```
10    FORMAT(1X, A2, I2, A2, F4.1)
```

C is paired with A2; L with I2; D with A2; and R(L) with F4.1 each time the range of the implied DO is executed. Thus each time the range of the implied DO is executed, the computer prints a new line, as shown in Fig. 8.13b; e.g., the first line is

```
R( 1)= 1.1
```

Note we could have dispensed with A format and the alphanumeric constants and have written the WRITE and FORMAT as

```
      WRITE(6,10) (L, R( L), , L=1,4)
10    FORMAT(1X, 2HR(, I2, 2H)=, F4.1 )
```

USING THE IMPLIED DO INDEX TO LABEL ARRAY ELEMENTS

```
C   USING THE IMPLIED DO INDEX TO LABEL ARRAY ELEMENTS
         DIMENSION R(4)
         DATA R / 1.1, 6.2, 3.4, 7.2 /
C
         WRITE(6,10)
 10      FORMAT(4X, 'L', 2X, 'R(L)' )
C
         WRITE(6,20) ( L, R(L), L=1,4)
 20      FORMAT(1X, I4, F6.1)
         STOP
         END
```

Figure 8.12a. Placing L, the index of the implied DO, in the range L, R(L). This allows us to label the elements of an array.

```
   L  R(L)
   1   1.1
   2   6.2
   3   3.4
   4   7.2
```

Figure 8.12b. Running the program of Fig. 8.12a.

USING THE IMPLIED DO WITH ALPHANUMERIC CONSTANTS

```
C   USING THE IMPLIED DO WITH ALPHANUMERIC CONSTANTS
         DIMENSION R(4)
C
         DATA R / 1.1, 6.2, 3.4, -7.2 /
         DATA C, D / 2HR(, 2H)= /
C
         WRITE(6,10) ( C, L, D, R(L), L=1,4)
 10      FORMAT(1X, A2, I2, A2, F4.1)
         STOP
         END
```

Figure 8.13a. Using variables to which alphanumeric constants have been assigned, in an implied DO. Each time the range of the implied DO is executed, the same values of C and D are printed. Thus R( ) is printed for each line.

```
 R( 1)= 1.1
 R( 2)= 6.2
 R( 3)= 3.4
 R( 4)=-7.2
```

Figure 8.13b. Running the program of Fig. 8.13a.

We now discuss a nested implied DO

```
WRITE(6,10) ((I,J, J=1,3), I=1,2)
```

shown in Fig. 8.14a. The inner implied DO is

```
(I,J), J=1,3)
```

This is also the range of the outer implied DO. Thus for each value of I (the index of the outer implied DO), the inner DO will be completely executed. The WRITE is paired with

```
10   FORMAT(1X, 2I2, 2X, 2I2, 2X, 2I2)
```

Since the range of the inner DO is I,J, three pairs of I,J will be printed, and because of the FORMAT, these pairs are printed all on one line (Fig. 8.14b). When the value of I is 1

```
1 1   1 2   1 3
```

is printed, and when the value of I is 2

```
2 1   2 2   2 3
```

is printed.

The next program, shown in Fig. 8.15a, prints and labels the elements of the array X

$$\begin{pmatrix} 1.1 & 2.3 & 2.4 \\ 3.4 & 7.6 & -3.2 \end{pmatrix}$$

The elements of the array are assigned to the array in

```
DATA X / 1.1, 3.4, 2.3, 7.6, 2.4, -3.2 /
```

We want each element to be labeled, e.g., X(1 1) = 1.1, so we assign the alphanumeric constants X(and)= to C and D, respectively in another DATA statement. The statement

```
WRITE(6,10) ( ( C, I, J, D, X(I,J), J=1,3) ,I=1,2)
```

will produce the desired result. The range of the inner DO is C, I, J, D, X(I,J). When, for instance, the value of I is 1 and the value of J is 2, the range produces X(1 2) = 2.3.

The FORMAT that produces the results shown in Fig. 8.15b is quite cumbersome. We note that the FORMAT is simply a group of field specifications A2,2I2,A2,F4.1 repeated three times. In the next section we will learn a way to indicate repetitions of field specifications and thus simplify the appearance of this FORMAT.

USING THE NESTED IMPLIED DO

```
C  USING THE NESTED IMPLIED DO
      WRITE(6,10) ( ( I, J, J=1,3), I=1,2)
 10   FORMAT(1X, 2I2, 2X, 2I2, 2X, 2I2)
      STOP
      END
```

Figure 8.14a. A nested implied DO. I is the index of the outer implied DO. (I, J, J=1,3) is the inner implied DO. Its range is I,J. The first time the inner DO is executed, the value of I is 1, so the computer interprets it as (1, J, J=1,3) and prints the first line of results. The second time, the computer interprets it as (2, J, J=1,3) and prints the second line.

```
 1 1   1 2   1 3
 2 1   2 2   2 3
```

Figure 8.14b. Running the program of Fig. 8.14a.

LABELING THE ELEMENTS OF A TWO-DIMENSIONAL ARRAY

```
C LABELING THE ELEMENTS OF A 2-DIMENSIONAL ARRAY
      DIMENSION X(2,3)
      DATA X / 1.1, 3.4, 2.3, 7.6, 2.4, -3.2 /
      DATA C, D / 'X(', ')=' /
      WRITE(6,10) ( ( C, I, J, D, X(I,J), J=1,3) ,I=1,2)
 10   FORMAT(1X, A2,2I2,A2,F4.1,  2X,A2,2I2,A2,F4.1,
     1         2X,A2,2I2,A2,F4.1)
      STOP
      END
```

Figure 8.15a. Printing and labeling the elements of an array. Each time the inner DO is executed, the same values of C and D are printed. Thus each element of the array is printed with X(   )=.

```
X( 1 1)= 1.1  X( 1 2)= 2.3  X( 1 3)= 2.4
X( 2 1)= 3.4  X( 2 2)= 7.6  X( 2 3)=-3.2
```

Figure 8.15b. Running the program of Fig. 8.15b.

We should remember that an implied DO can be placed anywhere in a READ or WRITE statement that a variable can be placed. Examples of use of implied DOs are

```
WRITE(6,10) A, B, (A(I), I=1,7,2),R
WRITE(6,10) ( M, (A(I), R, I=1, 7, M)
WRITE(6,10) (A(I), I=1,5), (( B(I,J), I=L1,L2,L3),J=M1, M2, M3)
WRITE(6,10) ( M(J), J=L1,L2,L3)
READ(5,10) L, M, N, (KOUNT(I), I=L,M,N )
```

In the last example, the values of L,M,N are the parameters of the index of the implied DO. Note, they must precede the implied DO, so the parameters of the DO are defined. Obviously they are, and should only be, read once. It would be illegal to write this statement as

```
READ(5,10) (L,M,N,KOUNT(I), I=L,M,N)
```

for the following reason. Every time an element of KOUNT is read, then a set of values for L,M,N would also be read. We would therefore be trying to redefine the parameters of the implied DO. This is illegal.

One last remark on implied DO loops applies to their use in both READ and WRITE statements; we will discuss it only in relation to WRITE statements, as shown in Fig. 8.16a.

```
WRITE(6,10) ( K(I), L(I), I=1,4)
```

prints the elements in the following order K(1), L(1), K(2), L(2), K(3), L(3), K(4), L(4); whereas, as shown in the first line of results in Fig. 8.16b,

```
WRITE(6,20) (K(I), I=1,4), ( L(I), I=1,4)
```

prints the elements in the following order: K(1), K(2), K(3), K(4), L(1), L(2), L(3), L(4), as shown in the second line of results of Fig. 8.16b.

TWO WAYS OF USING THE IMPLIED DO

```
C  TWO TYPES OF IMPLIED DO LOOPS
      DIMENSION K(4), L(4)
      DATA K / 4*1 /
      DATA L / 4*2 /
C     ...K AND L IN THE SAME IMPLIED DO
      WRITE(6,5)
 5    FORMAT(1X, 'PRODUCED BY ( K(I), L(I), I=1,4) '      )
      WRITE(6,10) ( K(I), L(I), I=1,4)
 10   FORMAT(1X, 8I3)
C
C     ...K AND L IN DIFFERENT IMPLIED DO LOOPS
      WRITE(6,15)
 15   FORMAT(1X, 'PRODUCED BY (K(I), I=1,4), ( L(I), I=1,4)'     )
      WRITE(6,20) (K(I), I=1,4), ( L(I), I=1,4)
 20   FORMAT(1X, 8I3)
      STOP
      END
```

Figure 8.16a. The implied DO (K(I), L(I), I=1,4) prints the values of K(1), L(1), K(2), L(2), etc., whereas (K(I),I=1,4), (L(I), I=1,4) prints all the values of K first and then all the values of L.

```
PRODUCED BY ( K(I), L(I), I=1,4)
  1  2  1  2  1  2  1  2
PRODUCED BY (K(I), I=1,4), ( L(I), I=1,4)
  1  1  1  1  2  2  2  2
```

Figure 8.16b. Running the program of Fig. 8.16a.

8.8. Using Arrays Without Subscripts in READ and WRITE Statements

In Fig. 8.17a, we instruct the computer to read the entire array A by writing READ(5,10) A. Since we have dimensioned A as having six elements, the computer reads all six elements. Thus this READ is equivalent to READ(5,10) (A(I),I=1,6) or in more expanded form

```
READ(5,10) A(1), A(2), A(3), A(4), A(5), A(6)
```

The format 10 FORMAT(F10.0) instructs the computer that it can read only one element from a card. Thus six data cards are required—they are shown in Fig. 8.17b. If we had written the format as 10 FORMAT(3F10.0), the computer would expect to read two cards with three elements per card. Had we written it as 10 FORMAT(6F10.0), the computer would expect to read all six elements from one card. In the table of Fig. 8.17a we see how the constants are assigned to the elements of A.

We print the results by first using

```
      WRITE(6,20) (A(I), I=1,6)
20    FORMAT(1X, 6F10.0)
```

This prints the results, as shown in Fig. 8.17c, on one line, as we expect. We can produce the same result by using WRITE(6,30) A. Because A is dimensioned to have six elements, this is equivalent to WRITE(6,20) (A(I), I=1,6). Thus the computer prints all 6 elements. Because the format is 30 FORMAT(1X, 6F10.0), the results are printed in one line, the same as the results for the WRITE with the implied DO, as we see in Fig. 8.17c.

In WATFOR and WATFIV you can place an unsubscripted array in an unformatted READ or PRINT statement. Thus if the program of Fig. 8.17a were written using the unformatted READ statement, you would replace READ(5,10) A with READ, A and you would eliminate the FORMAT statement; you would replace WRITE(6,30) A with PRINT, A and eliminate the FORMAT statement. The computer would read all the data cards until all six elements of the array A were defined—if you punched all six constants on one card, the program would read only one card; if you punched two cards with three constants per card, the computer would read two cards. Thus the situation is similar to that when you use a formatted READ—you can determine how many data cards should be used. For an unformatted READ you do this by how you punch the cards; whereas for a formatted READ you determine how many cards should be used by how you write the FORMAT.

USING ARRAYS IN READ/WRITE **WITHOUT SUBSCRIPTS**

```
C  USING ARRAYS IN I/O WITHOUT
C  USING SUBSCRIPTS
       DIMENSION A(6)
       READ(5,10) A
 10    FORMAT(F10.0)
C
C      ...WRITE USING SUBSCRIPTED ARRAY
       WRITE(6,15)
 15    FORMAT(1X, 'WRITTEN USING SUBSCRIPTED ARRAY')
       WRITE(6,20) (A(I), I=1,6)
 20    FORMAT(1X, 6F10.0)
C
C      ...WRITE USING UNSUBSCRIPTED ARRAY
       WRITE(6,25)
 25    FORMAT(1X, 'WRITTEN USING NON-SUBSCRIPTED ARRAY')
       WRITE(6,30) A
 30    FORMAT(1X, 6F10.0)
       STOP
       END
```

Figure 8.17a. Since A is dimensioned to have 6 elements, when the computer encounters READ(5,10) A it reads all 6 elements of A. Since only one field specification appears in 10 FORMAT(F10.0), the computer reads 6 data cards.

1.0	2.0	4.0	−4.0	62.0	4.0
A(1)	A(2)	A(3)	A(4)	A(5)	A(6)

Table for Fig. 8.17a. How the constants on the data cards are assigned to A.

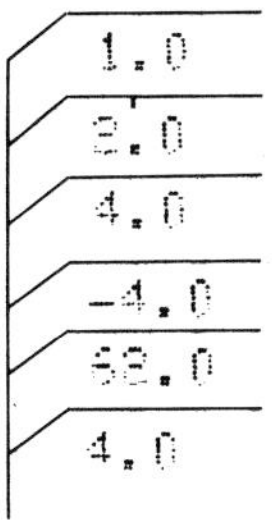

Figure 8.17b. The data cards the program of Fig. 8.17a reads.

Printed by WRITE(6,20) (A(I), I=1,6)

```
WRITTEN USING SUBSCRIPTED ARRAY
        1.        2.        4.       -4.       62.        4.
WRITTEN USING NON-SUBSCRIPTED ARRAY
        1.        2.        4.       -4.       62.        4.
```

Printed by WRITE(6,30) A

Figure 8.17c. Running the program of Fig. 8.17a. WRITE(5,30) A is equivalent to WRITE(5,20) (A(I),I=1,6).

We now return our discussion to formatted READ and WRITE statements.

The one restriction to using an array without subscripts in a READ or WRITE statement is that you must read all the elements or write all the elements of an array; you have no control over how many elements you want to read or write. This can, of course, create an error if you have miscounted the number of data cards and have consequently dimensioned the array incorrectly. The computer will then either want to read more or read fewer data cards than there actually are, depending on how you miscounted.

Using an array without subscripts is useful when you want to print characters on an entire line (or on part of it), as we will show in the next program. In Fig. 8.18a we present a program that will help you to determine how many columns you can use on the line printer. We will do this by repetitively printing 1234567890. across the page until the computer stops printing.

In the loop

```
      DO 10 J=1,150
         N=J-10*(J/10)
         M(J)=N
10    CONTINUE
```

we continually store the number 1, 2, 3, 4, 5, 6, 7, 8, 9, and 0 in successive elements of the array M as the subscript J varies from 1 to 150. The table for Fig. 8.18a shows what the statement N=J−10*(J/10) does. As the value of J varies from 1 to 9, so does the value of N. For instance, when the value of J is 9, then J/10 is 0, so the value of N is also 9. As the value of J varies from 10 to 19, the value of N varies from 0 to 9. For instance, when the value of J is 19, then J/10 is 1, so the value of N is 19−10, i.e., it is again 9. As the value of J varies from 20 to 29, then J/10 is 2, so the value of N is 29−20, i.e., it is again 9. From all this we see, for example, that the value of M(9) is 9, M(19) is 9, and M(29) is also 9. The results of running the program are shown in Fig. 8.18b. We see that the number of columns on the line printer is 132. When the program tries to print in the 133rd column, the computer prints an error message

```
IHC212I IBCOM - FORMATTED I/O, END OF RECORD ON UNIT    6
```

It then recovers and continues executing and prints the rest of the numbers.* If this program were run on the WATFOR/WATFIV compiler, the compiler would consider the use of 150I1 a compilation error.

* The 3 is not printed since it is used as a control character.

DETERMINING HOW MANY COLUMNS THERE ARE ON A PAGE

```
C   PROGRAM DETERMINES HOW MANY COLUMNS
C   THERE ARE ON A PAGE
      DIMENSION M(150)
C     ...GENERATE 1234567890 ETC.
      DO 10 J=1,150
         N=J-10*(J/10)
         M(J)=N
 10   CONTINUE
C     ...WRITE 1234567890 ETC.
      WRITE(6,20) M
 20   FORMAT(1X, 150I1 )
      STOP
      END
```

Figure 8.18a. The elements of the array M contain the numbers 1, 2, 3, 4, 5, 6, 7, 8, 9, 0, 1, 2, 3, 4. . .etc. By printing the elements of M across the page, the program determines how many columns there are on a page.

J	J/10	N
1	0	1
2	0	2
.		
.		
.		
9	0	9
10	1	0
11	1	1
12	1	2
.		
.		
.		
19	1	9
20	2	0
21	2	1
22	2	2
.		
.		
.		
29	2	9

Table for Fig. 8.18a. Shows what N=J−10*(J/10) does. Since M(J)=N, the elements of M in ascending order are 1, 2, 3, 4, 5, 6, 7, 8, 9, 0, 1, 2, 3, 4, 5 . . . etc.

```
123456789012345678901234567890123456789012345678901234567890123456789012345678901234567890123456789012345678901234567890123456789012
IHC212I IBCOM - FORMATTED I/O, END OF RECORD ON UNIT    6
45678901234567890
```

Figure 8.18b. Running the program of Fig. 8.18a.

We now discuss using a two-dimensional array without subscripts in READ and WRITE statements. In the program of Fig. 8.19a, the statement READ(5,10) A because of the appearance of DIMENSION A(2,3), instructs the computer to read the elements of a two-dimensional array. The computer reads the elements of the array in the same way a two-dimensional array is stored in the computer's memory: the computer reads the elements by column. Thus it will read the elements in the following order: A(1,1), A(2,1), A(1,2), A(2,2), A(1,3), A(2,3). Since the format is 10 FORMAT(2F10.1), the computer reads the elements two per card. The first data card is

```
1.0          4.0
```

Thus 1.0 is assigned to A(1,1) and 4.0 is assigned to A(2,1). This and the other two data cards are shown in Fig. 8.19b. How all the constants on the data cards are assigned to the elements of A is shown in the table of Fig. 8.19a.

USING TWO-DIMENSIONAL ARRAYS IN READ/WRITE WITHOUT USING SUBSCRIPTS

```
C   USING 2-DIMENSIONAL ARRAYS IN
C       I/O WITHOUT USING SUBSCRIPTS
        DIMENSION A(2,3)
C
        READ (5,10) A
 10     FORMAT(2F10.1)
C
        WRITE(6,15)
 15     FORMAT(1X, 'PRINTED BY ( (A(I,J), J=1,3), I=1,2)'              )
        WRITE(6,20) ( (A(I,J), J=1,3), I=1,2)
 20     FORMAT(1X, 3F10.0'
C
        WRITE(6,25)
 25     FORMAT(1X, 'PRINTED BY ( (A(I,J), I=1,2), J=1,3)'  )
         WRITE(6,30) ( (A(I,J), I=1,2), J=1,3)
 30     FORMAT(1X, 2F10.1)
C
         WRITE(6,35)
 35     FORMAT(1X, 'PRINTED BY WRITE(6,40) A   '     )
        WRITE(6,40) A
 40     FORMAT(1X, 2F10.0)
        STOP
        END
```

Figure 8.19a. The elements of a two-dimensional array used without subscripts in a READ are read by column; i.e., the order is A(1,1), A(2,1), A(1,2), A(2,2), A(1,3), A(2,3). Similarly, the elements of a two-dimensional array used without subscripts in WRITE are printed by column. Thus WRITE(6,40) A and WRITE(6,30) ((A(I,J), I=1,2), J=1,3) produce the same results.

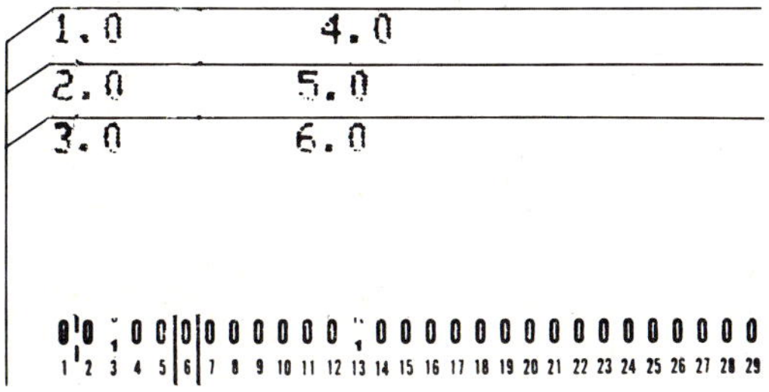

Figure 8.19b. The data cards read by the program of Fig. 8.19a.

1.0	4.0
A(1,1)	A(2,1)
2.0	5.0
A(1,2)	A(2,2)
3.0	6.0
A(1,3)	A(2,3)

Table for Fig. 8.19a. How the constants on the data cards are assigned to the elements of A.

We print the results by first using

```
      WRITE(6,20) ( (A(I,J), J=1,3), I=1,2)
20    FORMAT(1X, 3F10.0'
```

This prints the elements of the array in the form that arrays (or matrices) are used, i.e., by rows (Fig. 8.19c). We print the rows across the page, i.e., the values of A(1,1), A(1,2), A(1,3)

1. 2. 3.

We then print A(2,1), A(2,2), A(2.3)

4. 5. 6.

We then print the array in the form in which the array is stored in the computer's memory; we print the columns across the page. We do this by using

```
      WRITE(6,30) ( (A(I,J), I=1,2), J=1,3)
30    FORMAT(1X, 2F10.1)
```

The computer thus prints A(1,1), A(2,1); followed by A(1,2), A(2,2); followed by A(1,3), A(2,3).

We finally use

```
      WRITE(6,40) A
40    FORMAT(1X, 2F10.0)
```

When the computer executes this WRITE statement, it prints the elements of the array in the form in which the array is stored in memory. Thus, because FORMAT statements 30 and 40 are identical, the computer prints the elements in the same way that the preceding WRITE statement WRITE(6,30) ((A(I,J), I=1,2), J=1,3) does. It prints the elements by columns across the page. Because the computer handles arrays in the "nonconventional" manner, care should be taken in using unsubscripted arrays in READ and WRITE statements.

In WATFOR and WATFIV you can use unsubscripted two-dimensional arrays in both unformatted READ statements and PRINT statements. The only difficulty is that, as we mentioned with respect to printing one-dimensional arrays, you have no control over how the results are printed. The results are printed across the page without any regard for the form of the array.

```
PRINTED BY ( (A(I,J), J=1,3), I=1,2)
        1.          2.          3.
        4.          5.          6.
PRINTED BY ( (A(I,J), I=1,2), J=1,3)
        1.0         4.0
        2.0         5.0
        3.0         6.0
PRINTED BY WRITE(6,40) A
        1.          4.
        2.          5.
        3.          6.
```

Figure 8.19c. Running the program of Fig. 8.19a. When WRITE(6,40) A is used, you have no control over the order in which the elements are printed. When an implied DO is used, you do have control.

8.9. Repeating Groups of Field Specifications

In the program of Fig. 8.20a we present a program in which the group of field specifications I2,F5.1,4X is repeated 3 times. The results of running this program are shown in Fig. 8.20b.

Writing the FORMAT statement of Fig. 8.20a is not only tedious, but also open to error and hard to read. An easier way of writing this FORMAT is to place the group of field specifications in parentheses and precede the parentheses with the number indicating how many times you want the group of field specifications repeated. This number—here we have used 3—is called the *repetition factor* or *repeat count digit*. We thus write the FORMAT as

```
10    FORMAT(1X, 3(I2, F5.1, 4X), 'END')
```

as shown in Fig. 8.21a; we thus indicate that we want to use I2, F5.1, 4X three times. The results are shown in Fig. 8.21b; they are the same as in Fig. 8.20b. This same technique can be used to repeat groups of field specifications in a FORMAT used with a READ statement.

MOTIVATING REPEATING GROUPS OF FORMATS

```
C  MOTIVATING REPEATING GROUPS OF FORMATS
      DATA A, B, C / 1.1, 2.2, 3.3 /
      DATA I, J, K / 1, 2, 3 /
      WRITE(6,10) I, A, J, B, K, C
 10   FORMAT(1X, I2,F5.1,4X, I2,F5.1,4X, I2,F5.1,4X, 'END')
      STOP
      END
```

Figure 8.20a. We want I, A printed using I2,F5.1,4X; J, B printed using I2,F5.1,4X; and K, C printed using I2,F5.1,4X, so we repeat the group I2,F5.1,4X three times.

```
1  1.1       2  2.2       3  3.3      END
```

Figure 8.20b. Running the program of Fig. 8.20a.

REPEATING GROUPS OF FORMATS

```
C  REPEATING GROUPS IN FORMATS
      DATA A, B, C / 1.1, 2.2, 3.3 /
      DATA I, J, K / 1, 2, 3 /
      WRITE(6,10) I, A, J, B, K, C
 10   FORMAT(1X, 3(I2, F5.1, 4X), 'END')
      STOP
      END
```

Figure 8.21a. Same as Fig. 8.20a except that we signify that we want I2,F5.1,4X repeated three times by writing 3(I2,F5.1,4X). Whenever we want a group of formats repeated, we enclose the group in parentheses and precede the left parenthesis with a digit indicating how many times we want the group repeated.

```
1  1.1       2  2.2       3  3.3      END
```

Figure 8.21b. Running the program of Fig. 8.21a. As we expect, the results shown here are identical to those shown in Fig. 8.20b.

Parenthesizing field specifications in a FORMAT has another effect, as we now see. The program of Fig. 8.22a uses

```
         WRITE(6,10) (ARRAY(I), I=1,4)
   10    FORMAT(1X, 'RESULTS' / 1X, F5.1)
```

with the hope that the program would first print RESULTS and then the elements of ARRAY printed in a column, i.e., what is shown in Fig. 8.23b. Instead of printing this, it prints the results shown in Fig. 8.22b. The reason is as follows: The program first prints RESULTS. It then skips to the next line and prints the value of ARRAY(1). In order to print the value of ARRAY(2), it uses the FORMAT again from the beginning. It thus prints RESULTS on the next line and, only then, the value of ARRAY(2) on the following line. This process continues until all the elements of ARRAY are printed.

The way to obtain the desired results is to place the 1X,F5.1 in parentheses, as shown in Fig. 8.23a

```
         WRITE(6,10) (ARRAY(I), I=1,4)
   10    FORMAT(1X, 'RESULTS' / (1X, F5.1) )
```

If there are parenthesized field specifications in the FORMAT statement—here (1X, F5.1)—and if there are more variables—here A(2), A(3), and A(4)—in the WRITE (or READ) then there are field specifications in the FORMAT, then the program instead of using the entire FORMAT statement again, starts with the right-most parenthesized field specification—here (1X, F5.1)—and continues to the end of the FORMAT, matching field specifications with variables. If there are still more variables in the WRITE (or READ), the program uses the field specifications, starting again with this right-most parenthesized one—here (1X, F5.1)—and continues to the end of the FORMAT. This process continues until all the variables have been matched with a field specification.

Each time but the first that the parenthesized field specifications are used, the computer interprets the "(" not only as a left parenthesis, but also in effect as a slash, i.e., it uses the field specification—here 1X—that follows the left parenthesis, to determine how to advance the page on the line printer. If the field is a blank—as it is here when 1X is used—the computer prints on the next line the fields indicated within the parentheses. Thus in the program of Fig. 8.23a, the first time (1X, F5.1) is used, the parentheses are ignored. Therefore when the value of ARRAY(1) is printed, the computer associates the 1X with the preceding slash and uses it for the control character. For all values of succeeding elements of ARRAY, the 1X is associated with the parenthesis and is again used as a control character, so each of these elements is printed on a new line (Fig. 8.23b).

MOTIVATING THE USE OF PARENTHESES WITH REPEAT COUNTS OF ONE

```
C  MOTIVATING THE USE OF PARENTHESIS
C  WITH REPEAT COUNT OF ONE
      DIMENSION ARRAY(4)
      DATA ARRAY / 1.1, 2.2, 3.3, 4.4 /
      WRITE(6,10) (ARRAY(I), I=1,4)
 10   FORMAT(1X, 'RESULTS' / 1X, F5.1)
      STOP
      END
```

Figure 8.22a. The program was an attempt to first print RESULTS and then the elements of the ARRAY. Since there are 4 elements in ARRAY the FORMAT is used 4 times. However, each time the FORMAT statement is used, it is used from its beginning and thus RESULT is printed 4 times.

```
RESULTS
  1.1
RESULTS
  2.2
RESULTS
  3.3
RESULTS
  4.4
```

Figure 8.22b. Running the program of Fig. 8.22a.

USING PARENTHESES WITH A REPEAT COUNT OF ONE

```
C  USING PARENTHESES WITH A REPEAT COUNT OF ONE
      DIMENSION ARRAY(4)
      DATA ARRAY/ 1.1, 2.2, 3.3, 4.4 /
      WRITE(6,10) (ARRAY(I), I=1,4)
 10   FORMAT(1X, 'RESULTS' / (1X, F5.1) )
      STOP
      END
```

Figure 8.23a. If the FORMAT has to be used again, the computer scans the FORMAT from right to left for a parenthesized group of field specifications. When it finds the first such group—here (1X, F5.1)—the computer uses the part of the FORMAT from this group to the right end of the FORMAT, over and over again until the WRITE list is satisfied.

```
RESULTS
  1.1
  2.2
  3.3
  4.4
```

Figure 8.23b. Running the program of Fig. 8.23a. Since 1X, F5.1 is parenthesized, it is used over and over again until all the elements of ARRAY are printed.

We now discuss what happens if the slash is omitted and the FORMAT is written as 10 FORMAT(1X,'RESULTS', (1X, F5.1)) as is shown in Fig. 8.23c. When the value of A(1) is printed, the parentheses in (1X, F5.1) are ignored. Thus the 1X is not used for the control character; it is simply used to separate 'RESULTS' and the next field by one blank. Therefore the first line printed is

```
RESULTS   1.1
```

When the value of A(2) is printed (1X, F5.1) is used again and the 1X is used this time for the control character. Thus the value of A(2) is printed on the next line. This process continues—each successive element of A being printed on a new line—until all the elements are printed, as is shown in Fig. 8.23d.

We now discuss what happens when a repeat count digit precedes a parenthesized group of field specifications that is used more than once to satisfy the list in the accompanying READ (or WRITE), as is the case in the program of Fig. 8.24a. This program produces the labeled elements of the array X as is shown in Fig. 8.24b using 10 FORMAT (3 (1X, A2, I2, A1, I2, A2, F4.1), 3X)).

When the values of X(1, 1) and the strings that label it are all printed, the 1X is used for the control character. Because the repeat count digit is 3, the group of field specifications is used twice more, printing the values of X(1,2) and X(1,3) and the strings that label them, all on the same line as the value of X(1,1) is printed. However, the second and third time, the 1X is not used for the control character but simply to separate fields. Since the value of X(2, 1), X(2, 2), and X(2, 3) remain to be printed, 3 (1X, A2, I2, A1, I2, A2, F4.1, 3X) is used again (since this is the right-most parenthesized group of field specifications) producing its results on the next line.

```
C   SHOWS THAT IF SLASH IS OMITTED, THE '1X' IS
C   NOT USED AS A CONTROL CHARACTER
        DIMENSION ARRAY(4)
        DATA ARRAY/ 1.1, 2.2, 3.3, 4.4 /
        WRITE(6,10) (ARRAY(I), I=1,4)
 10     FORMAT(1X, 'RESULTS',   (1X, F5.1) )
        STOP
        END
```

Figure 8.23c. Same as the program of Fig. 8.23a, except that now the FORMAT has no slash; i.e., it is written as FORMAT(1X, 'RESULTS', (1X, F5.1)). The first time the computer encounters a parenthesized group that has no repeat count digit, the computer ignores the parentheses. Consequently, it does not treat the first field described by the group as a control character. Thus the first element of ARRAY is printed on the same line as RESULTS. However, after this, the 1X in (1X,F5.1) is used for carriage control.

```
RESULTS    1.1
  2.2
  3.3
  4.4
```

Figure 8.23d. Running the program of Fig. 8.23c.

MORE VARIABLES IN THE LIST THAN ARE INDICATED IN REPEATED GROUP FORMAT

```
C   MORE VARIABLES IN THE LIST THAN ARE
C   INDICATED IN THE REPEAT GROUP FORMAT
        DIMENSION X(2,3)
        DATA X/ 1.1, 3.4, 2.3, 7.6, 2.4, -3.2 /
        DATA C, COMMA, D / 'X(', ',', ')=' /
        WRITE(6,10) ( ( C, I, COMMA, J, D, X(I,J), J=1,3), I=1,2)
 10     FORMAT( 3( 1X, A2, I2, A1, I2, A2, F4.1, 3X)   )
        STOP
        END
```

Figure 8.24a. Same as Fig. 8.15a, except that now, instead of repeating the group of field specifications three times, we parenthesize it and precede it with a 3. Since a 3 precedes the group, the first three elements of X are printed on the first line. The computer then encounters the last parenthesis in the FORMAT. It then uses 3(1X, A2, I2, A1, I2, A2, F4.1, 3X) to print the next three elements of X on the next line.

```
X( 1, 1)= 1.1     X( 1, 2)= 2.3     X( 1, 3)= 2.4
X( 2, 1)= 3.4     X( 2, 2)= 7.6     X( 2, 3)=-3.2
```

Figure 8.24b. Running the program of Fig. 8.24a.

In the program of Fig. 8.25a, we show a program in which a group of parenthesized field specifications 2(1X, I2, F6.2, 3X) is not the last field specification in the FORMAT, here

```
10    FORMAT(1X, 2( I2, F5.1, 3X), 2( 1X, I2, F6.2, 3X), I2, E15.3)
```

When the program is run, the values of M(1), A(1); M(2), A(2); M(3), A(3); M(4), A(4); and M(5), A(5) are all printed on the same line. However, the remaining elements of M and A (for the subscript having the values 6 through 8) have yet to be matched with field specifications, so the computer uses the right-most parenthesized group of field specifications, 2(1X, I2, F6.2, 3X) to print the values of M(6), A(6) and of M(7), A(7) on the next line, as shown in Fig. 8.25b. Since I2 and E15.3 appear to the right of 2(1X, I2, F6.2, 3X), they are also used again. Thus the values of M(8) and A(8) are also printed on the second line.

Some systems allow you to place parenthesized field specifications within a parenthesis, e.g., in the FORMAT statement of Fig. 8.25a. We could place 1X, 2(I2, F5.1, 3X), 2(1X, I2, F6.2, 3X) in an outer set of parentheses, writing

```
10    FORMAT( (1X, 2(I2, F5.1, 3X), 2(1X, I2, F6.2, 3X), I2, E15.3))
```

Now this outer set is considered the right-most pair of parentheses. After the field specifications in the FORMAT are used for the first time, they are used again, starting with the outer set of parentheses which bracket 1X, 2(I2, F5.1, 3X), 2(1X, I2, F6.2, 3X).

PARENTHESIZED GROUP OF FORMATS IS NOT THE LAST SPECIFICATION IN THE FORMAT

```
C  PARENTHESIZED GROUP OF FORMATS IS NOT THE
C  LAST SPECIFICATION IN THE FORMAT
      DIMENSION A(8), M(8)
      DATA A / 1.1, 2.2, 3.3, 4.4, 5.5, 6.6, 7.7, 8.8 /
      DATA M / 1, 2, 3, 4, 5, 6, 7, 8 /
      WRITE(6,10) ( M(I), A(I), I=1,8)
 10   FORMAT(1X, 2( I2, F5.1, 3X), 2( 1X, I2, F6.2, 3X), I2, E15.3)
      STOP
      END
```

Figure 8.25a. Since 2(1X, I2, F6.2, 3X) is the right-most parenthesized group in the FORMAT, the computer uses it and the field specifications to its right, i.e., I2, E15.3, again until the WRITE list is satisfied.

```
M (1)        M (2)          M (3)            M (4)          M (5)
 ↓            ↓               ↓                ↓              ↓
 1  1.1      2  2.2         3  3.30          4  4.40        5        0.550E 01
 6  6.60       7  7.70        8         0.880E 01
 ↑             ↑              ↑
M (6)         M (7)          M (8)
```

Figure 8.25b. Running the program of Fig. 8.25a.

In the program shown in Fig. 8.26a, we use a parenthesized field specification in a FORMAT associated with the READ statement

```
      READ(5,10) N, (X(I), I=1,N)
   10 FORMAT( I3 / (F10.0) )
```

The value of N—which is the limit of I, the index of the implied DO—is read from the first card. Because of the slash, the value of X(1) is read from the next card; since F10.0 is being used for the first time, the parentheses around it are ignored. However, since F10.0 is parenthesized, each successive element of X is read using F10.0 and is read from a new card (Fig. 8.26b). We note that, although the technique used here is legal, it is not considered good programming style because it is error prone: We have no way of checking whether the value of N exceeds the dimension of X. Thus, what one should do is read the value of N in a preceding READ statement and first check that its value does not exceed the dimensions of X specified, before using it in an implied DO.

If, for some reason, the reader uses the technique shown in the program of Fig. 8.26a, he should note that placing N within the implied DO, i.e.,

```
      READ(5,10) (N, X(I), I=1,N)
```

would create an error. The reason is that we would be redefining the value of the index within the loop. He should also note that placing the slash in the parentheses, i.e.,

```
   10 FORMAT( I3, (/F10.0) )
```

would also create an error. The reason is that each time (/F10.0) is reused, the (/ has the effect of two slashes, and thus a card is skipped. For example, the third data card would be skipped and the value of X(2) would be read from the fourth instead of the third card.

A PARENTHESIZED FIELD SPECIFICATION USED WITH A READ

```
C   READ THE IMPLIED DO INDEX AND AN ARRAY
C   USING THE SAME FORMAT STATEMENT
       DIMENSION X(100)
       READ(5,10) N, (X(I), I=1,N)
 10    FORMAT( I3 / (F10.0) )
C
       WRITE(6,20) ( X(I), I=1, N)
 20    FORMAT(1X, 'ARRAY X' / (1X, F10.0) )
       STOP
       END
```

Figure 8.26a. A parenthesized group used in a FORMAT matched with a READ. After the computer uses the FORMAT for the first time, it scans the FORMAT from right to left for the first parenthesized group—here (F10.0). Each time but the first that it uses this group, the computer reads a new card. Thus if the FORMAT were written without a slash, i.e., FORMAT(I3,(F10.0)), the computer would expect to read the value of N and X(1) from the first card.

```
ARRAY X
        10.
         4.
         7.
        -6.
```

Figure 8.26b. Running the program of Fig. 8.26a.

8.10. The DATA Declaration Statement

All the variables need not be grouped at the beginning of the DATA statement. Thus, although in the first DATA statement of Fig. 8.27

```
DATA A, B, C, I / 1.2, 2*6.2, 41 /
```

we have indeed grouped all the variables together, in the second DATA statement

```
DATA A/ 1.2 /, B, C / 2*6.2 /, I / 41 /
```

we have placed the constants immediately after the variables to which they will be assigned. Thus 1.2 is assigned to A; 6.2 is assigned to B and C; and 41 to I. Note that when the list is continued after a slash, e.g., B,C and I, the list must be preceded by a comma. Thus we type /, B, C/ and /, I/ in the DATA statement. This form of the DATA statement may be easier for someone reading the program to understand. In order to further promote readability, it is advisable to leave one blank space between a constant and the next slash, e.g., between 1.2 and /, B, C.

Using an implied DO loop in a DATA statement is not allowed in ANS Standard FORTRAN. However, on many compilers (e.g., WATFOR/WATFIV), implied DO loops can be used in DATA statements, as shown in Fig. 8.28; DATA (X(I), I=1,4) / 4*0.0 /. If we use an implied DO in a DATA statement, we do not have to initialize all the elements of an array. Thus here we only initialized the first four elements of the array dimensioned in DIMENSION X(10). Another advantage is that even if you initialize the entire array, e.g., write

```
DATA (X(I), I=1, 10) / 10*0.0 /
```

it is immediately obvious to the person reading the program that you are initializing an array. This is as opposed to writing DATA X / 10*0.0 /, which requires the reader to search for the DIMENSION statement. Note that whether you use the implied DO or use the array without subscripts, you must always dimension the array in another declaration statement.

The form of the implied DO used here is the same as that used in a WRITE or READ statement except that the parameters of the DO index (the initial value, the limit, and the increment) cannot be variables—they must be constants—on most compilers which allow the implied DO in a DATA statement. For example, DATA (X(I), I=1,N) / 4*0.0 / would be illegal on these compilers; however, it would be allowed in WATFIV if N has been defined earlier in the program.

DIFFERENT FORMS OF THE DATA **STATEMENT**

```
DATA A, B, C, I / 1.2, 2*6.2, 41 /
DATA A/ 1.2 / ,B, C / 2*6.2 / ,I / 41 /
```

Figure 8.27. The two DATA statements shown here are equivalent. Note that a comma must precede the B and the I in the second DATA statement since the list is being continued.

USING AN IMPLIED DO **LOOP IN A** DATA **STATEMENT**

```
DIMENSION X(10)
DATA ( X(I), I=1,4 ) / 4*0.0 /
```

Figure 8.28. On many compilers (e.g., WATFOR/WATFIV) we can use an implied DO in a DATA statement. It has the same interpretation here as it does in a READ or WRITE statement. This makes it more explicit that, for example, here X is an ARRAY. Here zeros are assigned to all 4 elements of X.

On some systems you can use nested implied DO loops in a DATA statement as is shown in Fig. 8.29.

DATA

The form of the DATA statement is: DATA followed by a list of one or more variables—if there is more than one variable, the variables must be separated by commas. The list is followed by a "/", which is followed by the constants that will be assigned to the variables in the list. A "/" follows the list of constants. If you wish to, you may follow this slash with another list of variables. You then bracket the constants that will be assigned to these variables, with slashes; and a comma must follow the first of these slashes. This procedure may then be continued, if you wish. The constants must agree with the variables both in number and mode. Examples of three of the possible ways you can write one DATA statement are:

1.
```
DATA A, B, (M(I), I = 1,4)† / 6.4, 120.6, 10, 11, 2*6/
```
2.
```
DATA A/6.4 /, B / 120.6 /, (M(I), I=1,4)† / 10, 11, 2*6/
```
3.
```
DATA A / 6.4
DATA B / 120.6
DATA (M(I), I=1,4)† / 10, 11, 2*6/
```

Other examples are:

```
DATA A, B, C, D, E / .TRUE., .FALSE., 3* .TRUE. /
DATA STRIN1, STRIN2, INDEX/ 4HFOUR, 3HTWO, 8/
```

Note that declaration statements (e.g., LOGICAL, REAL, INTEGER, and DIMENSION statements must precede DATA statements.

† Not allowed on ANS Standard FORTRAN.

USING NESTED IMPLIED DO **LOOP IN A** DATA **STATEMENT**

```
DIMENSION IN(5,5)
DATA( ( IN(I,J), I=1,3), J=1,2 ) / 6*1 /
```

Figure 8.29. On some systems, nested implied DO loops can be used. It has the same interpretation here as it does in a READ or WRITE statement.

8.11. Using G Format

The G format allows you to read or write any type of variable except alphanumeric. Its general form is G*w*.*d*. The *w* stands for the field width and *d* represents the number of digits we want printed in the answer. When used with I and L (LOGICAL) format, the *d* has no meaning.

In the program of Fig. 8.30a we calculate 10.0^{I} where I varies from -3 to 5. We print the value of I using G3.1; and the value of 10.0^{I} using G15.1, G15.2, and G15.3. When the value of I is printed, the .1 in G3.1 has no meaning and the result is printed as if we were using I3 format. When we use G format to print the value of a REAL constant—here 10.0**I—the computer will print the result either with or without an exponent, depending on the constant's size. The field width should be large enough to accommodate, besides the room normally needed to print a constant in F format, the four characters used in exponential notation, e.g., E+02. Thus we have provided for ample room by using a field width of 15 here.

If a constant is REAL and its value is equal to or less than 0.1 (on some systems, just less than), G format instructs the computer to print the result in exponential form. If its value is equal to or greater than 10^{d} (on some systems, just greater than), the constant will also be printed in exponential form. However, for values of the constant between 0.1 and 10^{d} the constant will be printed in nonexponential form.

The first value of I is -3, so the value of 10^{I} is less than 0.1; consequently it is printed in exponential form. Since we are using G15.1, G15.2, and G15.3, the number of digits to the right of the decimal point in the mantissa of the result is 1, 2, and 3, respectively, 0.1E−02, 0.10E−02, 0.100E−02, as shown in Fig. 8.30b. For the next two values of I (-2 and -1) the values of 10^{I} are again less than or equal to 0.1, so the results are again printed in exponential form. When the value of I is zero, the value of 10^{I} is greater than 0.1, so the results are printed in nonexponential form.

1.   1.0   1.00

Again, the number of digits printed is the value of *d* in G*w*.*d*. The constant is printed in nonexponential form until its value is equal to or greater than 10^{d}. Thus, for the fields described by G15.1, G15.2, and G15.3, the constant is printed in exponential form when its value is equal to or greater than 10^{1} 10^{2} and 10^{3}, respectively, as we see from Fig. 8.30b:

```
1      0.1E 02      10.          10.0
2      0.1E 03      0.10E 03     100.
3      0.1E 04      0.10E 04     0.100E 04
4      0.1E 05      0.10E 05     0.100E 05
```

When G format is used with a READ statement, the *d* has no meaning for an INTEGER constant and has the usual meaning for REALs. A REAL constant inputted in a field described by G format can be written either in exponential or nonexponential form.

USING G FORMAT

```
C   USING G FORMAT
C        ...PRINT POWERS OF 10
         WRITE(6,5)
 5       FORMAT(1X, 'G3.1', T14, 'G15.1', T29, 'G15.2', T44, 'G15.3' )
         DO 20 J=1,9
            I=J-4
            B=10.0**I
            WRITE(6,10) I, B, B, B
 10      FORMAT(1X, G3.1, G15.1, G15.2, G15.3 )
 20      CONTINUE
         STOP
         END
```

Figure 8.30a. Program shows how G format works in printing REAL and INTEGER values. The general form of G Format is G*w*.*d*; when reading or writing INTEGERs, the *d* has no meaning. The value of a REAL variable R is printed in exponential form unless $0.1 < R < 10^d$ (on some systems, $0.1 \leq R \leq 10^d$), then the value is printed in nonexponential form.

```
G3.1      G15.1          G15.2           G15.3
 -3     0.1E-02       0.10E-02       0.100E-02
 -2     0.1E-01       0.10E-01       0.100E-01
 -1     0.1E 00       0.10E 00       0.100E 00
  0     1.            1.0            1.00
  1     0.1E 02       10.            10.0
  2     0.1E 03       0.10E 03       100.
  3     0.1E 04       0.10E 04       0.100E 04
  4     0.1E 05       0.10E 05       0.100E 05
  5     0.1E 06       0.10E 06       0.100E 06
```

Figure 8.30b. The program prints 10^I. In the first column the value of I is printed in I format. In the second column 10^I is printed using G15.1. So for $.1 < 10^I < 10^1$, the result is printed in nonexponential form; otherwise it is printed in exponential form. In the third column, 10^I is printed using G15.2. So for $.1 < 10^I < 10^2$ the result is printed in nonexponential form. In the fourth column, 10^I is printed in G15.3. So for $.1 < 10^I < 10^3$ the result is printed in nonexponential form.

8.12. T Format

As we have previously said, when T format is used, the fields that follow the T format (up to those described by the next T format) are printed starting in the column indicated by 1 minus the integer that follows the T. For instance, in the program of Fig. 8.31a, the string COLUMN 21, since it is preceded by T21, should be printed starting in column 20. Since '–END' follows 'COLUMN 21' in the FORMAT, it also follows it in the results, as shown in Fig. 8.31b. Since T2 follows '–END' and no T format follows T2, everything else in the FORMAT will be printed starting in column 1. Thus the computer first prints the string 'COLUMN1- - -'. The next string consists of ten "1"s. This is printed after COLUMN1- - - and ends in column 20. The last "1" occupies the same columns as the C of COLUMN 21. The "1" is printed but the C is not. We thus obtain

```
1OLUMN 21
```

as is shown in Fig. 8.31b.

T format can be used to advantage in FORMATs associated with READ statements. Thus in

```
      READ(5,20) NUM, NUM1, NUM2
20    FORMAT( I2, T1, I1, T2, I1 )
```

First NUM is assigned the value of the INTEGER constant punched in the first two columns of the data card. Then because of T1, I1, the computer in effect goes back to column 1 and assigns the digit punched in it to NUM1; and because of T2,I1, it assigns the digit in column 2 to NUM2.

USING T FORMAT

```
C  USING T-FORMAT IN OUTPUT
      WRITE(6,10)
 10   FORMAT(1X, T21, 'COLUMN 21', '-END', T2, 'COLUMN1---',
     1          '1111111111'  )
      WRITE(6,20)
 20   FORMAT(1X, '123456789-123456789-123456789-')
      STOP
      END
```

Figure 8.31a. Using T format in output. Everything between T21 and the next T format is printed starting in column 20. Everything after the T2 is printed starting in column 1. The string in statement 20 labels the columns.

```
COLUMN1---11111111110LUMN 21-END
123456789-123456789-123456789-
```

Figure 8.31b. Running the program of Fig. 8.31a. Since the strings that follow T2 in the FORMAT have 20 characters, the last character, a "1", occupies the same column as the first character of 'COLUMN 21'. Thus "1" is printed instead of the C.

8.13. Hollerith Fields

As we have previously explained, a Hollerith field enables you to define strings and alphanumeric constants in a way other than enclosing the characters within single quotes. If an integer followed by the letter H precedes a group of characters, it is equivalent to enclosing the characters within single quotes. Thus 4HLAMB is equivalent to 'LAMB'.

The comma is not a signal to the compiler that you have completed the Hollerith field; it is, however, the means by which you separate field specifications. The integer which precedes the H, determines how many characters will be in the Hollerith field. Thus you may follow the H field by any number of blanks before you write the comma, (e.g., 3HEND ,F10.3) as is shown in Fig. 8.32a.

If you are using a Hollerith field at the end of a FORMAT, you do not place a comma at the end of the H field. Thus you would write

```
10    FORMAT(1X, F10.3,   3HEND )
```

as is shown in Fig. 8.32b, but not 10 FORMAT(1X, F10.3, 3HEND,).

If we use a digit whose value is less than the number of characters in the string that follows the H, a compile-time error will occur. For example, in 10 FORMAT(1X, 4HTHINGS, F10.3), as is shown in Fig. 8.33a, the 4H includes only the characters T, H, I, and N in the Hollerith field. The G and the S are not included; the compiler thus considers them to be part of a field specification. So, it interprets the FORMAT as 10 FORMAT(1X, 4HTHIN, GS, F10.3). Since GS does not comprise a valid field specification, a compile-time error results.

We now discuss the situation in which the value of the digit that precedes the H is greater than the number of characters in the string.

In that case, an error may or may not arise, depending on what extra characters are included. For instance in 10 FORMAT (IX, 7HTHINGS, F10.3) the 7 includes the comma as well as THINGS. Since a comma does not have to separate a Hollerith format from other field specifications, an error does not occur; when the program is run, the string would simply be printed as THINGS,.

On the other hand, if we write 10 FORMAT (IX, 9HTHINGS, F10.3) the 9 includes the comma, the blank that follows it, and the F in F10.3. Thus the computer interprets the FORMAT as 10 FORMAT (IX, 'THINGS, F' 10.3), as shown in Fig. 8.33b. Since 10.3 is not a valid field specification, an error occurs.

As we have previously stated, if there are any blanks in the Hollerith field, they must be included in the character count. Thus since THE END has 7 characters including the blank, it would be written in Hollerith format as the 7HTHE END. Because using the Hollerith field requires an accurate character count, using quoted strings is not as error prone. You can use a repeat count digit with Hollerith fields. Thus FORMAT (1X, 20(1H*)) prints twenty asterisks ********************. FORMAT (1X, 20('*')) produces the same result. The 1H* and the '*' must be parenthesized, otherwise a compile-time error will result.

THE COMMA DOES NOT TERMINATE A HOLLERITH FIELD

```
10     FORMAT(1X, 3HEND    , F10.3 )
```

Figure 8.32a. The comma does not signal the end of an H field; it simply separates fields. Thus you may follow an H field by any number of blanks before you write the comma.

AN H FIELD TERMINATING A FORMAT

```
10     FORMAT(1X, F10.3,   3HEND )
```

Figure 8.32b. When an H field terminates a FORMAT, you do not follow the H field with a comma.

TOO MANY CHARACTERS IN HOLLERITH FIELD

10 FORMAT(1X, 4HTHINGS, F10.3) ⇒ 10 FORMAT(1X,4HTHIN,GS,F10.3)

Figure 8.33a. If the value of the integer which precedes the H is too small, the characters at the end of the string—here G and S—will not be included in the Hollerith field; the compiler will view them as an invalid field specification and will produce a compile-time error.

TOO FEW CHARACTERS IN HOLLERITH FIELD

10 FORMAT(1X, 9HTHINGS, F10.3) ⇒ 10 FORMAT(1X,9HTHINGS,F 10.3)

Figure 8.33b. If the value of the integer which precedes the H is too large, the Hollerith field will include the characters that follow the intended end of the Hollerith field—here F—and a compile-time error will occur.

8.14. Control Characters

As we have previously said, the character in the left-most column of the first field is not printed; it is used as a control character. If this column is left blank, as is the case when 1X is the first field in the FORMAT, the computer advances the line printer page one line. If we use the digit 1 as the control character, the line printer will skip to the next page.

If we use the digit 0 as the control character, the computer advances the line printer 2 lines. If the character "+" is used, the computer does not advance the line printer at all; the computer prints the results on the same line that the preceding WRITE statement stopped writing on. The control character can be defined by a Hollerith field (e.g., 1HO) or by quotes (e.g., '0') as we show in Table 8.6.

It is important to note that the control character has meaning only when it is placed in a position in the FORMAT where (and when) the computer looks for a control character. Thus in

```
FORMAT(1X, F10.3, 1H1, F10.3 )
```

the 1H1 is not interpreted as a control character, and the computer would just print the digit 1 between the next to the last and the last field. For a character to be interpreted as a control character, it must either come directly after FORMAT (, or after a slash, or when the FORMAT is rescanned and the control character appears directly after the left parenthesis at which the rescanning begins.

The control character does not have to stand alone. It can be at the beginning on a blank field as in the 10X in FORMAT(10X, F10.2), or the first character in a string as the 0 in FORMAT ('0 RESULTS'), or the first character in the Hollerith field as the 1 in FORMAT(8H1RESULTS).

Control character	Effect on line printer	Example of use in FORMAT with Hollerith	Example of use in FORMAT with quotes
Blank	Advances page 1 line	FORMAT(1X, I10)	FORMAT(' ', I10)
0	Advances page 2 lines	FORMAT(1H0, I10)	FORMAT('0', I10)
1	Skips to top of next page	FORMAT(1H1, I10)	FORMAT('1', I10)
+	Line printer not advanced	FORMAT(1H+, I10)	FORMAT('+', I10)

Table 8.6. The different control characters.

8.15. Using Strings in FORMATs Used with READ Statements

When a string is used in a FORMAT associated with a READ statement, the characters on the data card that are punched in the columns corresponding to the string will replace the characters in the string when the data card is read. Thus in Fig. 8.34a, since 10 FORMAT(11H12345678901) is used when READ(5,10), the characters in the Hollerith field will be replaced by the characters on the data card read. The data card is shown in Fig. 8.34b:

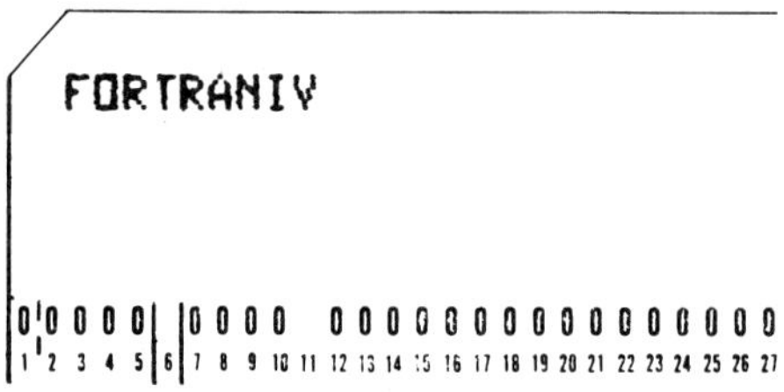

Thus the Hollerith field becomes 11H FORTRANIV. Since the first column on the card is blank, a blank is the first character in the redefined H field. When this FORMAT statement is used with WRITE(6,10), the blank serves as a control character. When the results are printed

```
FORTRANIV
1234567890
```

since the second column on the data card is also blank, the printing begins in column 2, as is shown in Fig. 8.34c. Had we wanted to, we could have written the FORMAT used with the READ statement as 10 FORMAT('   '); i.e., replace the H field with a quoted string as is shown in Fig. 8.34d. The results of running the program would be the same, as shown in Fig. 8.34e

USING H FIELD TO READ A DATA CARD

```
C  USING H FIELD FOR INPUT
       READ(5,10)
 10    FORMAT(11H12345678901)
C
C      ...PRINT WHAT HAS JUST BEEN READ
       WRITE(6,10)
C
C      ...PRINT COLUMNS
       WRITE(6,20)
 20    FORMAT(1X, 10H1234567890)
       STOP
       END
```

Figure 8.34a. Since the FORMAT of statement 10 is used with a READ, the characters in the string are replaced by the corresponding characters in the data card.

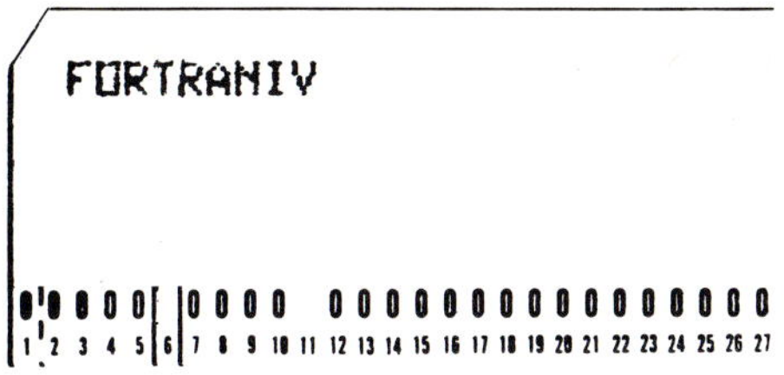

Figure 8.34b. The data card used with Fig. 8.34a. The character (a blank) in the first column will be used as a control character when the FORMAT in statement 10 is used with the WRITE statement.

```
 FORTRANIV
1234567890
```

Figure 8.34c. Running the program of Fig. 8.34a, we see that FORTRANIV is printed starting in column 2. This is because the first blank in column 1 on the data card was used for a control character; and column 2 was also a blank.

USING A QUOTED STRING TO READ A DATA CARD

```
C  USING QUOTED STRINGS FIELDS FOR INPUT
       READ (5,10)
 10    FORMAT('           ')
C
C      ...PRINT WHAT HAS JUST BEEN READ
       WRITE(6,10)
C      ...PRINT COLUMNS
       WRITE(6,20)
 20    FORMAT(1X, 10H1234567890)
       STOP
       END
```

Figure 8.34d. The same program as Fig. 8.34a, but now a quoted string is used in the FORMAT which is used to read the data card shown in Fig. 8.34b

```
 FORTRANIV
1234567890
```

Figure 8.34e. The results of running the program of Fig. 8.34d.

8.16. Reading Using X Format

As we have learned, X format can be used to separate fields when printing output. It can also be used with input, as we now show in Fig. 8.35a. The 2X instructs the compiler to skip the first 56 on the data card,which is shown in Fig. 8.35b. Thus the six characters that follow, i.e., 789012, will be described by F6.0. The 6X instructs the computer to skip the second 345678 on the data card. Thus the four characters that follow, i.e., 9012, will be described by I4. The results of running the program are shown in Fig. 8.35c.

8.17. More on the READ and WRITE Statements; the END Option

If you wish, you can let the unit number on the READ and WRITE statements be an INTEGER variable. Thus you can write, for instance, READ(N,10) A, B, C and WRITE(M,20) A, B, C. If all the READ and WRITE statements in a program are written this way, then when you run your program on a system where the reader is unit 7 and the line printer is unit 8, all you have to do in the beginning of the program is set N equal to 7 and M to 8.

On all systems, the data cards are followed by a control card indicating that no more data cards follow. We will call this card an *end of file* card. If the program reads this end of file card, the system prints an error message like END OF FILE ENCOUNTERED. In order to detect this end of file and then transfer control to another statement in the program instead of causing an error condition, we may use the following nonstandard READ statement:

```
READ(5,10,END=100) A, B, C, D, E
```

where 10 is the format. When an end of file is encountered, control is transferred to the statement number that follows END=, here statement 100. On WATFOR/WATFIV system, if we want to use an unformatted READ statement that also detects an end of file, we would substitute an asterisk for the FORMAT statement number, thus writing

```
READ(5,*END=100) A, B, C, D, E
```

USING X FORMAT TO SKIP FIELDS

```
C   PROGRAM SHOWS HOW X-FORMAT IS USED TO SKIP
C   FIELDS ON A DATA CARD
        READ(5,10) I, A, J
 10     FORMAT( I4, 2X, F6.0, 6X, I4)
C
        WRITE(6,20) I, A, J
 20     FORMAT(1X, I5, 10X, F10.3, 10X, I5 )
        STOP
        END
```

Figure 8.35a. A program in which X format is used to skip fields.

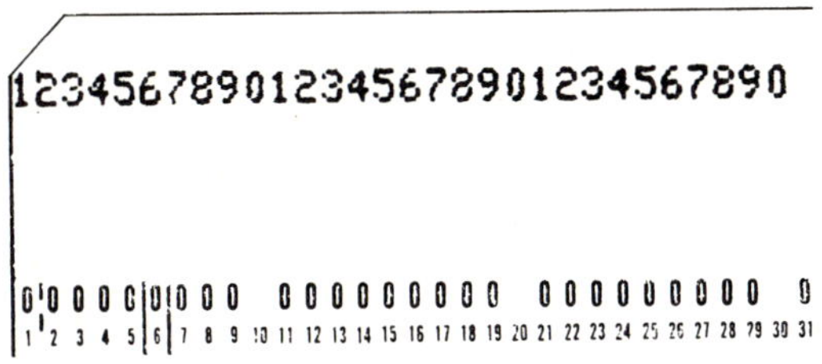

Figure 8.35b. The data card for Fig. 8.35a. The 2X enables the computer to skip the first 56; the 6X enables it to skip the second 345678.

```
1234              789012.000              9012
```

Figure 8.35c. Running the program of Fig. 8.35a.

PROBLEMS

1. A data card has the integer 1 punched in each of the first 5 columns. How will the constant punched on this card be read by F5.1, by F5.3, by F5.5, and by F5.7?

2. A data card has 1111E+02 punched in the first 8 columns. How will the constant punched on this card be read by E8.0, by E8.1, by E8.3, and by E8.4?

3. How many lines will be skipped between the results produced by the following two FORMAT statements: 10 FORMAT (1X, 2F10.0 //) and 20 FORMAT (1X, // 1X, 2F10.0).

4. Given the following paired READ and FORMAT statements: READ (5,10) A,B,C,D and 10 FORMAT(// 1X, 2F10.0, // 1X, 2F10.0), how many data cards are needed to satisfy this READ? What data cards should the values of A,B,C and D be printed on?

5. Write a program in which the letters in FOUR SCORES are assigned to variables in a DATA statement and then the values of these variables are printed.

6. Write a program that reads any array that has up to 3 rows and 3 columns and then prints the results in matrix form with each element labeled. Thus an array that has 2 rows and 3 columns would be printed, for instance, as

```
A (11) =6        A (12) = 3        A (13) = 6
A (21) =4        A (22) = 9        A (23) = 7
```

The first data card should indicate how many rows and columns the array has.

7. Given that *A* has the value 1.2345, what would the following program segment produce?

```
     DIMENSION A (10)
     DATA A/ 10*1.2345/
     WRITE (6,10) A
10   FORMAT (1X, 2F6.2, 3(1X, F6.3), F5.0)
```

8. What does the following program segment produce?

```
     LOGICAL TRUTH (10)
     DATA TRUTH / 4* .TRUE., 6* .FALSE./
     WRITE (6,10) TRUTH
10   FORMAT (1X, 4L5, (1X, L5))
```

Note that the first 4 elements of the array TRUTH have the value .TRUE. and the next 6 elements of the array TRUTH have the value .FALSE.

9. What does the following produce?

```
      WRITE (6,10)
10    FORMAT (1X, T15, 'WE HOLD THESE', T2, 'TO BE SELF-EVIDENT')
```

10. We have the following program segment:

```
      INTEGER ARRAY (10)
      READ (5,10) ARRAY
10    FORMAT (1X, 2I1, (3X, 3I1))
```

The first data card read has 1234567890 punched in the first 10 columns; the second one has 0987654321 punched in the first 10 columns. What are the values of the elements of ARRAY after the READ is executed?

9

Functions, Subprograms, and Subroutines

9.1. Statement Functions

The functions that we have used until now were built into the system; as we have previously mentioned, they are called library functions. In this and the next section we show how you can write your own functions. To facilitate defining the terms associated with a function and describing how to use a function, we will briefly discuss functions as they are treated in mathematics.

In mathematics we could define a function

$$S(X) = X + X^2 + 3$$

The expression $X + X^2 + 3$ is called the function; X is called the argument of the function, as we remember from our discussion of library functions; and S is called the function's name. If we replace the argument in the function name with another argument, the argument is changed in the function as well. Thus if we replace X with 2 in the function name, i.e., write S(2), then we must replace each occurrence of X in the function, with 2. We thus write

$$S(2) = 2 + 2^2 + 3$$

Similarly, if we replace X with Y in the function name, we have

$$S(Y) = Y + Y^2 + 3$$

Using functions allows us to write expressions in terser and, therefore, clearer form. Thus given

$$T = 3(X + X^2 + 3) + Z(Y + Y^2 + 3)^2$$

we could write it as

$$T = 3 \cdot S(X) + Z \cdot S(Y)^2$$

If we had wished to, we could have called the function, F. The function F would be defined as $F(X) = X + X^2 + 3$. We would then replace $F(X)$ by $X + X^2 + 3$ every time we saw F in an expression. Thus given

$$Y = 4 \cdot F(X)$$

USING A STATEMENT FUNCTION

```
C  USING STATEMENT FUNCTIONS
C
      FUN(T) = A + A1*T + A2*( T**2 ) + A3*( T**3 )
      READ(5,10) A, A1, A2, A3
 10   FORMAT( 4F10.0 )
      WRITE(6,20) A, A1, A2, A3
 20   FORMAT(1X, 'A=', F10.3, '  A1=', F10.3, '  A2=', F10.3,
     1       '  A3=', F10.3/)
C     ...CALCULATE POLYNOMIAL
      DO 40 J=1,10
         T=J
         FUNCT=FUN(T)
         WRITE(6,30) J, FUNCT
 30      FORMAT(1X, 'FUN(', I2, ')=', E15.7)
 40   CONTINUE
      STOP
      END
```

Figure 9.1a. We can define our own functions in the beginning of the program using one statement called a function statement. Here T is the argument of the function FUN. The function statement is not executed; it is referred to when the function is used in FUNCT = FUN(T). At that time, A, A1, A2, A3, and T must have been previously defined. They have been, in fact, defined in the READ.

we would interpret it as $Y = 4 \cdot (X + X^2 + 3)$. We learn from this that the name we give a function is immaterial; what is important is how we define the function. However, once we have named a function, we must always refer to the function by that name.

The FORTRAN functions we now describe are used the same way as algebraic functions. Since these FORTRAN functions are defined in one statement in the program, they are called *statement functions*. In the program of Fig. 9.1a we use the statement function named FUN to calculate a polynomial. The function is defined in FUN(T)=A + A1*T + A2* (T**2) + A3 * (T**3) where T is the argument of the function. In the function definition, the argument can only be a nonsubscripted variable. We have parenthesized T**2 and T**3 to make the expression more readable. This statement is not executed but is referred to when the function FUN is used later in the program. Statement functions must be defined in the beginning of the program before the appearance of any executable statement. Thus the variables used in the definition of the function—here A, A1, A2, A3, and T—are not defined until later in the program. However, before the function is used in the program, i.e., in

```
FUNCT=FUN(T)
```

all the variables used in the definition of the function must be defined. Thus the variables A, A1, A2, and A3 are defined in

```
READ(5,10) A, A1, A2, A3
```

The argument T is just the floated value of the DO loop index J. Since the DO statement which begins the DO loop, is

```
DO 40 J=1,10
```

the argument T assumes the floated values of the integers from 1 to 10. The first time FUNCT = FUN(T) is executed, since the value of T is 1.0, the computer interprets the function as FUN(1). It then refers to the function definition, and evaluates FUN(1) as A + A1*1.0 + A2*(1**2) + A3*(1**3). All of this is shown in the first line of the table for Fig. 9.1a.

Time executed	T	Form of FUN(T)	Value of FUN(T)
1st	1.0	FUN(1.0)	A+A1*1.0+A2*(1.0**2)+ A3*(1.0**3)

Each time the WRITE in the DO loop is executed, the computer evaluates FUN(T) for the current value of T. The results for the values of A, A1, A2, and A3 read from the data card shown in Fig. 9.1b are shown in Fig. 9.1c.

The reason that we did not write WRITE (6,30) J, FUN(T) is that in ANS Standard FORTRAN, you cannot use a function in a WRITE statement; in WATFOR/WATFIV, however, you can.

Time executed	T	Form of FUN(T)	Value of FUN(T)
1	1.0	FUN(1.0)	A + A1*1.0 + A2*(1.0**2) + A3*(1.0**3)
2	2.0	FUN(2.0)	A + A1*2.0 + A2*(2.0**2) + A3*(2.0**3)
3	3.0	FUN(3.0)	A + A1*3.0 + A2*(3.0**2) + A3*(3.0**3)

Table for Fig. 9.1a. The value of T is substituted into the definition of the function. This is shown for the first three values of T.

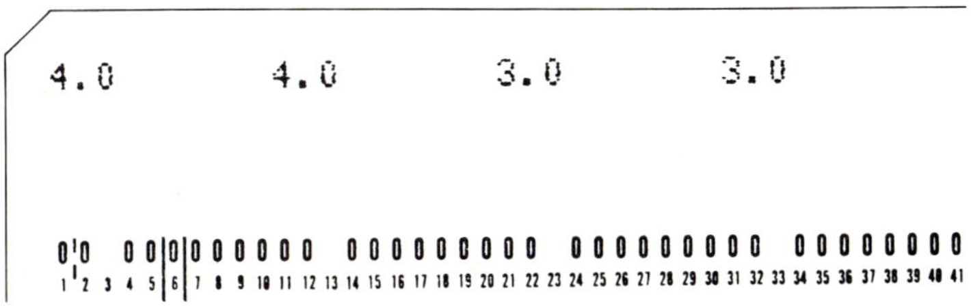

Figure 9.1b. The data card for Fig. 9.1a.

```
A=        4.000   A1=        4.000   A2=        3.000   A3=        3.000

FUN( 1)=   0.1400000E 02
FUN( 2)=   0.4800000E 02
FUN( 3)=   0.1240000E 03
FUN( 4)=   0.2600000E 03
FUN( 5)=   0.4740000E 03
FUN( 6)=   0.7840000E 03
FUN( 7)=   0.1208000E 04
FUN( 8)=   0.1764000E 04
FUN( 9)=   0.2470000E 04
FUN(10)=   0.3344000E 04
```

Figure 9.1c. Running the program of Fig. 9.1a.

The rule for forming the function name is the same as for forming a variable: on most systems it can consist of up to 6 letters or digits and the first character must be a letter. A statement function must come after DIMENSION and type declaration statements but may precede a DATA statement.

When a function is evaluated in the program, the *value* of the variable used as the argument is important. The name of the variable used as the argument is immaterial as long as it is the same mode as the mode of the argument used in the definition of the function. Since in the program of Fig. 9.1a FUN is defined using the REAL argument T, when we use the function later in the program we may use any REAL variable or constant as the argument. In order to show this, we have rewritten the program of Fig. 9.1a as is now shown in Fig. 9.2a, employing X as the function's argument when the function is used in

```
FUNCT=FUN(X)
```

although the function is still defined using T as the argument

```
FUN(T)  =  A  +  A1*T  +  A2*( T**2 )  +  A3*( T**3 )
```

The table for Fig. 9.2a shows how the function is evaluated for different values of X. Since we are using the same values of A, A1, A2, and A3 in this program as in the last, the results of this program as shown in Fig. 9.2b are the same as those of the last.

The argument of the function used in the definition of the function is called a *dummy argument*; no memory location is reserved for T in the program of Fig. 9.2a because the appearance of T in the function definition simply indicates where the value of X should be substituted when the function is executed. When a function is used in a program, its argument is called the *actual* argument—here X—of the function. As opposed to a dummy argument, a memory location is always reserved for an actual argument.

In ANS Standard FORTRAN, you cannot use subscripted variables in the definition of a statement function. Thus

```
FUN(T)=A(1) + A(2)*T + A(3)*(T**2)
```

would cause a compilation error on most systems. In WATFOR/WATFIV, however, this is allowed.

USING AN ACTUAL ARGUMENT WHICH IS DIFFERENT FROM THE DUMMY ARGUMENT

```
C   USING STATEMENT FUNCTIONS
C   DUMMY AND ACTUAL ARGUMENTS HERE ARE DIFFERENT VARIABLES
C
        FUN(T) = A + A1*T + A2*( T**2 ) + A3*( T**3 )
        READ(5,10) A, A1, A2, A3
 10     FORMAT( 4F10.0 )
        WRITE(6,20) A, A1, A2, A3
 20     FORMAT(1X, 'A=', F10.3, '  A1=', F10.3, '  A2=', F10.3,
      1         '  A3=', F10.3/)
C       ...CALCULATE POLYNOMIAL
        DO 40 J=1,10
           X=J
           FUNCT=FUN(X)
           WRITE(6,30) J, FUNCT
 30        FORMAT(1X, 'FUN(', I2, ')=', E15.7)
 40     CONTINUE
        STOP
        END
```

Figure 9.2a. The argument—here T—used in the function definition is a dummy argument; i.e., no location in memory is reserved for T. Only when a function is used in the program, e.g., herein FUNCT = FUN(X), is a memory location reserved for its argument—here X. Since FUN(X) is defined by FUN(T), X corresponds to T in the definition—X is called the actual argument of the function.

Time executed	X	Form of FUN(X)	Value of FUN(X)
1	1.0	FUN(1.0)	A + A1*1.0 + A2*(1.0**2) + A3*(1.0**3)
2	2.0	FUN(2.0)	A + A1*2.0 + A2*(2.0**2) + A3*(2.0**3)
3	3.0	FUN(3.0)	A + A1*3.0 + A2*(3.0**2) + A3*(3.0**3)

Table for Fig. 9.2a. The value of X is substituted into the definition of the function, i.e., since the real argument X corresponds to the dummy argument T. Every place where T appears in the function, the value of X is substituted.

```
A=      4.000  A1=      4.000  A2=      3.000  A3=      3.000

FUN( 1)=  0.1400000E 02
FUN( 2)=  0.4800000E 02
FUN( 3)=  0.1240000E 03
FUN( 4)=  0.2600000E 03
FUN( 5)=  0.4740000E 03
FUN( 6)=  0.7840000E 03
FUN( 7)=  0.1208000E 04
FUN( 8)=  0.1764000E 04
FUN( 9)=  0.2470000E 04
FUN(10)=  0.3344000E 04
```

Figure 9.2b. Running the program of Fig. 9.2a. We use the data card shown in Fig. 9.1b.

A function may be defined in terms of a library function and may have practically as many arguments as you want to use. The program of Fig. 9.3a uses the statement function

```
C(X,Y) = X / SQRT( X**2 + Y**2 )
```

which has two arguments—X and Y—to simplify the expression*

$$\cos AB = \frac{Ax}{\sqrt{Ax^2 + Ay^2}} \cdot \frac{Bx}{\sqrt{Bx^2 + By^2}} + \frac{Ay}{\sqrt{Ax^2 + Ay^2}} \cdot \frac{By}{\sqrt{Bx^2 + By^2}}$$

Using the definition† of C, we see that

```
C(AX,AY)= AX / SQRT(AX**2 + AY**2 )
```

as is shown in the table for Fig. 9.3a. Similiarly if we interchange AX and AY in the function name, we obtain

```
C(AY,AX) = AY/ SQRT( AY**2 + AX**2 )
```

as is also shown in the table. Note that we have also interchanged AX and AY in the function itself; but since SQRT(AY**2 + AX**2) is the same as SQRT(AX**2 + AY**2), then C(AY,AX) = AY/SQRT(AX**2 + AY**2).

Using the statement function C(X,Y), we can now simplify the expression for cos *AB* and write it as

```
COSAB = C(AX,AY) * C(BX,BY) + C(AY,AX) * C(BY,BX)
```

as is shown in Fig. 9.3a. We thus see that we can use a statement function to simplify a complex expression so that the expression's structure is more apparent to a person reading the program.

* COS AB is the cosine of the angle between the vectors **A** and **B**. AX is the X-component of **A**, and AY is the Y-component. Similarly, BX is the X-component of **B**, and BY is the Y-component.

† The Cs represent the directional cosines. Thus C(AX,AY) is the directional cosine of A with the *X*-axis; whereas C(AY,AX) is the directional cosine with the *Y*-axis.

USING FUNCTIONS TO SIMPLIFY EXPRESSIONS

```
C   USING FUNCTIONS TO SIMPLIFY AN EXPRESSION
        C(X,Y) = X / SQRT( X**2 + Y**2 )
C
        READ(5,10) AX, AY, BX, BY
 10     FORMAT( 4F10.0 )
        WRITE(6,15) AX, AY, BX, BY
 15     FORMAT(1X, 'AX=', F10.2, '   AY=', F10.2, '   BX=', F10.2,
       1       '   BY=', F10.2)
C
        COSAB = C(AX,AY) * C(BX,BY) + C(AY,AX) * C(BY,BX)
C
        WRITE(6,20) COSAB
 20     FORMAT(1X, 'COS(A,B) = ', F10.5)
        STOP
        END
```

Figure 9.3a. A statement function can be used in an expression in the same way as a library function can. We use the function C(X,Y) to simplify the expression in

$$\cos AB = \frac{Ax}{\sqrt{Ax^2 + Ay^2}} \cdot \frac{Bx}{\sqrt{Bx^2 + By^2}} + \frac{Ay}{\sqrt{Ax^2 + Ay^2}} \cdot \frac{By}{\sqrt{Bx^2 + By^2}}$$

We thus write:

```
COSAB = C(AX,AY)*C(BX,BY) + C(AY,AX)*C(BY,BX)
```

X	Y	Form of C(X,Y)	Value of C(X,Y)
AX	AY	C(AX,AY)	AX/SQRT(AX**2 + AY**2)
AY	AX	C(AY,AX)	AY/SQRT(AY**2 + AX**2)
BX	BY	C(BX,BY)	BX/SQRT(BX**2 + BY**2)
BY	BX	C(BY,BX)	BY/SQRT(BY**2 + BX**2)

Table for Fig. 9.3a. In C(AX,AY), AX is substituted for X and AY for Y in the function definition; whereas in C(AY,AX), the reverse procedure is followed: AY is substituted for X and AX for Y.

The data card for the program is shown in Fig. 9.3b; and the results of running the program, are shown in Fig. 9.3c.

All the functions we have used until now have been REAL since the function names did not begin with the letters I through N. Thus their values were also REAL. In the first three programs in this section, if we had called the function NFUN(T) instead of FUN(T), then the values of the function would have been truncated. In Table 9.1 we present this and some other aspects of statement functions.

Example 1

```
N(X) = X + X**2
```

The function name N is an INTEGER variable, so the value of the function is always truncated. Thus N(1.5) = 1.5 + 2.25, which is truncated to 3.

Example 2

```
F(J) = J + J**2
```

Since the function name is a REAL variable, the value of the function is floated. Thus F(2) = 2 + 4 which is floated to 6.0.

Example 3

```
REAL MIN
MIN(A,B) = A**2 + B**2
```

By declaring MIN to be REAL, the value of MIN will be REAL. Thus MIN(1.0,1.5) = 1.0 + 2.25, which is 3.25. As we have mentioned, declaration statements—e.g., REAL, INTEGER, LOGICAL—must precede function definitions.

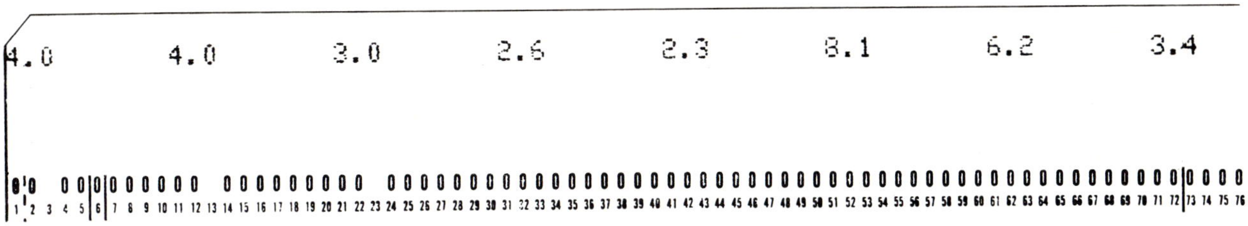

Figure 9.3b. The data card for the program of Fig. 9.3a.

```
AX=         3.00  AY=         4.00  BX=         5.00  BY=         6.00
COS(A,B) =       0.99869
```

Figure 9.3c. Running the program of Fig. 9.3a.

EXAMPLES OF STATEMENT FUNCTIONS

	Example statements	Comment
1	N(X) = X + X**2	Since the function name is an INTEGER variable, the value of the function is always truncated.
2	F(J) = J + J**2	Since the function name is a REAL variable, the value of the function is floated.
3	REAL MIN MIN(A,B) = A**2 + B**2	MIN has REAL values even though the function begins with the letter M.
4	INTEGER HYPOT HYPOT(X,Y) = SQRT(X**2 + Y**2) .	HYPOT has INTEGER values even though the function name begins with the letter H.
5	F(X,I,J) = X**I + X**J	A function which has REAL and INTEGER arguments. When the function is used, its arguments must be the same mode as that of the corresponding argument used in the function definition. Thus F(3.2,1,2) is allowed but F(4,2,3.0) is not.
6	F(X) = X**2 + SQRT(X) G(X) = F(X) + 4.0	It is allowable to define a function—here G—in terms of another function—here F.
7	G(X) = F(X) + 4.0 F(X) = X**2 + SQRT(X)	When a function—here G—is defined in terms of a second function—here F—the second function may follow the first.
8	LOGICAL GREAT GREAT(A,B) = A .GT. B	GREAT is a LOGICAL function. It has the value TRUE or FALSE.

Table 9.1. Different ways of using functions.

Example 4

```
INTEGER HYPOT
HYPOT(X,Y) = SQRT(X**2 + Y**2)
```

By declaring HYPOT to be INTEGER, the value of HYPOT will be an INTEGER. Thus HYPOT(1.0, 1.5) = SQRT(1.0**2 + 1.5**2); this equals SQRT(3.25), which is 1.8. This is truncated to 1.

Example 5

```
F(X, I,J) = X**I + X**J
```

When this function is used, its arguments must be the same mode as the mode of the corresponding argument in the function definition. Thus F(1,2,3) would be illegal since the INTEGER 1 corresponds to the REAL X; whereas F(1.0,2,3) would be acceptable.

Example 6

```
F(X) = X**2 + SQRT(X)
G(X) = F(X) + 4.0
```

It is allowable to define a function—here G—in terms of another function—here F. The order in which the functions appear in the program is not important. Thus the definition of G could have preceded the definition of F, as shown in Example 7.

Example 7

```
G(X) = F(X) + 4.0
F(X) = X**2 + SQRT(X)
```

Example 8

```
LOGICAL GREAT
GREAT(A,B) = A .GT. B
```

GREAT is declared to be a LOGICAL variable. Note that GREAT appears without arguments in the LOGICAL declaration statement, just as do HYPOT and MIN in the previous examples. Thus it would be an error to write LOGICAL GREAT(A,B).

Just as you cannot use the same variable name as an array name and as a non-subscripted variable name, so too you cannot use the same variable name for both a function and a variable. Doing so will lead to an error.

Although the dummy arguments of a function can only be nonsubscripted variables, the actual arguments of a function can be as follows (see Table 9.2):

1. A simple variable or constant, e.g., Y=FUN(6.41).
2. A subscripted variable, e.g., Y=FUN(X(3)).
3. Another function, be it a library or statement function, e.g., Y=FUN(SQRT(X))
4. A mathematical expression Y=FUN(A**2 + B**2)

EXAMPLES OF VALID ACTUAL ARGUMENTS OF STATEMENT FUNCTIONS

Type	Examples	Use in function
Simple variable or constant	X, Y, J, 3	G(X,3)
Subscripted variable	A(3), B(1,3)	F(I,B(1,3))
Function	F(X,2), SQRT(X)	G(F(X,2),R)
Expression	X*J + SIN(X)	G(X*J + SIN(X), 4)

Table 9.2. Valid actual arguments of statement functions.

9.2. Subprogram Functions

If you want to, you can define a function in a separate program called a *subprogram function*. The program we write that refers to the subprogram function is now called the *main program*. The main program is just the same type of program we have written until now. A subprogram is very much like the programs we have studied until now except that it can be executed only when it is referred to by the main program. We have partitioned Fig. 9.4a into a main program and a subprogram. The main program is

```
      T=6.1
      FUNCT = FUN(T)
      WRITE(6,10) T, FUNCT
10    FORMAT(1X, 'FUN(', F4.1,')=', E15.7)
      STOP
      END
```

and the subprogram function is

```
      FUNCTION FUN(T)
C  THIS IS THE FUNCTION SUBPROGRAM
      WRITE(6,10) T
 10   FORMAT(1X, 'VALUE PASSED TO SUBPROGRAM', F10.2)
      FUN= 1.2 + 5.1*T + 4.2*T**(-2)
      RETURN
      END
```

The main program refers to subprogram function FUN in FUNCT = FUN(T). When the main program refers to the subprogram function, we say it *calls* the function subprogram. Remember, a subprogram cannot be executed unless it is called.

Under normal conditions, the first statement in a function subprogram begins with the word FUNCTION. Next we punch in this statement the function's name—here FUN—and the arguments enclosed in parentheses—here (T). When the main program calls the function, control is transferred to the first executable statement in the function subprogram—here

```
WRITE(6,10) T
```

The value of T is the value of the argument of FUN; when the subroutine function is called, we say that the value of the argument has been *passed* to the subprogram. Since the value of the argument of FUN in the main program is 6.1, this is the value of T used in evaluating FUN. The value assigned to FUN here is the one that is returned to the main program. Control is transferred back to the main program when the RETURN statement is executed. It is transferred to the statement that contains the function; and if there are any remaining terms in the statement to be evaluated, they are. In our case there are no remaining terms, so the next statement is executed. Here, it is the STOP statement. If you forget to include a RETURN in a function subprogram, on most compilers a compile-time error will result. Note, a function subprogram must end with an END statement.

In the subprogram, the function being called can be subscripted only in the very first statement—here FUNCTION FUN(T); it cannot be subscripted in any subsequent statement. Thus it would have been a mistake to write FUN(T) = 1.2 + 5.1*T + 4.2*T**(−2) instead of FUN = 1.2 + 5.1*T + 4.2*T**(−2).

USING FUNCTION SUBPROGRAMS

```
C   USING SUBPROGRAM FUNCTIONS
        T=6.1
        FUNCT = FUN(T)
        WRITE(6,10) T, FUNCT
 10     FORMAT(1X, 'FUN(', F4.1,')=', E15.7)
        STOP
        END
```

Figure 9.4a. *Main program.* We can define a function in a separate program called a function subprogram. The original program is called the main program. Information is passed from the main program to the subprogram via the function's argument. The argument used in the function in the main program is an actual argument, and the one used in the function subprogram is a dummy argument; i.e., no memory location is reserved for it. When the computer executes FUNCT = FUN(T), it passes 6.1 to the subprogram, and 6.1 is used in calculating FUN. A subprogram function can be used in the program the same way a library or statement function can.

```
        FUNCTION FUN(T)
C   THIS IS THE FUNCTION SUBPROGRAM
        WRITE(6,10) T
 10     FORMAT(1X, 'VALUE PASSED TO SUBPROGRAM', F10.2)
        FUN= 1.2 + 5.1*T + 4.2*T**(-2)
        RETURN
        END
```

Subprogram. Normally the first statement of a subprogram function begins with the word FUNCTION followed by the function name and its arguments—a function subprogram must have at least one argument. After this statement, the function name cannot appear with an argument in the subprogram. Since 6.1 is the value passed to the subprogram, FUN is evaluated as FUN = 1.2 + 5.1*6.1 + 4.2*6.1**(−2). The RETURN statement returns control to the statement in the main program in which the function appears.

As in the case with statement functions, under normal circumstances the first letter of the function name determines the mode of the function's value. Thus the value of FUN(T) is REAL. Had we written the function name as NFUN, then the value of the function would be truncated to an INTEGER value.

Functions defined in a function subprogram can be used in the main program in the same way that statement functions and library functions can. Thus they can be used in expressions in assignment statements and IF statements. In this program we have used the function in an assignment statement and have thus written FUNCT = FUN(T). The results of running the program are shown in Fig. 9.4b.

In order to check that the program has passed a value properly to a subprogram, it is a good idea to echo-print such values. Thus in Fig. 9.4b we see

```
VALUE PASSED TO SUBPROGRAM        6.10
```

and consequently we know that the proper argument was indeed passed. Passing incorrect values to subprograms is one of the most common errors made.

The reason we did not eliminate the assignment statement and simply write WRITE (6,10) T, FUN(T) is that in ANS Standard FORTRAN you cannot include a function or any expression in a WRITE statement; in WATFOR/WATFIV, you can.

It is not necessary to use the same variable as the argument in the subprogram as you do when you call the function in the main program, as long as both arguments have the same mode. Thus we could have written the subprogram using X as the argument as is shown in Fig. 9.5a. When the subprogram is called, the value of the argument used in the main program is in effect assigned to the variable used as the argument in the function subprogram. We should not understand by this that a separate memory location has been reserved for X. The argument—here T—used in the function when the function is written in the main program, is called the actual argument because a memory location is reserved for it by the compiler. The argument—here X—used in the first line of the function subprogram is called a dummy argument.* No additional memory location is reserved for it; it is just the name we use in the subprogram to refer to the location already named by the actual argument. We have indicated this in the table for Fig. 9.5a.

	Memory location 6.1
Actual argument name	T
Dummy argument name	X

Since they label the same memory location, an actual argument and its corresponding dummy argument must have the same mode. Thus here T and X are both REAL. If they were not the same mode, a run-time error would result.

When the computer evaluates 1.2 + 5.1*X + 4.2*X**(−2), the computer interprets it as though it appeared in the main program as 1.2 + 5.1*T + 4.2*T**(−2). However, the RETURN is needed to return control to the main program.

If we had wanted to, we could have called FUN by writing FUNCT=FUN(6.1), i.e., by using a constant, not a variable, as the actual argument. Then the dummy argument would be the name used in the subprogram to refer to the location in the memory reserved for the constant 6.1. The results of running the program are shown in Fig. 9.5b.

* Note that this is the same terminology we used in the section on statement functions (Section 9.1).

```
VALUE PASSED TO SUBPROGRAM          6.10
FUN( 6.1)=  0.3242287E 02
```

Figure 9.4b. Running the program of Fig. 9.4a.

DUMMY AND ACTUAL ARGUMENTS ARE DIFFERENT

```
C   USING SUBPROGRAM FUNCTIONS
C   HERE DUMMY AND ACTUAL ARGUMENTS ARE DIFFERENT
        T=6.1
        FUNCT = FUN(T)
        WRITE(6,10) T, FUNCT
 10     FORMAT(1X, 'FUN(', F4.1,')=', E15.7)
        STOP
        END

        FUNCTION FUN(X)
C   THIS IS THE FUNCTION SUBPROGRAM
        WRITE(6,10) X
 10     FORMAT(1X, 'VALUE PASSED TO SUBPROGRAM', F10.2)
        FUN= 1.2 + 5.1*X + 4.2*X**(-2)
        RETURN
        END
```

Figure 9.5a. Since the arguments of a function subprogram are dummy arguments, we have rewritten the subprogram of Fig. 9.4a using X as the argument. Since the function in the main program has the form FUN(6.1), the value 6.1 is substituted for X, i.e., FUN is evaluated as FUN = 1.2 + 5.1*6.1 + 4.2*6.1**(−2).

	Memory location
	6.1
Actual argument name	T
Dummy argument name	X

Table for Fig. 9.5a. No memory location is reserved for a dummy argument—here X. It is simply the name used in the subprogram to refer to memory location of the actual argument—here T. Thus a dummy argument and its corresponding actual argument must have the same mode.

```
VALUE PASSED TO SUBPROGRAM          6.10
FUN( 6.1)=  0.3242287E 02
```

Figure 9.5b. Running the program of Fig. 9.5a.

In Fig. 9.6a we rewrite the function so that the coefficients of the polynomial are now the variables A, A1, and A2; i.e.,

```
FUN= A + A1**T + A2*T**(-2)
```

Although these variables are assigned values in the main program in

```
READ(5,10) A, A1, A2
```

these values must be communicated to the subroutine. This is done by making these variables arguments of the function. We thus write

```
FUNCT=FUN(T, A, A1, A2)
```

The term used to describe the arguments of a subprogram is *argument list*. Thus T, A, A1, A2, constitutes the actual argument list. The corresponding list used in the subprogram is called the dummy argument list. We have written the subprogram so that the dummy argument list is the same as the actual argument list, i.e., FUNCTION FUN(T, A, A1, A2).

When more than one argument is used, the first actual argument and the first dummy argument label the same memory location. The second actual argument and the second dummy argument label the same memory location, etc. The values of the variables A, A1, and A2 are given on the data card shown in Fig. 9.6a. We have echo-printed the dummy

USING A FUNCTION SUBPROGRAM WHICH HAS MANY ARGUMENTS

```
C  USING FUNCTION SUBPROGRAMS WITH
C  MORE THAN ONE ARGUMENT.
C  MAIN PROGRAM
        READ(5,10) A, A1, A2
 10     FORMAT( 3F10.0 )
        WRITE(6,15) A, A1, A2
 15     FORMAT(1X, 3F10.2 )
C       ...CALL AND EVALUATE FUNCTION
        DO 30 J=1,5
           T=J
           FUNCT=FUN(T, A, A1, A2)
           WRITE(6,20) J, FUNCT
 20        FORMAT(1X, 'FUN(', I2,  ')=', E15.7 )
 30     CONTINUE
        STOP
        END
```

Figure 9.6a. *Main program.* Fig. 9.4a rewritten so that the coefficients of the polynomial in the subprogram are now the variables A, A1, A2. These variables are defined in the READ statements, and their values are passed to the subprogram because the variables are arguments of the function, i.e., we have written FUNCT = FUN(T, A, A1, A2).

```
      FUNCTION FUN( T, A, A1, A2  )
      WRITE(6,10) T, A, A1, A2
10    FORMAT(1X, 'ARGUMENTS PASSED TO SUBPROGRAM' /  1X, 4F10.2)
      FUN= A + A1**T + A2*T**(-2)
      RETURN
      END
```

Subprogram. Since the subprogram is a separate program from the main program, any variable used in the subprogram must either be defined there or passed to the subprogram as one of the arguments of the function. All the variables in FUN = A + A1**T + A2*T**(−2) are defined since A, A1, A2, and T are all arguments of the function. It is always a good idea to echo-print the values of the arguments passed to the subprogram so that you can be sure the correct values have indeed been passed.

```
 4.0        4.0        3.0

1 2 3 4 5 6 7 8 9 10 11 12 13 14 15 16 17 18 19 20 21 22 23 24 25 26 27 28
```

Figure 9.6b. The data card for Fig. 9.6a.

argument list so that we are sure that the correct values have been passed. We see that their values are 4.0, 4.0, and 3.0, respectively. The table for Fig. 9.6b shows the contents of the memory locations labeled by the arguments. The value of T shown is for the first time the function is called.

	Memory locations			
	1.0	4.0	4.0	3.0
Actual actual name	T	A	A1	A2
Dummy actual name	T	A	A1	A2

Had we written the first line in the subprogram FUNCTION FUN(A, A1, A2, T), then the value of A in the subprogram would be 1.0; the value of A1 would be 4.0; the value of T would be 4.0; and the value of A2 would be 3.0. Again we note that an actual argument in the calling function must be the same mode as the corresponding dummy argument. Thus, if we called the function FUN with FUN(K, A, A1, A2), a run-time error would result since K is not the same mode as T in FUNCTION FUN(T, A, A1, A2).

In the program we calculate the FUN(T) for values of T determined by the loop index J. The results of running the program are shown in Fig. 9.6c.

We note here that as in the case of a statement function, a subprogram function must have at least one argument. The reason for this is that, if a function is written without an argument, then when the function is used in the main program, the compiler will treat the function as a simple variable and will not call the function.

If in the main program we had called the function as we did in the previous program, i.e., FUNCT = FUN(T), and correspondingly had written the subprogram

```
FUNCTION FUN(T)
FUN = A + A1*T + A2*T**(-2)
RETURN
END
```

as is shown in Fig. 9.6d, then A, A1, and A2 would have been undefined in the subprogram. The reason for this is that if we use the same variable in both the main program and the subprogram and if the variable is not passed to the subprogram, then the same variable will represent one memory location when it is used in the main program and a second memory location when it is used in the subprogram. Thus, for example, when A1 is used in the main program of Fig. 9.6a, it is defined when READ(5,10) A, A1, A2 is executed and its value is 4.0, whereas when A1 is used in the subprogram of Fig. 9.6d, since it represents a different variable, it is undefined in the subprogram. All of this is shown in the table for Fig. 9.6d.

	Memory locations			
	1.0	4.0	4.0	3.0
Actual variable name	T	A	A1	A2
Dummy variable name	T	A	A1	A2

Table for Fig. 9.6a. The value of the arguments the first time the function is called.

```
        4.00          4.00          3.00   <-- Printed by WRITE (6,15) A, A1, A2
ARGUMENTS PASSED TO SUBPROGRAM
        1.00          4.00          4.00          3.00
FUN( 1)=  0.1100000E 02
ARGUMENTS PASSED TO SUBPROGRAM
        2.00          4.00          4.00          3.00
FUN( 2)=  0.2074998E 02
ARGUMENTS PASSED TO SUBPROGRAM
        3.00          4.00          4.00          3.00
FUN( 3)=  0.6833331E 02
ARGUMENTS PASSED TO SUBPROGRAM
        4.00          4.00          4.00          3.00
FUN( 4)=  0.2601873E 03
ARGUMENTS PASSED TO SUBPROGRAM
        5.00          4.00          4.00          3.00
FUN( 5)=  0.1028120E 04
```

Figure 9.6c. Running the program of Fig. 9.6a.

A SUBPROGRAM WITH UNDEFINED VARIABLES

```
      FUNCTION FUN(T)
C  NOW A, A1, & A2 ARE UNDEFINED
      FUN = A + A1*T + A2*T**(-2)
      RETURN
      END
```

Figure 9.6d. *Subprogram.* If a variable is not used as a dummy argument in the subprogram, it must be defined there. Thus A, A1, and A2 are undefined.

Main program			Subprogram		
A	A1	A2	A	A1	A2
4.0	4.0	3.0	Undef	Undef	Undef

Table for Fig. 9.6d. Since A, A1, and A2 are no longer dummy arguments, their values are not passed to the subprogram. Thus they represent a different set of variables in the subprogram than in the main program.

You might very well ask at this point: Why use subroutine functions when statement functions accomplish the same thing with fewer statements? The answer is that many times a function requires more than one statement. For instance, if we want to calculate $N!$, we would need the statements

```
          FACT=1
          DO 10 J=1,N
             FACT = FACT * J
10        CONTINUE
```

Obviously we could not do this in a statement function, but we can do it in a subprogram function. Since we want FACT to be an INTEGER, we begin the subroutine function with the word INTEGER

```
INTEGER FUNCTION FACT(N)
```

as is shown in Fig. 9.7a. In the main program we must also specify that FACT will be an INTEGER, so we write INTEGER FACT. We can use the same procedure to specify that a subprogram function is REAL or LOGICAL. The value of FACT returned to the main program is the value of FACT the last time FACT = FACT * J is executed. The results of running the program are shown in Fig. 9.7b.

FUNCTION SUBPROGRAM

> The form of the first statement in the function subprogram is FUNCTION; followed by the function name; followed by (; followed by the argument list; followed by). If there is more than one argument in the argument list, the arguments must be separated by commas. The rule for forming the function name is the same as for forming a variable: on most systems it can consist of up to 6 letters or digits and the first character must be a letter. We may declare the function to be any mode,* i.e., INTEGER, REAL, or LOGICAL. Examples:
>
> FUNCTION NAME (A,B,C,K)
> REAL FUNCTION NAME (A,B,C)
> INTEGER FUNCTION FIRST (R,S,I,T)

If the value of N passed to the subprogram is zero or negative, then the DO statement would be, for example

```
DO 10 J=1,0
```

Since this would create an error on most systems, we have written the first executable statement in the subprogram as

```
IF( N .LE. 0 ) STOP
```

Thus the execution of the program would terminate in the subprogram. This is an example of program integrity because it checks the validity of the data. Of course, it would be preferable to have added a statement which prints a message informing us what

* The mode can also be COMPLEX or DOUBLE PRECISION.

CALCULATING N! USING AN INTEGER SUBPROGRAM

```
C   PROGRAM USES FUNCTION SUBPROGRAM
C   TO CALCULATE FACTORIAL
        INTEGER FACT
C
        READ(5,10) N
 10     FORMAT( I10 )
        WRITE(6,15) N
 15     FORMAT(1X, 'N=', I4 )
C
        M = FACT(N)
C
        WRITE(6,20) N, M
 20     FORMAT(1X, I3, '!=', I10)
        STOP
        END
```

Figure 9.7a. *Main program.* The function name determines the mode of the function's value. Since we want FACT to be INTEGER, we have to declare it as such in the main program.

```
        INTEGER FUNCTION FACT(N)
C   CALCULATES N!
        WRITE(6,5) N
 5      FORMAT(1X, 'VALUE PASSED TO SUBPROGRAM', I3 )
C       ...CHECK FOR NEGATIVE VALUE OF N
        IF( N .LE. 0 ) STOP
           FACT=1
C          ...CALCULATE N!
           DO 10 J=1,N
              FACT = FACT * J
 10        CONTINUE
           RETURN
        END
```

Subprogram. Since we want FACT to be an INTEGER, we write INTEGER FUNCTION FACT(N). We can terminate execution in a subprogram by placing a STOP there, as we have done in the IF. The value of FACT the last time FACT = FACT * J is executed is the value of FACT, which is returned to the main program.

```
N=   5
VALUE PASSED TO SUBPROGRAM  5
  5!=        120
```

Figure 9.7b. Running the program of Fig. 9.7a.

happened, i.e., if we should have preceded this statement with

```
      IF( N .LE. 0 ) WRITE(6,5) N
5     FORMAT(1X, 'THE VALUE OF N IS', I5)
```

However, since this might obscure more important features of the subprogram from the reader, we have omitted it.

Note that since the function subprogram is a separate program, we do not have to worry about using the same statement numbers in the subprogram as we do in the main program. Thus we have used the statement number 10 in both places.

We now use the same subprogram function to calculate the binomial coefficient

$$\binom{M}{N} = M!/[N! \cdot (M-N)!]$$

The symbol $\binom{M}{N}$ is also called a combination symbol. As an example $\binom{52}{5}$ tells how many different ways we can choose 5 objects from a total of 52 objects, regardless of the order in which we choose the 5 objects. Thus we can use this symbol to determine how many different 5-card hands we can obtain from a deck consisting of 8 cards. Here $N = 5$ and $M = 8$ so

$$\binom{M}{N} = \binom{8}{5} = 8!/[5!*3!] \text{ or } 56$$

In the program of Fig. 9.8a, we calculate $M!/[N! \cdot (M-N)!]$ by writing

```
C = FACT(M) / (FACT(N)*FACT(M-N) )
```

This is the first time we have shown the use of a subprogram function in a calculation. It is also the first time we have used a subprogram to evaluate the same function for different arguments. The subprogram function is used 3 times.

The values of M and N read are 8 and 5, respectively, as shown in Fig. 9.8b, and thus the value of M−N = 8−5 or 3. The program is run in Fig. 9.8c. The statement

```
C = FACT(M) / (FACT(N)*FACT(M-N) )
```

is executed like any other statement that contains a mathematical expression. Thus since FACT(N)*FACT(M−N) is parenthesized, this part of the expression is executed first.

The steps followed are:

1. FACT(5), i.e., FACT(N), is evaluated and the subprogram returns 5!
2. FACT(3), i.e., FACT(M−N) is evaluated and the subprogram returns to 3!
3. Then 5! is multiplied by 3!
4. FACT(8), i.e., FACT(M), is evaluated and the subprogram returns 8!
5. Finally, 8! is divided by the product of 3! times 5! and the result is assigned to C.

USING A SUBPROGRAM IN A CALCULATION

```
C  PROGRAM CALCULATES (M,N)
      INTEGER FACT, C
C
      READ(5,10) M, N
10    FORMAT( 2I10 )
      WRITE(6,15) M, N
 15   FORMAT(1X, 2I10 )
C
      C = FACT(M) / (FACT(N)*FACT(M-N) )
C
      WRITE(6,20) M, N, C
 20   FORMAT(1X, '(', I2, 2X, I2, ')=', I6 )
      STOP
      END
```

Figure 9.8a. *Main program.* We calculate $M!/[N! \cdot (M - N)!]$ in C = FACT(M) / (FACT(N)*FACT(M−N)).

```
      INTEGER FUNCTION FACT(N)
C  CALCULATES N!
      WRITE(6,5) N
 5    FORMAT(1X, 'VALUE PASSED TO SUBPROGRAM', I3 )
C     ...CHECK FOR NEGATIVE VALUE OF N
      IF( N .LE. 0 ) STOP
         FACT=1
C        ...CALCULATE N!
         DO 10 J=1,N
            FACT = FACT * J
 10      CONTINUE
         RETURN
      END
```

Subprogram. This is the same as the subprogram in Fig. 9.7a.

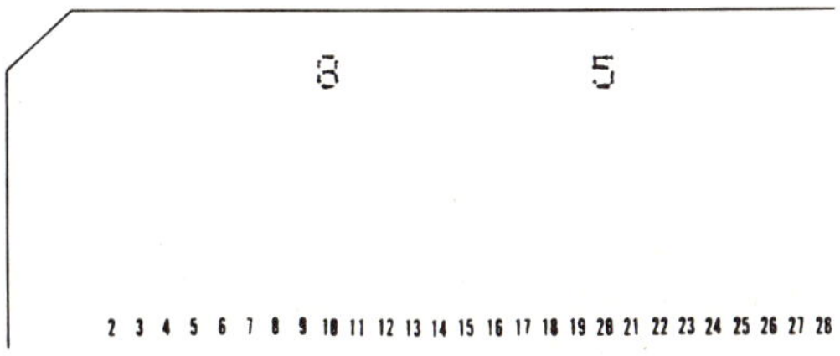

Figure 9.8b. The data card for Fig. 9.8a.

```
         8         5
VALUE PASSED TO SUBPROGRAM  3
VALUE PASSED TO SUBPROGRAM  5
VALUE PASSED TO SUBPROGRAM  8
( 8   5)=    56
```

Figure 9.8c. Running the program of Fig. 9.8a.

We see that each time the subprogram is called, FACT is assigned the value 1 in the subprogram, because of FACT = 1. If we had used in place of this statement, the DATA statement DATA FACT/1/ in the subprogram, then FACT would have had the value 1 in the beginning of the subprogram only the first time the subprogram is called. The second time the subprogram is called, the value of FACT would not be initialized to 1—the reason is that a DATA statement is not executed. Thus the second time subprogram FACT is called, the value of FACT would be the same as the last value assigned to FACT, the first time the program was called, i.e., 5! This would lead to an error.

The subprogram as presently written stops when the value of N is zero. However, 0! is defined as 1. In order to accommodate this result, we have rewritten the subprogram as is now shown in Fig. 9.8d. We have rewritten the first three executable statements as

```
IF( N .LT. 0 ) STOP
   FACT=1
   IF( N .EQ. 0 ) RETURN
```

Thus if the value of N is zero, the subprogram does no further calculation, but returns the value of 1 to the main program. We have thus increased the integrity of the program. We therefore see that you can use more than one RETURN in a subprogram.

ALTERING THE PROGRAM SO THAT IT CALCULATES 0!

```
      INTEGER FUNCTION FACT(N)
C  USES MORE THAN ONE RETURN
      WRITE(6,5)N
 5    FORMAT(1X, 'VALUE OF N PASSED TO SUBPROGRAM' ,I3)
C     ...TEST FOR INVALID N
      IF( N .LT. 0 ) STOP
         FACT=1
         IF( N .EQ. 0 ) RETURN
      DO 10 J=1,N
         FACT = FACT * J
 10   CONTINUE
      RETURN
      END
```

Figure 9.8d. The subprogram of Fig. 9.8a rewritten so that 0! is set equal to 1. If the value of N is zero, the value of FACT returned to the main program is 1. We thus see that we can have more than one RETURN in a subprogram.

9.3. Using Arrays in Subprograms

We can write the program of Fig. 9.6a so that the coefficients of the polynomial, A, A1, A2, are now elements of an array A. The array A must be dimensioned in the main program as is shown in Fig. 9.9a main program. The elements of the array are read from the data card shown in Fig. 9.9b. The elements of the A are then used as the arguments when the function is called in the main program

```
FUNC = FUN( T, A(1), A(2), A(3) )
```

We can only use nonsubscripted variables as the dummy arguments in the subprogram that will correspond to these elements of A. Thus we write

```
FUNCTION FUN(T, A, B, C)
```

as is shown in Fig. 9.9a subprogram. Thus A corresponds to A(1); B to A(2); and C to A(3), as is shown in the table for Fig. 9.9a.

In the subprogram, since T, A, B, and C are dummy arguments, no additional memory locations are reserved for them (see table for Fig. 9.9a).

	Memory locations			
	1.0	4.0	4.0	3.0
Actual argument name	T	A(1)	A(2)	A(3)
Dummy argument name	T	A	B	C

PASSING THE ELEMENTS OF A ONE-DIMENSIONAL ARRAY

```
      DIMENSION A(3)
      READ(5,10) ( A(I), I=1,3 )
10    FORMAT( 3F10.0 )
      WRITE(6,15) ( A(I), I=1,3 )
15    FORMAT(1X, 3F10.2  )
C     ... CALL & PRINT FUNCTION
      DO 30 J=1,10
         T=J
         FUNC = FUN( T, A(1), A(2), A(3) )
         WRITE(6,20) J, FUNC
20       FORMAT(1X, 'FUN(',I2, ')=', E15.7 )
30    CONTINUE
      STOP
      END
```

Figure 9.9a. *Main program.* We may pass elements of arrays as argument. Thus we write FUNC=FUN(T, A(1), A(2), A(3)). Of course the array A must be dimensioned in the main program.

```
FUNCTION FUN(T, A, B, C)
FUN = A + B*T + C*T**(-2)
RETURN
END
```

Subprogram. In FUN(T, A, B, C) the arguments are, as usual, all dummy arguments. The variable A here corresponds to A(1) in the main program; B corresponds to A(2) and C to A(3). A subscripted variable cannot be used as a dummy argument.

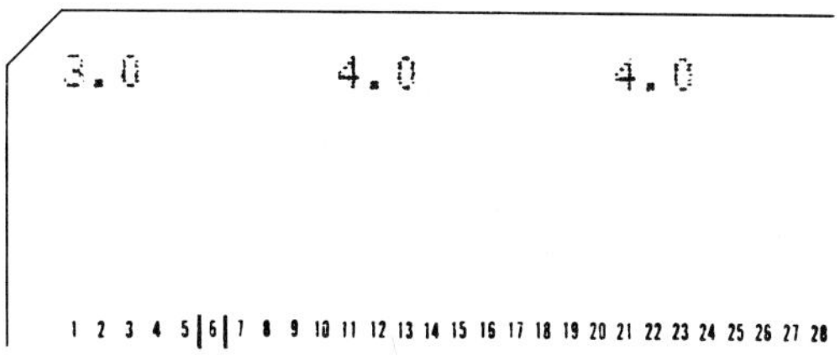

Figure 9.9b. The data card for Fig. 9.9a.

	Memory locations			
	1.0	4.0	4.0	3.0
Actual argument name	T	A(1)	A(2)	A(3)
Dummy argument name	T	A	B	C

Table for Fig. 9.9a

The value of T shown here, is the value the first time the subprogram is called. We remember that the dummy names are the names we use in the subprogram to refer to the locations that have already been labeled by the actual variable names in the main (or calling) program. Thus when the computer evaluates A + B*T + C*T**(−2), it interprets it as if it appeared in the main program as A(1) + A(2)*T + A(3)*T**(−2). However, the RETURN is still needed to return control to the main program. The results of running the program are shown in Fig. 9.9c.

We cannot use elements of an array, i.e., subscripted variables, as the dummy arguments in the function subprogram. Thus if we write

```
FUNCTION FUN( T, A(1), A(2), A(3) )
```

as is shown in Fig. 9.9d subprogram, a compile-time error will result. The subprogram shown was compiled on a WATFIV compiler. The error messages begin with asterisks.

```
        3.00         4.00          4.00   <———— Printed by WRITE (6,15) (A(I), I=1,3)
FUN( 1)=  0.1100000E 02
FUN( 2)=  0.1200000E 02
FUN( 3)=  0.1544444E 02
FUN( 4)=  0.1925000E 02
FUN( 5)=  0.2315999E 02
FUN( 6)=  0.2711110E 02
FUN( 7)=  0.3108162E 02
FUN( 8)=  0.3506250E 02
FUN( 9)=  0.3904938E 02
FUN(10)=  0.4303999E 02
```

Figure 9.9c. Running the program of Fig. 9.9a.

```
      1            FUNCTION FUN( T, A(1), A(2), A(3) )
***ERROR***     EXPECTING OPERATOR BUT ( BEFORE                1 WAS FOUND
***ERROR***     EXPECTING END-OF-STATEMENT,BUT , BEFORE A       WAS FOUND
      2            DIMENSION A(3)
      3            FUN = A(1) + A(2)*T + A(3)*T**(-2)
      4            RETURN
      5            END
```

Figure 9.9d. You cannot use elements of an array as the dummy arguments of the subprogram. Thus the subprogram represented here would not compile. The error messages begin with asterisks.

If we used an array with many elements, it would be tedious to enumerate them all as arguments. We can pass all the elements of the array from the main program to the subprogram by simply using the array name A—unsubscripted—as an argument, as shown in Fig. 9.10a main program.

```
FUNC = FUN(T, A)
```

Since A is dimensioned to have 3 elements, when the computer encounters A in FUN(T, A) in the main program, it knows that A has 3 elements. It is tempting for beginners to specify that A has 3 elements when using the function in the main program, i.e., write FUN(T, A(3)). But, as we have seen, this would instruct the computer that the second argument of the function is A(3).

In the subprogram, we use the name of a dummy array—here B—as the second argument

```
FUNCTION FUN(T,B)
```

The array B must be dimensioned in the subprogram, e.g., DIMENSION B(3). Since B is a dummy array, this does not reserve 3 memory locations for B. It simply informs the computer that B is an array. The dummy element B(1) corresponds to A(1); B(2) to A(2); and B(3) to A(3), as is shown in the table for Fig. 9.10a.

	Memory locations			
	1.0	4.0	4.0	3.0
Actual argument name	T	A(1)	A(2)	A(3)
Dummy argument name	T	B(1)	B(2)	B(3)

PASSING AN ENTIRE ARRAY

```
C   USING ARRAYS IN SUBPROGRAM FUNCTIONS
        DIMENSION A(3)
        READ(5,10) ( A(I), I=1,3)
 10     FORMAT(3F10.0)
        WRITE(6,15) ( A(I), I=1,3 )
 15     FORMAT(1X, 3F10.2 )
C       ...CALL & PRINT FUNCTION
        DO 30 J=1,5
           T=J
           FUNC = FUN(T, A)
           WRITE(6,20) J, FUNC
 20        FORMAT(1X, 'FUN(', I2, ')=', E15.7 )
 30     CONTINUE
        STOP
        END
```

Figure 9.10a. *Main program.* We can pass entire arrays from the main program to the subprogram (or in the opposite direction). We do this by using the array name as an argument of the function, e.g., FUNC = FUN(T, A) where A is an array.

```
      FUNCTION FUN(T,B)
      DIMENSION B(3)
      WRITE(6,10) T, B
10    FORMAT(1X, 'VALUES PASSED TO SUBPROGRAM' / 1X, 4F10.2)
      FUN = B(1) + B(2)*T + B(3)*T**(-2)
      RETURN
      END
```

Subprogram. In FUNCTION FUN(T,B), B is, of course, a dummy argument. In order to show that B is any array, we dimension it. The DIMENSION statement does not allocate 3 locations for array B.

	Memory locations			
	1.0	4.0	4.0	3.0
Actual argument name	T	A(1)	A(2)	A(3)
Dummy argument name	T	B(1)	B(2)	B(3)

Table for Fig. 9.10a. The elements of B are dummy arguments; they simply refer to locations already reserved for the elements of A in the main program.

Thus, when the computer evaluates B(1) + B(2)*T + B(3)*T**(−2) it evaluates it as if it appeared in the main program as A(1) + A(2)*T + A(3)*T**(−2). However, the RETURN is needed to return control to the main program. The results of running the program are shown in Fig. 9.10b.

On most FORTRAN systems, since B is a dummy argument, you may dimension it simply as DIMENSION B(1) in the subprogram.* This will inform the computer that B is an array; and the fact that we correctly dimensioned the actual array it corresponds to in the main program will suffice.

* In WATFOR/WATFIV, the system checks to see whether the dimensions of an array have been exceeded. It also does this in subprograms. So dimensioning an array to have one element on this system when the array had more than one element, would cause an error.

```
      4.00      4.00      3.00
VALUES PASSED TO SUBPROGRAM
      1.00      4.00      4.00      3.00
FUN( 1)=  0.1100000E 02
VALUES PASSED TO SUBPROGRAM
      2.00      4.00      4.00      3.00
FUN( 2)=  0.1275000E 02
VALUES PASSED TO SUBPROGRAM
      3.00      4.00      4.00      3.00
FUN( 3)=  0.1633333E 02
VALUES PASSED TO SUBPROGRAM
      4.00      4.00      4.00      3.00
FUN( 4)=  0.2018750E 02
VALUES PASSED TO SUBPROGRAM
      5.00      4.00      4.00      3.00
FUN( 5)=  0.2412000E 02
```

Figure 9.10b. Running the program of Fig. 9.10a.

We now write a program that uses a subprogram to sum the elements of a two-dimensional array. We will write two versions of the program. In the first version we will pass each of the elements of the array to the subprogram. In the second version, we will pass the entire array to the subprogram.

The first version is shown in Fig. 9.11a. In the main program, we first dimension the array in DIMENSION A(2,3). We then read the elements of the array from the card shown in Fig. 9.11b. We then call subprogram ADD which does the addition. We call it by listing all the elements of the array in the argument list:

```
SUM=ADD( A(1,1), A(1,2), A(1,3), A(2,1), A(2,2), A(2,3)  )
```

As we have mentioned before, we cannot use subscripted variables as arguments of the subprogram, so we write the first statement in the subprogram as

```
FUNCTION ADD( A, B, C, D, E, F)
```

PASSING THE ELEMENTS OF A TWO-DIMENSIONAL ARRAY

```
C   PROGRAM ADDS THE ELEMENTS OF A 2 X 3 ARRAY
C   BY PASSING EACH OF THE ELEMENTS TO A SUBPROGRAM
        DIMENSION A(2,3)
C       ...READ THE ARRAY
        DO 20 I=1,2
           READ(5,10) (A (I,J), J=1,3)
 10        FORMAT(3F10.0)
           WRITE(6,15) (A(I,J), J=1,3)
 15        FORMAT(1X, 3F10.2 )
 20     CONTINUE
C
        SUM=ADD( A(1,1), A(1,2), A(1,3), A(2,1), A(2,2), A(2,3)  )
C
        WRITE(6,30) SUM
 30     FORMAT(1X, 'SUM=', F10.3)
        STOP
        END
```

Figure 9.11a. *Main program.* We pass the elements of the two-dimensional array A to the subprogram. The subprogram sums the elements of A.

```
        FUNCTION ADD( A, B, C, D, E, F)
C   ADDS THE ELEMENTS OF AN ARRAY
        WRITE(6,10) A, B, C, D, E, F
10      FORMAT(1X, ' THE ELEMENTS PASSED TO THE SUBPROGRAM'/ 1X,
     1         6F10.2 )
        ADD = A + B + C + D + E + F
        RETURN
        END
```

Subprogram. In ADD(A, B, C, D, E, F) the elements are all dummies. The variable A corresponds to A(1,1) in the main program; B corresponds to A(1,2); C corresponds to A(1,3), etc.

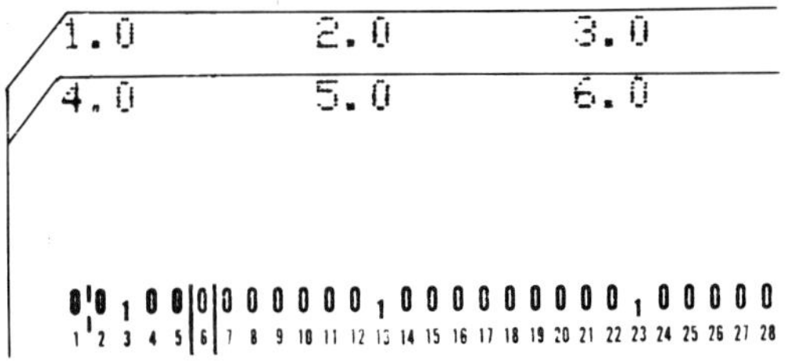

Figure 9.11b. The data cards for the program of Fig. 9.11a.

The dummy arguments are just the names we use in the subprogram to refer to the locations we have already labeled by the actual array name elements in the main program, as is shown in the table for Fig. 9.11a.

	Memory locations					
	1.0	2.0	3.0	4.0	5.0	6.0
Actual argument name	A(1,1)	A(1,2)	A(1,3)	A(2,1)	A(2,2)	A(2,3)
Dummy argument name	A	B	C	D	E	F

Thus when the computer evaluates A + B + C + D + E + F the computer interprets it as if it appeared in the main program as A(1,1) + A(1,2) + A(1,3) + A(2,1) + A(2,2) + A(2,3). However, the RETURN is needed to return control to the main program. The results of running the program are shown in Fig. 9.11c.

	Memory locations					
	1.0	2.0	3.0	4.0	5.0	6.0
Actual argument name	A(1,1)	A(1,2)	A(1,3)	A(2,1)	A(2,2)	A(2,3)
Dummy argument name	A	B	C	D	E	F

Table for Fig. 9.11a. The variables A, B, C, D, E and F are dummy arguments. They simply refer to locations already reserved for the elements of A in the main program.

```
        1.00        2.00        3.00
        4.00        5.00        6.00
 THE ELEMENTS PASSED TO THE SUBPROGRAM
        1.00        2.00        3.00        4.00        5.00        6.00
SUM=     21.000
```

Figure 9.11c. Results of running the program of Fig. 9.11a.

In the second version, shown in Fig. 9.12a, we pass the entire array to the subprogram in

```
SUM = ADD(A)
```

We write the first statement of the subprogram as

```
FUNCTION ADD(B)
```

where B is now a dummy array. When we dimension a dummy array, in order to avoid any errors, we should dimension it the same as the actual array it corresponds to in the main program. Since the actual array A is dimensioned as A(2,3) in DIMENSION A(2,3), we dimension B as B(2,3) in DIMENSION B(2,3). The fact that B is an array allows us to sum its elements in

```
      DO 20 I=1,2
         DO 10 J=1,3
            ADD = B(I,J) + ADD
10       CONTINUE
20    CONTINUE
```

where ADD was initialized in ADD = 0.0.

PASSING A TWO-DIMENSIONAL ARRAY

```
C   PROGRAM ADDS THE ELEMENTS OF A 2 X 3 1RR1Y
C   BY PASSING THE ENTIRE ARRAY TO THE SUBPROGRAM
        DIMENSION A(2,3)
C       ...READ THE ARRAY
        DO 20 I=1,2
           READ(5,10) (A (I,J), J=1,3)
 10        FORMAT(3F10.0)
           WRITE(6,15) (A(I,J), J=1,3)
 15        FORMAT(1X, 3F10.2 )
 20     CONTINUE
C
        SUM = ADD(A)
C
        WRITE(6,30) SUM
 30     FORMAT(1X, 'SUM=', F10.3)
        STOP
        END
```

Figure 9.12a. *Main program.* We have rewritten the program of Fig. 9.11a so that now we pass all the elements of the array A to the subprogram simply by using the array name as an argument.

```
        FUNCTION ADD(B)
C   ADDS THE ELEMENTS OF AN ARRAY
        DIMENSION B(2,3)
        WRITE(6,5) B
 5      FORMAT(1X, 'ELEMENTS PASSED TO SUBPROGRAM'/
     1         1X, 6F10.2 )
        ADD = 0.0
C       ...PERFORM THE SUM
        DO 20 I=1,2
           DO 10 J=1,3
              ADD = B(I,J) + ADD
 10        CONTINUE
 20     CONTINUE
        RETURN
        END
```

Subprogram. We use the array name B as the dummy argument. In the nested DO loops, the program sums the elements of B.

The dummy array elements are just the names we use in the subprogram to refer to the locations we have already labeled in the main program by the actual array name elements, as is shown in the table for Fig. 9.12a.

	Memory locations					
	1.0	2.0	3.0	4.0	5.0	6.0
Actual argument name	A(1,1)	A(1,2)	A(1,3)	A(2,1)	A(2,2)	A(2,3)
Dummy argument name	B(1,1)	B(1,2)	B(1,3)	B(2,1)	B(2,2)	B(2,3)

Thus when the computer executes the nested DO loop in the subprogram it interprets it as

```
      DO 20 I=1,2
         DO 10 J=1,3
            ADD = A(I,J) + ADD
10       CONTINUE
20    CONTINUE
```

However, the RETURN is needed to return control to the main program. The data cards for the program are shown in Fig. 9.12b; the results of running the program are shown in Fig. 9.12c.

	Memory locations					
	1.0	2.0	3.0	4.0	5.0	6.0
Actual argument name	A(1,1)	A(1,2)	A(1,3)	A(2,1)	A(2,2)	A(2,3)
Dummy argument name	B(1,1)	B(1,2)	B(1,3)	B(2,1)	B(2,2)	B(2,3)

Table for Fig. 9.12a. The elements of B are dummy arguments. They simply refer to the locations already reserved for the elements of A in the main program.

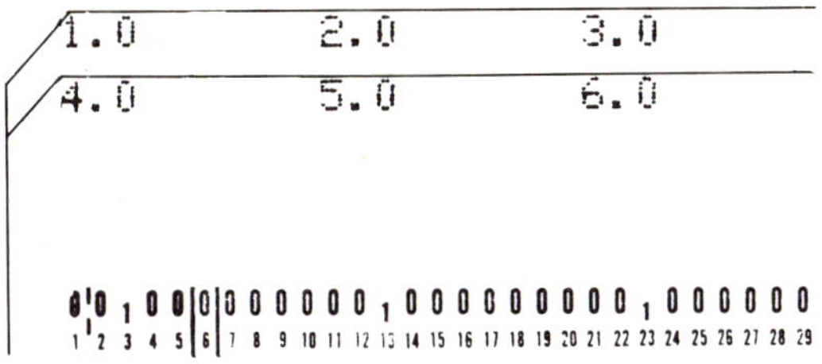

Figure 9.12b. The data cards for the program of Fig. 9.12a.

```
          1.00         2.00         3.00
          4.00         5.00         6.00
ELEMENTS PASSED TO SUBPROGRAM
          1.00         4.00         2.00         5.00         3.00         6.00
SUM=       21.000
```

Figure 9.12c. Running the program of Fig. 9.12b.

9.4. Redefining Dummy Arguments in Function Subprograms

On most systems it is possible to return information from the function subprogram to the calling program through one of the arguments.* Thus in the function subprograms of Fig. 9.13a, the dummy argument D, appears on the left-hand side of an assignment statement

```
D=T
```

This means that since D corresponds to the real argument B, when the main program statement WRITE(6,10) X, A, B is executed, the following will happen: the value of B printed will not be the one assigned to B in the main program, i.e., 2.0, but will be the value calculated in the subprogram at D=T, which is subsequently returned to the main program, i.e., 3.0. The results of running the program are shown in Fig. 9.13b.

* On Standard Basic FORTRAN, you cannot do this.

REDEFINING VARIABLES IN A SUBPROGRAM

```
C  REDEFINING VARIABLES IN SUBPROGRAMS
      A=1.0
      B=2.0
      X=T(A,B)
      WRITE(6,10) X, A, B
 10   FORMAT(1X, 'X=', F6.1, '   A=', F6.1, '   B=', F6.1)
      STOP
      END
```

Figure 9.13a. *Main program.* We can not only pass information from the main program to the subprogram via the arguments, but we can also go in the opposite direction.

```
FUNCTION T(C,D)
T = C + D
D=T
RETURN
END
```

Subprogram. When an argument of subprogram appears on the left side of an assignment statement, its value will be passed back to the main program. Thus since B corresponds to D, and since D = 3.0, then the value of B returned to the main program is 3.0.

```
X=    3.0  A=    1.0  B=    3.0
```

Figure 9.13b. Running the program of Fig. 9.13a. Since B is redefined as 3.0 in the subprogram, the value of B printed when the program is run is 3.0 and not 2.0.

On many systems you can redefine a dummy argument so that the compiler will produce an incorrect result. In Fig. 9.14a, we rewrite the program of Fig. 9.13a so that we now call the function with X=T(1,2.0). Then the value that the dummy argument D will return is still 3.0, but this will be put in the location where 2.0 had been placed, i.e., the location labeled by 2.0, as is shown in the second line of the table for Fig. 9.14a. Thus when the computer executes C=2.0 + 4.0, it will be adding the constant just placed into the location labeled by 2.0—i.e., 3.0—to 4.0 and would obtain the result 7.0 instead of 6.0. Results of running the program are shown in Fig. 9.14b. The WATFIV compiler would detect this error. It would stop the program during execution and print an error message. This analysis also applies to subroutines, a type of subprogram that we describe in Section 9.6.

CHANGING THE VALUE OF A CONSTANT

```
C  CHANGING THE VALUE OF A CONSTANT
      A=1.0
      X=T(A, 2.0 )
      C= 2.0 + 4.0
C
      WRITE(6,10) X, A, C
 10   FORMAT(1X, 'X=', F6.1, '   A=', F6.1, '   C=', F6.1 )
      STOP
      END
```

Figure 9.14a. *Main program.* By using 2.0 in X=T(A,2.0), we will cause the value of 2.0 to be redefined in the subprogram.

```
FUNCTION T( C, D)
T=C + D
D=T
RETURN
END
```

Subprogram. Since D, an argument of the subprogram, is redefined, the value of the actual argument which corresponds to D is also redefined. Since in the main program the actual argument is 2.0, the value of 2.0 is redefined.

Statement	A	2.0	C
A=1.0	1.0	2.0	Undef
C=2.0+4.0	1.0	3.0	7.0

Table for Fig. 9.14a. Before 2.0 is used in X = T(A,2.0), its value is 2.0. After the subprogram is called, the value of 2.0 is 3.0.

```
X=    3.0  A=    1.0  C=    7.0
```

Figure 9.14b. Running the program of Fig. 9.14a. Since the value of 2.0 was redefined to be 3.0, the value of C is 7.0 instead of 6.0.

9.5. Subprograms Calling Other Subprograms

A subprogram can call another subprogram. Thus we could for instance write

```
      FUNCTION FUN(A,B,C)
C  FUN CALLS ADD
      Y= ADD(A,B,C)
      RETURN
      END
```

where subprogram FUN calls subprogram ADD, as shown in Fig. 9.15a.

A subprogram cannot call itself. Thus,

```
      FUNCTION FUN(A,B,C)
C  FUN CALLS ITSELF
      Y=FUN(A,B,C) + FUN(C,B,A)
      RETURN
      END
```

as is shown in Fig. 9.15b, is illegal, since FUN calls itself in

```
Y=FUN(A,B,C) + FUN(C,B,A)
```

Similarly a subprogram cannot call a series of subprograms that eventually calls the original subprogram. When a subprogram calls itself, we say that it is *recursive*.

SUBPROGRAMS CALLING OTHER SUBPROGRAMS

```
      FUNCTION FUN(A,B,C)
C  FUN CALLS ADD
      Y= ADD(A,B,C)
      RETURN
      END
```

Figure 9.15a. A subprogram can call another subprogram. Thus FUN calls ADD.

```
              FUNCTION FUN(A,B,C)
         C  FUN CALLS ITSELF
              Y=FUN(A,B,C) + FUN(C,B,A)
***ERROR***  ATTEMPT TO USE PREVIOUSLY DEFINED NAME FUN    AS A FUNCTION OR AN ARRAY
              RETURN
              END
```

Figure 9.15b. A subprogram cannot call itself. The system prints an appropriate error message.

9.6. Subroutines

A subroutine is a subprogram in which information cannot be returned to the main program—or calling program—via the subprogram name. Thus a subroutine name cannot be used in an expression in a statement. Information is transferred to and from the main program through the arguments* of the subroutine.

In the program of Fig. 9.16a, we use a subroutine called FACT to calculate $N!$ We transfer control from the main program to the subroutine by using a CALL statement

```
CALL FACT(M,N)
```

Thus all we have to do is to precede the subroutine name with the word CALL. The value of N is the number of which we want to find the factorial. After the subroutine has been executed, the value of M will be the required factorial.

When we write the subroutine, the first card must contain the word SUBROUTINE followed by the subroutine name—here FACT. If the subroutine has any arguments, they are listed to the right of the subroutine name and are enclosed in parentheses (just as we would do for a subprogram function). Thus, in the first card of the subroutine in Fig. 9.6a,

```
SUBROUTINE FACT(L,N)
```

L and N are dummy arguments. The variable L corresponds to M in the main program, and we have used N in both the main program and the subroutine. Since subroutine names are not used in expressions, we do not have to concern ourselves with whether to make them REAL or INTEGER. Had we named the subroutine NFACT, the results would have been the same. The rule for forming a subroutine name is the same as the rule for forming a variable name. Note that you cannot use the same name for a subroutine and for a variable.

The structure of the subroutine is quite similar to that of a subprogram function. A RETURN statement transfers control back to the main (or calling) program. But instead of control returning to the statement that called the subprogram—as in the case of subprogram functions—control is returned to the first executable statement that follows the calling statement. Thus in Fig. 9.16a control is returned to

```
WRITE(6,20) N, M
```

Note that, as opposed to a function subprogram, we do not use the name of the subroutine in the subroutine itself. Thus the factorial desired will be assigned to L the last time L = L * J is executed, and this value of L will be returned to the main program. Just as in a subprogram function, a subroutine must end with an END. This informs the compiler that there are no more statements in the subroutine. The data card read by the program is shown in Fig. 9.16b. The results of running the program are shown in Fig. 9.16c.

* We will learn that we can also use a COMMON statement to transfer information to and from a subprogram.

USING A SUBROUTINE

```
C  PROGRAM USES SUBROUTINE TO CALCULATE FACTORIAL
      READ(5, 10) N
 10   FORMAT(I10)
      WRITE(6,15) N
 15   FORMAT(1X, 'VALUE OF N READ IS ', I3)
C
      CALL FACT(M,N)
      WRITE(6,20) N, M
 20   FORMAT(1X, I3, '!=', I10)
      STOP
      END
```

Figure 9.16a. *Main program.* This program calls a subroutine. This is done by using the statement CALL FACT(M,N). A subroutine's name cannot be used in a calculation. A subroutine is similar to a function subprogram except that all information passed from the subroutine back to the main program must be passed via the arguments. Also, a subroutine may have no argument at all.

```
      SUBROUTINE FACT(L,N)
C  CALCULATES N!
      WRITE(6,5) N
 5    FORMAT(1X, ' THE VALUE OF N PASSED IS :', I3 )
      IF( N .LE. 0 ) STOP
            L=1
         DO 10 J=1,N
            L=L * J
 10      CONTINUE
      RETURN
      END
```

Subroutine. In the present subroutine, the value of N is passed to the subroutine and the value of L (which is *N!*) is passed back to the main program. The variable L is a dummy argument and corresponds to M in the main program. If N were redefined in the subroutine, that value would be passed back to the main program and would be redefined there as well. When the RETURN is executed, control is transferred to the first executable statement following the CALL.

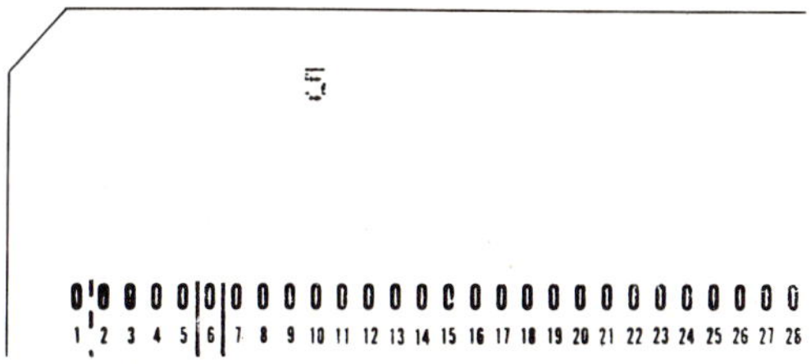

Figure 9.16b. The data card for Fig. 9.16a.

```
VALUE OF N READ IS    5
 THE VALUE OF N PASSED IS :    5
  5!=         120
```

Figure 9.16c. Running the program of Fig. 9.16a.

As we learned, a subprogram must have at least one argument; a subroutine, however, may have no arguments. In Fig. 9.17 we rewrite the program of Fig. 9.16a so that the main program of Fig. 9.16a is now a subroutine called MAIN. The main program in Fig. 9.17a consists of just three executable statements

```
CALL MAIN
STOP
END
```

Subroutine MAIN itself calls a subroutine, namely FACT. After FACT is executed, control returns to WRITE(6,20)N,M in subroutine MAIN. After the results are printed by the WRITE statement, control is transferred to the STOP statement in the main program. The data card for the program is shown in Fig. 9.17b. The results are shown in Fig. 9.17c.

A SUBROUTINE WITHOUT ANY ARGUMENTS

```
C   USING A SUBROUTINE WITHOUT ANY ARGUMENTS
       CALL MAIN
       STOP
       END
```

Figure 9.17a. *Main program.* In call MAIN we call a subroutine that has no arguments.

```
       SUBROUTINE MAIN
       READ(5,10) N
 10    FORMAT( I10 )
       CALL FACT(M,N)
       WRITE(6,20) N, M
 20    FORMAT(1X,  I3, '!=', I10)
       RETURN
       END
```

Subroutine MAIN. This subroutine itself calls a subroutine in CALL FACT(M,N). Since MAIN does the printing of the results, there is no need to return any arguments to the main program. After the results are printed, control is transferred to the STOP statement in the main program.

```
       SUBROUTINE FACT(L,N)
C   CALCULATES N!
       WRITE(6,5) N
 5     FORMAT(1X, 'VALUE PASSED:', I4)
       IF( N .LE. 0 ) STOP
          L=1
          DO 10 J=1,N
             L=L*J
 10       CONTINUE
          RETURN
       END
```

Subroutine FACT. This is the same as was shown in Fig. 9.16a.

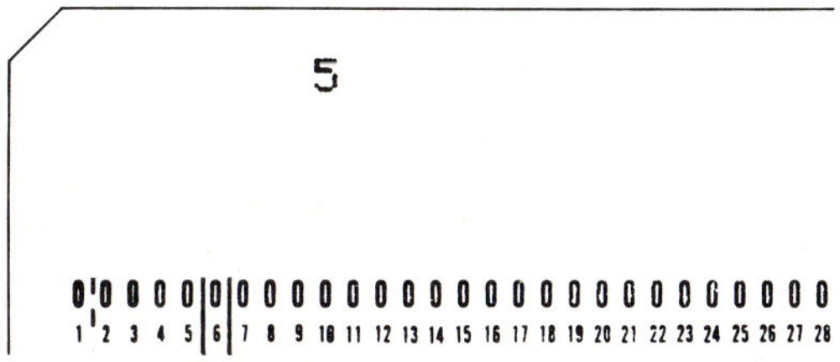

Figure 9.17b. The data card for the program of Fig. 9.17a.

```
VALUE PASSED:   5
  5!=         120
```

Figure 9.17c. Running the program of Fig. 9.17a.

9.7. The Arguments of Subroutines and Function Subprograms

The form that actual arguments of a subroutine or subprogram can take are given in Table 9.3. The form that dummy arguments of a subroutine can take are given in Table 9.4. You cannot use a constant or subscripted variable as a dummy argument. Thus SUBROUTINE FACT(3) and INTEGER FUNCTION FACT(8) would both produce compile-time error; and thus also, SUBROUTINE FUN(T, A(1), A(2)) and INTEGER FUNCTION FUN(T, B(3,2), C(1)) would produce compile-time errors.

As we have mentioned, corresponding dummy and actual arguments must have the same modes. For instance, if NUMB is an actual argument and has been declared to be REAL in the calling program, i.e., it appears in

```
REAL NUMB
```

then if NUMB is the corresponding dummy argument used in a subroutine or function subprogram, it must also be declared REAL there. However, if XNUMB is the corresponding dummy argument, it does not have to be declared REAL. The reason is that XNUMB is explicitly REAL, i.e., it begins with an X.

9.8. Differences between Subroutines and Function Subprograms

We now review the differences between subroutines and function subprograms. Subroutines and functions are identical except for the following:

1. A function subprogram must have at least one argument whereas a subroutine does not have to have any.
2. A function subprogram's name is used in expressions in the main program. Thus its name is used to return information to the main program and has a specific mode. An argument of a function subprogram can also be used to return information to the main program. On the other hand, a subroutine's name is not used to return information to the main program, only an argument of the subroutine can be used for this.
3. A function subprogram is called when the function is used in an expression; whereas a subroutine is called when the word CALL precedes the subroutine name.

Both subroutines and subprogram functions can call other subroutines and function subprograms, but they cannot call themselves.

PERMISSIBLE ACTUAL ARGUMENTS OF FUNCTION SUBPROGRAMS OR SUBROUTINES

Type	Examples	Use in calling subprogram
Constants	4, 3.0	M = FACT(4)
Nonsubscripted variable	X, N	M = FACT(N)
Array names	A, B	R = FUN(T,A)
Subscripted variable	A(4,2), B(3)	CALL G(T, A(4,2), B(3), B(2))
Expression	I*K+2	M = FACT(I*K+2)
	3.0+SQRT(X)	CALL FUN(T, 3.0+SQRT(X))
	A .GT. B	CALL SUB(R, A .GT. B)

Table 9.3. We will see in Chapter 10 that a function subprogram name or a subroutine name can also be an actual argument.

PERMISSIBLE DUMMY ARGUMENTS OF SUBPROGRAMS OR SUBROUTINES

Type	Examples	Use in subprogram
Nonsubscripted variable	X, N	FUNCTION FACT(N)
Array names	B, A	SUBPROGRAM SQRT(T, B)
		DIMENSION B(40)

Table 9.4. We will see in Chapter 10 that a function subprogram name or a subroutine name can also be a dummy argument.

9.9. Modularizing Programs

We can use subroutines and subprograms to make programs easier to follow. In Fig. 9.18a we write a program that calculates $N!$ We have partitioned the program into sections (subroutines and function subprograms) called *modules*; they are also called *segments*. Here, each of the modules performs one set of distinct operations. Subroutine READ reads the value of N for which we wish to calculate the factorial. Subroutine CHECK checks whether the value of N is negative; if it is, the subroutine prints an error message. (CHECK gives the program integrity.) The INTEGER function subprogram FACT calculates the factorial for the value of N. Finally, subroutine WRITE writes the results.

MODULARIZING A PROGRAM

```
C   PROGRAM CALCULATES N!
      INTEGER FACT
      CALL READ(N)
      CALL CHECK(N)
      M=FACT(N)
      CALL WRITE(N,M)
      STOP
      END
```

Figure 9.18a. *Main program.* A program that calculates N! We have partitioned or modularized the program so that each step is done in a different subroutine or subprogram.

```
      SUBROUTINE READ(N)
C   THIS SUBROUTINE READS DATA
      READ(5,10) N
 10   FORMAT( I10 )
      WRITE(6,20) N
 20   FORMAT(1X, 'N=', I4 )
      RETURN
      END
```

Subroutine READ. This reads the value of N.

```
      SUBROUTINE CHECK(N)
C   CHECKS WHETHER N IS ZERO OR NEGATIVE
C   SO THAT NFACT FUNCTION WILL EXECUTE WITHOUT ERRORS
      WRITE(6,5) N
  5   FORMAT(1X, ' N PASSED TO CHECK', I4)
      IF( N .LT. 0 ) WRITE(6,10) N
 10   FORMAT(1X, 'ZERO OR NEGATIVE ARGUMENTS: N=', I4 )
         IF( N .LT. 0 ) STOP
      RETURN
      END
```

Subroutine CHECK. Checks whether N is negative. If it is, the subroutine prints error message and then stops.

```
      INTEGER FUNCTION FACT(N)
C   CALCULATES N!
      FACT=1
      IF( N .EQ. 0 ) RETURN
         DO 10 J=1,N
            FACT=FACT * J
 10      CONTINUE
      RETURN
      END
```

Subprogram FACT. Calculates N!

```
      SUBROUTINE WRITE(N,M)
      WRITE(6,10) N,M
 10   FORMAT(1X, I3, '!=', I20)
      STOP
      END
```

Subprogram WRITE. Writes the results.

The best way to partition a program is so that it can be read from the top to the bottom. The flow chart for Fig. 9.18a is shown in Fig. 9.18b. Notice that the main program is very similar to the flow chart. The data card for the program is shown in Fig. 9.18c, and the results of running the program are shown in Fig. 9.18d.

When you submit the deck of cards to be compiled and executed it does not matter what order the subroutines are in as long as the main program comes first. Thus the order could be: Main program, WRITE, FACT, CHECK, and finally READ.

Once a program is modularized into subroutines, each subroutine can be debugged and checked out separately. This is advantageous if you are working with a large program that has many subroutines. Various subroutines can be given to different people to work on, thus shortening the time required to debug the entire program.

Even if all the subprograms are not yet debugged or perhaps not even written, you can test how the ones that are written interact. This is done by substituting dummy subprograms (they are also called program stubs) for the ones not yet completed. Thus in Fig. 9.18a, if we had not completed subprogram FACT but had completed all the other subprograms, we could make certain initial tests on the overall program by substituting the dummy subprogram

```
INTEGER FACT(N)
FACT=N
RETURN
END
```

This subprogram, as we see, returns the constant that was passed to it. This would allow us to test how the overall program reads, checks, and finally, prints the data.

We see that a dummy subprogram is one that has not been developed to the point that it does the task of the subprogram that will be substituted for it when the entire program is complete. However, the dummy subprogram allows arguments to be passed to and from it.

In order to facilitate the design and writing of modules, in practice a module should not be longer than 50 lines of programming code, i.e., the amount of code that can fit onto one page. The word *code* when used as a noun is a synonym for "programming statement"; when used as a verb—as in "to code"—it is a synonym for the verb "program".

Modules should be as independent of each other as possible. Thus a change that has to be made in one module, should have minimal effects on the other modules in the program—something that is easy to say but in fact may be difficult to do.

When deciding how to modularize a program, you should choose statements that naturally go together. For instance, you would not normally place READ and data validation statements and part of a calculation in one subroutine and then place the second part of the calculation in another subroutine. Rather, you would place the READ and data validation statements in one subroutine and the entire calculation in another subroutine. If a segment of a program is very likely to require changes in the future, the segment should be isolated by placing it in a subroutine. Thus corrections can be made to that segment without explicitly altering other parts of the program.

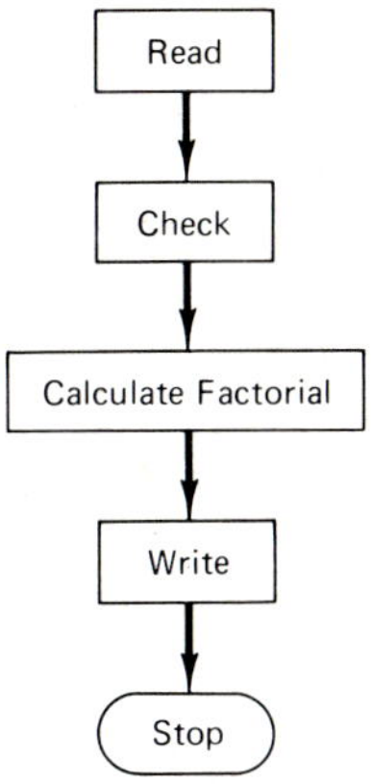

Figure 9.18b. Flow chart for Fig. 9.18a. Since the program has been modularized, the flow chart reads just as the main program does.

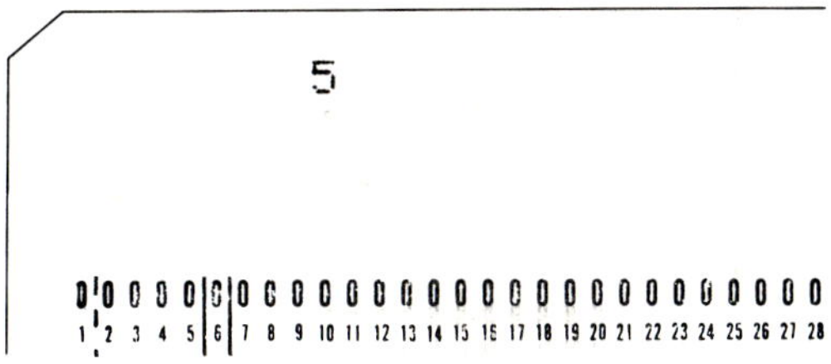

Figure 9.18c. The data card for the program of Fig. 9.18a.

```
N=    5
 N PASSED TO CHECK    5
  5!=                  120
```

Figure 9.18d. Running the program of Fig. 9.18a. When running the program, the main program must come first. The subroutines and subprograms can follow in any order.

9.10. Using Arrays as Arguments of Subroutines

The use of arrays as arguments of subroutines is the same as when arrays are used as arguments of function subprograms. In Fig. 9.19a, we write a program that histograms the values of X read from cards shown in Fig. 9.19b. In the main program, we zero all the elements of array M—the array which we will use to histogram X—in the DATA statement. We then call subroutine PARAM.

A HISTOGRAMMING PROGRAM

```
C   PROGRAM USES SUBROUTINE TO HISTOGRAM
        DIMENSION M(100)
        DATA M/ 100*0 /

C       ... READ LIMITS & INTERVAL SIZE FOR HISTOGRAM
        CALL PARAM( XMIN, DX, XMAX, K)
C
C       ...HISTOGRAMS VALUES READ FROM CARDS
        DO 30 I=1, 1000
           READ(5,10) X
 10        FORMAT( F10.0 )
           WRITE(6,15) X
 15        FORMAT(1X, 'X=', F12.2)
C          ...TEST FOR TRAILER
           IF( X .EQ. -12345678.0 ) CALL WRITE(M,K)
C
              CALL HISTO( XMIN, XMAX, DX, X, M )
 30     CONTINUE
C
C       ...USE IF TOO MANY CARDS ENCOUNTERED
        WRITE(6,40)
 40     FORMAT(1X, '1000 DATA CARDS ENCOUNTERED' )
        CALL WRITE(M,K)
        STOP
        END
```

Figure 9.19a. *Main program.* This program histograms values of X read from cards. The reading and histogramming is done in the DO loop. The trailer has the value −12345678.0. When the trailer is encountered, or if more than 1000 cards are read, subroutine WRITE is called. The entire array M is passed to both HISTO and WRITE.

Figure 9.19b. The data cards for Fig. 9.19a.

Subroutine PARAM reads XMIN, the minimum value of X; DX, the interval or bin width; XMAX, the maximum value of X for all the data. It then determines K, the number of intervals that will be required to histogram all the values of X.

```
K=(XMAX - XMIN)/DX + 0.1
```

For instance, if the value of XMAX is 10.0, of XMIN is 0.0, and of DX is 2.0, then K = 10.0/2.0 + 0.1, or 5.1, which is truncated to 5. The reason for the "0.1" is to correct for possible round-off errors. Since K is an argument of the subroutine, it is passed back to the main program. However, if the value of K exceeds the dimension of array M, or if it is less than or equal to zero, subroutine PARAM prints an appropriate error message and then stops.

The DO loop in the main program first reads and echo-prints the value of X, and if it's value is not equal to 12345678.0—the value punched on the trailer—the computer histograms it in subroutine HISTO. In subroutine HISTO, we calculate the value of the LOGICAL variable LIMIT in

```
LIMIT = (X .LT. XMIN) .OR. (X .GE. XMAX)
```

If the value of X is not within the limits of the histogram, the value of LIMIT is "true." If the value of LIMIT is true, the subroutine prints IS OUT OF RANGE on the same line that the main program echo-printed the value of X. The subroutine does this by using a "+" as the control character in

```
      IF( LIMIT ) WRITE(6,10)
 10   FORMAT(1H+, 15X, 'IS OUT OF RANGE' )
```

The reason for the 15 X is that we want IS OUT OF RANGE to be printed to the right of the echo-printing of X. Thus, for instance, when the value of X is −2, the computer prints

```
X = -2 IS OUT OF RANGE
```

(see Fig. 9.19c) and returns to the main program.

```
      SUBROUTINE PARAM(XMIN, DX, XMAX, K)
C  READS HISTOGRAMS PARAMETERS
      READ(5,10) XMIN, DX, XMAX
 10   FORMAT(3F10.0 )
      WRITE(6,20) XMIN, DX, XMAX
 20   FORMAT(1X, 'XMIN=', F10.2, '  DX=', F10.2, '  XMAX=', F10.2)
C
C     ...CALCULATE # OF INTERVALS
      K=(XMAX - XMIN)/DX + 0.1
      WRITE(6,15) K
 15   FORMAT(1X,'# OF INTERVALS =', I4)
C     ...CHECK FOR LIMITS ON # OF INTERVALS
      IF(K .GT. 100 ) WRITE(6,30) K
 30   FORMAT(1X, 'TOO MANY BINS. K=', I5 )
      IF( K .GT. 100) STOP
         IF( K .LE. 0 )  WRITE(6,40) K
 40      FORMAT(1X, 'BAD VALUE OF K. K=', I5 /
     1          1X, 'CHECK HISTOGRAM PARAMETERS' )
         IF( K .LE. 0 ) STOP
      RETURN
      END
```

Subroutine PARAM. This reads XMIN, the minimum value of X to be histogrammed; DX, the interval size; XMAX, the maximum value of X to be histogrammed. It calculates K, the number of intervals required to histogram X.

```
      SUBROUTINE HISTO ( XMIN, XMAX, DX, X, M )
C  HISTOGRAMS X
      DIMENSION M(100)
      LOGICAL LIMIT
C        ...TEST THAT X IS WITHIN LIMITS
      LIMIT = (X .LT. XMIN) .OR. (X .GE. XMAX)
      IF( LIMIT ) WRITE(6,10)
 10   FORMAT(1H+, 15X,  'IS OUT OF RANGE' )
      IF( LIMIT ) RETURN
C        ...CALCULATE BIN NUMBER
         J = (X - XMIN) / DX + 1.0
         WRITE(6,20) J
 20      FORMAT(1H+, 18X, 'INTERVAL', I3 )
C        ...DO THE HISTOGRAMMING
         M(J) = M(J) + 1
         RETURN
      END
```

Subroutine HISTO. After the proper interval to place the number just read is calculated in J = (X − XMIN) / DX + 1.0, the counting statement M(J) = M(J) + 1 is executed. After each time the subroutine is executed, the present value of each of the elements of M is returned to the main program.

The reason we calculated the value of LIMIT is that if X is out of the range of the histogram, then the value of J will be equal to or less than zero (this would cause an execution error) or the value of J would be greater than the number of intervals. (If there were 100 intervals, this could cause the dimension of M to be exceeded since the dimension of M is 100.) Either of these cases would cause difficulty. We used the GE operator in the (X .GE. XMAX) part of LIMIT instead of using GT for the following reason: If the value of X were equal to XMAX, then the value of J would equal 1 plus the number of intervals* in the histogram. Again, if there were 100 intervals in the histogram, this would cause the dimension of M to be exceeded.

If the value of X falls within the range of the histogram, we determine in which interval the value of X falls—as we explained in Chapter 7—by calculating

```
J = (X - XMIN) / DX + 1.0
```

Thus if X is 1.1, then J = (1.1 − 0.0)/2.0 + 1.0, or 1.55, which is truncated to 1. Thus 1.1 is placed in the first bin. The computer then prints the value of J on the same line that the main program echo-printed the value of X (see Fig. 9.19c).

```
X=            1.10      INTERVAL  1
```

The subroutine then histograms X when it executes

```
M(J) = M(J) + 1
```

Then the array M is passed back to the main program.

The range of the DO loop in the main program is executed again. This process continues until the trailer is encountered. Then subroutine WRITE is called. The array M and K, the value of the number of intervals used, are passed to WRITE. In this subroutine WRITE (6,10) (M(I), I=1,K) prints the results. Then the program stops.

If 1000 cards are encountered, the range of the DO loop in the main program is executed 1000 times. The program prints a message indicating this, and then calls WRITE, in which it prints the results.

The flow chart for the program is shown in Fig. 9.19d. The results of running the program are shown in Fig. 9.19c. On the line beneath RESULTS we see the contents of each interval (bin). Interval 1 has 1 event; interval 2 has 2 events; interval 3 has 3 events; interval 4 has 0 events; and interval 5 has 1 event. This agrees with the echo-printing of the values of X.

* In this case J = (XMAX − XMIN)/DX = 1.0, but (XMAX − XMIN)/DX is the value of the number of intervals, K. Thus in this case J = K + 1.

```
      SUBROUTINE WRITE(M,K)
C   WRITES RESULTS
      DIMENSION M(100)
      WRITE(6,10) ( M(I), I=1,K)
 10   FORMAT(1X, 'RESULTS'/ 10( I6, 2X)  )
      STOP
      END
```

Subroutine WRITE. When the trailer has been encountered, or if 1000 cards have been read, the latest value of each of the elements of M and the value of K are passed to subroutine WRITE. Here the results are printed and the program terminates.

```
XMIN=        0.00   DX=        2.00  XMAX=       10.00
# OF INTERVALS =    5
X=          1.10      INTERVAL  1
X=          2.30      INTERVAL  2
X=          4.20      INTERVAL  3
X=          3.10      INTERVAL  2
X=          5.20      INTERVAL  3
X=         -2.00 IS OUT OF RANGE
X=          5.40      INTERVAL  3
X=         12.00 IS OUT OF RANGE
X=          8.50      INTERVAL  5
X=          9.20      INTERVAL  5
X=-12345670.00
RESULTS
1        2        3        0        2
```

Figure 9.19c. Running the program of Fig. 9.19a. Subroutine HISTO prints the interval number on the same line that the main program echo-printed the value of X; or if the value of X is out of range, subroutine HISTO prints an error message on the same line that the main program echo-printed the value of X. It can do both of these things because of the "+" in the FORMAT statements.

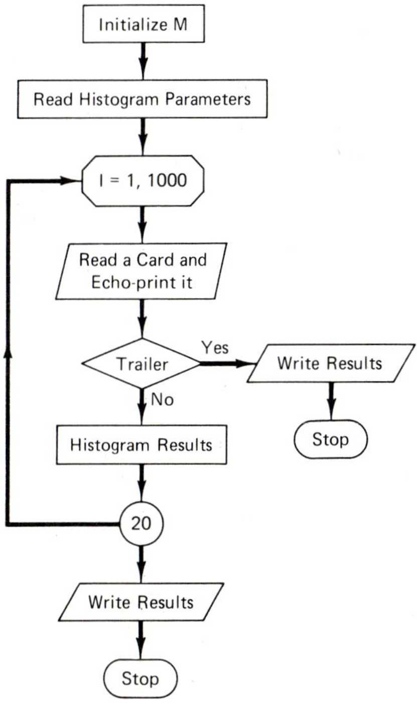

Figure 9.19d. The flow chart for Fig. 9.19a.

9.11. Plotting Histograms

In Fig. 9.20a we present a program which, given the INTEGER array BIN which is initialized in

```
DATA BIN / 3, 8, 6, 4, 0, 7 /
```

produces the horizontal histogram shown in Fig. 9.20b. The number of asterisks in each horizontal line corresponds to the value of an element array BIN: The number of asterisks in the first line corresponds to the value of the first element; in the second line, to the second element, etc.

We will use the variable ASTER to print the horizontal lines. We assign an asterisk to ASTER in

```
DATA ASTER / '*' /
```

The first time the computer executes the range of the DO loop, BINAMT equals BIN(1) and therefore its value is 3. Since the value of BINAMT is not zero, the condition in

```
IF( BINAMT .NE. 0 ) WRITE(6,10) J, BINAMT, (ASTER, I=1,BINAMT)
```

is true. The computer interprets the WRITE part of this statement as

WRITE(6,10) 1, BIN(1), (ASTER, I=1,3)

and prints three asterisks as is shown in Fig. 9.20b.

```
BIN# 1 FREQ=  3 ***
```

Because we are printing alphanumeric characters, we use A FORMAT as the field specification for ASTER. Since the location ASTER contains only one character, i.e., an asterisk, we have used A1 in the FORMAT. We have written the A format as 20A1 to accommodate the possibility that all 20 asterisks will be printed.

The reason we used BINAMT as the index limit in the implied DO is that using a subscripted variable as the index limit is illegal. Thus

WRITE(6,10) J,BINAMT, (ASTER, I=1, BIN(J))

would cause a compile-time error.

If for a given value of J, the value of BIN(J) and therefore the value of BINAMT is zero, then the computer would interpret the implied DO as (ASTER, I=1,0). Since the maximum value of the loop index I is zero, the implied DO is illegal and would cause an execution time error. In order to avoid this error, we include a WRITE statement which has no implied DO and which is executed only if the value of BINAMT is zero.

```
IF( BINAMT .EQ. 0 ) WRITE(6,10) J, BINAMT
```

PLOTTING A HISTOGRAM

```
C   DEMONSTRATES HOW TO PLOT A HISTOGRAM
      INTEGER BIN(6), BINAMT
C     ...PLACE VALUE IN HISTOGRAMMING ARRAY
      DATA BIN / 3, 8, 6, 4, 0, 7 /
      DATA ASTER / '*' /
C     ...PLOT HISTOGRAM
      DO 20 J=1,6
      BINAMT=BIN(J)
         IF( BINAMT .EQ. 0 ) WRITE(6,10) J, BINAMT
         IF( BINAMT .NE. 0 ) WRITE(6,10) J, BINAMT, (ASTER, I=1,BINAMT)
 10      FORMAT(1X, 'BIN#', I2, 1X, 'FREQ=', I3, 1X, 20A1)
 20   CONTINUE
      STOP
      END
```

Figure 9.20a. Program plots a histogram. If the value of BINAMT is zero, the program prints no asterisks but executes WRITE(6,10) J, BINAMT. If the value of BINAMT is not zero, the computer executes WRITE(6,10) J, BINAMT, (ASTER,I=1,BINAMT) and prints asterisks. The reason for the two WRITE statements is that (ASTER, I=1,0) would cause an execution-time error. The field specification for each asterisk is A1.

```
BIN# 1 FREQ=  3 ***
BIN# 2 FREQ=  8 ********
BIN# 3 FREQ=  6 ******
BIN# 4 FREQ=  4 ****
BIN# 5 FREQ=  0
BIN# 6 FREQ=  7 *******
```

Figure 9.20b. Running the program of Fig. 9.20b.

Now, because there are only two items, J and BINAMT, in the WRITE list, the field specification 20A1 in the corresponding FORMAT

```
10        FORMAT(1X, 'BIN#', I2, 1X, 'FREQ=', I3, 1X, 20A1)
```

is not used. An example of how the FORMAT is used in this case occurs when the program prints the line of results for BIN(5). Since the value of BIN(5) equals zero, the program executes

```
BIN# 5 FREQ=  0
```

thus printing no asterisks (see Fig. 9.20b).

In Fig. 9.21a, we have rewritten the histogramming program of Fig. 9.20a so that it now plots the results. In order to do this, we have replaced subroutine WRITE with a modified version of the plotting program we just discussed (Fig. 9.20a). The subroutine can accommodate up to 100 bins and can print a line consisting of up to 100 asterisks. We thus have written INTEGER BIN(100).

We remember that the variable K calculated in subroutine PARAM determines how many bins the histogram has and that M is the array in which the results of the histogram are stored. Since these two items are the ones that have to be passed on to the PLOT, we write

```
CALL  PLOT(M,K)
```

In the subroutine PLOT, the dummy array BIN corresponds to M, and the dummy variable NMAX corresponds to K. Since the array M is passed on to the subroutine PLOT and is represented by BIN, we have eliminated from the plotting program shown in Fig. 9.20a the DATA statement that initialized BIN. The data cards for the program are shown in Fig. 9.21b and the results of running the program are shown in Fig. 9.21c.

HISTOGRAM PROGRAM WHICH PLOTS RESULTS

```
C       PROGRAM HISTOGRAMS & PLOTS
        DIMENSION M(100)
        DATA M/ 100*0 /
        LOGICAL LIMIT
C       ... READ LIMITS & INTERVAL SIZE FOR HISTOGRAM
        CALL PARAM( XMIN, DX, XMAX, K)
C
C       ...HISTOGRAMS VALUES READ FROM CARDS
        DO 30 I=1, 1000
           READ(5,10) X
 10        FORMAT( F10.0 )
           WRITE(6,15) X
 15        FORMAT(1X, 'X=', F12.2)
C          ...TEST FOR TRAILER
           IF( X .EQ. -12345678.0 ) CALL  PLOT(M,K)
C
              CALL HISTO( XMIN, XMAX, DX, X, M )
 30     CONTINUE
C
C       ...USE IF TOO MANY CARDS ENCOUNTERED
        WRITE(6,40)
 40     FORMAT(1X, '1000 DATA CARDS ENCOUNTERED' )
        CALL  PLOT(M,K)
        STOP
        END
```

Figure 9.21a. *Main program*. Histograms and then plots results.

```
      SUBROUTINE PLOT( BIN, NMAX)
C  PLOTS HISTOGRAM
C  NMAX = # OF INTERVALS
      INTEGER BIN(100), BINAMT
      DATA ASTFR / '*' /
      DO 20 J=1, NMAX
      BINAMT=BIN(J)
         IF( BINAMT .NE. 0 ) WRITE(6,10) J, BINAMT, (ASTER, I=1,BINAMT)
         IF( BINAMT .EQ. 0 ) WRITE(6,10) J, BINAMT
 10      FORMAT(1X, 'BIN#', I2, ' FREQ=', I3, 1X, 100A1 )
 20   CONTINUE
      STOP
      END
```

Subroutine *PLOT.* Makes a horizontal plot consisting of lines of asterisks. The dummy arguments BIN and NMAX correspond to the actual arguments M and K respectively. For zero values of BIN(J), no asterisks are printed.

```
      SUBROUTINE PARAM(XMIN, DX, XMAX, K)
C  READS HISTOGRAMS PARAMETERS
      READ(5,10) XMIN, DX, XMAX
 10   FORMAT(3F10.0 )
      WRITE(6,20) XMIN, DX, XMAX
 20   FORMAT(1X, 'XMIN=', F10.2, '  DX=', F10.2, '  XMAX=', F10.2)
C
C     ...CALCULATE # OF INTERVALS
      K=(XMAX - XMIN)/DX + 0.1
      WRITE(6,15) K
 15   FORMAT(1X,'# OF INTERVALS =', I4)
C     ...CHECK FOR LIMITS ON # OF INTERVALS
      IF(K .GT. 100 ) WRITE(6,30) K
 30   FORMAT(1X, 'TOO MANY BINS. K=', I5 )
      IF( K .GT. 100) STOP
         IF( K .LE. 0 )  WRITE(6,40) K
 40      FORMAT(1X, 'BAD VALUE OF K. K=', I5 /
     1          1X, 'CHECK HISTOGRAM PARAMETERS' )
         IF( K .LE. 0 ) STOP
      RETURN
      END
```

Subroutine PARAM. Reads XMIN, X, and XMAX then determines the number of bins, K.

```
      SUBROUTINE HISTO ( XMIN, XMAX, DX, X, M )
C  HISTOGRAMS X
      DIMENSION M(100)
      LOGICAL LIMIT
C        ...TEST THAT X IS WITHIN LIMITS
      LIMIT = (X .LT. XMIN) .OR. (X .GE. XMAX)
      IF( LIMIT ) WRITE(6,10)
 10   FORMAT(1H+, 15X,  'IS OUT OF RANGE' )
      IF( LIMIT ) RETURN
C        ...CALCULATE BIN NUMBER
         J = (X - XMIN) / DX + 1.0
         WRITE(6,20) J
 20      FORMAT(1H+, 18X, 'INTERVAL', I3 )
C        ...DO THE HISTOGRAMMING
         M(J) = M(J) + 1
         RETURN
      END
```

Subroutine HISTO. Histograms the quantity X.

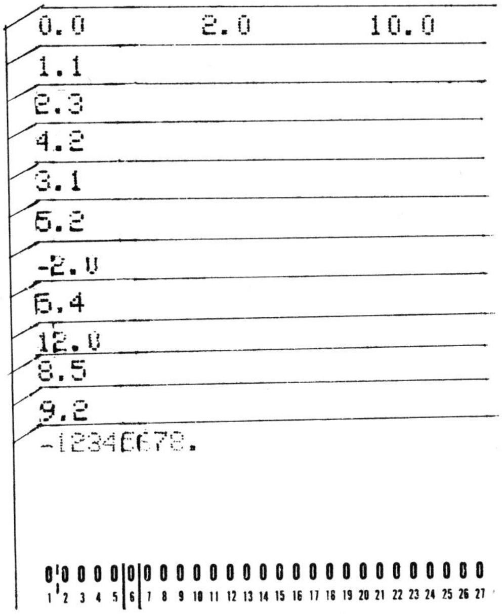

Figure 9.21b. The data card for Fig. 9.21a.

```
XMIN=          0.00   DX=         2.00   XMAX=          10.00
# OF INTERVALS =   5
X=          1.10      INTERVAL   1
X=          2.30      INTERVAL   2
X=          4.20      INTERVAL   3
X=          3.10      INTERVAL   2
X=          5.20      INTERVAL   3
X=         -2.00 IS OUT OF RANGE
X=          5.40      INTERVAL   3
X=         12.00 IS OUT OF RANGE
X=          8.50      INTERVAL   5
X=          9.20      INTERVAL   5
X=-12345670.00
BIN# 1 FREQ=  1 *
BIN# 2 FREQ=  2 **
BIN# 3 FREQ=  3 ***
BIN# 4 FREQ=  0
BIN# 5 FREQ=  2 **
```

Figure 9.21c. The results of running the program of Fig. 9.21a.

9.12. Matrix Multiplication Using Subroutines (Optional Section)

We now, by using subroutines, rewrite the program of Fig. 7.14a, which multiplied a two-dimensional matrix A by a one-dimensional matrix B and obtained as the result of a one-dimensional matrix C. The present program is shown in Fig. 9.22a. It performs matrix multiplications of the form C(K)=A(K,I)*B(I) where K is the number of rows in the matrices C and A, and I is the number of columns in matrix A and the number of rows in matrix B. The maximum value of K and I that the program can accommodate is 10, since we have used the dimension statement:

```
DIMENSION A(10,10), B(10), C(10)
```

We have modularized the program so that

1. The reading of the dimensions of the matrices and the checking that they do not exceed the dimensions specified in the DIMENSION statement are done in the subroutine PARAM.
2. The reading of the one-dimensional matrix is done in subroutine READ1.
3. The reading of the two-dimensional matrix is done in subroutine READ2.
4. The printing of the one-dimensional matrix is done in subroutine WRITE1.
5. The printing of the two-dimensional matrix is done in subroutine WRITE2.
6. The matrix multiplication is done in subroutine MULT.

We have called subroutine WRITE1 twice—once to print the matrix B; and once to print the matrix C, the result of the matrix multiplication B*A.

MATRIX MULTIPLICATION

```
C   PFRFORMS MATRIX MULTIPLICATION
        DIMENSION A(10,10), B(10), C(10)
        DATA C / 10*0.0 0  /
C       ...THE FOLLOWING IS USED IN THE MATRIX LABELING
        DATA MATA, MATB, MATC / 1HA, 1HB, 1HC /
C       ...PERFORMS MATRIX MULTIPLICATION OF THE FORM
C       ...C(K)=A(K,I)*B(I).
C       ...IN A(K,I): K=# UF ROWS; I=# U6 30LUMNS
C
C       ...READ AND CHECK I AND K
        CALL PARAM(K,I)
C       ...READ 1-DIMENSION MATRIX
        CALL READ1(B,I)
C       ...READ 2-DIMENSION MATRIX
        CALL READ2(A, K, I)
C
C       ...WRITE 1-DIMENSIUN MATRIX
        CALL WRITE1(B, I, MATB )
C       ...WRITE 2-DIMENSIUN MATRIX
        CALL WRITE2(A, K, I, MATA )
C
C       ...PERFORM MATRIX MULTIPLICATION
        CALL MULT(A, B, C, K, I )
C
C       ...WRITE RESULT MATRIX
        CALL WRITE1(C, K, MATC )
        STOP
        END
```

Figure 9.22a. *Main program.* Multiplies a one-dimensional matrix by a two-dimensional matrix.

```
      SUBROUTINE PARAM(K,I)
C   READS AND CHECKS DIMENSION OF MATRICES
      LOGICAL TESTHI, TESTLO
C     ...READ DIMENSIONS OF MATRICES
      READ(5,10) K, I
 10   FORMAT( 2I10 )
      WRITE(6,15)  K, I
 15   FORMAT(1X, 'K=', I5, '  I=', I5)
      TESTHI = (K. GT. 10) .OR. (I .GT. 10)
      TESTLO = (K .LT. 1) .OR. (I .LT. 1)
      IF( TESTHI .OR. TESTLO) WRITE(6,20) K, I
 20   FORMAT(1X, 'DIMENSIONS OUT OF RANGE: ROWS=', I3, ' COLUMNS=', I3)
      IF( TESTHI .OR. TESTLO ) STOP
         RETURN
      END
```

Subroutine PARAM. Reads the dimensions of the matrices and checks them for validity.

In CALL PARAM(I,K) the values of the number of rows, K, and the number of columns, I, are read. The constants on the first card shown in Fig. 9.22b are assigned to these variables. Thus 2 is assigned to K and 3 to I. The LOGICAL variable TEST HI assumes the value "true", if either the value of I or K is greater than 10. If this is the case, then the dimensions of A would be exceeded, so the subroutine prints an error message and then stops. The logical variable TESTLO assumes the value "true", if the value of I or K is less than 1. If this is the case, an execution-time error would occur, so the subroutine prints an error message and then stops. If the values of TESTHI and TESTLO are both "false", the RETURN is executed and control is returned to the main program.

In CALL READ1(B,I) we pass I the number of rows that B will have to subroutine READ. Since the value of the actual argument I is 2, when the READ statement in this subroutine is executed, the computer interprets it as

```
READ(5,10) (B(J), J=1,2 )
```

and because of the FORMAT, the computer reads the constants on the first card: 1.0, 2.0, and 3.0. Since the dummy array B corresponds to the actual array B, the constant 1.0 is assigned to the actual element B(1); 2.0 to B(2); and 3.0 to B(3).

In CALL READ2(A, K, I) we pass K (the number of rows A will have) and I (the number of columns A will have) to the subroutine. Since the value of the actual argument K is 2 and I is 3, the computer interprets the first two statements of the DO loop as

```
DO 20 M=1,2
   READ(5,10) ( A(M,J), J=1,3 )
```

Since the dummy array A corresponds to the actual array A, the elements of A are defined here.

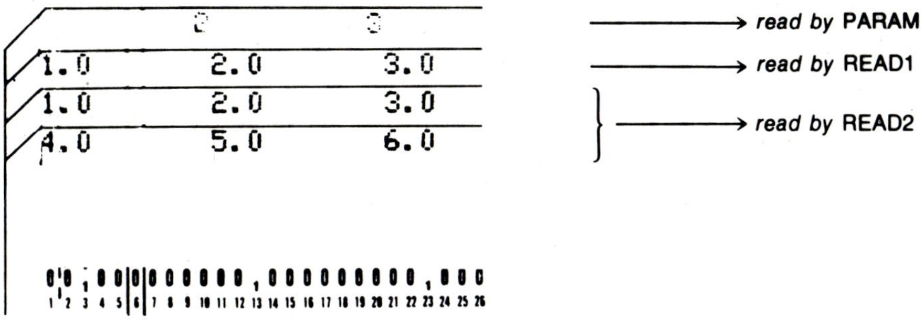

Figure 9.22b. The data card for Fig. 9.22a.

```
      SUBROUTINE READ1( B, I )
C   READS 1-DIMENSION MATRIX. I=# OF ROWS
      DIMENSION B(10)
      READ(5,10) (B(J), J=1, I)
 10   FORMAT( 8F10.0 )
      WRITE(6,20) (B(J), J=1,I)
 20   FORMAT( /1X, 8F10.2)
      RETURN
      END
```

Subroutine READ 1. Reads the one-dimensional matrices.

```
      SUBROUTINE READ2( A, K, I)
C   READS 2-DIMENSIONAL MATRICES
C   K= # OF ROWS; I= # OF COLUMNS
      DIMENSION A(10,10)
      DO 20 M = 1,K
         READ(5,10) (A(M,J), J=1,I )
 10      FORMAT( 8F10.0 )
         WRITE(6,15) ( A(M,J), J=1,I )
 15      FORMAT(    1X, 8F10.0)
 20   CONTINUE
      RETURN
      END
```

Subroutine READ 2. Reads two-dimensional matrices.

Subroutines WRITE1 and WRITE2 are similar to subroutines READ1 and READ2, respectively, except for essentially one obvious difference: a WRITE statement replaces a READ statement. When CALL WRITE1(B,I) is executed, the elements of the one-dimensional array B are printed. Since the value of the actual argument I is 2, the computer interprets the WRITE statement of the subroutine as

```
WRITE(6,10) (B(J), J=1,2)
```

and since the dummy array B corresponds to the actual array B, the elements of the actual array B are printed. Similarly when CALL WRITE2(A, K, I) is executed, the elements of A are printed.

This is the first time we have passed alphanumeric constants to a subroutine (or subprogram). Thus the constants 'A', 'B', and 'C' in

```
DATA MATA, MATB, MATC / 1HA, 1HB. 1HC /
```

are passed to subroutines which print the arrays. For instance, when

```
CALL WRITE1(B, I, MATB )
```

is executed, the alphanumberic constant 'B' that is stored in MATB (as well as the array B and the variable I) is passed to WRITE1. Since the actual argument MATB happens to be an INTEGER variable, the corresponding dummy argument must also be an INTEGER variable. Because we have used TITLE as this dummy argument, we must declare it to be an INTEGER in the subroutine. We could have used 'B' as the actual argument, thus writing CALL WRITE1 (B, I, 'B'). In that case, TITLE would not have to be declared INTEGER.

When CALL MULT(A, B, C, K, I) is executed, the matrix multiplication is performed. This multiplication is performed using dummy variables and arrays. The DO loop indices N and J are defined only in the subroutine

```
      DO 20 N=1,K
         DO 10 J=1,I
            C(N)=C(N)  + A(N,J)*B(J)
10       CONTINUE
20    CONTINUE
```

```
      SUBROUTINE WRITE1( B, I, TITLE )
C   WRITES 1-DIMENSION MATRIX.   I = # OF ROWS
      DIMENSION B(10)
      INTEGER TITLE
      WRITE(6,5) TITLE
 5    FORMAT(1X, 'MATRIX ', A1 )
C
      WRITE(6,10) (B(J) , J=1,I )
 10   FORMAT(1X, F10.1)
      RETURN
      END
```

Subroutine WRITE 1. Prints one-dimensional matrices.

```
      SUBROUTINE WRITE2(A, K, I, TITLE )
C   WRITES 2-DIMENSIONAL MATRICES
C   K= # OF ROWS, I = # OF COLUMNS
      DIMENSION A(10,10)
      INTEGER TITLE
      WRITE(6,5) TITLE
 5    FORMAT(1X, 'MATRIX ', A1 )
C
      DO 20 M=1,K
         WRITE(6,10) ( A(M,J), J=1,I )
 10      FORMAT(1X, 8F10.1)
 20   CONTINUE
      RETURN
      END
```

Subroutine WRITE 2. Prints two-dimensional matrices.

```
      SUBROUTINE MULT( A, B, C, K, I )
C   MULTIPLY MATRIX: C(K)=A(K,I)*B(I)
C   K= # OF ROWS; I= # OF COLUMNS
      DIMENSION A(10,10), B(10), C(10)
      DO 20 N=1,K
         DO 10 J=1,I
            C(N)=C(N) + A(N,J)*B(J)
 10      CONTINUE
 20   CONTINUE
      RETURN
      END
```

Subroutine MULT. Multiplies a two-dimensional matrix by a one-dimensional matrix.

However, each of the dummy variables (K and I) and arrays (A, B, and C) corresponds to one of the actual arguments passed to the subroutine. Thus since the dummy array C corresponds to the actual array C, after the DO loop is executed, the elements of the actual array C are defined. When the RETURN is executed, control is transferred to the main program. There, CALL WRITE1(C,K) is executed, and the elements of C are printed. The results of running the program are shown in Fig. 9.22c.

```
K=      2  I=      3

        1.00        2.00        3.00
          1.          2.          3.
          4.          5.          6.
MATRIX B
         1.0
         2.0
         3.0
MATRIX A
         1.0         2.0         3.0
         4.0         5.0         6.0
MATRIX C
        14.0
        32.0
```

Figure 9.22c. Running the program of Fig. 9.22a.

PROBLEMS

1. Write a program that produces a trigonometric table. The SINE, COSIN, and TANG should be statement functions that have arguments measured in degrees not radians.

2. Write a program that uses a function subprogram to sum the odd numbers from 1 to N.

3. Write a program that uses a function subprogram to find the smallest element in a one-dimensional array that has up to 10 elements.

4. Write a program that uses a function subprogram to find the product of the elements of a one-dimensional array that has up to 10 elements.

5. Write a program that uses function subprograms to find the sum of all the elements in an array that has 5 rows and 5 columns.

6. Write a program that uses function subprograms to find the product of all the elements in an array that has 5 rows and 5 columns.

7. Generalize the program of problem 5 for an N row, M column array.

8. Generalize the program of problem 6 for an N row, M column array.

9. Given an array that has 10 elements, write a program that places a number between the 3rd and the 4th element. In order to do this, the 4th element of the original array becomes the 5th element of the altered array, etc. Use one array for the original array and another array for the altered array; use a subroutine in writing the program.

10. Do problem 9 using only one array.

11. Generalize problem 9 so that you place the number between the Nth and $N +$ 1th element. Use one array for the original array and another for the altered array.

12. Do problem 11 using only one array.

13. Alter the program of Fig. 9.21a so that when it prints the histogram, it labels the minimum and maximum value for each bin.

14. Write a program that plots a histogram consisting of blanks plotted on a background of asterisks, e.g.,

```
          *********
BIN #1        *****
BIN #2         ****
          *********
```

Thus the first bin contains 4 events and the second bin contains 5 events.

15. Write a program that plots a sine curve. Do this by defining an array LINE which has blanks in all 101 elements, i.e., use DATA LINE / 101 * ' ' / to do this. Then place an asterisk in the appropriate element of LINE. The appropriate element I is given by I = 51 + 50*SIN(X). Thus when the value of X is zero an asterisk should be placed in the 51st element of LINE. The amplitude of the curve is 50. Plot the curve so that the X-axis is vertical. Note: If we use DATA ASTER / '*' / to define the character we will use for plotting, we must define ASTER as INTEGER (since the array LINE is INTEGER). If we do not declare ASTER to be INTEGER, LINE(I) = ASTER will produce an error.

16. Do problem 15 so that the X-axis is horizontal. Hint: use a two-dimensional array to do this.

17. Write a program that produces a histogram with vertical bars.

18. Using subroutines, write a program that performs any type of matrix multiplication.

10

Structured Programming

10.1. Introduction to Structured Programming

Structured Programming is based on a few concepts: GO TO-less programming; modularization of programs, and the top-down design of programs;* Professor E. W. Dijkstra introduced† the concept of avoiding GO TO statements in programs. GO TO statements make it difficult to follow the logic of a program and hence difficult to debug. Other languages (for instance PL/I) are better suited for writing GO TO-less programs. In previous chapters we have discussed how to avoid (when possible) GO TO statements in a FORTRAN program.

The introduction of the IF-THEN-ELSE into the proposed revision of ANS Standard FORTRAN will make GO TO-less programming in FORTRAN easier. Moreover, the IF-THEN-ELSE in conjunction with the WATFIV-S WHILE loop can make GO TO-less programming in FORTRAN as easy as it is in some other high level languages.

The top-down design of a program, including the modularization of programs along with programming management techniques, such as the Chief Programming Team (introduced by F. T. Baker), were employed at IBM in implementing a large information retrieval system for *The New York Times*. Because structured programming techniques were used, this job was done in record time, very few errors being generated along the way (one error was detected per 10,000 lines of code). One of the foremost proponents at IBM of top-down design is Harlan D. Mills,‡ who emphasizes the hierarchical structure of program development. This is part of top-down design, as we shall explain.

Flow charts are not the end-all for program design. In fact, a flow chart for any involved program is difficult to understand. Thus it is not surprising that at a meeting sponsored by the IEEE Computer Society at which 20% of the participants were from universities, 15% from government agencies, and 65% from industry, no one advocated the flow-charting of programs, or even mentioned it.§ Two approaches, each of which replaces flow charting and both of which are used in structured program design, are

* It also includes the concept of *levels of abstraction*; this means writing a module in several stages, each successive stage being less abstract. The final stage is the actual programmed module.

† E. W. Dijkstra, Programming considered as a human activity, *Proceedings of IFIP Congress 65*, Spartan Book, Washington, D.C. 1965.

‡ H. D. Mills, Top-down programming in logic systems, *in* "Debugging Techniques in Large Systems" (R. Rustin, ed.), pp. 41–55. Prentice-Hall, Englewood Cliffs, New Jersey, 1971.

§ William F. Ross, 1974 Lake Arrow Workshop, *Computer* Vol. 8, No. 6, p. 21 (1975).

MOTIVATION FOR PSEUDO LANGUAGE FLOW CHART FOR HISTOGRAMMING PROGRAM

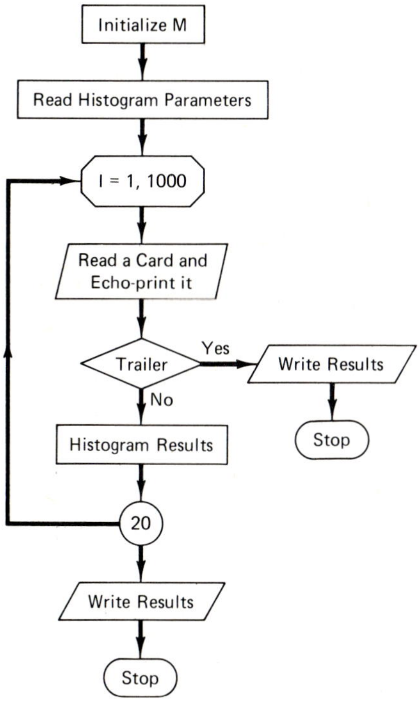

Figure 10.1. Flow chart for histogramming program. Although this flow chart is not complicated, it is harder to follow than the pseudo language equivalent in Fig. 10.2.

HIPO* (Hierarchical Input Process Output) diagrams and pseudo language (also known as Program Design Language abbreviated PDL). We first describe what a pseudo language is.

10.2. Program Design Aids: Pseudo Language

Before we write the program in a given language (here FORTRAN), we can write a description of the program using English phrases that are structured somewhat like the different programming statements but afford the writer more flexibility;† however, the different calculations are referred to simply by names. Thus a matrix multiplication would be referred to as PERFORM MATRIX MULTIPLICATION. The reason why such a language is called a pseudo language is that it does not actually have to correspond to any computer language. We now see how we would write the pseudo language equivalent of the histogramming program shown in Fig. 9.19a. We redisplay the flow chart for the program (originally shown in Fig. 9.19d) in Fig. 10.1 and the pseudo language equivalent in Fig. 10.2. There we show the beginning of a DO loop by writing START DO; and the end of a DO loop by writing END DO.

The way you indicate the beginning and the end of a loop is purely a matter of personal preference; what we have just presented here is but one of many ways of doing it. If you want to, you can indicate the parameters of the DO loop, e.g., you can write:

```
START DO :  VARY INDEX FROM 1 TO 1000 INCREMENTING BY 1
```

The following is one way of writing the test for the trailer and what the program should do when the trailer is detected:

```
IF TRAILER IS ENCOUNTERED THEN
    WRITE RESULTS AND STOP
```

What the program should do if the trailer is not encountered, we write as:

```
ELSE
    HISTOGRAM RESULTS
END IF
```

We have indented in this pseudo language version of the loop as we would have if we had written a DO loop and an IF statement. When we write the FORTRAN program, the pseudo language

```
IF TRAILER IS ENCOUNTERED THEN
    WRITE RESULTS AND STOP
ELSE
    HISTOGRAM RESULTS
END IF
```

* *HIPO-Hierarchical Input Process Output Documentation Technique*, IBM Corporation, Form No. SR-20-9413.

† The statements we will use are similar to constructions used in other high level languages and WATFIV-S.

PSEUDO LANGUAGE DESCRIPTION OF THE HISTOGRAMMING PROGRAM

```
INITIALIZE M
READ HISTOGRAM PARAMETERS
START DO.
   READ A CARD
   ECHO-PRINT IT
   IF TRAILER IS ENCOUNTERED THEN
      WRITE RESULTS AND STOP,
   ELSE
      HISTOGRAM RESULTS
   END IF
END DO.
WRITE RESULTS
STOP
```

Figure 10.2. Pseudo language equivalent of Fig. 10.1. This language resembles a computer language but does not have any particular grammar. A pseudo language program is used only in the planning stages of a program.

translates into

```
IF( TRAIL ) CALL PLOT(M,K)
   CALL HISTO( XMIN, DX, X, M)
```

since the program terminates in PLOT. If you are using WATFIV-S you can use the IF-THEN-ELSE to do this.

```
IF (TRAIL) THEN
    CALL PLOT(M,K)
ELSE
    CALL HISTO (XMIN, DX, X, M)
END IF
```

In conclusion, if you find using a flow chart easier than writing and using a pseudo language version of a program, then by all means use flow charts; however, remember that the trend is leading away from flow charts and to pseudo language formulations.

10.3. Top-Down Design and the Hierarchical Diagram

Top-down design is a tool, which, when properly used, makes program writing somewhat easier. William F. Ross characterizes* it as "code a little, test a little." When you write a program that has any degree of complexity, if you code the entire program and try to debug it, you will encounter a great deal of difficulty. If you use top-down design, you first write the main program in the proper code, but write only the program stubs (dummy modules) for the modules it calls. You then test the entire system—the main modules along with the program stubs. Next, you replace the program stubs one at a time with the proper code. Each time you substitute a coded module for a program stub, you test the entire system.

The order that you should follow in coding the modules is suggested by what is called a hierarchical diagram. For instance, if you follow the hierarchical diagram in Fig. 10.3 to write a program, you first write the main program and program stubs for subroutines A, B, C, and D and then test the system. You then have your choice of whether to write program A or B first, since both directly descend from the main program. Once you have written the program for A and B, you can then write the program for either C or D. You thus program from the top of the hierarchical diagram, down; hence the term top-down design. As we have said, after each new module is written, the newly modified system is tested. This allows us to detect errors resulting from the way the separate modules interact early in the writing of the program. It also allows us to localize where a difficulty occurs, because we know which module we have just added to the system.

In one version of top-down design, you program and test down a given branch of the diagram, before you program other modules. Thus the order that you would follow in programming the modules for the hierarchical diagram in Fig. 10.3 for this version of top-down design is: MAIN, A, C, D, and then B.

* See § footnote, page 488.

A HIERARCHICAL DIAGRAM (TOP-DOWN DESIGN)

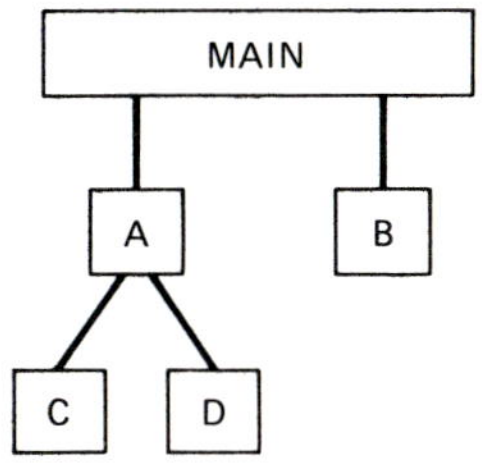

Figure 10.3. Hierarchical diagram for a program; A, B, C, and D represent modules. The diagram indicates what order should be followed in top-down writing of the program. One possible order is A, B, C, and then D. When we use top-down design, we first write the program for MAIN and program stubs (dummy modules) for A, B, C, and D. As we substitute a program for a program stub, we test the entire system (main program stubs and modules).

The hierarchical diagram for the histogramming program we studied in Fig. 9.21a is shown in Fig. 10.4a, and the order we will employ in coding and testing the program is shown in Fig. 10.4b.

CODE MAIN
CODE PARAM stub
CODE HISTO stub
CODE PLOT stub
TEST (MAIN with all stubs)
CODE PARAM
TEST (MAIN, PARAM with HISTO stub and PLOT stub)
CODE HISTO
TEST (MAIN, PARAM, HISTO and PLOT stub)
CODE PLOT
TEST (MAIN, PARAM, HISTO, PLOT)

The difference between, for example, "CODE PARAM Stub" and "CODE PARAM" is that "CODE PARAM" entails writing the program for PARAM; whereas "CODE PARAM Stub" obviously only involves writing the program stub. Whenever it is possible to make a subroutine a separate program without drastically changing its structure, it is a good idea to test a given subroutine even before we test how it interacts with the main program. In Fig. 9.20a we saw that subroutine PLOT can be made a separate program quite easily; similarly subroutine PARAM can be made a separate program. We will thus test these two subroutines as separate programs. Making HISTO a separate program requires drastically changing the structure of the subroutine (we leave this as an exercise for you to do). So we will not test it separately. Adding the testing of PARAM and PLOT to Fig. 10.4b, we obtain Fig. 10.4c.

HIERARCHICAL DIAGRAM FOR THE HISTOGRAMMING PROGRAM

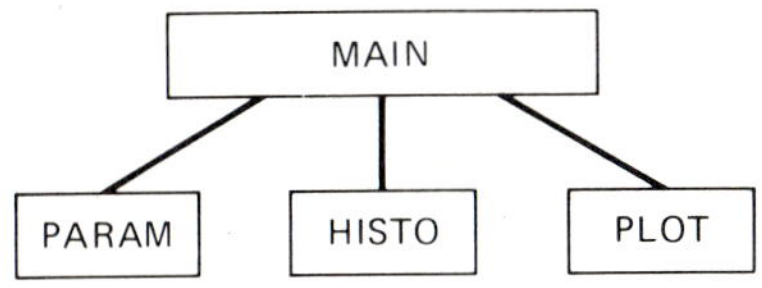

Figure 10.4a. Hierarchical diagram for histogramming program.

ORDER OF TOP-DOWN WRITING AND TESTING OF THE HISTOGRAMMING PROGRAM

CODE MAIN
CODE PARAM stub
CODE HISTO stub
CODE PLOT stub
TEST (MAIN with all stubs)
CODE PARAM
TEST (MAIN, PARAM with HISTO stub and PLOT stub)
CODE HISTO
TEST (MAIN, PARAM, HISTO and PLOT stub)
CODE PLOT
TEST (MAIN, PARAM, HISTO, PLOT)

Figure 10.4b. The order we will follow in the top-down writing and testing of the modules.

CODE MAIN
CODE PARAM stub
CODE HISTO stub
CODE PLOT stub
TEST (MAIN with all stubs)
CODE PARAM
TEST PARAM
TEST (MAIN, PARAM with HISTO stub and PLOT stub)
CODE HISTO
TEST (MAIN, PARAM, HISTO and PLOT stub)
CODE PLOT
TEST PLOT
TEST (MAIN, PARAM, HISTO, PLOT)

Figure 10.4c. The order which should be followed in the top-down writing and testing of a program, if the individual subroutines can be tested individually before they are used with the main program. Here we can test PARAM and PLOT separately.

10.4. Top-Down Testing

We now investigate how we test the histogramming program in a top-down manner. In Fig. 10.5a we present the main program and the program stubs for the three subroutines. Note at this stage that, insofar as the subroutines are concerned, we are only testing how the main program passes arguments to, and receives arguments from, the subroutines. The process of passing arguments to and from subroutines is called *interfacing*.

TOP-DOWN WRITING OF HISTOGRAMMING PROGRAM, STEP I (MAIN AND STUBS)

```
C  HISTOGRAMS AND PLOTS
      DIMENSION M(100)
      DATA M/ 100*0 /
C     ... READ LIMITS & INTERVAL SIZE FOR HISTOGRAM
      CALL PARAM( XMIN, DX, XMAX, K)
      WRITE(6,5) XMIN, XMAX, DX, K
 5    FORMAT(1X, ' MAIN' / 1X,
     1       'XMIN=', F15.3, '  XMAX=', F15.3, '  DX=', F15.3,
     2       'K=', I10)
C
C     ...HISTOGRAMS VALUES READ FROM CARDS
      DO 30 I=1, 1000
         READ(5,10) X
 10      FORMAT( F10.0 )
         WRITE(6,15) X
 15      FORMAT(1X, 'X=', F15.3 )
C        ...TEST FOR TRAILER
         IF( X .EQ. -12345678.0 ) CALL PLOT(M,K)
            CALL HISTO (XMIN, XMAX, DX, X, M, J )
            WRITE(6,25) J, ( M(L), L=1,10 )
 25            FORMAT(1X, ' MAIN.  BIN#', I3 / 1X, (5I5) )
 30   CONTINUE
C
C     ...USE IF TOO MANY CARDS ENCOUNTERED
      WRITE(6,40)
 40   FORMAT(1X, '1000 DATA CARDS ENCOUNTERED' )
      CALL  PLOT(M,K)
      END
```

Figure 10.5a. *Main Program.* The program echo-prints the value of all arguments passed to it from the program stubs. Since PLOT does not pass any arguments back to MAIN, its arguments are not echo-printed in MAIN.

In each of the subroutines, even when they are just stubs, we have printed the arguments that have been passed to it; e.g., in subroutine HISTO we have inserted

```
      WRITE(6,5)  XMIN, XMAX, DX, X , (M(I), I=1,10)
5     FORMAT(1X, 10('*') /
     1          1X, 'HISTO: XMIN=', F12.2, '  XMAX=', F12.2, '  DX=',
     2         F12.2, '  X=', F12.2 / (5I5) )
```

as is shown in Fig. 10.5a HISTO stub. We have started the printing with 10 asterisks so that the printing done by HISTO can be differentiated from the printing done by the other modules; similarly, before we return to the main program, we print 10 asterisks. Moreover, the string HISTO indicates the module doing the printing. We have followed this practice in the other modules (including the main program) except that PARAM (since it is called first) simply ends with 10 asterisks and PLOT (since it is called last) begins with 10 asterisks. We have printed only the first 10 elements of M since we want the output of this program to fit onto one page of this book. Under actual conditions, we would print all elements of the array. In each stub we have also inserted statements that assign values to the variables that are passed back to the main program and had previously not been defined (i.e., those variables whose values are either read or calculated in the module). Thus in subroutine PARAM we have written

```
XMIN=-10.0
XMAX=10.0
DX=2
K=10
```

and in HISTO stub we have added J=2 (this sets the bin number to two). In order to check that the arguments have been properly passed from the subroutines to the main program, we have inserted WRITE statements in the main program directly after the calling statements. Thus after PARAM is called, we have inserted

```
WRITE(6,5) XMIN, XMAX, DX, K
```

We have indicated in the accompanying FORMAT statement that these arguments were printed in the main program. Similarly after HISTO is called, we insert

```
WRITE(6,25) J, ( M(L), L=1,10 )
```

in the main program, where J and the array M are passed from HISTO to MAIN. Note, since PLOT does not pass any arguments back to MAIN, we do not echo-print their values in MAIN after PLOT is called. To test the operation of the main program itself, as usual, we have instructed the computer to echo-print each card it reads. Although it is impractical, for one set of test data we could have 1001 data cards. We could then test whether the program prints 1000 DATA CARD ENCOUNTERED in the case that the DO loop is completely executed.

```
SUBROUTINE PARAM( XMIN, DX, XMAX, K )
XMIN=-10.0
XMAX=10.0
DX=2
K=10
RETURN
END
```

Program stub for PARAM. Generates the values of the arguments that it will pass to MAIN.

```
      SUBROUTINE HISTO (XMIN, XMAX, DX, X, M, J)
      DIMENSION M(100)
      WRITE(6,5)  XMIN, XMAX, DX, X , (M(I), I=1,10)
5     FORMAT(1X, 10('*') /
     1         1X, 'HISTO: XMIN=', F12.2, '  XMAX=', F12.2, '  DX=',
     2        F12.2, '  X=', F12.2 / (5I5) )
      J=2
      WRITE(6,10)
10    FORMAT(1X, 10('*') )
      RETURN
      END
```

Program Stub for HISTO. Echo-prints all arguments passed to it from the MAIN program.

```
      SUBROUTINE PLOT( BIN, K)
      INTEGER BIN(100), BINAMT
      WRITE(6.5) K, (BIN(L), L=1, 10)
5     FORMAT(1X, 10('*') / 1X, 'PLOT.  # OF INTERVALS', I5 /(5I5) )
      STOP
      END
```

Program Stub for PLOT. Plots the values of the array the MAIN program passed to it.

In Fig. 10.5b we show a set of test data for the program in the stage of development shown in Fig. 10.5a. In Fig. 10.5c we show the results of running the program with these test data. We see from the first lines of results

```
MAIN
XMIN=          -10.000  XMAX=          10.000  DX=          2.000K=          10
```

that the arguments of PARAM are passed correctly to the main program. The program then reads the first data card and prints its value X=−11.000.

The printing that occurs after the first row of asterisks

```
HISTO: XMIN=       -10.00  XMAX=        10.00  DX=         2.00   X=       -11.00
   0     0     0     0     0
   0     0     0     0     0
```

shows that all the arguments were correctly passed to HISTO. Note that all the elements of M were set equal to zero in the main program, and we see that the array still contains zeros in HISTO.

The first three lines of printing that occur after the second row of asterisks

```
MAIN.  BIN#  2
   0     0     0     0     0
   0     0     0     0     0
```

indicate that the bin number (J=2) and the array M were correctly passed to the main program. The fourth line

```
X=          -6.000
```

indicates that a new card has been read. This entire process is repeated again and again, until the trailer is encountered and the program prints*

```
X=  -12345670.000
```

which occurs in Fig. 10.5c immediately before the last row of asterisks. Control is then transferred to PLOT, and the following is printed:

```
PLOT.  # OF INTERVALS   10
   0     0     0     0     0
   0     0     0     0     0
```

and we see that the number of intervals and the array M were correctly passed to PLOT. We thus see that the program does the correct thing when it encounters the trailer.

* This program was run on the IBM 360 using WATFIV. Thus the computer only prints the first 7 digits and follows it with zeros.

TEST DATA FOR STEP I

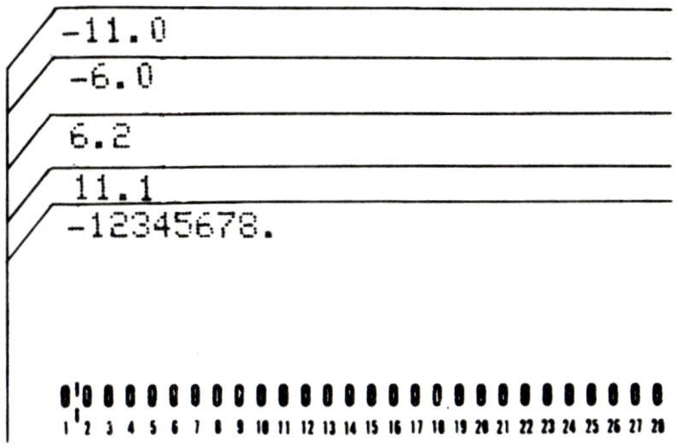

Figure 10.5b. Data that will test how the main program treats data, especially how it detects the trailer −12345678.0.

```
MAIN
XMIN=          -10.000   XMAX=             10.000  DX=             2.000K=          10
X=         -11.000
**********
HISTO: XMIN=         -10.00   XMAX=          10.00   DX=          2.00   X=        -11.00
   0     0     0     0     0
   0     0     0     0     0
**********
 MAIN.  BIN#  2
    0     0     0     0     0
   0     0     0     0     0
X=            -6.000
**********
HISTO: XMIN=         -10.00   XMAX=          10.00   DX=          2.00   X=         -6.00
   0     0     0     0     0
   0     0     0     0     0
**********
 MAIN.  BIN#  2
    0     0     0     0     0
   0     0     0     0     0
X=              6.200
**********
HISTO: XMIN=         -10.00   XMAX=          10.00   DX=          2.00   X=          6.20
   0     0     0     0     0
   0     0     0     0     0
**********
 MAIN.  BIN#  2
    0     0     0     0     0
   0     0     0     0     0
X=            11.100
**********
HISTO: XMIN=         -10.00   XMAX=          10.00   DX=          2.00   X=         11.10
   0     0     0     0  '  0
   0     0     0     0     0
**********
 MAIN.  BIN#  2
    0     0     0     0     0
   0     0     0     0     0
X=  -12345670.000
**********
PLOT.  # OF  INTERVALS    10
   0     0     0     0     0
   0     0     0     0     0
```

Figure 10.5c. Running the program of Fig. 10.5a, we see how the MAIN program interfaces (passes arguments to and from subroutines) with the other modules.

In Fig. 10.6a we show the program that will become the subroutine PARAM. All we have done is remove

```
SUBROUTINE PARAM ( XMIN, DX, XMAX, K )
```

from subroutine PARAM, which was shown in Fig. 9.19a. We have also replaced the RETURN with a STOP and made some printing modifications. In Fig. 10.6b we show the data that test whether PARAM correctly tests in

```
IF(K .GT. 100 ) WRITE(6,30) K
```

whether the value of K as calculated in

```
K=(XMAX - XMIN)/DX + 0.1
```

exceeds the dimension of array M (which is 100). The test data shown here have the value of 0.00 for XMIN, 0.10 for DX, and 20.0 for XMAX. This causes the program to write

```
TOO MANY BINS. K=  200
```

as is shown in Fig. 10.6c.

In Fig. 10.6d, we show the data that test whether PARAM correctly tests in

```
IF( K .LE. 0 )  WRITE(6,40) K
```

whether the values of XMAX and XMIN were by mistake interchanged during the keypunching. The test data have a higher value for XMIN than for XMAX, as shown in Fig. 10.6e.

```
XMIN=       20.00   DX=        1.00   XMAX=          0.00
# OF INTERVALS = -19
```

This causes the program to print also:

```
BAD VALUE OF K. K=  -19
CHECK HISTOGRAM PARAMETERS
```

The reason why K is −19, not −20, is that K = −20 + 0.1 or K = −19.9, and this is truncated to −19. The program PARAM was also tested to see that it accommodated correct data; however, we will show how it does when we combine the main program with subroutine PARAM (and stubs for HISTO and PLOT) as is shown in Fig. 10.7a.

In WATFIV-S, the first two IF statements in Fig. 10.6a could be replaced with

```
      IF(K .GT. 100 ) THEN
        WRITE(6,30) K
30      FORMAT(1X, 'TOO MANY BINS. K=', I5 )
        STOP
      END IF
```

A similar IF-THEN statement could replace the second two IF statements in Fig. 10.6a.

TOP-DOWN WRITING OF HISTOGRAMMING PROGRAM, STEP II (TESTING *PARAM*)

```
C   READS HISTOGRAMS PARAMETERS
      READ(5,10) XMIN, DX, XMAX
 10   FORMAT(3F10.0 )
      WRITE(6,20) XMIN, DX, XMAX
 20   FORMAT(1X, 'PARAM' /
     1       1X, 'XMIN=', F10.2, '  DX=', F10.2, '   XMAX=', F10.2)
C
C     ...CALCULATE # OF INTERVALS
      K=(XMAX - XMIN)/DX + 0.1
      WRITE(6,25) K
 25   FORMAT(1X,'# OF INTERVALS =', I4,
     1       / 1X, 10('*') )
C     ...CHECK FOR LIMITS ON # OF INTERVALS
      IF(K .GT. 100 ) WRITE(6,30) K
 30   FORMAT(1X, 'TOO MANY BINS. K=', I5 )
      IF( K .GT. 100) STOP
         IF( K .LE. 0 )  WRITE(6,40) K
 40      FORMAT(1X, 'BAD VALUE OF K. K=', I5 /
     1          1X, 'CHECK HISTOGRAM PARAMETERS' )
         IF( K .LE. 0 ) STOP
      STOP
      END
```

Figure 10.6a. The program that will become the subroutine PARAM.

TEST DATA FOR PARAM

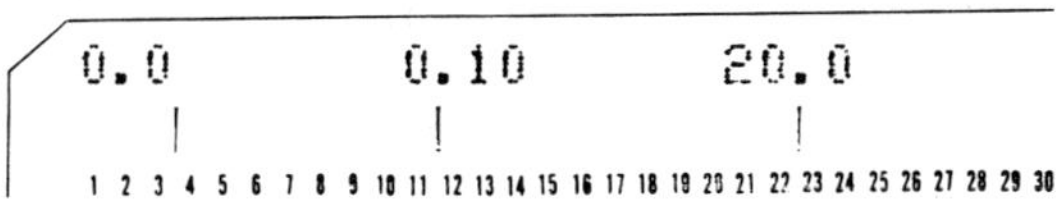

Figure 10.6b. Test data that will cause the dimensions of array M to be exceeded.

```
PARAM
XMIN=         0.00  DX=          0.10   XMAX=        20.00
# OF INTERVALS = 200
**********
TOO MANY BINS. K=  200
```

Figure 10.6c. Running the program of Fig. 10.6a with the data of Fig. 10.6b.

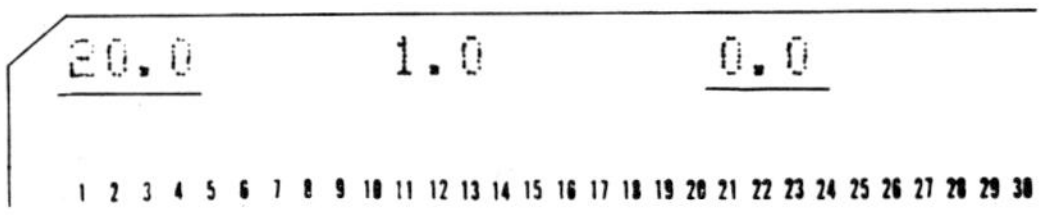

Figure 10.6d. Test data in which the values of XMAX and XMIN are by mistake interchanged. This produces a negative value of K.

```
PARAM
XMIN=        20.00  DX=          1.00   XMAX=         0.00
# OF INTERVALS = -19
**********
BAD VALUE OF K. K=  -19
CHECK HISTOGRAM PARAMETERS
```

Figure 10.6e. Running the program of Fig. 10.6a with the data of Fig. 10.6d.

TOP-DOWN WRITING OF THE HISTOGRAMMING PROGRAM, STEP III (MAIN, PARAM **AND STUBS)**

```
C  HISTOGRAMS AND PLOTS MOD. II
      DIMENSION M(100)
      DATA M/ 100*0 /
C     ... READ LIMITS & INTERVAL SIZE FOR HISTOGRAM
      CALL PARAM( XMIN, DX, XMAX, K)
      WRITE(6,5) XMIN, XMAX, DX, K
 5    FORMAT(1X, ' MAIN' / 1X,
     1        'XMIN=', F15.3, '   XMAX=', F15.3, '   DX=', F15.3,
     2        'K=', I10)
C
C     ...HISTOGRAMS VALUES READ FROM CARDS
      DO 30 I=1, 1000
         READ(5,10) X
 10      FORMAT( F10.0 )
         WRITE(6,15) X
 15      FORMAT(1X, 'X=', F15.3 )
C        ...TEST FOR TRAILER
         IF( X .EQ. -12345678.0 ) CALL PLOT(M,K)
            CALL HISTO (XMIN, XMAX, DX, X, M, J )
            WRITE(6,25) J, ( M(L), L=1,10 )
 25            FORMAT(1X, ' MAIN.  BIN#', I3 / 1X, (5I5) )
 30   CONTINUE
C
C     ...USE IF TOO MANY CARDS ENCOUNTERED
      WRITE(6,40)
 40   FORMAT(1X, '1000 DATA CARDS ENCOUNTERED' )
      CALL  PLOT(M,K)
      STOP
      END
```

Figure 10.7a. *Main Program.*

```
      SUBROUTINE PARAM(XMIN, DX, XMAX, K)
C   READS HISTOGRAMS PARAMETERS
      READ(5,10) XMIN, DX, XMAX
 10   FORMAT(3F10.0 )
      WRITE(6,20) XMIN, DX, XMAX
 20   FORMAT(1X, 'PARAM' /
     1        1X, 'XMIN=', F10.2, '  DX=', F10.2, '  XMAX=', F10.2)
C
C      ...CALCULATE # OF INTERVALS
      K=(XMAX - XMIN)/DX + 0.1
      WRITE(6,25) K
 25   FORMAT(1X,'# OF INTERVALS =', I4,
     1        / 1X, 10('*') )
C      ...CHECK FOR LIMITS ON # OF INTERVALS
      IF(K .GT. 100 ) WRITE(6,30) K
 30   FORMAT(1X, 'TOO MANY BINS. K=', I5 )
      IF( K .GT. 100) STOP
         IF( K .LE. 0 )  WRITE(6,40) K
 40      FORMAT(1X, 'BAD VALUE OF K. K=', I5 /
     1            1X, 'CHECK HISTOGRAM PARAMETERS' )
         IF( K .LE. 0 ) STOP
      RETURN
      END
```

Subroutine PARAM.

```
      SUBROUTINE HISTO (XMIN, XMAX, DX, X, M, J)
      DIMENSION M(100)
      WRITE(6,5)  XMIN, XMAX, DX, X , (M(I), I=1,10)
5     FORMAT(1X, 10('*') /
     1        1X, 'HISTO: XMIN=', F12.2, '  XMAX=', F12.2, '  DX=',
     2       F12.2, '  X=', F12.2 / (5I5) )
      J=2
      WRITE(6,10)
10    FORMAT(1X, 10('*') )
      RETURN
      END
```

Stub HISTO.

```
      SUBROUTINE PLOT( BIN, K)
      INTEGER BIN(100), BINAMT
      WRITE(6,5) K, (BIN(L), L=1, K )
5     FORMAT(1X, 10('*') / 1X, 'PLOT.  # OF INTERVALS', I5 /(5I5) )
      STOP
      END
```

Stub PLOT.

In Fig. 10.7b we show the test data for this run of the program. In Fig. 10.7c we show the results. The only way it differs from the results of running the program of Fig. 10.5a is that now the results start with

```
PARAM
XMIN=      -10.00   DX=          2.00   XMAX=         10.00
# OF  INTERVALS =  10
```

This is the echo-printing and the calculation of the number of intervals, all of which is done in subroutine PARAM. We see that the histogram parameters and the value of K are properly passed to the main program and then onto subroutine HISTO.

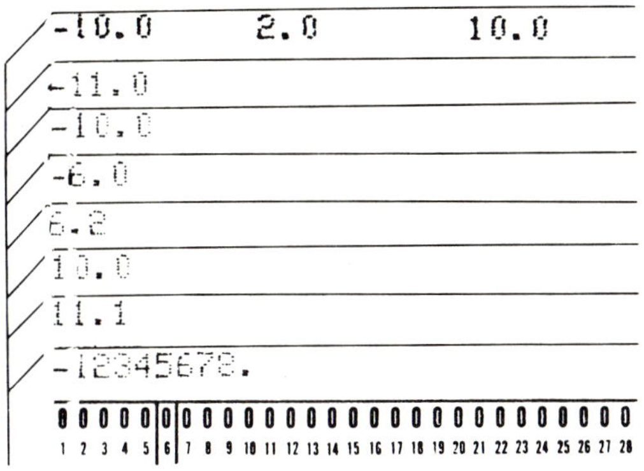

Figure 10.7b. Test data to check out the programs in Fig. 10.7a.

```
PARAM
XMIN=     -10.00  DX=         2.00   XMAX=        10.00  <——— Echo-printing done in PARAM
# OF INTERVALS =   10
**********
 MAIN
XMIN=           -10.000   XMAX=           10.000   DX=           2.000K=          10
X=          -11.000
**********
HISTO: XMIN=         -10.00   XMAX=         10.00   DX=         2.00   X=        -11.00
   0     0     0     0     0
   0     0     0     0     0
**********
 MAIN.  BIN#  2
    0     0     0     0     0
   0     0     0     0     0
X=          -6.000
**********
HISTO: XMIN=         -10.00   XMAX=         10.00   DX=         2.00   X=         -6.00
   0     0     0     0     0
   0     0     0     0     0
**********
 MAIN.  BIN#  2
    0     0     0     0     0
   0     0     0     0     0
X=           6.200
**********
HISTO: XMIN=         -10.00   XMAX=         10.00   DX=         2.00   X=          6.20
   0     0     0     0     0
   0     0     0     0     0
**********
 MAIN.  BIN#  2
    0     0     0     0     0
   0     0     0     0     0
X=          11.100
**********
HISTO: XMIN=         -10.00   XMAX=         10.00   DX=         2.00   X=         11.10
   0     0     0     0     0
   0     0     0     0     0
**********
 MAIN.  BIN#  2
    0     0     0     0     0
   0     0     0     0     0
 X=  -12345670.000
 **********
 PLOT.  # OF INTERVALS    10
    0     0     0     0     0
    0     0     0     0     0
```

Figure 10.7c. Running the program of Fig. 10.7a with the data of Fig. 10.7b. The only way this differs from the running of the main program with only stubs (Fig. 10.5c) is that now the echo-printed from PARAM is included.

In Fig. 10.8a, we show subroutine HISTO. When it is substituted for its stub, the histogramming program will consist of programs for MAIN, PARAM and HISTO and a program stub for PLOT. Because of lack of space we do not show all these programs assembled together; however, the results shown are for the running of the entire program. The test data shown in Fig. 10.8b test, among other things, whether a value of X that falls out of range will be detected in IF(LIMIT) WRITE (6,10) where LIMIT = (X .LT. XMIN) .OR. (X .GE. XMAX). Thus since the value of XMIN is -10.0 and the value of the first X is

TOP-DOWN WRITING OF THE HISTOGRAMMING PROGRAM, STEP IV (MAIN, PARAM, HISTO **AND STUB)**

```
      SUBROUTINE HISTO (XMIN, XMAX, DX, X, M, J)
C   HISTOGRAMS X
      DIMENSION M(100)
      LOGICAL LIMIT
      WRITE(6,5)  XMIN, XMAX, DX, X , (M(I), I=1,10)
 5    FORMAT(1X, 10('*') /
     1     1X, 'HISTO: XMIN=', F12.2, '  XMAX=', F12.2, '  DX=',
     2       F12.2, '  X=', F12.2 / (5I5) )
C          ...TEST THAT X IS WITHIN LIMITS
      LIMIT = (X .LT. XMIN) .OR. (X .GE. XMAX)
      IF( LIMIT ) WRITE(6,10)
 10   FORMAT(1H+, 25X,  'IS OUT OF RANGE'
     1      / 1X, 10('*') )
      IF( LIMIT ) RETURN
C          ...CALCULATE BIN NUMBER
         J = (X - XMIN) / DX + 1.0
         WRITE(6,20) J
 20      FORMAT(1H+, 25X, 'INTERVAL', I3 )
C          ...DO THE HISTOGRAMMING
         M(J) = M(J) + 1
         WRITE(6,30)
 30      FORMAT(1X, 10('*') )
         RETURN
      END
```

Figure 10.8a. *Subroutine HISTO*, which will be included with the main program, subroutine PARAM, and stub PLOT when the program is run.

```
-10.0      2.0        10.0
-11.0
-10.0
-6.0
6.2
10.0
11.1
-12345678.
1 2 3 4 5 6 7 8 9 10 11 12 13 14 15 16 17 18 19 20 21 22 23 24 25 26 27 28 29 30
```

Figure 10.8b. Test data. The values −11.0, 10.0 and 11.0 are outside the limits of the histogram; −10.0, −6.0 and 6.2 are within the limits.

−11.0, the computer, as we expect, prints IS OUT OF RANGE as is shown in Fig. 10.8c. Since the computer prints this in HISTO and previous information has been printed in HISTO, this message is no longer printed on the same line as X = −11.0, as it was in Chapter 9 when the complete program was run. Since the bin number J is not calculated in HISTO for a value of X that is out of range, the value of J is undefined. Since this program was run on a WATFIV system, when the main program prints the arguments passed to it from HISTO

```
MAIN.   BIN#UUU
    0      0      0      0      0
 0      0      0      0      0
```

it prints the value of the BIN # as being undefined, i.e., UUU. Also since the value of X was not histogrammed, the array M still contains only zeros when it is passed to the main program. The next value of X, which equals −10.000, is the minimum value of X which should be histogrammed. It should be placed in the first bin. Thus HISTO, after it prints the arguments passed to it, prints INTERVAL 1. Note that HISTO prints the contents of the array M before the present value of X has been added to it. After the array has been passed to the main program it has the present value of X added to it. Thus we see that the information is correctly passed to the main program when

```
MAIN.   BIN#   1
    1      0      0      0      0
 0      0      0      0      0
```

is printed, as is shown in Fig. 10.8c. We see here that the value of X is placed in the first element of the array.

We see that the values of X equal to −6.000 and 6.200 are histogrammed correctly. The next value of X is 10.000. This value is at the upper limit of the histogram. The value of J, if it were calculated in

```
J = (X - XMIN) / DX + 1.0
```

would be (10.0 + 10.0)/2.0 + 1.0, or 11. Thus it is not histogrammed and is eliminated by the test for LIMIT before J is calculated. Thus when the array M is printed when control is returned to the main program, the value of J is still 9 (as calculated for the previous value of X, i.e., 6.200), and the array M is not changed

```
MAIN.   BIN#   9
    1      0      1      0      0
 0      0      0      1      0
```

as compared to what was previously printed (in HISTO)

```
HISTO: XMIN=          -10.00          . . .          X=          10.00
  1      0      1      0      0
  0      0      0      1      0 IS OUT OF RANGE
```

The next value of X is 11.000; this is also out of range and is not histogrammed. Finally the trailer is encountered and the final histogram is printed

```
PLOT.   # OF INTERVALS    10
    1      0      1      0      0
    0      0      0      1      0
```

```
PARAM
XMIN=      -10.00   DX=        2.00   XMAX=        10.00
# OF  INTERVALS  =   10
**********
 MAIN
XMIN=          -10.000   XMAX=          10.000   DX=          2.000K=          10
X=         -11.000
**********
HISTO: XMIN=        -10.00   XMAX=        10.00   DX=        2.00   X=        -11.00
   0     0     0     0     0
   0     0     0     0     0  IS OUT OF RANGE
**********
 MAIN.   BIN#000
   0     0     0     0     0 <---- Since x = -11.0 is out of range, it is not histogrammed.
   0     0     0     0     0
X=         -10.000
**********
HISTO: XMIN=        -10.00   XMAX=        10.00   DX=        2.00   X=        -10.00
   0     0     0     0     0
   0     0     0     0     0  INTERVAL   1 <---- Interval for x = -10.0
**********
 MAIN.   BIN#   1
   1     0     0     0     0 <---- x = -10.0 is correctly histogrammed.
   0     0     0     0     0
X=          -6.000
**********
HISTO: XMIN=        -10.00   XMAX=        10.00   DX=        2.00   X=         -6.00
   1     0     0     0     0
   0     0     0     0     0  INTERVAL   3 <---- Interval for x = -6.0
**********
 MAIN.   BIN#   3
   1     0     1     0     0 <---- x = -6.0 is correctly histogrammed.
   0     0     0     0     0
X=           6.200
**********
HISTO: XMIN=        -10.00   XMAX=        10.00   DX=        2.00   X=          6.20
   1     0     1     0     0
   0     0     0     0     0  INTERVAL   9 <---- Interval for x = 6.2
**********
 MAIN.   BIN#   9
   1     0     1     0     0
   0     0     0     1     0 <---- x = 6.2 is correctly histogrammed.
X=          10.000
**********
HISTO: XMIN=        -10.00   XMAX=        10.00   DX=        2.00   X=         10.00
   1     0     1     0     0
   0     0     0     1     0  IS OUT OF RANGE
**********
 MAIN.   BIN#   9
   1     0     1     0     0 <---- Since x = 10.0 is out of range, it is not histogrammed.
   0     0     0     1     0
X=          11.100
**********
HISTO: XMIN=        -10.00   XMAX=        10.00   DX=        2.00   X=         11.10
   1     0     1     0     0
   0     0     0     1     0  IS OUT OF RANGE
**********
 MAIN.   BIN#   9
   1     0     1     0     0 <---- Since x = 11.0 is out of range, it is not histogrammed.
   0     0     0     1     0
X=  -12345670.000
**********
PLOT.   # OF INTERVALS    10
   1     0     1     0     0
   0     0     0     1     0
```

Figure 10.8c. Running the program of Fig. 10.8a with the data of Fig. 10.8b. Shown in HISTO is the array before the histogramming is done; shown in MAIN is the array after the histogramming is done. Whenever a value of X is out of range, the computer indicates this by printing a message in HISTO. Then the array printed in MAIN is not changed. When the value of X is within range, the array printed in MAIN is changed.

In Fig. 10.9a we show the program for PLOT. We have inserted NMAX = 6 to correspond with the dimensions of BIN and thus also with DATA BIN / 3, 8, 6, 4, 0, 7 /.

Thus we write

```
NMAX = 6
DO 20 J=1,NMAX
```

When this stub becomes subroutine PLOT, NMAX will be passed to it as an argument. Thus we will remove NMAX = 6. Since we already presented this program in Fig. 9.21a we will not discuss it further here; however, we again present the results of running it (see Fig. 10.9b).

In WATFIV-S, the two IF statements in Fig. 10.9a could also be written as

```
      IF ( BINAMT .EQ. 0) THEN
         WRITE(6,10) J,BINAMT
      ELSE
         WRITE(6,10) J,BINAMT, (ASTER,I=1, BINAMT)
10       FORMAT(1X, 'BIN#', I2, 1X, 'FREQ=', I3, 1X, 20A1)
      END IF
```

TOP-DOWN WRITING OF HISTOGRAMMING PROGRAM, STEP V (TESTING PLOT)

```
C   TESTING SUBROUTINE PLOT
      INTEGER BIN(6), BINAMT
C     ...BINAMT = # OF INTERVALS
C     ...PLACE VALUE IN HISTOGRAMMING ARRAY
      DATA BIN / 3, 8, 6, 4, 0, 7 /
      DATA ASTER / '*' /
C     ...PLOT HISTOGRAM
      NMAX = 6
      DO 20 J=1,NMAX
      BINAMT=BIN(J)
         IF( BINAMT .EQ. 0 ) WRITE(6,10) J, BINAMT
         IF( BINAMT .NE. 0 ) WRITE(6,10) J, BINAMT, (ASTER, I=1,BINAMT)
 10      FORMAT(1X, 'BIN#', I2, 1X, 'FREQ=', I3, 1X, 20A1)
 20   CONTINUE
      STOP
      END
```

Figure 10.9a. The program that will become subroutine PLOT. This program was tested in Chapter 9.

```
BIN# 1 FREQ=  3 ***
BIN# 2 FREQ=  8 ********
BIN# 3 FREQ=  6 ******
BIN# 4 FREQ=  4 ****
BIN# 5 FREQ=  0
BIN# 6 FREQ=  7 *******
```

Figure 10.9b. Running the program of Fig. 10.9a.

In Fig. 10.10a we show the complete program without any stubs. The sample set of data is shown in Fig. 10.10b and the results in Fig. 10.10c.

TOP-DOWN WRITING OF HISTOGRAMMING PROGRAM, STEP VI (MAIN, PARAM, HISTO AND PLOT)

```
C  HISTOGRAMS AND PLOTS MOD. IV
      DIMENSION M(100)
      DATA M/ 100*0 /
C     ... READ LIMITS & INTERVAL SIZE FOR HISTOGRAM
      CALL PARAM( XMIN, DX, XMAX, K)
      WRITE(6,5) XMIN, XMAX, DX, K
 5    FORMAT(1X, ' MAIN' / 1X,
     1        'XMIN=', F15.3, '  XMAX=', F15.3, '  DX=', F15.3,
     2        'K=', I10)
C
C     ...HISTOGRAMS VALUES READ FROM CARDS
      DO 30 I=1, 1000
         READ(5,10) X
 10      FORMAT( F10.0 )
         WRITE(6,15) X
 15      FORMAT(1X, 'X=', F15.3 )
C        ...TEST FOR TRAILER
         IF( X .EQ. -12345678.0 ) CALL PLOT(M,K)
            CALL HISTO (XMIN, XMAX, DX, X, M, J )
            WRITE(6,25) J, ( M(L), L=1,10 )
 25            FORMAT(1X, ' MAIN.  BIN#', I3 / 1X, (5I5) )
 30   CONTINUE
C
C     ...USE IF TOO MANY CARDS ENCOUNTERED
      WRITE(6,40)
 40   FORMAT(1X, '1000 DATA CARDS ENCOUNTERED' )
      CALL  PLOT(M,K)
      STOP
      END

      SUBROUTINE PARAM(XMIN, DX, XMAX, K)
C  READS HISTOGRAMS PARAMETERS
      READ(5,10) XMIN, DX, XMAX
 10   FORMAT(3F10.0 )
      WRITE(6,20) XMIN, DX, XMAX
 20   FORMAT(1X, 'PARAM' /
     1        1X, 'XMIN=', F10.2, '  DX=', F10.2, '  XMAX=', F10.2)
C
C     ...CALCULATE # OF INTERVALS
      K=(XMAX - XMIN)/DX + 0.1
      WRITE(6,25) K
 25   FORMAT(1X,  'PARAM' /
     1        1X,'# OF INTERVALS =', I4,
     2        / 1X, 10('*') )
C     ...CHECK FOR LIMITS ON # OF INTERVALS
      IF(K .GT. 100 ) WRITE(6,30) K
 30   FORMAT(1X, 'TOO MANY BINS. K=', I5 )
      IF( K .GT. 100) STOP
         IF( K .LE. 0 )  WRITE(6,40) K
 40      FORMAT(1X, 'BAD VALUE OF K. K=', I5 /
     1           1X, 'CHECK HISTOGRAM PARAMETERS' )
         IF( K .LE. 0 ) STOP
      RETURN
      END


      SUBROUTINE HISTO (XMIN, XMAX, DX, X, M, J)
C  HISTOGRAMS X
      DIMENSION M(100)
      LOGICAL LIMIT
      WRITE(6,5)  XMIN, XMAX, DX, X , (M(I), I=1,10)
 5    FORMAT(1X, 10('*') /
     1        1X, 'HISTO: XMIN=', F12.2, '  XMAX=', F12.2, '  DX=',
     2      F12.2, '  X=', F12.2 / (5I5) )
C        ...TEST THAT X IS WITHIN LIMITS
      LIMIT = (X .LT. XMIN) .OR. (X .GE. XMAX)
      IF( LIMIT ) WRITE(6,10)
 10   FORMAT(1H+, 25X, 'IS OUT OF RANGE'
     1       / 1X, 10('*') )
      IF( LIMIT ) RETURN
```

(Continued)

(Fig. 10.10a continued)

```
C          ...CALCULATE BIN NUMBER
           J = (X - XMIN) / DX + 1.0
           WRITE(6,20) J
 20        FORMAT(1H+, 25X, 'INTERVAL', I3 )
C          ...DO THE HISTOGRAMMING
           M(J) = M(J) + 1
           WRITE(6,30)
 30        FORMAT(1X, 10('*') )
           RETURN
       END

       SUBROUTINE PLOT( BIN, NMAX)
C   PLOTS HISTOGRAM
C   NMAX = # OF INTERVALS
       INTEGER BIN(100), BINAMT
       DATA ASTER / '*' /
       DO 20 J=1, NMAX
       BINAMT=BIN(J)
           IF( BINAMT .NE. 0 ) WRITE(6,10) J, BINAMT, (ASTER, I=1,BINAMT)
           IF( BINAMT .EQ. 0 ) WRITE(6,10) J, BINAMT
 10        FORMAT(1X, 'BIN#', I2, ' FREQ=', I3, 1X, 100A1 )
 20    CONTINUE
       STOP
       END
```

Figure 10.10a. Complete program without stubs. In subroutine PLOT, we have deleted the DATA statement and NAMX = 6 from Fig. 10.9a.

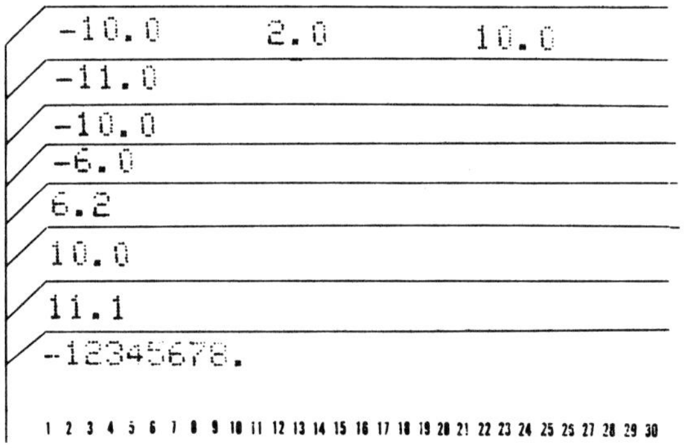

Figure 10.10b. The test data for Fig. 10.10a.

```
          $ENTRY
PARAM
XMIN=     -10.00   DX=       2.00   XMAX=      10.00
PARAM
# OF INTERVALS =  10
**********
 MAIN
XMIN=          -10.000   XMAX=           10.000   DX=            2.000K=          10
X=        -11.000
**********
HISTO: XMIN=        -10.00   XMAX=         10.00   DX=          2.00   X=        -11.00
   0     0     0     0     0
   0     0     0     0     0  IS OUT OF RANGE
**********
 MAIN.   BIN#000
     0     0     0     0     0
   0     0     0     0     0
X=        -10.000
**********
HISTO: XMIN=        -10.00   XMAX=         10.00   DX=          2.00   X=        -10.00
   0     0     0     0     0
   0     0     0     0     0  INTERVAL   1
**********
 MAIN.   BIN#   1
     1     0     0     0     0
   0     0     0     0     0
X=          -6.000
**********
HISTO: XMIN=        -10.00   XMAX=         10.00   DX=          2.00   X=         -6.00
   1     0     0     0     0
   0     0     0     0     0  INTERVAL   3
**********
 MAIN.   BIN#   3
     1     0     1     0     0
   0     0     0     0     0
X=          6.200
**********
HISTO: XMIN=        -10.00   XMAX=         10.00   DX=          2.00   X=          6.20
   1     0     1     0     0
   0     0     0     0     0  INTERVAL   9
**********
 MAIN.   BIN#   9
     1     0     1     0     0
   0     0     0     1     0
X=         10.000
**********
HISTO: XMIN=        -10.00   XMAX=         10.00   DX=          2.00   X=         10.00
   1     0     1     0     0
   0     0     0     1     0  IS OUT OF RANGE
**********
 MAIN.   BIN#   9
     1     0     1     0     0
   0     0     0     1     0
X=         11.100
**********
HISTO: XMIN=        -10.00   XMAX=         10.00   DX=          2.00   X=         11.10
   1     0     1     0     0
   0     0     0     1     0  IS OUT OF RANGE
**********
 MAIN.   BIN#   9
     1     0     1     0     0
   0     0     0     1     0
X=  -12345670.000
BIN# 1 FREQ=   1 *
BIN# 2 FREQ=   0
BIN# 3 FREQ=   1 *
BIN# 4 FREQ=   0
BIN# 5 FREQ=   0
BIN# 6 FREQ=   0
BIN# 7 FREQ=   0
BIN# 8 FREQ=   0
BIN# 9 FREQ=   1 *
BIN#10 FREQ=   0
```

Figure 10.10c. Running the MAIN program with subroutines PARAM, HISTO, and PLOT. When we run the program in production we will delete many of the print statements in the program.

10.5. Program Design Aids: the HIPO Diagram

Ideally, the Hierarchical Input Process Output (HIPO) diagram should precede the writing of a program; however, it can become somewhat involved. We present it here so that the student can see how the professional programmer plans a program. For the programs required in an introductory course, the student can dispense with HIPO diagrams.

In Fig. 10.11a we again show the hierarchical part of the HIPO diagram for the histogramming program shown in Fig. 10.5 through Fig. 10.10. The difference between a flow chart and a hierarchical diagram is that the latter shows the procedure that should be followed in top-down programming whereas the former shows the flow of logic in a program.

In Fig. 10.11b we show the IPO (Input, Process, Output) part for subroutine PARAM. The input part is on the extreme left of the diagram. It shows the variables that are the input to the subroutine: XMIN, DX, XMAX and how they are inputted—here via the card reader. An arrow points to the step in the subroutine where these variables are first entered. The process part indicates what the subroutine does; each step in the subroutine is described in a given line in pseudo language. On the right of each line is the number of the step in the process that will be executed next. To the right of the process part is what the subroutine outputs either as information to an output unit (here K is printed if the number of bins is too large) or as arguments that are returned to the calling program (here XMIN, DX, and K).

In order to explain the process part, each step is explained in a comment, as shown in Fig. 10.11c. Thus the comment for step 3 explains that "COMPUTE # OF BINS" is coded as K=(XMAX − XMIN) / DX + 0.1 and that 0.1 is included because of round-off error. On top of the process part are the modules that call the modules under discussion thus MAIN calls PARAM. On the bottom of the process part is the module to which control is returned—here back to MAIN.

HIERARCHICAL DIAGRAM FOR THE HISTOGRAMMING PROGRAM

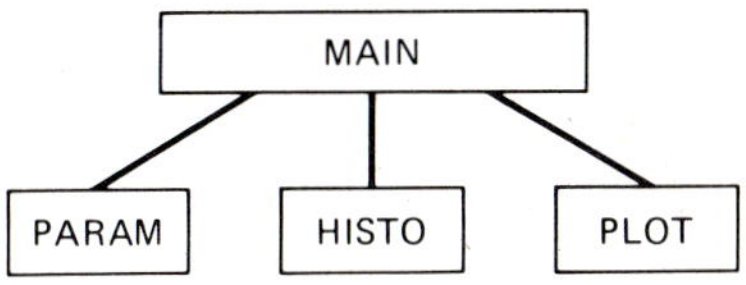

Figure 10.11a. Hierarchical diagram for the histogramming program.

INPUT-PROCESS-OUTPUT FOR PARAM

From MAIN

Input	Step	Process	Next Step	Output
XMIN DX XMAX →	1	READ	2	
	2	WRITE	3	
	3	COMPUTE # OF BINS	4	
Card reader	4	IF # OF BINS > 100 THEN WRITE MESSAGE AND STOP	5 →	K and message Printer
	5	IF # OF BINS ≤ 0 THEN WRITE MESSAGE AND STOP	6 →	K and message Printer
	6	RETURN	→	XMIN DX XMAX Subroutine arguments

To MAIN

Input **Process** **Output**

Figure 10.11b. INPUT-PROCESS-OUTPUT diagram for PARAM. The INPUT shows the variables either passed to PARAM or read by PARAM. The OUTPUT shows the variable either passed back to MAIN or printed. The PROCESS shows what the module does. On the right of the PROCESS we see the step executed next.

Step	Comment	
1	Variable read	Relation to X
	XMIN	Minimum value
	XMAX	Maximum value
	DX	Bin width
2	Echo-print what was read	
3	K = (XMAX − XMIN)/DX + 0.1 The 0.1 is in case of round-off error	
4	Prevents exceeding dimensions; Message is: TOO MANY BINS, K =	
5	Prevents zero or negative argument; Message is: BAD VALUE OF K. K = CHECK HISTOGRAM PARAMETERS	

Figure 10.11c. Comments for each step of the PROCESS part.

In Fig. 10.12a we show the IPO diagram for HISTO. Here, in the input part we show that XMIN, DX, and X are passed as arguments to the subroutine. In Fig. 10.12b we show the comments for Fig. 10.12a. We leave it to the reader as an exercise to write the HIPO diagrams for MAIN and PLOT.

10.6. Management-Programming Techniques

In a *structured walk through* (also called "team debugging"), the programmer of a certain module brings his part of the HIPO diagram (or the HIPO for a specific task he has been assigned to program), to a meeting of programmers including programmers whose modules will interface with his, and they go through each step of the program (hence the term "walk through") trying to find errors. At each step in the development of the program, from the pseudo language design stage to the finished code, and finally to the testing of the module, the programming team looks for, among other things, internal inconsistencies between interfacing modules and checks all facets of the program in order to see that the original specifications have been included.

The Chief Programmer Team* is a team centered around an expert programmer who designs the program and either designates parts of the task to other programmers or does the coding himself. The purpose of the other people on the team is to give the chief programmer the opportunity to concentrate on the design and perhaps the coding of the program without having to worry about such things as punching and testing code and documenting the program. As an example, a group librarian takes care of such things as running and documenting programs.

* F. T. Baker and Harlan D. Mills, Chief Programmer Teams, *Datamation*, Vol. 19, p. 58 (1973).

INPUT-PROCESS-OUTPUT FOR HISTO

From MAIN

Input	Step	Process	Next Step	Output
XMIN →	1	IF X OUT OF RANGE THEN	2/R →	Message
DX		WRITE MESSAGE AND RETURN		Printer
XMAX	2	COMPUTE CORRECT BIN AND	3 →	J
X		PRINT IT		Printer
Subroutine	3	INCREMENT PROPER BIN	4	
arguments	4	RETURN	→	M
				Subroutine arguments

To MAIN

Input **Process** **Output**

Figure 10.12a. INPUT-PROCESS-OUTPUT diagram for HISTO. In step 1 the subroutine either goes on to step 2 or returns to the main program. We thus have 2/R in the next step column.

Step	Comment
1	Use logical variable LIMIT LIMIT = (X .LT. XMIN)) .OR. (X .GE. XMAX) to determine if the value of X is out of RANGE. Then the computer prints OUT OF RANGE
2	J = (X − XMIN)/DX + 1.0
3	M(J) = M(J) + 1

Figure 10.12b. Comments for the PROCESS part of Fig. 10.12a.

10.7. Internal Documentation

There are two types of documentation used to describe a program: *external documentation* and *internal documentation*. External documentation is the term used to describe explanatory material that is not included in the program. It can include HIPO's and pseudo language descriptions of the program, as we have already described, and also other written material describing the program, its input and output. On the other hand, the term internal documentation is used to describe explanatory material punched on comment cards in the program and other aids used to clarify what the program is doing. Although external documentation is certainly useful, it is not always at the disposal of the person running the program. Therefore internal documentation should be as complete as possible; however, it should not overwhelm the reader or obscure the programming statements from him. The remainder of this section describes internal documentation.

The comment cards in the beginning of a program should briefly describe what the program does and the variables and arrays that will be used. It should indicate the compiler you ran the program on, whether you have followed ANS conventions, your name, and the date on which you write the program. If there are any subroutines, you should also list their names in the beginning of the program so that the person running the program can check that all the subroutines are in the deck. All of this is shown in Fig. 10.13.

The variable and array names should be chosen so that they indicate what the variables and arrays will be used for. All lists should be written so that the variable and array names in it are in alphabetical order. An exception to this is input and output lists, since clarity might demand that the input and output might be in nonalphabetical order. Output should be labeled so that it is immediately obvious what the output represents.

If certain data will cause an error in the program, then the program should produce an error message indicating the error and the portion of the program in which the error occurred. If you have subdivided your program into subroutines, then the subroutine name should be sufficient to localize the error.

PROPER DOCUMENTATION

```
C       PROGRAM HISTOGRAMS VALUES OF X
C
C                  VARIABLES AND ARRAYS USED
C       XMIN               IS THE MINIMUM VALUE OF X
C       DX                 IS THE BIN WIDTH
C       XMAX               IS THE MAXIMUM VALUE OF X
C       NUM                IS THE NUMBER OF BINS
C       BIN                IS THE HISTOGRAMMING ARRAY
C
C       SUBROUTINES USED:
C                  PARAM, HISTO, PLOT
C
C       WRITTEN BY S. MARATECK MAY 1976
C       RUN ON THE FORTRAN H COMPILER NYU IBM/370
C       ANS STANDARD FORTRAN FOLLOWED
```

Figure 10.13. Documentation that should be used in the beginning of a program; defining the variables, subroutines used, when written and by whom.

10.8. Generality, Independence, and Integrity

We now discuss three attributes a program can have that will prevent the need for altering the program sometime in the future.

A program exhibits one facet, *generality*, if it will do a task not only for one specific value of a variable but for any value of the variable. Thus a program that calculates 5! lacks generality as opposed to a program that calculates N! This type of generality is easy to incorporate into a program, as we have seen in preceding chapters.

A program exhibits another facet of *generality*, if it will perform many related tasks. For instance, a program that can produce a graph for any type of function exhibits a high degree of generality. This is harder to incorporate into a program and may not be worth the extra effort if you are designing a program solely for your own use.

Independence is the quality that makes it possible to run a program on many compilers. If you want to ensure that program has independence, you should limit your choice of statements to those prescribed by ANS Standard FORTRAN. Some other techniques that can be used include limiting A formats to A1, using INTEGER variables to specify the input/output units, e.g.,

```
READ( IN, 100) LIST
WRITE(NOUT, 100) LIST
```

where IN and NOUT are defined in the beginning of the program.

This last technique allows you to change the input and output units in the beginning of the program so that they match the unit numbers used on another computer on which you may want to run your program.

As we have explained previously, *integrity* is the quality that enables a program to accommodate any type of data, whether valid or not. The degree of integrity in a program can vary from the ability of a program to detect data that has been entered in the wrong mode—we use the ERR option* in the READ statement for this—to the ability of the program to detect data that will cause an overflow or cause the dimensions of an array to be exceeded, to the ability of the program to calculate a result for any valid data. An example of a program that does not exhibit this last quality is one written to calculate the solution to the quadratic equation $AX^2 + BX + C = 0$, but which produces an error if the value of A is zero. The subroutine PARAM, as shown in Fig. 10.6a, does not really exhibit the properties of integrity, since if we leave the field for DX blank (on the first input card) as shown in Fig. 10.14a the value of DX is zero. Thus the computer could not calcuiate the value of K as given by

```
K=(XMAX - XMIN)/DX + 0.1
```

Since neither the computer (nor anyone else, for that matter) can divide by zero, an error condition occurs, as is shown in Fig. 10.14b when the program of Fig. 10.6a is run with the data.

* By writing READ(5,10, ERR = 100) *list*, we instruct the program to transfer control to statement 100 if any input errors are detected on the data card whose values will be assigned to the variables in the list.

INCORPORATING INTEGRITY INTO A PROGRAM

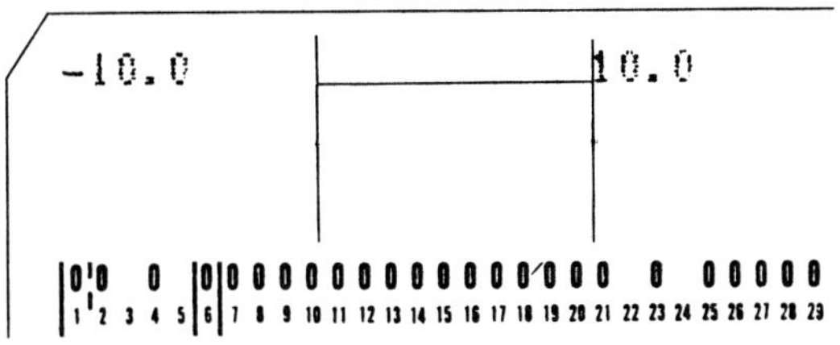

Figure 10.14a. Test data for PARAM in which the value of DX (the second field) is blank. Thus DX will be assigned the value zero.

```
PARAM
XMIN=     -10.00  DX=       0.0   XMAX=      10.00

IHC209I IBCOM - PROGRAM INTERRUPT (P) - DIVIDE CHECK OLD PSW IS  FF95000FA215EA34 .

TRACEBACK  ROUTINE  CALLED FROM ISN   REG. 14   REG. 15   REG.  0   REG.  1
```

Figure 10.14b. Running PARAM with the data of Fig. 10.14a. Since K = (XMAX − XMIN)/DX + 0.1 the computer would divide by zero when it evaluates K. Thus it prints the error message. Thus PARAM did not have integrity.

In Fig. 10.14c we rewrite the program with the inclusion of

```
      IF( DX .EQ. 0.0 ) WRITE(6,22)
22    FORMAT(1X, 'DX WAS READ AS 0.0' /
     1        1X, 'CHECK FOR BLANK FIELD ' )
      IF( DX .EQ. 0.0 ) STOP
```

Then when the program is run with the data of Fig. 10.14a, the program detects the errors as is shown in Fig. 10.14d.

In WATFIV-S, this IF could be rewritten as

```
      IF( DX .EQ. 0) THEN
          WRITE (6,22)
22        FORMAT(1X, 'DX WAS READ AS 0.0' /
     1               1X, 'CHECK FOR BLANK FIELD')
          STOP
      END IF
```

```
C   DEMONSTRATES INTEGRITY
C   READS HISTOGRAMS PARAMETERS
       READ(5,10) XMIN, DX, XMAX
 10    FORMAT(3F10.0 )
       WRITE(6,20) XMIN, DX, XMAX
       20   FORMAT(1X, 'PARAM' /
           1        1X, 'XMIN=', F10.2, '   DX=', F10.2, '   XMAX=', F10.2)
C
C      ...CHECK FOR ZERO INTERVAL WIDTH
       IF( DX .EQ. 0.0 ) WRITE(6,22)
 22    FORMAT(1X, 'DX WAS READ AS 0.0' /
      1        1X, 'CHECK FOR BLANK FIELD ' )
       IF( DX .EQ. 0.0 ) STOP
C
C         ...CALCULATE # OF INTERVALS
          K=(XMAX - XMIN)/DX + 0.1
          WRITE(6,25) K
 25       FORMAT(1X,'# OF INTERVALS =', I4,
      1           / 1X, 10('*') )
C         ...CHECK FOR LIMITS ON # OF INTERVALS
          IF(K .GT. 100 ) WRITE(6,30) K
 30       FORMAT(1X, 'TOO MANY BINS. K=', I5 )
          IF( K .GT. 100) STOP
             IF( K .LE. 0 )  WRITE(6,40) K
 40          FORMAT(1X, 'BAD VALUE OF K. K=', I5 /
      1              1X, 'CHECK HISTOGRAM PARAMETERS' )
             IF( K .LE. 0 ) STOP
       STOP
       END
```

Figure 10.14c. The PARAM rewritten so that it checks for a zero value of DX.

```
PARAM
XMIN=    -10.00  DX=       0.00  XMAX=      10.00
DX WAS READ AS 0.0
CHECK FOR BLANK FIELD
```

Figure 10.14d. Running Fig. 10.14c with the data of Fig. 10.14a. Zero values of DX are now detected in the program.

PROBLEMS

1. Write a pseudo language program for subroutine PARAM.
2. Write a pseudo language program for subroutine HISTO.
3. Write a pseudo language program for subroutine PLOT.
4. Write a pseudo language program to find the largest element in a one-dimensional array.
5. Write a pseudo language program to find the largest element in an array that has 10 rows and 10 columns.
6. How would you test the subroutines in problem 5 in a top-down manner?
7. Write the HIPO diagram for the main program in the histogramming program.
8. Write the HIPO diagram for subroutine PLOT.
9. How would you test the matrix multiplication program shown in Fig. 9.22a in a top-down manner.
10. Write the HIPO diagrams for problem 9.

11

The COMMON Statement and The EQUIVALENCE Statement

11.1 The COMMON Declaration Statement

We have learned that, in order to pass information to and from a subroutine, we must place the variables that represent this information as arguments of the subroutine. For instance, in the histogramming program shown in Fig. 9.16a, we used the subroutine calls:

```
CALL PARAM(XMIN, DX, XMAX, X, K)
CALL HISTO( XMIN, DX, XMAX, X, M)
CALL WRITE(K,M)
```

There is an alternative way of transmitting information to and from subroutines PARAM, HIST, and WRITE; we can use what is called a COMMON statement. The easiest way of using a COMMON statement is to list in a COMMON statement in the main program all the variables and arrays you want to transmit (or pass) between the main program and all the subroutines. For the above discussion—the program of Fig. 9.16a—this list would consist of: XMIN, DX, XMAX, X, K, M. We would thus write the COMMON statement as

```
COMMON XMIN, DX, XMAX, X, K, M
```

What this statement does is to establish an area in the computer's memory in which the variables and arrays mentioned in the COMMON list will be stored. This area of the memory is "held in common" by all the sections of the program—the main program and subroutines—in which the COMMON statement is used. We will explain this by referring to Fig. 11.1a.

USING THE COMMON STATEMENT

```
C   PROGRAM USES SUBROUTINES TO HISTOGRAM
C   SHOWS USE OF COMMON
       COMMON XMIN, DX, XMAX, X, K, M
       DIMENSION M(100)
C      ...SINCE M IS IN COMMON, YOU CAN'T ZERO IT IN A DATA STATEMENT
       DO 5  J=1,100
          M(J) = 0
 5     CONTINUE
       CALL PARAM
C
C      ...HISTOGRAMS VALUES READ FROM CARDS
       DO 30 I=1, 1000
          READ(5,10) X
 10       FORMAT( F10.0 )
          WRITE(6,15) X
 15       FORMAT(1X, 'X=', F15.3 )
C         ...TEST FOR TRAILER
          IF( X .EQ. -12345678.0 ) CALL PLOT
             CALL HISTO
 30    CONTINUE
C
C      ...USE IF TOO MANY CARDS ENCOUNTERED
       WRITE(6,40)
 40    FORMAT(1X. '1000 DATA CARDS ENCOUNT5R54' )
       CALL  PLOT
       STOP
       END
```

Figure 11.1a. *Main Program.* Every variable and array that appears in the COMMON statement is passed to every subroutine that has the COMMON statement in it. We have zeroed the array M in a DO loop, not in a DATA statement, because a variable that appears in a DATA statement cannot be used in a COMMON list.

```
       SUBROUTINE PARAM
       COMMON XMIN, DX, XMAX, X, K, M
C   READS HISTOGRAMS PARAMETERS
       READ(5,10) XMIN, DX, XMAX
 10    FORMAT(3F10.0 )
       WRITE(6,20) XMIN, DX, XMAX
 20    FORMAT(1X, 'XMIN=', F10.2, '  DX=', F10.2, '  XMAX=', F10.2)
C
C      ...CALCULATE # OF INTERVALS
       K=(XMAX - XMIN)/DX + 0.1
       WRITE(6,25) K
```

(Continued)

In this program we have rewritten the program of Fig. 9.16a by using COMMON statements. The fact that COMMON XMIN, DX, XMAX, X, K, M appears in all the subroutines as well as in the main program means that the variable names and array names used in the COMMON list are the same ones that are used in all the subroutines and in the main program. For instance, since XMIN, DX, XMAX, and K are defined in subroutine PARAM, and since they all appear in the COMMON list, they are defined in the main program as well after the RETURN is executed.

```
 25     FORMAT(1X,'# OF INTERVALS =', I4 )
C       ...CHECK FOR LIMITS ON # OF INTERVALS
        IF(K .GT. 100 ) WRITE(6,30) K
 30     FORMAT(1X, 'TOO MANY BINS. K=', I5 )
        IF( K .GT. 100) STOP
           IF( K .LE. 0 )  WRITE(6,40) K
 40        FORMAT(1X, 'BAD VALUE OF K. K=', I5 /
     1            1X, 'CHECK HISTOGRAM PARAMETERS' )
           IF( K .LE. 0 ) STOP
        RETURN
        END
```

Subroutine PARAM. Uses XMIN, DX, XMAX to determine the number of bins, K. In order to avoid errors, the COMMON lists in all the subroutines and in the main program should be the same.

```
        SUBROUTINE HISTO
        COMMON XMIN, DX, XMAX, X, K, M
C   HISTOGRAMS X
        DIMENSION M(100)
        LOGICAL LIMIT
C          ...TEST THAT X IS WITHIN LIMITS
        LIMIT = (X .LT. XMIN) .OR. (X .GE. XMAX)
        IF( LIMIT ) WRITE(6,10)
 10     FORMAT(1H+, 25X,  'IS OUT OF RANGE' )
        IF( LIMIT ) RETURN
C          ...CALCULATE BIN NUMBER
           J = (X - XMIN) / DX + 1.0
           WRITE(6,20) J
 20        FORMAT(1H+, 25X, 'INTERVAL', I3 )
C          ...DO THE HISTOGRAMMING
           M(J) = M(J) + 1
           RETURN
        END
```

Subroutine HISTO. Uses XMIN, DX, X to histogram values into the array M.

```
        SUBROUTINE PLOT
        COMMON XMIN, DX, XMAX, X, K, M
C   PLOTS HISTOGRAM
C   K = # OF INTERVALS
        INTEGER M(100), BINAMT
        DATA ASTER / '*' /
        DO 20 J=1, K
        BINAMT=M(J)
           IF( BINAMT .NE. 0 ) WRITE(6,10) J, BINAMT, (ASTER, I=1,BINAMT)
           IF( BINAMT .EQ. 0 ) WRITE(6,10) J, BINAMT
 10        FORMAT(1X, 'BIN#', I2, ' FREQ=', I3, 1X, 100A1 )
 20     CONTINUE
        STOP
        END
```

Subroutine PLOT. Uses K and M to print the results of the histogramming procedure.

The COMMON statement must be placed in the beginning of a program before any executable statement and before any DATA statements—we have thus placed it in the beginning of all the subroutines and in the beginning of the main program. Once a variable or an array has appeared in a COMMON statement, it cannot appear in the argument list of a subroutine. Since we have placed all the arguments of all the subroutines in the COMMON statement, all the calls to the subroutines no longer contain any arguments. We thus write in the main program of Fig. 11.1a: CALL PARAM, CALL HISTO, CALL PLOT. Similarly, the first statement of each subroutine no longer contains any arguments. We thus begin the three subroutines with SUBROUTINE PARAM, SUBROUTINE HISTO, and SUBROUTINE PLOT, respectively. In Fig. 11.1b we show the data cards for the program and in Fig. 11.1c we show the results of running the program.

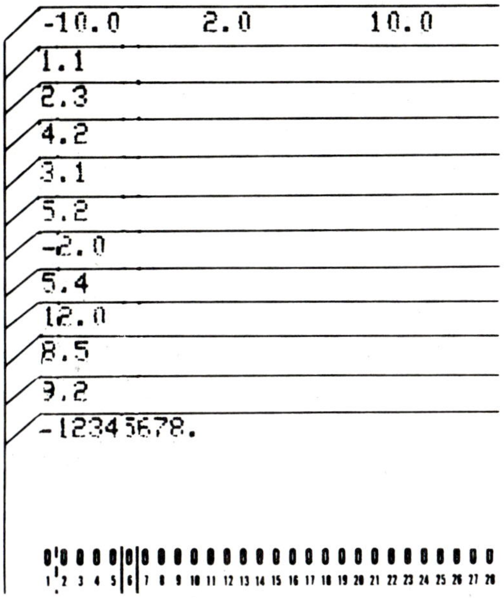

Figure 11.1b. The data cards for Fig. 11.1a.

```
XMIN=     -10.00  DX=       2.00  XMAX=      10.00
# OF INTERVALS =  10
X=             0.000          INTERVAL  6
X=             1.100          INTERVAL  6
X=             2.300          INTERVAL  7
X=             4.200          INTERVAL  8
X=             3.100          INTERVAL  7
X=             5.200          INTERVAL  8
X=            -2.000          INTERVAL  5
X=             5.400          INTERVAL  8
X=            12.000          IS OUT OF RANGE
X=             8.500          INTERVAL 10
X=             9.200          INTERVAL 10
X=  -12345670.000
BIN# 1 FREQ=  0
BIN# 2 FREQ=  0
BIN# 3 FREQ=  0
BIN# 4 FREQ=  0
BIN# 5 FREQ=  1 *
BIN# 6 FREQ=  2 **
BIN# 7 FREQ=  2 **
BIN# 8 FREQ=  3 ***
BIN# 9 FREQ=  0
BIN#10 FREQ=  2 **
```

Figure 11.1c. Running the program of Fig. 11.1a.

The COMMON list works in the same way as does the list of arguments used in subroutines. Used in its simplest form, a variable (or an array) in a COMMON list in a subroutine that occupies the same position in the list as a variable (or an array) in the main program, corresponds to that variable (or array). In other words, they label the same memory location. For instance, the main program of Fig. 11.1a has the statement COMMON XMIN, DX, XMAX, X, K, M (where M is an array). If a subroutine has the statement COMMON A, B, C, D, L, N (where N is an array), then the variable A in the subroutine would label the same memory location that XMIN does in the main program; B labels the same memory location as DX does; C as XMAX does; X as D does; L as K does; and the array N would label the same memory locations as the array M does (assuming that M and N have the same dimensions). All of this is shown in Table 11.1. As in the case of the argument lists in subroutines, the modes of the corresponding variables and arrays would have to agree. Thus here A, B, C, and D on the one hand, and XMIN, DX, XMAX, and X on the other, are all REALs. Whereas K and M on the one hand and L and N on the other are all INTEGERs.

The COMMON statement can also be used with function subprograms. Thus if you wanted to pass the variable *N* to the INTEGER function FACT, you could write the first two lines of the function as

```
INTEGER FUNCTION FACT
COMMON N
```

It is important to note that we initialized the array M in a DO loop in this program as opposed to initializing it in a DATA statement, as we did in the program of Fig. 9.16c. The reason is that in ANS standard FORTRAN and on many other systems, you cannot place a variable or an array in a DATA statement, if that variable or array appears in the list of the type of COMMON statement we have just studied. You must use what is called a BLOCK DATA subprogram—we will study this later on in this chapter. In WATFOR/WATFIV this restriction does not apply.

You can, if you wish, write the list of items in two or more COMMON statements. Thus if the COMMON in the main program is COMMON XMIN, DX, X, K, M, we can write the COMMON in the subroutine, as, for instance:

```
COMMON XMIN, DX
COMMON X, K, M
```

or

```
COMMON XMIN
COMMON DX, X, K, M
```

etc., as long as the order of the items in the combined list is not changed. Thus, it would be an error to write in a subroutine

```
COMMON X, K, M
COMMON XMIN, DX
```

since, for instance, X would correspond to XMIN in the main program.

Some examples of proper ways of partitioning the COMMON statement are shown in Table 11.2, and some improper ways of partitioning are shown in Table 11.3.

HOW COMMON **LISTS CORRESPOND**

		COMMON area									
COMMON XMIN, DX, XMAX, X, K, M (Main Program COMMON):	Memory locations										
	Main Program names	XMIN	DX	XMAX	X	K	M(1)	M(2)	M(3)		M(100)
COMMON A, B, C, D, L, N (Subroutine COMMON):	Subroutine names	A	B	C	D	L	N(1)	N(2)	N(3)		N(100)

Table 11.1. How variables and arrays in two COMMON statements correspond. Both COMMON statements label the same region of the memory even though the lists have different variable names.

CORRECT PARTITIONING OF COMMON **LISTS**

Equivalent statements to COMMON XMIN, DX, X, K, M		
COMMON XMIN, DX COMMON X, K, M	COMMON XMIN, DX COMMON X, K COMMON M	COMMON XMIN COMMON DX, X, K, M

Table 11.2. You can break up a COMMON list and write the portions of the list in different COMMON statements; however, the order of the items in the list must be preserved.

INCORRECT WAYS OF PARTITIONING A COMMON **LIST**

Improper ways of writing COMMON XMIN, DX, X, K, M		
COMMON X, K, M COMMON XMIN, DX	COMMON X, K COMMON XMIN, DX COMMON M	COMMON DX, X, K, M COMMON XMIN

Table 11.3. The partitionings of the COMMON list shown here are incorrect because the order of the items is not the same as in the original COMMON list.

There is a case in which the COMMON list in a subroutine can be shorter than the COMMON list in the main program. In the main program of Fig. 11.2 the COMMON statement is

```
COMMON XMIN, DX, XMAX, X, K, M
```

In the subroutine PARAM we can write the COMMON as

```
COMMON XMIN, DX, XMAX, X, K
```

i.e., we omit M. This is because the computer examines the list of items in the subroutine COMMON, starting from the left, and matches items one by one with the corresponding items in the main program COMMON. After it matches the last item in the subroutine list—here K—it stops. In subroutine PARAM, since the array M is not used and since it is to the right of the last item in the main program COMMON that is used, we can omit M from the COMMON statement in the subroutine.

If there were a subroutine that, for instance, used only the variables DX and X, it would be a mistake to write the COMMON for it as COMMON DX, X, since DX would be matched with XMIN in the main program and X would be matched with DX in the main program. For this reason, although subroutine PLOT only uses K and M out of all the items in the main program COMMON, it would create an error if we wrote the subroutine COMMON as COMMON K, M—so we use the same COMMON statement we used in the main program. Because of the possibility of making the type of error just discussed, it is best to duplicate the COMMON card you punched for the main program and use it as the COMMON statement for all the subroutines.

SHORTENING COMMON **LISTS**

```
C   USING VARIABLE LENGTH LISTS IN COMMON STATEMENTS
        COMMON XMIN, DX, XMAX, X, K, M
        DIMENSION M(100)
                .
                .
                .
        CALL PARAM
                .
                .
                .
        CALL HISTO
                .
                .
                .
        CALL PLOT
        STOP
        END

        SUBROUTINE PARAM
        COMMON XMIN, DX, XMAX, X, K
                .
                .
                .
        RETURN
        END
                .
                .
                .
        SUBROUTINE HISTO
        COMMON XMIN, DX, XMAX, X, K, M
        DIMENSION M(100)
                .
                .
                .
        RETURN
        END

        SUBROUTINE PLOT
        COMMON XMIN, DX, XMAX, X, K, M
        DIMENSION M(100)
                .
                .
                .
        RETURN
        END
```

Figure 11.2. You can shorten COMMON lists in subroutines only by dropping unneeded items that appear at the end of the COMMON list; e.g., we omit M in PARAM by writing COMMON XMIN, DX, XMAX, X, K.

It is possible to use both subroutine arguments and a COMMON statement. Thus we could have written all the COMMON statements as

```
COMMON XMIN, DX, K
```

and used M, X, and XMAX as subroutine arguments when appropriate. Thus we would have written the CALLs as: CALL PARAM(X, XMAX), CALL HISTO(X, XMAX, M), and CALL PLOT(M): and the SUBROUTINE statements as: SUBROUTINE PARAM(X, XMAX), SUBROUTINE HISTO(X, XMAX, M), and SUBROUTINE PLOT(M), as is shown in Fig. 11.3.

The restrictions on the list of variables in a COMMON statement are quite similar* to the restrictions on the list of dummy arguments (we remember that the dummy arguments are the ones that appear in the argument list of the subroutine itself). Only variables and array names can appear in a COMMON statement. An array element, for instance, cannot appear in a COMMON statement, as is shown in Table 11.4. One reason for this is that we can dimension an array in a COMMON statement. Thus

```
COMMON XMIN, DX, X, K, M(100)
```

means that the array M has 100 elements, not that the element M(100) shares the same location as the corresponding entry in another COMMON statement. If you dimension an array in a COMMON statement, you cannot dimension the array in a DIMENSION statement. Thus

```
DIMENSION M(100)
COMMON XMIN, DX, X, K, M(100)
```

would cause a compile-time error.

* The difference is that you cannot place an array that will have a variable dimension in a COMMON statement, whereas you can place such an array in an argument list.

```
C  SIMULTANEOUS USE OF COMMON AND ARGUMENTS
      COMMON XMIN, DX, K
      DIMENSION M(100)
          .
          .
          .
      CALL PARAM(X, XMAX)
          .
          .
          .
      CALL HISTO( X, XMAX, M)

      CALL PLOT( M )
      STOP
      END

      SUBROUTINE PARAM( X, XMAX)
      COMMON XMIN, DX, K
          .
          .
          .
      RETURN
      END

      SUBROUTINE HISTO( X, XMAX, M)
      COMMON XMIN, DX, K
      DIMENSION M(100)
          .
          .
          .
      RETURN
      END

      SUBROUTINE PLOT ( M )
      COMMON XMIN, DX, K
      DIMENSION M(100)
          .
          .
          .
      RETURN
      END
```

Figure 11.3. Any item that appears in an argument list cannot appear in the COMMON list. Note that all the COMMON lists are the same.

DIMENSIONING ARRAYS IN COMMON **LISTS**

DIMENSION M(100) COMMON XMIN, DX, X, K, M	Correct
⇕	
COMMON XMIN, DX, X, K, M(100)	Correct
⇕ (crossed out)	
DIMENSION M(100) COMMON XMIN, DX, X, K, M(100)	Incorrect

Table 11.4. You can dimension an array in a DIMENSION statement or in a COMMON list, but you cannot dimension one array in both.

11.2. Labeled COMMON

The type of COMMON statement we have previously discussed is called *unlabeled* COMMON—we will see the reason for this term shortly. As we have discussed, when we use an unlabeled COMMON statement, in most cases if we do not want any execution-time errors, we have to use COMMON statements that have the same number of items in the COMMON list in the main program as in all the subroutines. There is a type of COMMON statement that always allows you to partition the items that originally you would have placed in the unlabled COMMON so that now you do not have to repeat all the items in every COMMON statement list. In other words, it allows you to share only a few items with a given subroutine. The statement that allows you to do this is called a labeled COMMON statement.

In Fig. 11.4 we rewrite the program of Fig. 11.3 using labeled COMMON. One example of the labeled COMMON statements used is

```
COMMON / PARAMS / XMIN, DX, XMAX, X
```

PARAMS is the name or label of the region in the computer's memory that contains the variables XMIN, DX, XMAX, and X.

In the program of Fig. 11.4 we have used three labeled COMMON regions; PARAMS, BINS, and ARRAY. The labeled COMMONs do not have to appear in every subroutine, only in those in which a portion or all of the items in its list will be used. Thus PARAMS does not appear in subroutine PLOT; ARRAY does not appear in subroutine PARAM; and BINS does not appear in subroutine HISTO. It so happens that here all the labeled COMMONs are used in the main program, so they all appear there. In general, this need not be the case. In subroutine HISTO, we have written the list for the common region ARRAY as

```
COMMON / ARRAY / N
```

Thus array N here corresponds to array M in the main program. Consequently, we have dimensioned N in HISTO. The rule determining what names you can use for these labels are the same that apply to the formation of subroutine names: the name must start with a letter and may contain digits but no special characters. The maximum number of characters in the label name is the same as in a variable name—on most systems, six. Just as in the case of a subroutine name, a label does not have any mode. Thus it can start with any letter. The label name must appear between slashes. it is followed by the list of arrays and variables that will be held in COMMON in the labeled region. The label name can be the same as a variable name used in the program. The computer will make no connection between the two. You cannot use the same name for a label name as you do for a subprogram. Thus, it would have been an error to use PARAM instead of PARAMS as the label name because PARAM is a subroutine name.

LABELED COMMON

```
C   USE OF LABELED COMMON
      DIMENSION M(100)
      COMMON / PARAMS / XMIN, DX, XMAX, X
      COMMON / BINS / K
      COMMON / ARRAY / M
        .
        .
        .
      CALL PARAM
        .
        .
        .
      CALL HISTO
        .
        .
        .
      CALL PLOT
      STOP
      END

      SUBROUTINE PARAM
      COMMON / PARAMS / E, F, G, H
      COMMON / BINS / L
        .
        .
        .
      RETURN
      END

      SUBROUTINE HISTO
      DIMENSION N(100)
      COMMON / ARRAY / N
      COMMON / PARAMS / XMIN, DX, XMAX, X
        .
        .
        .
      RETURN
      END

      SUBROUTINE PLOT
      DIMENSION M(100)
      COMMON / BINS / K
      COMMON / ARRAY / M
        .
        .
        .
      RETURN
      END
```

Figure 11.4. By using labeled COMMON you can decrease the number of items that have to appear in a list. The name of the labeled COMMON appears between slashes. XMIN, DX, XMAX, X in the first appearance of labeled COMMON / PARAMS / correspond to E, F, G, H in the second appearance of PARAM; K in the first appearance of COMMON / BINS / corresponds to L in the second appearance of BINS; M in the first appearance of labeled COMMON / ARRAY / corresponds to N in the second appearance of ARRAY.

Any other time the label name—here PARAMS—appears as a label in another COMMON statement, the variable and arrays that follow it correspond to the original list—here XMIN, DX, XMAX, X. Thus when

```
COMMON / PARAMS / E, F, G, H
```

appears in subroutine PARAM, the variable E corresponds to XMIN; F to DX; G to XMAX; and H to X in the main program, all of which is shown in the table for Fig. 11.4. Note: As opposed to the items in the list, the label name cannot change. If you change the label name, you have defined a new COMMON region in the computer's memory. Also, as opposed to unlabeled COMMON, the number of memory locations indicated in the list for a given labeled COMMON must agree. Thus, under no circumstance could we have written COMMON / PARAMS / XMIN, DX, XMAX, X in the main program, for example, and COMMON / PARAMS / XMIN, DX in a subroutine.

		Labeled COMMON area (PARAMS)			
	Memory locations				
COMMON / PARAMS / XMIN, DX, XMAX, X (Main Program COMMON)	Main program names	XMIN	DX	XMAX	X
COMMON / PARAMS / E, F, G, H (Subroutine COMMON)	Subroutine names	E	F	G	H

Table for Fig. 11.4. Shows that XMIN, DX, XMAX, and X label the same locations as E, F, G, and H; this is because they comprise the list in labeled COMMON / PARAMS /.

Labeled COMMONs can be combined as shown in Fig. 11.5. Thus

```
COMMON / PARAMS / XMIN, DX, XMAX, X / BINS / K
```

combines labeled COMMON regions PARAM and BINS. Similarly,

```
COMMON / PARAMS / XMIN, DX, XMAX, X / ARRAY / N
```

combines labeled COMMON regions PARAMS and ARRAY.

In subroutine PARAM we see how we can partition a labeled COMMON statement into two labeled COMMON statements. Thus

```
COMMON / PARAMS / E, F
COMMON / PARAMS / G, H
```

is equivalent to COMMON / PARAMS / E, F, G, H. As in the case of unlabeled COMMON, the order of the COMMON statements in a given labeled COMMON will determine how the variables in the list will be associated with the variables in the list of the same labeled COMMON in another part of the program. Thus, had we reversed the order in labeled COMMON / PARAMS and written them:

```
COMMON / PARAMS / G, H
COMMON / PARAMS / E, F
```

this would be equivalent to COMMON / PARAMS / G, H, E, F.

As with unlabeled COMMON, you can dimension an array in labeled COMMON. Thus, for instance, in the program of Fig. 11.5, we could replace

```
DIMENSION M(100)
COMMON / ARRAY / M
```

with COMMON / ARRAY / M(100).

COMBINING AND PARTITIONING LABELED COMMON

```
C   COMBINING AND PARTITIONING LABELED COMMON
      DIMENSION M(100)
      COMMON / PARAMS / XMIN, DX, XMAX, X / BINS / K
      COMMON / ARRAY / M
              .
              .
              .
      CALL PARAM
              .
              .
              .
      CALL HISTO
              .
              .
              .
      CALL PLOT
      STOP
      END

      SUBROUTINE PARAM
      COMMON / BINS / L
      COMMON / PARAMS / E, F
      COMMON / PARAMS / G, H
              .
              .
              .
      RETURN
      END

      SUBROUTINE HISTO
      DIMENSION N(100)
      COMMON / PARAMS / XMIN, DX, XMAX, X / ARRAY / N
              .
              .
              .
      RETURN
      END

      SUBROUTINE PLOT
      DIMENSION M(100)
      COMMON / BINS / K / ARRAY / M
              .
              .
              .
      RETURN
      END
```

Figure 11.5. COMMON / PARAMS / E, F followed by COMMON / PARAMS / G, H are equivalent to COMMON / PARAMS / E, F, G, H. Also COMMON / PARAMS / XMIN, DX, XMAX, X/ BINS / K is equivalent to COMMON / PARAMS / XMIN, DX, XMAX, X followed by COMMON / BINS / K.

If we want to, we can use unlabeled COMMON together with labeled COMMON. Thus, we could have substituted unlabeled COMMON for labeled COMMON PARAM and have written COMMON XMIN, DX, XMAX, X, and have used it with labeled COMMON / BINS and labelled COMMON / ARRAY /, as shown in Fig. 11.6. Although there can be many labeled regions in a program—here BINS and ARRAY—there can only be one unlabeled COMMON region used in a program.

Since we are not using the variables in the unlabeled COMMON in subroutine PLOT, we have not used the unlabeled COMMON STATEMENT in this subroutine. However, it would not have been an error if we had placed the unlabeled COMMON there anyway.

COMBINING LABELED AND UNLABELED COMMON **IN ONE SUBROUTINE**

```
C      COMBINING LABELED AND UNLABELED COMMON
C   IN ONE SUBROUTINE
       COMMON XMIN, DX, XMAX, X
       COMMON / BINS / K
       COMMON / ARRAY / M
       DIMENSION M(100)
              .
              .
              .
       CALL PARAM
              .
              .
              .
       CALL HISTO
              .
              .
              .
       CALL PLOT
       STOP
       END

       SUBROUTINE PARAM
       COMMON XMIN, DX, XMAX, X
       COMMON / BINS / L
              .
              .
              .
       RETURN
       END

       SUBROUTINE HISTO
       COMMON XMIN, DX, XMAX, X
       COMMON / ARRAY / N
       DIMENSION N(100)
              .
              .
              .
       RETURN
       END

       SUBROUTINE PLOT
       COMMON / BINS / K
       COMMON / ARRAY / M
       DIMENSION M(100)
              .
              .
              .
       RETURN
       END
```

Figure 11.6. Labeled COMMON and unlabeled COMMON can be combined in the same program. The unlabeled COMMON does not have to appear in every subroutine.

Unlabeled COMMON is also called *unnamed* COMMON or *blank* COMMON. One reason why the term *blank* COMMON is used is that we can write COMMON XMIN, DX, X as

```
COMMON // XMIN, DX, X
```

i.e., unlabeled COMMON is equivalent to labeled COMMON except that a blank (or no space at all) is left between the two slashes.

In Fig. 11.7 we show how we can combine labeled and unlabeled COMMON in one statement.

Thus we can combine COMMON XMIN, XMAX, DX, X and COMMON / BINS / K in the statement COMMON XMIN, DX, XMAX, X / BINS / K. It is even permissible to place the labeled COMMON in the middle of the unlabeled COMMON list. Thus we can place labeled COMMON / BINS in the middle of the list XMIN, DX, XMAX, X, i.e., we can combine COMMON XMIN, DX, XMAX, X and COMMON / BINS / L in COMMON XMIN / BINS /L / / DX, XMAX, X as shown in Fig. 11.7 subroutine PARAM. The double slash indicates that the variables that follow them are in unlabeled COMMON. Thus the unlabeled COMMON list in subroutine PARAM is XMIN, DX, XMAX, X, as it is in the main program.

Certainly the type of combinations of unlabeled COMMON shown in Fig. 11.5, and especially those shown in Fig. 11.7, do not aid the reader in understanding the program. Thus, we do not consider them good programming techniques. In fact, they seem almost to test the reader's ability to decode a cipher. We have included these examples only to help the student read a program that for some unknown reason, uses these techniques.

COMMON

> The form of the COMMON statement is: COMMON followed by the list of variables and arrays. If there is more than one item in the list, the items must be separated by commas. An array may be dimensioned in a COMMON statement. If it is, you cannot also dimension it in a DIMENSION statement as well. Examples:
>
> COMMON A, B, C(100), D, I, J
> COMMON INTER(100), X, Y, Z(10)

LABELED COMMON

> The form of the labeled COMMON statement is: COMMON followed by /; followed by the labeled COMMON name; followed by /; followed by the list of variables and arrays. If there is more than one item in the list, the items must be separated by commas. An array may be dimensioned in a COMMON statement. If it is, you cannot also dimension it in a DIMENSION statement as well. Examples:
>
> COMMON / LAB1 / A, B, C(100), D, I, J
> COMMON / LAB2 / INTER(100), X, Y, Z(10)

COMBINING LABELED AND UNLABELED COMMON IN ONE STATEMENT

```
C   COMBINING LABELED AND UNLABELED COMMON
C   IN ONE STATEMENT
      COMMON XMIN, DX, XMAX, X / BINS / K
      COMMON / ARRAY / M
      DIMENSION M(100)
          .
          .
          .
      CALL PARAM
          .
          .
          .
      CALL HISTO
          .
          .
          .
      CALL PLOT
      STOP
      END

      SUBROUTINE PARAM
      COMMON XMIN / BINS / L /__/ DX, XMAX, X
          .
          .
          .
      RETURN
      END

      SUBROUTINE HISTO
      COMMON / ARRAY / N /____/ XMIN, DX, XMAX, X
      DIMENSION N(100)
          .
          .
          .
      RETURN
      END

      SUBROUTINE PLOT
      COMMON / BINS / K / ARRAY / M
      DIMENSION M(100)
          .
          .
          .
      RETURN
      END
```

Figure 11.7. Unlabeled COMMON is also called blank COMMON because it can be represented by two slashes. COMMON XMIN, DX, XMAX, X / BINS / K is equivalent to COMMON XMIN, DX, XMAX, X and COMMON / BINS / K. Similarly, COMMON / ARRAY / N / / XMIN, DX, XMAX, X is equivalent to COMMON / ARRAY / N and COMMON XMIN, DX, XMAX, X.

11.3. BLOCK DATA Subroutine

With most systems (not WATFOR/WATFIV), in a DATA statement you cannot initialize variables or arrays that appear in unlabeled COMMON—they must be in labeled COMMON. ANS Standard FORTRAN is even more restrictive than this: not only must the variables to be initialized in a DATA statement appear in labeled COMMON, but indeed they must be initialized in a separate subprogram called a BLOCK DATA subprogram. This subprogram can contain only declaration statements; it cannot contain executable statements (and thus no FORMAT statements), not even a RETURN.

In Fig. 11.8a we again present the program that shows how to plot a histogram. The array BIN used for the histogram is initialized in a DATA statement. If we wanted to write this program using subroutines and placing BIN in COMMON, in ANS Standard FOR-

MOTIVATING BLOCK DATA

```
C  DEMONSTRATES HOW TO PLOT A HISTOGRAM
      INTEGER BIN(6), BINAMT
C     ...PLACE VALUE IN HISTOGRAMMING ARRAY
      DATA BIN / 3, 8, 6, 4, 0, 7 /
      DATA ASTER / '*' /
C     ...PLOT HISTOGRAM
      DO 20 J=1,6
      BINAMT=BIN(J)
         IF( BINAMT .EQ. 0 ) WRITE(6,10) J, BINAMT
         IF( BINAMT .NE. 0 ) WRITE(6,10) J, BINAMT, (ASTER, I=1,BINAMT)
 10      FORMAT(1X, 'BIN#', I2, 1X, 'FREQ=', I3, 1X, 20A1)
 20   CONTINUE
      STOP
      END
```

Figure 11.8a. Program demonstrates plotting of a histogram.

TRAN we would have to use the BLOCK DATA subprogram to initialize BIN. We have done this in Fig. 11.8b.

The main program reads NMAX the number of lines of the histogram we want printed from the data card shown in Fig. 11.8c. NMAX is placed in unlabeled COMMON—although we could just have easily placed it in labeled COMMON. The main program calls subroutine PLOT.

If we had wanted to, we could have included in PLOT the DATA statement which initializes BIN. However, in order to show the use of BLOCK DATA, we have not done this. Again, if we had used BIN as an argument of PLOT, i.e., written SUBROUTINE PLOT(BIN), we could initialize BIN in a DATA statement in the main program or any subroutine. But since we have decided to place BIN in COMMON and since BIN will be initialized in another subprogram, we must place it in a labeled COMMON—we have placed it in labeled common A. BIN is then initialized in the BLOCK DATA subprogram.

```
BLOCK DATA
COMMON / A / BIN
INTEGER BIN(10)
DATA BIN / 3*1, 4*8, 3, 2, 4 /
END
```

We note that this subprogram must begin with the words BLOCK DATA. It is often tempting to include a RETURN in the subprogram, but this would be an error. The results of running the program are shown in Fig. 11.8d.

USING THE BLOCK DATA **SUBPROGRAM**

```
C   DEMONSTRATES USE OF BLOCK DATA
      COMMON NMAX
C     ...NMAX = # OF LINES IN THE HISTOGRAM
      READ(5,10) NMAX
 10   FORMAT( I10 )
      WRITE(6,20) NMAX
 20   FORMAT(1X, '# OF LINES IN THE HISTOGRAM = ', I3)
      CALL PLOT
      STOP
      END

      SUBROUTINE PLOT
C   PLOTS HISTOGRAM
      COMMON NMAX
      COMMON / A / BIN
      INTEGER BIN(10), BINAMT
      DATA ASTER / '*' /
      DO 20 J=1, NMAX
      BINAMT=BIN(J)
         IF( BINAMT .NE. 0 ) WRITE(6,10) J, BINAMT, (ASTER, I=1,BINAMT)
         IF( BINAMT .EQ. 0 ) WRITE(6,10) J, BINAMT
 10      FORMAT(1X, 'BIN#', I2, ' FREQ=', I3, 1X, 100A1 )
 20   CONTINUE
      STOP
      END

      BLOCK DATA
      COMMON / A / BIN
      INTEGER BIN(10)
      DATA BIN / 3*1, 4*8, 3, 2, 4 /
      END
```

Figure 11.8b. Program of Fig. 11.8a rewritten so that the values of BIN are initialized in another subprogram. A variable or array which is initialized in a DATA statement cannot appear in unlabeled COMMON; it can only appear in labeled COMMON and must be initialized in a special subprogram called BLOCK DATA.

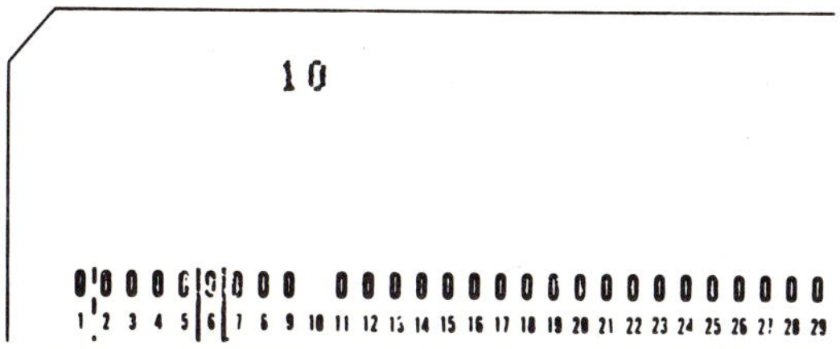

Figure 11.8c. The data card for Fig. 11.8b.

```
# OF LINES IN THE HISTOGRAM =   10
BIN# 1 FREQ=  1 *
BIN# 2 FREQ=  1 *
BIN# 3 FREQ=  1 *
BIN# 4 FREQ=  8 ********
BIN# 5 FREQ=  8 ********
BIN# 6 FREQ=  8 ********
BIN# 7 FREQ=  8 ********
BIN# 8 FREQ=  3 ***
BIN# 9 FREQ=  2 **
BIN#10 FREQ=  4 ****
```

Figure 11.8d. Running the program of Fig. 11.8b.

11.4. More on COMMON

It is possible to place in COMMON an array that is one part of the program, and have it correspond to nonsubscripted variables in another part of the program. In Fig. 11.9a, we want the 7-element array ARRAY in the main program to correspond to 5 nonsubscripted variables and a 2-element array F in subroutine MATCH. We thus write

```
COMMON ARRAY(7)
```

in the main program and

```
COMMON A, B, C, D, E, F(2)
```

in subroutine MATCH. We have elected to dimension the arrays ARRAY and F in the COMMON, although we could have dimensioned them in a DIMENSION statement. The correspondence between the two lists is shown in the table for Fig. 11.9a. Thus ARRAY(1) and A are the names of the same memory location. Similarly, ARRAY(2) and B correspond; ARRAY(3) and C correspond, ARRAY(4) and D correspond, ARRAY(5) and E correspond, ARRAY(6) and F(1) correspond, and finally ARRAY(7) and F(2) correspond. We can do the same thing with labeled COMMON lists, as is shown in Fig. 11.9b. The correspondence is the same as is shown in the table for Fig. 11.9a except that now the COMMON storage area is labeled SHARE.

ARRAYS IN COMMON LISTS CORRESPONDING TO VARIABLES IN COMMON LISTS

```
C   ARRAYS IN COMMON LIST CORRESPONDING TO
C   VARIABLES IN COMMON LISTS
          COMMON ARRAY(7)
          CALL MATCH
          STOP
          END

          SUBROUTINE MATCH
          COMMON A, B, C, D, E, F(2)
              .
              .
              .
          RETURN
          END
```

Figure 11.9a. The seven elements in ARRAY label the same memory locations as A, B, C, D, E and the two elements in F, since the elements of ARRAY appear in the unlabeled COMMON list and A, B, C, D, E and F appear in the unlabeled COMMON list in another part of the program.

	COMMON storage area						
Memory locations							
Main program names	ARRAY(1)	ARRAY(2)	ARRAY(3)	ARRAY(4)	ARRAY(5)	ARRAY(6)	ARRAY(7)
Corresponding subroutine names	A	B	C	D	E	F(1)	F(2)

Table for Fig. 11.9a. How the items in the two unlabeled COMMON lists label the same memory location.

```
C   AN ARRAY IN LABELED COMMON CORRESPONDING TO
C VARIABLES IN COMMON
          COMMON / SHARE / ARRAY(7)
          CALL MATCH
          STOP
          END

          SUBROUTINE MATCH
          COMMON / SHARE / A, B, C, D, E, F(2)
              .
              .
              .
          RETURN
          END
```

Figure 11.9b. The elements of the one-dimensional array ARRAY used in labeled COMMON SHARE label the same memory locations as A, B, C, D, E and the two-dimensional array F.

It is possible to place in COMMON a two-dimensional array that is in one part of a program (main program or subroutine) and have it correspond to a one-dimensional array in another part. In Fig. 11.10a we want the two-dimensional array TWO in the main program to correspond to the one-dimensional array ONE in subroutine BATCH. We will again be dimensioning the arrays in the COMMON statement. We thus write

```
COMMON TWO(2,3)
```

in the main program and

```
COMMON ONE(6)
```

in subroutine BATCH. The correspondence between the lists in the two COMMON statements are shown in the table for Fig. 11.10a. We remember that a two-dimensional array is stored in memory so that the first index varies more rapidly. Thus ONE(1) and TWO(1,1) are the name of the same memory locations. Similarly, ONE(2) and TWO(2,1) correspond; ONE(3) and TWO(1,2) correspond; ONE(4) and TWO(2,2) correspond; ONE(5) and TWO(1,3) correspond, and finally ONE(6) and TWO(2,3) correspond.

We can do the same thing with labeled COMMON lists, as is shown in Fig. 11.10b. The correspondence is the same as is shown in the table for Fig. 11.10a except that now the COMMON storage area is labeled SHARE2.

TWO-DIMENSIONAL ARRAY CORRESPONDING TO A ONE-DIMENSIONAL ARRAY IN COMMON LISTS

```
C   A 2-DIMENSIONAL LIST CORRESPONDING TO A 1-DIMENSIONAL
C   ARRAY IN COMMON LISTS
       COMMON TWO(2,3)
       CALL BATCH
       STOP
       END

       SUBROUTINE BATCH
       COMMON ONE(6)
       RETURN
       END
```

Figure 11.10a. The six elements in the two-dimensional array TWO label the same locations as the one-dimensional array ONE.

	COMMON storage area					
Memory locations						
Main program names	TWO(1,1)	TWO(2,1)	TWO(1,2)	TWO(2,2)	TWO(1,3)	TWO(2,3)
Corresponding subroutine names	ONE(1)	ONE(2)	ONE(3)	ONE(4)	ONE(5)	ONE(6)

Table for Fig. 11.10a. How the elements of the two dimensional array TWO and the elements of the one dimensional array ONE label the same memory location.

```
C   A 2-DIMENSIONAL ARRAY IN LABELED COMMON CORRESPONDING TO
C   A 1-DIMENSION ARRAY IN LABELED COMMON
       COMMON / SHARE2 / TWO(2,3)
       CALL BATCH
       STOP
       END

       SUBROUTINE BATCH
       COMMON / SHAPE2 / ONE(6)
       RETURN
       END
```

Figure 11.10b. The two-dimensional array TWO used in labeled COMMON / SHARE2 label the same memory locations as the elements of the one-dimensional array ONE which appears in unlabeled COMMON / SHARE2 in another part of the program.

The process we just described, of having a one-dimensional array in the COMMON list in one part of the program (main program or subroutine) correspond to variables in a COMMON list in another part of the program, is restricted to the use of COMMON statements. You cannot do the same thing with argument lists, as is shown in Fig. 11.11a. In the main program, we write

```
CALL MATCH( ARRAY )
```

where ARRAY is dimensioned as having 7 elements. We write the first statement of the subroutine as SUBROUTINE MATCH(A, B, C, D, E, F) where F is dimensioned in the subroutine as having 2 elements. We see that the number of items in the calling argument list in CALL MATCH(ARRAY), which is one, does not match the number of items in the subroutine list in SUBROUTINE MATCH(A,B,C,D,E,F), which is seven. Because of this, the compiler signals that an error has occurred when the program is run as is shown in Fig. 11.11b.

```
IHC900I EXECUTION TERMINATING DUE TO ERROR COUNT FOR ERROR
NUMBER 240
```

If, however, the number of actual arguments equals the number of dummy arguments, this type of error will not occur. For instance, we can have a two-dimensional array in one part of the program correspond to a one-dimensional array in another part. Thus in the main program of Fig. 11.11c, we call subroutine BATCH with

```
CALL BATCH( TWO )
```

where TWO is dimensioned in DIMENSION TWO(2,3). We write the first statement of the subroutine as SUBROUTINE BATCH(ONE) where ONE is dimensioned in DIMENSION ONE(6). Thus TWO(1,1) corresponds to ONE(1); TWO(2,1) corresponds to ONE(2); TWO(1,2) corresponds to ONE(3); TWO(2,2) corresponds to ONE(4); TWO(1,3) corresponds to ONE(5); and finally TWO(2,3) corresponds to ONE(6).

11.5. Comparison of Using Argument Lists and COMMON List

The advantage of using an argument list as opposed to a COMMON list is that it is immediately obvious which variables and arrays you are passing to the subroutine, especially if you use the same unlabeled COMMON for the main program and each subroutine.

Another advantage of using an argument list as opposed to a COMMON list is that it is easier to call a subroutine from different places in the program with different variables used for the same arguments if you use an argument list.

The advantage of using a COMMON list is that if there are many variables in the list it is tedious to punch them as arguments of subroutines whereas it is easier just to duplicate a COMMON statement which has a long list, for each subroutine. Another advantage is that items in a list are passed faster to a subroutine if they are in a COMMON statement than if they are arguments.

THE NUMBER OF ACTUAL ARGUMENTS MUST EQUAL THE NUMBER OF DUMMY ARGUMENTS

```
C   ARRAYS IN ARGUMENT LIST CORRESPONDING TO
C   VARIABLES IN ARGUMENT LIST
      DIMENSION ARRAY(7)
      CALL MATCH( ARRAY )
      STOP
      END

      SUBROUTINE MATCH(A, B, C, D, E, F )
      DIMENSION F(2)
      RETURN
      END
```

Figure 11.11a. If the number of items in the actual argument list does not equal the number of items in the dummy argument list, an error occurs.

```
IHC900I EXECUTION TERMINATING DUE TO ERROR COUNT FOR ERROR
    NUMBER  240
```

Figure 11.11b. Running the program of Fig. 11.11a.

TWO-DIMENSIONAL ARRAY CORRESPONDING TO A ONE-DIMENSIONAL ARRAY IN ARGUMENT LISTS

```
C   2-DIMENSIONAL ARRAY CORRESPONDING TO
C   A 1-DIMENSIONAL ARRAY IN ARGUMENT LIST
      DIMENSION TWO(2,3)
      CALL BATCH( TWO )
      STOP
      END

      SUBROUTINE BATCH( ONE )
      DIMENSION ONE(6)
      RETURN
      END
```

Figure 11.11c. The elements of the two-dimensional array TWO used as an actual argument label the same memory locations as the one-dimensional array ONE used as a dummy argument. Since the number of actual arguments equals the number of dummy arguments, an error would not occur if the program were run.

11.6. The EXTERNAL Statement

It is sometimes necessary to write a subroutine or function subprogram which itself uses one of several possible subroutines or functions (library, statement, or subprogram functions). What we do is to pass to the subroutine or function subprogram the name of the specific subroutine or function we want it to use. However, ordinarily when a name is passed to a subroutine or subprogram, the computer interprets the name as either a variable name or an array name. In order to signal the computer that we are passing a function or subroutine name, we must declare the name in an EXTERNAL statement in the main (or calling program).

In Fig. 11.12a we present a program that produces a trigonometric table. The DO loop of the main program produces an angle in degrees, but, as we remember, the trigonometric functions require the argument to be in radians. We pass the name of the trigonometric function—SIN, COS, or TAN—as well as the angle in degrees (THETA) on to subroutine CONVER. For instance, for the SIN we write

```
CALL CONVER( SIN, Y1, THETA )
```

where the value of Y1 will be the sine of THETA returned by the subroutine. The first line of the subroutine is

```
SUBROUTINE CONVER( FUN, Y, X )
```

where FUN is used in the statement

```
Y=FUN( CONST * X )
```

and where CONST converts angles to radians. We would like the computer to calculate the sine of CONST * X: i.e., we want the computer to interpret this statement as Y = SIN(CONST * X) and to call the library function SIN to evaluate it. In order to instruct the computer that SIN is a function, not a variable name, we must place SIN in an EXTERNAL statement in the main program. Since we will pass the COS and TAN functions to CONVER, we have to declare them in the EXTERNAL statement, as well; we thus write:

```
EXTERNAL SIN, COS, TAN
```

When the computer executes CALL CONVER(COS, Y2, THETA) it calculates

```
Y= COS(CONST*X)
```

in subroutine CONVER using the COS library function. CALL CONVER(TAN, Y3, THETA) applies for the TAN. The results of running the program are shown in Fig. 11.12b.

It is important to note that if a function is used with an argument and is passed onto a subprogram function or subroutine, we do not use an EXTERNAL statement. Thus the use of SIN(X) in CALL SUB(SIN(X), Y) does not require an EXTERNAL statement. The reason is that the compiler immediately recognizes that SIN(X) is a function, and it passes the *value* of SIN(X) onto the subprogram.

USING THE EXTERNAL STATEMENT

```
C  SHOWS USE OF THE EXTERNAL STATEMENT
C  PROGRAM CALCULATES TRIG TABLE
      INTEGER ANGLE, ANG
C
      EXTERNAL SIN, COS, TAN
C
      WRITE(6,10)
 10   FORMAT(1X, 'ANGLE', T15, 'SINE', T30, 'COSINE', T48, 'TANGENT'
C     ...GENERATE TRIG TABLE
      DO 30 ANGLE=1,91,10
         THETA=FLOAT( ANGLE - 1 )
         CALL CONVER( SIN, Y1, THETA )
         CALL CONVER( COS, Y2, THETA )
         CALL CONVER( TAN, Y3, THETA )
         ANG = THETA
         WRITE(6,20) ANG,   Y1, Y2, Y3
 20      FORMAT(1X, I5, T13, F10.7, T28, F10.7, T43, E15.7 )
 30   CONTINUE
      STOP
      END
```

Figure 11.12a. *Main program.* The functions SIN, COS, and TAN are passed to subroutine CONVER. In order to identify SIN, COS, and TAN as functions instead of variables, you must place them in an EXTERNAL statement.

```
      SUBROUTINE CONVER( FUN, Y, X )
C RETURNS THE SIN, COS, OR TAN OF AN ANGLE
C  RETURNS ANSWER IN DEGREES
      CONST=3.14159/180.0
      Y=FUN( CONST * X )
      RETURN
      END
```

Subroutine CONVER. The dummy argument FUN correspond to each of the functions SIN, COS, and TAN.

```
         $ENTRY
ANGLE       SINE           COSINE           TANGENT
    0    0.0000000       1.0000000       0.0000000E 00
   10    0.1736479       0.9848078       0.1763268E 00
   20    0.3420198       0.9396927       0.3639698E 00
   30    0.4999995       0.8660256       0.5773495E 00
   40    0.6427870       0.7660449       0.8390985E 00
   50    0.7660438       0.6427883       0.1191751E 01
   60    0.8660248       0.5000010       0.1732046E 01
   70    0.9396922       0.3420212       0.2747467E 01
   80    0.9848074       0.1736503       0.5671208E 01
   90    0.9999999       0.0000022       0.4501939E 06
```

Figure 11.12b. Running the program of Fig. 11.12a.

11.7. Execution-Time Dimensioning

In the programs of preceding sections we have made the number of locations that a dummy argument or arguments occupy equal to the number of locations that the corresponding actual argument or arguments occupy. In this section we investigate this concept. We begin with a discussion of one-dimensional arrays.

The purpose of dimensioning a dummy argument in a subroutine is to inform the computer that the argument is an array. If the array is a one-dimensional array, the subroutine DIMENSION statement on most systems serves no other purpose—only the DIMENSION statement in the main program allocates space in the computer's memory for the actual array that corresponds to the dummy array. For this reason, on most systems we can use any arbitrary positive INTEGER constant to dimension the dummy array in the subroutine. Thus in the program of Fig. 11.13a—which simply uses subroutine READ1 to read a one-dimensional array and then prints the results—we dimension the dummy array B as

```
DIMENSION B(1)
```

Although A, the actual array which corresponds to B, is dimensioned as

```
DIMENSION A(5)
```

The data card read by the program is shown in Fig. 11.13b. When the program is run, the values on the data card are assigned to the locations in the memory labeled by the elements of A when

```
READ(5,10) ( B(I), I=1,5 )
```

is executed as is shown for the table for Fig. 11.13a. Although B was dimensioned to have only one element, the execution of the READ statement does not cause the dimensions of the array to be exceeded. The reason is that A, the actual argument to which B corresponds, was dimensioned as having 5 elements in the main program. When the WRITE statement in the main program

```
WRITE(6,10) ( A(I), I=1,5)
```

is executed, the results are printed as is shown in Fig. 11.13c.

DIMENSIONING A DUMMY ARRAY AS HAVING ONE ELEMENT

```
C   CORRECT USE OF DIMENSIONS
      DIMENSION A(5)
      CALL READ1( A )
      WRITE(6,10)  ( A(I), I=1,5)
 10   FORMAT(1X, 'PRINTED IN MAIN PROGRAM' / 1X, 5F10.1 )
      STOP
      END

      SUBROUTINE READ1( B )
      DIMENSION B(1)
      READ(5,10)  ( B(I), I=1,5 )
 10   FORMAT( 5F10.0 )
      WRITE(6,20)  ( B(I), I=1,5)
 20   FORMAT(1X,  'PRINTED IN READ1' / 1X, 5F10.1 )
      RETURN
      END
```

Figure 11.13a. Program uses subroutine READ1 to read elements of an array. In the subroutine any one-dimenional array—here B—can be dimensioned as having one element. The printing of the elements are done in the main program.

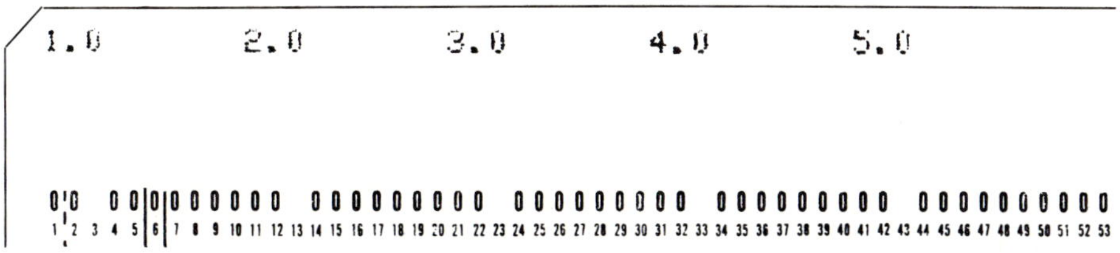

Figure 11.13b. The data card for Fig. 11.13a.

	1.0	2.0	3.0	4.0	5.0
Subroutine READ1 elements	B(1)	B(2)	B(3)	B(4)	B(5)
Main program elements	A(1)	A(2)	A(3)	A(4)	A(5)

Table for Fig. 11.13a. How the elements of array A correspond to the elements of array B even though the array was dimensioned to have one element in the subroutine.

```
PRINTED IN READ1
        1.0          2.0          3.0          4.0          5.0
PRINTED IN MAIN PROGRAM
        1.0          2.0          3.0          4.0          5.0
```

Figure 11.13c. Running the program of Fig. 11.13a.

On the WATFOR/WATFIV system, the compiler checks to see whether the dimensions of an array have been exceeded—and when it executes the statements in a subroutine, the compiler uses the subroutine DIMENSION statement to perform this check. For this reason, on these systems the dummy array must be dimensioned the same as the actual array is.

Even on systems on which it is allowed, in the following case it is not advantageous to dimension the dummy array as having one element. If in a program like the one shown in Fig. 11.13a, you simply used the array name in the READ in the subroutine, i.e., READ(5,10) B, the number of elements read would be determined by how B is dimensioned in the subroutine. Thus only one element and not the correct number of elements would be read.

Many is the time when a specific subroutine is called at different times by the main program to process arrays of various sizes. For instance, in the main program of Fig. 11.14a, we first use subroutine READ1 to read the 5-element array A and then use it again to read the 3-element array C. We then use subroutine WRITE1 to write array A (it has 5 elements) and then use it again to write array B (it has 3 elements). If we want to use the WATFOR/WATFIV capabilities for checking the dimensions of A and C, we would want the DIMENSION statement in READ1 to be interpreted as

```
DIMENSION A(5)
```

when A is processed, and the same dimension statement to be interpreted as

```
DIMENSION C(3)
```

when C is processed. The same applies to subroutine WRITE1. In other words, we would like the dimension of B to be a variable. What we do is to use an INTEGER variable as the dimension of B. We thus write the DIMENSION statement as

```
DIMENSION B(N)
```

as is shown in the subroutines of Fig. 11.14a. Both the variable N and the array B must be arguments of the subroutine. The array cannot appear in a COMMON statement,

EXECUTION-TIME DIMENSIONING

```
C   USING 1-DIMENSIONAL EXECUTION-TIME DIMENSIONING
C   USEFULL FOR COMPILERS LIKE WATFOR/WATFIV
      DIMENSION A(5), C(3)
C     ...READ ARRAYS
      CALL READ1( A, 5 )
      CALL READ1( C, 3 )
C     ...WRITE ARRAYS
      CALL WRITE1( A, 5 )
      CALL WRITE1( C, 3 )
      STOP
      END

      SUBROUTINE READ1( B, N )
C   USES EXECUTION-TIME DIMENSIONS
      DIMENSION B(N)
      READ(5,10) ( B(I), I=1,N )
 10   FORMAT( 5F10.0 )
      WRITE(6,20) ( B(I), I=1,N )
 20   FORMAT(1X, 'PRINTED IN READ1' / 1X, 5F10.2 )
      RETURN
      END

      SUBROUTINE WRITE1( B, N )
C   USES EXECUTION TIME DIMENSIONING
      DIMENSION B(N)
      WRITE(6,10) ( B(I), I=1,N )
 10   FORMAT(1X, 'PRINTED IN WRITE1' / 1X, 5F10.2 )
      RETURN
      END
```

Figure 11.14a. In the subroutines the dimensions of an array can be an INTEGER variable that is evaluated at execution time. This allows some compilers, like WATFOR/WATFIV, to check that the dimensions of an array used in a subroutine are not exceeded for an array of arbitrary size. The main program uses subroutine READ1 to read arrays and subroutine WRITE1 to write arrays.

instead. Again, the actual array(s) to which B corresponds must be dimensioned in the main program. The data cards for the program are shown in Fig. 11.14b, and the running of the program is shown in Fig. 11.14c.

The dimensioning process we have used here is called by the following terms: *execution-time dimensioning*, *adjustable dimensioning*, or *variable dimensioning*. Execution-time dimensioning cannot be used to dimension an array in the main program. Remember, execution-time dimensioning does not reserve memory locations, it is used only in subroutines by the compiler to further process a dummy array that must correspond to an actual array dimensioned in the main program.

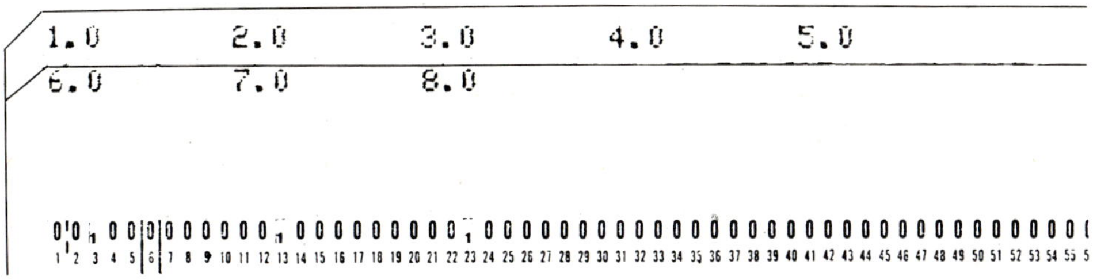

Figure 11.14b. The data cards for Fig. 11.14a.

```
PRINTED IN READ1
        1.00         2.00         3.00         4.00         5.00
PRINTED IN READ1
        6.00         7.00         8.00
PRINTED IN WRITE1
        1.00         2.00         3.00         4.00         5.00
PRINTED IN WRITE1
        6.00         7.00         8.00
```

Figure 11.14c. Running the program of Fig. 11.14a.

We note that execution-time dimensioning for one-dimensional arrays is useful for WATFOR/WATFIV systems and other systems that check for exceeded dimensions. It is also useful if we just use the array name (unsubscripted) in a READ or WRITE statement in a subroutine, as shown in Fig. 11.14d. Thus in subroutine READ1, the value of N in DIMENSION B(N) determines how many constants will be read by READ(5,10) B. Similarly, in subroutine WRITE1, the value of N in DIMENSION B(N) determines how many constants will be written by WRITE(6,10) B. The data cards for the program are shown in Fig. 11.14e and the running of the program is shown in Fig. 11.14f.

When you pass a two-dimensional array to a subroutine, the actual array and the dummy array must, of course, both be dimensioned. The first dimension of the dummy array must equal the first dimension of the actual array. The second dimension of the dummy array can be an arbitrary positive INTEGER constant. Another way of saying this is that the number of rows in the dimensioning of both arrays must be equal, whereas the number of columns need not. Thus if A is the actual array, and B the dummy, and A is dimensioned as DIMENSION A(3,2) in the main program, then the first dimension of B must be 3; whereas the second dimension of B can be, for instance, 1. In other words, we could dimension B as DIMENSION B(3,1) in the subroutine.

EXECUTION-TIME DIMENSIONING USED WITH READ AND WRITE STATEMENTS HAVING UNSUBSCRIPTED ARRAYS

```
C   EXECUTION-TIME DIMENSIONING USED WITH
C   READ AND WRITE STATEMENTS WHICH HAVE UNSUBSCRIPTED ARRAYS
        DIMENSION A(5), C(3)
C       ...READ ARRAYS
        CALL READ1( A, 5 )
        CALL READ1( C, 3 )
C       ...WRITE ARRAYS
        CALL WRITE1( A, 5 )
        CALL WRITE1( C, 3 )
        STOP
        END

        SUBROUTINE READ1( B, N )
        DIMENSION B(N)
        READ(5,10) B
 10     FORMAT( 8F10.0 )
        WRITE(6,20) B
 20     FORMAT(1X, 'PRINTED IN READ1' / 1X, 8F10.2 )
        RETURN
        END

        SUBROUTINE WRITE1( B, N )
        DIMENSION B(N)
        WRITE(6,10) B
 10     FORMAT(1X, 'PRINTED IN WRITE1', / 1X, 8F10.2 )
        RETURN
        END
```

Figure 11.14d. Execution-time dimensioning can be used in a subroutine to determine how many elements should be read or printed if an unsubscripted array name appears in a READ or WRITE statement.

```
  1.0          2.0          3.0          4.0          5.0
  6.0          7.0          8.0

1 2 3 4 5|6|7 8 9 10 11 12 13 14 15 16 17 18 19 20 21 22 23 24 25 26 27 28 29 30 31 32 33 34 35 36 37 38 39 40 41 42 43
```

Figure 11.14e. The data cards for the program of Fig. 11.14d.

```
PRINTED IN READ1
      1.00      2.00      3.00      4.00      5.00
PRINTED IN READ1
      6.00      7.00      8.00
PRINTED IN WRITE1
      1.00      2.00      3.00      4.00      5.00
PRINTED IN WRITE1
      6.00      7.00      8.00
```

Figure 11.14f. Running the program of Fig. 11.14d.

In Fig. 11.15a—the program simply reads an array and prints it—we investigate what happens when the first dimension of the dummy array does not equal the first dimension of the corresponding actual array. In the main program we have written DIMENSION A(3,3). In the subroutine, we have dimensioned the corresponding dummy array as DIMENSION B(2,2). We remember that elements of an array are stored by rows. Thus when the data cards shown in Fig. 11.15b are read by subroutine READ2, the elements are stored in the following order: B(1,1), B(2,1), B(1,2), and B(2,2), as shown in the table for Fig. 11.15a. However, since the actual array A is dimensioned as DIMENSIQN A(3,3), the actual elements are stored in the following order: A(1,1), A(2,1), A(3,1), A(2,1), etc., as is shown in the table for Fig. 11.15a.

1.0	3.0	2.0	4.0	Undef	Undef
B(1,1)	B(2,1)	B(1,2)	B(2,2)		
A(1,1)	A(2,1)	A(3,1)	A(1,2)	A(2,2)	A(3,2)

Thus, although A(1,1) corresponds to B(1,1), and A(2,1) to B(2,1), because array A has a third row, A(1,2) does not correspond to B(1,2), and A(2,2) does not correspond to B(2,2). What happens is that A(3,1) corresponds to B(1,2); A(1,2) corresponds to B(2,2); and A(2,2) and all the other elements of A are undefined. Thus when the main program prints the results, since the values of A(1,1) and A(1,2) are printed on the first line, and the values of A(2,1) and A(2,2) on the second, the program produces the results shown in Fig. 11.15c.

```
1.0  4.0
3.0  0.0
```

The 0.0 results from the fact that A(2,2) is undefined. If this program were run on the WATFOR/WATFIV compiler, a U would be printed here.

INCORRECT DIMENSIONS IN SUBROUTINE

```
C   INCORRECT DIMENSIONING IN SUBROUTINE
        DIMENSION A(3,3)
        CALL READ2( A )
        WRITE(6,5)
 5      FORMAT(1X, 'PRINTED BY MAIN PROGRAM ' )
        DO 20 I=1,2
           WRITE(6,10) ( A(I,J), J=1,2 )
 10        FORMAT(1X, 2F10.1 )
 20     CONTINUE
        STOP
        END

        SUBROUTINE READ2( B )
        DIMENSION B(2,2)
        WRITE(6,5)
 5      FORMAT(1X, 'PRINTED BY READ2 ' )
        DO 30 I=1,2
           READ(5,10) ( B(I,J), J=1,2 )
 10        FORMAT( 2F10.0 )
           WRITE(6,20) ( B(I,J), J=1,2 )
 20        FORMAT(1X, 2F10.2 )
 30     CONTINUE
        RETURN
        END
```

Figure 11.15a. If the number of rows in a two-dimensional dummy array do not equal the number of rows in the two-dimensional actual array it corresponds to, you will get incorrect results. The number of columns is arbitrary. Subroutine READ2 reads arrays, and the main program prints them.

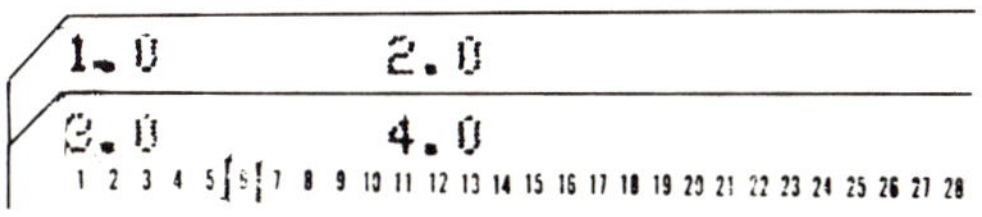

Figure 11.15b. The data cards for Fig. 11.15a.

Memory Locations	1.0	3.0	2.0	4.0	—	—	—	—	—
Subroutine READ Elements	B(1,1)	B(2,1)	B(1,2)	B(2,2)					
Main program elements	A(1,1)	A(2,1)	A(3,1)	A(1,2)	A(2,2)	A(3,2)	A(1,3)	A(2,3)	A(3,3)

Table for Fig. 11.15a. Since the number of rows in B do not equal the number of rows in A, elements like A(3,1) are assigned values they should not be assigned; whereas A(2,2), which should be assigned the value of B(2,2), is assigned an arbitrary value instead.

```
PRINTED BY READ2
      1.00      2.00
      3.00      4.00
PRINTED BY MAIN PROGRAM
       1.0       4.0
       3.0       0.0
```

Figure 11.15c. Running the program of Fig. 11.15a. The 0.0 is an arbitrary number. It occurs because A(2,2) does not correspond to an element of B and is thus undefined. The 4.0 occurs where it does because A(1,2) corresponds to B(2,2).

If B also had three rows, then no matter how many columns it had, A(1,2) would correspond to B(1,2); and A(2,2) would correspond to B(2,2). In the program of Fig. 11.16a, we rewrite the preceding program so that both arrays A and B are dimensioned to have the same number of rows, i.e., DIMENSION A(3,3) appears in the main program and DIMENSION B(3,2) appears in the subroutine. The data cards read by the subroutine are shown in Fig. 11.16b. How the elements of the dummy and actual array correspond is shown in the table for Fig. 11.16a. The results of running the program are shown in Fig. 11.16c; they duplicate the values read in.

CORRECT DIMENSIONS IN SUBROUTINE

```
C     CORRECT DIMENSIONING IN SUBROUTINE
      DIMENSION A(3,3)
      CALL READ2( A )
      WRITE(6,5)
 5    FORMAT(1X, 'PRINTED BY MAIN PROGRAM ' )
      DO 20 I=1,3
         WRITE(6,10)  ( A(I,J), J=1,2 )
 10      FORMAT(1X, 2F10.1 )
 20   CONTINUE
      STOP
      END

      SUBROUTINE READ2( B )
      DIMENSION B(3,2)
      WRITE(6,5)
 5    FORMAT(1X, 'PRINTED BY READ2 ' )
      DO 30 I=1,3
         READ(5,10)  ( B(I,J), J=1,2 )
 10      FORMAT( 2F10.0 )
         WRITE(6,20)  ( B(I,J), J=1,2 )
 20      FORMAT(1X, 2F10.2 )
 30   CONTINUE
      RETURN
      END
```

Figure 11.16a. The number of rows of the dummy array B equals the number of rows of the actual array it corresponds to, i.e., A. The number of columns do not have to agree. Subroutine READ2 reads arrays, and the main program prints them.

Memory Locations	1.0	3.0	5.0	2.0	4.0	6.0	—	—	—
Subroutine READ2 elements	B(1,1)	B(2,1)	B(3,1)	B(1,2)	B(2,2)	B(3,2)			
Main program elements	A(1,1)	A(2,1)	A(3,1)	A(1,2)	A(2,2)	A(3,2)	A(1,3)	A(2,3)	A(3,3)

Table for Fig. 11.16a. Since the number of rows in the actual and dummy arrays are the same and since the elements are stored by columns, the proper elements of each correspond.

```
PRINTED BY READ2
      1.00      2.00
      3.00      4.00
      5.00      6.00
PRINTED BY MAIN PROGRAM
       1.0       2.0
       3.0       4.0
       5.0       6.0
```

Figure 11.16c. Running the program of Fig. 11.16a. The results mirror the input because the number of rows in the actual and dummy arrays are the same.

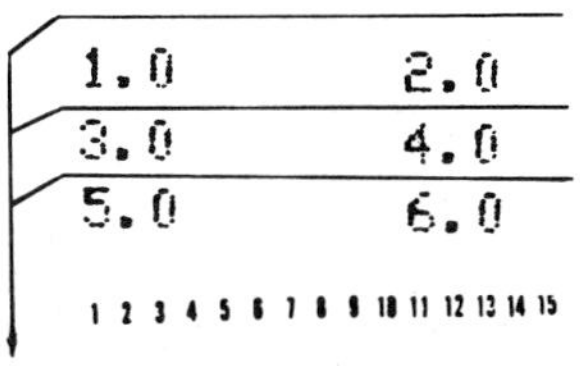

Figure 11.16b. The data cards for Fig. 11.16a.

If we wrote a subroutine that contained two-dimensional (dummy) arrays that would be passed to and from it, and we wanted the subroutine to have the capability of being used by many different main programs, it would be advantageous to let the dimensions of the dummy arrays be variables. Again, all we would require is that the first dimension of the dummy array and the first dimension of the actual array be the same. Thus, in the subroutines of Fig. 11.17a we have written

```
DIMENSION B(L,1)
```

where both B and L must be in the argument list of the subroutines. The array B cannot appear in a COMMON statement. Subroutine READ reads a two-dimensional array which has L rows and K columns and subroutine WRITE prints the same two-dimensional array. The first statements in these subroutines are SUBROUTINE READ(B,L,K) and SUBROUTINE WRITE(B,L,K), respectively. In the main program which would call these subroutines, the value of the variable that L (the number of rows) corresponds to should be set equal to the first dimension of the actual array that B corresponds to. We now explain this.

The main program of Fig. 11.17a first reads and then prints the array A. Since A is dimensioned as DIMENSION A(4,4), the first dimension of the dummy array B in both subroutines should be 4. We thus write the CALLs as CALL READ(A,4,4) and CALL WRITE(A,4,4). Since the dummy variable L corresponds to the first 4 in the argument list of these CALLs, the computer interprets DIMENSION B(L,1) in the two subroutines as

```
DIMENSION B(4,1)
```

The second 4 in the argument list becomes the value of K in the subroutines. Thus, in subroutine READ the READ statement READ(5,10) (B(I,J), J=1,K) is interpreted as READ(5,10) (B(I,J), J=1,4), and in subroutine WRITE, the WRITE statement is interpreted as WRITE(6,10) (B(I,J),J=1,4). The main program, by calling READ and WRITE again, next reads and then prints the array C. Since C is dimensioned as DIMENSION C(3,3), the first dimension of the dummy array B when both subroutines are called, should now be 3. We thus write the CALLs as CALL READ(C,3,3) and CALL WRITE(C,3,3). The computer now interprets the DIMENSION statement in these subroutines as DIMENSION B(3,1).

DIMENSION-**TIME DIMENSIONING FOR TWO-DIMENSIONAL ARRAYS**

```
C   DEMONSTRATES USE OF ADJUSTABLE DIMENSIONS
C   FOR 2-DIMENSIONAL ARRAYS
        DIMENSION A(4,4), C(3,3)
        CALL READ( A, 4, 4 )
        CALL WRITE( A, 4, 4 )
        CALL READ( C, 3, 3 )
        CALL WRITE( C, 3, 3 )
        STOP
        END

        SUBROUTINE READ(B, L, K)
C   USES ADJUSTABLE DIMENSIONS
C   FOR READING 2-DIMENSIONAL ARRAYS
        DIMENSION B(L,1)
        DO 20 I=1,L
        WRITE(6,5)
 5      FORMAT(1X, 'PRINTED BY READ' )
            READ(5,10) ( B(I,J), J=1,K )
 10         FORMAT( 8F10.0)
            WRITE(6,15) ( B(I,J), J=1,K )
 15         FORMAT(1X, 8F10.1 )
 20     CONTINUE
        RETURN
        END

        SUBROUTINE WRITE( B, L, K)
C   USES ADJUSTABLE DIMENSIONS FOR
C   PRINTING 2-DIMENSIONAL ARRAYS
        DIMENSION B(L,1)
        WRITE(6,5)
 5      FORMAT(1X, 'PRINTED BY WRITE ' )
        DO 20 I=1,L
            WRITE(6,10) ( B(I,J), J=1,K )
 10         FORMAT(1X, 8F10.1 )
 20     CONTINUE
        RETURN
        END
```

Figure 11.17a. Program reads and writes two-dimensional arrays. The first dimension in the dummy array in the subroutines is a variable. This way, the number of rows in the dummy array will equal the number of rows in the actual array and no incorrect output will occur. Had we dimensioned the dummy array B as 4 by 1 we would have to dimension the actual array C as 4 by 3 also, since the number of rows in both arrays must be the same.

Let us now investigate what happens if we did not use adjustable dimensions. Assume that the array C being read was a 3 by 3 array, then the program would have to be written so that C would be dimensioned as C(4,3) in the main program, and the dummy array B would be dimensioned in the subroutines as

```
DIMENSION B(4,1)
```

The reason for this, of course, is that the number of rows in the dummy array B equals the number of rows in the actual arrays A and C. Thus besides the restriction that the number of rows in the real and actual arrays must be the same, we would have the added restriction that the number of rows in the actual arrays A and C would also have to be the same. Assuming that the CALLs using C remained CALL READ(C,3,3) and CALL WRITE(C,3,3), we would be using only 9 locations of the 12 allocated for C. Thus we would be wasting 3 locations. At this level, this waste would not be detrimental; but imagine if we were working with an array A that had 100 rows, then the dimension for C would also have 100 rows. We would then be wasting many locations. The number of locations wasted would be $100 \times 3 - 9$, or 291 locations. On a larger scale, this could mean that our program was so large that the computer could not accommodate it; or if it could be accommodated, the execution time could be drastically increased.

The data cards for the program of Fig. 11.17a are shown in Fig. 11.17b, and the results of running the program are shown in Fig. 11.17c.

If this program were written for the WATFOR/WATFIV system, it would be advisable to change the execution-time DIMENSION statements so that the number of columns would also be a variable; that is, change it to

```
DIMENSION B(L,K)
```

This would allow the computer to check that the dimensions of the dummy array B were not exceeded in the subroutines. This DIMENSION statement could as easily have been used in Fig. 11.17a, since on standard FORTRAN systems, the value of K can have any arbitrary positive INTEGER value.

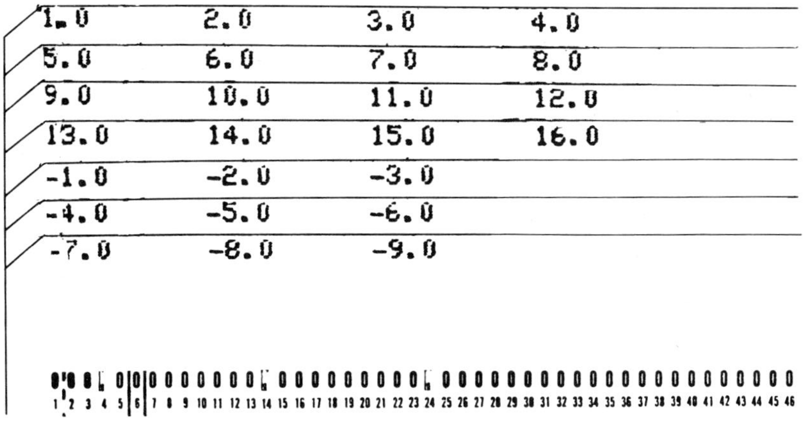

Figure 11.17b. The data cards for Fig. 11.17a.

```
PRINTED BY READ
        1.0          2.0          3.0          4.0
PRINTED BY READ
        5.0          6.0          7.0          8.0
PRINTED BY READ
        9.0         10.0         11.0         12.0
PRINTED BY READ
       13.0         14.0         15.0         16.0
PRINTED BY WRITE
        1.0          2.0          3.0          4.0 )
        5.0          6.0          7.0          8.0 }  A
        9.0         10.0         11.0         12.0 }
       13.0         14.0         15.0         16.0 )
PRINTED BY READ
       -1.0         -2.0         -3.0
PRINTED BY READ
       -4.0         -5.0         -6.0
PRINTED BY READ
       -7.0         -8.0         -9.0
PRINTED BY WRITE
       -1.0         -2.0         -3.0 )
       -4.0         -5.0         -6.0 }  C
       -7.0         -8.0         -9.0 )
```

Figure 11.17c. Running the program of Fig. 11.17a.

We now present the mathematical formulas that explain why we do not have to match the second dimension in a two-dimensional dummy array with the second dimension of the actual array. If we represent the maximum value of the first subscript of an array A as D1 and the maximum value of the second as D2, then we can construct an equivalent one-dimension array—call it E—such that the value of its subscript N is given as

```
N=I + D1*( J-1 )
```

where E(N) labels the same memory locations as A(I,J). In Table 11.5a we show how this works where A is dimensioned as DIMENSION A(3,2), thus the value of D1 is 3. As an example of the use of the formula, we see that when I is 3 and J is 1, then N is 3. So E(3) labels the same location as A(3,1), as shown in Table 11.5b. We note that the value of the second dimension of A—D2 has no effect on the subscript of the equivalent one-dimensional array. Since two-dimensional arrays are stored in contiguous memory locations (as is shown in Table 11.5b), having the elements of a dummy array correspond to those of the actual array is the same as having their one-dimensional equivalent arrays correspond. Thus the second dimension of the array does not affect this correspondence—as we have seen in Fig. 11.16a–c. On the other hand, if the first dimensions of the two arrays are not equal, the elements of the two arrays will not correspond, as we have seen in Fig. 11.15a–c. If we are using a three-dimensional array A where we represent the dimensions as DIMENSION A(D1,D2,D3), then E(N) labels the same location as A(I,J,K) where N is given by

```
N=I + D1*( J-1 ) + D1*D2*( K-1 )
```

We see that again the rightmost dimension—here D3—does not affect the value of N. Thus if we used an array C dimensioned in the main program as DIMENSION C(8,7,6), then the first two dimensions of the dummy array would have to be 8 and 7, respectively, and the last dimension could be any positive INTEGER. So if we used the dummy array B, we could dimension it in the subroutines B(8,7,1).

In general, the last dimension in a multidimensional dummy array can be any positive INTEGER; whereas all the previous dimensions of the dummy and actual array must correspond.

FOR DIMENSION A(D1,D2) **AND GIVEN**
A(I,J) **THEN** N = I + D1*(J−1)

I	J	D1	N
1	1	3	1
2	1	3	2
3	1	3	3
1	2	3	4
2	2	3	5
3	2	3	6

Table 11.5a. If a two-dimensional array A is dimensioned as D1×D2 then A(I,J) would occupy the same location as I + D1*(J−1) of an equivalent one-dimensional array. For a D1×D2×D3 array, A(I,J,K) occupies the same location as I + D1*(J−1) + D1*D2*(K−1) of the equivalent one-dimensional array.

DIMENSION A(D1,D2) ⇒ DIMENSION A(3,2)

A(1,1) E(1)	A(2,1) E(2)	A(3,1) E(3)	A(1,2) E(4)	A(2,2) E(5)	A(3,2) E(6)	Two-dimensional array A(I,J) Equivalent one-dimensional array E(N)

Table 11.5b. How E(N) corresponds to A(I,J) where N, I, and J are given in Table 11.5a. In a multiple-dimensioned array, the last (rightmost) dimension does not affect the location of an element in the equivalent one-dimensional array.

11.8. The EQUIVALENCE Statement

The EQUIVALENCE statement enables the two or more variables (or array elements) in the same part of the program—be it main program or subroutine—to share the same memory location. On the other hand, the COMMON statement allows two or more variables (arrays) in different parts of the program to share the same memory location.

One reason why we would want to use an EQUIVALENCE statement is shown in Fig. 11.18a. In this program, only the value of X is read. We have by accident changed the name of the variable X, and called it Y in

```
T = Y * (Y + 3 )
```

and then called it W in

```
Y = W + W**4 + 2
```

The data card for the program is shown in Fig. 11.18b. The results of running the program are shown in Fig. 11.18c. The program was written on a WATFOR/WATFIV system. During execution, as soon as the compiler detects the first undefined variable, here Y, it prints an error message. Thus it never gets a chance to detect that W is undefined. Instead of rewriting the two offending statements, we could instruct the compiler that X, Y and W label the same memory location. We do this by placing the EQUIVALENCE statement

```
EQUIVALENCE( X, Y, W )
```

in the beginning of the program, as shown in Fig. 11.18d. The EQUIVALENCE statement must be placed before all executable statements and before any DATA statements. The data card for Fig. 11.18d is the same one shown in Fig. 11.18b. The results of running the program are shown in Fig. 11.18e.

ONE REASON FOR USING THE EQUIVALENCE STATEMENT

```
C   USE FOR EQUIVALENCE STATEMENT ( I )
C   EQUIVALENCING TWO OR MORE VARIABLES WHICH HAVE THE SAME VALUE
        READ(5,10) X
 10     FORMAT(F10.0)
        Z = X + X**2 + X**3
        T = Y * (Y + 3 )
        Y = W + W**4 + 2
        WRITE(6,20) X, Z, T, Y
 20     FORMAT(1X, 'X=', F10.4, '   Z=', F10.4, '   T=', F10.4,
      1        '   Y=', F10.4 )
        STOP
        END
```

Figure 11.18a. In this program X, Y and W should be the same variable. Note that only the value of X was read, thus Y and W are undefined.

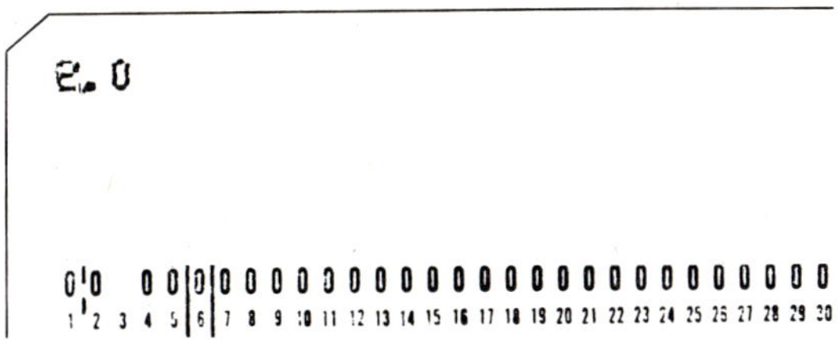

Figure 11.18b. The data card for Fig. 11.18a.

```
***ERROR***    VALUE OF Y          IS UNDEFINED
```

Figure 11.18c. Running the program of Fig. 11.18a. In the second assignment statement the compiler detects that Y is undefined. It thus prints the error message.

```
        EQUIVALENCE( X, Y, W )
        READ(5,10) X
 10     FORMAT(F10.0)
        Z = X + X**2 + X**3
        T = Y * (Y + 3 )
        Y = W + W**4 + 2
        WRITE(6,20) X, Z, T, Y
 20     FORMAT(1X, 'X=', F10.4, '   Z=', F10.4, '   T=', F10.4,
      1        '   Y=', F10.4 )
        STOP
        END
```

Figure 11.18d. By equivalencing X, Y, and W, they label the same memory location.

```
X=    20.0000   Z=     14.0000   T=     10.0000   Y=     20.0000
```

Figure 11.18e. Running the program of Fig. 11.18d with the data card shown in Fig. 11.18b.

The second reason for wanting to use an EQUIVALENCE statement is shown in Fig. 11.19. This is the same program that demonstrated the use of variable dimensioning (Fig. 11.17) in order to have actual array dimensions match the dummy array dimensions; however, here the dimensions of both A and C are larger than they were. The array A is used in the beginning of the program in CALL READ(A, 300, 300) and CALL WRITE(A, 300, 300) and then is no longer used. Then the array C is used. The statement DIMENSION A(300), C(200) reserves 500 memory locations. By including EQUIVALENCE(A(1), C(1)) in the program, we instruct the computer that the 200 elements of array C should label the same memory locations as the first 200 (corresponding) elements of A, as shown in the table for Fig. 11.19. The fact that A(1) and C(1) are in the EQUIVALENCE statement mean that A(1) and C(1) label the same memory location; A(2) and C(2) label the same memory location; . . .A(200) and C(200) label the same location. Since there are no more elements of C, the correspondence ends here. Thus, instead of using 500 memory locations for the arrays; we only used 300. Writing the EQUIVALENCE statement the way we did is not the only way we can obtain the correspondence shown in the table for Fig. 11.19. All we have to do is to place in the statement any pair of elements that label the same location; thus EQUIVALENCE (A(3), C(3)) would have the same effect. In fact on some compilers you can simply write EQUIVALENCE (A,C). Note, as opposed to the COMMON statement and type statements (INTEGER, REAL, etc.), you cannot dimension an array in an EQUIVALENCE statement; a subscripted variable in an EQUIVALENCE statement refers to a given element.

In Fig. 11.20 we show an EQUIVALENCE statement in which the first element of one of the arrays does not correspond to the first of the second array. The resulting correspondence is shown in the table for Fig. 11.20.

A SECOND REASON FOR USING THE EQUIVALENCE STATEMENT

```
C USE FOR EQUIVALENCE STATEMENT ( II )
C  DIFFERENT ARRAYS USING THE SAME LOCATIONS AT
C  DIFFERENT POINTS IN THE PROGRAM
      DIMENSION A(300), C(200)
      EQUIVALENCE( A(1), C(1) )
      CALL READ(A, 300, 300 )
      CALL WRITE(A, 300, 300 )
      CALL READ(C, 200, 200)
      CALL WRITE(C, 200, 200 )
      STOP
      END
```

Figure 11.19. The array C is used after the array A is used. In order to save space, we equivalence A and C. You cannot dimension an array in an EQUIVALENCE statement.

A(1) C(1)	A(2) C(2)	A(3) C(3)	A(200) C(200)	A(201)	A(202

Table for Fig. 11.19. We see that because of the EQUIVALENCE statement and since A is dimensioned as 300 and C as 200, the first 200 elements of C label the same locations as the first 200 elements of A.

EQUIVALENCING TWO ONE-DIMENSIONAL ARRAYS

```
DIMENSION X(6), Y(4)
EQUIVALENCE( X(4), Y(3) )
```

Figure 11.20. Equivalencing an arbitrary element—here Y(3)—of one array with an arbitrary element—here X(4)—of another.

X(1)	X(2) Y(1)	X(3) Y(2)	X(4) Y(3)	X(5) Y(4)	X(6)

Table for Fig. 11.20. The effect of the EQUIVALENCE in Fig. 11.20.

In Fig. 11.21 we show an EQUIVALENCE statement in which the first four elements of a two-dimensional array, A, label the same four memory locations, respectively, as do the first four elements of the two-dimensional array B. The resulting correspondence is shown in the table for Fig. 11.21. In the EQUIVALENCE statement, we can refer to the first element of any multidimensional array—call it A—as A(1), the second element as A(2), etc. We have thus written EQUIVALENCE (A(1), B(1)) as contrasted with EQUIVALENCE (A(1,1), B(1,1)).

In Fig. 11.22 we show an EQUIVALENCE statement EQUIVALENCE (A(1), B(2)) in which elements 2, 3, and 4 of the one-dimensional array B label the same three locations as the first three elements of the two-dimensional array A. The resulting correspondence is shown in the table for Fig. 11.22.

In Fig. 11.23a, we see an applications of equivalencing a one-dimensional and a three-dimensional array. By writing EQUIVALENCE (X(1), Y(1)), we equivalence the three-dimensional array X and the one-dimensional array Y, both of which are shown in DIMENSION X(3,3,3), Y(27). We can thus zero the three-dimensional array X by placing the one-dimensional array Y in a simple DO loop.

```
      DO 10 I=1, 27
         Y(I) = 0.0
10    CONTINUE
```

instead of in the triply nested DO loop shown in Fig. 11.23b.

```
      DO 30 I=1,3
         DO 20 J=1,3
            DO 10 K=1,3
               X(I,J,K)=0.0
10          CONTINUE
20       CONTINUE
30    CONTINUE
```

EQUIVALENCE

The form of the EQUIVALENCE statement is: EQUIVALENCE followed by sets of parentheses in which are placed the variables or array elements that you wish to equivalence. The variables and array elements are separated by commas. If there is more than one set of parentheses, the sets are separated by commas. Examples:

EQUIVALENCE (A, B, C, D), (A(1), B(3)), (R(3,2), G(1,2), Z)
EQUIVALENCE (A, B)

Dummy arguments of subroutines and of function subprograms cannot appear in an EQUIVALENCE statement.

EQUIVALENCING TWO TWO-DIMENSIONAL ARRAYS

```
DIMENSION A(2,3), B(2,2)
EQUIVALENCE( A(1), B(1) )
```

Figure 11.21. You can equivalence two two-dimensional arrays—here A and B—simply by equivalencing A(1) and B(1).

A(1,1)	A(2,1)	A(1,2)	A(2,2)	A(1,3)	A(2,3)
B(1,1)	B(2,1)	B(1,2)	B(2,2)		

Table for Fig. 11.21. The effect of the EQUIVALENCE in Fig. 11.21.

EQUIVALENCING A ONE-DIMENSIONAL AND A TWO-DIMENSIONAL ARRAY

```
DIMENSION A(2,3), B(4)
EQUIVALENCE( A(1), B(2) )
```

Figure 11.22. You can equivalence a two-dimensional array—here A—with a one-dimensional array—here B—simply by equivalencing A(1) and B(2).

B(1)	B(2)	B(3)	B(4)			
	A(1,1)	A(2,1)	A(1,2)	A(2,2)	A(1,3)	A(1,2)

Table for Fig. 11.22. The effect of the EQUIVALENCE in Fig. 11.22.

A THIRD REASON FOR USING THE EQUIVALENCE STATEMENT

```
C   USE FOR EQUIVALFNCE STATEMENT  ( III )
C   EQUATING MULTI AND 1-DIMENSIONAL ARRAYS
       DIMENSION X(3,3,3), Y(27)
       EQUIVALENCE ( X(1), Y(1) )
       DO 10 I=1, 27
          Y(I) = 0.0
 10    CONTINUE
```

Figure 11.23a. By equivalencing a three-dimensional array—here X—with a one-dimensional array—here Y—we can initialize all the elements of X simply by initializing Y in a DO loop.

```
      DIMENSION X(3,3,3)
      DO 30 I=1,3
         DO 20 J=1,3
            DO 10 K=1,3
               X(I,J,K)=0.0
10          CONTINUE
20       CONTINUE
30    CONTINUE
```

Figure 11.23b. If we did not equivalence X to Y as we did in Fig. 11.23a, then we would have to initialize X in a doubly nested DO loop.

PROBLEMS

1. Write a program that zeros an array that has 100 elements. In a subroutine it should place M constants in the array, starting at the Nth location. The values of N, M and constants are read from data cards by the main program. Use a COMMON statement to pass arguments to and from the subroutine.

2. Using COMMON statements, write a program that calculates $\binom{N}{M}$.

3. Which are the proper ways of subdividing COMMON A,B,C,D,E,F?

(a)	(b)	(c)
COMMON A,B,C	COMMON A,B	COMMON A
COMMON F	COMMON C,D	COMMON C,D
COMMON D,E	COMMON E,F	COMMON E,F

4. If COMMON A,B,I,J,C,D is the COMMON statement in the main program, which of the following can be used as COMMON statements in subprograms?

(a)	(b)	(c)
COMMON E,F,K	COMMON E,F,G	COMMON A,B
COMMON L,D	COMMON K,R,M	

5. Given the fact that COMMON A,B,C,D,E and COMMON /SUB/K,L,Z are in the main program, which of the following can be used in subprograms?

   (a) COMMON A,B/SUB/K,L//C,D,E
   (b) COMMON A,B/SUB/K,L,Z//C,D
   (c) COMMON /SUB/K,L,Z//A,B

6. Write the program in problem 1 so that the array is zeroed in a DATA statement and passed to the subroutine by a COMMON statement.

7. Using subroutines, write a program that zeros a three-dimensional array by only using one DO loop. Do not use an EQUIVALENCE statement in the program. Can you use either a COMMON statement or an argument list to do this problem?

8. Write a program that places 1s in all the elements on the left-hand side of a 10 by 10 matrix, and zeros in all the elements on the right-hand side. Hint: use a subroutine to initialize one-dimensional arrays. If you follow the hint, can you use either a COMMON statement or an argument list?

9. Write a program that uses a subroutine to plot either the SIN or the COS. Use an EXTERNAL statement to do this.

10. Using execution-time dimensioning, write a subroutine that multiplies matrices.

11. Given DIMENSION A (100), B (100), what are some of the ways you can equivalence each element of array A to the corresponding element in array B?

(a) EQUIVALENCE (A,B)
(b) EQUIVALENCE (A(4), B(3))
(c) EQUIVALENCE (A(1), B(1))
(d) EQUIVALENCE (A(100), B(100))

12. What does the following program produce?

```
      DIMENSION A(4,4)
      CALL SUB(A)
      CALL BUS(A)
      STOP
      END

      SUBROUTINE SUB (B)
      DIMENSION B (16)
      DO 10 J = 1 to 16
         B (J) = J
   10 CONTINUE
      RETURN
      END

      SUBROUTINE BUS (C)
      DIMENSION C(2,2)
      WRITE (6,10) C
   10 FORMAT (1X, 4F10.1)
      RETURN
      END
```

12

Significance, Double Precision, Complex Numbers

12.1. Converting Binary Numbers to Decimal Numbers

We recall that constants are stored in the computer's memory as binary digits. (The term binary digit is abbreviated, as *bit*). The group of bits used to store constants is called a *word*. On a given type of computer, each word has the same number of bits—on the IBM 360/370 a word has 32 bits. In order to understand how the contents of a word translates into decimal, we now describe how to convert a binary number to a decimal number. But first we comment on decimal numbers.

The number 123.45 in decimal is the same as

$$100 + 20 + 3 + .4 + .05$$

or

$$1 \times 100 + 2 \times 10 + 3 \times 1 + 4 \times (1/10) + 5 \times (1/100)$$

or

$$1 \times 10^2 + 2 \times 10^1 + 3 \times 10^0 + 4 \times 10^{-1} + 5 \times 10^{-2}$$

as is shown in Fig. 12.1a.

That this expression involves powers of 10 (i.e., 10^2, 10^1, 10^0, 10^{-1}, and 10^{-2}) results from the fact that the decimal system uses 10 as its base. The fact that the 3 is to the immediate left of the decimal point means that it multiplies 10^0. As you go to the left of the 3 in 123.45, the numbers multiply increasing powers of 10: thus the 2 multiplies 10^1 and the 1 multiplies 10^2. Similarly, since the 4 in 123.45 is to the immediate right of the decimal point, it multiplies 10^{-1}. The numbers in 123.45 to the right of the 4 multiply decreasing powers of 10. Thus the 5 multiplies 10^{-2}.

In any number system, the largest digit we can use in a number is the value of the base minus one. Thus the largest digit we can use in the decimal system is 9. Since the binary system uses 2 as its base, the largest digit we can use in a binary number is 1. Thus a binary number consists of zeros and ones. We convert the binary number 101.11 into its decimal equivalent by using the technique described in the preceding paragraph, but now we use powers of 2 instead of powers of 10. Thus since 101.11 is a binary number, we

EXPANDING A DECIMAL NUMBER

$$123.45 = \underline{1 \times 10^2 + 2 \times 10^1 + 3 \times 10^0 + 4 \times 10^{-1} + 5 \times 10^{-2}}$$

Figure 12.1a. How a decimal number can be expressed as the sum of powers of 10. The base of the decimal system is 10.

express it as the sum of powers of 2

$$101.11 = 1 \times 2^2 + 0 \times 2^1 + 1 \times 2^0 + 1 \times 2^{-1} + 1 \times 2^{-2}$$

or

$$4 + 0 + \tfrac{1}{2} + \tfrac{1}{4} \text{ or } 5\tfrac{3}{4}, \text{ i.e., } 5.75 \text{ in decimal}$$

as is shown in Fig. 12.1b. Thus we can see why decimal fractions which consist of the sum of powers of ½, can be expressed exactly on binary machines. For example, 0.50 is 2^{-1} and in binary is 0.1; 0.25 is ¼ or 2^{-2} and in binary is 0.01; 0.75 is ½ + ¼ or $2^{-1} + 2^{-2}$ and in binary is 0.11; and 0.125 is ⅛ or 2^{-3} and in binary is 0.001.

12.2. Significance

As we remarked when we discussed REAL constants, you may use a maximum of approximately 7 decimal digits in writing a REAL constant on the IBM 360 (on the CDC 6600 you may use a maximum of approximately 14 decimal digits in writing a REAL constant). We now explain why the maximum number of digits depends on the computer's hardware.

A word that stores a REAL constant, we recall, is subdivided into a sign bit, an exponent part, and a mantissa. The mantissa contains the fractional part of the REAL constant. Thus in 0.16345×10^{-5}, the binary equivalent of 0.16345 is stored in the mantissa. If the mantissa of each REAL word on a hypothetical machine contains six bits, then the maximum value of the mantissa expressed in binary occurs when all the bits are 1s: i.e., 11 11 11. In decimal, this corresponds to

$$1 \times 2^5 + 1 \times 2^4 + 1 \times 2^3 + 1 \times 2^2 + 1 \times 2^1 + 1 \times 2^0 = 32 + 16 + 8 + 4 + 2 + 1 = 63$$

as shown in Fig. 12.2. Thus, on our hypothetical machine the maximum number of decimal digits the mantissa could accommodate is approximately two; i.e., it could accommodate the two-digit numbers 11 through 63, but it could not accommodate the two-digit numbers 63 to 99. The number 63, which we obtained by adding the powers of two, is equivalent to 64–1 or 2^6-1 (where 6 is the number of bits in the mantissa). We can generalize this result by saying that the largest decimal number that can fit into an n bit mantissa is 2^n-1. Since the mantissa on the IBM 360/370 contains 24 bits, the largest decimal number the mantissa can accommodate is $2^{24}-1$ or 16777215. Any eight-decimal digit number larger than this cannot fit into the mantissa. On the other hand, any integer that has a maximum of seven decimal digits can fit into the mantissa.

Although the maximum number of decimal digits you can use in the mantissa on the IBM 360/370 is approximately 7, the machine can store decimal numbers that have many more than 7 digits, as we shall see in the analysis of the following program. We discuss the program in terms of the decimal system.

EXPANDING A BINARY NUMBER

$$101.11 = \underline{1 \times 10^2 + 0 \times 2^1 + 1 \times 2^0 + 1 \times 2^{-1} + 1 \times 2^{-2}} = 5.75$$

Figure 12.1b. How a binary number can be expressed as the sum of powers of 2. The base of the binary system is 2.

THE LARGEST REAL CONSTANT THAT CAN BE STORED IN A 6 BIT MANTISSA

2^5	2^4	2^3	2^2	2^1	2^0	
1	1	1	1	1	1	6 Bit Mantissa

$$1 \times 2^5 + 1 \times 2^4 + 1 \times 2^3 + 1 \times 2^2 + 1 \times 2^1 + 1 \times 2^0 = 63 = \underline{2^6 - 1}$$

Figure 12.2. The largest REAL constant that can be stored in a 6 bit mantissa is $\underline{2^6-1}$. In an N-bit mantissa, the largest constant than can be stored is 2^N-1. On a 24 bit mantissa, the largest REAL constant is $2^{24}-1$ (16,777,215) which has 7 digits in it.

In the program of Fig. 12.3a we multiply the decimal numbers 22222.0 by 123456.0 and assign the product to RESULT. If we do this multiplication by hand, we obtain 2743439232. This result contains 10 digits, but the computer can only accommodate approximately 7 decimal digits in the mantissa of a REAL word. Therefore the computer rounds the product to 7 digits. In other words, it takes the 7 most meaningful digits 2743439. It then multiplies this by 10^3 to compensate for the fact that it cannot accommodate the 232 part of the product. It thus in effect obtains 2743439000. In this number the digits 2743439 are said to be *significant*; the remaining 3 zeros are called *nonsignificant* digits. The computer stores the product as the binary equivalent of 2743439×10^3 or, in normalized form, the binary equivalent of 0.2743439×10^{10}. The binary equivalent of 2743439 is stored in the mantissa part of the REAL word, and the binary equivalent of the exponent 10 is stored in the exponent part.

In Fig. 12.3b we show the results of the program. We have used both E20.10 and F20.0 to print the results. Since there are only 7 significant digits in RESULT, the digits (104) following 2743439 in both answers are meaningless.

For this reason, once you learn what the maximum numbers of digits your machine can accommodate in the mantissa of a REAL word (by consulting the manufacturer's manual), you should not, in general, print more than that number of digits in your results.

12.3. Overflow and Underflow

The word length on the IBM system 360/370 is 32 bits. As we have mentioned for a REAL word 24 bits are allocated to the mantissa. Of the remaining 8 bits, 7 are allocated to the exponent and 1 to the sign of the constant, as we see in Fig. 12.4a. On the IBM 360/370 the decimal equivalent of exponent ranges from approximately -77 to approximately 76 where the base is 10. If a calculation produces an exponent greater than 76, the computer cannot store the result. Then what is called an *overflow* occurs. The most common cause of overflow is division by zero. If a calculation produces an exponent that is less than -77, the computer cannot store the result. Then, what is called an *underflow* occurs. On most systems, when a REAL underflow or overflow occurs, an execution-time error is printed.

On the IBM 360/370, in an INTEGER word 31 bits are allocated to the constant, and 1 to the sign of the constant, as is shown in Fig. 12.4b. Thus the largest positive value of an INTEGER constant is $2^{31}-1$ or 2,147,483,647. The largest negative value is $-2{,}147{,}483{,}647$. If an INTEGER calculation produces a constant larger than the former or smaller than the latter, then an overflow occurs. A program that calculates $N!$ using INTEGER products will produce an overflow for values of N greater than 13. Beware, many computers do not detect INTEGER overflows; when an INTEGER overflow occurs, the computer prints misleading results.

SIGNIFICANT VS NONSIGNIFICANT DIGITS

```
C   PROGRAM DEMONSTRATES THE USE OF
C   THE EXPONENT PART OF THE REAL WORD
       RESULT=123456.0 * 22222.0
       WRITE(6,10) RESULT, RESULT
 10    FORMAT(1X, 'RESULT=', F20.0, 2X, E20.10 )
       STOP
       END
```

Figure 12.3a. If the result of a calculation has more than 7 digits in it, the computer places the 7 most significant digits in the mantissa and drops the digits that follow it. The exponent is adjusted to compensate for this.

nonsignificant digits

```
RESULT=              2743439104.        0.2743439104E 10
```

Figure 12.3b. Running the program of Fig. 12.3a. The product is really 2743439232. The computer keeps 2743439, in the mantissa and drops the 232 part. The exponent is adjusted to compensate for this. In both results the last three digits (104) are meaningless: they are called nonsignificant digits.

THE REAL WORD

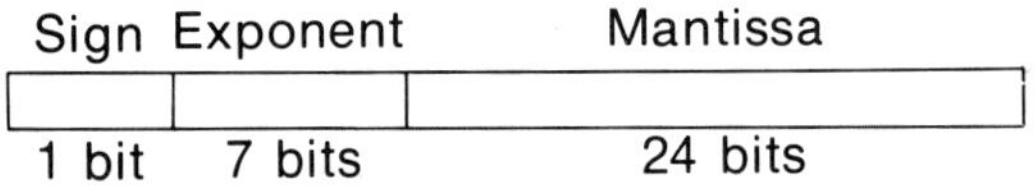

REAL Word

Figure 12.4a. How a REAL word is subdivided into the sign, exponent, and mantissa.

THE INTEGER WORD

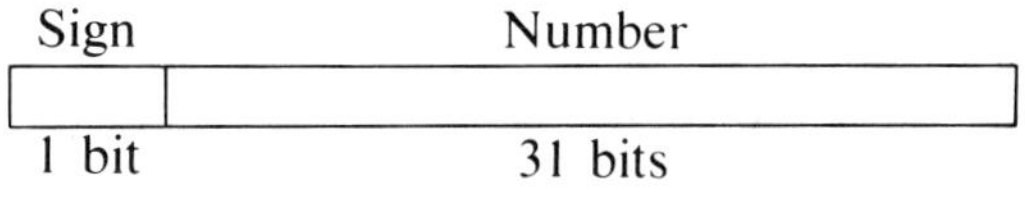

INTEGER Word

Figure 12.4b. How an INTEGER word is subdivided into the sign and a 31 bit part in which the constant is stored. Thus the largest INTEGER constant which can be stored $2^{31}-1$ or 2,147,483,647.

12.4. More on Significance

Before we discuss significance, we would like to remind the reader of the purpose of the exponent part of a REAL word. A decimal point is assumed to be at the left of the mantissa. The purpose of the exponent part of the REAL word is to shift the decimal point a given number of binary places to the left or the right. Thus if the computer wants to store the binary number 111111 in a REAL word, the computer places 111111 in the mantissa. Because the decimal point is assumed to be at the left of the mantissa, the computer—if it were not for the exponent—would interpret the number as .111111. Thus the computer adjusts the exponent part here so that it shifts the decimal point six places to the right. Thus the original .111111 becomes 111111. We also recall that all numbers are stored in the mantissa in normalized form, that is, no numbers are stored with leading zeros. Thus .00123 is stored as the binary equivalent of $.123 \times 10^{-2}$.

We now determine what is the maximum number of significant digits the computer can accommodate in a constant in which all the digits are to the right of the decimal point, i.e., numbers less than one. In order to do this we take the largest binary number less than 1.0 which the computer can accommodate—it is 0.1111111 . . . (i.e., all the bits in the mantissa are 1's)—and investigate how it translates into decimal. We would expect this number to translate into the largest decimal number less than 1.0—a decimal point followed by all 9's, i.e., .99999999 . . . We will now see that because the mantissa has a limited number of bits, the number of 9's we get when we translate into decimal is only approximately one-third the number of bits in the mantissa. In order to calculate the decimal equivalent of the binary 0.111111 . . . we must calculate $\Sigma_{N=1}^{N=NMAX} \frac{1}{2}^N$. For those not familiar with this notation, Σ stands for the sum of the expression to its right, where N—called the index of the summation—assumes all the integral values from 1 to NMAX. Thus $\Sigma_{N=1}^{4} \frac{1}{2}^N = \frac{1}{2}^1 + \frac{1}{2}^2 + \frac{1}{2}^3 + \frac{1}{2}^4$. It represents the decimal equivalent of the binary number .1111. In Fig. 12.5a we write a program that calculates $\Sigma_{N=1}^{N=NMAX} \frac{1}{2}^N$, where the value of NMAX is read by the program from a card shown in Fig. 12.5b. The computer calculates

```
SUM = SUM + 1.0/ 2.0**N
```

each time the range of the DO is executed. The first time the range is executed, SUM on the right of the equals sign is zero, so SUM = 1.0/2.0**1. Thus the second time the SUM

MAXIMUM NUMBER OF SIGNIFICANT DIGITS IN A REAL CONSTANT

```
C   PROGRAM DETERMINES THE MAXIMUM NUMBER OF
C   SIGNIFICANT DIGITS IN A CONSTANT
        SUM = 0.0
        READ(5,10) NMAX
 10     FORMAT( I10 )
        WRITE(6,20) NMAX
 20     FORMAT(1X, 'NMAX=', I5 / 1X,
     1        '(2**N)-1', 7X, 'N', 6X, '1/2**N', 27X, 'SUM OF 1/2**N' )
C
C       ...SUM 1/2**N
        DO 40 N=1,NMAX
           POWER = 1.0 / 2.0**N
           SUM = SUM + POWER
           DIGIT = ( 2.0**N ) - 1.0
           WRITE(6,30) DIGIT, N, POWER, SUM
 30        FORMAT(1X, F10.0, I7, 2F31.27 )
 40     CONTINUE
        STOP
        END
```

Figure 12.5a. How a binary constant of the form 0.111111 . . . transforms into decimal. If the mantissa of a word were infinite, then 0.11111 . . . (binary) would translate into 0.99999 . . . (decimal), a constant having all 9's.

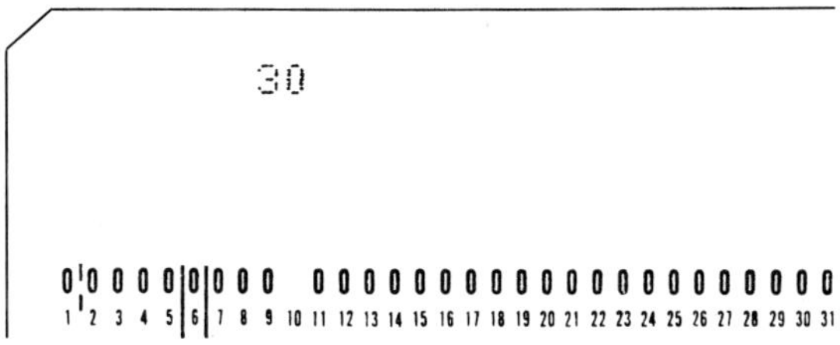

Figure 12.5b. The data card for the program of Fig. 12.5a.

on the right of the equals sign is 1.0/2.0**1 so SUM = 1.0/2.0**1 + 1.0/2.0**2; and the third time SUM = 1.0/2.0**1 + 1.0/2.0**2 + 1.0/2.0**3, etc. In Fig. 12.5c the values listed in the column labeled N represent the number of bits in the mantissa. The values in the column labeled SUM OF ½**N represent the sum of powers of $\frac{1}{2}^N$ from 1 to the value of N which is also printed. Thus, from the fifth line we see that $\Sigma_{N=1}^{5} \frac{1}{2}^N = .96875$.

If the mantissa has 24 bits, the largest binary number less than one that can be stored in the mantissa is represented by a decimal point followed by 24 ones. We see from the rightmost column in line 24 of the table that this corresponds to

.9999999403953552

in decimal. As we have mentioned, the largest decimal number less than 1 is represented by a decimal point followed by all 9's. We see that the closest we could get to this on a machine which has a 24-bit mantissa would be seven 9's. The digits following the 9's (i.e., 403953552) result from the fact that the mantissa has a finite number of bits.

In the DO loop we have also calculated 2^N-1 (the largest decimal digit that can fit into an N-bit mantissa.) For a given line of output, we see that when the number of digits in the value of 2^N-1 increases by 1, the number of 9's in the constants labeled by SUM OF ½**N also increases by 1. Thus the first 9 (i.e., 0.9375) appears when the value of 2^N-1 increases from 7 to 15. The second 9 (i.e., 0.9921875) appears when the value of 2^N-1 increases from 63 to 127. This correspondence continues until the value of N equals 24, the number of bits in the mantissa on the computer on which we ran the program (IBM 370). Thus for a given value of N, the number of 9's in the constant labeled by SUM OF ½**N equals the maximum number of digits you can use in a REAL constant.

Because we are dealing with constants obtained from raising 2 to a power, all the digits* listed in the columns labeled ½**N and SUM OF ½**N are significant. We remember that this program was run on a machine that has a 24-bit mantissa. We see that when N becomes 25, the constants listed under SUM OF ½**N do not change. However, the constants listed under ½**N, for N equal to and greater than 25, do change (and are in fact correct). Why then do the constants listed under SUM OF ½**N not change? The reason

* After N equals 22, the values of the trailing zeros are not significant.

NMAX= 30

(2**N)-1	N	1/2**N	SUM OF 1/2**N
1.	1	0.500000000000000000000000000	0.500000000000000000000000000
3.	2	0.250000000000000000000000000	0.750000000000000000000000000
7.	3	0.125000000000000000000000000	0.875000000000000000000000000
15.	4	0.062500000000000000000000000	0.937500000000000000000000000
31.	5	0.031250000000000000000000000	0.968750000000000000000000000
63.	6	0.015625000000000000000000000	0.984375000000000000000000000
127.	7	0.007812500000000000000000000	0.992187500000000000000000000
255.	8	0.003906250000000000000000000	0.996093750000000000000000000
511.	9	0.001953125000000000000000000	0.998046875000000000000000000
1023.	10	0.000976562500000000000000000	0.999023437500000000000000000
2047.	11	0.000488281250000000000000000	0.999511718750000000000000000
4095.	12	0.000244140625000000000000000	0.999755859375000000000000000
8191.	13	0.000122070312500000000000000	0.999877929687500000000000000
16383.	14	0.000061035156250000000000000	0.999938964843750000000000000
32767.	15	0.000030517578125000000000000	0.999969482421875000000000000
65535.	16	0.000015258789062500000000000	0.999984741210937500000000000
131071.	17	0.000007629394531250000000000	0.999992370605468700000000000
262143.	18	0.000003814697265625000000000	0.999996185302734400000000000
524287.	19	0.000001907348632812500000000	0.999998092651367200000000000
1048575.	20	0.000000953674316406250000000	0.999999046325683600000000000
2097151.	21	0.000000476837158203125000000	0.999999523162841800000000000
4194303.	22	0.000000238418579101562500000	0.999999761581420900000000000
8388607.	23	0.000000119209289550781200000	0.999999880790710400000000000
16777215.	24	0.000000059604644775390620000	0.999999940395355200000000000
33554416.	25	0.000000029802322387695310000	0.999999940395355200000000000
67108848.	26	0.000000014901161193847660000	0.999999940395355200000000000
134217712.	27	0.000000007450580596923828000	0.999999940395355200000000000
268435456.	28	0.000000003725290298461914000	0.999999940395355200000000000
536870912.	29	0.000000001862645149230957000	0.999999940395355200000000000
**********	30	0.000000000931322574615478600	0.999999940395355200000000000

Figure 12.5c. Running the program of Fig. 12.5a, we see that as the number of 9's in SUM increases, so do the number of digits in 2^N-1. This program was run on a 24-bit machine. For N greater than 24, the value of SUM does not change.

can be seen by examining a 4-bit mantissa. When N equals 1, the value of $2^{-N} = 0.1$ in binary. This is stored as $\boxed{1|0|0|0}$. When N equals 2, the value of 2^{-N} equals 0.01 in binary, but in normalized form this is stored as $\boxed{1|0|0|0}$, as shown in Table 12.1, where the exponent (in decimal) is −1. When 2^{-2} (or .01) is added in the arithmetic unit (in locations called *arithmetic registers*) to the previous sum, .1, the decimal points must be aligned. Thus, in the arithmetic unit, 2^{-2} (or .01) is represented as $\boxed{0|1|0|0}$ and when added to the previous sum $\boxed{1|0|0|0}$, the result is $\boxed{1|1|0|0}$. When N equals 3, the value of 2^{-N} equals .001 and is stored in normalized form as $\boxed{1|0|0|0}$, and the exponent (in decimal) is −2. When .001 is added in the arithmetic unit to the previous sum, .11, the decimal points must again be aligned. Thus in the arithmetic unit, 2^{-3} is represented as $\boxed{0|0|1|0}$ and when it is added to the previous sum $\boxed{1|1|0|0}$; the result is $\boxed{1|1|1|0}$. This process continues up to and including N equals 4.

When N equals 5, the memory location for 2^{-N} has no difficulty in storing .00001. It is stored as $\boxed{1|0|0|0}$, where the exponent (in decimal) is −4. Thus, as long as the exponent part of the word is large enough to store the shift in the decimal point, 2^{-N} for very large values of N can be represented. However, when it comes to adding 2^{-5} or .00001 to the previous sum, .1111, since the decimal points must be aligned the .00001 is represented as $\boxed{0|0|0|0}$ in the arithmetic unit. Thus the 1 of .00001 does not fit. Obviously when $\boxed{0|0|0|0}$ is added to the previous sum $\boxed{1|1|1|1}$, the result is the same as the previous sum. This result is repeated for each successive value of N: i.e., the sum does not change. All of this is shown in Table 12.1. We should now understand why in Fig. 12.5b the value of the constants labeled by SUM OF ½**N does not change after the value of N exceeds 24.

HOW THE NUMBER OF BITS IN THE MANTISSA AFFECTS ADDITION

	Memory locations		Memory location		Arithmetic registers		
N	2^{-N}		SUM		2^{-N}	+	Previous value of SUM
	exp.	mantissa					
1	0	1 0 0 0	1 0 0 0	=	1 0 0 0	+	0 0 0 0
2	−1	1 0 0 0	1 1 0 0	=	0 1 0 0	+	1 0 0 0
3	−2	1 0 0 0	1 1 1 0	=	0 0 1 0	+	1 1 0 0
4	−3	1 0 0 0	1 1 1 1	=	0 0 0 1	+	1 1 1 0
5	−4	1 0 0 0	1 1 1 1	=	0 0 0 0	+	1 1 1 1

Table 12.1. How SUM=SUM + 1.0/2.0**N works for a 4-bit mantissa. When 2^{-N} is added to the previous sum in the arithmetic unit, the decimal points must be aligned. Thus for N equals 5, 2^{-5}, cannot fit into a 4-bit location, and the 1 is dropped. Thus, from this point on, the value of the sum does not change. In Fig. 12.5b, we see that this happens for N equals 25 on a 24-bit mantissa.

12.5. Hexadecimal Representation

The hexadecimal system is a system that uses base 16; thus the largest digit that can be used in the hexadecimal system has the value 15. The IBM System 360/370 uses a hexadecimal representation. Four bits are represented by one hexadecimal digit.

2^3	2^2	2^1	2^0

Thus the largest numbers that can be stored in this grouping is $1 + 2 + 4 + 8 = 15$. Since the mantissa has 24 bits, it has 6 hexadecimal digits. The largest value of the constant that can fit into the mantissa is still $2^{24}-1$; and the results of the previous program (Fig. 12.5a) still apply. One of the few differences between a 24-bit mantissa that uses binary and one that uses hexadecimal is when the constant stored in the mantissa has digits both to the left and to the right of the decimal point. Thus 1.75 would be stored as follows:

0	0	0	1	1	1	0	0	0	0	0	0	0	0	0	0	0	0	0	0	0	0	0	0
			∧																				

as is shown in Fig. 12.6a.

The dark vertical lines indicate how the bits are grouped into hexadecimal digits. Note that the bit pattern is no longer normalized because the first 4 bits constitute the hexadecimal digit 1.

The exponent part indicates how many hexadecimal places the decimal point should be shifted. Thus for 1.75, the exponent would indicate that the decimal point should be moved 1 hexadecimal place (4 binary places) to the right. We have indicated this place with a caret. We can see that the range of a hexadecimal exponent is greater than the range of a binary exponent because 1 hexadecimal place equals 4 binary places.

We next investigate the hexadecimal representation of 19.999999. . . . The closest we can get to 19.9999999. . . . is

0	0	0	1	0	0	1	1	1	1	1	1	1	1	1	1	1	1	1	1	1	1	1	1
							∧																

as is shown in Fig. 12.6b, where the 8 bits (2 hexadecimal digits) to the left of the implied decimal point (the caret) represent 19, and the 16 bits (4 hexadecimal digits) to the right of the implied decimal point represent the .999999 . . . part of the constant. In this case the exponent would indicate that the decimal point should be shifted 2 hexadecimal places to the right. From the results shown in Fig. 12.5c, we see that by using 16 bits the closest to all 9's we can get is .9999847412 . . . . Thus we can only get four 9's. Therefore the closest we can get to 19.999999 . . . is actually 19.9999847412 which only has 6 significant digits in it. Thus, we see that sometimes 1 digit of significance is lost in hexadecimal representation.

THE HEXADECIMAL SYSTEM

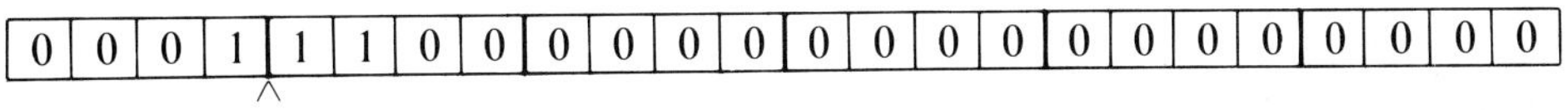

Figure 12.6a. How 1.75 is expressed on a hexadecimal (base 16) machine. In hexadecimal, bits are grouped into groups of 4; i.e., the maximum value of these 4 bits is 15. The exponent part shifts the decimal point 4 bits at a time. The solid lines show the partition into hexadecimal digits and the caret (∧) shows where the decimal point should be.

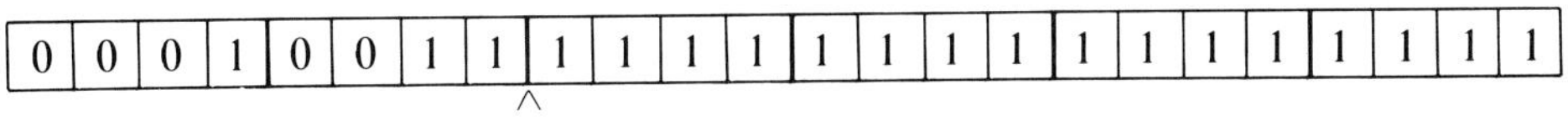

Figure 12.6b. How 19.999999 . . . is represented on a hexadecimal machine. Because the 19 requires 8 bits, now only 16 bits can be used to represent the 9's following the decimal point; thus we can only get four 9's, and the total number of significant digits we can get is only 6.

12.6. Double Precision*

By using what is called *double precision*, we in effect instruct the computer to double the number of bits in the mantissa—the computer actually uses the mantissas of two words. This allows us to approximately double the number of significant digits in a REAL constant. The range of the exponent, however, is the same as in a single-precision REAL word. Double precision on the IBM 360/370, uses the mantissa of one word (24 bits) and the mantissa, the sign, and the exponent part of the second word (32 bits) to store the bits of a double-precision constant. Therefore it can use 56 bits for the mantissa. Thus the largest REAL constant you can have in double precision on the IBM 360/370 is $2^{56}-1$. A double-precision constant on the IBM 360/370 can have a maximum of 16 decimal digits. We declare that a variable will be double precision by placing it in the list of a DOUBLE PRECISION statement. We declare that a REAL constant is DOUBLE PRECISION by following it by the letter D and then an exponent. Thus if we want 1.1 to be a DOUBLE PRECISION constant, we write it as 1.1 D0. Since the .1 part cannot be expressed exactly in binary, the computer internal representation of 1.1D0 is closer to the actual number 1.1 than the computer internal representation of the non-double-precision constant.

In Fig. 12.7a we investigate the use of DOUBLE PRECISION variables. In XDUB = .9D0 we assign the DOUBLE PRECISION constant .9D0 to the DOUBLE PRECISION variable XDUB. .9D0 is the DOUBLE PRECISION equivalent of .9E0, i.e., $.9 \times 10^0$.

* Not available in Standard Basic FORTRAN.

DOUBLE PRECISION

```
C   INTRODUCTION TO DOUBLE PRECISION
      DOUBLE PRECISION CALDUB, CALDB1, XDUB, YDUB, XDUB1, SUB
      XDUB = 0.9D0
      XSING = 0.9
      YDUB = 0.5D0
      XDUB1 = 0.9
      CALDUB = 0.9*0.9D0
      CALDB1 = 0.9D0*0.9D0
      SING = 0.9D0
      SUB = XDUB - SING
C
      WRITE(6,10) XDUB, XDUB, YDUB, XSING, XDUB1
 10   FORMAT(1X, 'XDUB = 0.9D0', 5X, D25.18 /
     1       1X, 'XDUB = 0.9D0', 5X, F25.18 /
     1       1X, 'YDUB = 0.50', 5X, F25.18 /
     1       1X, 'XSING = 0.9', 5X, F25.18 /
     1       1X, 'XDUB1 = 0.9', 5X, D25.18 )
C
      WRITE(6,20) CALDUB, CALDB1, SING, SUB
 20   FORMAT(1X, '0.9 * 0.9D0 =', 5X, D25.18/
     1       1X, '0.9D0 * 0.9D0 = ', 5X, D25.18 /
     1       1X, 'SING = 0.9D0', 5X, F25.18/
     1      1X, '0.9D0 - 0.9=', D25.18 )
      STOP
      END
```

Figure 12.7a. Usually in a DOUBLE PRECISION word, you combine the mantissas of two REAL words, thus you double the accuracy (precision). You declare a variable to be DOUBLE PRECISION by placing it in the DOUBLE PRECISION list in the beginning of the program. You declare a constant to be DOUBLE PRECISION by following it with a D and then the exponent. WATFOR/WATFIV compilers print 16 digits in DOUBLE PRECISION results.

When we print the results as shown in Fig. 12.7b, we see that there are 15 significant digits in the result. The 8 to the right of the string of 9's is not significant. We print the result using D25.18. This is the same as E format but is used for DOUBLE PRECISION variables. The D 00 in the result means 10^0. When we print the value of XDUB using F format (F25.18), we get the same result without the D 00. (We ran this program on a WATFIV compiler on the IBM 370; the WATFOR/WATFIV system prints 16 digits in DOUBLE PRECISION results, then if necessary it prints trailing zeros.) We contrast this with 0.9 in single precision, the value of XSING, and we see that we get only 7 significant digits. Since 0.9 cannot be expressed exactly in binary, the double precision result is more accurate than the single precision result. In YDUB = 0.5D0, we show that by declaring a constant that can be expressed exactly on the machine as a DOUBLE PRECISION variable, we do not gain any accuracy.

In XDUB1 = 0.9 we assign a single precision constant to a DOUBLE PRECISION variable and print its value using D format; we see that the value of XDUB1 is single precision and is printed as 0.899999976158142000D00, i.e., only the first 7 digits are significant. In CALDUB = 0.9*0.9D0 we multiply a single precision constant by a DOUBLE PRECISION constant and assign the result to a DOUBLE PRECISION variable. What happens is that the internal representation of .9 is expanded to two words, but the second word contains only zeros. Thus the result is not as accurate as a calculation done entirely in DOUBLE PRECISION, CALDB1 = 0.9D0*0.9D0, as shown in Fig. 12.7b, in which both constants are double precision.

Next we assign a DOUBLE PRECISION constant 0.9D0 to the single precision SING. The result only has 7 significant digits, and is thus only single precision.* Finally, we subtract the value (0.9) of the single precision variable SING from the value (0.9D0) of the DOUBLE PRECISION variable XDUB and assign the result to the DOUBLE PRECISION variable SUB. The internal representation of 0.9 is expanded to two words, but the second word contains only zeros. Thus the result of the subtraction is not zero, but the difference between 0.9D0 and 0.9.

We note that we can use F format to print the DOUBLE PRECISION results, if we make the field width large enough. However, we advise you to use D format to make it clear to anyone reading the program that the variable whose value was printed in the field was declared to be DOUBLE PRECISION.

In Fig. 12.7c we see the results when the program is run on the IBM 370 FORTRAN compiler. We see that the values of 0.9D0 and 0.9D0*0.9D0 are printed as exact numbers 0.9 and 0.81, respectively. This is misleading because the constants stored have the values shown in Fig. 12.7b.

* The result is not rounded, but the excess digits are dropped or chopped.

```
XDUB = 0.9D0          0.899999999999999800D 00  <---- Printed using D25.18
XDUB = 0.9D0              0.899999999999999800  <---- Printed using F25.18
YDUB = 0.50               0.500000000000000000
XSING = 0.9               0.899999900000000000
XDUB1 = 0.9           0.899999976158142000D 00
0.9 * 0.9D0 =          0.809999978542327800D 00
0.9D0 * 0.9D0 =            0.809999999999999800D 00
SING = 0.9D0               0.899999900000000000
0.9D0 - 0.9= 0.238418579046051300D-07
```

Figure 12.7b. Running the program of Fig. 11.7a on a WATFIV compiler. We see that since 0.5 can be expressed exactly in binary, making it DOUBLE PRECISION does not change its value; however, since 0.9 cannot be expressed exactly in binary, making it DOUBLE PRECISION increases its precision. Whenever we use D format to print a DOUBLE PRECISION variable its value is printed with a D. The value of a DOUBLE PRECISION variable when used with F format is not printed with a D.

```
XDUB = 0.9D0          0.900000000000000000D 00  <---- Printed using D25.18
XDUB = 0.9D0              0.900000000000000000  <---- Printed using F25.18
YDUB = 0.50               0.500000000000000000
XSING = 0.9               0.899999976158142100
XDUB1 = 0.9           0.899999976158142100D 00
0.9 * 0.9D0 =          0.809999978542327900D 00
0.9D0 * 0.9D0 =            0.810000000000000000D 00
SING = 0.9D0               0.899999976158142100
0.9D0 - 0.9= 0.238418579046051300D-07
```

Figure 12.7c. Running the program of Fig. 12.7c on the IBM 370 FORTRAN compiler. Although the values of 0.9D and 0.9D0*0.9D0 are printed as exact numbers, in reality they are stored as was shown in Fig. 12.7b.

The procedure for reading a DOUBLE PRECISION constant is the same as for reading a REAL constant in exponential mode. Thus if we want $0.12345671234567 \times 10^{-4}$ read by D25.12, we type 0.12345671234567D-4 on the card, as shown in Fig. 12.8. Just as in punching a constant to be read by E format, the exponent part must be right-justified; whereas if the mantissa is punched with a decimal point, the mantissa can be punched anywhere in the field.

The DOUBLE PRECISION library functions are shown in Table 12.2. The arguments of these functions must be DOUBLE PRECISION variables.

READING IN DOUBLE PRECISION

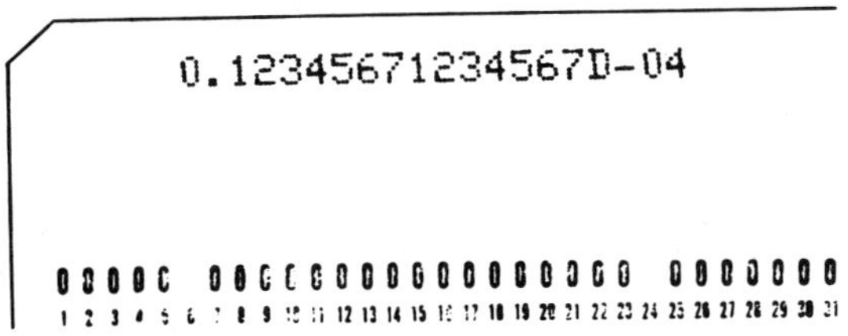

Figure 12.8. In order to read a DOUBLE PRECISION constant, you type it as you would an E (exponential) constant. This data card will be read by a D25.12 format.

DOUBLE PRECISION function	REAL function	Purpose
DSQRT (X)	SQRT (Y)	Square root (X)
DABS (X)	ABS (Y)	Absolute value (X)
DSIN (X)	SIN (Y)	Sine (X)
DCOS (X)	COS (Y)	Cosine (X)
DEXP (X)	EXP (Y)	e^X
DLOG (X)	ALOG (Y)	$\log_e (X)$
DLOG10 (X)	ALOG10 (Y)	$\log_{10} (X)$

Table 12.2. The DOUBLE PRECISION library functions. These functions are preceded by the letter D. In the second column are listed the REAL equivalents. The argument of a DOUBLE PRECISION function must be a DOUBLE PRECISION variable.

12.7. Newton's Method and DOUBLE PRECISION Functions

Newton's method for finding the square root of X, where A is the first approximation, is $Y = [A + (X/A)]/2.0$, where Y is the second approximation* to the square root of X. Thus if we wish to find the square root of 20.0, and our first approximation is 4.0, we obtain 4.5 as the answer for Y. If we want a better approximation, we now use 4.5 as the value of A. This process of substituting the result of a formula back into the formula to obtain a better answer is called *iterating*. Each time the formula is used, it is called an *iteration*.

In Fig. 12.9a we present a program that calculates the square root of X using a subprogram function that employs Newton's method. We use the statement

```
10   A = ( A + X/A ) / 2.0
```

to calculate the square roots where the first approximation is set equal to 1.0 in A = 1.0. In the IF statement we see how X/A^2 compares with 1.0. If A is a good approximation to X, then X/A^2 is close to 1.0. We do not know *a priori* whether A**2 is greater or less than X, thus we calculate ABS (X/A**2 − 1.0) and compare this with EPSIL. The value of EPSIL is a very small constant. We initially will set this constant equal to zero in order to see one of the ramifications of the iteration process. If the value of A does not satisfy the

* The derivation is as follows: if $X = (A + B)^2$, then $X = A^2 + 2AB + B^2$. If A is a good approximation to $\sqrt{X}$, then B is small, so we assume that B^2 is negligible. Thus $X = A^2 + 2AB$. Solving this for B, we obtain $B = (X - A^2)/(2A)$. But if $X = (A + B)^2$, then $\sqrt{X} = A + B$, but $A + B = A + (X - A^2)/(2A) = (X/A + A)/2$. Thus $\sqrt{X} = (X/A + A)/2$. If we had chosen A such that $A^2 > X$, then we would be squaring $A - B$, and we would solve $X = A^2 - 2AB$. Solving this for B, we obtain $B = (X + A^2)/2A$. Thus $A - B = (X + A^2)/2A$ or $A - B = (X/A + A)/2$. We thus obtain the same result for both cases.

NEWTON'S METHOD FOR FINDING SQUARE ROOTS

```
C  USES FUNCTION SUBPROGRAM TO CALCULATE SQRT(X)
      READ(5,10) X
 10   FORMAT(F10.0)
      Y = SQR(X)
      WRITE(6,20) X, Y
 20   FORMAT(1X, 'THE SQUARE ROOT OF', F10.3, '  IS', F10.7 )
C
      STOP
      END
```

Figure 12.9a. *Main program.* In Y = SQR(X) we call the function we have written in the function subprogram.

```
      FUNCTION SQR(X)
C  CALCULATES SQUARE ROOT USING NEWTON'S METHOD
      A = 1.0
      EPSIL = 0.0
 10   A = ( A + X/A ) / 2.0
      FRAC = X / A**2
C
      WRITE(6,20) X, A, FRAC
 20   FORMAT(1X, 'X=', F10.3, '   A=', E16.7, 3X,  'X/A**2=', E16.7 )
      IF(ABS( X/A**2 - 1.0 ) .GT. EPSIL ) GO TO 10
         SQR = A
         RETURN
      END
```

FUNCTION SQR. Program calculates the square root of *X* using Newton's method. The value of epsilon, EPSIL, is set to zero. Each time a value of A is calculated, it is substituted back into A = (A + X/A)/2.0.

condition in the IF, this value of A becomes the approximation in (A + X/A), and a new approximation is obtained. We see that the value of X on the data card shown in Fig. 12.9b, is 20.0. The results of running the program are shown in Fig. 12.9c.

Because A^2 is larger than X, then X/A^2 approaches 1.0 through the fractions which are less than 1.0, and therefore it approaches 0.9999. . . . (the probability of A^2 precisely equaling X is very small because of round-off error). We ran this program originally on a computer for which the largest number less than 1 has only 6 9's in it. After the value of X/A^2 reaches 0.999999, a number with six 9's in it, the program yields the same results for each subsequent iteration. This is in agreement with the results shown in Fig. 12.5c. Because of the limited number of bits in the mantissa, there is a limit to the number of 9's we can get in the largest constant less than 1.0. If we choose a value of EPSIL less than 1×10^{-6} (i.e., 1.0 − 0.999999), the program will never stop iterating.* In Fig. 12.9d we have rewritten the subprogram substituting 1×10^{-5} for EPSIL. We would thus be fairly certain that the program stops. To make absolutely certain that the program does stop, we could also limit the number of iterations to 20, for example.

The subprogram as currently written does not accommodate values of X that are zero or negative: A zero value of X would cause an overflow condition; a negative value would cause the program to iterate indefinitely. In order to give the subprogram integrity, we would have to test for these values of X and return a value of SQR equal to zero for X to equal zero, and an error message if X were negative.

The reader may ask why not write the condition in the IF statement so that we compare X with A^2 as opposed to comparing X/A^2 with 1.0, thus writing the IF statement as ABS(X−A**2) .GT. 1.0E −5. The reason is that this condition would always be true for very large values of X and the program would never stop iterating. For example, if the value of X were 123456., we would require A^2 to be .00001 away from 123456., and thus we would require A^2 to be expressed to 11 significant digits, i.e., 123456.00001. However, a machine that can accommodate a maximum of 7 digits could store only the 123456.0 part of this constant. Thus, when the machine evaluates ABS(X−A**2), the smallest result it can obtain is .1; thus the value of ABS (X − A**2) would always be greater than† 1.0×10^{-5}.

* When this program was run on the HP 3000 and the CDC 6600, the program continued to iterate. When run on the IBM 360, the program stopped after 6 iterations and produced an answer.

† We recall that because of round-off error, the probability of getting A^2 to exactly equal X is remote.

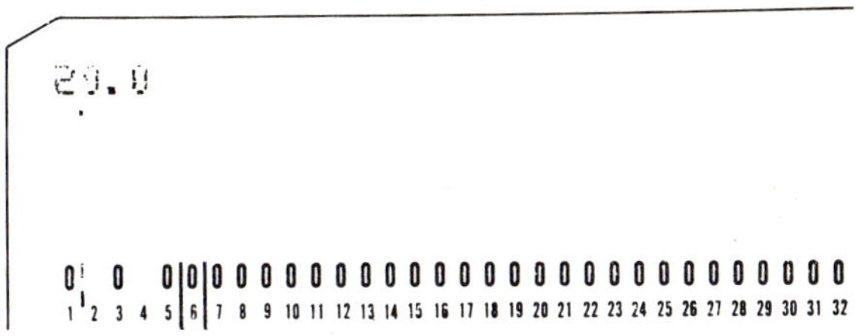

Figure 12.9b. Data card for Fig. 12.9a.

```
X=     20.000   A=    0.1050000E 02     X/A**2=     0.1814058E 00
X=     20.000   A=    0.6202380E 01     X/A**2=     0.5198922E 00
X=     20.000   A=    0.4713474E 01     X/A**2=     0.9002185E 00
X=     20.000   A=    0.4478314E 01     X/A**2=     0.9972427E 00
X=     20.000   A=    0.4472139E 01     X/A**2=     0.9999992E 00
X=     20.000   A=    0.4472136E 01     X/A**2=     0.9999998E 00
X=     20.000   A=    0.4472136E 01     X/A**2=     0.9999998E 00
X=     20.000   A=    0.4472136E 01     X/A**2=     0.9999998E 00
X=     20.000   A=    0.4472136E 01     X/A**2=     0.9999998E 00
X=     20.000   A=    0.4472136E 01     X/A**2=     0.9999998E 00
X=     20.000   A=    0.4472136E 01     X/A**2=     0.9999998E 00
```

↗ *Program was manually stopped here.*

Figure 12.9c. Running the program of Fig. 12.9a. We see that X/A^2 approaches 1.0 throughout the fractions less than 1.0. Because of the limited size of the mantissa, we get only six 9's in X/A^2. This dictates the minimum value of EPSIL we can use to stop the program: $1.0 - 0.999999$ or 1×10^{-6}. If we use a value of EPSIL less than this, the program will never stop iterating.

```
C   CALCULATES SQUARE ROOT USING NEWTON'S METHOD
       A=1.0
 10    A = ( A + X / A ) / 2.0
C
       IF( ABS( X/A**2 - 1.0 ) .GT. 1.0E-5 ) GO TO 10
          SQR = A
          RETURN
       END
```

Figure 12.9d. The subroutine of Fig. 12.9a rewritten so that the value of epsilon, EPSIL, is now 1.0×10^{-5}.

In Fig. 12.10a we write the program of Fig. 12.9a, but now we use a DOUBLE PRECISION function to calculate the square root. Since the computer can accommodate a maximum of approximately 16 significant digits in a DOUBLE PRECISION constant, we can now certainly safely use 1×10^{-10} as the computer constant. Since 1×10^{-10} cannot be expressed exactly on a binary computer, we write it as 1.0D−10. Since we want the function SQR to be DOUBLE PRECISION, we begin the function with DOUBLE PRECISION FUNCTION SQR(X), and we use DABS to find the absolute value of $X/A^2-1.0$. Also, in the main program we declare SQR to be DOUBLE PRECISION. The results of running the program are shown in Fig. 12.10b.

FINDING SQUARE ROOTS USING DOUBLE PRECISION

```
C   USES DOUBLE PRECISION FUNCTION
C   TO CALCULATE SQRT(X)
      DOUBLE PRECISION SQR, X, Y
      READ(5,10) X
 10   FORMAT( D25.0 )
      Y=SQR(X)
      WRITE(6,20) X, Y
 20   FORMAT(1X, 'THE SQUARE ROOT OF', D25.14, '  IS', D25.14 )
      STOP
      END

      DOUBLE PRECISION FUNCTION SQR(X)
      DOUBLE PRECISION A, X
      A=1.0
 10   A = ( A + X / A ) / 2.0
C
      IF( DABS( X/A**2 - 1.0 ) .GT. 1.0D-10 ) GO TO 10
         SQR=A
         RETURN
      END
```

Figure 12.10a. The program of Fig. 12.9a now written in DOUBLE PRECISION. Since the number of 9's in X/A^2 should now be doubled, we have also doubled the exponent in EPSILON. We now write it as 1.0D−10.

```
THE SQUARE ROOT OF       0.20000000000000D 02   IS      0.44721359550016D 01
```

Figure 12.10b. Running the program of Fig. 12.10a.

12.8. Complex Numbers

A complex number is one that has a real and imaginary part. In $10.3 + 16.2i$, the 10.3 is the real part and 16.2 is the imaginary part where i is $\sqrt{-1}$. If you multiply two complex numbers, the procedure is the same as for regular (real) multiplication. Thus $(2 + 2i) \cdot (3 + 4i)$ is $2 \cdot 3 + 2 \cdot 4i + 3 \cdot 2i + 2i \cdot 4i$. Since $i \cdot i$ is -1, then the product is $6 + 14i - 8 = -2 + 14i$. If we declare the variables A and B to be COMPLEX, we can then perform a complex multiplication by simply writing C = A*B, as shown in Fig. 12.11a. Since we want A to equal $2.0 + 2.0i$ and B to equal $3.0 + 4.0i$, we must read the four REAL constants which form these two complex numbers. We read the constants in READ (5,10) A, B. Since both these variables are declared to be COMPLEX in

```
COMPLEX A, B, C, D, E
```

we must use two fields to describe A and two to describe B.
We thus write the associated FORMAT as

```
10    FORMAT( 2F10.0, 2F10.0 )
```

The data card read is shown in Fig. 12.11b.

If we want to include a COMPLEX constant in the program without reading the constant, we must use the CMPLX function. For example D = CMPLX (1.0, 2.0) creates the constant $1.0 + 2.0i$ and assigns it to D which has been declared to be COMPLEX. In WRITE (6, 30) C, D, we print the values of C and D. Since both these variables are COMPLEX, we need two fields to describe each, as shown in the associated FORMAT

```
      WRITE(6,30) C, D
30    FORMAT(1X, 'C=', 2F10.1, 'I', 2X, 'D=', 2F10.1, 'I' )
```

where 'I' represents i. The results of printing this are shown in Fig. 12.11c.

If we want to find the real and the imaginary part of a complex number, we have to use the REAL and AIMAG functions, respectively. Thus REAL(E) finds the real part of E and AIMAG(E) finds the imaginary part, as is shown in Fig. 12.11a and the results in Fig. 12.11c. (Note AIMAG begins with an A since all library functions which return REAL results cannot begin with I, J, K, L, M or N.)

COMPLEX NUMBERS

```
C   SHOWS USE OF COMPLEX NUMBERS
        COMPLEX A, B, C, D, E
        REAL RE, IM
        READ(5,10) A, B
 10     FORMAT( 2F10.0, 2F10.0 )
        WRITE(6,20) A, B
 20     FORMAT(1X, 'A=', 2F10.1, '   B=', 2F10.1 )
C
        C= A * B
        D = CMPLX( 1.0, 2.0 )
C
        WRITE(6,30) C, D
 30     FORMAT(1X, 'C=', 2F10.1, 'I', 2X, 'D=', 2F10.1, 'I' )
        E = C * D
        RE = REAL(E)
        IM = AIMAG(E)
C
        WRITE(6,40) E, RE, IM
 40     FORMAT(1X, 'E=', 2F10.1, 'I   REAL PART=', F10.1, 2X,
      1        'IMAGINARY PART = ', F10.1 )
        STOP
        END
```

Figure 12.11a. Using complex numbers. All variables that are complex must be declared as such. When reading the value of a complex variable, two constants must be provided; the first for the real part and the second for the imaginary part. We produce 1 + 2*i* by writing CMPLX(1.0, 2.0). When writing the value of a complex variable, one field must be supplied for the real and one field for the imaginary part.

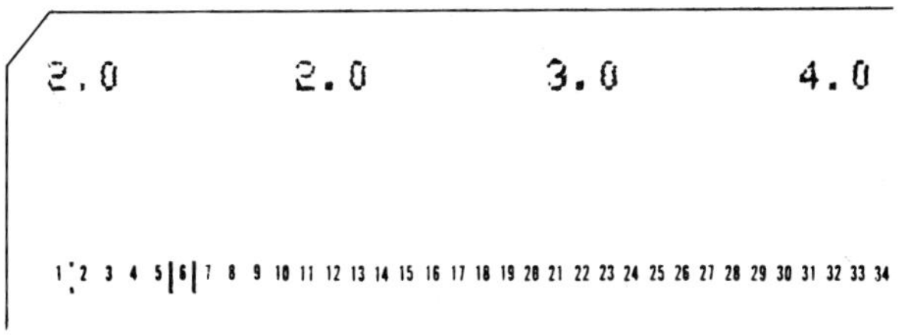

Figure 12.11b. The data card for Fig. 12.11a. For each complex variable, two constants must be supplied, the first for the real part and the second for the imaginary part.

```
A=        2.0       2.0  B=       3.0       4.0
C=       -2.0      14.0I  D=       1.0       2.0I
E=      -30.0      10.0I  REAL PART=     -30.0  IMAGINARY PART =      10.0
```

Figure 12.11c. Running the program of Fig. 12.11a. The function REAL obtains the real part of a complex variable, the function AIMAG obtains the imaginary part.

PROBLEMS

1. Convert the following binary numbers into their decimal equivalents:

(a) 1011.101
(b) 1100.001
(c) .0101

2. What is the maximum number of significant digits you can get if the mantissa has 20 bits?

3. Write a program that determines how many bits are in the mantissa of the computer you are using. Hint: use the results shown in Table 12.1.

4. How would the following numbers be represented in binary on a hexadecimal machine?

(a) 14.25
(b) 22.5
(c) 41.125

5. Write a program that determines how many bits there are in the effective mantissa of the DOUBLE PRECISION word on your computer.

6. Rewrite the subroutine of Fig 12.9 so that in case the value of EPSILON is too small to stop the program, the program will automatically stop after 20 iterations.

7. The program of Fig 5.14a which calculated e, the base of the natural logarithms, was written so that it only calculated the first nine terms in the series for e. The reason for this is that the following result was observed on the IBM 370: When the tenth term, and after that, succeeding terms, were added to the series, the value of the series did not change. The explanation of this result is the same one that explains why $\Sigma_N(\frac{1}{2})^N$ did not change when N became greater than 24 in the program of Fig. 12.5a—the tenth term was so small in comparison to the sum of the preceding terms that when the decimal points of the tenth term and the sum were aligned in the register, the value of the tenth term became zero. Write a program that sums the first 15 terms in the series for e but does the sum backward, i.e., adds the 15th and 14th terms, then adds this sum to the 13th term, then adds this new sum to the 12th term, etc. When you run this program see whether you get a better approximate e than was obtained in Fig 5.14c. What you are showing is that on a computer, addition is not always associative, i.e., $A + (B + C)$ does not always equal $(A + B) + C$. For the sake of comparison, the value of e to 16 figures is 2.71828 18284 59045.

8. Rewrite the program of 5.14a which calculated e, so that the sum is done in DOUBLE PRECISION. Sum the first 20 terms and compare the results to the answer you obtained in problem 7.

13

More INPUT/OUTPUT

13.1. More on A Format

As we have previously remarked, in ANS Standard FORTRAN and WATFOR, the only way you can assign an alphanumeric constant to a variable is by using a DATA statement, a READ statement or by using an alphanumeric constant as an actual argument of a subroutine; an alphanumeric constant cannot appear explicitly in a program except in a DATA statement or in a subroutine call. Thus on these systems the following statements would produce compile-time errors

```
A='STR'
IF ( R .EQ. 'G' ) GO TO 40
```

because the alphanumeric constants 'STR' and 'G' appear in non-DATA statements.

As you recall, you can assign an alphanumeric constant to either a REAL or an INTEGER variable. In the program shown in Fig. 13.1a, we use a DATA statement to assign the alphanumeric constants to the INTEGER variables NAME1 and NAME2 and to the four elements of the REAL subscripted variable STRING. We do this in

```
DATA NAME1, NAME2, STRING / 'JOAN', 'BILL', 'FRED', 3*'RITA' /
```

Just as in the case of repeated identical numerical constants, 3*'RITA' is equivalent to 'RITA', 'RITA', 'RITA'. To make the discussion of the program easier to follow, we have made all the constants 4 characters long, the maximum allowed under normal circumstances on the IBM 370/360. The program was run on this system. We now discuss the DATA statement.

The constants are assigned to the variables as shown in Fig. 13.1b

J O A N	B I L L	F R E D	R I T A	R I T A	R I T A
NAME1	NAME2	STRING(1)	STRING(2)	STRING(3)	STRING(4)

In order to print alphanumeric constants, we must use A format as shown, for instance in

```
30    FORMAT(1X, A3 )
```

The number that follows the A, as usual, indicates the field width. Thus A3 specifies an alphanumeric field 3 columns wide. To help the reader understand how A format operates, we have written the first WRITE statement in the program so that it prints

```
123456
```

This will enable us to determine which column a given character is printed in.

PRINTING USING A FORMAT

```
C  ASSIGNING ALPHANUMERIC CONSTANTS TO
C  VARIABLES IN A DATA STATEMENT
      DIMENSION STRING(4)
      DATA NAME1, NAME2, STRING / 'JOAN', 'BILL', 'FRED', 3*'RITA' /
C     ..LABEL COLUMNS
      WRITE(6,5)
 5    FORMAT(1X, '123456' )
C
      WRITE(6,10) NAME1
 10   FORMAT(1X, A1 )
      WRITE(6,20) NAME2
 20   FORMAT(1X, A2 )
      WRITE(6,30) STRING(1)
 30   FORMAT(1X, A3 )
      WRITE(6,40) STRING(2)
 40   FORMAT(1X, A4 )
      WRITE(6,50) STRING(3)
 50   FORMAT(1X, A5 )
      WRITE(6,60) STRING(4)
 60   FORMAT(1X, A6 )
      STOP
      END
```

Figure 13.1a. In the DATA statement, we assign alphanumeric constants to the variables NAME1 and NAME2 and to the array STRING. The results are printed using A format with different field widths. In the DATA statement 3*'RITA' is equivalent to 'RITA', 'RITA', 'RITA'. An alphanumeric constant can be stored in either a REAL or an INTEGER location.

J O A N	B I L L	F R E D	R I T A	R I T A	R I T A
NAME1	NAME2	STRING(1)	STRING(2)	STRING(3)	STRING(4)

Figure 13.1b. How the alphanumeric constants are assigned to the variables.

Since each of the alphanumeric constants we have used consists of 4 characters, each constant occupies the entire memory location allocated to the variable to which it is assigned. If the A field width is less than 4 (the maximum number of alphanumeric characters that can be stored in a memory location on the IBM 370), then the leftmost characters in the memory location which fit into the field, are printed. Thus since the contents of NAME1 (|J|O|A|N|) are printed in a field described by A1, only J is printed. Similarly, since the contents of NAME2 (|B|I|L|L|) are printed in a field described by A2, only BI is printed. Since the contents of STRING(1) (|F|R|E|D|) are printed in a field described by A3, only FRE is printed. Since the contents of STRING(2) (|R|I|T|A|) is printed by a field described by A4, all four characters are printed. All of this is seen in Fig. 13.1c.

If the A field width is greater than 4, then all the characters in the memory location are printed; moreover, they are printed right-justified in the field. Thus, since the contents of STRING(3) (|R|I|T|A|) are printed by a field described by A5, the leftmost column of the field is left blank. This is followed by RITA, as is shown

```
123456
 RITA
```

Similarly, since the constants of STRING(4) (|R|I|T|A|) are printed by a field described by A6, the two leftmost columns of the field are left blank. This is followed by RITA as is shown

```
123456
  RITA
```

If we had used a 3-character constant—such as TED—in the DATA statement and had assigned it to NAME1, then TED would be stored left-justified, i.e., |T|E|D| |.

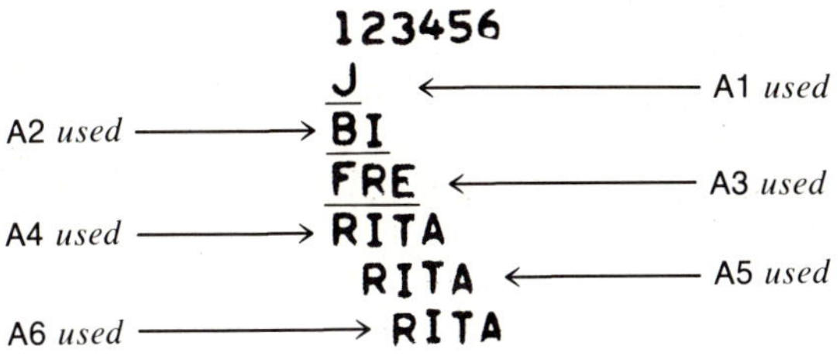

Figure 13.1c. Running the program of Fig. 13.1a. In using A format for printing, if the field width is less than the number of characters in a computer word—it is called the word length, and here it is 4—then the leftmost characters in the word are printed, e.g., J, BI, and FRE. If the field width is equal to or greater than the number of characters in a word, then the contents of the word are printed right-justified in the field.

In our next program, shown in Fig. 13.2a, we show how A format works when used to READ an alphanumeric constant from a data card. We use the format

```
10    FORMAT( A1, 1X, A2, 1X, A3, 1X, A4, 1X, A5, 1X, A6 )
```

to read the 6 constants that will be assigned to the 6 elements of STRING. The constants are punched on the card as is shown in Fig. 13.2b.

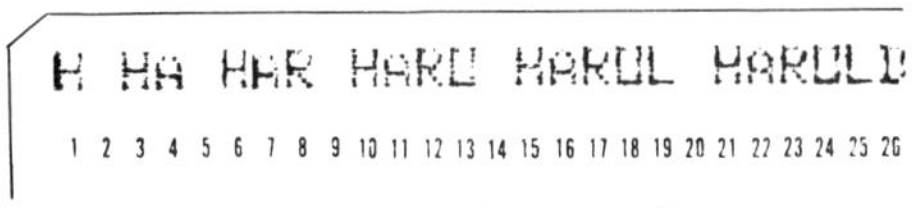

As long as the field width is smaller than 4 (the maximum number of characters that can be stored in a memory location), then the characters read are stored left-justified in the appropriate memory location. Thus since STRING(1) is read from a field described by A1 which contains H, the H is stored as [H][ ][ ][ ] in location STRING(1). Since STRING(2) is read from a field described by A2, which contains HA, the HA is stored as [H][A][ ][ ] in location STRING(2). Since STRING(3) is read from a field described by A3, which contains HAR, the HAR is stored as [H][A][R][ ] in location STRING(3). All of this is shown in Fig. 13.2c.

As you might expect, since STRING(4) is read from a field described by A4, which contains HARO, these characters are stored as [H][A][R][O] in the location STRING(4). We now see what happens if the field width is greater than 4. If this is the case, then the 4 rightmost characters are stored in the memory location. Thus, since STRING(5) is read from a field described by A5, which contains HAROL, then AROL is stored in STRING(5). And finally, since STRING(6) is read from a field described by A6, which contains HAROLD, the ROLD is stored in STRING(6).

The results of the program are shown in Fig. 13.2d. The contents of each of the locations described by the elements of STRING are printed starting in column 3. As we said in the discussion of Fig. 13.1a, the contents of an alphanumeric memory location are printed right-justified; the blanks that appear to the right of the word—as the three blanks in STRING(1), i.e., [H][ ][ ][ ] —are in effect printed. Thus the H instead of being printed in column 6, is printed in column 3 to allow for these three blanks.

READING USING A FORMAT

```
C  USING 'A FORMAT' IN READ STATEMENTS
      DIMENSION STRING(6)
C
      READ(5,10) STRING
 10   FORMAT( A1, 1X, A2, 1X, A3, 1X, A4, 1X, A5, 1X, A6 )
C     ...LABEL COLUMNS
      WRITE(6,20)
 20   FORMAT(1X, '1234567890' )
      WRITE(6,30) STRING
 30   FORMAT(1X, A6 )
      STOP
      END
```

Figure 13.2a. A format used in reading alphanumeric constants.

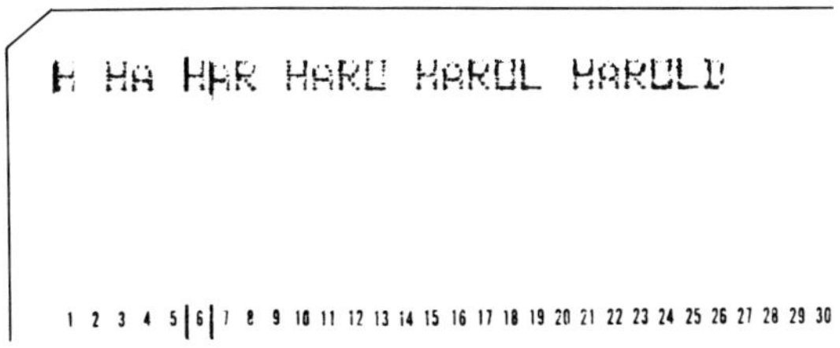

Figure 13.2b. The data card used for the program of Fig. 13.2a.

H	HA	HAR	HARO	AROL	ROLD
STRING(1)	STRING(2)	STRING(3)	STRING(4)	STRING(5)	STRING(6)

Figure 13.2c. How the alphanumeric constants are assigned to the variables. If the A field width used is smaller than word length, then the characters read are stored left-justified in the word, e.g., H, HA, and HAR. If the A field width used is greater or equal to the word length, then the 4 rightmost characters read are stored in the memory. Thus HARO, AROL, and ROLD are stored.

```
1234567890
   H
   HA
   HAR
   HARO
   AROL
   ROLD
```

Figure 13.2d. Running the program of Fig. 13.2a. Since the field width (6) used here, is larger than the word length (4), all results are printed right-justified.

The rules we have just discussed are hard to remember. Also the maximum number of characters that a memory location can accommodate varies with the type of computer you are using. Thus, if you want your program to be able to run on a variety of computers, and if you are simply reading alphanumeric characters and printing them, then you should read and write each character using the field specification A1. In Fig. 13.3a we have written a program that reads all 80 columns on the data card shown in Fig. 13.3b, in A format and copies this information onto the line printer as is shown in Fig. 13.3d.

Since CARD has 80 elements, we can read the information from all 80 columns using

```
      READ(5,10) (CARD(I), I=1,80 )
10    FORMAT( 80A1 )
```

How the first five characters are stored are shown in the Fig. 13.3c. A drawback of this method is that we do not use the 3 rightmost locations in a word, as we see from the table. We print the information using

```
      WRITE(6,20) (CARD(I), I=1,80)
20    FORMAT(1X, 80A1 )
```

READING THE 80 COLUMNS ON A DATA CARD

```
C   READING ENTIRE CARD USING 'A FORMAT'
        DIMENSION CARD(80)
        READ(5,10)  (CARD(I), I=1,80 )
 10     FORMAT( 80A1 )
C
        WRITE(6,20)  (CARD(I), I=1,80)
 20     FORMAT(1X, 80A1 )
        STOP
        END
```

Figure 13.3a. Each of the 80 elements of CARD is read using A1 format. This allows you to write a program using A format that will work on a machine with any word length.

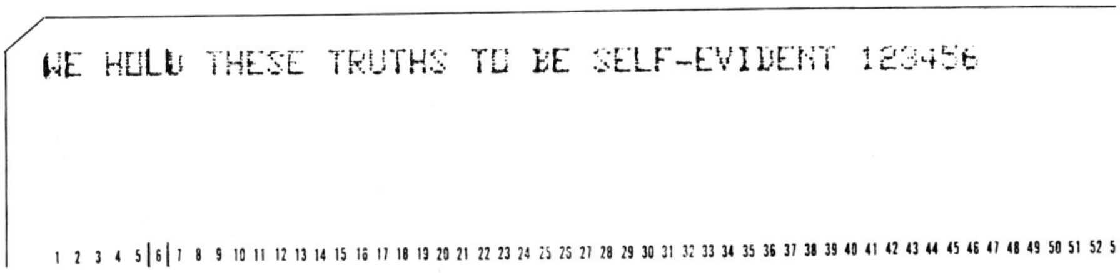

Figure 13.3b. The data card for Fig. 13.3a.

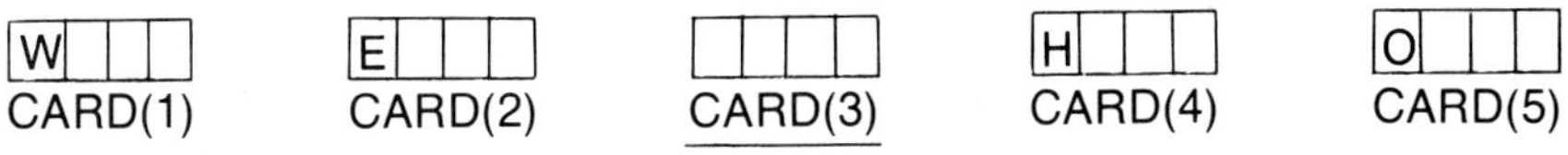

Figure 13.3c. How the first five characters on the data card are stored in memory. The contents of card (3) are all blanks.

```
WE HOLD THESE TRUTHS TO BE SELF-EVIDENT 123456
```

Figure 13.3d. Running the program of Fig. 13.3a.

We now write a program, shown in Fig. 13.4a, that searches an array to see whether a certain alphanumeric constant, which is read from a data card, is in the array. This constant is read* by

```
            READ(5,10) FIRST
     10     FORMAT( A4 )
```

The alphanumeric constants are assigned to the array NAME in

```
DATA NAME / 'JOAN', 'TED', 'JILL', 'BOB', 'JIM', 'RITA' /
```

We test to see whether the alphanumeric constant read is in the array when the inner DO loop

```
            DO 20 I=1,6
               IF( NAME(I) .EQ. FIRST ) GO TO 40
     20     CONTINUE
```

is executed. In order to compare the alphanumeric values of two variables—here NAME(I) and FIRST—the two variables must be the same mode; i.e., both must be either REAL or both INTEGER. Since NAME has been declared REAL, both NAME(1) and FIRST are the same mode. The data for the program are shown in Fig. 13.4b.

The last card of the data is a trailer and has the constant END typed on it. In DATA TRAIL/'END'/ we assign the constant 'END' to TRAIL. Thus in

```
            IF( FIRST .EQ. TRAIL ) STOP
```

we test each value of FIRST read, to see whether it equals 'END'. In order for this test to be made, the mode of FIRST and TRAIL must be the same, as they are here. Again, note that had we written the IF as

```
            IF( FIRST .EQ. 'END' ) STOP
```

a compile-time error would result on many systems, but not in WATFIV.†

The first constant read is JILL, and this is assigned to FIRST. Thus IF(FIRST .EQ. TRAIL) STOP is interpreted as IF('JILL' .EQ. 'END') STOP. Since the condition 'JILL' .EQ. 'END' is false, the computer executes the inner DO loop. The first time

```
        IF ( NAME(I) .EQ. FIRST ) GO TO 40
```

is executed, the values of the variables are as shown in the first line of the table for Fig. 13.4a

I	NAME(I)	FIRST	Next statement
1	JOAN	JILL	20

Consequently, the computer interprets this IF statement as

```
        IF ( 'JOAN' .EQ. 'JILL' ) GO TO 40
```

Since 'JOAN' does not equal 'JILL', the CONTINUE statement (statement 20) is executed so the statements in the range of the inner DO loop are executed again. When the range of

* Since all the constants will have 4 characters or less, we have used A4 format as opposed to reading in the characters individually as we did in the last program. In the next program, we will see that reading the characters individually makes the comparison of characters complicated.

† In WATFIV, FIRST would have to be declared to be CHARACTER mode.

SEARCHING AN ARRAY FOR AN ALPHANUMERIC CONSTANT

```
C   SEARCHES ARRAY 'NAME' FOR A GIVFN
C   ALPHANUMERIC CONSTANT
        REAL NAME(6)
        DATA NAME / 'JOAN', 'TED', 'JILL', 'BOB', 'JIM', 'RITA' /
        DATA TRAIL / 'END' /
C       ...READ CARDS
        DO 60 J=1,101
           READ(5,10) FIRST
 10        FORMAT( A4 )
           WRITE(6,15) FIRST
 15        FORMAT(1X, A4 )
           IF( FIRST .EQ. TRAIL ) STOP
C             ...SEARCH ARRAY 'NAME'
              DO 20 I=1,6
                 IF( NAME(I) .EQ. FIRST ) GO TO 40
20            CONTINUE
C             ...PRINT RESULTS
              WRITE(6,30) FIRST
 30           FORMAT(1X, A4, ' IS NOT IN THE ARRAY' )
              GO TO 60
 40           WRITE(6,50) FIRST
 50           FORMAT(1X, A4, ' IS IN THE ARRAY' )
 60     CONTINUE
        STOP
        END
```

Figure 13.4a. The program searches the DATA statement for the presence of an alphanumeric constant that was read from a data card. The last data card is a trailer and has END punched on it. An alphanumeric constant cannot be used in an assignment statement or in an IF statement. Thus we could not write IF(FIRST .EQ. 'END') STOP. Also in an IF or an assignment statement involving strings, all the variables must be the same mode. Thus, in IF(NAME(I) .EQ. FIRST) GO TO 40 both FIRST and NAME are REAL.

I	NAME(I)	FIRST	Next statement
1	JOAN	JILL	20
2	TED	JILL	20
3	JILL	JILL	40

Table for Fig. 13.4a. Shows how IF(NAME(I) .EQ. FIRST) GO TO 40 works. If the alphanumeric constant assigned to NAME(1) equals that assigned to FIRST, then the condition NAME(I) .EQ. FIRST is true, and the program prints that FIRST is in the array. Otherwise, the I loop is continued.

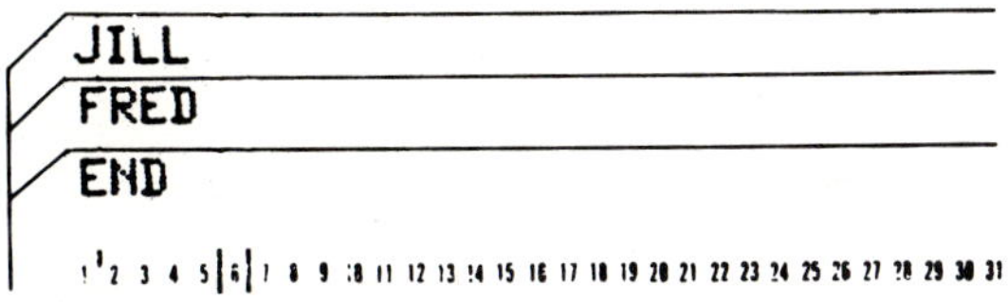

Figure 13.4b. The data cards for the program of Fig. 13.4a.

the inner DO is executed for the third time, the computer interprets the IF in the inner loop as

```
IF( 'JILL' .EQ. 'JILL' ) GO TO 40
```

Since the condition is true, the next statement executed is

```
40        WRITE(6,50) FIRST
```

which instructs the computer to print

```
JILL IS IN THE ARRAY
```

as is shown in Fig. 13.4c. The computer then reads the next card. Thus 'FRED' is assigned to FIRST. This time the condition in

```
IF ( NAME(I) .EQ. FIRST ) GO TO 40
```

is never true, so the DO loop is completely executed. The next statement executed after the loop, is WRITE(6,30) FIRST, which instructs the computer to print

```
FRED IS NOT IN THE ARRAY
```

Finally, the last card is read, and 'END' is assigned to FIRST. Now the condition in IF(FIRST .EQ. TRAIL) STOP is true, so the program stops.

The constant END must be punched starting in the first column of the data card, for the condition FIRST .EQ. TRAIL to be true. If it is punched starting in the second column, i.e.,

```
 END
1234
```

then it will be stored in the memory location FIRST as [ ][E][N][D]. The contents of TRAIL, on the other hand, are stored as [E][N][D][ ]. When the computer evaluates the condition FIRST .EQ. TRAIL, it checks whether corresponding positions* of both memory locations contain the same characters. Since TRAIL begins with an "E", whereas FIRST begins with a blank, the leftmost position in both memory locations do not contain the same character. The condition is therefore false.

* These positions are called *bytes*.

```
JILL
JILL IS IN THE ARRAY
FRED
FRED IS NOT IN THE ARRAY
END
```

Figure 13.4c. Running the program of Fig. 13.4a.

In the next program, shown in Fig. 13.5a, we read data cards on which are punched a person's name and his weight. The data cards are shown in Fig. 13.5b. We will read the alphanumeric constants representing the name, one character at a time using A1 format. This is done in

```
      READ(5,10) ( NAME(I), I=1,20 ), WEIGHT
10    FORMAT( 20A1, F10.0 )
```

If the person's last name begins with a letter between H and M (including H and M) we print his weight. Otherwise, we do not. Since a person's name is punched starting in column 1, the first letter of the name is assigned to NAME(1). We test to see whether this name is between H and M in

```
      IF( NAME(1) .GE. H .AND.
1        NAME(1) .LE. M ) WRITE(6,20) (NAME(I), I=1,20), WEIGHT
```

The variables H and M have been assigned the values 'H' and 'M', respectively, in the DATA statement. Whenever a test is made as to the alphabetical order of alphanumeric constants (i.e., using the operators GT, GE, LT, LE) the variables used in the test, on all systems but WATFIV,* must be INTEGER mode. Thus we have declared H to be INTEGER. Each character that appears on a keypunch key has been assigned a number in the compiler. The computer uses these numbers to determine whether a condition involving alphanumeric constants like NAME(I) .GE. H is true or false. Each successive letter of the alphabet has been assigned a higher number than the preceding letter.

We caution the reader here that the results of comparing strings using GE, GT, LE, or LT is highly computer-dependent. Thus a string comparison that works on one type of computer or compiler may not work on another. The reason for this is that part of the string is placed in the sign bit. Thus, depending on what binary value is given to a character, the value of the alphanumeric constant could be either positive or negative. Thus on a given machine, one constant could be less than a second constant; whereas on a different machine, the first constant could be greater than the second constant.

Another caveat to remember when using alphanumeric constants is not to mix modes in an assignment statement. Thus if we write DATA LINE, ASTER / ' ', '*' / and then write LINE=ASTER, we will obtain an error because LINE is INTEGER and ASTER is REAL. In order to make this assignment statement work, we must either declare LINE to be REAL or ASTER to be INTEGER.

* On WATFIV we can use CHARACTER mode.

COMPARING CONSTANTS FOR ALPHABETICAL ORDER

```
C     COMPARING ALPHANUMERIC CONSTANTS
C     PROGRAM SHOULD PRINT THOSE NAMES WHOSE FIRST LETTER
C     IS BETWEEN H AND M
      INTEGER NAME(20), TRAIL(3), H
      DATA H, M, TRAIL / 'H', 'M', 'E', 'N', 'D' /
C       ..READ AND FIND NAMES
      DO 30 J=1, 101
         READ(5,10)  ( NAME(I), I=1,20 ), WEIGHT
 10      FORMAT( 20A1, F10.0 )
         WRITE(6,15)  ( NAME(I), I=1,20 ), WEIGHT
 15      FORMAT(1X, 20A1, F10.0 )
         IF( NAME(1) .EQ. TRAIL(1) .AND.
     1       NAME(2) .EQ. TRAIL(2) .AND.
     2       NAME(3) .EQ. TRAIL(3) ) STOP
           IF( NAME(1) .GE. H .AND.
     1         NAME(1) .LE. M ) WRITE(6,20) (NAME(I), I=1,20), WEIGHT
 20        FORMAT(1X, 'SELECT ', 20A1, F10.0 )
 30   CONTINUE
      STOP
      END
```

Figure 13.5a. If you compare alphanumeric constants for alphabetical order, the constants must be assigned to INTEGER variables. Thus in NAME(I) .GE. H both variables are INTEGER since H was declared INTEGER. Beware that comparing for alphabetical order does not work on all computers. Since each name NAME is read using 20A1, we test for the trailer by comparing each of the first three characters of NAME with E, N, and D, respectively.

```
ABRAMS, S. L.         150.0
HOWARD, R.            180.0
MARTIN, J.            170.0
SMITH, J.             130.0
END
1 2 3 4 5 6 7 8 9 10 11 12 13 14 15 16 17 18 19 20 21 22 23 24 25 26 27 28 29 30
```

Figure 13.5b. The data card for Fig. 13.5a.

The trailer has the characters END punched in the first three columns. Because we have read the alphanumeric constants, using A1 format, we must test for the trailer by seeing whether the value of NAME(I) is E; NAME(2) is N, and NAME(3) is D. This is done in

```
      IF( NAME(1) .EQ. TRAIL(1) .AND.
     1    NAME(2) .EQ. TRAIL(2) .AND.
     2    NAME(3) .EQ. TRAIL(3) ) STOP
```

where 'E', 'N', and 'D' have been assigned to the first three elements of TRAIL, respectively, in

```
      DATA H, M, TRAIL / 'H', 'M', 'E', 'N', 'D' /
```

Since, when testing for equality in an IF, both variables must be the same mode, we have declared TRAIL to be INTEGER in

```
      INTEGER NAME(20), TRAIL(3), H
```

The results of running the program are shown in Fig. 13.5c. In order for this program to work, each person's last name must be punched starting in the first column of the data card. When the first card is read—ABRAMS, S.L. 150.—the value of NAME(1) is A, as is shown in the first line of the table for Fig. 13.5a. We see that the condition

```
NAME(1) .GE. H  .AND.
NAME(1) .LE. M
```

is false; therefore the computer only echo-prints the data card. When the next card—HOWARD, R. 180.0—is read the value of NAME(1) is H. This condition is true, and then, after the card is echo-printed, the computer prints SELECT followed by the contents of the card. For the third card, MARTUN, J. 170.0, the condition is again true so SELECT MARTUN J. 170 is printed. For the fourth card, the condition is false so only the echo-printing is done. Finally, the trailer is read and the program, after it echo-prints END, stops. The reason that 0.0 is printed on the same line as END is that when the trailer is read, the computer interprets the blanks in the field for WEIGHT, as zeros. So the value of WEIGHT is 0.0.

11.2. CHARACTER Mode in WATFIV (and the Proposed ANS FORTRAN Revision)

Before we proceed, we make the same warning concerning using GT, LT, GE, and LE operators with strings on a WATFIV compiler as we did for FORTRAN compilers. Although string comparisons will work the same way on all IBM 360/370 WATFIV compilers, they might work differently on WATFIV compilers on other machines.

We now rewrite the preceding program using the capabilities of the WATFIV compiler. If your program will be processed by this compiler, you can specify in a declaration statement called a CHARACTER statement which variables will be assigned alphanumeric constants. These variables are said to be written in CHARACTER mode. This will allow us to write the preceding program without a DATA statement since we can assign strings to CHARACTER variables in assignment statements and compare strings with CHARACTER variables in IF statements. The CHARACTER mode has also been included in the proposed ANS FORTRAN revision; so the reader should read this section with more than a casual interest.

```
ABRAMS, S. L.                    150.
HOWARD, R.                       180.
SELECT HOWARD, R.                          180.
MARTUN, J.                       170.
SELECT MARTUN, J.                          170.
SMITH, J.                        130.
END                                0.
```

Figure 13.5c. The results of running the program of Fig. 13.5a.

Card	NAME(1)
1st	A
2nd	E
3rd	M
4th	S

Table for Fig. 13.5a.

In a CHARACTER statement, you can specify the maximum number of characters you wish to be assigned to each CHARACTER variable. Thus in the program of Fig. 13.6a

```
CHARACTER NAME*20
```

the 20 is called the *length specifier*, and it indicates that up to 20 characters can be assigned to the variable NAME. You can assign a maximum of 256 characters to a CHARACTER variable.

By following a variable with an asterisk and an integer, we can specify the maximum number of characters that can be assigned to the variable. If a variable is not followed by an asterisk and an integer, then the maximum number of characters you can assign to it is 1. Thus in

```
CHARACTER A*2, B*6, C, D*3
```

the maximum number of characters you can assign to C is 1. However, if an asterisk followed by an integer follows the word CHARACTER, the integer specifies the length of each of the variables in the list that does not have its own length specifier. Thus in

```
CHARACTER *4, A*2, B, C, D*3
```

both B and C have a length of 4.

Just as arrays can appear in other types of declaration statements, arrays can also appear in a CHARACTER statement. If an array has not been dimensioned previously, it can be dimensioned in a CHARACTER statement. Thus

```
CHARACTER A*3(40)
```

declares that the array A has 40 elements and up to three characters can be assigned to each element.

Because of the CHARACTER statement, we can now use any field width (up to 155) we wish in writing an A format, knowing that all the characters in the field will be stored in the memory. Thus in order to be consistent with NAME*20 we have used A20 in the FORMAT statements paired with the READ and WRITE statements, e.g.,

```
          READ(5,10) NAME, WEIGHT
10        FORMAT( A20, F10.0 )
```

(although we could have also used any field width less than 20.) Thus all 20 characters punched in the first 20 columns of the data cards will be assigned to NAME. The data cards for the program are shown in Fig. 13.6b. In Fig. 13.6c we see how the alphanumeric constant on the first data card is stored in the memory.

As we have mentioned, in WATFIV you are permitted to use alphanumeric constants in IF and assignment statements, as long as the variable it appears with has been declared to be CHARACTER mode. Thus we can use the constant 'END' in the IF statement that tests for the trailer

```
IF( NAME .EQ. 'END' ) STOP
```

since NAME has been declared to be CHARACTER mode. Similarly, we can write the IF

USING CHARACTER MODE

```
      CHARACTER NAME*20
C     ...READ AND SEARCH FOR NAMES
      DO 30 J=1,101
         READ(5,10) NAME, WEIGHT
 10      FORMAT( A20, F10.0 )
         WRITE(6,15) NAME, WEIGHT
 15      FORMAT(1X, A20, F10.0 )
C        ...TEST FOR END OF FILE
         IF( NAME . EQ. 'END' ) STOP
         IF( NAME .GE. 'H' .AND. NAME .LT. 'N' )
     1         WRITE(6,20) NAME, WEIGHT
 20         FORMAT(1X, 'SELECTED ', A20, 2X, F10.0 )
 30   CONTINUE
      STOP
      END
```

Figure 13.6a. Same as the program of Fig. 13.5a, but written using the CHARACTER variable option in WATFIV. The CHARACTER statement specifies which variables will be assigned an alphanumeric constant. Using the CHARACTER statement allows us to use alphanumeric constants in IF and assignment statements. One of the benefits of the CHARACTER statement is that we can write the program without a DATA statement. CHARACTER NAME*20 declares that NAME can contain up to 20 alphanumeric characters.

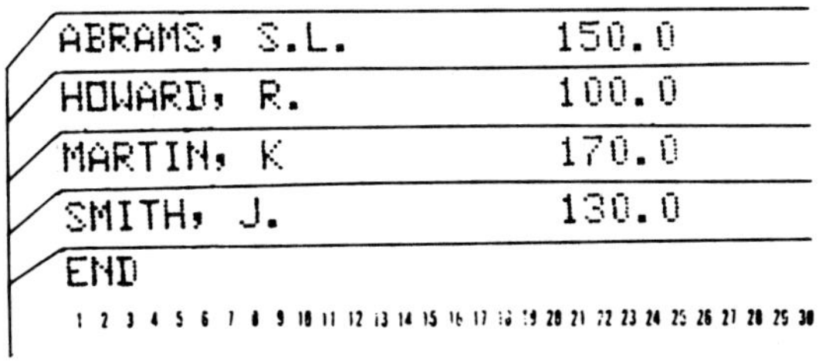

Figure 13.6b. The data cards for Fig. 13.6a.

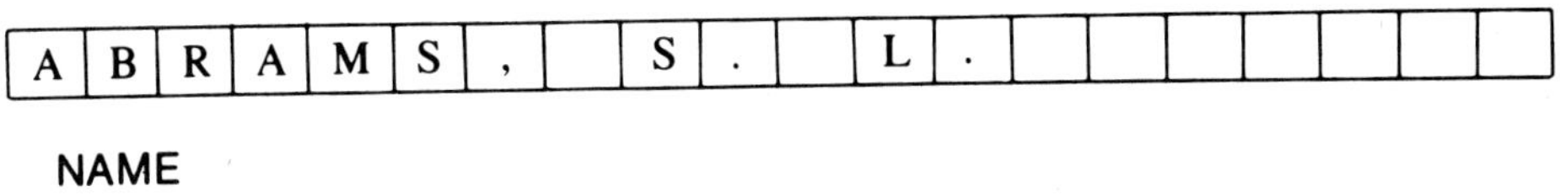

Figure 13.6c. How the constant on the first data card is assigned to NAME.

```
ABRAMS, S. L.                      150.
HOWARD, R.                         180.
SELECTED HOWARD, R.                           180.
MARTIN, K                          170.
SELECTED MARTIN, K                            170.
SMITH, J.                          130.
END                                  0.
```

Figure 13.6d. Running the program of Fig. 13.6a.

statement that determines whether or not to print the information on the data statement, using alphanumeric constants. We thus write

```
            IF( NAME .GE. 'H' .AND. NAME .LT. 'N' )
     1           WRITE(6,20) NAME, WEIGHT
```

We have thus been able to write the program without a DATA statement. The results of the program are shown in Fig. 13.6d. The reason why we have written the second part of the condition as

```
NAME .LT.'N'
```

not as

```
NAME .LE. 'M'
```

is that the latter comparison would eliminate a name like MARTINS, since 'MARTINS' is greater than 'M'. In the previous program (Fig. 13.5) we were able to use NAME(1) .LE. M in the IF statement, because we were only comparing the first letter of the word.

Had we wanted to, we could have written the program so that it reads all 80 characters on the card in A format be defining NAME as NAME*80, as we now show in Fig. 13.6e. The results of running this program are shown in Fig. 13.6f.

CHARACTER

The form of the CHARACTER statement is: CHARACTER followed by a list of variables and arrays. If the list is preceded by an asterisk followed by a length specifier, they must be separated from the list by a comma. If the list consists of more than one variable or array, these must be separated by commas. Example:

CHARACTER*10, FORM*4(10), MAT*3(5), A, CHAR(10)

The dimension of an array follows the array's length specifier. In the example above, FORM is an array that has 10 elements and each element has a length of 4; similarly, MAT has 5 elements and each element has a length of 3. Since A and CHAR(10) have no length specifier, their lengths are 10.

Note, when a CHARACTER variable is passed from a calling program to a subroutine (or subprogram), besides being declared CHARACTER in the calling program, it must be declared CHARACTER in the subroutine (or subprogram) as well.

USING CHARACTER MODE TO READ AN ENTIRE DATA CARD

```
C   WATFIV VERSION OF PROGRAM WHICH  PRINTS THOSE NAMES WHOSE
C   FIRST LETTER IS BETWEEN H AND M
C   READS BOTH NAME AND WEIGHT IN 'A FORMAT'
       CHARACTER NAME*80
C      ...READ AND SEARCH FOR NAME
       DO 30 J=1,101
          READ(5,10) NAME
 10    FORMAT( A80 )
          WRITE(6,15) NAME
 15       FORMAT(1X, A80 )
          IF( NAME .EQ. 'END' ) STOP
             IF( NAME .LT. 'N' .AND. NAME .GE. 'H' ) WRITE(6,20) NAME
 20          FORMAT(1X, 'SELECTED ', A80 )
 30    CONTINUE
       STOP
       END
```

Figure 13.6e. Same as Fig. 13.6a except that the entire data card is read using CHARACTER mode and A format.

```
ABRAMS, S. L.           150.0
HOWARD, R.              180.0
SELECTED HOWARD, R.              180.0
MARTIN, J.              170.0
SELECTED MARTIN, J.              170.0
SMITH, J.               130.0
END
```

Figure 13.6f. Running the program of Fig. 13.6e.

We could, of course, have written this program in WATFIV without using FORMATs, as is shown in Fig. 13.7a. Thus we have written READ, NAME, WEIGHT. When you read an alphanumeric constant in WATFIV using a nonformatted READ, you must enclose the constant between apostrophe marks as we show in Fig. 13.7b; i.e., the first card must be punched

```
'ABRAMS, S.L. ', 150.0
```

The comma which appears between the apostrophe marks is treated like any other character in an alphanumeric constant. Thus it is not considered to be a delimiter separating constants on a data card for an unformatted READ. The results of the program are shown in Fig. 13.7c.

READING ALPHANUMERIC CONSTANTS USING A FORMAT-FREE READ

```
C   WATFIV VERSION OF PROGRAM WHICH  PRINTS THOSE NAMES WHOSE
C   FIRST LETTER IS BETWEEN H AND M
C   USES FORMAT-FREE READ
       CHARACTER NAME*20
C      ...READ AND SEARCH FOR NAME
       DO 10 J=1,101
          READ, NAME, WEIGHT
          PRINT, NAME, WEIGHT
          IF( NAME .EQ. 'END' ) STOP
             IF( NAME .LT. 'N' .AND. NAME .GE. 'H' )
     1             PRINT, 'SELECT', NAME, WEIGHT
10    CONTINUE
      STOP
      END
```

Figure 13.7a. Same as Fig. 13.6a except that a format-free READ and PRINT are used.

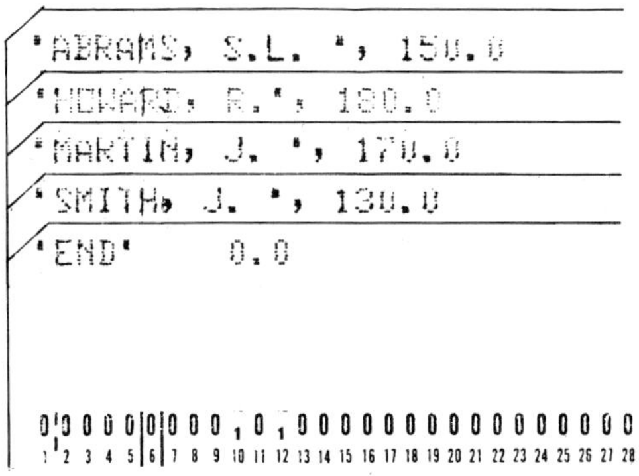

Figure 13.7b. Data cards for Fig. 13.7a. Alphanumeric constants must be enclosed in apostrophe marks.

```
ABRAMS, S.L.            0.1500000E 03
HOWARD, R.              0.1800000E 03
SELECT HOWARD, R.                0.1800000E 03
MARTIN, J.              0.1700000E 03
SELECT MARTIN, J.                0.1700000E 03
SMITH, J.               0.1300000E 03
END                     0.0000000E 00
```

Figure 13.7c. Running the program of Fig. 13.7a.

We conclude this section by discussing how we can refer to a specific character in a string. For instance, if the CHARACTER variable STRING contains the string '1234567890', how can we refer to the fourth character, i.e., 4. In the program of Fig. 13.7d we show how. In

```
CHARACTER STRING*10, ARRAY(10)
```

we declare the variable STRING to be a character variable 10 characters long; and the array ARRAY to be a CHARACTER array with 10 elements, each of which is one character long. In the EQUIVALENCE statement, we state that the first position of STRING should share the same memory location as the first element of ARRAY. Thus we get the following memory location correspondence.

ARRAY(1)	ARRAY(2)	ARRAY(10)
	STRING	

as is shown in the table for Fig. 13.7d.

This means that the first (leftmost) character of STRING is stored in ARRAY(1), the next character of STRING is stored in ARRAY(2), etc. So when the elements of ARRAY are printed in the DO loop using FORMAT (1X,A1), the characters in STRING are printed in a vertical line as is shown in Fig. 13.7e.

In the proposed revision of ANS FORTRAN, there is an easier and more powerful way of referring to characters in a string. We subscript the character variable with an INTEGER expression referring to the first character and one referring to the last character in the substring (a group of adjacent characters is called a substring). For instance, in the variable STRING used in Fig. 13.7d, STRING(3:5) would refer to the substring '345', i.e., the third to the fifth character in STRING. STRING (8:8) refers to the eighth character, namely, '8'. Another valid form would be STRING(I:J). You can refer also to substrings in arrays. Thus, if 'ABCD' is stored in the first element of the CHARACTER array LETTER, then LETTER(1) (3:4) refers to 'CD'.

SUBSTRINGS (GROUPS OF CHARACTERS WITHIN STRINGS)

```
      CHARACTER  STRING*10, ARRAY(10)
      EQUIVALENCE (ARRAY, STRING)
      STRING='1234567890'
C
      DO 20 J=1,10
         WRITE(6,10) ARRAY(J)
 10      FORMAT(1X, A1)
 20   CONTINUE
      STOP
      END
```

Figure 13.7d. By equivalencing the CHARACTER variable of length 10, STRING, to the CHARACTER array ARRAY, which has ten elements, we can refer to specific characters in STRING.

ARRAY(1)	ARRAY(2)	...	ARRAY(10)
STRING			

Table for Fig. 13.7d. Because of the EQUIVALENCE statement, the first character of STRING occupies the same location as ARRAY(1), etc.

```
1
2
3
4
5
6
7
8
9
0
```

Figure 13.7e. Running the program of Fig. 13.7d.

13.3. Execution-Time FORMAT

ANS Standard FORTRAN and most compilers, but not Standard Basic FORTRAN, allow you to read a FORMAT in during the execution of a program. For instance, if we wanted the variable VAR printed according to a FORMAT statement

```
FORMAT(1X, 'VAR=', F10.2 )
```

we would read the (1X'VAR=',F10.2) part, which would be punched on a data card as shown in Fig. 13.8a. We would store it in the array FORM, when READ(5,10) FORM is executed. Note that FORM is dimensioned to have 80 elements. Its associated FORMAT statement would be 10 FORMAT(80A1), as is shown in Fig. 13.8b. Then in order to print the value of VAR in the form described on the data card, we would type WRITE(6,FORM) VAR where FORM takes the place of the usual FORMAT statement number that appears in a WRITE statement. The results of running the program are shown in Fig. 13.8c. Execution-time format can be used for both reading and writing data. Thus we could write READ(5,FORM1) A,B,C, where FORM1 describes an appropriate format.

A disadvantage of using execution-time format is that the burden of writing the FORMAT statement is on the user of the program. Thus he not only has to punch data, but he also has to have some knowledge of programming.

EXECUTION-TIME FORMAT

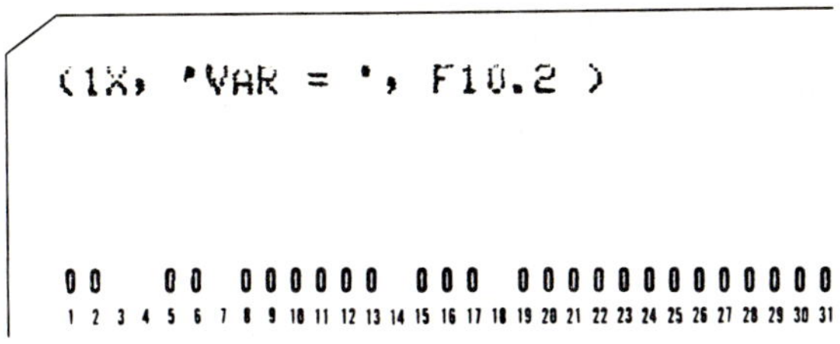

Figure 13.8a. A format that will be read during execution time. Note the word FORMAT does not appear on the card, but everything else which appears in the FORMAT statement, does appear.

```
C  SHOWS USE OF EXECUTION-TIME FORMAT
      DIMENSION FORM(80)
      READ(5,10) FORM
 10   FORMAT( 80A1 )
      VAR = 13.2
      WRITE(6,FORM) VAR
      STOP
      END
```

Figure 13.8b. Program reads a FORMAT during execution time. The FORMAT is read using A format and in this case stored in array FORM. Then WRITE(6, FORM) VAR is equivalent to WRITE(6,10) VAR where statement 10 is FORMAT (1X, VAR=1, F10.2)

```
V   A   R         =                  13.20
```

Figure 13.8c. Running the program of Fig. 13.8b.

13.4. The NAME LIST Statement

The NAME LIST declaration statement allows us to read data and to produce labeled results without using FORMAT statements. It is not available on ANS standard FORTRAN but is available on many compilers, including WATFIV but not WATFOR. In Fig. 13.9a we show how the NAME LIST is used. We place variables, arrays, and array elements in a NAME LIST statement, e.g.,

```
NAME LIST / ONE / A, C, K
```

where here ONE is the label we gave the list (here A, C, K) in the NAME LIST statement. The list is called the *class*. Thus the class called ONE consists of A, C, and K. We can instruct the computer to read all or some of the values of the variables in the class called ONE by writing

```
READ(5,ONE)
```

We have decided to read the values of the array A and of the variable K. In order to indicate that we want certain values assigned from a data card to the variables in the class, we must type, starting in column 2, an ampersand, immediately followed by the class name that starts in column 3, (Fig. 13.9b). The card reader will recognize only characters punched in columns 2 through 80 of the data card for the NAME LIST option. We then punch the name of a variable belonging to the class followed by an equals sign, followed in turn by the constant we want to assign to the variable. Thus we write K = 3, i.e., the same form we use in writing a simple assignment statement. The "assignment statements" on the data card must be separated for each other by a comma. They do not have to be in the order in which the variables appear in the NAME LIST statement. If we want to assign values to an array, we list the values in the order in which their values will be stored in the memory; each of these values must be separated by a comma, i.e.,

```
A= 1.0, 2.0, 3.0, 4.0
```

assign 1.0 to A(1), 2.0 to A(2), 3.0 to A(3), and 4.0 to A(4). If all the constants were the same, e.g., 3.0, we could write A = 4*3.0. We inform the computer that we have finished the assignments for the class by following the last assignment with &END. This may either appear on the same card as the last assignment (as we have done in the data cards for class TWO) or on the next card, where it is punched starting in column 2 (as is done in class ONE.) & END can have no imbedded blanks. A variable or an array can appear in more than one class. Thus C appears both in class ONE and class TWO. The classes must appear in the data cards in the order in which they will be read. Thus since READ(5,ONE) precedes READ(5,TWO) in the program the data cards for class ONE must precede those for class TWO.

In order to print the results, we have defined a class called OUT—and we write WRITE(6,OUT). First, & followed by the class name is printed. Then the values of all the variables and arrays listed in the class OUT are printed as shown in Fig. 13.9c. The elements of array A are printed in the order in which they were stored in the memory. The last line of output ends in &END. If we want to, we can have the output punched on cards.

13.5. The PUNCH Statement

By writing PUNCH 10, A, B, C, K, we instruct the computer to punch the values of the variables in the list onto cards. The format 10 FORMAT(2 F10.1, E15.4, I6) does not have a control character.

THE NAME LIST STATEMENT

```
C     SHOWS USE OF NAME LIST
      DIMENSION A(4), B(2)
      NAME LIST / ONE / A, C, K
      NAME LIST / TWO / K, J, B, C
      NAME LIST / OUT / TOTAL, A, I, K, J, B, S
      TOTAL = 0.0
      WRITE(6,10)
 10   FORMAT(1X, 'ECHO PRINT' )
      READ(5,ONE)
      WRITE(6,ONE)
      READ(5,TWO)
      WRITE(6, TWO)
C
C     ..SUM THE A'S
      DO 20 I=1,4
         TOTAL = TOTAL + A(I)
 20   CONTINUE
      S = C * B(2)
      I = K + J
      WRITE(6,OUT)
      STOP
      END
```

Figure 13.9a. Using the NAME LIST for unformatted READS and WRITES. READ(5,ONE) reads some or all of the variables in the list for class ONE, i.e., the array A, the variables C and K. WRITE(6,OUT) writes the labeled values of the variables listed for class OUT.

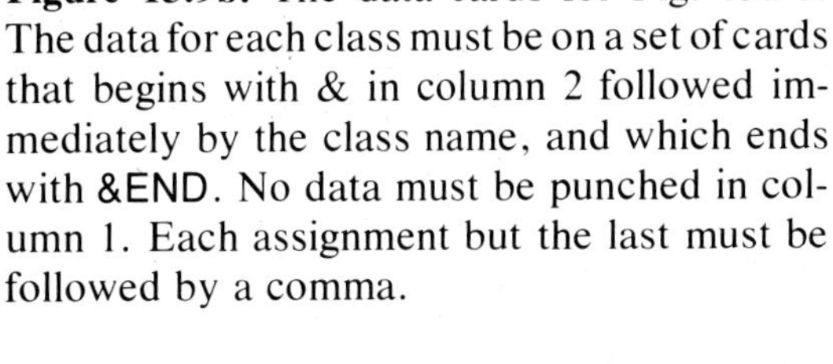

Figure 13.9b. The data cards for Fig. 13.9b. The data for each class must be on a set of cards that begins with & in column 2 followed immediately by the class name, and which ends with &END. No data must be punched in column 1. Each assignment but the last must be followed by a comma.

```
ECHO PRINT
&ONE
A=   0.1000000E 01,   0.2000000E 01,   0.3000000E 01,   0.4000000E 01,C=UUUUUUUUUUUUUUUU,K=           3,&END
&TWO
K=           3,J=           9,B=   0.3000000E 01,   0.4000000E 01,C=   0.2000000E 01,&END
&OUT
TOTAL=   0.1000000E 02,A=   0.1000000E 01,   0.2000000E 01,   0.3000000E 01,   0.4000000E 01,I=          12,K=           3,J=
           9,B=   0.3000000E 01,   0.4000000E 01,S=   0.8000000E 01,&END
```

Figure 13.9c. Running the program of Fig. 13.9a. The name of the array and then its values are listed.

13.6. The Scale Factor

13.6.1. Output

When nP (where n is an integer) precedes an F format, it has the effect of multiplying the result by 10^n. It thus shifts the decimal point in the result and is called a *scale factor*. For example, in Fig. 13.10a, the value of A is 1.234567. When A is printed using 1PF10.4, its value is multiplied by 10^1, and the results is printed as 12.3457 as is shown in Fig. 13.10b. When A is printed using 2PF10.4, its value is multiplied by 10^2 and the result printed as 123.4567. If A is negative, then n has the effect of multiplying the result by 10^{-n}.

When n precedes an E format, it does not affect the value of the result, only the form. If n is positive, then n digits are printed to the left of the decimal point. Thus when A is printed using 1PE16.7, the result is printed* as 1.2345660E 00. We have accomplished two things. The first is that the result instead of being printed in normalized form (.1234567E1) is now printed in more readable form; and the second is that we have increased the number of digits we see, since normally we would have seen 7 digits using E16.7 instead of the 8 now visible. Note that the exponent was decreased from 1 to 0 in order to compensate for the appearance of the extra digit to the left of the decimal point. On systems that do not print a leading zero to the left of the decimal point, we have to be sure that the field width is large enough to accommodate the extra digit which now appears to the left of the decimal point.

When A is printed using 2PE16.7, two digits appear to the left of the decimal point: The result is printed as 12.3456600E-01. Again the exponent was decreased to compensate for the appearance of two digits to the left of the decimal point. If the value of n in nP is negative, then n leading zeros appear to the right of the decimal point, and the number of significant digits printed by nPE$w.d$ is decreased to d-n. For this reason negative scale factors are rarely used with E formats.

Once a scale factor is used, it affects all subsequent field descriptors in the FORMAT statement until another scale factor is encountered. Thus in Fig. 13.10a.

```
20    FORMAT(/1X, 2PF10.5, F10.5, E16.7, 0PE16.7 )
```

the 2P applies to all specifications but the last. Therefore the computer interprets this statement as

```
20    FORMAT(1X, 2PF10.5,  2PF10.5, 2PE16.7, 0PE16.7)
```

as is shown in Fig. 13.10b when the results are printed.

The description which applies to E format also applies to D format. On G format, the scale factor has an effect only when the result is printed in exponential form.

13.6.2. Input

Scale factors are rarely used with READ statements, so you may very well want to omit this part of the section. When reading, a scale factor has no effect on E and D formats if the constant is punched with an exponent. When nP precedes E, F, and D formats and the constant is punched without an exponent, the value of the constant read

* The fact that the result is not printed as 1.2345670E 00, is the result of a peculiarity on the WATFIV compiler.

USING A SCALE FACTOR

```
C   USING THE SCALE FACTOR
      A = 1.234567
      WRITE(6,10) A, A, A, A
 10   FORMAT(1X, 'EFFECT OF 1P:', 1PF10.4, ' EFFECT OF 2P:', 2PF10.4 /
     1      1X, 'EFFECT OF 1P:', 1PE16.7, 'EFFECT OF 2P:', 2PE16.7 )
      WRITE(6,20) A, A, A, A
 20   FORMAT(/1X, 2PF10.5, F10.5, E16.7, 0PE16.7 )
      STOP
      END
```

Figure 13.10a. Using a scale factor. The specification *n*PF*w.d* has the effect of multiplying a constant by 10^n before it is printed. *n*PE*w.d* places *n* digits to the left of the decimal point before the result is printed. The exponent is correspondingly reduced by *n*.

```
EFFECT OF 1P:     12.3457  EFFECT OF 2P:   123.4567
EFFECT OF 1P:     1.2345660E 00EFFECT OF 2P:  12.3456600E-01

     2PF10.5     F10.5       E16.7              0PE16.7
123.45660 123.45660  12.3456600E-01     0.1234567E 01
```

Figure 13.10b. Running the program of Fig. 13.10a. The scale factor in 1PE16.7 produces 1.234567 instead of .123456E+1. When a scale factor is used, it applies to all subsequent field specification in the FORMAT until a new scale factor is encountered.

is multiplied by 10^{-n}. Thus if 123.4 is read using 2PF10.0, then its value is stored as 123.4×10^{-2} or 1.234. If it is negative, then the value of the constant read is multiplied by 10^{n}. When reading using G format, the effect of a scale factor is the same as for F format unless the constant is punched with an exponential—then the scale factor has no effect.

13.7. Files

The word *file*, as used in this section, means a collection of data which has been placed on a medium like magnetic tape or a magnetic disk, on which information can be written very quickly and in turn from which it also can be read very quickly.

If your program is going to process many sets of data, you can imagine that it is inconvenient always to have to read the information from cards—because cards are bulky and the process of reading them is time consuming. On the other hand, information can be stored in compact form on magnetic tape or disks and can be read from them very quickly. Most of what follows is devoted to a description of magnetic tape and how to use it.

In substance, the magnetic tape used for processing data is identical to that used on tape recorders—it is a plastic tape coated with iron oxide that enables the computer to magnetize spots on the tape. Magnetic tape used for data processing generally comes in reels that accommodate 2400 feet of tape. However, the same tape cassettes—two small reels housed in a plastic case—normally used for cassette tape recorders are also used for storing both data and programs on the very small, relatively inexpensive computers called minicomputers.

In general, in computer parlance the word *files* is used to describe any collection of information—be it data or programs. A subdivision of a file is called a *record*. Thus a data card and a line of output on the line printer can be considered a record. A magnetic tape file is subdivided into records.

In order to write information on a magnetic tape file, a unit number must be assigned to the tape unit you will be using. This may be done in one of the control cards that precede the program. For example, if we assign number 8 to the tape unit we are going to use, then if we wanted to write the information in array A on the magnetic tape using FORMAT 100, we would write WRITE(8,100)A. Each time we use a WRITE statement to write information on magnetic tape, the computer writes the information starting on a new record.

In any READ statement, one can instruct the computer to branch to a specific statement in the program by including END=, followed by that statement number. We will use this technique when we read a magnetic file.

In Fig. 13.11 we write a program that continuously takes the information from a set of four cards and places it on a record on the tape designated as unit 8. The first time the READ statement is executed, the computer interprets it as

```
READ(5,10,END=50) (A(I), I=1,8)
```

the second time as

```
READ(5,10,END=50) (A(I), I=9,16)
```

the third time as

```
READ(5,10,END=50) (A(I), I=17,24)
```

WRITING FILES

```
C   PROGRAM WRITES ON A MAG TAPE
       INTEGER BEGIN, END
       DIMENSION A(32)
       DO 40 K=1,100
C      ...READ FOUR CARDS
          DO 20 I=1,4
             BEGIN = 1 + 8*(I-1)
             END= 8*I
             READ(5,10,END=50) (A(J), J=BEGIN,END)
 10          FORMAT( 8F10.0 )
 20       CONTINUE
C         ...WRITE INFORMATION FROM FOUR
C         ...CARDS ON TO ONE RECORD
          WRITE(8,30) (A(I), I=1,32)
 30       FORMAT( 32E17.7 )
 40    CONTINUE
C
 50    END FILE 8
       REWIND 8
       STOP
       END
```

Figure 13.11. The program reads four cards and writes them on one record. Each time a WRITE statement is executed, the information is written starting on a new record. END FILE 8 places an end of file mark on the tape on unit 8, and REWIND 8 rewinds the tape on unit 8. When an end of file is encountered on the card reader, END=50 causes control to pass to statement 50.

and finally the fourth time as

READ(5,10,END=50) (A(I), I=25,32)

All this information is written on tape 8 by

```
WRITE(8,30) (A(I), I=1,32)
```

When the computer encounters the end of file on the INPUT because of END=50 in the READ, it branches to statement 50

```
50   END FILE 8
```

This instruction places a mark on the tape signifying that no more data follow. This mark is appropriately called an *end of file mark*. The next statement REWIND 8, rewinds the tape to its beginning, or load point. On most systems the operating system automatically rewinds all magnetic tapes used in a program to their load points after the execution of the program is complete.

In Fig. 13.12 we write a program that reads the magnetic tape and prints the information on it on the line printer. When the end of file we wrote on the tape is encountered, the program—because of the END=40 in the READ statement—branches to statement 40, where it prints END OF PRINTING.

If a piece of dust gets on the magnetic tape or if one of the spots becomes demagnetized, the computer will not be able to read the bit pattern correctly. In this case an error condition arises, and the system normally terminates the program. This could be avoided by having the READ statement branch to another statement in the program. If you wanted to branch to statement 100, you would add ERR=100. The READ statement would now appear as

```
READ(8,10, END=40, ERR=100) A
```

If you then wanted to backspace one record so that the computer could reread the record, you would write BACKSPACE8.

The ERR option can be used when reading cards and also when using the NAME LIST option. Thus we can write

```
READ(5,CLASS, END=10, ERR=100)
```

A considerable amount of time is spent formatting information when printing on a magnetic tape. Similarly when reading formatted information from tape, extra time is spent reading simply because the information is formatted.

A faster way both of writing information on and reading information from a magnetic tape is to use unformatted READ and WRITE statements. In an unformatted READ or WRITE no FORMAT is used. Thus we would write WRITE(8)A and READ(8)A. We could try to list the contents of a tape written using an unformatted WRITE by writing

```
WRITE(6) A
```

where 6 is the unit number for the printer. All we would get, however, is unrecognizable output.

A magnetic tape is called a *sequential file* since in order to read the tenth record you must read the previous nine. This is obviously an inefficient way of handling data. A magnetic disk is an example of a direct-access file. A magnetic disk is like a phonograph record. The information is stored in concentric rings, and the information is magnetized similarly to the way it is on magnetic tape.

When using a magnetic disk, you can instruct the computer to read or write a specific record. The computer goes directly to that record and performs the specified task, hence the magnetic disk is called a *direct-access device*.

READING FILES

```
C  PROGRAM READS A MAG TAPE
      DIMENSION A(32)
      DO 30 I=1,1000
         READ(8,10,END=40) A
 10      FORMAT( 32E17.7 )
         WRITE(6,20) A
 20      FORMAT(1X, 8E17.7 )
 30   CONTINUE
C
 40   WRITE(6,50)
 50   FORMAT(1X, 'END OF PRINTING' )
      STOP
      END
```

Figure 13.12. Reads information from a magnetic tape and writes the information on the line printer. The END=40 transfers control to line 40 when the end of file is sensed on the tape on unit 8.

PROBLEMS

1. Write a program that counts the number of blanks on a data card that has alphanumeric data on it.

2. Write a program that reads a data card that has alphanumeric data on it and substitutes dashes for blanks when it echo-prints what was read.

3. Write a program that counts the number of words in a sentence read from a data card. A sentence ends with a period and only one blank separates words.

4. Do problem 3 if the words are separated by more than one blank.

5. The form of a simple IF statement is IF (⟨variable⟩ . ⟨relational operator⟩ . ⟨variable⟩) STOP where the items in angular brackets can be any legal characters which satisfy the term in the brackets. Thus ⟨relational operator⟩ can be EQ, NE, GE, LE, GT, and LT. Write a program that tests whether an IF statement punched on a data card satisfies the requirements of the IF statement as defined here. To simplify matters, define ⟨variable⟩ as a letter of the alphabet.

6. The form of a simple READ statement is READ (5, 100) ⟨variable list⟩ where ⟨variable list⟩ = ⟨variable⟩ | ⟨variable⟩, ⟨variable list⟩. (The "|" means "or"). The definition of ⟨variable list⟩ is recursive, i.e., you can substitute ⟨variable list⟩ from the left-hand side into ⟨variable list⟩ on the right-hand side. If you do you get

   ⟨variable list⟩ = ⟨variable⟩ | ⟨variable⟩, ⟨variable⟩

   or

   ⟨variable list⟩ = ⟨variable⟩ | ⟨variable⟩, ⟨variable⟩, ⟨variable list⟩

   This recursive definition allows you to have as many variables in the list as you want. Write a program which tests whether a READ statement is grammatically correct.

7. One definition of an assignment statement is ⟨variable⟩ = ⟨variable⟩ | ⟨constant⟩. Write a program which tests for proper assignment statements. To simplify matters define ⟨constant⟩ as any digit from 0 to 9.

8. Using the approach of problems 5, 6, and 7 (it is called a BNF grammar—Backus Naur Form), write the definition of ⟨INTEGER constant⟩.

9. Using a BNF grammar write the definition of ⟨REAL constant⟩.

10. Using the results of problem 8, write a BNF definition of ⟨variable⟩.

11. Using the results of problems 7, 8, 9, and 10, write a program that checks if an assignment statement punched on a data card is written correctly.

12. Write a program that reads constants from one tape, sorts them in ascending order, and then writes the results on another tape.

13. Write a program that reads an array from one tape, places a constant read from a data card between the Nth and $N^{th} + 1$ elements of the array, and writes the altered array on another tape.

14. Write a program that histograms values read from an array. The values of X Max, X Min, and DX should be read from cards.

Appendix

A—Object Decks

If you wish to, you can instruct the computer to punch the object program on cards. This deck of cards is called an *object deck*. You cannot punch an object deck on WATFOR/WATFIV.

B—Control Cards for IBM System 360/370

On the IBM System 360/370 all control cards that have instructions on them and are not used for WATFOR/WATFIV begin with a slash in column 1 and in column 2. In column 3 we begin punching what is known as the *name field*; this is followed by one or more blanks and then the *operation field*; this is followed by one or more blanks and then the *operand field*. Not every control card which has an instruction on it has to have a name field, but each must have an operation and operand field. The operation field must contain one of the following codes:

```
JOB
EXEC
DD
```

The first control card is a JOB card, an example of which is

```
//TEST1 JOB (A101,6312),'ABRAMS'
```

A JOB card must have a name field. The name field here contains TEST1. This is the job name and identifies to the computer the program you are currently running. At N.Y.U., the job name is printed in large letters on the first page of your results. It must begin with a letter and contain either letters or digits, and has a maximum of eight characters. This is followed by one or more blanks and then by JOB. This is the operation. This is followed by one or more blanks and then by the operand field. On this particular card, the operand consists of the account number A101,6312 in parentheses (this is the number assigned to you by the computer center which allows you to run programs on the computer) followed by a comma and then by your name preceded and followed by an apostrophe. How you represent your name is restricted by the fact that you can use a maximum of 20 characters here. At times, more information about your job is punched on this card.

This card is followed by an EXEC control card. An EXEC card instructs the computer how to process your program. An EXEC card does not have to have a name field, so here we have omitted it. In order to inform the computer we have done this, we leave the third column blank. The operation field contains EXEC. This is followed by a blank and then the operand field. An example of an operand field for a FORTRAN program is FORTGCLG—it is called the *catalog procedure name*. FORTGCLG instructs the computer to compile and execute your FORTRAN program. The CLG stands for Compile, Linkage edit, and Go. Among other things "linkage edit" connects your program with auxiliary programs—such as input/output programs—which your program may require: *go* means execute. The FORTG which precedes these letters stands for the FORTRAN G compiler. Our EXEC card thus looks like

```
// EXEC FORTGCLG
```

If we wanted only to compile, we would follow FORTG with only the letter C. Thus our EXEC card would be

```
// EXEC FORTGC
```

If we were running an object program, i.e., a program already translated into machine language, we would want only to linkage edit and execute. We would thus follow FORTG with the letters LG. Our EXEC card* would now be

```
// EXEC FORTGLG
```

The EXEC card is followed by a DD card. A DD card instructs the computer that either a program or data cards follow. The name field here instructs the computer whether a program or data cards follow and from which input "unit" it will be read. If a program follows, the first part of the name field indicates whether the program is a FORTRAN source program (i.e., contains FORTRAN statements)—FORT is used for this: or an object program—LKED is used for this. If data cards follow, GO is used here. FORT, LKED, or GO is followed by a period, which in turn is followed by a name that indicates which input unit will be used to read the program. SYSIN indicates that the card reader will be used for this.

The operation field contains DD. This is preceded and followed by one or more blanks. The operand field here contains an asterisk. This indicates that a program or data cards immediately follow the DD card. Thus a DD card which indicates that a FORTRAN source program immediately follows and that it will be read from the card reader is

```
//FORT.SYSIN DD *
```

In Fig. B1, we show the control cards that will enable you to compile a source program. Thus the procedure name used here is FORTGC. This is followed by the //FORT.SYSIN DD * card, which is followed by the program. This in turn is followed by a /* card. This indicates that the job is complete.† It is called a delimiter.

```
//TEST1 JOB (A101,6312),'JONES'
// EXEC FORTGC
//FORT.SYSIN DD *
```

FORTRAN Source Program(s)

```
/*
```

Figure B1. Compiling a FORTRAN source program.

* At New York University if you want to compile and execute your program you write

// EXEC FORTRANG.

† At New York University a // card is used.

In Fig. B2, we show the control cards that will enable you to compile and execute a source program, which requires no data. Thus the procedure name is FORTGCLG. This is followed by the //FORT.SYSIN DD * card, which is followed by the program, which in turn is followed by a /* card. In the situations shown in both Figs. B1 and B2, if there is more than one source program, e.g., a main program and subroutines, then all the programs are sandwiched between the //FORT.SYSIN DD * card and the /* card. The main program must precede the subroutines.

```
//TEST1 JOB (A101,6312),'JONES'
// EXEC FORTGCLG
//FORT.SYSIN DD *

 FORTRAN Source Program(s)

/*
```

Figure B2. Compiling and executing a FORTRAN source program.

A DD card that indicates that an object program immediately follows is

//LKED.SYSIN DD *

In Fig. B3 we show the control cards that enable you to execute an object program which does not require data. Thus the procedure name used here is FORTGLG. This is followed by a //LKED.SYSIN DD* card, which is followed by the object program, which in turn is followed by a /* card. If there is more than one object program, the programs are sandwiched between the //LKED.SYSIN DD * card and the /* card.

```
//TEST1 JOB (A101,6312),'JONES'
// EXEC FORTGLG
//LKED.SYSIN DD *

 FORTRAN Object Program(s)

/*
```

Figure B3. Executing a FORTRAN object program.

If the source program requires data, then the source program is followed by a //GO.SYSIN DD * card. This is followed by the data which in turn is followed by a /* card, as shown in Fig. B4.

```
//TEST1 JOB (A101,6312),'JONES'
// EXEC FORTGCLG
//FORT.SYSIN DD *
```

FORTRAN Source Program(s)

```
//GO.SYSIN DD *
```

Data

```
/*
```

Figure B4. Compiling and executing a FORTRAN source program that has data.

If the object program requires data, then the object program is followed by a //GO.SYSIN DD * card. This is followed by the data which in turn is followed by a /* card, as shown in Fig. B5.

```
//TEST1 JOB (A101,6312),'JONES'
// EXEC FORTGLG
//LKED.SYSIN DD *
```

FORTRAN Object Program(s)

```
//GO.SYSIN DD *
```

Data

```
/*
```

Figure B5. Executing a FORTRAN object program that has data.

If you want to obtain an object program or a listing of the source program, you can specify this in the EXEC card. Thus, if you wanted to obtain an object program and a listing of the program while you were compiling and executing it, you would write

```
// EXEC FORTGCLG,PARM.FORT='DECK,LIST'
```

DECK means produce an object deck, and LIST means produce a listing of the program.

In Fig. B6, we show the control cards to compile a source program and to list the program and produce an object deck.

```
//TEST1 JOB (A101,6312),'JONES'
// EXEC FORTGCLG,PARM.FORT=' DECK,LIST'
//FORT.SYSIN DD *

 FORTRAN Source Program

/*
```

Figure B6. Producing an object deck and a listing of a FORTRAN source program.

If you only wanted to produce an object deck, but not a listing of the program, you would write

```
// EXEC FORTGCLG,PARM.FORT='DECK'
```

C—Control Cards for WATFIV

In Fig. C1 we show the control cards for a WATFIV job which requires data.

```
//TEST2     JOB     (A101,6312),'JONES'
// EXEC WATFIV
//GO.SYSIN DD *
$JOB

 FORTRAN Source Program(s)

$ENTRY

 Data

$STOP(1)
/*
```

Figure C1. Control cards for a WATFIV program requiring data.

If no data are required, simply omit the data but retain all other cards.

In Fig. C2 we show the control cards required at New York University for a WATFIV job requiring data.

```
//TEST1  JOB    (A101,6312),'JONES', CLASS=W
$JOB
```

FORTRAN Source Program(s)

```
$ENTRY
```

Data

```
$EOF
//
```

Figure C2. Control cards at New York University for a WATFIV program requiring data cards.

If no data are required, simply omit the data but retain all other cards.

D—Time Sharing

In a time-sharing environment we type our program on a teletypewriter that is attached to the computer either electrically ("hard wired" to it) or via a telephone line ("acoustically coupled" to it). After we have correctly identified ourselves to the computer and have indicated that we will be using the FORTRAN system, we type our program.

Each line of the program must have a line number. This is followed by at least one space and then the FORTRAN statement, as we would keypunch it on a card. The space is for typing a digit indicating you want to continue a statement. Each successive line of the program must have a higher line number, since unless we instruct it otherwise the computer follows the order of the line numbers when it executes the program. After each line we type, we depress the carriage return key. A program that sums the numbers read in a READ statement is shown in Fig. D1.

```
100         READ(5,10)A,B
200     10  FORMAT(2F10.0)
300         C=A+B
400         WRITE(6,20)A,B,C
500     20  FORMAT(1X, 'A=', F10.2, 'B=', F10.2, 'C=', F10.2)
600         END
```

Figure D1. A program written on a time-sharing system.

Note the FORMAT statements have both a line number and a statement number.

For statements that have statement numbers (e.g., FORMATs), some systems require you to type the statement number within the first 5 columns following the line number, then leave at least one space and then type the statement. If the statement has no statement number, then on these systems you must leave at least 6 spaces between the line number and the statement. Thus on these systems you have to maintain the structure of the FORTRAN statement card.

In order to execute the program you type RUN. The program then executes. Since the program requires data, the computer types a question mark on the next line. Then on the same line, you type the data as you would keypunch it on a data card, remembering to type the data in the proper fields. After you hit the carriage return, the computer prints the results and the word READY. If you want to change a line of the program, for instance, line 300, type 300 followed by the altered statement. If you want to delete a line, you simply type the line number and then hit the carriage return. If you want to include a new line in the program, for instance, between lines 500 and 600, you type that new line with a line number that is between 500 and 600. If you type LIST, the program will list the program with all modifications.

We now give an example. First we run the program shown in Fig. D1. Then we will alter line 300 so it calculates the product of A and B. When we LIST the program, the listing will reflect this change. All this is shown in Fig. D2.

```
RUN
?3.0            4.0
A=      3.00B=       4.00C=       7.00
READY
300             C=A*B
LIST
100             READ(5,10)A,B
200       10    FORMAT(2F10.0)
300             C=A*B
400             WRITE(6,20) A,B,C
500       20    FORMAT(1X, 'A=', F10.2, 'B=', F10.2, 'C=', F10.2)
600             END
READY
RUN
?3.00           4.0
A=      3.00B=       4.00C=      12.00
READY
```

Figure D2. Running the program of Fig. D1, then altering it, listing it, and finally running the altered version.

If a program contains a subroutine, the subroutine must have higher line numbers than the main routine has, as we show in Fig. D3.

```
100           CALL CALC
200           END

300           SUBROUTINE CALC
400           READ(5,10)A,B
500     10    FORMAT(2F10.0)
600           C=A*B
700           WRITE(6,20)A,B,C
800     20    FORMAT(1X,3F10.2)
900           RETURN
1000          END
```

Figure D3. A time-sharing program that contains a subroutine.

Subject Index

C 9
D 0
E 1
F 2
G 3
H 4
I 5
J 6